D0622491

# conservation and management
## of natural resources in
## the united states

# conservation and management of natural resources in the united states

Charles F. Bennett
university of california, los angeles

cartography
and illustrations by
Noël Diaz
university of california, los angeles

John Wiley & Sons
new york · chichester · brisbane · toronto · singapore

*Library of Congress Cataloging in Publication Data:*

Bennett, Charles F.
  Conservation and management of natural resources
in the United States.

  Bibliography: p.
  Includes indexes.
  1. Conservation of natural resources—United
States.  2. Conservation of natural resources.  I. Title.
S930.B46  1983      333.7′2′0973      82-21941
ISBN 0-471-04652-3

Printed in the United States of America

10 9 8 7 6 5 4 3 2 1

to ashley

# preface

This book provides the general college student in the United States with an introduction to a subject that is of central importance to our nation: the conservation and management of our nation's natural resources. Until fairly recently, public concern for conservation often appeared to be more or less restricted to a relatively few persons who had the leisure time to engage in "good works." While their efforts were often of great significance—indeed, it was they who often kept alive public concern for conservation—conservation is today the concern and responsibility of all citizens.

Some people see this democratization of conservation as an unhealthy development. Some see in it a threat to our economic system and others take the lofty, if not arrogant view, that the person who lacks in-depth instruction in chemistry, physics, and biology has no business becoming involved in matters relating to the conservation and management of natural resources.

Conservation and management of natural resources, in a democratic society, are too important to be left entirely to specialists and politicians to pursue alone—particularly with regard to the formulation of policy. One need not be a trained scientist to make responsible decisions respecting the many environmental questions one confronts almost daily. Because we are increasingly called on to make conservation decisions via the ballot, it is necessary that the formal education of college students in our nation include concepts that can provide the basis for continuing reasoned and insightful judgments relating to questions about the use of our nation's natural resources.

A look at the Contents will show that, for the most part, the topics treated are fairly conventional with the single major exception of Chapter 4. That chapter alerts the reader to the fact that while the major emphasis of this book is on the United States, we as a nation can no longer regard ourselves as self-sufficient in many natural resources and are now dependent on other nations—especially poor ones—for some of the most critical natural resources we consume in this country. Thus, our behavior vis-à-vis consumption of such resources must necessarily affect, in various ways, the nations from whom we import the resources.

The focus in Chapter 4 is on chance geological, biological, and historical events that have contributed largely to the poverty of those nations to which the term Third World has been given. Chapter 4 questions the still too frequently held assumption that underdeveloped nations are poor because of certain inherent flaws in their national characters and not because of factors over which the inhabitants of these nations have had no control. We need not be mystics to accept the view that our nation, at least insofar as natural resources are concerned, is bound up in mankind. I hope that this chapter will stimulate thinking that leads toward a more global view of natural resource conservation.

In most of the chapters there is a section that

presents some examples drawn from the Third World. Please note, however, that these sections are not intended to be encyclopedic and no attempt has been made to make them all-inclusive or even nearly so. These special sections merely introduce the reader to problems of natural resource conservation in the Third World and thus encourage the reader to include these countries in his/her thinking when reflecting on matters relating to natural resource conservation in the United States.

I wish to acknowledge the many contributions made by my students who directly or indirectly have helped to shape the conservation courses I teach and thus the content of this book. Thanks also to my editor, Katie Vignery, and to the production staff at John Wiley & Sons. To my wife, Carole, goes my gratitude for never-ceasing love, patience, and inspiration.

*Charles F. Bennett*
Los Angeles, California, 1982

# contents

Contents

# the concepts and language of conservation

This chapter defines and discusses many of the terms and concepts used in the field of conservation and management of natural resources. The chapter is divided into three sections. The first section is concerned with general terms and concepts, the second part includes biological terms and concepts, and the third section deals with human societal terms and concepts.

## GENERAL TERMINOLOGY

The first term requiring definition and discussion is the one about which this book has been written: conservation. Although widely used and certainly a part of the vocabulary of any college student one encounters such varied applications and meanings that it is important that the reader be made aware of the meaning the author gives to the word because this has greatly influenced the organization and content of this book.

The approach to a definition of conservation will be aided if it is recognized at the outset that conservation of natural resources is a human phenomenon. Conservation, however the word may be defined, has no meaning outside of the human context because it is only the human species, among the thousands of other living species, that exploits the earth's resources in culturally controlled fashions. All other living organisms have exploitive behav-

iors that are almost entirely governed by genetically inherited mechanisms. For living species other than humans, excess exploitation of resources is controlled by natural checks and balances. These checks and balances prevent or correct the uncontrolled growth of populations and hence the uncontrolled exploitation of available resources in an environment. Humans are cultural beings and thus we survive largely because of our inventiveness and ability to transmit our inventions to succeeding generations. A large part of this inventiveness has long been and continues to be directed toward obtaining ever-greater amounts of natural resources from the planetary resource pool. Not only has this inventiveness allowed us to achieve a large and still growing population and to become the dominant vertebrate animal in many parts of the earth, it has also provided the means to temporarily "correct" or "fix" the disturbances we have repeatedly caused in the earth's habitats that we use and have used. Our success, until recently, appeared to be phenomenal.

Natural checks and balances are as much a part of the human condition in the earth's environments as they are for other living creatures. We are discovering with increasing frequency that, in many cases, our technological fixes merely put off until another day problems that we thought we had solved forever. We are having to recognize that no amount of technical expertise will overcome the fact that the earth's resources are finite and therefore we must confront the need to devise methods of conservation and management of the earth's resources that do not threaten the future well-being—even the existence—of our species.

Conservation and management of natural resources has a large altruistic—moralistic, if you will—element. If concern for natural resources were only of the moment, there would be limited reason to devote much time and thought to the matter. The life span of a human is such that she or he can be an irresponsible exploiter of the earth's resources and entirely or largely escape most or all of the consequences of such behavior—although, to be sure, some unpleasantness might have to be experienced by the perpetrators. The ecological and economic consequences of many if not most of the undisciplined uses of the earth's resources are visited on succeeding generations. This concern for future generations of humans does not solely embrace those natural resources that supply energy, food and materials but also a myriad of living and nonliving entities for which there is little or no market value. It is a truism that we do not live by bread alone and so it is with natural resources. Some of the most cherished natural resources include those for which there is no market price. What monetary value can be placed on a stretch of wild river, the Yosemite Valley, or a rare butterfly? Yet these and similar things constitute, for some persons, the chief objects of conservation concern and effort. As our world becomes increasingly urbanized the few relatively wild areas left and the wild creatures within and outside of the urban areas will be ever more valued for themselves and money often has little or nothing to do with such valuation.

It is now possible to offer a definition of conservation. Conservation of natural resources is the scientifically disciplined and socially equitable utilization and, when indicated, preservation of the earth's natural resources. Conservation is aimed at maximizing the material and nonmaterial benefits from resource utilization and preservation commensurate with minimizing waste and environmental damage and assuring that unborn generations inherit a planet on which previous human use of natural resources has not attenuated the ability of the living systems to support the material and nonmaterial needs of the human population.

What is a natural resource? Carl O. Sauer, the American geographer, once observed that a natural resource is a cultural appraisal. There can be no single list of items that represent natural resources for every human society on earth today because the heterogeneity of human cultures assures that each society makes its own determination as to what constitutes a natural resource. Ask a college student in the United States or Western Europe to list what the most important natural resources are and it is likely that the list will contain iron, coal, petroleum, water, and clean air. Ask the same question of a Somali herder and the list might be headed by grass and followed by water and firewood. It is an important fact to keep in mind that as human societies add to their technologies they more or less constantly reappraise the components of the earth's living and nonliving elements with an eye toward discovering "new" natural resources. In the early part of this century, for example, aluminum was something of a curiosity and uranium was known to be a rare and useless element. One must be very careful not to fall into the common error of thinking that all natural resources are utilitarian in the sense that they have a market value, that is, that they can be bought and sold. While the greater share of conservation and management efforts are, of necessity, directed toward natural resources that comprise the material components of human support systems, conservation also properly includes items that are part of the psychic support systems of human societies. Thus, to summarize, a natural resource is any nonmanufactured component of the earth's environments deemed of value by one or more persons.

It is usual to divide natural resources into two large categories: renewable and nonrenewable. To the former belong water, air, soil, plants, and animals, while the latter includes fossil fuels and many metallic and nonmetallic minerals. This division is useful but its limitations must be noted. All natural resources are finite in quantity and all natural resources can be so overutilized or abused as to reach a point where they are, for all practical purposes, no longer renewable. One need only think of severe air and water pollution, massive losses of soil and destructive use or abuse of wild vegetation or animal life to see the point. With regard to the category of nonrenewable resources, it is now possible to recycle several metals, for example, copper, lead, iron, and aluminum. Thus, there may be a third category of resources developing, those that can be recycled. As metals become more scarce in the earth, greater attention will be given to recycling and one can foresee the day when most metals will be regularly recycled and not discarded as is often the case today.

In this general section there remains only the term *management* to be defined and discussed. When used in the context of conservation of natural resources, management refers to all the methods, techniques and strategies devised and used to achieve the sought-after conservation goals. Thus, management is the action part of conservation. To some readers, this distinction may appear unwarranted because it may be felt that the word conservation is sufficient. However, conservation has too often been a gloss for well-meant intentions but lacking the formulation and activation of methods to get the job done. By including the word management one is reminded that effective conservation requires action.

## BIOLOGICAL TERMINOLOGY

Among the most frequently used words to describe place are *habitat* and *environment*. These are both useful terms but there are many occasions when something more precise is required and the following terms serve the need: community, ecosystem, and biome. The term *community* refers to all the interrelated living entities in a given place and such a collection is distinctive as, for example, the tall-grass prairie community (Fig. 1.1). This word is very useful for description but is somewhat lacking in its usefulness for analytic studies and, too often, ignores except peripherally the important nonliving entities present in a community except to list them or to describe them in a general way. The term *ecosystem* is almost synonymous with community but with some very major differences. While the term community is descriptive of the plants and animals present in an area, *ecosystem* is a system of interacting living and nonliving entities that apportions the available energy and nutrients (Fig. 1.2).

It is much easier to define what an ecosystem is than it is to apply the concept in everyday management of natural resources, because any ecosystem is extremely complicated and thus difficult to study as a complete unit. However, great progress in this direction is being made with perhaps the most promising results thus far coming from studies of saltwater marshes and grasslands. The object of ecosystems studies, as they relate to conservation, is to develop computer models that will so accurately simulate the natural systems that a high degree of prediction can be achieved with regard to management.

You will sometimes encounter the word *habitat* in this book and it refers to that part or parts of an ecosystem required by a plant or animal species. The key to many aspects of biological conservation is proper management of habitats.

**Figure 1.1**  Remnant of tall-grass prairie said never to have been plowed.

The term *biome* is very useful for it refers to the largest nonaquatic ecosystems that conservationists, ecologists, and others find convenient to work with. Some examples of biomes are tropical savannas, rainforests, midlatitude coniferous forests, deserts, and Mediterranean scrub woodlands (Table 1.1). Although there is a fair degree of international agreement as to what the biomes are, there are still variations in terminology and thus there is no single list to which all scholars agree.

Ecosystems are dynamic entities and their living and nonliving components tend to vary with the passage of time. The term used to identify these orderly changes is ecological succession. There are short, middle- and long-term aspects to ecological succession. An ex-

Table 1.1
**Principal biomes of the world**

| |
| --- |
| Tropical rainforest[a] |
| Tropical cloud forest |
| Tropical deciduous forest |
| Tropical scrub forest |
| Tropical savanna |
| Mangrove forest[a] |
| Desert[a] |
| Mediterranean woodland and shrub[a] |
| Middle-latitude grassland[a] |
| Middle-latitude marshland[a] |
| Middle-latitude deciduous forest[a] |
| Coniferous forest[a] |
| Tundra[a] |

[a] Indicates a biome that occurs within the United States.

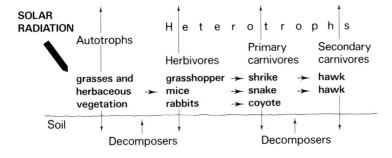

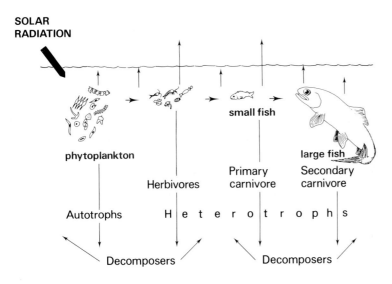

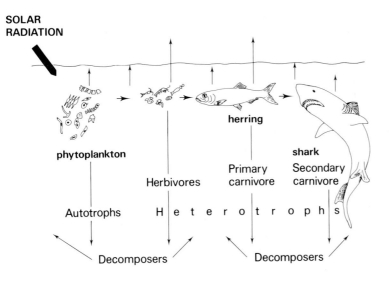

(Arrows indicate energy flows)

**Figure 1.2** Simplified examples of three kinds of ecosystems. (top) Prairie ecosystems, (middle) fresh-water ecosystems and (bottom) marine ecosystems.

ample of short-term ecological succession occurs when a farmer abandons a field and allows grass, shrubs, and trees (if the farm happens to be located where there are trees!) to invade the once-cultivated fields. The succession will follow a predictable order of plant, animal, and microclimatic changes. An example of a middle-term change can be seen (not in a single human's lifetime) when a tract of tropical rainforest that has been cut-over is abandoned and allowed to run wild. The succession from the time of abandonment back to maturity might take more than a century and a half. And, finally, an example of long-term ecological succession is that which occurs any place on earth over geological time and in response to climatic changes that involve many thousands of years, as for example the ecological changes that have occurred since the last major period of continental glaciation (glacial maximum) about 19,000 years ago.

Ecosystems appear to be always adjusting to maximize the utilization of the available energy, nutrients, and other materials. This is reflected by the presence of trophic levels in the system, that is, there are primary producers (the green plants), primary consumers (the herbivores), and the secondary consumers (the carnivores). A component of each trophic level are decomposers—plants and animals whose role it is to decompose the dead plants and animals and thus make chemical nutrients available to the living organisms in the system. The primary producers constitute the fundament of any ecosystem and ultimately determine what the total *biomass* (all the plants and animals) of the community will be. If physical conditions remain fairly stable within a community, that community—after a period of varying length that involves the aforementioned ecological succession—will attain a condition of approximate equilibrium that will be maintained until some perturbation upsets the "steady state" causing ecological succession to reoccur. These steady-state ecosystems are marked by

relatively little change in plant or animal species composition or in the respective populations of the species over what, to humans, appear to be considerable periods of time. Such an ecosystem may be called a mature community indicating that it represents the end of an ecological succession and will tend to maintain its composition barring disturbance or the evolutionary changes that occur over geological time spans.

It is important to reflect on this phenomenon of the mature community because it is the preservation of this type of ecosystem that many conservationists consider to be the sine qua non of conservation. That this cannot often be the case, however, must be obvious to anyone who recognizes that untouched ecosystems must often be a luxury in a world rapidly filling with people. This brings us to a consideration of a closely related term, *diversity*.

The term diversity as applied in ecology refers usually to the total number of life forms present in a given area or ecosystem. Until recently, it was widely believed that the greatest diversity occurred in mature communities, and since this is the most stable community it followed that retention or recovery of diversity must be a major aim of management of biological resources. However, some studies have shown that mature ecosystems may not always have the greatest diversity particularly if one looks at individual groups such as birds, mammals, or grass species, for example. It is also apparent that at least one mature ecosystem, mangroves, has a very low diversity of plant and animal species. It seems possible that in any mature ecosystem there is a certain degree of what might be called redundancy in that there may be more species present than are needed for the continued functioning of the ecosystem.

What was just said suggests that we may sometimes be overcareful in our efforts to prevent the simplification of ecosystems because we have based our efforts on the belief that the highest degree of diversity is a necessity.

However, the problem is that only rarely do we know which insect or which reptile or which bird or mammal or which plant is not required to keep a given system in good operating condition.

Biological resources that are the object of human exploitation must be managed in such a way as to assure that harvesting does not impair the ability of the resource to maintain an adequate breeding stock. This kind of harvesting strategy is termed *sustained yield* and means, essentially, that the "interest" is harvested without cutting into "capital" the latter being the needed reproducing population. It is much easier to talk about sustained yields than it is to put the concept into effective practice because of a frequent lack of information about the size of the populations to be harvested, their reproductive rates, and how much interference the organisms can tolerate before suffering what might be a precipitous decline in numbers.

It is somewhat easier to determine what the appropriate levels of forest harvests should be than it is for many animal populations but unexpected climatic changes or outbreaks of insect "pests" or fire can greatly alter the best-laid plans of sustained yield forest management. Animals can be extremely difficult to harvest on a sustained yield basis because their populations tend to fluctuate in response to many environmental factors such as predator pressure, food availability, disease outbreaks, and the like. The cyclic aspect of the population size of many animal species often sets up the basis for conflict between resource managers and resource harvesters. The former tend to be cautious and may try to keep the allowable harvests in harmony with the lower or middle range of population fluctuations while the latter often look only at the top of the population curves and attempt to harvest as though such is always the prevailing condition.

Somewhat related to the concept of sustained yield is that of *carrying capacity*. This term refers to the limit of a given area to maintain a certain number of wild and/or domesticated animals. This is one of the more important management concepts with respect to rangeland management for livestock but it applies equally to wildlands and wild animals. Carrying capacity is often difficult to assess and in the past was frequently determined less by scientific measure than by intuition and hope.

One of the ever-present dangers that exists when wild animals are harvested for commercial ends is that the numbers may be reduced below a level from which the animal population can make a recovery even if given complete and effective protection from further harvesting. This variable is termed the *biological potential* and refers to the lower population limit from which the animal can make a recovery to greater numbers. Some animals can be incredibly reduced in numbers, as was the American bison, and still make a comeback if protected. However, other animals do not possess such a high potential and once past the critical lower population size are doomed to extinction no matter what protection is given them.

## HUMAN SOCIETAL TERMS AND CONCEPTS

Because conservation and natural resources are anthropocentric concepts it follows that human values are central to conservation and management of natural resources. Human values, as we all know, are as varied as are the ways of life followed by human societies and even within any local group one is certain to find a variation of values. It is this great range of variations that converts much of resource management from what might be a rational scientific endeavor into what is often a gladiatorial arena. The "pure" preservationist may look on a given forest as something to be saved and protected from any and all exploitation saving sensory enjoyment. A lumber company executive may see the same forest as a harvestable resource. The resolving of these (as well as other views as how best to treat the forest) is a principal task of resource management. The difficulty of this task is greatest in those nations where there is a democracy.

The arena in which many value conflicts respecting natural resource use is fought consists chiefly of the legislative chambers of local, state, and national governments. In short, many if not most management decisions respecting natural resources are strongly influenced by political decisions. It is said that politics is the art of the possible and it follows, then, that conservation and management of natural resources is also the art of the possible and this holds true even in those nations where there is only limited political participation by the mass of citizens. In such centrally planned economies as that of the U.S.S.R. there are conflicts between natural resource managers and heads of factories and the conflicts appear to be resolved as often in response to political pressures as they are in response to environmental considerations. In a capitalist society, of which the United States is the remaining best example, many political constituencies exist and all but the most naive are versed in the uses of communication techniques and the political/legislative processes and are frequently effective in pressing their demands—values—on lawmakers. An example of this is the organization to which owners of off-road-vehicles (ORVs) belong. These people, many of whom are concentrated in the western United States, seek their recreation in the form of running their vehicles over the desert. The Bureau of Land Management (BLM), which has the legal responsibility to manage much of the nation's desert lands, must be responsive to the U.S. Congress. The latter, in turn, is responsive to the active lobbying of the persons whose pleasure it is to use ORVs in the desert. Thus, the BLM sets aside areas in the deserts for the use of these vehicle users and attempts to prevent such vehicular use in other parts of the desert. To a "purist" this may appear as a *reductio ad absurdum* and totally unworthy of BLM support. However, in a democracy it is necessary to attempt to accommodate almost all constituencies no matter how strange their ideas may appear to be.

American conservationists were comparatively slow to recognize the power of politics—and the courts of law—but this is no longer true and scarcely a day goes by without a news story of litigation being initiated to prevent some action thought by the plaintiffs to be detrimental to the environment. Although there was conservation/management legislation prior to World War II it has been chiefly since that time that legislation in this area has exploded. Resolving by law and litigation conflicts related to the use of natural resources, therefore, is now a major aspect of natural resource management. Only the naive visionary overlooks this essential truth.

Certain conflicts related to values are not likely to be resolved unless and until there are some major shifts in majority attitudes in the United States. Probably the largest growing area of value conflict at present, and certain to become very much more serious in the near future, is that which focuses opon growth versus a steady-state economy. Basically, the conflict is as follows: the advocates of growth argue that in a capitalistic economy it is necessary to the continued existence of such an economy that there be continued growth. Growth is defined in various terms but we may use the annual rate of increase of the gross domestic product (GDP) as the measure. The GDP is the sum of all the goods and services produced annually in a nation (unless otherwise indicated). It is argued that the very nature of capitalistic enterprise requires that there be growth—that a static situation will cause deterioration and ultimate destruction of the system. The advocates of a steady-state economy argue that our nation is rapidly approaching the time when there will not be sufficient energy and other resources to sustain continued growth.

The two positions briefly described above are heavily burdened with values and value judgments. The steady-state advocates are sensitive to the reality of a finite earth and an already very large human population relative to the total amount of natural resources and seek to stabilize the economy before overpopulation and overexploitation of resources causes great human suffering and even the collapse of human societies. The advocates of growth argue that the historical experience strongly supports the view that continued growth is possible this being due in large measure to human inventiveness that has repeatedly discovered new resources or new uses for old resources thus greatly extending the support base of our species. Only timidity, goes this line of argument, will prevent our species from continuing to increase its production and consumption of materials far into the future.

Both arguments have their strengths and weaknesses and for the individual, the decision as to which one is right is probably as likely to be determined by personally held values as by objective analysis. But make no mistake, the debate has only begun and before this century is over it may become the most important object of political and legislative action in the United States and many other nations as well.

In all industrial societies, regardless of their political-economic orientation, a natural resource required for industry can only be such if it can be obtained profitably (no matter where the profit goes). A resource for which there is no present profitable market but which may be marketable at some future time is called a *latent resource*. Uranium not very long ago was a latent resource as was aluminum. In many Third World nations there are natural resources that for them are partially latent in that they have neither the technical means nor the capital means to realize fully the value the resource(s) might have in the industrialized world. An example of this is petroleum. Many of the petroleum-exporting nations have lacked both the technology and the capital to build refineries and petrochemical factories. Today, some of these nations have the capital but still lack the technology to maximize the latent commercial values of the oil they export. Some Third World nations are beginning to adopt the policy of restricting export of certain nonrenewable resources in order to have a supply in the future when they may possess the capital and the technology to maximize financial returns from the exploitation of the resources.

The size of the reserves of many nonrenewable natural resources such as petroleum, iron, and copper is partly a function of the total amounts known or thought to exist and partly the function of market price. If the latter rises, certain deposits not previously thought to be usable because the cost of extraction was more than the market price may become a part of the proven reserves. Not many years ago, for example, so-called heavy oil deposits of immense size in parts of the Western Hemisphere were not counted as a part of the petroleum reserves because the costs of extraction and refining were far above the then prevailing price of more easily extracted and refined types of crude petroleum. Since the great rise in petroleum prices, these deposits are on the verge of being counted a part of the petroleum reserves. Thus it can be seen that a part of the cultural appraisal of a natural resource is the cost-to-benefit ratio. This ratio can be changed by market conditions as just illustrated by petroleum and it can be altered by a change in technology. An example of the latter was the development of techniques to utilize a relatively poor and once-uneconomic type of iron ore called taconite. As long as abundant high-quality iron ores were available in the United States it was not economically beneficial to attempt to exploit the low-grade ores. However, as the former became scarcer and the costs of importing iron ores increased, the latent taconite resource received the careful attention of engineers who developed a process that created what is essentially a new natural resource and one that is very important in the U.S. iron and steel industry.

Regardless where and under what form of economy it takes place, industry places various kinds of stress on local and distant ecological systems. We group many of these stresses under the general heading pollution. Until fairly recently, pollution was shrugged off as a necessary concomitant of economic growth. This acceptance led to few legal attempts to stop such activities and the ecological/economic damage could be and was ignored by the perpetrators and treated simply as an externality. An externality refers to any facet of a business agreement between contracting persons that does not affect them or their contractual relationship although it may affect a noncontracting person. This "person" doesn't have to be one person or society in general but may be a lake, river, shoreline, or the atmosphere, just to mention some possibilities. The latter, not being living persons, could not sue in a court of law because they had "no standing" to use the legal phrase. A human who was injured, say, by the pollution of the water flowing past his or her property had standing and could sue but this was often a futile effort because the courts often held to the view that such pollution was a necessary aspect of economic activity.

What we witness today is the rapid development of a body of law that requires entrepreneurs to be legally and hence economically responsible for what were once "cost-free" externalities. This is one of the most important recent gains in the effective conservation and management of natural resources. Unfortunately, many nations still accept the old view respecting pollution as well as other kinds of damages to natural resources and often because it is believed (or at least argued) that their economies cannot operate profitably if the control of pollution and other environmental impacts must be made a part of the costs of production. This is a completely false position because today's externalities, with regard to the environment, will most assuredly have to be paid for by someone and the payments tend to increase alarmingly in size with the passage of time.

## SUMMARY

Conservation and management of natural resources has a vocabulary of terms and concepts that must be grasped if a person is to be able to think and act effectively in this important area of human concern. It is convenient to divide the terms and concepts into three broad categories.

1 *General terminology.* Includes not only the term conservation and management of natural resources but also others such as renewable and nonrenewable resources. It is important to realize that a natural resource is basically a cultural appraisal, and related to this is the fact that the aims of conservation and management of natural resources are also often cultural appraisals.

2 *Biological terminology.* Includes terms and concepts relating to biology, which includes ecology and many other subareas. Examples of such terminology include ecosystem, biome, habitat, community, ecological succession, diversity, carrying capacity, and many others.

3 *Human societal terms and concepts.* This relates to the broad sphere of human values around which orbit virtually all aspects of conservation and management of natural resources. Among the extremely numerous terms and concepts are preservation, wilderness values, latent natural resource, externalities, steady-state versus growth economy, the role of the market in establishing the amount of a resource that is available at a given time, and multiple use versus preservation of wild lands.

# a brief history of conservation

## INTRODUCTION

One of the many vanities of our time is the commonly held assumption that comparatively little of importance with respect to human relationships with the environment occurred until this century and then only in the United States. Humans have a very long history and (in the strict use of terms) prehistory of concern with their natural resources.

One of the earliest evidences in the Old World of conservation are attempts to manage the game resource in Assyria at about 850 B.C. The Assyrian nobility established private hunting reserves in which only nobles were permitted to hunt. This idea diffused about the Mediterranean region and has been reported as a part of the ancient history of Egypt, Greece, and the Roman Empire. The idea of the private game reserve for the nobility is also old in China and may predate the appearance of the idea in the Mediterranean region.

It was the Romans who spread the game reserve idea into Western Europe along with other attributes of their culture during the many centuries in which they increased their empire through conquest. The concept of the private hunting (later to include fishing) reserve has been very persistent in parts of Europe and may be found today even in those nations claiming to have a classless society as, for example, Yugoslavia.

The formal promulgation of hunting and fishing regulations appear to have their beginnings in parts of Western Europe in the seventh century A.D. With the passage of time the early crude regulations (usually designed to keep commoners from hunting or fishing on royal reserves) became more biologically sophisticated although it was not until the nineteenth century that anything identifiable as scientific fish and game management can be discerned.

Early regulations were often incredibly cruel. An excellent example is afforded by the draconian regulations promulgated by William the Conqueror, the Norman victor of England (Battle of Hastings, 1066): "whoever shall kill a stag, wild boar, or even a hare, shall have his eyes torn out." William played an important role in the formulation of forestry laws with respect to what came to be known as the "New Forest." The so-called New Forest, located in southern England, is in fact very old and was old at the time under discussion here (Fig. 2.1). It received its name New Forest because it had a new owner—William. This forest had for some time previous to 1066 been the private hunting reserve of Saxon kings.

With the passage of time and the rising of a wealthy merchant class in England, the private preserve was extended to persons who possessed wealth but lacked a noble lineage. Although the regulations of William were superseded by less draconian measures they retained until recent times an element of vindictiveness that shocks persons long accustomed to a more relaxed (legal) reaction to illegal hunting and fishing on private property.

**Figure 2.1**  New Forest, England. The ponies are semi-wild.

However socially unsuitable this long history of unequal access to the fish and game of Britain is, it probably had the end result of preserving a share of the native fauna right down to the present day—the notable exceptions being wild boar, brown bear, wolf, beaver, and reindeer.

A major example of hunting preserves continuing into the present is afforded by Spain (Fig. 2.2). Such reserves are termed *cotos* and they have figured prominently in the social history of the nation. Again we confront a situation that has included a gross lack of social sensitivity but the biological result has been to preserve remnant populations of brown bears, wolves, and European lynx, for example.

Early forest laws in Europe appear to have been directed chiefly toward the animal resource and it was only later that interest and hence regulation began to focus on the trees.

As first one and then another European nation began to develop naval and merchant ships, oaks, ash and beech trees became of greater and greater importance. Indeed, these tree species were the iron and steel of the great fleets of the Mediterranean even in the time when Greece and later Rome ruled the civilized world. Later, beginning in the sixteenth century, these hardwoods became the most prized of resources because no nation could mount a credible naval presence without access to these trees. Oaks were the most highly prized and during Admiral Horatio Nelson's time a single major naval vessel (ship of the line) required a quantity of oak represented by 60 acres of nature oak forest. Forest laws during this time took chiefly the form of restricting who might cut the more valuable trees and limiting the uses to which the timber could be put.

**Figure 2.2** Coto Doñana, Spain. This important reserve also includes extensive marsh areas.

Forest management, as we understand the term today, did not come into being until the nineteenth century.

The first school of forestry of note was founded in Spain in the nineteenth century and provided at least a partial model for the later establishment of the great school of forestry at Oxford.

Turning to Africa, the search for early evidence of conservation is largely frustrated by a lack of written records. In Africa, south of the Sahara, there are fragmentary data suggesting that at least in some places and in some times there were comparatively formalized regulations enforced by a ranking chief. The available data also suggest that for at least some African societies, there was little or no man-and-nature dichotomy, and this tended to result in behavior that, if not exactly conservation oriented, had the same effect. Since this topic has received almost no attention from researchers up until now it may be that a great deal more

existed in sub-Saharan Africa vis-à-vis conservation than is now evident.

Prehistoric conservation activities in the Western Hemisphere are little known and are not likely to become better known since the available data (chiefly from reports written at the time of first European-Indian contacts) have been pretty well worked over and without eliciting very much information. Some exceptions to that statement, however, exist. The Inca peoples of the Andes of South America are reported to have divided their empire into what were hunting districts and in which the exploitation of the more valuable animals, such as vicuña, were strictly controlled by the ruling house. In addition, periodic roundups of predators were conducted during which times such animals were killed.

The Andean civilization is famous for the vast system of agricultural terraces that covers thousands of hectares of slopes (Fig. 2.3). These terraces may have been built with the

**Figure 2.3**  Agricultural terraces in the Andes.

idea of increasing the total area available for irrigated agriculture as well as making cultivation less arduous but the terraces had the effect of greatly reducing the loss of soil as would otherwise occur on steep slopes cleared of vegetation but not terraced.

Although the comments made above about some of the early history were brief they alert the reader to the fact that ideas about conserving natural resources have been present in at least some parts of the world for a rather long time. We will now direct attention to the United States and the development of ideas about conservation in that nation.

## UNITED STATES:
## PRE-TWENTIETH CENTURY

European settlement of that portion of North America that became the United States brought with it most of the attitudes and traditions held by Europeans' cultures with respect to natural resources. If there can be said to have been an attitude common to all of the culturally disparate peoples who formed the vanguard of settlers, it was an essentially unrestrained exploitive approach to the forests, soils, and animals. The reasons for this are several but chief among them must have been the extraordinary abun-

dance of trees, land for farming or pasture, and animal resources. By the early seventeenth century when English colonies were beginning to be founded on the East coast, most of the once-extensive hardwood forests of Western Europe were little more than a memory as was the even earlier wealth of wild game birds and mammals freely available to any hunter. Eastern North America appeared like a fabulous cornucopia of natural wealth of so great an extent that it could never be exhausted. The journals and reports of the early settlers are replete with accounts of great numbers of deer and other game, of bird flocks whose numbers darkened the noonday sky and of fish such as salmon so abundant as to defy adequate description. And land was there for the taking, an enormous expanse that, as exploration brought ever-increasing evidence of vast land resources to the west, made for what appeared to be a Garden of Eden without limit. Although drawn from many religious sects the overwhelming majority were Christians, many of whom were of the opinion that it was their religious duty to labor hard and grow rich.

Thus, natural resources were things that should be used and not things to be preserved or even managed. Few indeed are the bits of evidence that would indicate that the colonists were the slightest bit concerned about their responsibilities toward the natural resources of the continent. True, during the colonial period certain ordinances were issued by the British Crown that were designed to limit forest cutting and, in some few instances, to regulate hunting, but these are notable chiefly for the fact that they appear meager exceptions to the then prevailing laissez faire approach to the use of resources.

At the time the English colonies declared their independence of the Crown, European settlement had long since burst the bounds of the 13 colonies although the velocity of this westward expansion had been slowed both by British and French efforts. The fledgling United States rapidly added territory: 1803 saw the acquisition of the enormous Louisiana Purchase; Florida was added in 1819, Texas was acquired in 1845, Oregon in 1846, and most of what is now the American southwest in 1848. This rapid acquisition of vast new territory containing enormous stores of natural resources further reinforced the long-held notion of inexhaustible natural resources requiring little or no conservation.

If one is to find the roots of what was later to grow into the American conservation movement, one must seek it in the writings of the first American wilderness mystics, that is, the persons who perceived the wildlands as possessing mystical properties that would provide the models of the good life for those who sought values above and beyond those of the market place. The dean of such persons was Henry David Thoreau, whose book *Walden* is now a treasured American literary classic as well as the most eloquent early exposition of the cult of the wilderness.

Thoreau appealed not to the pragmatic conservationist but to those persons disturbed by the growth of cities and industry and weary of lives too much concerned "with getting and spending." Thoreau spoke in a manner that transcended his age and perhaps even the message he sought to convey. This may be illustrated by a quote from his essay "Walking." His words seem to carry a contemporary message to many of us in this last quarter of the twentieth century. "I wish," said Thoreau, "to speak a word for nature, for absolute freedom and wildness, as contrasted with a freedom and culture merely civil,—to regard man as an inhabitant, or a part and parcel of nature, rather than a member of society."

There is an aspect of Thoreau that makes him typical of most of the important figures of American conservation. He was a townsman who had received—for the time—an excellent education that would not have been obtainable in other than an urban area or one dependent on such an area. Throughout the history of American conservation it has been the urban person who has "discovered" nature and been able to articulate this discovery that has been in the vanguard of the conservation movement. Another aspect of Thoreau's appeal continues to be an important element of the conservation movement and that is the mystical belief that one must seek the nature of meaning and truth about existence in the wildlands because such is not to be discovered in the clutter and confusion of cultural and, particularly, urban landscapes. It was this view, expounded in his most famous book, *Walden: Or Life in the Woods,* that continues to motivate many persons involved in lay and even professional conservation work. Closely allied with the mystical attributes of *Walden* is a moralistic or ethical element that remains a highly visible component of many conservation efforts all over the world.

Something like an organized, recognizable, conservation movement did not appear in the United States until the beginning of the twentieth century but some important groundwork was laid in the previous half century—and one must not overlook the somewhat isolated efforts of those persons who even earlier brought attention to the loss of soils and other resources. The 35 years marking the period between the close of the American Civil War and the beginning of the twentieth century were not years to be identified by a marked increase in national concern for natural resources. This period was one of the most destructive of natural resources in this nation's history. Forest destruction reached a fearsom scale with unrestrained clearcutting and wildfires common features. The Sacramento River, in California, became clogged with sediments washed down from the Sierran foothills by hydraulic gold mining operations. The nation's game bird and mammal resources were subjected to virtually unrestricted slaughter by commercial market hunters. During the winter, when freezing temperatures held meat in a fresh condition, entire train carloads of ducks, pigeons, and other animals were sent to the large urban markets. Bison were slaughtered by the hundreds of thousands for their hides, which were in fashion for use in horsedrawn vehicles during the winter. Untold numbers of bison were left to rot on the prairies having only yielded up their hides although some also had their tongues cut out and shipped east to a market appreciative of this gourmand delight. The bones accumulating from this slaughter were so abundant that some persons made a profitable business of going over the grasslands and gathering them. These were later loaded onto railroad cars and sent to factories where they were reduced to bone-meal for fertilizer and other uses.

The legal claimants of the bison resource, the Plains Indians, were made the object of official U.S. Government concern which, in practice, led to the loss of land and resources as well as their own lives. One American Army officer, General W. T. Sherman, though not heretofore accorded a place in the field of applied ecology, perceived the central ecological position of the bison in Plains Indian cultures and encouraged the slaughter of the bison as being an efficacious means of bringing the Indians to heel. Sherman's characterization of these Indi-

ans as the "vermin of the Plains" was widely shared at the time by the whites who used every possible means to divest the Indians of their lands and other natural resources. The Indians proved not to be without their well wishers in the urban intellectual community and in 1881, Helen Hunt Jackson published her highly emotional polemic on behalf of the Indian, *A Century of Dishonor*. Like many publications of this genre, Jackson's book was often long on emotion and short on factual detail but it was influential in certain federal legislative circles. These persons sought to save the Indians by converting them from "savage hunting" to a life of settled agriculture. Then the whites decided that the best route to take would be to convert the Indians into whites or at least convert them from Indian culture to a white culture. The vehicle for this decision was the Dawes Act passed by Congress in 1887. Allowing for the well-meaning intentions of the Act's author, its chief effect was to hasten the destruction of the remaining Indian societies.

Although Sherman heralded the destruction of the bison as a means to subjugate the remaining Indians hostile to U.S. regulation there were a few persons who began to perceive the possibility that the commercial slaughter might result in extermination of this animal that once numbered in the millions. Most influential of these persons was William T. Hornaday who, in 1889, wrote *The Extermination of the American Bison* in which he emphasized the need to protect the remaining animals lest the species become extinct. Hornaday's was not the first publication by a reputable biologist pointing to the plight of the bison but his publication appears to have been the proximate stimulus leading to legislation that gave the remaining animals total federal protection.

In many respects, the most impressive person in this period was George Perkins Marsh, who in 1874 published *Man and Nature; or Physical Geography as Modified by Human Action*. This book detailed large parts of the history of human-induced environmental changes from classical times to his day. The book focused chiefly on parts of Europe but the message was clear: what has happened elsewhere can also happen here (and in fact had and was). This book greatly influenced the early identifiable conservation movement in the United States but it appears more likely that its message was not fully appreciated until that movement was well underway. In any event, the book can be read today for its content since it is still relevant to many contemporary conservation issues.

One of the most important of what might be termed the early pragmatic conservationists was John Wesley Powell. A seriously wounded veteran of the Civil War (he lost an arm in that conflict), Powell obtained the post of professor of geology at Illinois Wesleyan University. There he began a series of studies on the Grand Canyon and arid regions of the southwest. This work resulted, in 1878, in a report sent to the U.S. House of Representatives. The principal thrust of this report was that certain parts of the southwest could be developed for irrigation farming providing such development was made possible by federal financing. Powell's arguments were met with mixed responses with the result that little measurable movement was made in the direction he espoused. However, when he became Director of the U.S. Geological Survey (1881) he was in a better position to press his ideas and these efforts led, in 1902, to the still highly controversial Federal Reclamation Act (see Chapter nine).

The growing magnitude of natural resource destruction in the waning decades of the nineteenth century prompted private and government entities to begin efforts to save a part of America's natural heritage. In 1872 the federal government established Yellowstone National Park by an Act signed by President U.S. Grant. This was the first in what was to become a National Park Movement. These efforts were to be emulated by other nations and the United States is properly accorded the honor of having begun the now world trend of establishing national parks in which public use is restricted.

By the end of the nineteenth century the concept of governmental responsibility for much of the nation's natural resources had gained a measure of respectability and it was within this ambience that Theodore Roosevelt appeared and to whom is frequently accorded the honor of having started the modern conservation movement. Roosevelt's concerns covered both the pragmatic and moralistic aspects of conservation and thus protagonists of both views had his ear. He was sensitive to pleas that representative portions of the nation's wilderness areas be preserved for esthetic enjoyment as he was also aware of the need to develop conservation programs designed to permit the long-term utilization of the nation's natural resources. Gifford Pinchot, a forester, was selected by Roosevelt to launch the new conservation efforts.

Pinchot was admirably suited to the task of organizing a conservation movement being a person of great energy, possessed of considerable administrative ability and with a flair for publicizing his work and the work of his associates. Pinchot received his professional forestry training in France, there having been no advanced forestry training in the United States. It was Pinchot who founded the Yale University School of Forestry. Although Pinchot's work was based on a secure educational background, the fact that he was a skilled politician (as, of course, was Teddy Roosevelt) may well have been as instrumental in his having made conservation a popular and respected endeavor. Although his principal area of interest was forest conservation he was influential over much of the entire range of conservation concerns during his active life.

Pinchot was above all a member of the pragmatist school of conservationists and viewed forests as resources to be used with care and scientific guidance. This view early brought him into conflict with those who tended to view forests not in terms of resources to be harvested but as wilderness areas to be preserved. Most notable of the conflicts that arose was that which developed between Pinchot and John Muir. Often referred to as the "poet of the Sierras," Muir was the epitome of the mystic who viewed wilderness areas not as sources of raw materials but as being more akin to religious temples. It was Muir's persuasive writings and lectures that figured most prominently in getting Yosemite Valley set aside in 1890 as a national park. For Muir the wilderness was the manifestation of God's work and he more than once expressed the view that only through achieving rapport with the wilderness could humans attain heaven as the following quote illustrates, "The clearest way into the universe is through a forest wilderness." Not for Muir were works of humans in the wilderness for he firmly believed that only through our continued access to wilderness could a basic human need to commune with nature, be assured. Pinchot, though not entirely lacking in appreciation for the thoughts and ideals of Muir, looked on forests much as a farmer looks at fields, that is, as crops to be managed and harvested. The sharp dichotomy of views as evidenced by these two giants in the formative years of the conservation movement in the United States is often very much with the movement today.

## UNITED STATES: TWENTIETH CENTURY

Theodore Roosevelt, while being sympathetic to the ideas expressed by Muir and his adherents also shared with Pinchot the pragmatist view that our nation required natural resources and was going to get and use them one way or another. Thus, the principal task of conservation appeared to be one of devising intelligent constraints on the use of the nation's natural resources through the promulgation of legislation. First, however, it was necessary to obtain something of a consensus from representatives of the nation's leadership as it then existed. To this end, in 1908 Roosevelt convened a White House Conference of Governors. The Conference included far more than just the states' governors, however. Among the invited were the Supreme Court justices, the president and vice president of the United States, representatives of most of the major scientific and conservation groups, members of both houses of Congress, and certain leaders of U.S. industry and commerce. In the following year, a North American Conservation Conference was held in Washington, D.C., which was noteworthy chiefly because representatives of Mexico and Canada joined those from the United States in a declaration of the mutual interests of the three nations with regard to the conservation of forests, water, lands, minerals, game, and as the primary consideration, public health. Under the latter heading was water pollution. Indeed, in the Declaration, public health and clean water were treated as being synonymous. The Conference ended with the plea that a world conservation conference be held. These international aims and aspirations did not find fruition. However, recently there has been a trend toward international involvement in conservation and management of natural resources. Among some of the organizations so involved are the United Nations, the International Union for the Conservation of Nature and Natural Resources, and the World Wildlife Fund. These and other organizations sponsor activities designed to identify, study, and manage the natural resources of all nations.

The early governmental concern with forests has already been noted. Petroleum conservation was given some attention, especially with regard to the practice of "flaring off" natural gas in petroleum fields (allowing the gas to burn without making any use of it a practice that led to the loss of untold billions of cubic feet of what is now seen as one of our most valuable energy resources). There was also fear in the early years of this century that the petroleum resource was being used at such a rate that the nation would soon be without oil and its derived products. However, the discovery of enormous fields in Texas as well as the discovery of vast petroleum deposits in other parts of the world soon put to rest any concern about the need to conserve oil.

Soils and water were, however, different matters. The nation had a long history (unfortunately still not ended) of gross misuse of the soil resource in agricultural and pastoral activities (see Chapter six). The growing population, together with an almost explosive growth in industry and commerce, placed ever increasing demands on the nation's freshwater supplies and particularly so in the semiarid and arid region of the West and Southwest, the areas that occupied Powell's energies.

If there is a modern "father" of soil conservation it is surely Hugh Hammond Bennett. Although by no means the first American to be concerned for the nation's soils (see Chapter six), Bennett was the most important individual in this century with respect to the establishing of federal as well as state and local agencies designed to reduce soil loss and to improve soil use in general. The decade of the 1930s marked the establishment of a Soils Service as a part of the Department of Agriculture.

From at least the time of Powell's efforts in the West and the establishment by Congress of the 1902 Reclamation Act interest and attention was given increasingly to the matter of water conservation and development in the West. The 1930s, a decade of national and international economic depression, stimulated the federal government to spend large sums of money on major water impoundment schemes. The largest of these was the construction of Hoover Dam on the Colorado River. Other mammoth dam-building projects designed to conserve water against the years of drought as well as to provide drinking and irrigation water and hydroelectricity multiplied in the same region.

During World War II and in the years immediately after the conservation movement slowed for a time but then again gathered force as various writers began to inform the nation regarding the threatened state of its natural resources. Although this literary genre was not new, these writings also frequently carried a global message thus marking an important development in the twentieth-century conservation movement. Among the widely read books on these themes was *Road to Survival* by William Vogt, which appeared in 1948. This widely read book strongly detailed the growing ecological crises not only of America but of the entire planet. Although the message of Vogt and others reached many persons it appears that the implications of what they had to say were often rejected as being too pessimistic and downbeat in a time when the nation and much of the rest of the world were attempting to rebuild from the chaos of the war. Nevertheless, the evidence of ecological trouble continued to increase and even the most determinedly myopic had to recognize that there were some serious problems associated with the nation's natural resources and their patterns of utilization.

By 1960 a growing share of the public was becoming aware that soaring demand for manufactured goods and the explosive increases in the demand for and consumption of energy were creating some very serious environmental problems. Many of these problems were not at all new. Some, like air pollution, had been around in parts of the world for centuries. But the magnitude and the diversity of the problems led to a growing sense of unease among many persons who in earlier years had paid scant attention to the quality of the environment or how natural resources were exploited. Before the decade of the 1960s came to a close a new and major chapter in the history of American natural resource conservation and management had been written.

Many things contributed to making the decade of the 1960s the national decade of the environment and one seeks in vain for the single trigger mechanism that started what is now called "the environmental movement." The environmental movement, of course, is a continuation of the conservation movement and does not mark something entirely new. This phase of the conservation movement differs, however, in a very important respect from earlier phases. Until the 1960s, the U.S. conservation movement was chiefly the activity and concern of a comparatively small number of well-educated and affluent persons. More than one of the leading conservation organizations had few of any minority race members. Conservation was one of the "good works" in which the affluent person might engage. Of course, insofar as government agencies were concerned, there was a pragmatic and to a large degree democratic approach to conservation. Nevertheless, conservation did not become the people's concern until the 1960s.

What happened in that decade to take conservation out of the club rooms and into the more proletarian sectors of the nation? As indicated earlier, no one reason can be identified but among the several factors that appear to be important are the very large numbers of young people in high schools and colleges; a large groundswell of youthful dissatisfaction with many of the material values of their parents; the leisure available for millions of young people to reflect on their individual as well as collective prospects for the "good life" and a growing concern as to what that consisted of; the war in Vietnam, which threatened the young men of college age with the military draft and the prospect of service in a war that many of them as well as many of their elders rejected as being unnecessary and contrary to the nation's publicly stated love of peace; the publication in 1962 of Rachel Carson's *Silent Spring,* a book that provided the flame that ignited the environmental movement and whose impact was almost explosive. In a calm and only seldom pejorative prose Carson detailed what was then known about the biological effects of DDT and other insecticide applications on crop lands and wildlands. Her title bespoke the possibility that unless such applications were halted there would come a springtime made silent because all the birds would have died because of direct and indirect poisoning. A massive and often thoroughly unethical attack was mounted in some quarters against the book but it stood up fairly well and it was clear that its basic message could only be ignored to our peril.

Research on the biological effects of insecticides greatly increased as did research into a growing number of subjects that had to do with the impact of manufactured substances on the soil, water, and air as well as living organisms. As the data began to accumulate, it became increasingly clear that Carson, far from being an exaggerating prophet of ecological disaster, could be faulted, if at all, for having been too restrained. Before the close of the decade the huge dimensions of our past misuse and continuing misuse of natural resources was becoming clear and with this increasing clarity greater concerns were being expressed about how much of the nation's natural resources remained. Additional concern was being generated regarding human population growth. The demographic concerns of Malthus were exhumed leading to, among things, the founding of Zero Population Growth, Inc. in 1968, an organization that seeks to reduce the rate of human population growth of the nation (and the world) to zero. This group and many other persons see the growth of human numbers as being at or near the root of our resource problems (Chapter three).

Another very important attribute of this latest phase in the conservation movement is the concern for the quality of our environments. In previous decades attention was, as you have seen, focused on saving parts of the natural resources and/or management and utilization of the resources. To these historic concerns was added concern for quality with especial concern for air and water. Air, until just a few years ago, was seldom even mentioned in any book dealing with conservation but that is no longer the case. At present, improving air quality is a major concern of several federal and state agencies and the economic impact of these efforts is enormous. Until recently water conservation referred to quantity with the addition that water destined for domestic uses had to meet certain public health standard with regard to pathogenic organisms present. Today, water quality has emerged to be at least the coequal of the older concerns of water conservation.

The concern for environmental quality is frequently expressed as the quality of life. At this point it becomes almost impossible to identify and or follow the multitude of often conflicting views and values held by this or that protagonist as to the identifying criteria of a quality life insofar as such relates to the biological and physical environments. This present confusion may be due to the fact that we are living in an era when many time-honored value systems are being challenged but as yet no widely agreed on criteria for such a life have emerged. We ought to watch these developments carefully because it is from this area of human action, the area of values and value judgments, that the future trends of conservation will emerge.

In the meantime, environmentalism is politically respectable and even necessary. If one still harbors doubts as to the potential political power of the masses of citizens of our nation, that person need only look at the phenomenal political-legislative response at federal and other governmental levels. Before the decade of the 1960s concluded, Congress passed the Environmental Protection Act, which created the Environmental Protection Agency. This federal agency, although frequently beset by lobbying forces that threaten its very existence, has thus far withstood the pressures and is writing a major new chapter in the nation's efforts to conserve its natural resources.

The decade of the 1970s may prove to be the international decade of the environment. On April 22, 1970, the first observance of Earth Day took place, which has been described as the greatest concentration of environmental awareness in U.S. history. In February 1971, Richard Nixon presented a State of the World message in which he asked for the means to control environmental pollution and, in the same address, pledged the cooperation of the United States for the 1972 International Conference in Stockholm, Sweden, at which global environmental problems were to be the main items on the agenda. During that decade there was a growing awareness of the environmental limits of the planet leading to such characterizations as "spaceship earth." Scholars from many fields began research efforts designed to determine what, if any, are the limits to growth.

Perhaps the most significant development of that environmentally active decade was the increased awareness that the world's economies and hence its natural resources are intertwined. This heightened awareness owed itself to many factors of which the most important were the rise of a new international economic order of multinational corporations and the trauma sustained by the oil crisis. Also brought into far sharper focus than ever before was the economic and social situations of the Third World although it must be noted that this has thus far led to little alteration in the previously established relationships between the developed and underdeveloped nations.

It is not cynical to suggest that the oil crisis was the catalyst that galvanized the attention of millions of persons who had previously given little if any thought to energy resources. When the lifeblood of our industrial society was suddenly threatened, awareness of energy's central role in society moved to the fore. Conservation of energy became the key theme in conservation efforts at many levels but a more somber note was also being sounded, this being the growing threat to the environment if certain alternatives to oil—principally coal and nuclear power—were to be given a greatly increased role in national and international energy production. Energy sources seen as less damaging to the environment (e,g., solar) were strongly pushed by conservationists but often given little attention by others.

As the decade of the 1980s unfolds we are being increasingly reminded that the price of good conservation of our nation's natural resources is eternal vigilance. What Congress gives in one administration can be taken away in another. Thus, more than ever before, it becomes our responsibility to be informed and to vote our concerns and to legally express our concerns whenever opportunity is presented to do so.

## SUMMARY

Humans have a long history and prehistory of concerns for natural resources. The first efforts directed toward conservation seem to have been for the purpose of protecting wild animals like deer for the purpose of hunting them by elites. Although the place and time of origin of hunting preserves are not known they became widespread in the Mediterranean region more than 2000 years ago and it was the Romans who later spread the custom into Western Europe.

The development of formal hunting and fishing regulations appeared first in parts of Western Europe in the seventh century A.D. These early hunting and fishing rules carried extremely cruel penalties for noncompliance.

With the passage of time, not only the aristocracy had hunting preserves but also a developing wealthy merchant class, especially in England. Although private preserves still occur in Europe and many other parts of the world, the trend has been strongly toward democratizing hunting and fishing and to convert formerly private preserves into public areas.

Conservation of other than animal resources was much slower to develop at least insofar as serious management is concerned. For example, the first school of forestry was established in the nineteenth century in Spain.

Turning to the American experience, colonists encountered an extraordinary abundance of fish, game, forests and land. This gave rise to a widespread notion that these resources and others were inexhaustible: little if any thought was given to resource conservation.

The roots of what later came to be called the conservation movement are found in the nineteenth century and particularly in the writings of Henry David Thoreau who urged a mystical approach to the appreciation of nature. During the second half of the nineteenth century activities that are clearly identifiable as a nascent effort toward conserving some of the nation's natural resources were underway. Notable among these was the establishment of Yellowstone National Park in 1872.

By the end of the nineteenth century the idea that the federal government had a responsibility to conserve or manage at least some of the nation's natural resources had gained a measure of respectability, and in 1902 congress passed the Reclamation Act, which provided federal support for water development in the West. The amount of land, irrigated by such water, that a single person or married couple could own was limited to 160 acres and 320 acres, respectively.

The modern conservation movement is generally seen to have been launched during the presidential administration (1901–1909) of Theodore Roosevelt. His principal lieutenant in these conservation endeavors was the nation's first professionally trained forester, Gifford Pinchot.

Pinchot's concept of conservation was that resources were to be used "wisely" for the good of the nation. This clashed with the views held by such staunch "preservationists" as John Muir, who wished to *preserve* as much wilderness as possible including the National Forest lands then coming into existence. In general, Pinchot's position prevailed.

Although the nation's forests were on the way to receiving an important measure of conservation this was not the case with some other natural resources and especially the nation's soils. In spite of a long history of accelerated soil erosion, no organized attempt at the federal level to conserve and manage the soil resource was undertaken until well into the twentieth century. The pioneer figure in these efforts was Hugh H. Bennett and it was he who was chiefly instrumental in the founding of the Soil Conservation Service in the 1930s. That progress notwithstanding, major yet preventable losses of soil continue to the present.

The most recent major development in the conservation movement was the environmental movement that had began immediately after World War II. This most recent phase of the conservation movement is distinctive in being far more broadly based in American society than were the earlier phases. In addition, far more phenomena were brought under the umbrella of conservation as, for example, water quality, air pollution, concern for endangered species of plants and animals, the "quality" of life, energy consumption, and the protection of entire ecological systems.

The environmental movement has stimulated governmental bodies to pass much legislation aimed at achieving ecologically sound uses of natural resources. Not everyone agrees that this has been a desirable trend and there is an increasingly well-organized and well-financed opposition to further environmental legislation as well as frequent attempts to weaken legislation already enacted.

While it is apparent that significant conservation gains have been achieved during the past 125 years, much remains to be accomplished. One is often reminded that what one legislative body may enact to protect the nation's natural resources another, later, legislative body may undo. We are learning that the conservation of our natural resources requires, like liberty, eternal vigilance, unflagging energy, and a resolve to achieve and maintain needed conservation measures. Conservation also requires that there be an overwhelming majority of citizens who share the view that one has a moral obligation to treat the earth and all that lives on it with reverence and respect.

# human population and natural resources

The first U.S. Textbook on conservation *The Conservation of Natural Resources in the United States,* was by Professor Charles Richard Van Hise and was published in 1910. Van Hise's book consisted chiefly of a series of lectures he had previously delivered at the University of Wisconsin, Madison, on the subject of conservation of natural resources in the United States. The topics he covered would be familiar to all students today with the possible exception of the concluding chapter in which he spoke of a need to "conserve man himself" and to this end he focused his remarks on human disease and life expectancy. His basic argument was that human life expectancy was too short and that it was a desirable goal of conservation to extend the number of years the average person might live and this was to be accomplished chiefly through an improvement in the control of disease.

More than 70 years have passed and there is still great concern among many persons with respect to human population but the concern is usually stated in terms of a fear of too many people . . . of a population that strains the world's resource base. The control of disease that was Van Hise's hope has been extraordinarily successful. In his day diphtheria, whooping cough, poliomyelitis, typhoid, measles, streptococcus infections, and other diseases were common threats to children and contributed to a life expectancy at birth of about

48 years for males and 45 years for females. Today, in the age of antibiotics, the life expectancies at birth for males and females are approximately 69 and 77 years, respectively. In other industrialized nations the figures are even a bit higher but in the poor nations and in the poor regions of well-to-do nations the figures are sometimes even lower than those for the United States at the beginning of the twentieth century.

The widely felt concern in our day for the rapid growth of human numbers is not unique to our times but is a concern that dates back to 1798 when Thomas Robert Malthus, an English economist, published *An Essay on the Principle of Population as it Affects the Future Improvement of Society, With Remarks on the Speculations of Mr. Godwin, M. Condorcet, and Other Writers.* The principal idea expressed in this essay was that human population tends to increase geometrically (i.e., exponentially) whereas food production increases only arithmetically and therefore there is always present in human populations a tendency to increase in number beyond food production sufficient to feed the population unless the population growth is halted by disease, famine, warfare, or other population-limiting phenomena. In later editions, Malthus sharpened his arguments and brought to them more data to support his premises. His views were not well received by many of the educated persons of his day—although it appears that Charles Darwin found in Malthus the "key" to his theory of natural selection—and Malthus' prediction that it is the lot of humankind to suffer periodic catastrophes because of recurrent overpopulation became increasingly discredited as world agricultural production increased at rates that were occasionally exponential rather than arithmetic. This surge was due to major improvements on crop plants and agricultural methods and to the fact that hitherto unfarmed regions in North America and elsewhere became major contributors to the world's food supply.

In the midst of the great growth in food production the dreary prognostications of Malthus were quickly forgotten or recalled only as the eccentric maunderings of a pessimist. With the passage of the nineteenth century and well into the twentieth century it frequently appeared as though the only population problem was a lack of sufficient numbers of persons to staff all the jobs needed being done in an exploding industrialization. More than one nation's government expressed public alarm at what were perceived as being too-low birth rates. Some nations took the step of offering financial inducements to married people to produce children. Some nations still do this—including the United States. Although at present in the United States there is no official alarm that the birth rate is too low (such alarm *was* raised in the United States in the 1930s, however) the income tax policy of state and federal agencies allows a deduction for each child in a family.

A few years past the conclusion of World War II, however, some articles and an occasional book appeared that contained warnings of an impending population explosion. These publications generally directed their concern to the poor nations taking for granted, it seems, that the rich nations had no population difficulties. Informed persons throughout the world began to take a greater interest in global matters including interest in the numbers of humans present and the numbers being born and dying each year. The United Nations began to keep ever more accurate population data (although even today there are nations where a reliable census of humans is yet to be taken) and to make these data widely available. Besides national agencies, private groups came into being having as their object the monitoring of human population growth and the projecting of such growth into the decades ahead. The picture that emerged from all these efforts was world human population increasing at an unprecedented rate (at least for the time since written historical records have been kept) and the fact that the rates of annual increase for some regions (e.g., Latin America) were so high as to merit the adjective "explosive."

Although persons in a variety of professions became interested and concerned it was biologists who appear to have been particularly influential in creating a more general public concern for population growth than had been achieved before. This is not to say that professional demographers had not been active. Indeed it is the work of these professionals that provided the crusading biologists with most of the data they used and are using. It may be that biologists were effective in spreading the overpopulation message because it is fundamental to a biologist's education to be familiar with the explosive possibilities of exponential growth and it was the exponential growth of human numbers against a base of historically unprecedented size that captured the attention of many a biologist who previously had worked in subject areas seemingly far removed from the hurly burly of human demographic projections and analyses.

So many persons have been (and are) associated with the current concern for human population growth that it is difficult to select some for discussion without appearing to slight the contributions of others. However, three persons have been particularly active in the United States and these will serve to describe the concerns and activities of the much larger group.

First is William Vogt whose 1948 book, *Road to Survival,* was mentioned earlier. Although not a professional biologist, Vogt's major contribution in this and other publications was to identify the rapidly increasing rates of human population growth in various Latin American nations and to encourage those nations to embark upon population control programs. Vogt for years was the proverbial "voice in the wilderness" but he lived to see more and more persons in Latin America share his views and to see some efforts directed toward reducing fertility in that region.

Second is Paul Ehrlich, a biologist. In 1965 Ehrlich published *The Population Bomb,* a book that gained an enormous international readership and that had and still has considerable public impact. The fundamental message of the book is that the world's population is growing at such a rate against such a large base that, unless stabilized, it will lead to international chaos. Ehrlich's views while warmly received in some quarters were rejected in others as being alarmist. Although the book was written for a mass audience and thus does not always conform to scientific writing its fundamental data are sound. Ehrlich's concern with the growth of human numbers led him to help found the organization Zero Population Growth, Inc. As the title implies, the organization has as its chief object the stabilization of human population on a national and a world level.

The third person is Garrett Hardin, also a biologist. In 1964 Hardin published *Population, Evolution, and Birth Control: A Collage of Controversial Ideas,* in which he presented a collection of already published materials and commented upon them in articles and editorials of his own authorship. In 1977 *Managing the Commons,* a collection of original as well as previously published materials, appeared. In these publications Hardin's message is very clear: human population growth poses a major threat to humanity and world order and therefore no effort should be spared to bring the growth in human numbers under control. Most notable in Hardin's arguments is what some persons perceive as a hardboiled attitude vis-à-vis nations whose rates of population increase, in Hardin's view, are so high as to threaten the continued existence of the world's natural systems. Although the adjective fearless" is somewhat overworked it does apply most accurately to Hardin's unrelenting and unequivocal argument that humans are subject to the same biological laws as other living organisms and that not to take the necessary measures to check our population growth is wrong and derives largely from ignorance, superstition, and mores that no longer serve the best interests of humanity.

Arrayed against those who firmly believe that there is indeed a "population bomb" ticking away with ever greater urgency are many persons who are not persuaded that a population problem exists. Some of these people derive their positions from religious commitment. Others derive their views from Marxian positions that hold that the problem is not one of overpopulation but inadequate distribution of the world's resources. Still others interpret the human historical experience to be one of continued growth of productivity and human numbers and view the current concern about overpopulation as a peculiar aberration suffered by certain occupants of the academic "ivory tower." Let us examine some of these views.

Beginning with religion we encounter an area that is essentially impervious to argument directed along scientific lines. Not every religion contains dogma respecting human reproduction and even within some religious organizations there are widely varying responses to official positions respecting fertility control. The Roman Catholic Church has long been identified as the principal Western religious institution forbidding all but the most minimal (and most unreliable) techniques of birth control. Although the Vatican has scarcely wavered on this point it is clear that a wide variation of opinion exists among the Catholic clergy with respect to birth control and perhaps more important it is clear that significant (and growing?) numbers of the Catholic laity are ignoring papal pronouncements and practice birth control using methods that are officially prohibited by the Church. Among poor people and in the poorer nations, where population growth is often greatest and where the nominal faith is chiefly Roman Catholic there appears to be a somewhat greater willingness to comply with the official Church position vis-à-vis birth control. However, it may be that of equal or greater importance are the traditional mores and attitudes that tend to largely govern fertility in human societies. By this is meant such phenomena as the belief that it is a woman's natural destiny to have as many children as she is biologically capable, that a man's virility is best measured by the number of children he is responsible for begetting, that numerous children offer solace and economic security when their parents become aged, and not to be overlooked is that children are seen as a special delight. Thus, sometimes hidden within what may appear to be religious control are other factors that may be subject to modification through education. But in those instances where there is a conscious feeling of guilt with respect to religion and birth control practices it is extremely difficult to alter fertility.

The religious complex known as Hinduism does not expressly forbid the use of contraceptives and thus permits an avenue of approach to disseminating birth control information. Certain aspects of that religion, however, do tend to stimulate fertility and chief of these is the high value given to the production of male children with a contrasting low regard for the production of female children. One of the reasons for this attitude is the belief that a man's funeral pyre must be lighted by one of his sons if the deceased is to achieve his next incarnation.

With regard to the Marxist position it can best be summarized by the belief, noted earlier, that there can be no overpopulation, only a poor distribution of resources. Fortunately, reason sometimes does prevail as witness the example of China. With a population base of one billion the Chinese government has adopted many measures that have the aimed-for effect of reducing fertility. During the many post-1949 revolutionary throes in that nation there has been some vacillation with respect to the official government position on birth control, but at present little or no vacillation is evident and in spite of their commitment to Karl Marx the government makes it abundantly clear that population control is desired.

In the United States, particularly, arguments to control growth of human numbers and growth of resource use falls on many an unreceptive ear not because the person is religiously or politically turned away but from a conviction that we and the world are nowhere near the limits of natural resources nor near the limits of technological solutions. Population growth is seen not as a growing danger but in terms of larger and larger potential numbers of consumers of goods produced from what are seen as inexhaustible resources. Any problems we encounter can be "fixed" by the development of new technology and the discovery of new sets of resources. Before one rejects this position it is well to note the following: in terms of the human experience over thousands of years it has been the development of new technologies and the development of previously unperceived resources that have paved the way to achieving levels of material comfort and lengthened life spans undreamed of even a couple of centuries ago. Certainly, if one confines one's view to the past, the arguments of those predicting population explosions and ecological chaos appear ridiculous, fainthearted, and destructive.

It is the principal task, therefore, of all concerned with the current unprecedented growth in human numbers to show that much of the past success to which we point with pride has had a very limited run on earth. The great technical success we as a species have enjoyed has lasted but a tiny fraction of the total time *Homo sapiens* has been present and may be considered, in many of its aspects, to be essentially ephemeral especially if the carefully considered warnings raised by competent scientists and other scholars are ignored. What are the factual bases for these warnings? In the next section we will review some local and global aspects of human population and will suggest what the demographic conditions may be within the next 20 to 50 years.

It is one of the world's singular paradoxes that accurate head counts of our species are, in general, very recent and this in spite of the fact that at least since governments discovered taxation counting citizens has had a decided economic value. It appears that China was the first to produce a fairly accurate census this being in 2 A.D. under the Han dynasty. The next notable example of census taking is that of the Romans who gave us the word *census*. There was no continuation of the Roman census practices after the decline of the Empire and early European history provides only local and sporadic attempts to make head counts. In the eighteenth century, census taking became common in some parts of Europe although the first official *national* census of England was not taken until 1801 it having been resisted in previous centuries.

Something at least approaching the idea of the census of human numbers developed in at least two parts of the pre-Columbian New World. In the Mexican region tribes subject to the Aztecs were required to pay tribute in natural resources (e.g., feathers, honey) according to the number of households. These tribute lists were used at a later date by conquering Spaniards. In the central Andes of South America, the Inca more or less enumerated their subjects for tax and other purposes. In neither instance, however, should one confuse these head counts with accurate modern censuses.

In the United States the first federal census was taken in 1790 and it has been repeated every 10 years since. The principal reason for initiating this was to assure correct numerical representation in the House of Representatives. Over the years the range of data collected has been increased beyond head counts and the ages of persons censused.

Prior to 1900, Latin America was almost uncensused with the notable exception of New Spain (later Mexico). Toward the end of the eighteenth century a census was taken that indicated a population of approximately 6.5 million persons in New Spain. For most of the succeeding decades only estimates are available unitl 1920 when census taking became relatively accurate in Mexico and most of Latin America and has become increasingly so with each succeeding census.

Prior to the European colonial period in sub-Saharan Africa there are no known censuses. Modern counts are a very recent phenomenon and some countries have yet to conduct a census that is reliably accurate. Southern Asia, similarly, has only recently begun to make accurate head counts although one does find exceptions as for example in the former Dutch East Indies (Indonesia) where beginning early in the nineteenth century the Dutch on Java began to keep very accurate records of the population including births and deaths and other associated data.

In summary, deliberate counting of people including births and deaths and other pertinent demographic information is, with few exceptions, no more recent than the nineteenth century and for many large parts of the earth even more recent.

It is important, therefore, to realize that only very limited hard demographic data are available for most of the time humans have been present on earth. This situation has required some very sophisticated detective cum statistical work on the part of historical demographers to unravel the human demographic past.

Noting these difficulties, however, we may proceed to examine, briefly, the broad outlines of human demographic history prior to the twentieth century.

The first fact we confront and one that is of more than passing significance is that for most of the time that the genus *Homo* has been on earth it has been a comparatively rare creature. Various scholars have attempted to assess the total human population circa one million years ago and all conclude that the total was modest. In 1960 Edward S. Deevey, Jr. estimated that there was a world total of 125,000. A million years ago there were no humans in the Americas, Australia, and much of Eurasia. Continuing with Deevey's estimates, population growth was slow through long intervals of time but occasionally significant increases occurred with the advent of new technology, for example, the invention and diffusion of agriculture, the modern Industrial Revolution, and the invention and diffusion of modern medicine. Although the trend in total numbers through time continued upward there were many events over the years which temporarily reduced human numbers. Improved technology, particularly food-producing technology, provided much of the basis for the population increase but counterforces were at work to dampen what would have otherwise been explosive increments. Chief among these were diseases and particularly those affecting infants and children. Although we lack data directly relatable to most areas of the world prior to very recent times, it is possible to relate to the distant past certain recent conditions of infant mortality rates where poverty is great, education low, and medical facilities and health conditions are generally primitive. Infant mortality may seldom have been less than 300 per 1000 live births and a further toll was taken of children prior to puberty. Life spans (longevity) were apparently uniformly low—30 to 35 years on average until late in the nineteenth century.

The surge in population growth that began to occur in the nineteenth century owes itself to more than a single factor and one must be very cautious in attempting to relate cause to effect where these (and other) population statistics are concerned. However, there can be no doubt that one important cause of the accelerating increase was and is due to the medical revolution. Briefly, the medical revolution was the discovery that certain microorganisms play a basic role in disease and the development of techniques to combat the organisms and conditions in which the organisms proliferate and/or are transmitted to human hosts. Also included are scientific studies of human nutrition, human physiology in general, and the application of procedures designed to improve the conditions of human health in most parts of the world.

It is often overlooked that even in the early years of the twentieth century in technologically advanced nations such as the United States, infant mortality was still very high compared to modern standards. Infants, children, and adults regularly suffered from a wide range of serious diseases. Scarlet fever, diphtheria, whooping cough, human malaria, and other diseases were still commonplaces in the lives of many people in the United States. At the beginning of the twentieth century the life expectancy at birth in the United States was about 45 to 47 years. Today that expectancy is about 77 years for women and 69 years for men. Some women are still alive who lived through their childbearing years in the United States when it was not unusual to lose up to half of one's children to disease. If it be realized that the United States, Canada, and Western Europe were leading the world in the medical revolution at the beginning of this century one requires little imagination to conjure up the situation for the remaining greater part of humanity at that time.

The important fact to be noted here is that not only was *Homo sapiens* comparatively rare until recently but it has been only a matter of recent decades that our species has gained a series of major victories over disease. The human response to this enormous ecological change has lagged, perhaps understandably so, because the conventional wisdom vis-à-vis fertility for most of human time on earth required that we exert ourselves to multiply our numbers because we were, for a long time, an endangered species and fecundity was long our chief bulwark against extinction. Like the giant oil tankers that require many kilometers in which to stop and alter course because of their enormous inertia, the millenia-long habits respecting human fertility are not easily altered. *Mores,* religion, and other factors work to hold high the rate of human fertility even though the demographic charts indicate it is dangerous to do so.

The growth in human numbers in the years since 1850 have been truly astonishing. From an estimated 1.13 billion in 1850 the population increased in the next century to an estimated 2.49 billion in 1950. Since 1950 the increase has been as follows (estimated): 1960, 2.99 billion; 1970, 3.62 billion; 1980, 4.3 billion (Map 3.1, Table 3.1). Estimating future population growth is one of the most difficult tasks that demographers set for themselves because so many factors influence such growth. However, the United Nations (Concise Report) suggests that in the year 2000 the world's population will be 6.4 billion. It might be instructive (or perhaps shocking) to include here the U.N. projections for the first 75 years of the next century: 2025, 9.1 billion; 2050, 11.2 billion; 2075, 12.2 billion. With regard to the last estimate it can be noted that college students reading this will give birth to children who will live to experience that world of 12 billion people—about three times the current total.

Those total figures are difficult to comprehend and for many persons not trained to think in a global manner the figures relate to a geographical entity—the entire planet—which is of itself too large an entity to grasp easily and to think about as a unit (although global thinking must soon become a part of the intellectual equipment of every educated person). Thus it is important to note that insofar as population has an impact on resources, it is perhaps less the global total than the regional and national totals and rates of increase that are of the greater immediate concern.

Turning, then, to a consideration of regional population totals and rates of growth we can note the following important facts: the human population is very unevenly distributed over the earth and the rates of annual increase are also regionally and nationally varied. The regions having the greatest rates of increase are Latin

Table 3.1
**World population by major region, 1979 (est.)**

| Region | Population $\times 10^6$ | Annual Increase, % | Arithmetic Density (persons/km²) |
|---|---|---|---|
| World | 4336 | 1.8 | 32 |
| Africa | 456 | 2.7 | 15 |
| North America | 244 | 0.9 | 11 |
| Latin America | 359 | 2.6 | 17 |
| Asia | 2509 | — | 17 |
| Europe | 482 | 0.6 | 98 |
| Oceania | 22.5 | 1.8 | 3 |
| U.S.S.R | 264 | 0.8 | 12 |

*Source:* United Nations.

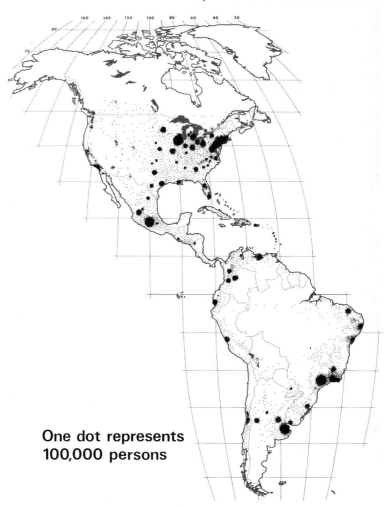

**One dot represents
100,000 persons**

America, Africa, the Middle East, and southern Asia. The United States, Canada, Western Europe, Japan, and the U.S.S.R. have lower rates of increase.

U.N. projections of future population growth indicate that Latin America, Africa, East Asia, and southern Asia are increasing much more rapidly than North America, the U.S.S.R., and Europe. To put this in perspective, it is the poorest nations that are having and are expected to continue having the highest rates of population increase at least until the year 2075. According to this U.N. projection, by the year 2000 the poor regions will have a total population only slightly less than the current world population. These projections ultimately may be shown to be wrong in either direction by some millions but given the care and caution that is generally exercised by the United Nations with respect to demographic projections, one can feel comfortable that these estimates are close to the actual mark, especially with respect to the year 2000 less than two decades distant.

We are still dealing with numbers alone and therefore must begin to refine our statements in order that population data can be related to

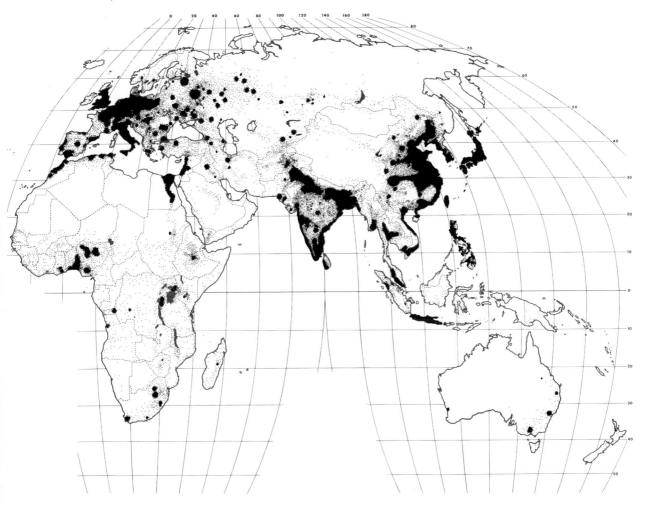

**Map 3.1** Human population distribution. One dot = 100,000 persons.

natural resources. One of the most frequently used measures is persons per unit of land area. This is the simple *arithmetic population density* arrived at by dividing the total human population into the total land area. Although such data provide one with a preliminary sense of population in relation to resources—in this case land area alone—it is in many ways misleading and geographically naive. A much better measure, for example, is the ratio of population to the total arable land. Refinements of this ratio are desirable, however, because it does not take into account such features as crop pro-

ductivity per hectare, numbers of people engaged in farming, percentage of food consumed in a nation compared to total food produced, and per capita nutritional characteristics. Be aware that crop production figures for almost all Third World nations are estimates because food produced for subsistence (not for sale) is seldom measured accurately even though it may constitute a very large share of the total agricultural production.

Great regional and national inequalities exist with respect to food production and per capita nutrition as well as the total quantity of arable land available. The greatest inequities are for the most part correlated with the Third World nations.

Consider the term *arable land,* for example. This seems quite clear as to meaning for it refers to land that is suited to cropping (sometimes land suited to pastures is included in this figure). A moment's attention to any map of the world's soils plus a little insight into the differences in crop producing potential among soils quickly leads one to correctly conclude that arable land is a rough generalization concealing the fact that some areas of the earth happen to be endowed with soils of great crop producing potential while other regions possess extremely limited soils.

Comparing, therefore, a map of the world's human population ranged against arable land to a map of soils will show that the physiological densities are far greater than is suggested by the person/arable land ratio.

Most of the current publications on population growth one encounters in the United States takes it as given that the chief areas of concern are the Third World nations because it is these that are presently experiencing the most rapid rates of growth on resource bases that are often deficient. The conclusion seems all too obvious. The poor nations are out–reproducing their resources and are thus posing a threat to the security and natural resources demanded by the wealthy nations. Taking this reasoning a step farther, it is argued in some quarters that we (the United States and presumably the other "have" nations) should withhold food shipments from those nations whose fertility is out of balance with their own food producing ability and resource bases. It has been suggested that certain nations ought to be considered nonsalvable and their pleas for food be ignored because they have gotten themselves into demographic conditions that no amount of outside help could alleviate. Other poor nations, whose demographic circumstances are judged to be not so catastrophic, are to receive food providing they adopt birth control measures deemed suited to whomever is going to make the judgments as to who shall starve and who shall not. Lest you think this kind of argument is little heard be assured that the opposite is the case and a virtual crescendo amounting to hysteria characterizes some of the proponents of this argument. Often overlooked in these presentations are the following counter arguments.

The developed world owes a significant part of its development to the natural resources it has acquired and continues to acquire from the poorer nations.

The developed countries have created much of the current and projected population-economic difficulties through a long history of purchasing resources at bargain prices, selling back manufactured goods at prices that have seldom if ever been a bargain.

Some nations in the developed world are themselves unable to feed their people from their own land—examples include Great Britain, the Netherlands, and Japan.

Many statements made regarding "overpopulation" are biased by ethnocentric value judgments.

There is the real possibility that the principal problem with respect to population and food is not one of production but in distribution of the world's annual food crop.

A large part of the apparent food shortfall in many of the poorer nations is due not to limited production but to inadequate protection against pests given to the harvested product.

If the emphasis is taken from food and placed on other resources such as petroleum, ferroalloys, and aluminum, the "overpopulated" nations are almost entirely the so-called developed nations.

Let us briefly take up some of these arguments and examine them.

**THE DEVELOPED WORLD OWES MUCH OF ITS DEVELOPMENT TO HAVING HAD ACCESS TO THE NATURAL RESOURCES OF THE THIRD WORLD** Europe, the United States, and Japan have had a history of acquiring an ever-increasing percentage of their raw materials as well as many agricultural products from Third World nations (or their colonial predecessors). Seldom have these resources been paid for at other than very low prices over which the individual exporting nations have had almost no control. The economic returns were and are seldom sufficient to permit change from an economic (and hence *socio*economic) situation that perpetuates economic uncertainty and subservience and which, for all intents and purposes, maintains social conditions in which high fertility continues to *appear* to be necessary. Lacking other than the minimal financial resources, social programs such as retirement benefits for the aged or increased capital investment to provide jobs are lacking and there is, understandably, little perceived value in limiting fertility.

The developed countries must also bear the responsibility for having energetically introduced virtually all the measures invented in the past 100 years that reduce human death rates among the young. The Third World nations have been and for the most part remain weak and politically ineffective in the international scene (with the major current exception of the Organization of Petroleum Exporting Countries—OPEC). Lacking organization and thus acting like myriad independent entrepreneurs in the "market place" they have been and remain vulnerable to the *limited number* of wealthy purchasers of their aluminum ore, bananas, coffee and other resources and productions. To aban-

don these people to famine by arguing that they alone got themselves into their demographic difficulties is a questionable proposition.

**SOME DEVELOPED NATIONS CAN'T FEED THEMSELVES** In the rhetoric of overpopulation and food production the fact that certain developed nations are parasitical with respect to food production is frequently ignored. Notable examples include Japan, Great Britain, the Soviet Union, and the Netherlands. None of those nations would survive long if shipments of basic foodstuffs—particularly grains—were denied them. The Netherlands, particularly among European nations, is dependent upon extranational sources to supply its food needs. According to one authority on Third World food supply problems, Georg Borgstrom, the Netherlands has been a *net* food importing nation for centuries. Are such nations, then, to be considered "basket cases" because they have not held their populations within acceptable bounds? Another extreme example is Japan's dependency on food imports. According to Borgstrom, Japan in the 1969 to 1970 period imported 99 percent of the corn (maize) it used, 80 percent of the wheat it used, 93 percent of the soybeans it used, and 39 percent of the meat it consumed. Even with respect to rice, 3 percent of its needs were imported. Should Japan, therefore be written off as a demographic pariah threatening the world's stability?

**THE ETHNOCENTRIC BIAS OF MANY STATEMENTS ABOUT OVERPOPULATION** Characteristic of much writing about the population "explosion" is the lack of any statement as to what constitutes overpopulation. Most of the publications on this topic appear to be authored by persons living in the affluent nations and the often-expressed idea one finds in their writings is that the population problem is largely associated with the Third World nations, that is, the poor countries. It is quite true that in terms of rates of increase at the present time these nations are in the forefront and some are also among the most densely populated with respect to people/farmland ratios. However, in terms of per capita annual drawdown on natural resources, it is the rich nations of the world who may be judged to be most heavily populated because these nations utilize a disproportionate share of natural resources and especially energy and minerals.

Perceptive persons in many Third World nations who are familiar with these facts may be forgiven if they conclude that concern in some quarters about population growth derives chiefly from the fear that the affluent ways of life for the few rich nations is being threatened by poor people in poor nations who wish a better sharing out of resources.

The foregoing comments must not be interpreted as meaning there is no population problem—there is. But one must also be aware that there is more than a degree of selfishness behind some of the published concerns vis-à-vis the growing world human population that derives from cultural biases that are not particularly pleasant to confront.

**IS THERE INADEQUATE DISTRIBUTION OF FOOD RATHER THAN INADEQUATE PRODUCTION?** Food production is still sufficient to feed the standing crop of humanity although it is obvious to even the most casual observer that the quality of diets in many parts of the world are inadequate and especially with regard to high-quality protein. There is disagreement as to whether or not the world's maldistribution of food is referable to an absolute inadequacy of production or because of inadequate distribution. One factor making the question almost impossible to answer is the fact that for quite large regions we have only the most general estimates of crop production, this being particularly true where much of the crop production does not enter commercial channels but is consumed by the producers or is bartered. Relatively few parts of the world enjoy regular agricultural surpluses that can be sold abroad. Chief among such limited instances are the United States and Canada, which usually have large amounts of wheat, corn, rice, and soybeans to sell abroad. More significant is the fact that the greater part of these surplus productions are fed to livestock rather than being consumed (in the United States and Canada) directly as human food. Were the meat-eating habits of North Americans to change to a lowered per capita consumption, greater quantities of high-quality plant food would become available for direct human consumption, of which a large percentage would be available for export. Increasing the quantity of grain available for export, however, would not necessarily result in increased exports because many nations in need of the food are unable to pay for it. It is this attribute of the distribution system—the marketplace—that many point to as evidence that the food problem is largely manufactured by economic forces rather than by any real limitations on production. As is the case with many arguments associated with human population there is an element of truth here. Food is usually seen as a commodity to be sold and not given away except under unusual circumstances and usually for very short time durations. Thus, it is possible to point to dietary habits (e.g., meat eating) and world marketing practices as being partly responsible for some of the maldistribution of food. Overlooked by many proponents of this position, however, is that there are upper limits on food production, and that no amount of goodwill with respect to the global allocation of food resources will negate the fact that human population growth, if unchecked, will render this goodwill little more than a magnanimous gesture. In the short run, it is probable that we as a species could largely ameliorate the observed conditions of maldistribution of food among the planet's billions of persons, but unless there is a concurrent effective limitation to population growth, efforts to improve the dietary lot of much of humanity would fail and perhaps produce a greater quantity of human misery into the bargain.

**FOOD PRODUCTION AND CROPS LOSSES IN POOR NATIONS** The widespread coverage of the "green revolution" in the popular and scientific media has tended to obscure another area of agriculture in the poor nations that, in many respects, is of· equal potential significance providing that some rather simple little miracles are performed. Large portions of the crop production in Third World nations are lost in the fields and in storage with such losses sometimes representing more than 50 percent of the potential quantity of food that might have been available for human consumption. Growing crops are attacked by a wide range of biological competitors ranging from viruses to elephants, and crops in storage are the focus of attacks by a host of insects and rodents as well as fungi. Comparatively simple adjustments made in the storage techniques could result in a major increase in available human food. Again, however, one must be cautioned that these would also prove to be little more than stopgap measures if population growth were not checked. Maybe these and other measures that are presently available to increase the world's food supply ought not be initiated until population growth has been checked so that there will be some options available to humanity should natural forces such as climate changes cause widespread crop failure. To attempt to maintain a standing crop of humanity at just about the level of maximal food production obtained under optimal technical, climatic, and biological conditions would be ecological folly of enormous proportions.

## SUMMARY

Early in this century, there was little if any concern that our nation or any nation might be overpopulated although such a concern had been raised by Malthus toward the end of the eighteenth century in his famous essay on human population growth. Malthus had no way of foretelling the great advances that were to take place in food production, especially in what was, at the time of his essay, a United States barely out of its colonial experience and not yet occupying lands that were to become enormously productive of food.

During the nineteenth century, the population "problem" was sometimes perceived as one of there being too few people to supply the labor needs of those parts of the world that were rapidly industrializing. Some governments enacted legislation to encourage an increase in births. The United States, for example, still encourages reproduction by allowing an income tax deduction for each minor child.

A renewed interest in the ideas expressed by Malthus surfaced after World War II. Often termed "neo-Malthusianism," this concern draws attention to the rapid world growth in human numbers in the twentieth century during which time the world human population, which was an estimated $1.6 \times 10^9$ persons in 1900 grew to approximately $3 \times 10^9$ in 1960 and $4.3 \times 10^9$ in 1980. It is interesting and significant that most of the concerns have been expressed by residents of the developed world and their remarks are most often directed toward the rates of population growth in the Third World, that is, the poorer nations.

Many factors influence human birth rates but chief among them are religious beliefs and mores. The latter refer to traditional ideas about the desirable number of children to have as well as other attitudes such as the "correct" male and female roles (e.g., the male demonstrates his "masculinity" by fathering a large number of children and a woman demonstrates her "femininity" by devoting her energies to being a fecund female and devoted mother).

Not everyone shares the view that there is such a phenomenon as human overpopulation. Marxists, for example, often argue that there are not too many people but that there is a maldistribution of wealth. Opposing views are also held by certain religious groups who argue that life is a gift of God and is not to be denied through the artificial control of births. Many biologists, and others as well, see humans as a biological species that can't forever expand its numbers without ultimately encountering a shattering loss of life by famine, disease, and other catastrophes. These people argue that if humankind is to survive, effective measures must be adopted to halt the increase in population.

If there are to be effective national and international efforts to decrease the human birth rate the size, sex and age structure as well as birth and death rates must be known with a fairly high degree of accuracy. However, it is only recently that relatively reliable population data have become available for much of the world and there remain nations where no reliable nationwide census of human numbers has ever been taken. These difficulties notwithstanding, demographers have a fairly sound grasp as to what is happening in a general way to human numbers worldwide and have made projections based on various assumed trends in infant mortality and other variables. These projections vary, but all agree that there will be some further large increases in the total world population. For example, it appears that in less than two decades, in the year 2000, there will be approximately $6.4 \times 10^9$ people on earth. The United Nations has made projections for the first 75 years of the twenty-first century as follows: 2025; $9.1 \times 10^9$ persons; 2050; $11.2 \times 10^9$ persons; 2075; $12.2 \times 10^9$ persons. Thus, in less than a century, there may be a near tripling of the 1980 population that was widely held to have been dangerously high.

The global population total can be misleading, for it ignores regional differences in population growth rates—highest in the poor countries—and national differences in per capita consumption of natural resources—highest in the rich countries. Thus, population growth rates as well as total regional or national numbers do not become meaningful unless they are related to such things as available farm land, per capita consumption of natural resources, and the like.

Food production is increasingly and correctly seen as one of the most basic indices to a nation's population situation. However, often overlooked is the fact that some of the most developed nations are also major importers of food (e.g., Great Britain, Holland, Japan, the Soviet Union, and some of its satellite nations).

What, if anything, do population numbers mean with respect to the conservation and management of the earth's natural resources? First, the great recent increase in the total human population has led to a major total increase in demand for the world's natural resources. Second, the population projections for the next 50 to 70 years assure that total demand for the world's natural resources will increase well beyond the current level. Thus, the problems associated with the conservation and management of natural resources will also increase beyond what are already difficult levels. The demands for natural resources will increasingly assume a more global aspect and Third World nations will demand a larger per capita share of natural resources as their populations continue to increase and the per capita demand for goods also increases. The industrialized nations will attempt to obtain increased quantities of natural resources from areas outside their national boundaries as this group of nations (1) continues to experience population increases albeit at rates below those of Third World nations, (2) increasingly reduces the quantities of natural resources once contained within their national boundaries, and (3) remains committed to and largely governed by an economic philosophy that requires that its respective economies must attempt to be in a perpetual state of growth.

The industrialized nations will increasingly

compete with each other for the many natural resources they must obtain from foreign sources. This competition is already dramatically evident with respect to petroleum and will increase markedly in the next three decades as the total supply shrinks and as demand increases.

The United States may be the best example of growing dependency on foreign sources for needed natural resources. In 1900 the United States was all but self-sufficient in the resources the nation required. Today, however, the United States is dependent on foreign sources for many of the most important of the natural resources used by our nation.

This change of the United States from being a largely self-sufficient nation vis-à-vis natural resources to a major importer of natural resources is one of the most important events in our nation's history. This shift not only increases the possibilities for economic disturbances in the American economy but, coupled with the increasing world demand for natural resources by other industrialized nations, is putting a rapidly growing pressure on resource managers in the Third World nations. In this economic climate, exacerbated by growing populations and growing internal demands for natural resources, one can see that the task of even the best-informed and intentioned conservationist/managers of natural resources in Third World nations is far from enviable. It is questionable that certain populous and economically weak nations possessing a natural resource demanded by the wealthy nations of the world can mount any but weak conservation programs unless given financial and technical assistance from the same nations seeking the natural resource.

These difficulties are not confined to nonrenewable or nonregenerating natural resources although it is the nonrenewable resources that often appear to be the more critically important. Human pressure is growing at a rapid rate on soil, forest, grassland, and water resources in all nations. It is with respect to these regenerating resources that one can most easily see the damaging relationship between population increase and natural resources. If we refer again to the population figures for Latin America, Africa, and Asia we not only see a projection of human population increase but also an implied increased damage to the just-named natural resources. This population increase will not be the only reason for the increased damage to natural resources. There is a growing per capita demand in Third World nations for manufactures that can only be obtained through export of natural resources, including farm products that draw on soil resources and often at the expense of forests that are cut to make way for increased farm or pasture lands.

No nation, however wealthy, can escape from the need to adjust its population size to fit the availability of resources. To this must be added that not only is availability a critical feature but the per capita level of consumption is equally so. Although the current human population of the United States is somewhat less than a third of the population of India the United States consumes resources at a per capita rate very much greater than in India. Perhaps the price our nation should be prepared to pay in order to retain these high levels of consumption is to reduce the size of our population? Certainly that suggestion is no more unreasonable than the one most commonly heard, that India (and many other Third World nations) halt population growth and even reduce the present level in order that there be a better ratio between population and natural resources.

Continued high per capita consumption of goods coupled with a continued commitment to economic growth in the developed world and human population increases currently prevailing in the Third World, if not soon altered, will increasingly destabilize the ecosystems in almost all parts of the globe and make futile most efforts to conserve and manage the world's natural resources.

# the tyranny of geography

## INTRODUCTION

One of the most cherished and seldom examined myths of the developed or industrialized world is that the condition of developedness is largely the result of hard-working and "right"-thinking people who by dint of their individual and collective efforts have achieved material rewards that are not possessed by the rest of the world's peoples because those peoples are lacking in the drive, ambition and general overall ability that have made the rich nations rich.

Hard work *has* played a role in the creation of the wealthy nations but equally hard work has not resulted in wealth for the poor nations often collectively termed the Third World (Map 4.1). How can this be so? Can it be that this great disparity is due to some inherent lack in these people or else wouldn't they too be sharing equally in the world's material benefits and rewards?

There are two fundamental reasons for this disparity of wealth among nations: (1) the accidents of biological and geological history causing inequitable global geographical distribution of natural resources and (2) the accidents of human history that have greatly benefited some nations and penalized others. To these phenomena I ascribe the term the tyranny of geography.

Tyranny of geography means that the global distribution of biological, geological, and cultural resources are the accidents of history and that no one living or dead has ever had any effect on the natural distributions of biological and geological resources and few living have had other than the most minute influence on human history as it relates to the wealth of nations. In order to appreciate better the magnitude of the cultural aspects of this tyranny it is necessary to examine briefly certain relevant aspects of human behavior as they relate to territoriality.

Territorial behavior, that is, the tendency of many animal species to occupy and defend a specific area for feeding and/or reproduction, is a much studied phenomenon. Most vertebrate species exhibit some form of such behavior and primates, the order of mammals to which *Homo sapiens* belongs, often have very complex territorial behavior. That *Homo sapiens* is also territorial in behavior has been a much-argued question but among biologists interested in the matter it is generally held that our species does show such behavior. However, this behavior is different from say, the territorial behavior of howler monkeys in that the monkey behavior is largely programmed through its genetic inheritance whereas human territorial behavior is generalized and is much influenced by culture. That is, humans learn what their territories are as for example what the individual's personal space is, his/her hometown, and his/her national identity. It is national identity that most interests us here.

National identity, that is, one's identification with a particular country, is a culturally ac-

quired trait. One is taught in childhood that this nation is one's native country. This lesson can be also "unlearned" later if the individual moves from one nation to another and then adopts the latter as his new "native" land.

By whatever means or time(s) the individual learns the identity of his native country (territory) he is then conditioned by a myriad of cultural means to believe that his native land is possessed of unique and wonderful attributes and that these attributes are in varying degree related to the superiority of himself and his fellow citizens and perhaps, as well, the result of a beneficent deity that has showered unequal gifts on the "chosen" and the "unchosen."

Nationalism therefore is culturally determined territorial behavior and the concept of the nation, that is, the *nation-state,* is currently the most generally accepted expression of human territorial behavior insofar as such behavior relates to the entire planet. There are, of course, other levels of territorial identification

**Map 4.1**   The Third World Nations.

such as the state or province in which one lives, one's hometown and, importantly, one's home or domicile.

Whatever its benefits may be, the nation-state tends to inculcate in the minds of its citizens mythical (and mystical) notions about the global distribution of natural resources. Thus one encounters frequent examples of an American sense of superiority with regard to the great wealth of natural resources that that nation has possessed and still possesses. Although sel-

dom articulated in other than oblique ways there is a general feeling in the United States that less well-endowed nations owe their condition to some human failing rather than to the fact that the nations simply had poor geographic fortune.

One of the common features of expressed nationalism is the view that one's own nation is culturally superior to all other nations. This view is commonly held not only by the well-paid worker in England but frequently also by the most poverty stricken landless peasant in a poor Third World country. This kind of an attitude may often be harmless and even, on occasion, beneficial, but when it becomes the *zeitgeist* of governments to justify global expansionsim or to justify maintaining traditional rich country-poor country relationships the view is not only not harmless but serves as a powerful sanction by which one part of the world remains in comparative poverty while the other part enjoys material comforts and security. Far too many persons in the wealthy nations have the opinion that at sometime in the past all peoples had an equal start in the race to acquire and/or control the world's natural resources and that, through some form of social Darwinism the more fit won and those less fit lost out. By this reasoning the losers have mostly themselves and their inadequate cultures to blame for the disparities in national wealth one sees in the world today. A comforting view, perhaps, but one that is at gross variance with the facts of biological, geological, and human history.

The truth is that time and chance have governed the biological, geological, and human past and the reluctance to recognize this obvious truth leads to the continuance of what was earlier characterized as the tyranny of geography. In order to assess the magnitude of this tyranny it is necessary to describe some of the more salient aspects of the global distribution of natural resources and to examine some of the historical processes that have created a global dichotomy characterized by powerful and wealthy "developed" nations and weak and "underdeveloped" Third World nations.

## GLOBAL DISTRIBUTION OF NATURAL RESOURCES

The geographical distribution of the major renewable and nonrenewable natural resources in the world is very uneven. To illustrate this fact the following resources will be discussed:

soils, softwoods, high-quality rangeland, energy resources, and metallic resources.

### Soils

High-quality soils capable of being farmed more or less continuously for decades or centuries (see Chapter six) are located chiefly in the middle latitudes in the Northern Hemisphere. In the middle latitude of the Southern Hemisphere there is relatively little land area as compared to the opposite hemisphere—hence the soils that tend to develop under the climatic regimes of such latitudes are scarce in the southern half of the globe. The low latitudes, that is, the region between 30 degrees north latitude and 30 degrees south latitude, are dominated by soils of low agricultural potential. There are exceptions but the overwhelming geographical reality is that in this region where a large part of the human population now resides and where rates of population increase are highest, enormous areas are overlain with exceedingly poor soils if they are evaluated in terms of their agricultural value.

The heartlands of Africa and South America contain enormous areas of soils that can be made to yield crops only at marginal levels of production. Almost all of the Sahara lies within this belt and agriculture is limited to local oases, the Nile River valley in Egypt and within some irrigation projects. Virtually all of the Arabian Peninsula lies within this belt and soil use is limited to tiny specks of land where life-giving water is available. India and Pakistan, too, are located almost entirely within this region. The soils are extremely varied and range from excellent in the Ganges River Plain to leached and agriculturally poor soils dominating much larger areas and to desert soils that require the greatest care if their already high salt content isn't so increased that no crop can be grown. Southeast Asia and the southern half of China contain locally excellent soils but the greater part of the region must grow its crops on steep slopes overlain (when not eroded) by soils of poor agricultural worth. Most of the people in this great global belt rely upon agriculture to produce the food they need and for the export products they sell in order to purchase manufactures they do not themselves produce. Somewhat over one-half of all living persons live in this region.

## Softwoods

Wood from trees that produce useful softwood for construction and manufacturing (e.g., paper pulp) is distributed chiefly in the middle and high latitudes. Of the various kinds of economically valuable softwoods that are harvested trees belonging to the genus *Pinus* (true pines) are the most important. This genus of trees is confined almost completely to the Northern Hemisphere (although introduced by humans to many places in the Southern Hemisphere). Besides pines there are fir (*Abies*), spruce (*Picea*), cedar (*Cedrus*), and redwood (*Sequoia*) to mention some of the more prominent examples.

The Southern Hemisphere is deficient in useful softwoods although there are some of importance such as the Parana "pine" (*Araucaria*) of South America, the tropical "cedars" (*Cedrella*) of tropical American and Australia, balsa (*Ochroma*) of tropical America as well as a few African and Asian softwoods.

## High-quality Rangeland

Rangeland, that is, natural pasture, plays an essential role in the production of meat. In a world that is suffering from a protein shortage in the diets of an estimated two-thirds of all persons, high-quality natural pasture is a valuable natural resource. This resource is distributed chiefly in the northern middle latitudes with lesser areas occurring in southern South America, New Zealand, South Africa, and Australia. Although cattle and other livestock animals figure importantly in the export economies of many nations located in the low latitudes

the natural pastures are generally poor and have very low carrying capacities.

## Energy Resources

Energy resources include those resources which when harnessed are used to power machinery of every description. Today, the principal energy resource is petroleum followed in order of importance by coal, natural gas, hydropower, and nuclear fuel.

Although all of the deposits of petroleum have not yet been located there is little likelihood that many discoveries such as those once made in the Persian Gulf region lie ahead. The world's petroleum map today, although subject to some changes in the next two decades, will remain essentially as it is until the day when petroleum is no longer the world's chief source of energy.

During the "gold rush" days in the western United States there was an oft repeated saying "gold is where you find it," which was the miner's way of saying that its discovery would be chiefly a function of chance. Petroleum prospecting, in its early days, was also on a "where you find it" basis but the prospecting has become more sophisticated and the risks of drilling dry holes is reduced over former times. However, as a glance at the map of producing petroleum fields indicates, the global geographical distribution of this complex and valuable fossil fuel appears to be almost random. Certainly the distribution is the chance result(s) of a collection of biological and physical events that began millions of years ago. Most of these geological and biological "accidents" occurred in the Northern Hemisphere but even there the distribution is anything but regular.

Principal winners in this geological lottery were the areas that are today the United States, Venezuela, Saudi Arabia (the biggest single winner), Iran, Kuwait, the U.S.S.R., Libya, Algeria, Nigeria, Mexico, and Canada. Of the 150 plus nations flying their flags over the U.N. building in New York fewer than two dozen are members of the elite club of major petroleum producers.

**COAL**  Like petroleum, coal is a "fossil" fuel in that the deposits were laid down millions of years ago. Also like petroleum, the distribution of coal is a reflection of geological and biological events that took place many millions of years ago. The great coal fields are (1) the result of abundant vegetation growth and (2) the preservation of same under conditions that presently occur only in areally restricted situations. The paleozoic coal producing conditions were located chiefly on land or in shallow freshwater. The chief winners in this lottery (in terms of remaining unmined coal deposits) are the United States, the U.S.S.R., China, and Western Europe. Lesser winners include India, and, in the Southern Hemisphere, South Africa and Australia. Among the major losers are most of Latin America, most of Africa, and most of Southeast Asia.

**NATURAL GAS**  Natural gas, a complex hydrocarbon in gaseous form, is distributed more or less the same as petroleum, that is, the major natural gas fields are located in the Northern Hemisphere and the distribution in that hemisphere (as well as in the few places where natural gas fields occur in the Southern Hemisphere) is fairly restricted in distribution. The United States has wasted much of this resource in the past (see Chapter fourteen) but sizable, albeit rapidly diminishing, amounts remain. On the North American continent it is Canada and Mexico that now appear to have the largest gas deposits although these are dwarfed by fields in the Persian Gulf and in the North African and Indonesian regions. Again, this valuable and versatile energy resource is absent from the territories of most the nations of the world.

**HYDROPOWER**  A distinction must be made between installed hydroelectric plants and hydroelectric potential. The installed capacity is overwhelmingly concentrated in the Northern Hemisphere led by the United States and followed by the U.S.S.R., Canada, and Japan. The world distribution of hydroelectric potential, however, is almost the reverse of the distribution of installed plants. The greatest potential is in Africa although Brazil also has a very important still-to-be developed resource. In the Northern Hemisphere China and the U.S.S.R. have a combined approximate 23 percent of the world's potential hydroelectric resources. The United States has about 4 percent of the undeveloped potential as compared with approximately 19 percent of the world's installed capacity.

**NUCLEAR POWER**  The materials from which nuclear power can be generated are chiefly uranium and thorium. Mineral exploration on a global basis for these valuable materials is still very incomplete and, because of the military importance of these materials, it is possible that all discovered deposits have not been made known to the public. Thus the present concentration of publicly known deposits is in part an artifact of intensity of mineral exploration efforts, and official governmental secrecy. Nevertheless, it appears that uranium and thorium are distributed widely over the world but the major *reported* concentrations of importance are chiefly in the United States, the U.S.S.R., Western Europe, and perhaps India. Principal reported deposits in the Southern Hemisphere are located in Australia, South Africa, southern Zaire, Gabon (which straddles the Equator), Brazil, and the Andes between Chile and Argentina. It is certain that the known geography of these radioactive materials will change in the years immediately ahead.

## Metallic Resources

Among the more important metallic resources in the industrialized world are iron, copper, aluminum, manganese, cobalt, nickel, chromium, tungsten, vanadium, molybdenum, niobium, tantalum, lead, zinc, tin, mercury, titanium, magnesium, gold, silver, and platinum.

Quantitative estimates of the size of almost any natural resource will tend to vary because each person working up the estimate will have a somewhat different view as to how best to estimate something that has not been measured carefully for the entire planet. Estimates of the size of still-to-be-exploited mineral deposits certainly are in the forefront of this phenomenon of widely differing estimates. Part of this is due to a lack of mineral exploration but an important part is due to economics. The size of a given resource such as an iron ore deposit will often depend upon the price per ton the mined metal will receive as compared with prevailing mining and transportation costs. Thus, the total iron ore resource reserve (and virtually all other metals as well) is, in part, a function of the relationship of production costs to the price obtained for the delivered ore. If prices for a given metal rise more rapidly than the costs of production ore deposits that previously may not have been counted as part of the world's reserves may be later included in such an estimation. This phenomenon is very important in the world and will become increasingly so in the years ahead.

Another factor that may influence the estimate is the development of new technology that makes a formerly uneconomic ore deposit economically feasible to exploit. Thus the map of the metal resources of the world is not a static one but changes with conditions in the market place that may cause the reserves to "grow" or to "shrink" independently of the amounts of metals being removed each year by mining activities. Of course, ultimately, no matter what the market price of a metal may be, the ore will be exhausted.

The Southern Hemisphere has very large known reserves of such important metals as iron, several of the ferroalloys, copper, tin, bauxite (the ore of aluminum), gold, and to a limited degree, lead and zinc. In this context also note that the United States is dependent to a major degree on foreign sources for a growing number of metals (see Chapter seventeen).

This brief review of the distribution of some of the world's important natural resources indicates that there is a lack of uniformity in the global distribution of every natural resource of significance. As was pointed out earlier, this lack of uniformity is the result of geological and biological occurrences over which no human living or who ever lived has had the slightest influence.

It is important for us to recognize that the world distribution of natural resources reflects *natural events* and do not reflect, as some persons still appear to believe, the relative level of worthiness of one nation's peoples over another. This leads now to a consideration of some of the aspects that comprise the other part of the tyranny of geography.

## HUMAN ASPECTS OF GEOGRAPHICAL TYRANNY

The most obvious feature of the world's political geography is that the planet is divided into almost 150 nation-states. These range in size from diminutive island nations such as Nauru (approximately 21 square kilometers) to the U.S.S.R. (approximately 22.4 million square kilometers). These two nations also illustrate differences other than just size: Nauru has a population of about 381 persons per square kilometer, has no fossil fuel or metallic resources nor a hydroelectric resource, but does have a large but rapidly diminishing phosphate resource. The U.S.S.R. has an average of 11 persons per square kilometer and has enormous fossil fuel, metallic and hydroelectric resources.

Another interesting contrast is afforded by the United States and Zaire. The population of the United States is now approximately 225 million persons and that of Zaire an estimated 23 million persons (no accurate census has yet been taken of that nation's population). The average population density of Zaire is approximately 10 persons per square kilometer while in the United States the ratio is approximately 22 persons per square kilometer. Like the United States, Zaire is rich in copper and has cobalt that the United States does not possess but requires for its steel industry. Although apparently lacking coal and petroleum Zaire has a hydroelectric potential far greater than that of the United States. Furthermore, Zaire has manganese (which the United States does not possess), tantalum (which the United States does not possess), niobium, tungsten, zinc, gold, and silver. Unlike the United States, Zaire does not possess other than limited soils of high agricultural potential. It does possess a great wealth of tropical hardwood forest but almost no softwood resources.

The per capita income per year in the United States (1977) was $7686.00. For the Republic of Zaire the estimated figure for per capita income in 1975 was $127.00. In the United States the illiteracy rate is less than 8 percent of the total adult population but the rate for Zaire is an estimated 75 percent. The infant mortality in the United States in 1976 was approximately 15 per 1000 live births. The estimated rate for Zaire is 104 per 1000 live births (1975). The United States enjoys one of the most stable and democratically elected governments in the world. Zaire does not have free elections and its current (1982) head of state has declared himself ruler for life. In the United States there are hundreds of four-year colleges and thousands of high schools. In Zaire there are no single four-year colleges and few high schools.

The United States is the archetypally developed industrial nation. Zaire serves very well as an example of a large albeit poor nation that does not share in the distribution of the world's wealth. Zaire belongs to the group of nations termed the Third World. It is to this group the remarks in the next section are principally addressed.

## The Third World

In the early part of the decade of the 1960s the term Third World was coined to describe those nations that were politically unaligned with either the capitalist or the centrally planned nations. What began as a political characterization soon changed to become an economic designation. Thus the term Third World now refers to nations that have little or no industry, sell raw materials and/or agricultural products to the industrialized nations, and are dependent on the latter for most of the manufactured goods the Third World nations purchase.

A more complete profile of a Third World nation might include the following factors.

Very low per capita income.

Very low average level of achieved grade level in formal education.

Relatively high illiteracy rate.

Continual lack of investment capital.

Frequent capital "flight" to the developed nations.

Poor distribution of income within the country.

Dependence on foreign exchange to pay for imports.

Export products into a world market that is often unstable and that usually does not offer stable nor adequate prices.

Discouraged from gaining access to the markets of the industrialized nations when the Third World nation does have a manufactured product to export.

Prevented or discouraged from profiting from the value added that comes with the capacity to turn a raw material like bauxite into something more valuable like aluminum and aluminum products.

How did these conditions come about? Although the individual history of each region and each nation in the Third World differs they have some attributes in common that explain, to an important degree, why there is such a phenomenon as the Third World.

What are some of the principal means by which human actions created the Third World? To answer that question requires going back to the end of the fifteenth century A.D.

The Ottoman Turks had succeeded in extending their empire in such a fashion as to cut off the ancient overland trade routes between Europe and the Middle and Far East. These regions (and particularly the latter) were the source of spices (important for meat preservation) and other raw materials treasured by Europe. One European response was to seek a sea route to the Indies, as the Far East was then generally known in Europe. The first successful voyage to India and return was made in 1498–1499 by Vasco de Gama, a Portuguese navigator. Just a few years earlier, in search of the same destination Christopher Columbus, a Genoan in the service of the Spanish monarchs, sighted land in October 1492 that proved not to be the Indies but what came to be called America. The voyages just mentioned were quickly followed up by other mariners from Spain and Portugal.

By the middle of the sixteenth century virtually all that is known as Latin America had fallen to the control of Spain and Portugal and certain local coastal sites in Africa (south of the Sahara, principally) and southern Asian had passed to the control of the same two nations. One aspect to be noted here is that in the Americas the areas of conquest were not confined to a few local shore sites but included the penetration and occupation of essentially the entire land masses whereas in the cases of Africa and Asia the interest appears to have been in acquiring ports where ships could be repaired and outfitted or where a trade entrepôt could be advantageously established. Although it was a mariner in the employ of Spain whose ships were first on the New World scene, he was quickly followed by the Portuguese, who discovered what is today Brazil. The collision of Spanish and Portuguese interests was anticipated by the Treaty of Tordesillas of 1494, which divided the western land hemisphere between Spain and Portugal (giving very little land to Portugal—the treaty allowed only what is now the northeastern region of Brazil to Portugal).

Spain sought to exercise iron fisted control over her New World dominions and tightly restricted all trade among the various colonial units and between them and the mother country. Although less restrictive than the Spaniards, the Portuguese also sought major control over the economic activities of what was to become Brazil.

Other European nations soon challenged Iberian control and the pages of history are replete with the names of mariners such as Dampier, Drake, Anson, Morgan (all British), L'Ollonais (a Frenchman), and Pret Heyn (Dutch) who ravaged the Spanish "treasure" fleets bound from the Caribbean to Spain or who pillaged and burned Spanish ports where there was chance for loot. Heroes to their countrymen and hated by the Spaniards, the exploits of these freebooters were symptomatic of the fact that for much of the sixteenth century the Iberian mariners and especially the Spaniards were masters of the seaways as well as the land of the Americas. However, in the seventeenth century, England, France, and Holland wrested bits and pieces of land from the Iberians.

The story unfolding on the African continent was very different in that only local parts of the periphery of the continent were being occupied by Europeans. The Cape Town region of South Africa fell early to the Dutch who in turn were forced to surrender to the British. The chief importance of this site was as a rest and refit stopover on the long sea route to Asia. By early in the sixteenth century there were European trade entrepôts at various points on the west coast of Africa chiefly for the purpose of dealing in human slaves destined to the Spanish and Portuguese colonies in the Americas. European interest in the east coast of Africa was relatively minor at that time this being due, in part, to the presence of Arab settlements at Zanzibar and Dar es Salaam, the former an island very close to the African mainland and the latter one of the best ship harbors along the entire east coast of Africa.

European penetration of the African continent was late beginning in earnest only in the second half of the nineteenth century. The Europeans who engaged in this exploration included, among others, Speke, Burton, Rohlfs, Livingstone, and Stanley. As recently as the beginning of the twentieth century large parts of the continent were still unknown to Europeans except through rumor and story.

The European colonization of the interior of the African continent, therefore, began almost half a century after much of the former American colonial empires of Spain and Portugal had achieved political independence (1820s for much of Latin America). The wish on the part of European nations to colonize Africa reached peak momentum at the end of the nineteenth century and by the beginning of the twentieth century virtually all of the continent had been claimed by European powers. The European nations represented at or near the beginning of this century included England, France, Belgium, Germany, Italy, Portugal, and Spain. The only independent entity was Liberia, which had been created, in 1848, through the influence of the United States as a place to which persons of African ancestry might go from the United States. However laudable this might have been it did result in the usurpation of the territory of native Africans who ever since have been forced to accept a second-class status in their native land. Although Egypt and the Sudan were nominally free they in fact were under the de facto control of Great Britain; and Ethiopia, although nominally a kingdom, had its sovereignty repeatedly compromised by Italy.

The objectives of this African colonization were varied but generally fell into two categories: (1) the desire to obtain on-the-spot locales for the purpose of trade with the Africans and (2) the desire to acquire land as well as other valuable natural resources particularly minerals although animal products (e.g., ivory), and forest products, were sometimes of major interest. Not to be overlooked is the possibility that the acquisition of some African colonies was perceived as a necessary cachet of European power. Certainly some of the territories acquired seem hardly worth the effort if such be measured in terms of potential or actual economic benefit to the imperial power that claimed the land.

Political independence for the African colonies is, of course, a twentieth-century phenomenon, in fact, a phenomenon of the last half of the century. Ghana (formerly Gold Coast colony of Great Britain) led off in 1957 and the process continues with the only holdout remaining being Southwest Africa. The near term fate of Southwest Africa is presently unclear but it will acquire political independence before another half decade passes.

The Republic of South Africa should be included in this discussion of ongoing moves to achieve political independence. Although that nation is independent and is so recognized in the world, the black majority (blacks outnumber whites by 70 to 17.5 percent) is disenfranchised. The policy of apartheid pursued by South Africa is all too well known to require explication here. The black South African majority may be seen as a Third World people being subjugated by a minority population.

As noted earlier, the object of the first European voyages to the Far East was for the purpose of trade. The Portuguese, though first on the scene, were quickly followed by the British, Dutch, Spaniards (the latter to the Philippines), and the French. The Portuguese were well established along the west coast of India by the middle of the sixteenth century, were established on the island of Ceylon (the nation of Sri Lanka today) by 1510 and were on the southwest coast of the Malay Peninsula one year later. Just past the midpoint of the sixteenth century Spain had established trade with Manila in the Philippines via the famed Manila Galleon.

Near the beginning of the seventeenth century the Dutch began to establish themselves in what was to become, until the conclusion of World War II, the Dutch East Indies and what is now Indonesia. Later, in the seventeenth century, Great Britain began its bid for territorial acquisition by directing its efforts to coastal India. Great Britain was soon followed by France, this on the east coast of the Indian subcontinent where they quickly came into conflict. The two nations extended their territorial acquisition often at the expense of the Dutch and the Portuguese. By 1900 all other European powers but the Portuguese, in the tiny west coast colony of Goa, had been dispersed from the Indian subcontinent by Britain. The British had by then also gained control or major influence over Ceylon, parts of northern Borneo, and the Malay Peninsula. The Dutch were ensconced in their Indonesian colony and the French were consoling themselves with a tenuous foothold in parts of southeast Asia (French Indo-China).

The chief object of most of this colonial expansion was in the interest of trade although one also finds an interest in acquiring control of certain valuable natural resources including land. The British system of colonial government did not often encourage permanent settlement and its British governmental servants were usually rotated back to England on retirement. There was a greater degree of permanent settlement among the Dutch and Portuguese, but actual land displacement was usually nominal.

Independence for this region came after World War II. The Philippines, which had fallen as spoils of war to the United States in the Spanish-American War was given its freedom in 1946. This event was quickly followed by India (1948), Indonesia (1949–1950), Vietnam (formerly a French colony) in 1976 and only after a war that lasted for many years, the last 10 of which were pursued by the United States in the belief that this would prevent the spread of communism.

One recurrent theme in the brief description of the colonial era of Latin America, Africa, and Asia is the interest in trade. The term *trade* requires some brief discussion.

By trade one refers, in the context of this chapter, to the acquisition of a wide variety of natural resources by the representatives of the imperial powers, which in turn were paid for by what the powers wished to sell to their colonies (or to territories they controlled). Thus, the colony was often viewed by the mother country as a supply yard, a place where valuable raw materials could be cheaply obtained in exchange for whatever manufactured goods the locals could be induced to purchase. The means by which these exchanges were formalized varied. In the Spanish colonies this was controlled by a vast and distant bureaucracy based in Spain. The Portuguese experimented with allowing individuals to set up what were more or less personal fiefdoms (captaincies-general) along the coast of Brazil. Somewhat later, European nations developed an international political philosophy called mercantilism, which rested on the premise that it was the chief purpose of the nation-state to engage in trade designed to enrich the mother country at the expense of the colonies on which the mercantile system depended.

Thus, there came to be a blending at the highest political levels of the interests of private entrepreneurs and of the state. It was this mercantilist philosophy of government that motivated much if not most of the European colonial expansion after the beginning of the sixteenth century until the colonies severed themselves from home countries. The early mercantilists often sought precious metals (gold and silver) in exchange for that which was sold to the colonies. This came directly from mines as was the case with Spain or from the sale of raw materials, obtained from the colonies, which were marked up and sold or transformed into manufactured goods and sold back to the colony from which the raw materials had been first obtained at extremely advantageous prices.

Essentially, the end of mercantilism is marked by the times when former colonies became politically independent. Although not a part of this discussion, it may be noted that the 13 English colonies that became the original United States of America rebelled chiefly because of exasperation with the subservient economic role imposed by an England that still insisted on forcing a restricted mercantilist role on its American colonies.

The term "independence" also requires some discussion. As it has been used above in this brief treatment of colonial history it refers to achieving de jure political independence, that is, the achievement of what is generally called legal political sovereignty. However, independence does not necessarily extend to economic sovereignty especially with regard to control of a nation's natural resources.

Dozens of nations have achieved their political independence without gaining meaningful control, that is, sovereignty, over their natural resources. Thus, the process of national independence movements may be seen as multistaged with the beginning stage sometimes marked by achievement of political sovereignty (which may be seriously compromised for varying periods of time) to be followed later by efforts to gain de jure and de facto control of the nation's patrimony of natural resources. Many examples of this exist: Mexico gained political independence from Spain in 1821 but it was not until 1938 under the presidency of Lázaro Cárdenas that the nation began to regain de facto control of its land and mineral and fossil fuel resources that had, in previous years, passed largely into the hands of foreign investors; Panama, which became independent from Colombia in 1903 became, in many respects, a colony of the United States, which not only exerted a peculiarly strong control of Panama's pass route between oceans but also for many years dominated the internal and external affairs of that tiny nation—only in 1978 was Panama able to obtain from the United States a treaty that will, at the end of 1999, give to Panama control over its principal natural resource—the narrow isthmian pass route.

After the dust of independence settled on more than one African nation it was found that the most valuable natural resources were still owned or controlled by Europeans. Gaining de facto control of the natural resources is not easy and is often complicated by a lack of trained technicians and capital and by being blocked from access to foreign markets.

The colonial experience resulted in the development of social and economic structures that have often persisted far after the time of colonialism. This development is due to a number of factors of which the more important appear to be the ease by which the industrial nations could and often still can enforce their terms in the marketplace, such terms frequently bearing a close resemblance to those that prevailed during the merchantilist age.

Why don't the former colonial nations industrialize and challenge this old pecking order? The answers to this question are many and varied but most important are the geographical realities of unequal distribution of natural resources as discussed earlier in this chapter.

The serious scholar often does not like to entertain the possibility that luck is an important factor in human events but the word describes much of what has happened to nations with respect to their relative positions vis-à-vis wealth in natural resources.

Certainly one is justified in characterizing as a geographical lottery that which resulted in the uneven world distribution of natural resources, and one is further justified in speaking of a global cultural lottery that resulted in the territorial spread of certain European nations at the expense of peoples who at the time did not possess the armaments and other resources required to resist successfully such advances. And luck played an important role in the fact that some former colonial entities dominated by Europeans benefited from the Industrial Revolution that developed in Europe while the citizens of the former Iberian colonies in Latin America remained culturally tied to an Iberia that, after the close of the sixteenth century, fell into a technological-scientific decline that has only recently begun to be arrested.

Highly relevant to that decline is that Spain and Portugal had not participated in some of the important social and economic changes that were occurring elsewhere in Europe during the fifteenth century. This was due, in part, to Spanish preoccupation with what Spanish historians term the *reconquista,* that is, the reconquest of Spain from the Moors, who had successfully invaded the Iberian peninsula at the beginning of the eighth century and had thereafter obtained control of much of what is now Spain. The *reconquista* extended through virtually all the time between the Moorish invasion and the Spanish conquest, in 1492, of Granada, the last Moorish state remaining in Spain. This long war moved by fits and starts and was motivated, to a major degree, by religious convictions (i.e., the reconquest was a war fought by Catholics against those of Moslem faith). Elsewhere in Europe during the fifteenth century the long-standing feudal system was beginning to disintegrate but in Spain, and also Portugal, the old semifeudal system of land tenure (ownership) and land use still prevailed without significant alteration. This was particularly true for southern Spain where some very large landholdings (*latifundia*) had been created in the wake of Spanish reconquest. Such estates were sometimes awarded to persons or families who had made important contributions to achieving victory over the Moors.

This system of large estates controlled by a minority of the population together with a much larger landless and therefore dependent rural labor force, that is, a landless peasantry, was transferred to the Spanish colonies of the New World. Although it is now more than a century and a half since most Latin American nations gained independence, the colonial patterns of land tenure and land use still widely persist. Land reform has occurred in some nations, for example, Mexico, but the demand for such reform continues to provide fuel for revolution in several other Latin American nations.

Many observers of Latin America are of the opinion that continued maldistribution of land together with antiquated attitudes vis-à-vis land use lie close to the center of the problems that are making difficult the rational development, conservation and management of natural resources in many parts of that region.

Luck, insofar as the present inhabitants of most of the former colonies of Latin America and Africa are concerned, played a major role in the determination of national boundaries. The phenomenon of national boundaries is one of the most unfortunate legacies of colonialism in Africa and Latin America (and in some parts of Asia). The boundaries were seldom drawn with an idea to containing natural, cultural, and physical geographical units nor were they drawn with an eye to a future when the colonies would become independent and therefore dependent to a major degree on the natural resource base contained with a given colonial territory. Thus, we see a "Balkanized" Central America, that is, a region consisting of ministates too small vis-à-vis individual resource bases to have more than a forlorn hope for achieving a stable economy in today's era of high per capita demand for manufactured goods. In Africa we see new nations struggling with boundaries, some of which are certain to produce military strife. Some examples of this are the boundary between Ethiopia and Somalia, the boundary between Kenya and Somalia, and the boundary between Tanzania and Kenya, to name a few. These boundaries cut across territories that had been occupied, or at least seasonally utilized, by cultures that had no influence whatever at the time the boundaries were established.

Former colonies, now independent, are sometimes not above exploiting this situation, as for example the case of Indonesia, which forced itself on the western half of the island of New Guinea (this was formerly a part of the Dutch East Indies) even though this area is culturally non-Indonesian and the native people feel as burdened by the colonial power of Indonesia as they did under Dutch power in an earlier day. In Africa there is scant evidence that the now-independent nations have any intention of rectifying the colonial boundaries if such rectification includes the loss of national territory to a neighbor nation.

How does geographical tyranny relate to conservation of natural resources? Third World nations must often adopt measures with respect to the exploitation of natural resources that are at variance with sound ecological and long-term economic practices. Pressured by the forces of geographical tyranny these nations too often mine rather than manage their natural resources. Thus, the development of the natural resources too often tends toward destruction, and the distinction between renewable and nonrenewable resources, under such conditions, fade to the point of obscurity. Even the richest of these nations, that is, nations like Nigeria, possessed of abundant and extremely valuable natural resources, do not find it an easy matter to progress from a colonial to an independent and stable economic status. The old colonial social and economic infrastructures remain almost intact and seem impregnable to change. As the industrialized world's demand for raw materials increases and as the population of the Third World explodes, conservation and management of natural resources becomes increasingly the dream of only a few.

## SUMMARY

Many, indeed a majority, of the world's nations are victims of the accidents of biological and geological history that have produced an inequitable global distribution of natural resources. These nations are also the victims of the accidents of human history that have greatly benefited some nations and penalized others. These phenomena of accident and chance are termed tyranny of geography.

Greatly exacerbating the effects of this uneven geographical distribution is the fact that the earth's land—and some ocean—surface is divided into nation-states of which the citizens of the more powerful nations view the contained natural resources as theirs and theirs alone to use as deemed desirable. Nations that happened to win in this biological, geological, and historical lottery tend to look on the losers as being more or less responsible for their situation.

Third World nations have many features in common, some of which are low rates of literacy, poor income distribution within the country, dependency on foreign exchange to pay for imports, often discouraged from developing industry that might compete with the products of developed nations, frequently subject to flights of capital, and having inadequate numbers of people trained to do technical jobs. Third World nations often have a colonial history that ended only in the twentieth century, or if it ended earlier, had previously had imposed on them socially inadequate political and economic systems that have been extremely difficult to alter short of violent revolution. This holds true for recently independent nations who may discover that after the advent of political independence they remain under the political control of foreigners who retain control of a usually limited range of natural resources. Pressed increasingly by the demands of a rapidly expanding human population, Third World nations seldom are able to adopt measures that assure that their natural resources will be conserved and managed in the best possible way. On the contrary, too often these nations tend to mine rather than manage their resources.

Some argue that however unfortunate these conditions are and however lamentable it is that these conditions appear to persist, it is not the problem of the developed world. This however is a naive and incorrect understanding of the matter. This attitude ignores the growing dependence of the industrialized world on the natural resources contained in the Third World; it ignores the fact that even the poorest of these nations might possess the means to bring great suffering to other parts of the world through atomic or biological blackmail; and it ignores the fact that the currents now running swift in the stream of international relations move not toward maintenance of the *status quo ante* independence of the Third World nations, but toward a reordering of the world's international relationships. At the base of the relationships today are forms of international behavior that have outlived their time, and this includes attitudes about the global distribution of natural resources that have never had a validity.

There is no longer a conservation and management of natural resources that is strictly nation-state oriented. Increasingly the informed persons of this world must begin to think about resource conservation and management on a global scale and in terms of international cooperation. True international cooperation lies rather far down the road, it would seem, but long before that time has arrived there must be a well-developed awareness among the world's educated that there is one set of global resources and however these are apportioned the conservation and management—or lack of such—of natural resources are not just nation-state concerns but the concerns of all.

The reader should be sufficiently informed to appreciate the nature and dimensions of the problems that the Third World nations face with respect to the conservation and management of their natural resources. Prerequisite to such an appreciation is an understanding that the great disparity of wealth, which now prevails between the developed nations and the Third World, has been brought about not by human virtue or its lack but by a geographical factor that owes its persistence to human affairs.

# the atmosphere

## INTRODUCTION

The thin envelope of gases (comprised chiefly of nitrogen and oxygen) that surrounds the earth has, until very recent times, been seen as a resource so abundant and impervious to human influence as to be dismissed as irrelevant in any discussion of conservation and management of natural resources. No longer is this true as more and more people on our planet tearfully and coughingly become aware that the atmosphere is a finite resource and one that requires the greatest care if it is to continue to provide us and other living things with air of required purity and abundance.

Before discussing the problems we have with the atmosphere and how we must manage this resource we will examine some of the important features of the earth's atmosphere.

The layer of gases in contact with the earth has been appropriately characterized as an ocean of air. Such a simile draws attention to the dynamic properties of the atmosphere which, like the oceans, is in constant motion and is involved in a variety of actions particularly energy transfers and movement of gases. The atmosphere has a vertical structure the components of which vary in depth from latitude to latitude and from one season to another in any particular latitude. The air strata with which we are chiefly concerned, in their order of proximity to the earth are the *troposphere* and *stratosphere*—the latter including the ozone layer.

The troposphere extends upward from between 8 and 16 kilometers in altitude and contains most of the mass of gases surrounding this planet. The most abundant gases in clean air near sea level are nitrogen, about 78 percent, and oxygen, about 21 percent. The remainder is comprised of traces of such gases as argon, neon, helium, krypton, hydrogen, xenon, water vapor, carbon dioxide, methane, carbon monoxide, ozone, sulfur dioxide, and other gases. With increasing altitude from sea level the concentration of any one of these gases in a given volume of air decreases. This is very noticeable in regard to oxygen when attempting to perform strenuous exercise at elevations about 1.5 or 2 kilometers. Insofar as humans and most other living things on this planet are concerned, only the lower 3 kilometers of the troposphere contains sufficient oxygen to meet life needs.

Not only is there a decrease in the number of molecules of any gas per given volume of air with increasing altitude in the troposphere, there is also a reduction of temperature with altitudinal increase. This latter phenomenon is termed the *lapse rate* and is a highly variable phenomenon and often plays important roles in atmospheric pollution. On the average, in still air, the laspe rate of temperature is approximately 1°C per 100 meters of altitude. Such average conditions seldom occur because the air is frequently in motion and because air moisture frequently varies and this alters the lapse rate. In some instances instead of a decrease

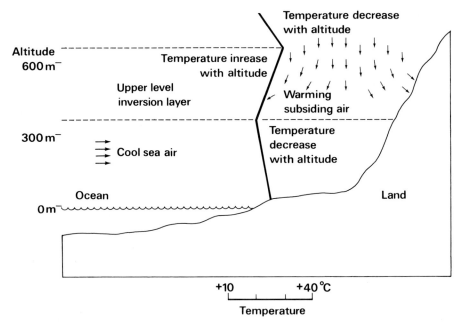

**Figure 5.1** Upper-level air temperature inversion such as frequently occurs in central and southern California.

in temperature with an increase in altitude, there is an *increase* in temperature, this condition being termed a *temperature inversion.* Temperature inversions play major roles in air pollution and will be discussed later in the chapter (Fig. 5.1).

At the top of the troposphere the atmostpheric temperature ceases to decrease but begins to rise, albeit moderately, with increasing altitude: this point or level is the tropopause. Then begins the stratosphere that extends to varying altitudes but an average maximum of approximately 30 kilometers near the equator is to be expected with lower altitudes near the poles. Although possessing far too little oxygen to support life as well as having extremely low temperatures—far below freezing—the stratosphere contains most of the *ozone layer* which, as its name suggests, is a layer of gases characterized by the relatively high concentration of triatomic oxygen (ozone), $O_3$. Close to the earth's surface, ozone is an undesirable gas

but its presence in the stratosphere is of singular importance because it functions to screen out large quantities of ultraviolet solar radiation which, if not so absorbed, would reach the lower levels of the troposphere causing a heightened incidence of skin cancers.

The atmosphere extends beyond the stratosphere to a total distance from the earth's surface of approximately 500 kilometers. Although it is possible that all this considerable volume can be impacted by human actions, at present concern for atmospheric conservation and management is directed to the troposphere and the stratosphere including the ozone layer.

## POLLUTION AND OTHER MODIFICATIONS

Atmospheric conservation and management consists chiefly in controlling human actions that result in air pollution. Air pollution may be defined as all human induced, i.e., anthropogenic, changes in the atmosphere that are found to be medically, biologically, or esthetically undesirable. Therefore, in this book non-anthropogenic sources of air pollution will not be considered.

Air pollution will be discussed under the following broad categories: gaseous, particulates, odor, noise, climatic modification, and ionizing radiation.

## Gaseous Pollution

In today's technologically complex world a wide range of gaseous materials is sent into the atmosphere as a result of human activities. Although the list is rather long only activities that are known to be major elements in air pollution will be discussed here. Specifically, the following gases will be examined in terms of their principal sources, effects in the atmosphere, and the measures taken and/or needed to reduce their quantities in the air: carbon dioxide ($CO_2$), nitrogen oxides ($NO_2$, $NO_3$ and others), ozone ($O_3$), sulfur dioxide ($SO_2$), carbon monoxide ($CO$), and gaseous hydrocarbons.

**CARBON DIOXIDE** Carbon dioxide is a natural component of the troposphere and were it totally absent, most life on this planet would cease to exist. Green plants depend on this source for the carbon they fix as a part of photosynthesis, and it follows that consumers would cease to exist were green plants unable to function. Carbon dioxide also plays a central role in maintaining the heat balance of the earth's atmosphere at levels high enough to support life. This latter occurs because the earth radiates heat in relatively long waves (as contrasted with the short-wave radiation received from the sun) and these waves are impeded from being immediately lost to space principally by the presence of $CO_2$ and water vapor in the troposphere. This retarding effect on terrestrial radiation is critical because were this mechanism not present the earth atmosphere

near the surface would be too cold to support life as we know it.

However, too much of a good thing, as we well know, can be undesirable and this is the case with carbon dioxide in the earth's atmosphere. Until the industrial revolution got well underway humans added only relatively minor quantities of carbon dioxide to the earth's atmosphere. True, by the eighteenth century there had been extensive clearing of woodlands in Europe, which released large amounts of $CO_2$ into the atmosphere and it may also be noted that for several thousands of years prior to the eighteenth century, fire had been used as a means to rapidly remove unwanted cut vegetation as a part of the agricultural system called slash and burn. Also, hunters, for many thousands of years, used fire as a means to drive animals past hunters, into traps, or over cliffs and these activities contributed to the total of $CO_2$ in the atmosphere. However, it is believed that only since the fossil fuels, coal, natural gas, and petroleum have come into widespread use that there has been an anthropogenic addition of $CO_2$ to the atmosphere of sufficient magnitude to possibly influence the heat balance of the troposphere. Quite recently it has also been suggested that the extensive forest destruction now occurring in the tropics may be contributing importantly to $CO_2$ buildup in the atmosphere. We will first examine fossil fuel combustion and then turn to the question of forest destruction and other biological sources of atmospheric carbon.

The advent of the Industrial Revolution marked the advent of power production through the combustion of fossil fuels the first being coal and followed, beginning late in the nineteenth century, by petroleum and then by natural gas. That this combustion might increase atmospheric $CO_2$ was first suggested in the nineteenth century. The concern then, as now, was that this change in carbon dioxide content might cause climatic changes. Almost no research followed from the early conjectures, however, and it was not until recent years that interest in the question of $CO_2$ buildup and climatic change began to receive significant attention from the scientific community.

A major difficulty in determining how much $CO_2$ has been added to the atmosphere, or put another way, in determining what fraction of the total $CO_2$ now present in the atmosphere is from anthropogenic causes, is hampered by a lack of data from the early years of the Industrial Revolution. However, attempts have been made to estimate the increases since the middle nineteenth century. The contribution made by the burning of fossil fuels was apparently rather modest in the middle of that century but later climbed steeply. We can safely assume that the curve is still steeply upward and probably will remain so until the world shifts away from fossil fuels as its major source of energy. Actual observation of $CO_2$ content in the atmosphere is quite recent and is still very limited. The primary source of information to date is from an observatory located on the volcano, Mauna Loa, on the island of Hawaii. Observations made there beginning in 1958 indicate two major phenomena: (1) that there is a seasonal fluctuation in the $CO_2$ content of the atmosphere and (2) that the trend has been upward with respect to the total amount of $CO_2$ present in the atmosphere in comparable seasons. If the trends were to continue until all (assumed) recoverable fossil fuel were combusted, the total $CO_2$ in the atmosphere would reach levels high enough to cause significant temperature changes and hence climatic changes in the troposphere.

Recently, it has been suggested by some scientists that forest destruction (see Chapter eight) may be a significant contributing factor to increased $CO_2$ in the troposphere. There is considerable merit to this suggestion. Vegetation, and particularly trees, is a major carbon "sink" in that carbon is held out of atmospheric circulation for varying lengths of time. The longer lived a particular type of vegetation is,

and the larger the total mass of that vegetation, the greater amount of carbon there is in that sink. As forests are cut and the wood either burned or allowed to decompose, carbon is released to the troposphere. If the rate of forest removal is increased over the "normal" rate resulting from senility, disease, and storms, then the amount of carbon in the air will increase.

Note that whatever the source of atmospheric carbon, there is a considerable lag between the time when the carbon enters the atmosphere and when it passes into one of the several known "sinks." The most important such sink are the oceans of the earth but the behavior of carbon in this great sink is only partially understood at present. There is, however, general agreement among experts that were all increases of atmospheric $CO_2$ stopped today it would require close to 100 years before significant decreases in tropospheric $CO_2$ would occur.

Returning to wood, an important forest-related carbon sink are buildings containing wood. The millions of wooden structures in the world have the effect of withholding carbon in very large quantities from the troposphere. It might be worthwhile to extend the life spans of wooden structures in order to prolong their value as carbon sinks.

What is the basis for concern that an increase in atmospheric $CO_2$ could alter the world's climates? Carbon dioxide is known to be highly absorbent of electromagnetic radiation at about 15 microns wavelength and this just happens to be the wavelength of most of the radiation from the earth's surface (some radiation is reflection from the earth of solar radiation, which is of shorter wavelengths and this tends to pass directly back into space). Therefore an increase in atmospheric $CO_2$ might raise the average temperature of the troposphere, which could cause some important changes in precipitation amounts and distribution. These in turn might have far-reaching effects on agricultural production and many other human activities. In addition, it has been suggested that even a modest warming of the troposphere in the middle and high latitudes could cause the release of enormous quantities of carbon now locked up in another "sink," this being *peat.* Peat is partially decomposed and partially preserved vegetal matter that is in the incipient stages of becoming coal. Peat is soft, contains much moisture, and occurs at or near the surface of the land. Vast areas of the northern hemisphere are overlain with peat beds. A warming of climate would cause peat to decompose more rapidly (rather than tend toward preservation) and thus to release large amounts of $CO_2$ into the air. It appears that climatic warming due to increased carbon dioxide would be greatest in the higher latitudes—just where peat is most abundant.

Experts do not always agree on what the directions of climatic change will be with an increase in atmospheric $CO_2$. Most incline to the view that a general warming will occur and that regional precipitation patterns will be altered. However, others are inclined to the belief that so much *particulate matter* is being released into the troposphere that it might cause a greater amount of solar radiation to be immediately reflected back from the troposphere into space before reaching the earth's surface thus more than compensating for the warming influence of the increased $CO_2$.

Perhaps the most significant effect of a warming of the troposphere would be to melt the polar ice caps and the remaining glaciers in the world. This would raise sea levels everywhere and, depending on the total amount of melting, would submerge parts of coastlines. Cities located near coasts and with elevations only a little above current sea level would be threatened with partial or complete inundation by seawater.

Given the growing concern about $CO_2$ increase in the troposphere, what are the options available for reducing $CO_2$ of anthropogenic origins? To answer that question we must look at the major sources of this pollution and the places in the world where they occur.

The combustion of fossil fuels ranks as the principal source of tropospheric $CO_2$ pollution. The United States is far and away the largest national consumer of fossil fuels and thus this nation represents the world's principal source of carbon dioxide pollution. Western Europe is also important as are Japan and the U.S.S.R. All of the Third World nations combined probably do not equal the combusion of fossil fuel in the United States. More petroleum is consumed annually in one state, California, than is consumed annually in all of the nations south of the Sahara in Africa (excluding South Africa).

What are the possibilities that the industrialized nations of the Northern Hemisphere will reduce their consumption of fossil fuel in order to decrease $CO_2$ contamination of the atmosphere? The answer is that until there is (1) conclusive evidence that climatic changes will occur and (2) that such changes will produce highly disruptive economic and social changes on a global scale there is not likely to be any but token efforts made to alter the flow of carbon dioxide into the air.

What are the possibilities of retarding forest destruction in the Third World in order to reduce added $CO_2$ from this source? Even if points (1) and (2) in the last paragraph were met this would not be sufficient motivation to significantly retard forest removal in most of the Third World because many of these nations do not have the means of obtaining a living except by farming or pastoralism. In addition, and this is extremely important, wood is the major fuel in many Third World nations and there is no economically suitable substitute (see Chapter eight). The pressure on wood as a fuel resource is growing very fast this being caused by rapid population growth and the high cost of petroleum. If forest destruction is determined to be a major source of atmospheric $CO_2$ contamination, it would require the transfer of huge sums of money from developed nations for an indefinite period of time to compensate for any significant reduction of forest cutting. This transfer of money is not likely to occur and therefore one may expect added $CO_2$ from this source over a long term and an all-but-permanent major loss of the functioning of what is known to be a major carbon sink.

It might be expected that as petroleum becomes scarcer and more expensive that this source of $CO_2$ pollution wil! diminish. However, increased combustion of coal may be expected to make up for some of the loss of energy derived at present from petroleum (and natural gas). It would appear that for the next two or three decades, at least, $CO_2$ of anthropogenic origin will increase in the troposphere and that whatever climatic influence this phenomenon produces will continue for many decades into the future. We confront here an aspect of air management and conservation having a potential for great environmental and social impacts but one that has scant chance of being acted on because of enormous national, economic, and social constraints.

**SULFUR DIOXIDE** Sulfur dioxide ($SO_2$) as well as certain other oxides of sulfur are normal components of the troposphere. However, human activities, chiefly the burning of fossil fuels, frequently add large quantities of sulfur compounds to the air. That this is an aspect of air pollution is not arguable, but considerable controversy exists with regard to the medical and other biological effects of air so polluted. Thus far, the medical case against $SO_2$ is equivocal with opposing parties often citing similar data in order to "prove" quite different positions! In England and the United States, national governmental agencies charged with health and other environmental matters generally accept that even relatively minor increases in atmospheric $SO_2$ are dangerous to human health and have adopted regulations governing the combustion of fossil fuels—particularly

coal—possessing a high sulfur content. Because there is a lack of scientific data unequivocally identifying sulfur compounds in the air as being serious medical threats it is understandable that some industrial interests vigorously resist governmental regulation requiring expensive installations of devices designed to remove ("scrub") sulfur from smoke stacks before the smoke is allowed to escape. Although the case for such regulation rests largely on circumstantial evidence this has been sufficient for many to adopt the view that the prudent thing to do is reduce sulfur emissions. This is not the place to examine the statistical evidence that has been brought to bear on this question but it should be noted that in some instances the same data could be used to prove that other contaminants are the culprits or that none is and that the observed morbidity (illnesses) may be due to non atmospheric causes. It is extremely important that the issue of $SO_2$ pollution as it relates to human health be settled.

Recently, attention has been directed to a phenomenon called acid rain, rain containing measurable quantities of sulfuric acid ($H_2SO_4$). Such "rain" has been reported for a number of locations in the Northern Hemisphere and appears to be associated with the combustion of fossil fuels containing large amounts of sulfur. It is being suggested that such acid rain is or will have adverse effects on human health and on various ecosystems particularly lakes and ponds. Normal rain or snow is moderately acid having a pH of about 5.7. However, very acid precipitation (pH between 2.0 and 3.0) has been reported in parts of the northeastern United States. These acid rains owe their $H_2SO_4$ principally to sulfur emissions from a large number of old coal-fired generating plants that have not been subject to the same legal control of emissions as have new plants. Fish life is threatened and forest production will probably decrease as soils become contaminated with sulfur materials.

Sulfur compounds are often abundant components of a type of air pollution called sulfurous smog. The term *smog* was originally used to describe a combination of smoke and fog but has been now extended to include all types of situations where the air is so polluted that visibility is altered and where some irritation if not actual biological morbidity is present. Sulfurous smogs most often occur in the major industrial areas of the northern hemisphere and anywhere coal is burned and fog is present.

Sulfur pollution can be reduced by burning only low sulfur fossil fuels, by washing coal before burning it, by devices that remove these compounds from emissions before they enter the troposphere, and by reducing the total quantities of fossil fuel that are combusted. Because of the enormous dependence of the world on fossil fuels it is unlikely that the total quantities burned will be reduced because of concern with $SO_2$ and its related compounds. The international price for petroleum has risen sharply and great pressure is being exerted in the United States to relax government regulations governing the allowable rate of emission of sulfur compounds. Because the United States is growing ever more dependent on foreign sources for petroleum it will be quite surprising if the regulations are not significantly relaxed, for not to do so would cause loss of economic production, loss of jobs, and hence, enormous pressure to accept what many already believe is an unacceptable level of sulfur-related air pollution. If it be kept in mind that, in general, coal, which the United States has in large supply, contains significantly more sulfur than most of the petroleum we burn and that the contribution of coal to the nation's energy production is expected to rise markedly in the coming decades, we may expect a significant increase in sulfur pollution of the air.

Another fossil fuel—natural gas—produces relatively little sulfur dioxide when combusted (there being relatively little sulfur in natural gas) and thus this fossil fuel is in high demand in areas where sulfur would otherwise be a major element in air pollution. Unfortunately, natural gas is no longer abundant in the United States, is becoming very expensive, and perhaps ought not be burned at all except in rare instances because of its great value in the chemical industry (see Chapter fourteen).

**NITROGEN OXIDES** When petroleum is combusted in internal combustion engines nitrogen oxides are produced. These are very important with respect to air pollution.

In Los Angeles, California, particularly, but by no means exclusively, a kind of air pollution called photochemical smog owes its existence principally to nitrogen oxides being acted on by sunlight (Fig. 5.2). The problem in Los Angeles is exacerbated by the fact that air temperature inversions (which prevent vertical dispersal) are frequent during much of the year and the passage of contaminated air to lee-

**Figure 5.2** Temperature inversion with accompanying smog, Los Angeles area, California.

ward of the region is retarded by high mountains and relatively high passes. A temperature inversion traps the pollutants within the inversion layer and holds them sometimes for days. The top of the inversion layer is usually so low in altitude in Southern California as to be well below all but a few "escape" routes in the mountains lining the eastern edge of the South-

ern California air basin. Temperature inversions occur most frequently in spring, summer, and fall. The winter months are usually characterized by clean air maintained by a usual lack of temperature inversion and the through-flow of winds and particularly during and just after winter storms (Map 5.1).

Although unequivocal evidence that this type

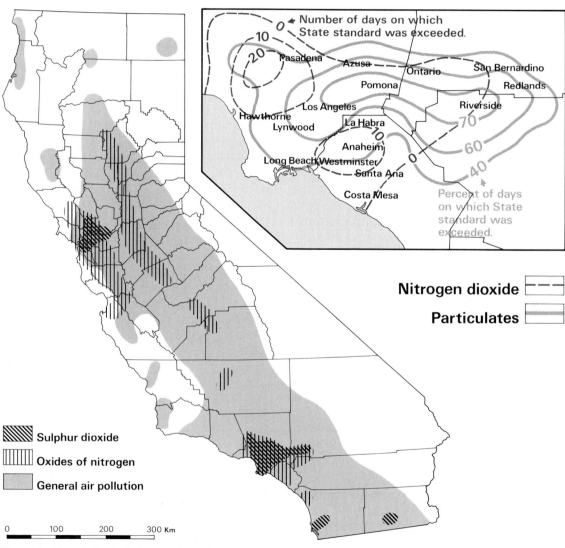

**Map 5.1** Air pollution in California (South Coast Air Quality Management District, California, 1980).

of smog causes human illness does not yet exist there is no question that great eye irritation is associated with it. There is abundant evidence of severe damage to wild and cultivated vegetation. Among other detrimental aspects of this photochemical smog are PAN (an acronym for peroxyacetyl nitrates) and ozone ($O_3$), which is not a nitrogen oxide. Although ozone plays a critical role in the stratosphere in screening out ultraviolet radiation it is an undersirable compound in the lower parts of the troposphere. Ozone is known to be harmful to the lungs of animals and this includes humans, of course. It is not yet clear as to what the lethal levels of $O_3$ are in the atmosphere with respect to human health. Laboratory studies suggest that the lungs of some animals can adapt to rather high concentrations of ozone providing the initial concentrations are low. Like many questions about air pollution and human health it is difficult to determine exactly what medical problems are associated with this particular pollutant. Again, the prudent course to follow requires that efforts be directed toward reducing the level of gaseous ozone in the troposphere.

The PAN component (and other nitrogen oxide components) of photochemical smog is known to cause severe plant damage. Some plant species are particularly sensitive as, for example, many row-crop vegetables. In several parts of California where photochemical smog contains PAN as well as other oxides of nitrogen, it has become impossible to continue production of certain crops.

In summary, the oxides of nitrogen are known to be detrimental to plant life and to the lungs of test animals and are suspected of being detrimental to human health. Although unequivocal data supporting the last view are lacking it is nevertheless felt by many public health officials that the trheat is real and that measures taken to reduce these oxides in the atmosphere are entirely necessary.

The principal source of the added nitrogen oxides is from automobiles and trucks. Both gasoline and diesel engines produce these pollutants and special equipment is required to prevent their being released into the air.

**CARBON MONOXIDE** Carbon monoxide (CO) is always produced in association with the combusion of any carbon-containing material. It is because of this that care must be taken to properly vent gas heaters and furnances in homes lest a buildup of this ordorless gas cause the death of the inhabitants. Vast quantities of CO are produced by automobile engines, and in large urban areas this will result in appreciable temporary increases in the CO content of the air. This can be a serious matter on expressways during the peak hours of use when vehicles spend a great deal of time inching along or coming to complete stops. As vehicles emit CO the gas is sucked into automobiles through their air vents and, at the very least, produce a reduced reflex response time on the part of many drivers. This problem was ignored until recently but no longer and CO is recognized as a serious facet of air pollution. There is not the slightest question regarding the potential lethality of CO—the principal issue is what are the levels of concentration that actually occur and whether such constitute a hazard. It has been determined that the concentrations, under certain situations, do reach levels where human performance is impaired. Fortunately, CO does not remain for long periods of time in the air but is fairly rapidly transformed to $CO_2$. Nevertheless, this pollutant deserves—and is receiving—attention as a potential cause of automobile accidents.

**HYDROCARBONS** Once petroleum is brought to the surface of the land (or water) and is exposed to the air it begins to evaporate its volatile components. At every step along the way from well-head to final passage through an internal combustion engine, there are opportunities for some of the materials to evaporate into the air. Two major sources of evaporated hydrocarbons are petroleum refineries including petrochemical factories and gasoline engines. Gaseous hydrocarbons play an important role in the development of photochemical smog—in fact they tend to initiate the entire chain of events (in the presence of sunshine) that we call photochemical smog. Thus, it is of the utmost importance that every effort be made to reduce the amount of hydrocarbons allowed to enter the atmosphere and particularly in the locations where climate and topography combine to heighten the effects of photochemical smog.

The internal combustion engine, unless modified to control hydrocarbon emissions, allows the leakage of these gases from the fuel tank, carburator, crankcase vent, and exhaust system. Attempts to control such emissions have resulted in special engine designs that cause a better "burn" of gasoline in the combustion chamber, the cycling of crankcase vapors back through the combustion chambers rather than directly out into the air, and devices in the exhaust system that convert unburned hydrocarbons to more acceptable compounds. At present, catalytic converters using platinum are in compulsory use on most newer automobiles in the United States. At this writing, diesel engines are exempt because they meet the hydrocarbon emission standards. However, diesel engines may find the going more difficult in future years because they tend to be fairly heavy emitters of oxides of nitrogen (as well as particulates, which will be discussed later).

Control of stationary sources of hydrocarbon emissions require adoption of different practices of handling volatile hydrocarbons to prevent their escape into the air. This is accomplished by redesign of plants and such things as delivery hoses at gasoline stations. It was discovered that one of the major sources of hydrocarbon pollution in the Los Angeles region was the thousands of gasoline pumps, which, in the course of servicing automobiles, allowed

large quantities of gaseous hydrocarbons to escape. New regulations are causing a shift to vending equipment that greatly reduces this source of hydrocarbon emissions.

**GENERAL COMMENTS ABOUT SMOG** All types of smog are now to be found in the industrialized parts of the world. As some Third World nations become more industrialized their problems with smog grow to rival if not exceed those with already-existing smog problems. Examples in the Western Hemisphere include the basin in which Mexico City is located, São Paulo, Brazil, and Santiago, Chile.

Much of the African continent is yet to experience other than localized smoggy conditions. Of course, any city having automobiles may be expected to experience an occasional attack of air pollution but for most of Africa such events are still rare.

Western Europe has long experienced smog associated with coal burning. Few persons will ever forget, for example, the choking and eye-irritating conditions that sometimes are encountered in the winter in such cities as Madrid, Spain, when atmospheric conditions, coal burning, and internal combustion engines combine to making breathing conditions most unpleasant.

Japan's major cities live with very high levels of air pollution quite like conditions one is likely to encounter in many parts of California during most of the year.

As China becomes more industrialized one may expect smog to increase significantly, which is already the situation in many parts of the U.S.S.R.

Combating the conditions that produce smog (and other types of air pollution) is costly, and because the relationships of smog to human health are sometimes difficult to demonstrate beyond question there is a tendency in many parts of the world to accept smog as a necessary condition for economic advance. The United States is almost alone among nations in

**WEATHER MODIFICATION** Some of the aspects of air pollution discussed earlier such as $CO_2$ result in weather modifications and there are other accidental and deliberate human actions that also cause changes in the weather and climate.

A potentially significant accidentally caused atmospheric change is that of *albedo* alteration at the earth's surface. The term albedo refers to the reflective characteristics of a surface. A dark surface has a low albedo and a light-colored surface such as snow has a high albedo. Green vegetation has a relatively low albedo but bare land or dry grass have relatively high albedos. This being the case it follows that human-induced changes in the local albedos of the earth's surface might result in changes in temperatures, precipitation, and wind velocities. Concern for possible climatically related changes associated with human-induced albedo changes are in the early stages of discussion among scientists but there appears to be fairly general agreement that this is an area for concern as, for example, ever-larger tracts of low-albedo tropical forests are destroyed and are replaced by vegetation having significantly higher albedos. It will take some years, perhaps, before the dimensions of this problem can be established.

Great attention has sometimes been given to the possibilities of deliberately changing the weather. Such interest includes suppression of hurricanes and other destructive storms originating in the low latitudes, hail suppression (hail is one of the most destructive natural phenomena that farmers have to face in the middle latitudes—entire crops can be destroyed in a few minutes), and the production of rain in places where rainfall is always or occasionally inadequate for agricultural or other needs.

This is not the place to describe in detail the methods proposed to achieve the just-named types of weather modifications. For our purposes it is sufficient to point out that atmospheric science has not yet developed to the level where it is safe to experiment at any but very local scales with the dynamics of the troposphere. In fact, given the present state of the art it can be said that meddling with the atmosphere might be foolhardy. Certainly, any experimentation must be done with all the care possible to limit undesirable effects and to restrict effects to the territory of the nation performing the experiments. Although exciting in concept, efforts to suppress hurricanes, for example, may not be wise because many of the possible effects of hurricane suppression or modification have not been studied. It is known that the eastern part of the United States receives up to one-third of its annual precipitation from storms that originate as hurricanes in the Caribbean Sea and the Gulf of Mexico. Hurricanes are also instrumental in maintaining the heat balance of the earth. Thus, tampering with hurricanes may have far-reaching impacts.

## AIR QUALITY LEGISLATION IN THE UNITED STATES

Woven into many of the discussions in the previous parts of this chapter are comments on rules and laws governing the conservation and management of the air resource. However, it will be an aid to the reader if more concise and focused attention is paid this topic with respect to the United States so that the reader can better judge the progress that has been made and the tasks that lie ahead.

The fundamental federal legislation is the Clean Air Act of 1963 and amended in 1970 and 1977. The legislation is detailed and complex but has at its principal intent the reduction of emissions that endanger the health or welfare of humans. The presumption is that emissions are hazardous unless the persons responsible for the emissions can prove otherwise. The Act and its amendments are so written as to include almost all aspects of air pollution (noise pollution is governed by other legislation). Enforcement has increasingly focused on emissions from automobile engines (for which there is now a complex set of regulations) and emissions from fixed points such as power-generating plants, factories of all kinds, and refuse dumps where refuse was burned rather than covered with earth. Federal legislation permits individual states to enact regulations more stringent than those imposed by the federal government. California has been notable in adopting air pollution standards far more restrictive than those imposed by Washington with the result that automobiles sold in that state are subject to emission controls exceeding those required elsewhere in the nation.

In spite of California's more stringent controls on automobile and other sources of emissions the state is still subject to major episodes of air pollution and particularly so in Southern California. Why is this so? Unfortunately for the people of California, the answer to that question has not been determined to everyone's satisfaction. Many people are understandably irritated to find that after being subjected to added automobile costs that are higher than in other states not having similar auto emission rules there are still many days each year with heavy photochemical smog. Many suspect that a major source of this pollution are automobiles whose smog control divices are no longer functioning properly. The catalytic converters required on new automobiles (since 1975) can be ruined if leaded gasoline is burned in the engine; it is estimated that only two tanks of leaded gasoline are sufficient to ruin the converter. An engine with a nonfunctioning catalytic converter emits more pollutants than did older engines before catalytic converters came into use. Why is leaded gasoline used? The answers are lower price per gallon for leaded regular gasoline and a sometimes short supply of available unleaded gasoline. Although it is

illegal to put leaded gas into a car whose motor is designed to use unleaded gas (there are printed notices fixed next to the gas tank spouts), people disobey the law. No one knows just how many hundreds of thousands of cars are operating in southern California with damaged (accidentally or deliberately) catalytic converters but some believe the number to be so large as to be the principal reason for the continued major photochemical smog episodes.

Control of air pollution produced by the automobile has been a long and difficult struggle and that struggle is not yet won. The American automobile industry has not been a particularly inspiring sight with reference to attempts to clean up auto emissions. The federal government has been fought almost every step of the way and the auto industry has used every legal device available to it to prolong production of "dirty" engines. The plea has often been that great engineering difficulties stand in the way of producing less polluting engines. The catalytic converter is little more than a compromise and does not merit one's admiration for the feats of U.S. automobile engineering. In this context it might be noted that one of Japan's auto manufacturers produced a stratified charge engine that, without a converter, meets the clean air standards of California. Japan, it may be remembered, has far less experience with automobile manufacture than does the United States.

A final comment about the catalytic converter is in order. Not only is this device easily ruined and, in any case, must be replaced more than once during the life span of an automobile, but it also results in lowered fuel milage, and particularly so in California where the emission standards are most severe.

It is unfair to single out the automobile manufacturers alone for comment. It is, after all, the consuming public that votes for air pollution when it accepts the product offered—not to mention tampering with smog control devices or using improper fuel.

## SUMMARY

The thin envelope of atmospheric gasses surrounding this planet and on whose lowest stratum (the troposphere) most life on earth depends, until recently was generally thought to be invulnerable to major human distrubances. In recent years, and particularly since the explosive growth in the numbers and geographical dispersion of automobiles, we have discovered that the atmosphere is a limited and fragile resource that must be protected from changes resulting from human activities.

Atmospheric alterations take many forms including gaseous pollution, particulate pollution, human-induced increases in pollen content, aerosols, odors, noise increases, and weather modifications that may be deliberate or accidental.

Most of the more serious aspects of atmospheric alterations occur in urban and industrial areas but, increasingly, sparsely settled agricultural areas are experiencing air pollution caused by the intensive use of machinery, dust, the application of a variety of chemicals, and increased pollen content.

Smog, a general term applied to polluted air when there is a human-induced reduction in atmospheric visibility, is caused frequently by a combination of high atmospheric humidity, the combustion of fossil fuels, and local atmospheric conditions that trap, for varying periods of time, the combination of combustion products and moist air. In some regions, as in Southern California, where the automobile is a major if not the major source of air pollutants, engines emit nitrogen oxides that are acted on by sunshine to produce a brown-tinted pall termed photochemical smog. This type of smog is extremely irritating to the eyes and to persons with respiratory difficulties. However, it has been almost impossible to prove statistically that this or most any other type of smog is damaging to healthy persons—a fact that has made laws to control the causes of air pollution difficult to enact.

Nevertheless, the U.S. government began to move in the direction of conserving the nation's air with the passage, in 1963, of the federal Clean Air Act. Amended in 1970 and 1977, this Act is designed to reduce many of the pollutants spewed into the air from a variety of sources. This legislation was and continues to be opposed by certain commercial interests, the most notable of which has been the American automobile industry, which repeatedly claimed it could not meet the emission control standards established by the legislation. One need not be cynical to note that while the giant and long-experienced U.S. auto industry pleaded its inability to meet auto emission standards, the Japanese were doing so and selling their cars in the U.S. market, and that one of the Japanese makes of automobile had an engine so designed that it did not require any special smog-control device to meet U.S. emission control standards.

California, which has some of the most serious automobile-caused air pollution problems in the nation, has passed legislation even more restrictive than the federal law. Detractors point to continued air pollution problems in the state as evidence that smog control devices on autos are not doing the job of reducing auto-caused smog. The answer appears to be that there is a legion of faulty and/or illegally disconnected smog control devices among the state's millions of registered cars.

It is well within the technical capability of our nation to reduce to modest quantities many of the substances we are now sending into the atmosphere to the detriment of its quality. The problem is a political/economic one and thus extremely difficult to resolve.

There is at least one major atmospheric alteration for which, at present, there are no means of controlling and that is the increase in carbon dioxide. Carbon dioxide is a normal component of the troposphere but humans have been adding to the atmospheric content of $CO_2$ since early in the Industrial Revolution. Since the beginning of this century, the amounts of $CO_2$ sent into the air worldwide have been increasing rapidly and it is widely feared that this will cause significant changes in the earth's climates, which may have a negative impact on global food production. At present, there is scant evidence that there will be any global diminution in the amounts of fossil fuels burned worldwide for decades to come and even if such were to begin at once many decades must pass before world atmospheric levels of $CO_2$ would begin to decrease.

Atmospheric conservation has many geographical facets if effective control of air quality is to be achieved. This holds true for individual nations and their political divisions and it holds true internationally. The atmosphere, as it has been characterized, is an ocean of air, and it moves about quite independently of political boundaries. The day must soon arrive when effective international efforts are mounted to conserve what is a golbal natural resource.

# conservation and management of soils

## INTRODUCTION

It is a curious fact, that of all the topics comprising the subject of conservation and management of natural resources, soil is often ranked by urban readers as the least interesting. One can marshal an army of potential protectors if the word is passed that some animal species is in danger, but public notice that the soil is in danger will scarcely elicit comment except from those few who are informed as to its critical ecological and economic significance.

This general indifference to soil may be chiefly a result of the shift from rural to urban life but, whatever the cause, it is a short-sighted and even dangerous indifference because our species—plus hundreds of thousands of other living species—are immediately dependent for life on that substance we call soil.

## WHAT IS SOIL?

Soil is defined as the collection of chemical and biotic materials mixed with varying amounts of air and water that forms a relatively thin and discontinuous layer on the nonaquatic surface of this planet. True soil is a living entity, being both biologically and chemically dynamic and is almost continuously in a state of change. The kinds and rates of changes depend on the climate, chemical composition of the rocks from which part of the soil is derived, and on the nature of the plants and animals living within and on top of the soil. Although material removed from the moon's surface was referred to as moon "soil," that material is not true soil because it lacks a biotic component—it is moon mineral matter. It is important that we realize that soil is a living dynamic entity because that realization marks the departing point for understanding not only how soils come into being but also provides some of the important insights necessary for an understanding of soil conservation and management techniques.

Soils provide the nutrients and support for the grasslands, shrublands, woodlands, and forests of the world. Soils act as sponges that soak up part of the precipitation that would otherwise run off directly to streams, lakes, and oceans. And soils provide the growth medium for most food and fiber crops and also support the primary production that is later converted by many domesticated (and wild) animals into food and raw materials used by humans.

In short, soils constitute the ecological foundation of human existence and, all of our superb technological and scientific achievements notwithstanding, we as a species are as dependent on the soil for our existence and well-being as were our ancestors hundreds of thousands of years before agriculture was invented.

It is important that we recognize that the agriculture and animal husbandry on which our species now depends for life are cultural inventions and are not phenomena we inherited with the genes that determine the color of our eyes or of our skins. To some persons reading these words this may appear overly portentious but so few persons ever reflect on the origins of agriculture and animal husbandry that the feeling is general among the public that agriculture and animal husbandry are somehow "natural" phenomena and thus inherently sound from a soils-use point of view. This feeling is so widespread that it hides the important fact that, at best, agriculture and animal husbandry systems are ecological compromises and, at worst, may lead to destruction of ecosystems. It must be kept in mind that when agriculture and animal husbandry began no one was present to pass out a guarantee that these activities were not, in the long run, going to prove to be ecological dead ends. We still have no such guar-

antee and thus one thing is certain: only through the most careful soil conservation and management can we guarantee that agriculture and animal husbandry will still be ecologically viable activities 11,000 years from now (a time span roughly equal to the total time that agriculture has been present at some place on this planet).

It will aid our understanding of some aspects of soil conservation if we briefly review the more common agricultural systems and relate them to some changes they cause in the soil.

## AGRICULTURAL SYSTEMS

The oldest organized agricultural system about which we have information is slash-and-burn cultivation (Fig. 6.1). This system (actually many variations are known to exist or to have existed) is based on cutting down woody vegetation, al-

**Figure 6.1** Slash and burn cultivation, Amazon region, Brazil.

lowing the cut debris to dry, setting fire to the debris when it has dried sufficiently, and then planting on the cleared and ash-covered soil. This type of agriculture is, today, largely confined to the low latitudes but formerly was much more widely distributed and included such areas as the northeastern United States (prior to European settlement) and northwestern Europe. An important attribute of this system is that a given cleared parcel will be cultivated for a relatively short time, that is, approximately two or three years in the moist tropics. (In the middle latitudes, individual fields were sometimes cultivated up to a decade but this required a tool such as a hoe to remove weeds.)

Where human populations are small so that there is always a large quantity of unfarmed land compared to the amount of land being farmed at any given time, this system appears to produce only modest alterations in the soils, such as a brief raising of soil temperature in the upper 5 to 10 centimeters of the soil at the time the slash is burned. There is a greater daily range of temperature in the upper 15 to 20 centimeters than which prevailed prior to the removal of woody vegetation, some loss of soil nutrients taken up by the part of the crops plants that are harvested and some accelerated soil loss.

The next agricultural system we can easily recognize is termed hoe cultivation. Unlike slash-and-burn cultivation, this system tends to use the same pieces of land for many years although some parcels may be fallowed (rested) for varying intervals of time. Typically, this system is labor-intensive (requires the labor of many persons) and wild vegetation is continually suppressed with varying degrees of success. Some of the impacts on soils include the following.

Temperatures in the upper centimeters of the soils will show greater daily and seasonal ranges than temperatures under wild vegetation.

Where fertilizer is used (this always being nonfactory manufactured in traditional hoe-cultivation systems) some chemical changes may occur.

Nutrients are removed by the crop plants but most or all are returned through use of plant and animal manures (the latter sometimes including human feces).

On sloping land accelerated soil erosion may become a serious problem. Hoe cultivation is principally distributed in parts of Latin America, in Ethiopia, and in China although it is found locally in many other parts of the world.

In this general and very simplified typology of agricultural systems we may next list plow cultivation (Fig. 6.2). Most available evidence indicates that the plow was invented in or near the valley of the Nile River in Egypt. The earliest plows did little more than disturb the upper few centimeters of the soil, and so limited was this disturbance there have been suggestions made that the real purpose of early plowing was less to prepare the soil for planting than a ritual copulation with the earth to ensure high production of crops. In any case, the idea of the plow, an instrument pulled by animals to break up the topmost layer of the soil to make planting easier, spread to various parts of the world and in the course of this diffusion underwent many modifications in response to differing soils and the differing needs of the people using the plow. Over time, many other animal-drawn agricultural tools were developed whose purposes was to either work the soil itself, to control unwanted vegetation, or to plant, fertilize, or harvest crops. For the sake of convenience all of these additions can be considered a part of the changing picture of plow cultivation through time.

There can be no question that modern plow cultivation with its myriad tools drawn or moved by the internal combustion engine (and ani-

**Figure 6.2** Plow cultivation in the Middle West.

mals in many parts of the world) today provides humans with a quantity of food undreamed of only a few centuries ago. However, such cultivation has profound effects on the soil, of which some of the more important are the following.

Increased erosion.

Loss of fertility.

Changes in the vertical distribution of soil particles and plant nutrients.

Changes in water infiltration.

Changes in water retention characteristics because of soil compaction.

Thus, as agriculture has become more complex and more productive over the past 11,000 years it also has acquired a heightened capacity to alter soil characteristics of which some represent great concern vis-à-vis conservation and management of soils.

## SOIL CLASSIFICATION AND MAPPING

Given the transcendental significance of the soil resource it would seem that some gener-

ally agreed on classification has long been in worldwide use. Unfortunately, that is not the case, and at present there are several classifications from which to choose. Russian soil specialists did much, if not most, of the pioneering work in the latter part of the nineteenth century: this work was dominated by the view that soils are best understood and therefore classified if the structure and form of soils are compared with the chief factors of soil formation (e.g., climate, vegetation, and mineral "parent" material). This is a particularly attractive approach to geographers but insofar as the U. S. Soil Service is concerned the feeling is that emphasis should be given to the appearance (morphology) soils and that the genesis of a soil should receive less emphasis than has been given to it by the Russians. Because the Russians were the pioneering pedologists (soil scientists) it is still common practice to employ pedologic terms coined by the Russians (e.g., chernozem, podsol, and gley, to mention only a few). Of course other nations have made contributions to soil science so there are also German terms such as bodensol (bog soil) and a plethora of English terms since both the United

States and other English-speaking countries have been busy in this century with the scientific study of soils (there might also have been included French terms, Spanish terms, and the terms derived from still other languages). The result has been a considerable confusion of terminology and efforts are now underway to bring order out of confusion. One such effort of great value and growing international acceptance is the soils classification termed the Seventh Approximation developed by soil scientists working in the United States. The primary feature of this classification is that it groups the soils of the world into 10 soil orders (Map 6.1).

For the purposes of soil conservation and management, however, it is necessary to have a scheme or schemes that allow depiction of detailed local variations in soils. Again, we find a large number of classifications but little agreement between one country and another as to which one is best. Therefore it is often all but impossible to transfer the data from a detailed soils map drawn in one country to conform with the criteria for drawing such maps in another country.

The U.S. Soil Survey, a unit of the U.S. Department of Agriculture, provides us with an example of an agency engaged in detailed soils mapping. The efforts of this government agency have not only produced outstanding maps and other publications for soil conservation and management in the United States but these are increasingly effective abroad. This influence notwithstanding, there is still a broad array of mapping/classification procedures and criteria found even in those countries where the U.S. soils publications have been translated and made available to the populace.

Maps of soil orders tend to be small-scale maps showing large areas (e.g., 1:1,000,000 is a scale commonly used), and one sometimes encounters maps of world distributions of the soil orders at a scale of 1:12,000,000 or even smaller. At the opposite end of this spectrum are maps that depict local soil conditions and/or distributions. Such maps, to be effectively used by farmers and soil conservationists, must be of sufficiently large scale to permit the inclusion of the varied data required for good soil management. Thus, map scales of 1:100,000 or larger are necessary. Best are maps of 1:50,000 or larger—maps of the U.S. Soil Survey are commonly of the scale 1:24,000 (one that is also commonly employed by the U.S. Geological Survey). A soils map of 1:50,000 or larger provides the opportunity to include an enormous amount of detail and information. Some of the kinds of such information are described in the following paragraphs.

Mature soils have fairly well-defined horizontal layers called *soil horizons*. Each soil horizon is distinct in its physical and biological properties as compared to all other soil layers (horizons) located above or below it at a given place. The total collection of soil horizons in a locality is called a *soil profile*. Figure 6.3 depicts a soil profile that represents a typical situation in parts of the more fertile parts of the U.S. Midwest. This example, however, is not representative of all soils because some do not have all the horizons shown in the example or may even lack them entirely. In the latter case, the soil is likely to be judged immature, that is, too young to have developed soil horizons and thus a soil profile.

The presence or absence of soil horizons and profiles are important criteria in those soil classifications related to local situations. Detailed soils maps include not only the above features but also others such as color; clay, sand, and silt content; size and amount of stones present; organic (including humus) content; slope; and drainage. These, and other, criteria form the data base required to determine the best uses to which a given soil should be put as well as to establish the best management practices for it.

In local, that is, large scale, soil studies conducted by the U.S. Soil Survey, the emphasis is upon the series and class. The series consists of soils that have a very similar sequence of horizons and other features such as those listed above. Part of a series name is the same as some geographical feature—natural or cultural—located adjacent to the place where the given series was first described. Thus, the soil series designated as Yolo clay loam was first described in Yolo County, California, and the designation "clay loam" is the class of soil and in this case refers to a relatively high clay content but with sufficient sand and other materials to impart good cultivation properties (tilth). Even though the designation Yolo clay loam may seem to be a very restricted one it is possible to recognize still further refinements such as soil phase or some other term that recognizes extremely local differences in the physical, biological, and other features in a given series and class of soils (see Map 6.2 for a part of a typical U.S. Soil Survey map).

Among the things one is likely to discover in one's first attempt to conduct a soil survey of some small region is the extraordinary range of soil classes and phases that can occur in even

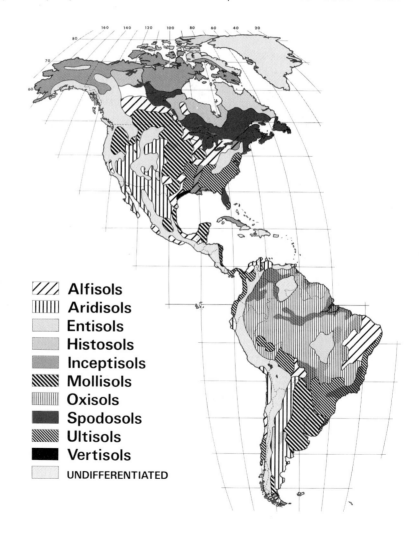

| | |
|---|---|
| ⫽⫽⫽ | **Alfisols** |
| ‖‖‖‖ | **Aridisols** |
| | **Entisols** |
| | **Histosols** |
| | **Inceptisols** |
| ▨▨▨ | **Mollisols** |
| ‖‖‖‖ | **Oxisols** |
| ▮▮▮ | **Spodosols** |
| ▨▨▨ | **Ultisols** |
| ▮▮▮ | **Vertisols** |
| | UNDIFFERENTIATED |

a very limited area. It is just such variation that must be discovered and mapped, however, if adequate soil management is to be achieved in most farming areas of the world. Soil surveys (and resultant maps) are costly and it is chiefly for this reason that vast portions of the farmed lands of the world still lack detailed soil surveys. Even in the United States, where extraordinary progress has been achieved with soils mapping at large scales, there remain many areas for which maps are not yet available (such mapping is done not only by the U.S. Department of Agriculture Soil Survey but also by state and county agencies).

Although the Seventh Approximation soil classification has very much to recommend it and should become widely adopted, thus greatly simplifying communications among the soils scientists, that day appears to be far off in the future. The current international trend is to employ a part of the system and to modify or even discard the rest in favor of local (national) schemes. Perhaps, however, it is less important to achieve uniformity of classification than

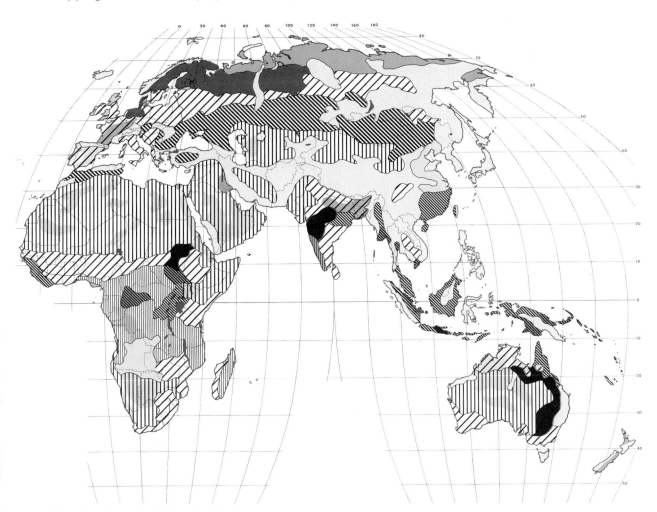

**Map 6.1** World distribution of soil orders.

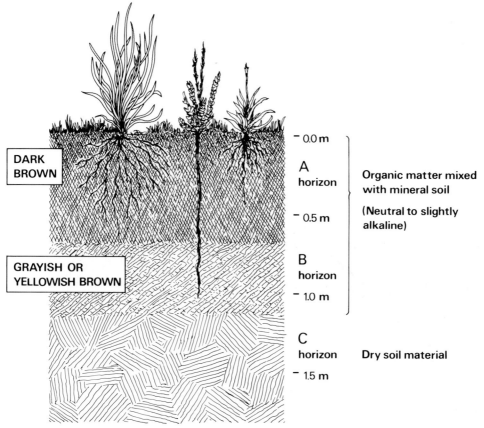

DARK
BROWN

GRAYISH OR
YELLOWISH BROWN

— 0.0 m

A
horizon          Organic matter mixed
                 with mineral soil

— 0.5 m          (Neutral to slightly
                 alkaline)

B
horizon

— 1.0 m

C
horizon          Dry soil material

— 1.5 m

**Figure 6.3**  Generalized profiled of a mollisol.

it is to get to work with whatever classifications are available thereby making maps available for soil management as quickly as possible.

## SOILS RESOURCES OF THE UNITED STATES

One of the greatest of our natural resources treasures is the range of the kinds of soils we possess. Nine of the 10 soil orders included in the Seventh Approximation are to be found within our nation's boundaries and, more importantly, we have an abundance of extremely fertile soils as well as an abundance of soils that can be brought into production if sufficient

water and/or fertilizer are made available to farm them.

In a general treatment such as this, it is not possible to detail local soil conditions (i.e., soil series and classes). Therefore, descriptions of the soils resources will be limited to a brief overview of the soil orders (see Map 6.3 for distributions).

### Entisols

Entisols lack soil horizons because such soils are either too young to have developed vertical structures (soil horizons) or because they consist of materials such as sand, which does not tend to evolve onto the structures characteris-

**Map 6.2** Portion of a typical United States Soil Survey map. The first capital letter represents the soil series, the lower case letter represents the principal physical nature of the soil and the last letter represents the degree of slope. Ex.: MaD = Mariposa series, gravelly silt loam, 3 to 30 percent slope. (United States Soil Survey)

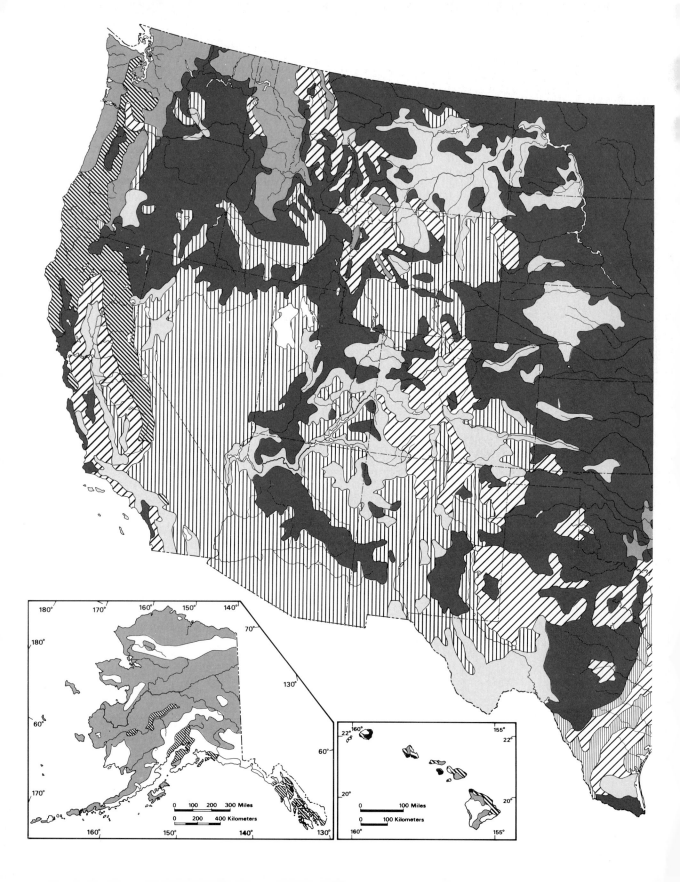

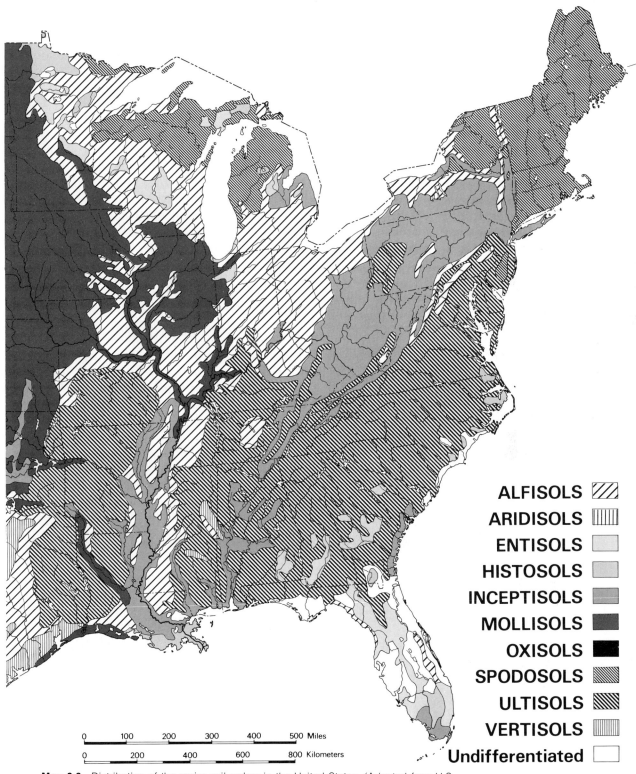

| ALFISOLS | |
|---|---|
| ARIDISOLS | |
| ENTISOLS | |
| HISTOSOLS | |
| INCEPTISOLS | |
| MOLLISOLS | |
| OXISOLS | |
| SPODOSOLS | |
| ULTISOLS | |
| VERTISOLS | |
| Undifferentiated | |

0    100    200    300    400    500 Miles

0        200       400       600       800 Kilometers

**Map 6.3**  Distribution of the major soil orders in the United States. (Adapted from U.S. Atlas, 1968).

tic of mature soils. Some entisols in the United States are located adjacent to flowing streams and are the result of seasonal deposits of sediment. Since entisols are usually restricted in area it is often impossible to show their presence on small-scale maps. Some *extensive* areas of entisols comprised chiefly of sandy material are located in parts of the Midwest. Other entisols lie above rocks and are so shallow that their use for crops is restricted.

Entisols that are well drained—or can be drained by artificial means—and that are deep enough to provide adequate room for the roots of crop plants are among the more fertile of our soils.

## Vertisols

Vertisols are mature soils that have features making them difficult to either farm or build on because they contain so much clay they are subject to alternate swelling during rainy seasons and shrinkage during dry periods. However, because vertisols do possess rather good quantities of organic material as well as nutrients for certain crops they can be made agriculturally productive if measures are taken to adjust to the considerable movement characteristic of this soil order. The geographical distribution is limited chiefly to the Gulf Coast region.

## Inceptisols

Inceptisols are young soils that have just begun to show the development of horizons and other features associated with mature soils. Their geographical distributions in the United States is extensive and includes not only widely disjunct locations in the 48 conterminous United States but also Alaska and Hawaii. No simple generalization about soil quality is possible other than to say that relatively few of the soils in this order are useful for agriculture. Some of those that occur in Hawaii have been found suited to the cultivation of sugar cane and pineapples. In many cases, however, inceptisols are too thin to support intensive agriculture and their best use is for pasture, woodlands, or forests.

## Aridisols

Aridisols, as the prefix may suggest, are located in regions where there is limited precipitation, that is, in arid or semiarid regions. Such conditions are widely distributed in the Western approximate one-third of our nation. These soils possess horizons and are low in organic content but have unusually high mineral contents—sometimes so high that their use for farming is extremely difficult if not impossible. In those places where adequate water is available and the soils are not overly mineralized agricultural production can be very important.

## Mollisols

As the prefix to the name of this soil order suggests, mollisols are soft, i.e., friable, soils easily worked by agricultural implements. This soil order includes some of the most fertile soils in our nation. They are characterized by well-developed horizons, a high organic content, good but usually not excessive mineral content, and have excellent tilth. Most of these soils are located in the Midwest although there are some extensive areas of mollisols elsewhere. If one were required to identify the most valuable of the soil orders relative to American agriculture mollisols would likely be given that designation.

## Spodosols

Spodosols comprise a group of soils that have developed in cool, moist climates and chiefly under coniferous forest cover. These soils tend to be quite acid and present difficulty if one wishes to farm them. However, spodosols can be highly productive of some crops if the soils are limed, that is, have $CaCO_3$ added to them to counteract the acid conditions. These soils are located chiefly in the Great Lakes and Northeastern regions but some examples occur elsewhere as, for example, southwest Florida.

## Alfisols

Many soils in this order are moderately acidic and require the addition of lime to make them suitable for crop production. However, if this measure is taken together with fertilization as needed, these soils may be adjudged to be among the best we possess. Although widely distributed in the conterminous United States, the areas of principal importance lie east of the Great Plains and west of the Appalachian Mountains.

## Ultisols

Ultisols are soils that have been exposed to extreme conditions of precipitation leading to the leaching out of much of the soluable mineral content. These soils tend to have low fertility relative to potential agricultural use. Ultisols can, in some instances, be made productive with the addition of fertilizer although in some instances the best use is to allow them to remain in natural tree cover. Soils belonging to this order occur in many parts of the conterminous United States and in Hawaii.

## Oxisols

Oxisols comprise soils characterized by having high concentrations of iron and silica in the upper horizons, by being highly acid, and by having other properties that often seriously limit their utility for agriculture. Such soils are typically poor in phosphorous, magnesium, and nitrogen. Their presence in the United States is arguable but they are included here chiefly in order to present a complete listing of the 10 soil orders. Oxisols develop under conditions of abundant rainfall and warm temperatures and require a long time span to fully mature. Thus, while the necessary climatic conditions occur in parts of the United States—and especially in parts of Hawaii—there has not been sufficient time for such soils to have developed.

## Histosols

Histosols are characterized by having a large organic content, being poorly drained, and being very acid. These characteristics notwithstanding, soils of this order can be highly productive of certain vegetable crops. However, in most cases the soils must be drained before they can be farmed. Histosols are located in many places but often have such limited local distribution that they are difficult to show on small-scale maps. A major problem with these soils, in addition to those just noted, is that some have such a high organic content they tend to dry and blow away when they are drained. These soils are also subject to fire and it is not unusual to encounter signs warning against fire when passing through a region of farmed histosols.

# HISTORY OF SOIL CONSERVATION AND MANAGEMENT IN THE UNITED STATES

Although published histories of colonial America are often preoccupied with political matters, it ought to be remembered that among the foremost activities of the colonies were agriculture and animal husbandry. Merchants and other entrepreneurs constituted a small minority among the farming majority and even the town dweller was likely to have a farm and engage in farming at least on a part-time basis. Colonial America was a collection of farmers, and thus a discussion of American soil conservation must begin with this early period.

Unfortunately, the picture is almost uniformly bleak. Farmers usually didn't understand until too late the limitations inherent in the soils they sought to cultivate. The first problems encountered were accelerated soil erosion that came a decade or so after clearing the forest for pastures and cultivation. The second most serious problem was loss of fertility. At the time, there was no such thing as a soil science nor anything but the most rudimentary concepts of scientific farming anywhere in the world. The farmers were not completely devoid of any notions of ecological cause and effect relationships of the lands they farmed but they were greatly disadvantaged compared with farmers today in not possessing anything but the most speculative kind of scientific guidelines to follow. The colonial farmer did not generally recognize that his field practices could cause his soil to wash away and even if he did it is not likely that it would have resulted in more than a modest response in agricultural practices. This was because of the generally held attitude that cheap land was so readily available there was no reason to worry if the land one happened to be farming became worn out and had to be abandoned. This attitude toward soils resources (and many other natural resources) was embedded early in the thinking of North Americans and even today surfaces at times when the topic of natural resource shortages is mentioned.

There was at least one person, however, who not only perceived the relationship between land use and soil erosion and fertility decline but who also sought to enlighten his fellow farmers. This man, Jared Eliot, a country preacher, physician, and part-time farmer, deserves to be better known to our generation but the style of much historical writing limits mention to the leading politicians of an era. Eliot lived, worked, and died in New England (1685–1763) and, although largely forgotten nowadays, deserves an honored place in the ranks of American soil conservationists. He was chiefly concerned with accelerated soil erosion and he appears to have been the first to have made the connection between accelerated soil loss and ground surfaces kept bare as a part of tillage practice.

Jared Eliot's discovery today sounds almost naive for it is hard to believe that most farmers had not made the connection between bare soil and soil loss long before. In addition, Eliot noted that the loss of topsoil correlated with diminishing crop yields. He read widely and was aware of the advances then being made in English agriculture and sought to get some of the English innovations adopted by farmers in the New England area. Chief among the latter was the planting of crops whose chief purpose was to restore soil fertility. Some farmers in England observed that certain crops such as the clovers tended to improve soil fertility while growing and also later when the plants were plowed under into the soil (this latter is known as *green manuring*) (Fig. 6.4). The biological basis of clover and soil fertility was not then known and did not become known for more than a century but today we understand that it is the presence of certain species of nitrogen-fixing bacteria (*Rhizobium* being one very important genus) living in the roots of the clover plants. The clovers belong to the plant family Leguminosae and most of the members of this very large group of plants have nitrogen-fixing bacteria associated with their roots.

Eliot's greatest contribution was to perceive the relationship between land use and soil loss and to propose means to prevent or reduce such loss. He argued that a farmer should plow his land in such a way that a maximum amount of water would be absorbed rather than allowed to run off carrying the topsoil with it.

By the end of the eighteenth century there was a growing interest among farmers for the development of better soil management practices. Although several names are prominent, those of Samuel Deane and Thomas Jefferson stand out.

Deane wrote a detailed account of what he perceived to be the best farming practices applicable in New England (1790) and his book, *The New England Farmer,* is said to have been of some influence. Deane proposed that land should be plowed on the contour, meaning that the furrow should be more or less at right angles to the slope. However, few farmers adopted the practice even though no less an influential

**Figure 6.4** Plowing under a cover crop of sweet clover for green manure.

figure than Thomas Jefferson advocated such practice.

Thomas Jefferson, perhaps best known for his political roles in the early history of the United States, was also a serious farmer. Indeed, it could be fairly argued that Jefferson was among the first of the scientific American farmers in that he saw the need for experimentation and testing of crops, animals, and farming practices if American agriculture was to advance. For Jefferson, farming was the very essence of "the American dream" and we owe him a great deal with respect to the introductions of crops plants and farming practices from Europe.

Although there were additional discoveries of sounder soil management practices, these discoveries did not have measurable effects on the larger picture of American agriculture. Careless and wasteful cultivation practices that characterized the colonial period continued throughout the nineteenth century. As time passed there was less and less excuse for this because a considerable body of data had been accumulated that pointed the way to proper soil management. The frontier mentality prevailed all too frequently, however, and soils continued to be washed away to streams, lakes, and the oceans in ever-increasing quantities.

By no means was all the loss due to water erosion for wind erosion had become a part of the dismal picture even as early as the colonial period. The nineteenth century did not lack for voices crying out against this loss of soil but their impact was too modest to staunch the flow. Here we confront one of the most astonishing aspects of U. S. history. We were a nation that until the early part of the twentieth century was chiefly rural, deriving most of its income from farms or farm-related enterprises and treating its basic natural resource, the soil, as though that resource were limitless. For the most part, those who were calling for a major overhaul of the cultivation and land-use practices that were bleeding off the nations' resources were ignored.

One cannot report that suddenly there was a national recognition of a soil erosion crisis. What did happen was that in 1914 the U. S. Department of Agriculture began its first recorded studies of soil erosion that were linked to specific types of slope and land-use practices. Then, slowly, some states began similar or related studies. It was not until 1927 that national attention was effectively focused on the seriousness of soil loss. Thanks largely to the efforts of American pioneer soil scientist, Hugh Hammond Bennett, plus the efforts of his colleagues, the United States belatedly set about providing the legislative and financial means required to reverse the destructive uses of the nation's soils. It was not until well into the 1930s that effective federal and state-sponsored soil conservation efforts got underway. Many of the serious erosion problems confronted nationally in the 1930s are still with us and to these must be added many other soil problems still awaiting solution.

At the national level, the starting point for soil conservation was the creation of the Soil Conservation Act of 1935. This Act also created the Soil Conservation Service (SCS), which was attached to the U.S. Department of Agriculture. A perhaps too enthusiastic and ambitious SCS promptly began to exasperate and irritate many other agencies, particularly at the state levels, whose personnel sometimes felt pushed aside. This led to several legislative modifications among which was the proposal that each state should set up its own soil conservation districts and that the SCS would work by invitation through these districts. Almost all of the nation's farmlands are now within such districts (often termed soil and water conservation districts).

At the outset of the establishment of the SCS there was conflict between other federal and state and local agencies as to which one had prime authority. Certain farm organizations were especially intransigent and spared no opportunity to impede the work of the SCS. The federally funded Tennessee Valley Authority (TVA), for example, sought to prevent the formation of soil conservation districts in the areas under TVA control, believing that to allow the formation of such would lead to the reduction of TVA authority. However, in spite of all the difficulties, gains have been made in soil erosion control and generally improved management of some of the nation's soils.

The war against mismanagement of the soil is far from won, however, and the greater part of the farms of the United States is still not managed in ways that would best preserve the quality (and thus long-term productivity) of the soil. In addition, problems not of great concern in the 1930s have recently appeared and have become quite serious and will be discussed later in this chapter.

## CONTEMPORARY SOIL CONSERVATION AND MANAGEMENT IN THE UNITED STATES: PROBLEMS AND SOLUTIONS

The principal soil conservation problems requiring attention in our nation are as follows.

1  Accelerated soil erosion.
2  Loss of soil fertility.

**3** Mineral accumulation in soils.

**4** Soil compaction.

**5** Covering good soils with buildings, roads, and other constructions.

In the following section these will be taken up and discussed in the foregoing order.

### Accelerated Soil Erosion

The first soil management problem encountered in the earliest colonial times—accelerated erosion—remains the most important soil management problem today (Figs. 6.5, 6.6, and 6.7). This is particularly ironic in view of the fact that it was recognition of the seriousness of this phenomenon that led to the establishment of the Soil Conservation Survey in the 1930s. Today, more than 40 years later, after spending billions of dollars in attempts to reduce and/or prevent such soil loss, there is concern that during the past couple of decades the situation has not only not improved but that soil loss has worsened during that time. Why has there been so limited success in the control of soil erosion in the United States?

There is no single or simple answer to that question and essential elements of a complete answer must include the following factors.

**Figure 6.5** Severe gully erosion.

There are no national, and only a few state or local laws that require a farmer or farm operator to prevent loss of soil.

The economics of farming tend to emphasize short-run economic decisions that often tend to cause deterioration of the soil.

Money appropriated for soil conservation has sometimes been spent to increase annual crop yields rather than improve soil use to prevent or lessen soil loss.

There has been limited actual cooperation between the SCS and the farmers for whom the SCS prepares land-use plans.

There is general suspicion on the part of some farmers of any and all governmental interference in their activities.

One of the most treasured of American folkways is the right to hold private land and to act thereon with a maximum degree of freedom. This cherished custom has been much impinged on by legislation over the years but there remain several areas with respect to agriculture where the operator can act with a high degree of independence from any control other than those instituted by himself or herself. These areas include decisions on what crops to plant, what animals to raise, and what cultivation or husbandry methods are to be used. True, these and other farming decisions are very much influenced by federal legislation regarding price supports for farm products, import controls, or lack thereof and other items that may encourage or discourage a farmer from acting in one

**Figure 6.6** Severe sheet erosion occuring on exposed soil.

**Figure 6.7** Wind erosion. The man is walking where a four foot deep creek was filled with wind-blown soil.

fashion or another. But as of this date few states have laws designed to restrict farming activities that will produce an abnormal loss of soil. At present, the federal government can do no more than persuade farmers to treat the soil in their care with sound management techniques.

The results of this situation are to be seen in a report issued in 1977 by the Office of the Comptroller General (OCG) of the federal government and in the statements of some of the officials of the United States Department of Agriculture, (USDA). The OCG looked at nearly 300 farms in the corn belt, the Great Plains, and the Northwest and found that about 84 percent of them were losing more than 12 metric tons of soil per hectare per year and that there was little discernible difference between farms that were being aided by the SCS and those which did not receive such assistance and advice (Table 6.1). Secretary of Agriculture Robert Bergland (1978), in his confirmation hearings before the U.S. Senate said that "we are losing 15 tons of soil out of the mouth of the Mississippi River every second." But the Secretary went on to observe that ". . . we have only begun to scratch the surface of our conservation activities."

How to prevent accelerated soil erosion on our nation's farms is, to a major degree, a political rather than a technical question. Although there are undoubtedly still new things to be learned about the causes of accelerated soil erosion as well as the development of new techniques to prevent such losses, it is overwhelmingly evident that until there is national legislation backed up by effective enforcement to require that farmers adopt approved soil management practices the bleak situation will continue and possibly worsen.

Most farmers are not ignorant self-serving destroyers of the soil's resource. Farmers are placed in extremely difficult economic and ecological circumstances, many of which are seldom if ever faced by entrepreneurs in other

Table 6.1
**Recent examples of accelerated soil erosion in the United States**

| Region, *State* County | Number of Farms in Sample | Number of Farms With Estimated Soil Losses in Various Ranges (tons/acre) | | | | |
|---|---|---|---|---|---|---|
| | | 0–5 | 5.1–10 | 10.1–20 | 20.1–40 | Over 40 |
| **Pacific Northwest** | | | | | | |
| *Washington* | | | | | | |
| Benton | 20 | — | 11 | 8 | 1 | — |
| Whitman | 30 | 5 | 14 | 11 | — | — |
| **Great Plains** | | | | | | |
| *Kansas* | | | | | | |
| Finney | 35 | 1 | 23 | 2 | 9 | — |
| *New Mexico* | | | | | | |
| Roosevelt | 28 | 2 | 7 | 9 | 10 | — |
| *North Dakota* | | | | | | |
| Burleigh | 11 | 7 | 4 | — | — | — |
| Walsh | 16 | 12 | 4 | — | — | — |
| *Texas* | | | | | | |
| Gaines | 39 | 1 | — | 2 | 5 | 31 |
| **Midwest** | | | | | | |
| *Illinois* | | | | | | |
| Adams | 36 | — | 6 | 16 | 9 | 5 |
| *Iowa* | | | | | | |
| Webster | 34 | 4 | 11 | 19 | — | — |
| *Wisconsin* | | | | | | |
| Grant | 34 | 12 | 15 | 5 | — | 2 |

*Source:* Comptroller General of United States, Report to Congress, 1977.

sectors of the economy. For one thing, effective soil management programs are frequently expensive to initiate and to maintain. Naturally these programs add to the cost of the farm product and thus the farmer must raise his/her price to recover the investment. If, however, only some farmers follow the suggested soil management practices they will find themselves at an economic disadvantage because the farmers who have not made such investments can produce their product at a lower cost. Farming, collectively, provides a textbook example of an economic activity that has so many producers that each individual producer has very little market influence (as compared with a monopoly situation where a single producer may be able to set the price for the product). Most farmers are not happy to follow practices that lead to the loss of their soil but farmers cannot afford—in view of the economic inflation that raises the cost of farm equipment, labor, and supplies at a rate considerably greater than the farmers can recover from the sale of their products—to comply fully. Under such conditions it is perhaps unreasonable to expect the individual farmer to pay the cost of soil management even though it might be argued that his or her long-run interests are best identified with such practice.

The nation's best interests are involved in the issue of controlling accelerated soil erosion. It is past time when we as a nation should demand that the same requirements to protect the environment be made of farmers as they are increasingly being made of urban industry. The same tax and income incentives must be made available and, the bottom line, we the consumers of farm products must realize our responsibility to pay the added cost that will come from an effective national soil conservation/management program.

**Figure 6.9** Grain (corn) stubble left in field to help retain moisture and reduce soil erosion.

**Figure 6.8** Stubble mulching. Note that the grain stubble remains at the surface to reduce wind erosion and water loss by evaporation.

The principal methods and techniques employed to reduce accelerated loss of soils include avoiding cultivation on steep slopes, plowing on the contour, trying as much as possible to keep some plant cover or mulch on the soil at all times and particularly during fallow periods (Figs. 6.8 and 6.9), giving quick attention to the development of any new gully, preventing overgrazing, reducing intensivity of soil use so that the soil structure doesn't degrade to easily eroded dust, permanently removing some current crop land from cultivation, and putting this crop land into low-intensity pasture or woodland/forest-use, depending on the situation.

Many of the foregoing items above are familiar to the reader but a brief review may nevertheless be in order. In earlier years the cultivation of very steep slopes was much more common than it is today. It is now too expensive to cultivate steep slopes except for a relatively few crops (e.g., wine grapes). However, it is still very common to encounter overgrazed pastures located on steep slopes and such situations, if they are not new, will usually present obvious evidence of soil loss. It should be noted, in this context, that much good farmland is not level but is best described as "rolling," that is, having gentle slopes. In irrigated regions where furrow or flood irrigation is practiced, land will be artificially leveled in order to manage the water. Where sprinkler irrigation is used the land may receive none or only limited artificial leveling.

Plowing on the contour means plowing more or less at right angles to the slope (Fig. 6.10). This seems like such an obvious adjustment it may surprise many that this is a comparatively recent practice, one that, unfortunately, is still not universally employed in the United States. By plowing with the contour the soil tends to either stay in place or to move only short distances over long periods of time.

Intensive cultivation often leads to the surface of the soil being uncovered for varying periods of time. Bare soil is especially prone to being eroded by moving water or by wind. It is absolutely essential that soil be left in an exposed condition for only the briefest of times and never over a winter, something that is still too often done in parts of the United States. Effective ways by which soils can be covered is to plant cover crops of grass or legumes or to mulch the surface of the soil. The latter can include leaving grain stubble in the ground until it becomes time to plow and plant the next crop. Another way is to spread crop residues such as straw on the ground; however, the best procedure is to grow a cover crop, preferably one that will add to soil fertility (e.g., legumes).

Gullying may result when improper soil management practices are followed on even fairly gentle slopes. This condition may be corrected by altering the practices that created the gully and by taking the gully and the adjacent area out of crop cultivation and planting appropriate shrubs or other permanent vegetation that will

**Figure 6.10** Contour plowing and cultivation to reduce soil erosion.

prevent the further accelerated loss of soil. It may also be appropriate to construct small soil-check dams in the bottom of the gully as a further hindrance to soil loss.

The prevention of overgrazing is one of the most important of all efforts directed toward the prevention of accelerated soil erosion. Although it is not very difficult to determine the *carrying capacity* (the maximum number of animals that may be stocked on a given pasture without causing damage to the pasture eco-system) of a given area it is often difficult for the cattle or sheep rancher to avoid overstocking. Also, the carrying capacity of a given area will fluctuate from year to year, sometimes dramatically so. Conditions for stocking may hover around average conditions for a number of years only to be sharply lessened by a severe drought. Ideally, the number of animals being grazed in such an area should be reduced to the new and much lower carrying capacity. However, this may be very difficult for a rancher to do without taking serious economic losses. If drought conditions are widespread this might force abnormally large numbers of animals onto the market, causing prices to be depressed below the level at which the producer can show a profit. Under such conditions it is common for the rancher to hold the animals off the market hoping for better prices.

In the meantime the animals must be fed, and purchased feed (alfalfa and other types of hay) generally becomes more expensive and in any case is always more costly than range grasses. Thus, the rancher will find himself or herself overgrazing his or her pastures and hoping that climatic and market conditions will change for the better. It can be seen, therefore, that even under the best managed situations climatic conditions can intervene to upset sound soil management practice. It is unrealistic to expect livstock ranchers to stock at rates that represent the carrying capacity for the dryest years on record. If such measures were practiced (and they would be only if so required by gov-ernment edict) the price of meat and other animal products would rise dramatically. In this context it should be pointed out that on U.S. government-owned lands rented or leased pasture land is subject to frequent modifications of allowable stocking levels.

The intensivity of soil use is affected by many factors among which market conditions are the most potent. In times when the prices (and profits) of agricultural products are high there is a tendency to work the land as hard as possible to take advantage of the favorable market conditions. But even in times when prices are comparatively low and perhaps still falling there is a common tendency to work the soil as hard as possible in an attempt to compensate for low prices with added production. Perhaps of even greater significance with respect to economics is the growing influence of large corporations that include farming as one of their many and diversified interests. Under these conditions, the soil may become simply an element of production.

Accelerated soil erosion is a national problem and requires a greater effort at the national level to lessen and, ultimately, bring under control. It would appear that only legislation at the national level could bring about the desired changes in the use of the nation's soils.

Bringing federal legislation forward as a solution is to open a subject that is one of the most emotionally charged in the field of American conservation and resource management. Our nation has long been committed to the concept that private ownership of resources is the most desirable way by which the resources of the nation can be apportioned. However, over the years and particularly at present, there has been and is a growing debate about the responsibilities of the owners of natural resources. With respect to soils, in most places in the United States the owner of a farm or ranch may use the land in such a way as to lead to its total ruin without being subject to legal sanctions.

With the now general recognition that there are no more new lands to be discovered, is it not time for the nation to assume a greater degree of legal responsibility for the protection and management of its soil resources? Our nation has for sometime been accustomed to federal regulation in many areas of our national economy, for example, the Interstate Commerce Commission (ICC), which regulates the interstate movement of goods, and the Federal Communications Commission (FCC), which regulates radio and television. These agencies and many others have been established where it was shown that national interest required governmental regulation. There is no such agency regulating the use of the nation's soils because the political conditions have worked against such a move. Recall, if you will, the comments made earlier in this chapter about what happened when the Soil Conservation Service (SCS) was established and how eventually the SCS had to back off and await invitation by the states through the Soil Conservation Districts of the state's own devising. The "farm bloc," as it is known in Washington, remains a potent element in American politics and rightfully so. But soil is too important a national problem to be left to the country's farmers alone to solve. The urban dweller must become better informed about soil erosion in the United States and must take more active roles in influencing legislation at state and national levels. It is ridiculous for there to exist a widespread belief that while city people can grasp the intricacies of an industrial society, questions about soil erosion are too difficult for them to understand.

## Loss of Soil Fertility

As we have seen in the brief descriptions of the soil orders that occur within the United States, fertility varies greatly from one order to another and also among the soils within individual orders. However, no matter how great the natural fertility of a soil may be, once it is farmed or grazed the fertility will tend to decrease with the passage of time. The rates of loss of plant nutrients will depend on many factors including climate, the soil itself, the kinds of crops grown, and the intensivity of the agricultural and grazing practices.

Under natural conditions, soil fertility may remain approximately static, may increase over time or, under conditions such as always high temperatures and high soil moisture, may lose fertility. In any case, farming and grazing will cause a loss of soil nutrients if the crop—plant or animal—is not left in place but is harvested. Thus, a decline in production will ensue in time unless fertilizers are added to compensate for the nutrient losses that accompany a harvest.

Farmers have been adding fertilizer to their fields for centuries in different parts of the world and the practice was commonly followed from the earliest colonial days in the United States. The principal fertilizers used were animal manures and, to a lesser degree, green manures. Animal manures differ in their nutrient contents especially with regard to nitrogen. However, compared with fertilizers produced in factories, manures generally have a far smaller percentage not only of nitrogen but also of other important nutrients such as phosphorus and potassium. Moreover, unless manures are given special care to prevent loss of nutrients, especially nitrogen, the nutrient content will be decreased. For these reasons, as well as the matter of limited availability in an era when animals no longer supply much of the energy on our nation's farms, the fertilizers most used on American farms are factory manufactured. These usually have greater nutrient contents than do manures and also the concentration of each nutrient is controlled so that the farmer is able to apply the quantities and combinations required by the crops being grown.

Contrary to much current opinion, there is nothing inherently wrong with the use of factory-produced fertilizer. Adherents of the "organic school" of cultivation are in error when they suggest that nitrogen that comes from a factory is inferior to nitrogen that is contained in animal manure. However, there is a serious problem that must be guarded against when using factory fertilizers: relying on increased applications of fertilizer to compensate for soil problems induced by unsound cultivation practices. Not only is this a costly procedure that can create further problems by causing a buildup of chemicals in the soil detrimental to some crops, it may also contaminate ground-water resources (see Chapter 9).

Loss of soil fertility may not always be solely attributable to the loss of nutrients. Cultivation practices that alter the soil's capacity to make the nutrients available to crops may also be partly to blame.

In general, today, loss of soil fertility is less a problem than it was prior to World War II when farming intensity often outstripped the then ex-isting available sources of fertilizer. The heavy and widespread applications of factory-made fertilizers are phenomena that have arisen since World War II.

## Mineral Accumulation in Soils

In the preceding section we noted that too-heavy applications of fertilizers may result in the accumulation of minerals to the detriment of crop plants. Of even greater significance are problems arising from the application of con-trol chemicals and the mineral changes asso-ciated with irrigated agriculture.

There are few more charged subjects than that of insecticides and pesticide applications on our nation's farms and grazing lands. Much, if not most, of the concern arose when it was brought to the public's attention that certain in-secticides such as DDT (dichlorodiphenyl-trichloroethane) produced widespread and long-lasting impacts in the ecosystems into which they were applied for insect pest control. These particular insecticides belong to a group called chlorinated hydrocarbons and they all not only persist in the soil for a long time but

they also often degrade into lethal and highly persistent compounds. It is now illegal to apply these kinds of insecticides in the United States unless a special permit is obtained and this is rarely given. Unfortunately, there is no ban on the continued manufacture of chlorinated hy-drocarbon insecticides nor on their sale to other nations.

A wide range of chemicals are employed for weed, fungal, and annual pest control. Al-though these appear to be less dangerous than many that were in use only a few years ago, it is too soon after their adoption to make any statements as to the long-run impacts, if any, that chemicals will have on soils.

In many parts of the West where irrigation is practiced, problems arise because soils often tend to become so impregnated with addi-tional minerals that soil productivity is either reduced or destroyed altogether. This phe-nomenon, called *salination,* is particularly common where aridisols are farmed, although the condition may arise wherever either the ir-rigation water is highly charged with dissolved minerals and/or where the soil naturally has a relatively high mineral content (Fig. 6.11). This subject is discussed in detail in Chapter 9, so suffice it to say here that these problems can be largely avoided by adopting correct irriga-tion methods and recognizing the limitations inherent in the water quality and mineral con-tent of the soil.

## Soil Compaction

Closely associated with the mechanization of American agriculture has been the rise in the incidence of soil compaction or increased bulk density, as it is also known. When heavy agri-cultural machinery is run repeatedly over a field the soil tends to become compacted, reducing the soil's capacity to absorb water, reducing air spaces in the soil, and thus reducing the soil's crop production capacity. In addition, farmers all too seldom return sufficient organic

**Figure 6.11** Soil salination in an irrigated field in California.

material to the soil in the form of crop residues and manure.

Soil compaction can be largely avoided by not running heavy machinery over the same routes time after time and also by taking care to add organic material to the soil. Unfortunately, in many parts of our nation, the trend is toward heavier farm machinery. Nevertheless, this problem is well known and understood by farmers and there appears to be a growing emphasis on returning organic wastes to the land.

Closely related to soil compaction are practices that lead to the impairment of drainage. Chief among these is plowing at the same depth year after year, which may create a *plow pan*. A plow pan is a layer of hard clay located at shallow soil depths which, when well devel-

oped, may be impervious to the passage of water. Thus, fields that may once have had good drainage may become waterlogged, a condition that will limit crop production. Most crop plants won't grow in a water-logged environment, and, should such a condition be created, the solution is to plow at varying depths after first having plowed sufficiently deep to break up the plow pan. The latter can be expensive and the entire problem can be avoided by adopting, at the outset, the practice of varying the depths at which the fields are plowed.

## Covering Good Soils with Buildings and Roads

Although given last place in this discussion of soil management and conservation, the practice of covering our soils with roads and buildings ranks only a little behind the seriousness of accelerated soil erosion. Various estimates are available as to the number of hectares of farmland taken out of production in the United States each year because of road construction or "development," but there does not yet exist a detailed study for the United States as to how much of our best and next to best agricultural soils have been covered over by construction. However, it does not require that such a study be done in order to become aware of the fact that one of the most senseless of American practices is the casual manner in which Americans allow their urban areas to encroach on highly productive soils. Examples are to be found in every farming region of the nation. In many places the phenomenon has gone on essentially unchecked for decades and few voices have been raised against it.

Although most cities employ one or more city planners, planning seldom, if ever, includes serious considerations about soil conservation in terms of keeping good soils under cultivation. The pressures to convert farmland to urban land are often enormous as cities seek more tax revenues and as "developers" seek to realize large profits on their land speculations adjacent to urban areas. Also, the farmers themselves frequently share in the search for profits to be realized on lands that might be converted to an urban-use tax classification. There are states where farmers have been the group most opposed to any attempt by the state legislature to pass laws that would have the effect of preserving the best soils of the state for agricultural use.

Here, again, is the classic conflict between concepts of private land ownership and the general public good. An important aspect of the conflict is that too many people think that there is so much land that urban spread makes scarcely a dent in the overall quantity of soil available for agriculture. The problem, of course, is the quality of the soil covered over by urban spread, and again, a large part of the urban spread has been at the expense of some of the best soils in many states.

The city person has the responsibility to learn how to prevent the entombment of fine agricultural soils. The issue is primarily economic and political. Most attempts to preserve soils for agriculture lead to proclamations about the sanctity of private property and property rights, but in no sector of our natural resources is the public interest more paramount, even though at present the general public has little influence over urban encroachment upon the nation's high-quality soils.

Roads, highways, parking lots, and similar construction features to accommodate the automobile have taken an enormous amount of formerly productive soils out of production. The vast interstate highway system slashes its multilaned paths across the nation with little regard for the soils that have been sacrificed so that we can drive in larger numbers and at greater speeds. In urban areas it is common for parking lots at factories to occupy more land (i.e., soil) than the factory structure occupies.

A wise nation would require a careful examination of all the trade-offs with a bias in favor of soil protection before any new construction were permitted and before any urban sprawl were allowed. A wise and mature nation would recognize that it is responsible for the future as well as the present and would temper the thirst for land profits. That we are not yet such a nation is only too evident but we can become such a nation when we recognize the central position that soil occupies in our nation's diminishing wealth of natural resources. Then the day might arrive when the term "developer" might in fact allude to a person whose activities are motivated in the direction of proper and responsible management of the soil resources adjacent to urban areas.

## SOIL CONSERVATION AND MANAGEMENT IN THE THIRD WORLD: SOME EXAMPLES

One phenomenon common to most Third World nations is their reliance on their soil resources to produce a major share of the products they export to obtain foreign exchange. Moreover, the human populations are chiefly rural and they depend far more on agriculture for a livelihood than on any other economic activity. Thus, it can be seen that the soil resources in the Third World have a singular importance making the conservation and management of the soils a matter of transcendental importance and necessity.

Contrary to the evident need to manage these life-sustaining resources properly, soils have been generally neglected and abused to the point that many Third World nations now must rely on far less good soils than they once possessed within the historical past.

Not only is there a preponderance of rural inhabitants in most of the Third World but this population, as noted before, has been increasing rapidly in recent years. This puts added pressure on what is often an already overtaxed and abused soils resource, thus further exacerbating already-existing soil problems.

## Latin America

All 10 soil orders we discussed are represented in the Latin American region but this diversity is overshadowed by the fact that almost one-half of the area is overlain with oxisols and ultisols. These soils have their greatest areal spread in South America and particularly in Brazil, Venezuela, Colombia, Guyana, Surinam, and French Guiana plus eastern Peru and eastern Bolivia. Soils that belong to these relatively infertile soil orders are also common in much of Central America, southern lowland Mexico, and parts of the Caribbean islands.

Mollisols, to go the opposite extreme in terms of soil quality, have a limited distribution in Mexico but are fairly well represented in parts of Argentina, Uruguay, Paraguay, southern Brazil, and Chile. Alluvial soils and soils derived from volcanic materials are locally distributed, and although they represent only a small percentage of the total soil cover of the region, they constitute an extremely valuable soil resource.

## Accelerated Soil Erosion in Latin America

Since early in the colonial era the chief problem with respect to soil use in Latin America has been *accelerated soil erosion* (Fig. 6.12). This problem has long been associated with livestock overgrazing and poor tillage practices, coupled with a rapidly growing rural-farm

**Figure 6.12**   Accelerated soil erosion in Mexico.

population that has been increasingly destructive of the soil. In more recent years forest removal on slopes has advanced to the point where it threatens to be a more serious cause of soil erosion than overgrazing.

H. H. Bennett was the first person to attempt an overall survey of soil erosion in Latin America, and in 1945 he estimated that some countries such as Mexico, Venezuela, and Ecuador had experienced accelerated soil losses of up to 50 percent or more on their farmlands and grazing lands. The soils of most Andean countries have been especially damaged because a large percentage of the agricultural population cultivates relatively steep slopes. The latter often results due to the nature of land tenure in parts of the Andean region. Since the early days of the colonial era the more level and hence less erodable land has been held in large estates (latifundias) by a few landowners. The rural population has been progressively forced up on the slopes. Much of these slopes is suitable only for poor pasture at best but is pressed into growing the food crops needed by the descendants of those who once worked the better land. Even the private estates are rarely the object of adequate soil management. This is due in part to ignorance but also to absentee ownership, a common practice throughout the region.

In other parts of Latin America, accelerated soil erosion has occurred on relatively modest slopes where tillage practices and soil characteristics combined to lead to rapid soil loss. One notable example is the region of *terra roxa* (red soil) in Brazil. This region, centered in the state of São Paulo, is the site of most of the commercial coffee production in Brazil. This crop has long played a fundamental role in the export economy of that nation and even today, after several decades of increased economic diversification, coffee remains of critical importance to Brazil's economy.

*Terra roxa* is an example of a soil that may be judged either good or poor depending on the crop one wishes to grow on it. This soil is particularly well adapted to coffee production because it is very porous, allowing for deep penetration of the roots of the coffee bushes. This allows the bush to obtain maximum moisture during dry periods as well as to exploit effectively the modest but (almost) sufficient nutrients available. However, for high nitrogen-demand crops such as cotton, *terra roxa* is totally unsuited and when planted to cotton the soil tends to erode very rapidly. Note, however, that growing coffee on these soils does not protect against rapid soil erosion. One of the principal problems of this coffee-growing region has been large-scale accelerated soil loss extending over many years. The chief response, for a long time, was to clear and plant new land rather than to care for land already under cultivation but suffering a heavy loss of soil.

It became apparent, during the past 10 years, that there was, after all, a limit to the total area suitable for coffee and this led to significant government-encouraged efforts to set up soil management programs. These programs focus on planting on the contour, using fertilizer, using cover crops and, in general, taking the measures already found elsewhere to be effective in slowing or preventing soil loss.

The coffee "frontier" has recently moved southward into Paraná state where there are extensive areas of *terra roxa* but also where killing frosts occur during the Southern Hemisphere winter. These frosts sometimes destroy a large part of the coffee crop and kill large numbers of coffee bushes. This, in turn, produces wild fluctuations in the world price for coffee and creates unstable conditions in the coffee-growing region of Brazil. These phenomena increase the difficulties associated with establishing and maintaining stable soil management programs.

Effective soil erosion control programs in Latin America must first of all be sensitive to the complex social realities of the region. Chief among these are the systems of land tenure that often produce wasteful soil practices. Absentee ownership of land and the misuse of poor soils on steep slopes by the rural poor population to grow their food and pasture their animals are ecological as well as social evils. However, land reform alone will not necessarily improve soil-use practices. On the contrary, breaking up large estates (latifundias) into small peasant holdings may hasten the loss of the remaining soil. Land reform must always include the establishment of a government-scientific infrastructure that assures the new landowners will manage the soil correctly. Unfortunately, this has seldom been the case in Latin America.

Land reform is too frequently seen as having relatively narrow political and social parameters and too often the government that has brought about reform in land tenure is content to rest on its laurels and to ignore the need to protect the soil resource against further loss by erosion. Another aspect of land reform having negative results is giving away to peasants soils that ought never to be placed under cultivation but ought to be planted with trees or turned into pasture with a controlled low-grazing pressure. Mexico, for example, has been particularly remiss in giving lands to *ejidos* (communal farms) that ought never be cultivated.

In the longer run, land reform can only be seen as a temporary solution to rural land tenure. In many, if not most, nations of Latin America there is now insufficient soil of farmable quality to be distributed to all the landless persons clamoring for it. Most of these nations will sooner or later have to face up to their demographic pressures and realize that however politically desirable land redistribution may be, it will result in national impoverishment of the soils resources if (1) a limit to such redistribution is not established and (2) if there is not a major soil erosion control program mounted to go along with the redistribution of land. Accelerated soil erosion is politically blind. That

is, political ideology whether left, right, or center will avail a nation nothing if it substitutes such ideology for sound soil management practices.

## Loss of Soil Fertility in Latin America

With comparatively few local, albeit important, exceptions, loss of soil fertility is ubiquitous in Latin America and may be growing worse in many parts of the region because of the explosive increase in the prices of factory-made fertilizers that has occurred since the rise in petroleum and natural gas prices. The principal exceptions to this generalization are found where there are intensive "modern" agricultural enterprises engaged in growing crops destined chiefly for export. In contrast to this are the countless farms whose proprietors can't afford to purchase fertilizer or, if they are able, care not to do so for various reasons. The need for much greater applications of fertilizer in Latin America is well known and thus the problem of fertility loss is widely recognized. On the other hand, is the small proprietor (i.e., the small landholder) in many of the nations of this region aware of the need to fertilize and if so, does he have the financial means to do so?

We must not think that with all soils of low fertility the problem is solely one of applying the needed chemicals. It may be that in many instances, and with particular reference to oxisols and ultisols, the application of costly fertilizers will not necessarily result in added crop production owing to the chemical and physical nature of these soils. Soils belonging to these two orders frequently possess properties that limit their capacity to move chemical nutrients from the soil to plant roots (limited cation exchange capacity). Thus, a well-meaning farmer or farm advisor might apply fertilizer only to find that the resultant crop production does not justify the economic costs involved. This does not mean that these and other soils can't be successfully fertilized but it indicates that considerable scientific soils investigations may be required before a good fertilizer program can be developed.

Although increased use of fertilizers is no panacea for inadequate agricultural production in Latin America, means must be found to permit farmers, and especially small landholders, to obtain the fertilizers they require at prices they can afford to pay.

### Soil Salination

Soil salination occurs in many parts of Latin America where agriculture is practiced in arid or semiarid climates. The places where such conditions are most significant include the northern part of the Mexican state of Baja California adjacent to the lower end of the Colorado River, north-central Mexico, parts of northeastern Brazil, intermontane basins in the Andes, and northeastern Argentina.

In all instances the problems are caused chiefly by a limited water resource containing large quantities of dissolved minerals and soils—often aridisols—having a high mineral content. Very understandable is the desire on the part of the farmers to irrigate as many hectares as possible but, unfortunately, this desire all too often exceeds the ecological limitations dictated by soil and water quality.

In concluding this discussion of soil management issues and needs in Latin America, it must again be stressed that the still-too frequent neglect of the soil resource threatens the ecological and economic foundations of the region. Although most if not all the national governments of the region are intent on achieving industrialization they often appear to adopt a myopic view vis-à-vis proper soil conservation and management.

### Africa

Most Africans, whether they be citizens of Libya or Mozambique, work on the land as farmers or herders or combinations of both. Furthermore, most African nations depend heavily on the soil not only to produce the daily food for their peoples but also for exports to obtain the foreign exchange required to pay for imported goods.

Most of the farmed or grazed areas are still subject to traditional practices, which are labor intensive with little use made of machinery, plant and animal genetics, commercial fertilizer, and pesticides. However, there are some areas where agriculture is very capital intensive and where livestock is managed according to the latest scientific precepts but these do not presently represent more than a small fraction of African agriculture and animal husbandry.

### Accelerated Soil Erosion

The overwhelming soil problem in most of Africa is accelerated soil erosion (Fig. 6.13). Although it is not yet established that most African soils are inherently more subject to erosion than are soils located elsewhere in similar lat-

**Figure 6.13** Extreme gully soil erosion in Kenya, Africa.

itudes it appears that this might be the case. Whatever may prove correct, accelerated soil erosion is far and away the most serious and pressing environmental problem that must be addressed on this continent.

The chief causes of this loss are deforestation, overgrazing, and cultivation practices that lead to lowered humus content plus other soil changes that result in a more easily eroded soil. There is also a growing conviction on the part of some observers that the plow may not be a suitable instrument for cultivation in many parts of the continent south of the Sahara because the plow hastens soil loss.

Chemical changes including salinization are to be found in many parts of Africa. As agriculture becomes more modern there is an associated increase in the use of chemicals to improve soil fertility (seldom high to begin with) and to control crop pests and unwanted wild vegetation. A unique aspect of herbicide application is the use of defoliants as a means to reduce the total brush-shelter available to the tsetse fly (*Glossina* sp.), the vector of African sleeping sickness.

Many African soils south of the Sahara contain a multitude of tiny sharply angular particles. These contribute to soil compaction when motorized agricultural equipment is used. In some instances, the soil surface becomes similar to the graded and compacted surface of roads.

## Salination

Salination is a threat wherever irrigation is pursued. Thus, salination has emerged as a problem in parts of the Sudan and other African nations where irrigation schemes have been undertaken. The Nile valley in Egypt has largely escaped salination problems even though this is one of the most ancient and continuously irrigated agricultural regions on earth. This has been due, in the past, to the annual flushing of the soil by the Nile flood and by the extremely porous alluvial soils (entisols) that floor the flood plain of the Nile River as it passes northward through Egypt to the Mediterranean Sea.

When Egyptian agriculture switched from a rhythm based on the annual Nile flood to water control made possible by the gigantic Aswan dam, the annual flushing (as well as annual increment of water-deposited fertile sediments) came to a halt. Now, commercially manufactured nitrogen must be applied to the fields since fertility would otherwise decline. Unless the greatest care is taken, salination may become a problem, and pesticide, herbicide, and other chemical residues may also be expected to accumulate in the soil in some parts of the Nile valley in Egypt.

## Desertification

The phenomenon whereby non–desert land is converted to desert by natural or human means (or a combination of both), is now recognized as one of the continent's most serious environmental problems. This phenomenon does not fit comfortably into a single category of soil, water, or plant conservation. Desertification is mentioned here because it entails, among other things, changes in the soil. These changes include lowered moisture content, lowered humus content, and a greater tendency to be eroded by wind. Much of the desertification presently taking place in Africa is occurring in the northern edge of the semiarid region adjacent to the southern Sahara. Thus, desertification is moving along a very broad front and each year hundreds of thousands of hectares of soil are being converted to desert conditions under which plant growth (primary productivity) is sharply diminished.

The causes of desertification are not yet understood in their entirety. It appears that part of the phenomenon is related to secular changes in the climate but it is also very apparent that human activities such as overgrazing livestock and overexploiting the available and always very limited water resources exacerbate what may, at base, be natural climatic phenomena. Recently a large region along the southern edge of the Sahara known as the Sahel, experienced a prolonged drought that resulted in the destruction of most of the carrying capacity of the always very poor pastures in the region (Fig. 6.14). Thousands of persons, formerly following the life of nomadic herders (with some agricultural activity when circumstance permitted) became the recipients of support from international food relief programs. It is unlikely that many of these people will ever be able to return to their former way of life because of the massive and apparently long-lasting damage sustained by the plants and soils of the Sahel. As noted, drought in the Sahel is a frequent occurrence but what makes this most recent drought so destructive is the overgrazing of livestock that developed during a few comparatively good rainfall years plus the added water resource made available by well-meaning foreign aid efforts that caused a number of wells to be driven to provide a more reliable supply of water. Herds of cattle increased as a result of this alteration of the frag-

ile semiarid ecology causing an overstocking of the available pasture. When the drought arrived, the area, having been over–exploited, was unable to withstand the lack of water and the Sahelians watched helplessly as their livestock, their only valuable possessions, perished by the thousands.

Although an accurate census of Africa's peoples is yet to be taken, enough is known to state that the rate of population increase in most parts of the continent is rising and that it may be expected that the annual increase may soon match the approximately 3 percent that presently characterizes much of Latin America. A map of the human population of Africa can be misleading because rather vast areas are shown to be almost devoid of human settlement. This is seldom an indication of great potential for pioneers to settle, however, but reflects, instead, the fact that the soils of enormous portions of the continent cannot support other than a modest number of persons. By the same token, some of the more densely settled nations, for example, Nigeria (the most

**Figure 6.14**  Drought conditions in the Sahel, Africa.

populous African nation south of the Sahara), and Uganda, do not necessarily indicate a particularly rich soil resource base. In the case of Uganda, the relatively high population density has developed on what, in the main, is a rather mediocre soil resource.

A major international effort is required in order to inventory Africa's soils and thus provide part of the data base for critically needed soil management programs. It is unfortunate that international groups in Africa such as the Organization for African Unity (OAU) have not found the means whereby such an effort could be mounted. Perhaps more than on any other continent the fate of present and future millions depends to a major extent on giving top priority to soil conservation.

## SUMMARY

It is comparatively easy, in a thoroughly urbanized society, to forget the central role played by the soils resource in our nation's well-being. Soils provide the nutrients for grasslands, forests, and croplands and while we often think first of other resources when evaluating the nation's natural wealth the United States would find itself immeasurably less wealthy were it not for the magnificent soil resources it possesses.

The scientific study, including the classification of soils, is of comparatively recent development worldwide: in the United States the time span of such work can be measured in decades. This recent start, however, should not obscure the fact that, at present, American soil scientists are among the most active in the world and their contributions have had great impact not only on soil conservation and management in the United States but in many foreign nations as well.

With respect to the federal government, a large share of soil studies is accomplished by the U.S. Soil Survey, a unit of the U.S. Department of Agriculture. Building first on the work of foreign soil scientists and later modifying that

work, the U.S. Soil Survey has devised a soil classification that focuses on the structure of soil as contrasted with systems of classification which focus upon the genesis, that is, the origin of soil. The U.S. Soil Survey soil classification now widely employed in the U.S. is termed the Seventh Approximation, a designation that draws attention to the fact that the classification is the result of an evolving study and that the final refinement has not yet been achieved. The Seventh Approximation recognizes 10 major soil orders of which nine occur within the boundaries of the conterminous United States, further evidence of the soil wealth alluded to above.

Although important strides have been made in soil science in the United States it is unfortunately not similarly true of the effective application of soil conservation measures to a large percentage of the nation's farmlands. The results of this appear frequently in published statistics, which point up the large-scale loss of soil that continues to occur in this country. There is a curious history of limited concern for accelerated soil erosion and other soil problems in the United States. It was not until 1927 that any serious national attention was focused on our soil resource and it was not until 1935 that the federal government passed a soil conservation act. This created the Soil Conservation Service (SCS), a unit of the Department of Agriculture. However, this agency finds itself unable to do the total job intended originally because principal legal responsibility for soil conservation is retained by the states and the SCS may operate in a given state only if an invitation is received to do so. This limitation, however, has not prevented the SCS from accomplishing valuable work but soil conservation problems are far greater than is the legal ability of the SCS to correct them.

Of the varied problems associated with soil conservation, accelerated soil loss is by far the most important in the United States. Yet, huge quantities of some of the nation's finest soils are washed away or blown away annually because farmers do not adopt what are well-known and readily applicable soil management practices. The reasons for this situation are several, of which economic limitations and carelessness are the most significant. The major economic problem is that good soil management costs money and the economic return, in the short run, may not justify the expenditure unless all farmers make similar investments and thus all add these costs to the product they grow or produce. A conscientious farmer may find that he or she is placed at a competitive disadvantage by making soil conservation investments if other farmers do not do so. Of course, in the long run, good soil management practices will have a positive economic return, but farmers, like most persons, make the most of their decisions in terms of the short run.

It is one of the hallowed beliefs in our nation that private land is not and should not be subject to more than the very minimum of governmental control. However, a quick examination of the actual legal situation shows that governments have often interfered with private landholders through taxation, application of eminent domain (whereby the state is able to seize land if it is required for a "higher" public need), legal constraints on how land may be used (land zoning), and other constraints. Thus, to suggest that there is ample legal precedent for a greater legal role to be played by the federal government with regard to conserving the nation's soils is not outrageous.

It does not appear that many state governments have the political will to do the necessary job of achieving proper soil conservation. It would appear to some that just as the nation views the air as a national resource whose quality is a federal matter of concern, so too, should be the soil resources. As long as soil conservation is left up to individuals and to state governments, our nation will continue to waste this resource.

Although most Third World nations depend to an extraordinary degree on their soils to provide not only the food required for their citizens but also the export crops often desperately needed to obtain foreign exchange, these nations commonly mistreat their soils with an abandon that is ecological suicide. This is only too well illustrated in many parts of Latin America and Africa as well as in virtually every other part of the Third World.

Latin American nations, with few exceptions, still have the greater share of their active labor force working the land (as compared with the United States where less than 5 percent of the labor force is so employed). Yet one can scarcely travel more than a few kilometers in any direction in rural areas and not encounter evidence of accelerated erosion, loss of fertility, salination, or some other problem or group of problems. Some of this condition is related to the recent explosive growth in the human population but many of the soil problems antedate this by centuries. What we encounter is the collision of a centuries-old mismanagement of the soil with the recent and current major expansion of human numbers.

Unfortunately, many of the governments of this region prefer to allocate government funds to the urban industrial sector and to ignore the rural farming sector. Accepting the argument, almost universally advanced by Third World nations, that they must increase their industry, to accomplish this at the continued cost of major damage and loss of soil is an ecologically untenable course yet one that is generally followed throughout the region.

One must, however, note the fact that progress of a sort is being made in some of these nations with respect to demonstrating the techniques of soil management to more and more farmers. However, many economic constraints limit the adoption of these techniques not least of which is the large number of economically marginal peasant farmers in this region.

The problems of soil loss in Africa are as

great if not greater than those occurring in Latin America. This is owing to many factors among which are population growth, an overwhelmingly large percentage of the total population striving to farm or herd animals for a living, and what appears to be a singular lack of high-quality soils and, particularly, soils that do not rapidly deteriorate when put under the plow. There do not yet exist any reliable measures of the rates of soil loss for most of the African continent but general written accounts are sufficient to attest to an enormous and growing loss due to poor tillage and herding practices.

Of almost equal seriousness is the rapid en-croachment of the desert on lands formerly productive of crops and animals. This phenomenon, termed *desertification,* is marching unchecked across several parts of the African continent leaving in its wake ecological desolation.

It is another of the bitter ironies of our age that while an international organization exists in Africa, the Organization for African Unity, which could provide the political infrastructure for mounting an international program to save the continent's soils, the organization has been far more interested in military matters.

# grassland resources

## INTRODUCTION

The prophet Isaiah observed that "all flesh is grass," which is the same idea expressed by ecologists when they say that grass and other green plants are primary producers. Grasslands are among the most important of the world's natural resources because they provide food for many of our domesticated herbivores, provide habitat and food for many nondomesticated animals, stabilize soils, contribute to soil development, and provide us with recreational areas. However, scientific management of grasslands is still in its early stages.

It is difficult to say precisely what the most important aspect of grasslands is insofar as this ecosystem relates to human use. However, it is certain that among the most important aspects is that of providing the food required by cattle, sheep, and the domesticated herbivores. These animals provide us with meat, milk, hides, and fleece whose total economic value, worldwide, is enormous. Of particular value is the protein these animals supply to human diets. Protein, that is, the amino acids, is essential to the growth and healthy functioning of humans. A lack of sufficient quality protein between the age of weaning and the age of seven or eight tends to cause the affected child to be smaller than children receiving adequate protein. There is also accumulating evidence that protein deficiency occurring during early childhood may result in permanent mental retardation. It is true that adequate protein can be obtained from a vegetarian diet but this is often difficult to

achieve and it appears that most of the world's people prefer animal protein if it can be obtained. It can therefore be appreciated that when we speak of the grassland resource, we speak of one of the principal actual or potential sources of protein production to satisfy human needs and this indicates that grasslands must be among the high priorities for correct management. In wealthy countries, and particularly in the United States, grasslands when used for cattle pastures are viewed as only a step toward meat production because it is the prevailing practice to "finish" beef in feedlots. This finishing process consists of fattening the cattle with grains and other foods before sending them to market. This is a high-energy consumption activity and there are already moves underway to encourage the public to accept beef as it comes off the grass rather than demanding the more energy-costly feedlot beef. This suggests that, in the future, greater attention will be given to finishing beef on grass. This would tend to make our grasslands even more important than they are at present.

## GRASSLAND TYPES

The thousands of years of human association with grasslands has given rise to a varied folk-taxonomy of which some of the more widely used will be discussed as follows.

The terms used for grasslands in the United States in past years tended to reflect the differing nationalities of the Europeans who have lived in the region. Today, however, the vocab-

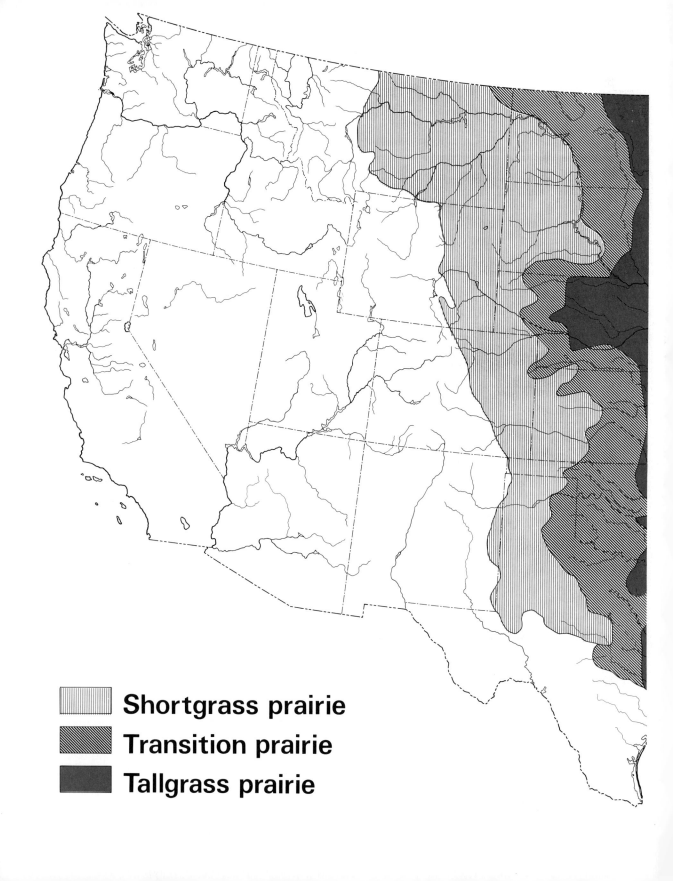

Shortgrass prairie

Transition prairie

Tallgrass prairie

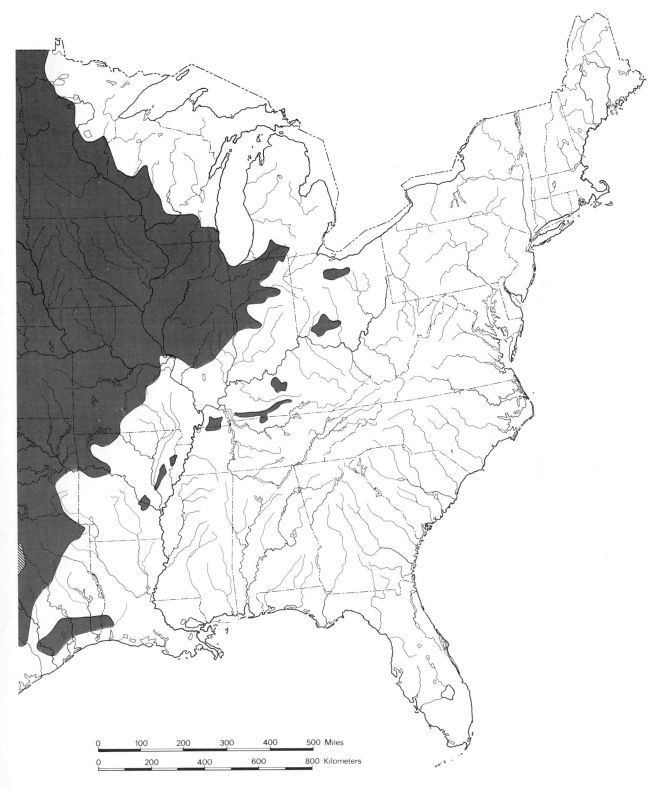

**Map 7.1** Approximate distributions of tall grass, transitional grass and short grass prairie in the United States prior to European settlement and disturbance.

ulary is fairly limited and the words *rangeland, prairie* and *grazing type* are the most frequently used to describe nonirrigated grasslands west of the Mississippi River. Sometimes the term Great Plains is used to describe not only a physiographic region but also the grassland as well.

Rangeland, or simply range, is the term most frequently used by livestock raisers and grassland managers. The term prairie is used frequently by biologists, ecologists and naturalists when they write about the grassland between the Rocky Mountains and the western edge of the eastern woodlands.

Rangelands embrace subtypes that may be recognized on the basis of the extent to which they have been deliberately modified or by the kind of grazing they provide. The former may be divided into unimproved rangeland, which is grassland that has not been the object of attempts to increase its production of plant species palatable to domesticated livestocks, improved rangeland, which is grassland that has been reseeded to desirable grass species and perhaps given some fertilizer as well, and desert rangeland, which is a special type of unimproved grassland but set apart because it almost never pays to attempt to improve such grasslands due to limited potential primary productivity. Grazing types are usually described on the basis of the dominant vegetation and therefore rangeland in this classification includes a lot of situations where grass is not the dominant vegetation.

Turning to prairies, three types are usually recognized: tall grass, transition and short grass. Tall-grass prairie is almost completely gone now because its distribution coincided with soils and climates suited to growing corn and other valuable crops. Much of the transition prairie has also gone under the plow but a fair amount remains and provides valuable grazing areas. The short-grass prairie still occurs over large parts of the high plains. Tall-grass prairies attained heights of nearly 2 me-

ters by the end of the summer growing season, the short-grass prairie peaks out at well under 1 meter high while the transition prairie attains heights between the two just mentioned parameters (Map 7.1).

Outside of North America but in latitudes similar to those occupied by the North American grasslands, other names are employed for this biome (Map 7.2). In parts of Eastern Europe and widely over Asia the word *steppe* is more or less synonymous with our use of rangeland. In the Southern Hemisphere in analogous latitudes one encounters the word *pampas* in Argentina and *veld* in Africa.

Some of the terms frequently encountered in low latitudes in the Western Hemisphere are the following: *savanna,* which is applied to a wide range of grass-shrub-tree-palm combinations. The word is of American Indian origin and has been applied to tropical grasslands in many parts of the world: *potrero,* which means pasture in Spanish and *llano,* which means a plain in Spanish but often is used synonymously with potrero; in Brazil, *campo* is widely used to designate a grassland. Many combinations are used each referring to the relative density of grass, shrubs, trees, or palms.

In the Asian tropics one encounters terms familiar to North American and European usage. However, one local name, *kogón,* of possible Tagalog origin, bears mentioning. This term refers to grasslands dominated by *Imperata* spp. that frequently occupy soils that have been damaged by unsound farming practices. Great expanses of *kogonales* occur in the Philippine Islands, Indonesia, and mainland Asia. These grasses are tough and have a very low nutritive value.

## ORIGIN OF THE NORTH AMERICAN GRASSLANDS

One of the long-standing controversies in geographical and biological circles swirls around the origin of the once great area of grasslands

that lay between the Rocky Mountains and the eastern woodlands and that extended from the Gulf of Mexico well into central Canada. Long assumed to be a climatically controlled climax ecosystem it has been shown that some of the areas covered by grass receive more than enough precipitation to support trees or other woody vegetation.

It has come to be widely recognized that fire has contributed to the establishment and maintenance of the grassland biome. Evidence for this consists of the frequency of lightning caused fire and recorded observations of Plains Indians using fire to drive game mammals past bowmen or, in a few special situations, over cliffs where the animals fell to their deaths or were injured so severely that they could be killed easily. With both lightning and human-set fire, the flames might range over a great area before a natural break such as a river or escarpment would bring them to a halt. The comparatively low relief of the region offers only limited natural obstructions to flames.

Although fire contributed to the total areal extent of the grasslands and to the plant-species content, vertebrate and invertebrate animals also played and still play significant roles with particular regard to plant-species composition. The importance of herbivores is particularly important because most of them, vertebrate or invertebrate, are selective feeders—in the case of the larger vertebrates one says

selective grazers—and thus exert pressures that collectively result in much of the plant species diversity that occurs in the biome. Changes in the population size of any one of these herbivores can result in changes in the plant species composition.

Recognizing this phenomenon, rangeland managers describe vegetation responses brought about by grazing mammals in terms of decreasers, increasers and invaders (Fig. 7.1). Decreasers are grass species that are easily depleted under even modest grazing pressure. Increasers are the grass species that can stand up fairly well to grazing pressure. Invaders are the grass and other plant species that tend to invade a grassland that has been severely overgrazed. Many invaders are of limited value for livestock and many wild animals as well. The particular species belonging to the decreaser and increaser categories will vary within a given grassland depending on the particular animal species involved in the overgrazing. Although the term properly includes wild mammal grazing it is usually confined to cattle and other domesticated livestock. However, prior to the introduction of domesticated animals, the North American grasslands were grazed by millions of bison and by lesser but still large numbers of antelope and deer. In addition, vast numbers of rodents exerted pressure on these biomes. An example of the latter is the black-tailed prairie dog (*Cynomys ludovi-*

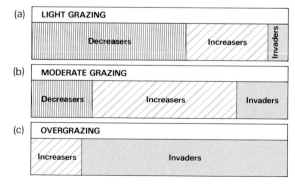

**Figure 7.1** The relative behavior of three major rangeland components when subjected to varying degrees of grazing pressure.

*cianus*) (Fig. 7.2). This prolific rodent, now reduced to what is only a few remnant populations, once ranged from northern Mexico to the United States-Canada border. A highly social animal, these rodents sometimes occurred in huge concentrations called "dog towns," adjacent to which they were undoubtedly the single most important biological force exerted on the grass.

To summarize, the North American grassland east of the Rocky Mountains owes its former areal extent to climate, fire, and a variety of biological factors of which selective feeding was the most important.

## HISTORY OF RANGELAND USE IN THE UNITED STATES

Until the arrival of Europeans there were no domesticated grazing animals on any of the grasslands of North America. The arrival of Spaniards in the sixteenth century marked the beginning of a series of ecological events that have resulted in changes in the plant and ani-

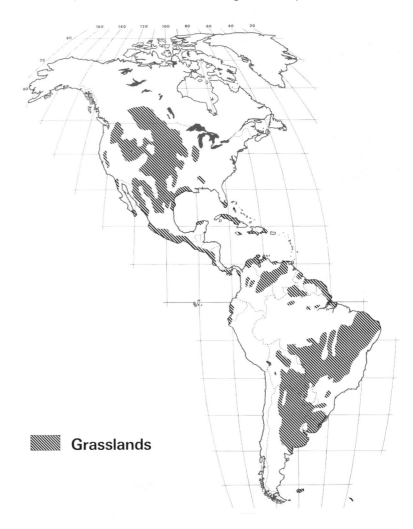

███ **Grasslands**

mal species composition of the native grasslands. Spaniards introduced cattle, horses, sheep, and burros and, with few exceptions, these animals were allowed to multiply and to wander with little or no restriction. Cattle were usually the most important, economically speaking, because they provided hides and tallow for which there was a large market demand. Meat production, in the early decades, was of limited economic importance. Although we have no documented record we may nevertheless correctly assume that as livestock

numbers increased the structures of the grasslands also began to change and especially with regard to the numerical frequency of individual plant species.

Spanish-introduced livestock ranged over much of what is now called the southwestern United States. No accurate counts were kept of animal numbers but general descriptions made at the time indicate that, locally, cattle sometimes numbered in the thousands and that overgrazing was frequent.

However, it was after the U.S. Civil War, that

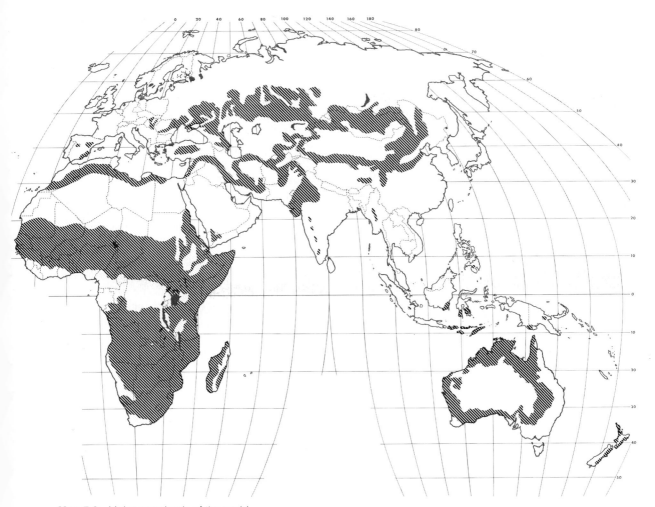

**Map 7.2**  Major grasslands of the world.

**Figure 7.2** Prairie Dog colony in North Dakota. The mounds of earth were excavated by animals.

livestock, cattle, and sheep really became ecologically important on most of the prairie rangelands. Although Americans (as distinct from Mexicanos) had begun to raise cattle almost with the founding of the East Coast colonies, the *range cattle industry* was a product of the prairie rangeland. The early, post-Civil War range cattle industry depended on unlimited access to grass and water. This was the era of "cattle barons" and "cowboys." The former included U.S. citizens as well as various foreigners and particularly French and English investors. The cowboys included many young men and boys who worked under miserable conditions for miserable wages not guessing that they were establishing the most durable regional literary genre in the nation's history.

Fortunes were occasionally made in this business and this attracted some men who had more money than good ecological sense. The fever to get rich with beef—for now the emphasis was on meat and not hides although the latter continued to be valuable—led to the overstocking of many parts of the range. Virtually none of these entrepreneurs had any detailed understanding of the ecology of the grasslands they had preempted and this ignorance applied with special vigor to the climates. Al-

though some of this region receives abundant and reliable precipitation, other parts are not so well watered and in these areas "average" precipitation has little meaning because there is often a large range of total precipitation between one year and another. This remark about the "average" also applies to the length and severity of winters.

For almost 20 years, environmental conditions were such as to lull many into overextending themselves at the bank and to overstocking the range. Some of the advertisements of the era designed to attract investors to this "sure-fire" opportunity to become wealthy are almost painfully amusing in their ecological and biological naivete. Then came the winter of 1885 which was so severe—and particularly in the southern prairie region—that a large percentage of the cattle perished and many of those animals that survived did not gain back all their strength during the following spring and summer. The animals were in no condition to stand up the next winter, that of 1886–1887, which in its severity made the previous winter appear almost benign. This time the loss of animals was disastrous and attended by many financial failures. Although winter severity was the proximate cause of the losses this problem was exacerbated by the poor condition of overgrazed lands that were unable to provide the survivors of the 1885 winter with sufficient quality food to help them get through the following winter.

Damage to the range because of overgrazing was apparent some years prior to the winters just mentioned but there was really no legal mechanism available to put a halt to the practice of overgrazing. Much of the land claimed by ranchers was not theirs legally and was held by voiced claim and sometimes by force of arms. At base, this great expanse of grass was a "commons" to which many claimed grazing "rights" but for which no one was held responsible to see that the biome was not misused. There were virtually no fences in the region and when a farmer attempted to put one up to protect his crops it was almost certain to be destroyed. This, then, was the era of the open-range cattle industry, a period that lasted little more than two decades.

Cattle and sheepmen were not the only settlers to spread themselves upon the grasslands after the Civil War. In 1862, the Congress of the United States passed the Federal Homestead Act, which made it possible to obtain 160 acres (approximately 65 hectares) of government land at little more than the cost of a man's labor for a relatively brief time. Unfortunately, the Act was ecologically blind and made no distinction between humid, semiarid, and arid lands. Thus, when the homesteaders attempted to take up land in the region of the short-grass prairie, they encountered problems for which they were unprepared except that many displayed a degree of courage and fortitude in the face of hardship that evokes one's admiration today. Among the problems encountered were grasshopper plagues, drought, severe winters, lack of transport, lack of a market for the crops they did succeed in raising, financial stress, and the almost continuous opposition of cattlemen who resented this invasion of "their" grassland. Many of the would-be

homesteaders failed and their land was often acquired for a pittance by ranchers but often not before the homesteader's foredoomed efforts had disturbed the ecosystems and damaged them in various ways.

Homesteaders who had the good fortune to stake their claims in areas humid enough to bring in a crop faced the problems listed above plus the one of a lack of economical fencing material. As noted earlier, stockmen wanted an open range and bitterly resented any attempt to fence the grass away from their animals—even though the men had no legal claim to the grass. Most farmers found that without adequate fencing they stood to lose all or part of their hard-earned crops to cattle. The all-but-treeless plains made wood prohibitively expensive and stone was rare or nonexistent. Untold person-hours were spent in the task of guarding crops from cattle.

Finally, in the 1870s, an effective and inexpensive fencing material became available, this being barbed wire. Farmers were soon fencing their properties with this and the response of the stockmen was immediate and sometimes violent. Fence cutting reached such levels of physical violence and property damage that some states passed laws making wire cutting a felony. In some instances mere possession of wire cutters could get a man into serious difficulties that might end in his life being taken. Without barbed wire there could have been no effective agricultural settlement on much of the plains. Thus, barbed wire can be viewed as an ecological factor of major importance in the grassland biome we call the prairie.

Vast tracts of prairie land, however, continued to elude settlement by stockman and farmer alike because of a lack of surface water. Without readily available water, cattle and sheep could not be grazed nor land homesteaded. This problem was particularly pronounced west of the 100th meridian where annual precipitation tends to be modest and there are often considerable distances between streams and springs. Coupled with the just-mentioned conditions is a water table that is often too deep for the hand digging of wells. Well digging was finally solved by the use of well-drilling rigs but there remained the problem of getting the water to the surface. This last was solved with the introduction of the windmill, which makes use of the wind that is such an ubiquitous feature of the Great Plains. Water is pumped into tanks and troughs and thus made available for humans and their beasts. According to the historian Walter Prescot Webb, it was the railroads who introduced the windmill to the plains, after which it was adopted by cattlemen and then by farmers.

Barbed wire was first seen by stockmen as an enemy but they later came to adopt it for their own use because they found it all but impossible to upgrade herd quality and to manage the grasslands unless they had some means of controlling their livestock. However, the advent of fencing in the now closed-range cattle and sheep industries did not mark the beginning of a more careful use of the grass resource. The same fundamental lack of understanding of the ecological limitations of this region prevailed and thus overstocking was general. The effects of such practice often became clearly visible only after severe damage to the grass cover and soil had occurred.

Farmers also affected the grassland in a number of ways not the least of which was destroying the sod by plowing areas too dry to support nonirrigated agriculture. Many a homestead had to be abandoned but the regrowth of a soil-stabilizing grass cover was often slow and serious loss of soil frequently occurred as well as a general lowering of grazing quality. Farmers also played a role in the larger picture of overgrazing livestock. Many farmers tried to fatten a few steers for market and this often was attempted on too little land and the result was badly overgrazed pastures.

By the early years of the twentieth century an abundance of reports had accumulated in various government archives attesting that much of the rangeland—including desert rangelands—had been damaged because of a lack of proper management. The reports also made it clear that actions causing such damage had by no means ceased but it was not until 1936 that a detailed quantitative evaluation of rangeland conditions was published. The report told how fine grazing lands were reduced to a small fraction of their former carrying capacity. This report owed its existence to the passage, in 1934, of the Taylor Grazing Act—named for a congressman, Edward T. Taylor, from Colorado. This legislation was bitterly opposed by many livestock interests in the West as well as proponents of states rights, who saw in the legislation a means for the federal government to usurp what some felt were rights belonging to the individual states. The Act had been devised for the purpose of halting overgrazing on public lands and to bring some order to the often economically chaotic livestock industry—particularly the large sector that depended on the public domain for grass. The Act has been of enormous importance in providing a basis for the development and application of sound range management practices on the public lands in the western United States.

Administration of the Taylor Grazing Act fell to a succession of federal agencies until 1946 when the responsibility was given to the then newly established Bureau of Land Management (BLM) (Map 7.3). The government rangelands were divided into grazing districts (numbering 52 at present) and grazing is controlled in order to allow previously damaged land to recover and, in all cases, to prevent overgrazing.

Persons not owning land adjacent to a grazing district may not rent land from the BLM. This was thought necessary in order to prevent itinerant and landless herders from misusing the range. The BLM controls the grazing rights to approximately 178 million acres (about 72 million hectares), an area approximately equal to 1.75 times the size of California. Although the numbers fluctuate, approximately 9 million head of livestock, mostly cattle and sheep, graze these lands each year.

The early 1930s were also marked by other federal legislation designed to conserve and better manage the range resource. An example of this was legislation allowing development of a program permitting the federal government to purchase lands that had been seriously damaged by cultivation and/or overgrazing and to retire such lands from further cultivation. Approximately 2.5 million acres (one million hectares) were obtained and are now under careful management of the BLM. Some land, in 1960, was designated as National Grasslands. Totaling about 3.8 million acres (1.54 million hectares) these are located chiefly in the high plains although Idaho and Oregon have some National Grasslands. The National Grasslands are administered by the U.S. Forest Service and grazing is permitted under terms contained in the Taylor Grazing Act.

As noted earlier, damage to the plains was not confined to the pioneering era in that region. Although 160-acre homesteads were ecological and economic impossibilities in some of the region, it was discovered that wheat could be grown providing there was sufficient precipitation at least in some years. Wheat growing in this region has always been something of a gamble against the weather. Fortunes have been made in years when there has been ample rain or snow coupled with high grain prices. But wheat prices have varied almost as much as the weather in this region and crop-destroying droughts and low prices have also been common features of the wheat-growing industry. In economically good times and bad there has been a strong tendency to plant wheat on what at best is marginal land—marginal in the sense that precipitation is rarely adequate to bring in a harvestable crop. This sometimes led to the degradation of parts of the short-grass prairie and soil losses in mammoth quantities.

The most dramatic soil erosion was by wind transport. In the decade of the 1930s, after a prolonged drought coupled with great areas from which all plant cover had been removed by human agency, the dust began to blow resulting in what has come to be known as the "dust bowl." Millions of tons of topsoil were picked up by the wind and transported eastward. Although most of the dust fell well within the borders of the United States some fell into the Atlantic Ocean. This ecological and economic calamity set in motion a human migration composed of the people who had not the means to repair what decades of misuse had wrought on the land. This migration, dramatized by John Steinbeck in his novel, *The Grapes of Wrath,* was nature's means of collecting on an ecological debt long overdue, a debt that had begun to accumulate when the first stockman allowed his animals to overgraze a part of the range and from the time the first homesteader broke the sod on prairie that ought never to have been disturbed.

As indicated in chapter six, accelerated soil erosion remains a major problem in this region even after the expenditure of huge sums of money to correct the problem. Although now provided with a rich data base and an impressive number of available management techniques and access to all kinds of expertise, too many private landowners persist in practices that year by year reduce the quality of the nation's privately held rangeland resource.

## OBJECTIVES OF RANGE MANAGEMENT

The chief objectives of range management in the United States are few and straightforward. These objectives are also applicable to other places in the world but sometimes there are cultural or other variations that must be taken

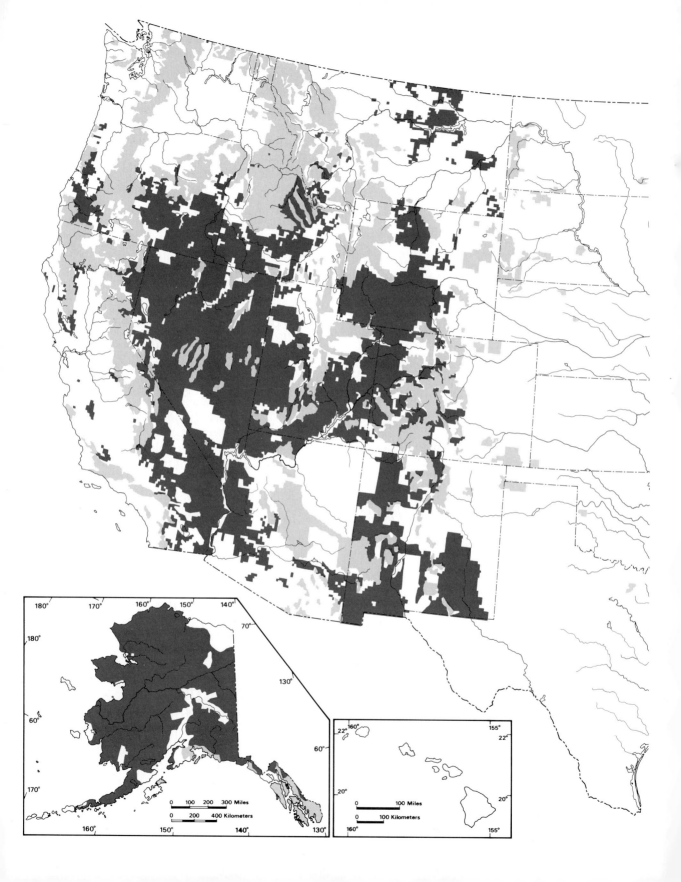

**Bureau of Land Management**

**National Forest**

**Map 7.3**  Land administered by the Bureau of Land Management (U.S. Atlas).

into consideration and these will be discussed later in this chapter.

1  To limit the harvest (either by direct grazing or by cutting for hay) to only that part of the productivity that does not degrade the grassland quality, that is, does not lead to conditions suited to *invaders* nor to accelerated soil erosion.

2  To achieve the just-stated objective of proper stocking-rates the following must be done:

**(a)** The carrying capacity must be determined and not exceeded.

**(b)** Animals should be moved from one pasture to another never allowing stock to remain long enough to degrade the grassland.

**(c)** When indicated, grasslands should be reseeded to palatable species of native grasses.

**(d)** Fertilizer should be applied at least during the time degraded grassland is in the process of being restored to higher levels of primary productivity.

**(e)** When indicated, there should be control of undesirable weedy and woody plant species.

The key to almost all sound range management is the determination of the carrying capacity and to translate this into the permissible *stocking rate*. The latter is usually expressed in terms of an animal unit. One such unit is the "animal unit month," which is the amount of forage required to support one cow or five sheep for one month. One frequently encounters "cow-calf unit," which refers to a mother cow and its calf. This last named unit is often seen in advertisements of ranches for sale in which the reader is informed as to the number of cow-calf units the ranch is capable of carrying throughout the year. In this context, it might be pointed out that relatively few bulls are required to impregnate a herd of cows and some ranching operations run no bulls at all but rely instead on artificial insemination.

Determination of the stocking rate is difficult and requires, at a minimum, an intimate and detailed knowledge of the species composition of the range, how the given range vegetation responds to grazing and at what grazing pressure woody species or other invaders can be expected to appear. A knowledge of *local ecological succession* is of critical importance as this is no task for armchair resource managers. At present, such determinations are often highly idiosyncratic and intuitive, based as they are on the individual experience of the range manager. It is a major aim of range management to shift as much as possible of this work to computers but until better rangeland models are developed there is no substitute for the "person on the spot"—and perhaps never will be because the models will always require further refinement and this can come only if there is an input of field-derived data.

Raising livestock is not only an ecological activity it is also an economic activity and thus decisions respecting stocking rates on privately owned range are certain to be influenced by short-run economic conditions as well as by long-run ecological considerations. Although motion pictures and television often make the raising of livestock to appear romantic and exciting this is one of the more difficult means by which people attempt to earn their daily bread. The vagaries of climate, animal health and livestock market prices seldom combine for long to convey a sense of comfort and safety to the men and women who follow this way of life.

In the United States relatively few cattle and sheep (lambs) are sold to the retail markets directly from the range. Most of the animals destined for the dinner table are purchased by feed-lot operators who fatten the stock and then send it to market. The livestock raiser often operates on a small profit margin and frequently suffers financial loss. Thus, for many stock raisers, doing the kinds of things they should such as keeping the stocking rate within the ecological limits of their pastures may appear financially impossible. So, the tendency is to hope that each year will be a good year of abundant grass—although this is a gamble that clearly cannot be won because the dry years will inevitably arrive and the rancher will be forced to reduce herd size and probably increase the debt load by borrowing to purchase hay for the stock he or she retains. By the time the excess stock is sold off the range is damaged and it is not unusual to see pastures almost as bare of grass as a city sidewalk. A pasture so stressed will not return to a quality grassland unless a considerable amount of money is spent on seed and fertilizer and stocking rates are held very low to allow recovery—all of which is often beyond the means of the rancher or he/she wouldn't have allowed the deterioration to have occurred in the first place.

Stocking rates on BLM and other government-owned and managed rangeland is more easily controlled and hence the potential for damage is lessened. However, we deal here with a real-world situation in which the dictates of sound ecological practices are frequently the object of adverse pressure by stockmen who, understandably, want to get as many animals as possible on the public domain. Relatively few livestock ranches are self-sufficient in land. Most ranchers have a "home" ranch comprising the private land they own and then lease land from the BLM or some other government agency.

The leases are arranged in such a way that a rancher can depend on having access to the public range for what is, in effect, perpetuity. As long as the rancher obeys the restrictions respecting stocking rates and the like he or she operates on the leased land as though it were his or her own. When ranches are offered for sale it is usual practice to include the area of leased land in the description of the property.

Knowing and adhering to correct stocking rates is not enough to assure correct use of grass. It is necessary that the animals be moved from place to place in order to prevent local damage. Livestock, if left to their own ways, tend to overgraze some pastures and to underutilize others. Sheep, particularly, must be grazed with considerable skill and must always be accompanied by a shepherd lest grave damage be caused by these animals. Sheep crop grass very close to the surface of the ground and if not kept moving slowly over the grass will even uproot the grass and cut up the soil surface with their sharp hooves. Cattle do not require such close supervision and it is usually sufficient to drive animals from one pasture to another without continued surveillance by a herder. Cattle ranches are usually fenced and cross-fenced to facilitate range management but the leased land has few fences, as a rule, and stock must be watched somewhat more closely and herded from one place to another as conditions dictate.

Reseeding range is an excellent means of improving carrying capacity. There are business firms that specialize in the sale of wild grass seeds and ranchers may obtain the expert help and advice of farm agents in order to maximize the returns from reseeding efforts. It might be objected that reseeding is not natural but one is reminded that neither is the grazing of cattle and sheep on North American grasslands nor, for that matter, is much of the rangeland itself. These lands have been so modified by human acts that there is little of the pristine remaining. Livestock ranching is only a division of agriculture and as such can profit by the acceptance of certain management concepts long ago adopted by farmers.

Sometimes extraordinary increases in grassland productivity can be achieved by the application of fertilizer including not only nitrogen but other elements that may be present in too limited a quantity to assure a vigorous stand of high-quality grass species. Unfortunately, this is a costly process and the recent rise in the price of nitrogen fertilizer has made its application to grasslands very expensive. If a trend should develop for a widespread retail acceptance of grass-finished beef perhaps the economics of fertilizer application to rangeland would improve.

The invasion of overgrazed grassland by invaders can be such a gradual process that a rancher, if not alert, may overlook what is happening until he or she suddenly discovers that beef production is falling. Removal of unwanted plants can be expensive and if not conducted with the utmost care, can further add to the ecological difficulties. The ideal way to remove unwanted woody vegetation (from an ecological point of view) is to use hand labor but this is usually too expensive. Brush invasion has caused the partial loss of grass production over hundreds of thousands of hectares of the western rangelands. Perhaps in the future if there is a shift to acceptance of grass-finished beef in the retail market it will then be economical to employ nonchemical means to remove brush and restore the range to higher levels of productivity of grass and beef or sheep.

Grass-finished beef and lamb have been mentioned before in this chapter and perhaps there is a question in the reader's mind as to what the differences are that makes them less marketable than feedlot-finished meat. The latter, of course, is fatter than range finished meat as already noted but the grass fed animals also have fat as well. However, the latter tends to be yellower than feedlot-finished fat and to have a different flavor. Also the fat of feedlot-finished animals tends to be distributed in a way that produces a "marbled" effect and hence is called marbled beef or lamb. The American consuming public has developed a taste for the feedlot-finished meat. The energy costs involved in the whole complex business of producing feedlot-fed animals are very high and these may be increasingly difficult to justify

given the increasing cost and scarcity of available energy.

A shift to grass-finished beef and lamb meat would work a hardship upon feedlot operators but would benefit many ranchers who might then be in a financial position to manage their range better. There would also be a saving in energy and very likely some improvement in human health as such relates to fat intake.

## GRASSLAND MANAGEMENT IN LATIN AMERICA AND AFRICA

In the following section grassland use and management in Latin America and Africa will be examined. Although the underlying ecological "rules" are more or less the same as for the United States, the problems, both environmental and societal that are present in much of the Third World requires that different approaches sometimes be adopted to achieve sound grassland management.

### Latin America

Ever since cattle were introduced into the Western Hemisphere by Columbus, the grasslands of Latin America have been of economic importance. The relative value of the grasslands varies greatly with latitude and altitude. The most valuable regions, beyond question, are the pampas of Argentina and Uruguay. The least valuable, insofar as native grasslands are concerned, are found in the low latitudes and although some of these grasslands cover large areas their carrying capacities are very low by middle latitude standards.

**MIDDLE LATITUDE GRASSLANDS** These grasslands occur in Argentina, Uruguay, Southern Brazil, central Chile, and northern Mexico. Relatively few of the native grasses still figure importantly in some of these areas they having been subject to the accidental and deliberate introduction of many grass and legume species. The areas of greatest economic significance are in Argentina and Uruguay although northern Mexico's rangelands are important to that nation.

Two major grassland units are recognized in Argentina. These are the already mentioned pampas and the Patagonian steppe. The pampas were once expanses of grass that began in the east just a short distance from the Atlantic shoreline and extended westward almost to the foot of the Andes, where a very pronounced rain shadow produces a desert rangeland of low carrying capacity. Pampas also cover most of Uruguay although they are not quite as productive in Uruguay as in Argentina due, probably, to soil conditions that impede drainage.

Southward, in Argentina, the pampas merges slowly into a short-grass range, the Patagonian steppe. This is a region of cool summers and cold winters and subject to strong winds most of the year.

Although the invading Spaniards—who came on the pampas in the sixteenth century—filled letters and reports with panegyrics describing the grass and how well adapted to the raising of cattle it was, later generations were not satisfied with the beef production that could be achieved on the native grasses, and toward the end of the nineteenth century alfalfa (lucerne—*Medicago* spp.), a legume of high palatability and high in protein, was introduced. Great areas of grassland were converted to alfalfa as well as to other introduced forage plants and with great economic success. Argentina came to be synonymous with beef export—chiefly to Great Britain—and even today beef production and export remains one of the foremost economic activities of that nation.

The Patagonian region has been given over to sheep ranching on large properties. The carrying capacity of this range is less than that of the pampas but is well suited climatically to sheep that are grown mostly for wool.

The principal conservation needs of the pastures of Argentina and Uruguay has long been to put a halt to what is frequently serious overstocking. In parts of Argentina, during this century, range management has led to sounder practices in the pampas although less attention has been paid to the steppes in the south.

Uruguay has had a particularly sorry history of overgrazing and this has been due in large measure to the fact that sheep rather than cattle were and remain the principal livestock animal. As noted earlier in this chapter, sheep grazing must be managed with care least the animals ruin good pasture. Degradation of the native grasslands by invaders of low value for livestock feed and accelerated soil erosion have hurt the economy of a nation that has perhaps overdepended on a single product—wool—to maintain itself. Recognition of what has occurred is leading to better practices and while much remains to be done, there is reason to believe that Uruguay is now on the path to bringing back an appreciable share of the former high wool production of its grasslands.

In the northern rangelands of Mexico traditional practices tend to prevail. That is, there is only a limited amount of what might be called range management. Almost anywhere in this region one encounters glaring examples of accelerated soil erosion and pastures rendered almost useless by the invasion of woody plants like mesquite (*Prosopis* spp.) and prickly pear cactus (*Opuntia* spp.). This is a region where rainfall is both scarce and unreliable and drought years are frequent. When droughts occur it is common to read in Mexico City newspapers of cattle dying in large numbers because of lack of feed and water. Some of the ranches with sufficient capital and oriented toward exporting their cattle to the U.S. market attempt to manage their land along the lines developed in the United States. Unfortunately, such ranches are in the minority and centuries of abuse too often show no signs of reversal. It is in Mexico's best self-interest to pay greater attention to these rangelands and to provide the technical and financial assistance required to restore them to higher productivity. A nation, such as Mexico, that is unable to provide sufficient protein in the diet of large numbers of its citizens ought to give great emphasis to grassland management. Perhaps the wealth Mexico hopes to obtain from its petroleum will lead to more attention to the grasslands in the north of the nation.

**LOW LATITUDE GRASSLANDS** Grasslands presently cover a large part of Central America, parts of tropical South America, and occur on most islands in the Caribbean. Many local names are used to designate the grasslands but the term savanna will be used here for the sake of simplicity.

The origin of the tropical savannas has been a source of controversy. Some argue that they are climatically controlled climax ecosystems while others point to the role of human-set fire and argue that this may be the chief factor controlling the occurrence of savannas. Without taking space to examine both of these positions in detail it can be noted that climate does appear to play a role and particularly in the areas where there is, each year, a dry season during which there is little or no rainfall and that human-set fires also have played and still play a role that has been extensively documented. Within recent years, the total area of savanna has been increased in order to provide pasture for cattle.

The native grass species of most of the savannas are low in nutrients with respect to cattle feed and, moreover, these grasses tend to lose most of the little food value they have during the dry season. Thus, the carrying capacity of the savannas is almost always low.

During the centuries up to the present, cattle were raised on almost all the savannas but often were of limited economic value. This was due to very slow rates of growth on the poor grass, limited markets for meat, and poor transportation to what might have been fairly lucrative markets. There were a few exceptions but these are not of interest to us in this general appraisal. Cattle breeds were derived chiefly from animals introduced from Spain and, later, the humped cattle—"zebu"—of Asia. These breeds, although adapted to poor pasture and hot and moist climates, make only slow growth on the available forage and an animal often requires four or more years to attain a weight achieved in 18 months by cattle in the United States.

Events occurring chiefly within this century and, in some instances, only within the last few decades, have altered the previous poor economic position of cattle raising. Chief among these changes is the growth of the human population, which has created better market opportunities in the region and a growing world demand for meat. A particularly lucrative market is provided by the United States and it is to this market most of the beef exported from Central America is directed.

Not all savanna areas are proving profitable for beef production. Some are still too distant from markets and some areas are infected with livestock disease, particularly hoof-and-mouth disease, that precludes entry of fresh beef into the United States.

The low carrying capacity of tropical savannas is being countered with the introduction of a host of exotic grasses most of which are of African origin. This trend is so pronounced in Central America and some parts of South America that a geographer, James Parsons, has characterized the phenomenon as the "Africanization" of the tropical American grasslands. In Central America (although the process did not begin in this region) the process has advanced to the degree that it is very difficult to locate any but small areas still dominated by native grass species.

These exotic pastures have helped to increase beef production but there are some troubling aspects to the long-run prospects. Chief among these is the question of how long the soil will retain fertility and thus the ability to provide the grasses with the nutrients they require. While it is possible to apply fertilizer to these grasslands the cost is high and will go higher in the future. Most of these pastures are lacking phosphorus and nitrogen and both of these elements are costly and require great skill in application so that maximum returns in primary production are obtained. Another major problem is related to the fact that the area of grassland is being extended in Central America and the Amazon Basin of Brasil. In both instances the forest is being removed causing major ecological changes whose consequences are only being guessed at. One question involves how long the exotic grasslands, grown where forests once stood, will remain productive. Certainly many of the soils do not contain sufficient nutrients to support quality tropical pastures for more than a few years at the most.

Although savannas have fed cattle for centuries, little is known about how such grasslands should best be managed. Overgrazing is almost universal and data to determine the productivity trends are all but nonexistent for most of the areas. At present, in Central America, something akin to speculative fever has captured the thoughts of too many persons trying to get rich on export beef at the expense of the region's ecosystems.

All of the Central American nations are in difficult financial condition and seek, almost desperately, for any means that will earn the foreign exchange needed to pay their petroleum and other import bills and to service an already overlarge and growing foreign debt.

There are no easy answers to this problem. One cannot, however, escape the conclusion that until some rational relationship between human population and natural resources in the region is achieved, it may be futile to talk about grassland and forest management (see chapter eight).

## UPLAND AND MOUNTAIN GRASSLANDS
Geographers and others still do not agree on what highlands and mountains are. In this discussion the former refer to elevations generally between 1000 and 2000 meters and the latter to elevations over 2000 meters.

The upland and mountain grasslands of this region are important resources. In Central America, the upland area is frequently devoted to coffee plantations but one also encounters high-quality pastures of native and exotic grass species where dairy cattle are raised. Dairying is of increasing importance, economically, in Central America partly as a result of improved knowledge regarding infant and child nutritional needs. Like lowland savannas, many of the upland pastures have been created at the expense of forest. Unfortunately, trees have often been removed from steep slopes and this has caused massive losses of soil. Only the least steep slopes should be turned into pasture, but alas, little attention has been given to this. Overstocking is very common and particularly on the smaller landholdings. Soil loss in some instances has been so great that the land has had to be abandoned.

In South America, the Andes Mountains offer many locations where animals may be grazed. It was in this region that domesticated livestock was grazed in pre-European times, the animals being llamas and alpacas, the only large herbivores to have been domesticated in the Western Hemisphere. Spaniards introduced the usual collection of domesticated animals of which cattle, sheep, horses, and goats became established in mountain grasslands. In almost all parts of the mountains there is a centuries-long history of overgrazing and although this fact is well-known there is little at present that can be termed grassland management.

## African Grasslands
Cattle and other domesticated animals have shared African ecosystems with hordes of native mammalian herbivores for 5000 or more years. The cattle, sheep, and goats that have long been dominant in African herding are not native to the region south of the Sahara but were introduced by humans whose identities are not

known. Domesticated livestock animals, and especially cattle, play a social role in traditional African pastoral societies quite unlike the economic role that livestock plays in industrial societies. For most black African herders the mere possession of livestock, and especially cattle, confers status on the owner and the level of this status is determined not by the quality of the animals but the number of animals the herder possesses.

It might be argued that there is an economic aspect to African herding and this is true but it is different from the economic role of livestock in a cash economy. In Africa, cattle and other livestock animals are used to settle various debts and obligations such as the dowry required to obtain a bride (the so-called bride price of ethnographic literature). But to emphasize the economic is to risk obscuring the overwhelming psychic content of cattle ownership. It is this noneconomic element of cattle and other livestock ownership that lies at the root of some of the most serious environmental problems in Africa. Because it is quantity rather than quality that interests the traditional herder it is almost inevitable that grasslands will frequently be stocked above their carrying capacity. This not only results in seriously accelerated soil erosion but also degradation of pasture quality and poor quality livestock—as measured from a nontraditional African vantage point.

There is also another important tradition in this region although it's of much more recent inception: the livestock introductions and management by Europeans mostly in the southern part of the continent. As might be expected, the Europeans orientation has been toward meat, hides, draft animals, and, recently, dairying.

For traditional African herders the chief grassland management tool has long been fire and it may be taken for granted that human-set fires have been a part of the dynamics of the tropical savanna for at least as long as domesticated livestock have been present. In south-

ern Africa Europeans were quick to adopt the use of fire to control unwanted vegetation and to encourage the growth of grass. Fire, therefore, must be included in any discussion of grasslands and grassland management in Africa south and east of the Sahara.

## Grassland Types

A universally agreed-on classification of African grasslands has not yet been developed. However, several terms are widely used and will serve our purposes quite well. Extending east-west along the southern edge of the Sahara and into the "horn" of Africa is a belt of short-grass called the Sudanese steppe. This belt has a low carrying capacity and is subject to prolonged droughts. Merging with this on its southern edge is a slightly denser and higher grassland intermixed with shrubs and trees. This belt, like its neighbor to the north, receives scanty rainfall and rainfall reliability is low. Together these two units is sometimes called the Sahel.

South of the Sahel and forming almost a semicircle around Africa's forested heart is a vast area of relatively tall grass interspersed with bushes and various trees. This is the *African savanna*. This grassland is controlled by numerous factors of which rainfall is only one and then only in certain parts. No person presently knows exactly how much of the contemporary savanna in Africa is "natural" and how much has been brought into existence through human action of forest clearing and burning. This latter grassland is termed *derived savanna* referring to its having been derived from what had been woodland or forest prior to tree removal by humans. It is generally agreed that some of the savanna that has not been derived within historic times may nevertheless be savanna that was at least modified as to plant species content by herdsmen beginning several thousand years in the past. This is most certainly the case in many parts of East Africa where it was discovered that unless fires were set at fairly frequent intervals the grassland would give way to the invasion of woody plants, that is, fire is necessary to prevent ecological succession to a vegetation complex dominated not by grass but by trees and shrubs.

The grasslands of the southern end of the continent are divisible into three broad categories: desert, steppe or short-grass, and veld. The latter requires a few words of discussion.

The veld resembles middle latitude grasslands in the Northern Hemisphere. Although fairly well studied there remains much to be learned about veld ecology. It does appear that fire has played a part in its maintenance but much of the veld area had been so impacted by the livestock of Europeans as well as European-set fire—not to mention an unknown length of time when African herders dominated this region—it is now all but impossible to render a judgment as to the "naturalness" of a given part of the veld.

Management, therefore, of virtually all of Africa's grasslands requires an understanding of the use of fire. Recognition of the last is evidenced by a growing body of scientific literature reporting the results of experimental burning projects.

Important as it is, one must not think that fire is always the best tool for managing wild grasslands in Africa. If not used with great care pastures may be badly injured by fires that are too hot and that destroy more vegetation than desired. This may lead not only to a situation where invader species gain a foothold but also to accelerated soil erosion. Other methods employed to control woody vegetation include ring barking, hand cutting, mixed grazing-browsing by cattle and goats and the use of chemicals.

To ring bark a tree one makes a wide cut or cuts entirely around the trunk. Some of the most undesirable species take more than three years to die thus detracting from the usefulness of this method. Since this is a very labor-intensive operation it is also too expensive except in areas where very low wages are paid. Hand cutting can be very effective because there is no waiting time for a tree to die but this, too, is labor intensive and thus costly.

Mixing cattle (grazers) with goats (browsers) in the same pasture has produced some attractive results in terms of repressing woody vegetation and increased meat production per hectare. However, goats require careful management if they are not to become a threat to the vegetation through their propensity to overexploit an area unless kept moving and their numbers kept well within the carrying capacity of the available leaf forage. A further difficulty is that goat meat and milk are not always very acceptable especially in southern Africa where the experiments have been conducted.

The use of chemicals to control vegetation is a controversial method because it is not yet determined what the total impact of such chemicals is in the ecosystems where they are employed. To be "safe," a herbicide ought to have a very short life after application and its breakdown products should be harmless. Until such a product is available it does not appear wise to adopt chemical control as a significant element in any vegetation control or modification project in Africa.

If there is one universal grassland problem in Africa that one is overgrazing. There has as yet been no detailed study made of all the grasslands of Africa and thus it is difficult to list precisely the areas that have been most damaged. However, available information tends to support the view that overgrazing is most often associated with traditional African herders for reasons noted above.

It is very difficult to convert traditional herders from their old ways to new ways that focus on the cash value of animals and with the level of such value being determined by body conformation, meat quality, milk production levels, butterfat content of milk, and other considerations not a part of the traditional picture. To shift from the traditional to the "modern" involves more than a simple reorientation. It requires some alterations in the very structure of a herding society. That this can be accomplished is attested to by the fact that some of Africa's most famous traditional herders, the Masai of East Africa, are now engaged in modern scientific animal husbandry. The cultural change involved in this is a major one, however, and for a long time to come traditional ways will prevail in Africa.

Contributing to the problem is the growth of human population that requires more cattle and other animals to satisfy social requirements. This not only is impacting already established pastures but contributes to further tree cutting.

It has been suggested that the best way to obtain meat from the grasslands of Africa is to herd the large wild herbivores. Cattle, goats, and other domesticated animals are all exotic south of the Sahara and though these animals have been selected over the centuries to survive in these ecosystems they seldom produce the quantities of meat per unit of land area that the wild animals do.

There is already a long-standing cultural acceptance in much of Africa of "game" meat, as is evident from the fact that illegal killing of game by meat hunters is a frequently reported event. What holds back this idea of game ranching?

A major difficulty is that wild animals require different management techniques than do, say, cattle. Where herders mix with their livestock and take pride of ownership in the animals this would be nearly impossible to duplicate with beasts that do not tolerate close human contact. Game ranching is almost an intellectual exercise—coupled with some very hard and dirty work—in that the herded animals would scarcely be aware of the fact they were being managed by humans. Culling (harvesting) the herds would require shooting and the meat would be subjected to government inspection. This meant that installations to process meat would have to be established in many locali-

ties and a transport system developed to get the mean to market. All of this means added costs and it is not yet clear that there is a market for such a sanitized product.

## SUMMARY

Grasslands are among the world's most important resources. They provide food for many of our domesticated herbivores, provide habitat for many wild animals, contribute to soil development, and provide us with recreational areas.

The terminology applied to grasslands in general and to specific grassland types varies considerably from one part of the world to another. In the United States, although a variety of names is applied, the most commonly encountered are range or rangeland, prairie, or simply grasslands.

The origin of the North American grasslands has long been an object of controversy but it seems certain that fire set by lightning as well as by Indians played a major role in the total areal extent of this biome. In addition, climate and native animal life played important roles in the plant species composition of the grasslands.

Domesticated livestock, like wild herbivores, tend to be selective grazers and thus they impact the species composition as well as the overall ecological condition of rangelands. Cattle, horses, and sheep were first introduced onto the North American grasslands by Spanish explorers. Much later, after the United States gained control of much of the North American grassland biome, large-scale cattle and sheep ranching became widespread. Beginning shortly after the close of the Civil War, large cattle herds were assembled on parts of the Great Plains. In other parts of the West, sheep herding also became important chiefly for the wool the animals produce. There then ensued repeated major episodes of overgrazing and attendant degradation of the grasslands leading not only to lowered carrying capacities but to graver problems of which accelerated soil erosion was perhaps the most serious.

Although the importance of the grasslands to U.S. food production was well known for many decades after the Civil War it was not until 1936 that the first detailed quantitative evaluation of our nation's rangelands was published. This landmark publication owed its existence to passage, in 1934, of the Taylor Grazing Act, which for the first time brought order to the long history of chaotic misuse of our publicly owned grassland resources. Responsibility for administering the provisions of the Taylor Grazing Act fell successively to several federal agencies until 1946 when the then newly established Bureau of Land Management (BLM) assumed responsibilities.

The basic objectives of range management are straightforward—to control grazing pressure so that the quality of the range is not degraded but maintained at a level of productivity that permits a prolonged maximum sustained yield of grass and hence of animal biomass. To achieve this, careful and repeated examinations of the grassland condition must be made to assure that unwanted invaders (i.e., deleterious plant species) are not allowed to gain dominance or even modest abundance. In many instances, it is desirable to reseed the grassland although whether or not to follow this course of action may be determined by the size of the economic return to be expected. It is also not unusual that grassland productivity can be increased by the application of fertilizer but, again, economic considerations will be important in making this decision.

The market price for grass-fed livestock is extremely volatile and this tends to have a negative influence on range management and particularly so where private land is concerned. It is relatively easy for the Bureau of Land Management to reduce the number of livestock units allowed per hectare when conditions of the range so indicate but a private rancher may feel that it is economically necessary to overstock in order to make a profit in a weak market.

Similar thinking also applies to options such as reseeding or the use of fertilizer. If a rancher could be certain that such economic inputs would yield a profit then he or she might be willing to make the investments. However, such assurances are never available and thus much desirable upgrading of private grassland does not occur.

Another market factor influencing range management is that most cattle and lambs are "finished" in feedlots. The public has been educated to demand fat meat and many persons do not like the appearance nor the taste of grass "finished" meat. Were these tastes to be altered, greater profitability to the rancher might ensue. By assuring the rancher a better return on investment an incentive would be created to achieve improved private rangeland management.

Grasslands resources are important in many Third World nations and particularly so in the Latin American and African regions. Unfortunately, little is being done to manage these resources and almost everywhere one encounters examples of accelerated soil loss and other serious problems brought on by overgrazing. Since many of these grasslands occur under conditions of relatively high temperatures throughout the year, seasonally heavy precipitation followed by dry periods and soils that are often poor in nutrient content, correct management of these grasslands requires that great care be taken with the stocking rate. Unfortunately, the generally poor quality of cattle together with traditional but often inadequate pasture management practices combine to exacerbate already long-standing, human-induced ecological problems.

Given the fact that increasing numbers of people and especially children, suffer from protein deficiencies in their diets, it seems self-evident that sound grassland management is a highly desirable goal. This holds true not only for a developed nation like the United States but even more so for the Third World where protein deficiency has reached epidemic proportions in many areas.

The political decision makers of the Third World must direct more of their attention and their nation's financial resources to conserving the grasslands. The intimate relationship between good grassland management and improved protein availability should be more widely appreciated there than it now is. Far too little attention is given to the importance of good childhood nutrition and especially with regard to the intake of animal protein. Good grassland management practices, if widely adopted in the Third World, would go far toward helping overcome the physical and mental limitations imposed by a childhood deficient in protein.

# forests, woodlands, and shrublands

## INTRODUCTION

Of all the natural resources discussed in this book it may be that forests and woodlands are the most highly regarded. However, it is also true that trees have often been the objects of dislike, fear, and abuse.

A brief examination of the history of human attitudes toward trees, reveals that humans have often had ambivalent feelings about them. In some traditional societies certain tree species have been the object of worship and were given careful protection. In other traditional societies certain tree species have been viewed as harboring dangerous evil spirits able to harm persons who lived near such trees. Examples of the latter feelings about trees can be found in many traditional fairy tales of Europe and Asia.

Some of these ambivalent feelings about trees may be due to the fact that our species requires large areas of nonforested land in order to produce most of the food we like to eat. Forests have very low human carrying capacities and we grow a large share of our food in what are pioneer ecosystems dominated by domesticated grasses. Of course, not all forest clearing has been for the purpose of food production and large areas of forest in our nation have been subjected to abuse by persons whose interest was in getting out as much lumber as possible at the lowest economic costs.

We have changed from a nation that was seldom concerned about its forest resources to a nation that may sometimes be so protective of its trees that it hinders the application of sound management techniques. Some of these issues and problems will be discussed later in this chapter.

Although not able to support large human population densities, forest and shrubland ecosystems are of major ecological and economic importance. They regulate the flow of water, retard soil erosion, provide habitats for other living organisms and function as important parts of the global carbon cycle. The economic values include watershed protection, lumber, fuel, chemicals, paper pulp, and recreational values whose monetary worth cannot always be ascertained.

**WHAT IS A TREE, A SHRUB, A PALM?** A tree is any woody dicotyledon that when mature is at least 6 meters high. A shrub is any woody dicotyledon that when mature is less than 6 meters high. Some shrubs attain tree height under extremely favorable conditions of soil moisture and fertility. The distinction between trees and shrubs, therefore, is somewhat arbitrary but is useful for discussions of woody vegetation. A palm (or palm tree) is a monocotyledon distinguished by usually having a columnar trunk surmounted by a spray of very large long leaves. Although often growing alone as single individuals some palm species form clumps from which several trunks emerge. Unlike trees and shrubs all palms are evergreen. They vary greatly in height: mature individuals of some species scarcely reach a meter while other species may attain more than 30 meters in height. Most palm species are found in the low latitudes.

The terms forest, woodlands, and shrublands are encountered frequently in print but they do not have precise meanings. However, in general, a forest refers to a stand of trees whose crowns (tops) touch and form a closed canopy during all or part of the year. A woodland is an area where trees are abundant but whose crowns do not form a closed canopy (although such may indeed occur here and there in a woodland). Shrubland is applied to any situation where shrubs predominate. Some shrublands form dense closed canopies but others consist of shrubs, which occur separately with open space between individuals.

Forests and woodlands are often classified according to locational, botanical, phenological (seasonal), and phytophysiognomic (physical appearance of vegetation) criteria. For example, on the western slope of the Sierra Nevada of California between the elevations of approximately 1000 and 2000 meters the dominant vegetation consists of a midlatitude (location), evergreen (phenology), needleleaf coniferous forest (phytophysiognomy) in which the most important commercial species (species referring to botanical characteristics) are western yellow pine (*Pinus ponderosa*), sugar pine (*P. lambertiana*), and Douglas fir (*Pseudotsuga menziesii*).

Shrublands may be classified according to height but may also be named according to other criteria. For example, in the Mediterranean regions of the world there are several recognized types of shrublands to which the following names have been given: maqui, garrigue, jarral, matorral, chaparral, and coastal sage (to name only some of the more frequently used terms). Some of the terms refer to the phytophysiognomy (e.g., matorral, which refers to a thick mass of woody vegetation), and some terms are chiefly botanical (e.g., coastal sage,

which refers to the dominant shrub, which in this case includes members of such plant genera as *Salvia* and *Artemisia*).

**COMMERCIAL     CONSIDERATIONS** For commercial purposes trees are frequently grouped into two very broad categories: softwoods and hardwoods. The former are relatively light in weight and comparatively easy to saw, plane or carve. Hardwoods are, by comparison with softwoods, heavy—some even have a specific gravity greater than 1—and are generally more difficult to saw, plane, or carve. Although most hardwoods are stronger than softwoods there are exceptions and some softwoods possess great strength. Most of the world's commercially valuable softwoods are located in the northern hemisphere and most softwoods are conifers. Commercially valuable hardwoods have a broader world distribution and some of the most important commercial species are found in the low latitudes.

Although many softwood species have relatively high rates of growth this is not true for all. In addition, while many softwood species have life spans of less than a century, other species do not attain maturity until after 300 to 600 years although they may attain a harvestable size within 50 to 60 years. Pines (*Pinus* spp.) include some very rapidly growing species with relatively short life spans but it is also a pine species (*P. aristata*) that attains an age of more than 4000 years, thus making them possibly the oldest living things on earth.

Few hardwood species attain a harvestable size in the time that many softwood species do. For this reason reforestation (replanting of trees) of most former hardwood forests and woodlands is done with fast-growing softwood species. An important exception is the tree genus *Eucalyptus,* native to Australia, which is a hardwood but grows as fast as many softwood species.

The palms (Arecaceae) are distributed

chiefly in the low latitudes because most palm species are intolerant of frost. Palms are often components of forests and woodlands and occasionally form pure stands themselves.

## TREE STRUCTURES AND FUNCTIONS

The major structural units of a tree are the roots, trunk, and crown. Roots provide architectural stability and function to absorb water and nutrients required by the tree. Roots may grow only laterally or they may also include a tap root that grows downward. A major component of any root system are minute root hairs, which do most of the work of water and nutrient absorption. The trunk is complex in cross-section and contains the following concentric divisions beginning at the center of a mature tree: heartwood, sapwood, cambium, bastwood, and bark.

Heartwood is usually much denser than sapwood and does not contain living tissue. Its chief function is to supply structural strength to the mature trunk. Some tree species lose their heartwood when the trees reach an advanced age but this may not cause the death of the tree. Intact heartwood of some species is highly valued commercially for special applications. The sapwood contains living tissue through which sap—termed phloem—transports carbohydrates and other materials produced by photosynthetic activities in the leaves, downward to the root zone. The cambium consists of a very thin but critically important layer of cells that produce sapwood, bastwood, and bark. Complete circumferal destruction of the cambium will cause the death of the tree. Bastwood provides the passageway for water and nutrients picked up by the roots. Bark provides insulation and critical protection against attack by insects, fungi, diseases, and fire. Bark is porous and a tree does a certain amount of "breathing" through it.

The crown consists of branches and leaves. This is the zone in which almost all the photosynthesis occurs. Some species if deprived of the crown will die but others can stump sprout (*coppice*). In general, stump sprouting is most commonly found among hardwoods and some hardwood forests are managed in such a way as to produce a maximum of coppice wood. The most important elements in the crown are the leaves, which perform the photosynthetic tasks and regulate the rate at which a tree or shrub gives up moisture to the surrounding atmosphere. The discharge of water to the atmosphere—termed transpiration—is under the immediate control of minute openings in the leaves called stomata (sing., stoma) that open and close in response to external and internal conditions of temperature and moisture.

Trees are frequently described in terms of their tolerance. Used in the forestry context the term refers to a tree's ability to grow in shade. Intolerant trees are species that find it difficult to grow in the shade and, therefore, these are usually pioneer species, or they typically occur

**Figure 8.1** Bristle-cone Pine.

in woodland situations where there is sufficient sunlight reaching the ground to assure germination of seeds and growth of the seedlings. That a given tree species is intolerant does not imply that it must be shortlived. The oldest known living tree species, the bristle cone pine (*Pinus aristata*) (Fig. 8.1) is very intolerant and some of the more important commercial species such as western yellow pine (*P. ponderosa*) (Fig. 8.2) attains ages exceeding 600 years even though it is intolerant. Dominance in a forest by intolerant species raises some interesting questions as to how this can come about if the seed and seedlings are not adapted to shady conditions. No single answer to this can be given but it seems that fire and blowdowns by wind expose the surface to sunlight for sufficient periods to allow for germination of

the seeds of shade intolerant species and if these species happen to be fast growing—as is the case with a number of commercially important intolerant, albeit long-lived, softwood species—this may be all that is necessary to maintain forests dominated by "pioneer" species.

**THE FOREST ENVIRONMENT** Trees and shrubs not only require certain independently existing conditions of air temperature, light, water and soil in which to grow but trees and shrubs themselves modify all of these conditions. A forest canopy reduces soil temperatures and reduces the amount of light reaching the ground surface. Trees and shrubs remove nutrients from the soil—and contribute some, also—and draw on the available soil moisture. Atmospheric humidity may be significantly higher under the canopy than above. Trees and shrubs also provide a multitude of habitats for other plants as well as for many animal species.

**Figure 8.2** Stand of mature Western Yellow Pine (Ponderosa Pine).

## HISTORY OF FOREST USE AND MANAGEMENT IN THE UNITED STATES

### The Past before European Settlement

The history of the forests of North America is still unclear at several critical points and particularly so with regard to the events that occurred during the Pleistocene era when a large part of North America was repeatedly covered by ice. This continental glaciation extended into the northern United States, chiefly in the area midway between the coasts and never farther south than parts of Kansas, Missouri, and southern Illinois. The Great Lakes were sculpted during the Pleistocene era by continental glaciation and some of the mountains of the West were subjected to the modeling effects of mountain glaciers.

There is no debate that forests and other

vegetation were totally removed from all areas covered by ice but there is controversy regarding the effects of glaciation (and all associated climatic phenomena) on the vegetation in areas not covered by ice. Available evidence indicates that vegetation changes occurred but were mostly contractions of the total area a given vegetation type (phytophysiognomy) rather than, say, the complete disappearance of desert vegetation, chaparral, or pine forests in the southeast. Holocene (recent) time has been marked by the reinvasion of vegetation into the glaciated portions of the United States and elsewhere. With regard to the latter, correlation of a given vegetation reinvasion with climatic change is complicated by the fact that *Homo sapiens* was present in North America prior to the end of the last major ice advance (Wisconsin glaciation, approximately 17,000 years ago) and may have played a role in plant succession through accidental or deliberate setting of fire. Fire was used to drive animals past armed hunters and perhaps fire was used in warfare. In the East fire was used by some Indians as a means of clearing away slash to permit planting of crops. Although study of the role of the American Indian in modifying the vegetation of parts of North America has received some emphasis in recent years there is still great difficulty in separating those activities from natural fires and other nonanthropogenic environmental events.

It is important that more be learned about the role of fire (natural or anthropogenic) in ecosystems dominated by woody vegetation in North America because data are being accumulated that strongly point toward the need to incorporate fire as a management tool in many tree and brush ecosystems. Fire will be discussed in greater detail later but it is important that its ecological importance be stressed early in this chapter.

Are the present forests (where not disturbed by humans) climax forests or are they undergoing slow ecological succession in response to slow and all but imperceptible post-Pleistocene climatic changes? It has been suggested that we are living at present in an interglacial period. If environmental conditions with particular regard to climates are not stable but are undergoing change is it reasonable to believe that wild vegetation is also changing slowly, in response to the changes in climate? This conjectural note has been introduced here to point up the fact that there are some important questions respecting North American forest ecology that remain to be answered.

## European Settlement to the Early Nineteenth Century

At the time of the first recorded European contacts in the area that is the conterminous United States, much larger forest areas existed than do at present. Forest came almost to the shore along much of the Atlantic seaboard and extended, with relatively few interruptions, to and sometimes beyond the Mississippi River. West of the Great Plains the Rocky Mountains contained a vast store of coniferous forests as did the mountain ranges of the Pacific Coast.

The Eastern forests were amazingly varied in hardwood and softwood species and many of these were and still are of great commercial value. The Southeast was dominated by coniferous forests as were the areas now the States of Michigan, Wisconsin, and Minnesota. To people coming from a Europe that had centuries before destroyed most of its forests to make way for agricultural and pastoral activities this sylvan abundance must have been overwhelming. The resource abundance seems to be responsible for giving rise to the belief that the trees were without end and could be used and abused without concern for the future.

During pioneer settlement in forested land the chief reaction to trees seems to have been to remove the trees as rapidly as possible so that crops could be planted and pastures developed. The theme of tree removal as being synonymous with the spreading of civilization and taming the wilderness is a well-established genre in American literature and pictorial art. Not having foreknowledge of the soils and climates much forest was cleared on land that proved difficult or even impossible to farm and such areas were later abandoned. Trees were also cut for their timber and for fuel. A great historian of the American frontier, Frederick Jackson Turner, perceived this clearing of the forest in almost Homeric terms stating in his influential monograph, *The Frontier in American History,* that the settler "waged a hand-to-hand war upon the forests cutting and burning a little space to let in the light upon a dozen acres of hard-won soil and year after year expanding the clearing of new woodlands against the stubborn resistance of primeval trunks and matted roots."

Although few will suggest that the spread of farms in forested areas was wrong per se, a protest *can* be made of the first decades of major commercial timber exploitation. Commercial logging can be traced back into the colonial period but such activity did not emerge as truly destructive until the nineteenth century when loggers turned their attention to the pine forests of the upper Midwest. Timber cutting in this region was extremely wasteful and destructive. Enormous quantities of debris—"slash"—were left by the loggers that when dry became highly flammable. Fires were frequently ignited through human carelessness and resulted in forest fires that raged unchecked over large areas and caused human deaths numbering in the hundreds. One of the worst of these occurred in Wisconsin in 1871 and resulted in the loss of more than 1100 lives and the destruction of an untold quantity of timber and wildlife resources.

The next area to feel the brunt of this *raubwirtschaft* (robber economy) were the coniferous forests of the Southeast although fires as destructive of human life as had occurred in the Great Lakes states did not occur here. The

last chapter of this tale of forest destruction was written in the West and particularly in the three Pacific States: Washington, Oregon, and California.

In the second half of the nineteenth century informed persons in positions to influence public and governmental opinion began to draw attention to the terrible waste that had been taking place in the nation's forests. Among the several important personages during this era, Carl Schurz, Secretary of the Interior during the presidency of Rutherford B. Hayes (1877–1881), is particularly notable. In 1877, Schurz recommended to the Congress that all forest lands in the public domain should be withdrawn from being homesteaded (or otherwise transfered to private hands) and be retained and managed by the federal government. However, he was ahead of the times and the action he proposed was not taken until 1891 when the first of several Timber Land Reserves were set aside in parts of the West. These were essentially "paper" reserves because money was not immediately appropriated to guard and manage them. There was also the problem as to what the reserves were to be, that is, were they to be carefully *preserved* areas or areas in which there would be a managed harvest of trees. Two influential persons, well-known today in the annals of American conservation, Gifford Pinchot and John Muir, pressed opposing concepts. The former, the first scientifically trained forester in the United States believed that the reserves should be harvested albeit along scientific lines. The latter, the "poet laureate of the Sierras of California" and wilderness preservationist, saw in the Forest Reserve Act the legal means by which wilderness could be preserved forever. This issue, insofar as federal legislation was concerned, was decided in 1897 with the passage of the Forest Management Act, which made it clear that the forest reserves were for the purpose of supplying a "continuous supply of timber for the use and necessities of citizens of the United States."

In 1896, the year prior to passage of the Forest Management Act, the prestigous National Academy of Sciences was requested by the federal government to provide the conceptual basis for a national forest policy. This request led the Academy to appoint a committee—referred to in most references as the National Forest Commission although it never had this as an official title—which included Gifford Pinchot, and seven other persons. The committee's report had a helpful influence on the forest conservation movement but conflicts among the members reduced some of the report's potential influence. However, Gifford Pinchot emerged as an expert on the condition of the forests of the United States and particularly those that had been placed into the reserves. These were being administered by the Department of the Interior but this was little more than a paper operation since essentially neither money nor organization had been made available by the Congress for de facto management.

In 1898 Pinchot was made head of a new Division of Forestry in the Department of Agriculture and assumed his job even though all the forest reserves were still under the jurisdiction of the Department of the Interior! This being the situation, the Division of Forestry directed its attention toward the owners of private forests. The fortune's of the nation's forests as well as those of Pinchot changed markedly with the inauguration of Theodore Roosevelt as president of the United States. Having come to Roosevelt's admiring attention before the presidential years, Pinchot found himself head of the Bureau of Forestry (the new name for his Division) and he was given a much wider range of responsibility for the nation's forest reserves. In 1905 an Act of Congress created the National Forest Service as a division of the Department of Agriculture, where it remains to the present day. Pinchot was made the first head of the National Forest Service and his views respecting forest management were to establish the pattern of operation for the Forest Service that survive, albeit modified, to the present day. Pinchot emphasized, whenever possible, that the credo of his agency would be service and that the prime object of his efforts were not to preserve wilderness intact but to manage forests for timber and other purposes. To bring public attention to this he had the name forest *reserves* changed, in 1906, to National Forests. Gifford Pinchot went on to play a major role in the development of forest policy in the United States.

Landmark federal forest legislation since 1906 includes The Weeks Act (1911), which enabled the federal government to purchase forest land located at the head of navigable streams—this allowed acquisition of vast tracts in the western United States and also in the East; the Fulmer Act (1935), which provided for federal assistance to states wishing to purchase land for state forests; the Multiple-Use Sustained Yield Act (1960), which formalized what had for decades been the operating credo of the Forest Service; the revised Endangered Species Act (1973), which for the first time gave protection to threatened plant species; and the National Forest Management Act (1976), which spells out in detail the legal meaning of some earlier legislation. The Acts just listed are by no means the sum total of important federal forest legislation but they are examples of the central role played by the federal government in the management of the nation's forest lands.

In a free-market economy it is not surprising that there should be points of friction between the National Forest Service and those who wish to use the nation's forests for timber harvest. While there can be little doubt that federal legislation has been required to protect our nation from further wanton destruction of our forest and other wood resources it is also true that too much such legislation and the complex web of policy decisions such legislation creates can be counterproductive. As federal legislation regarding forests becomes more intricate and subject to varied legal interpretations there is a growing and serious danger that, sometimes, basically scientific questions are brought into courts for litigation and judgment may be rendered wholly or in part on the basis of emotion or layperson opinion rather than upon the scientific merits of the problem. Paradoxically, then, federal legislation may sometime have effects on forests contrary to the intent of the legislation.

A certain degree of conflict between public and private interests with regard to the nation's public-owned forests may be a healthy thing. However, there is some indication that the legislative burden may be increasingly counterproductive to the application of scientific management techniques. It is important that citizens be informed of the nature of scientific forest management and thus be in a position to intelligently influence the behavior of government and private sectors involved in forest use and management.

## FOREST, WOODLAND, AND SHRUBLAND RESOURCES OF THE UNITED STATES

### Resource Types

The tree and shrub resources of the United States can be grouped in a number of ways depending on the interest one has in these resources. It will be helpful if the reader frequently consults Map 8.1.

At a broad level of generalization we can recognize the following units: western forest types and eastern forest types. The area of the former includes the Rocky Mountains to the Pacific Ocean and the area of the latter includes all forest types east of the Great Plains. Western forests are mostly softwoods but eastern forests contain large quantities of hardwood species of commercial value as well as extensive and important softwood resources.

### Western Forest Types

With regard to harvestable timber, western forests are dominated by coniferous species of which pines and Douglas fir are the most important commercially although spruce, *Picea*, is also important as is redwood, *Sequoia sempervirens* (Fig. 8.3). Many other species of trees including some hardwoods are harvested in this region but their economic importance is much less than the softwood genera and species just noted.

Chaparral covers a considerable area of California (Fig. 8.4). This is considered as a forest type by the Forest Service but is actually a type of shrubland in which there are very few species having commercial timber value. However, chaparral plays an extremely important role in watershed management and therefore is a very important resource (see chapter nine).

### Eastern Forest Types

With regard to harvestable species, eastern forests contain both hardwoods and softwoods in great diversity. In the Southeast there are extensive areas dominated by several species of pines and especially longleaf pine (*Pinus palustris*), loblolly pine (*P. taeda*), and slash pine (*P. elliottii*) (Fig. 8.5).

Adjacent to the pine-dominated region is an area dominated by a mixture of oak (*Quercus*) and pine species. This region is in turn bordered by a very extensive area of mixed hardwood forest including oaks, chestnut (*Castanea*), and yellow poplar or tulip tree (*Liriodendron*). To the north and east of the Great Lakes there is an area dominated by birch (*Betula*), beech (*Fagus*), maple (*Acer*), and hemlock (*Tsuga*). In the western part of the Mississippi valley extending from eastern Texas north to the Great Lakes region there are vast areas dominated by oaks and hickory (*Carya*). In the Great Lakes region of Michigan, Wiscon-

**Figure 8.3** Stand of old-growth Redwood trees.

sin, and Minnesota there are complex assemblages of pines with some hardwoods. Some parts of New England have relatively large areas dominated by spruce, or fir (*Abies*) mixed with hardwoods.

## OWNERSHIP

Of the approximately 307 million hectares (758 million acres) of forest land in the United States about 101 million hectares (250 million acres) are classified as noncommercial. Noncommercial forests include great areas of shrublands or woodlands containing few species of commercial timber value but some of these areas include forests that would be considered commercially useful except that they have been put into parks in which commercial timber harvests are not allowed. Commercial forest lands include approximately 206 million hectares (509 million acres) of which the greater share, about 148 million hectares (367 million acres) are privately owned. That is, something on the order of 72 percent of the total area of commercial forest lands of the United States is in private hands. The way the kinds of wood is

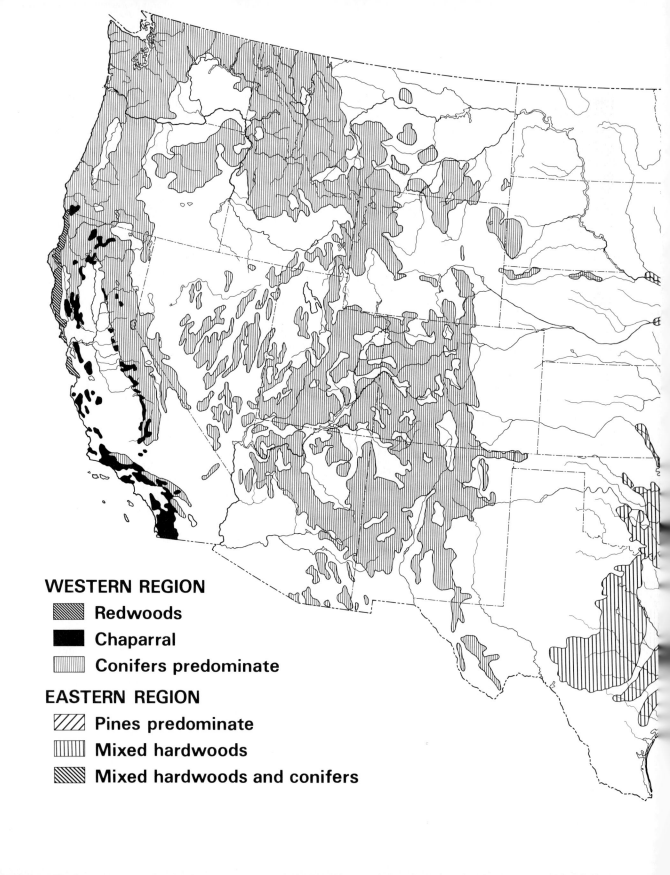

**WESTERN REGION**

▧ Redwoods

■ Chaparral

▥ Conifers predominate

**EASTERN REGION**

▨ Pines predominate

▥ Mixed hardwoods

▨ Mixed hardwoods and conifers

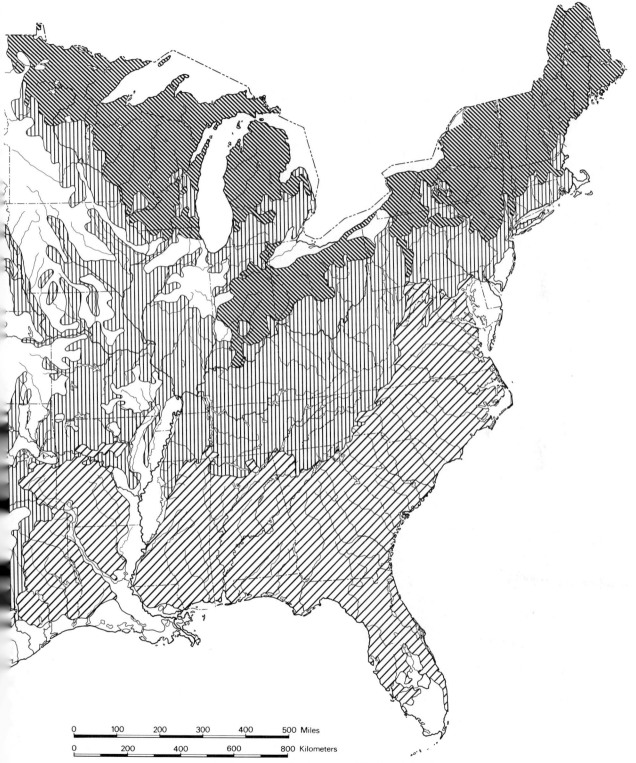

**Map 8.1** Forest types of the United States. (Modified from the U.S. Forest Service).

0     100     200     300     400     500 Miles

0       200       400       600       800 Kilometers

**Figure 8.4**  Chaparral in southern California. The blooming shrub is *Ceanothus*.

**Figure 8.5**  Stand of mixed hardwood trees in the Eastern United States.

distributed among private and public ownership is interesting. The National Forest Service, in 1965, owned the greater share of the nation's growing softwood resource amounting to approximately 6.5 million cubic meters (230 million cubic feet) as compared to approximately 5 million cubic meters (176 million cubic feet) of growing softwoods owned by the private sector. The picture for hardwoods is markedly different with the private sector owning almost 4.9 million cubic meters (173 million cubic feet) of growing hardwoods as compared to the National Forest's approximately one-half a million cubic meters (18 million cubic feet). Even if all of the publicly owned hardwood forests are counted one finds that more than 90 percent of the hardwood forest area is in private hands.

The differences between private versus public ownership of softwood and hardwood stands can be accounted for by geography and history. Most of the hardwood forests, as already noted, are located in the eastern part of the United States where pioneer settlement proceeded with little involvement of the federal government and thus the hardwood resources tend to be mostly in private hands. Also note that a sizable part of the privately held softwood resource is also located in the east and particularly in the southeastern region (Fig. 8.6). It is in the western United States (and Alaska) that the federal government has had the greatest areas to either surrender to the private sector or to retain. This also being a region in which softwoods are of much more commercial importance than hardwoods it has followed that it is in the National Forests that a large share of the nation's growing softwood resource is to be found. Privately held forest land in the western United States is not insignificant but, nevertheless, federal and state owned forest lands are dominant in this region.

Federal ownership of forests is not entirely lacking in the East. Although most of the National Forest lands lie west of the Mississippi River, there are some eastern National Forests of which some are on land that was once farmed and then abandoned because the farms could not be made to return a profit.

Private ownership of forest varies enormously in terms of the size of the individual holdings. In general, privately held softwood forests tend to be large properties and may represent large sums of invested capital. Hardwood holdings tend to be modest in size and sometimes can best be characterized as woodlots rather than forests. Many of the hardwood forest holdings in private hands are parts of farms and are harvested to augment farm income. The forest economics of small-forest holders, especially with regard to hardwoods, is usually significantly different from the economics of largeholdings. Because of this, and other factors, there is and has long been conflict in the ranks of professional foresters as to

**Figure 8.6** 70-year-old White Pine plantation in North Carolina.

where the emphasis ought to be put with respect to forest management efforts. The big timber companies, of course, are in a financial position to hire the expertise required and the federal government tends to emphasize management of the National Forests for which it is responsible. Thus, the small-forest holders who collectively own an important share of the nation's wood resources—particularly hardwoods—sometimes feel left out and even discriminated against with respect to federal advice and help. This is an important issue and will be discussed later under management techniques.

## PRINCIPAL USES OF THE WOOD RESOURCE

So numerous and varied are the uses to which our forests are put that only a very lengthy table could do justice to this subject. This may come as a surprise because we live in an era when metals and plastics may appear to have all but driven wood from the scene but nothing could be less true. House and other construction annually consumes millions of cubic meters of lumber and the paper industry annually uses millions of cubic meters of softwoods. In addition to those two giants are hundreds of other uses to which the wood resource is put. We must also add to the list of major uses watershed control, recreation, wilderness preservation, and wildlife conservation.

One of the oldest and yet one of the newest uses of the wood resource is for the production of energy. Until coal came into wide use at the beginning of the Industrial Revolution, wood provided the most important nonanimal source of energy for many manufacturing activities (water power was sometimes locally important). Charcoal made from hardwood was especially important to iron and steel manufacture and its use gave way only slowly to coal. Later, the supremacy of coal was challenged by liquid hydrocarbons and natural gas. As en-

ergy demands soared, wood fuel, in the United States became almost forgotten by industry. However, now that the liquid hydrocarbons are becoming ever more costly, wood is again being viewed as an important source of energy for the nation. The technology that appears to be most useful at this time involves converting logs to small chips which, after some moisture is removed, can be fed into furnaces to produce high heat levels, which can produce steam to generate electricity. Although wood chipping is still in the early stages of development with respect to power generation it offers both good and bad prospects for the future (Fig. 8.7). The good prospects relate to the fact that by using wood as an energy source we move toward an economy geared to solar energy. The bad prospects relate to the possibility that careless overexploitation of the wood resource might occur resulting in serious impacts on forest ecosystems. It may be expected that most wood chipping operations will take place on private lands since it is unlikely that conservation groups would allow other than minimal harvest from public lands of wood chips destined for electricity generating plants. Therefore, the private sector will require advice and guidance lest it mismanage the wood-energy resources it controls.

Besides the possibility of growing trees principally for power production there is presently a large available supply of waste wood and bark that is produced as a regular part of forest harvest and lumber mill operations. One sometimes sees estimates of the size of this resource so huge as to suggest that it might almost make up for all the petroleum we import! However, even though the supply is undeniably great it is not all located in places and concentrations as to make its use economically feasible. Nevertheless, this waste wood is definitely a significant actual and potential source of energy and perhaps if harvest and mill operations were modified a greater quantity of useful wood waste would become avail-

**Figure 8.7** Wood chipping machine in operation. Chips may be seen going into the truck beside the "chipper."

able. A not inconsiderable quantity of such wood "waste" is already being used to produce energy.

## MANAGEMENT OF FORESTS, WOODLANDS, AND SHRUBLANDS

There are so many marked differences between the aims and strategies of publicly owned forests and shrublands as compared to privately owned forests that it will be useful to treat these two entities separately. Of course, ecological "rules" apply equally to all forms of tree or shrub ownership although the aims of management may vary.

The National Forests of the United States are managed in such a way as to conform to the acts of Congress that stipulate that there be multiple use of such lands. Over the years this concept of multiple use has been subjected to greater and greater legislative refinement but even with the passage of the Forest Management Act of 1976, which was supposed to detail the legal and operative meanings of multiple use, confusion remains. However, the fundamental aim of multiple use is very clear: to respond to as many constituencies as possible commensurate with sound ecological use of the National Forests. These constituencies are varied and range from commercial timber interests to advocates of total preservation of forested areas. Hunters, fishermen and fisherwomen, backpackers, bird-watchers, weekend campers requiring permanent campground facilities, white-water rafters, canoe enthusiasts, off-road vehicle enthusiasts, public utilities, cattle ranchers, and other groups comprise a complex collection of constituencies, all of which have a legal claim to the use of the forests.

The first thing that must be made clear is that commercial timber harvest is not the paramount concern of the National Forest Service. While it is true that there is great interest in such harvests on the part of commercial timber companies the Forest Service is legally bound to operate in such a way that commercial harvests do not conflict with the other uses of the forests.

Each year the Forest Service, through its many regional offices, determines what the allowable cut will be for each regional forest unit. This amount is determined after an in-field assessment has been made of the quantity of mature trees that can be harvested without causing environmental and esthetic damage to the forest. Actual harvesting may be on a selective cut basis, that is, only designated trees may be felled. However, clear-cutting, that is, removal of all trees from an area, is also permitted in some National Forests. Private firms are required to bid for the rights to these trees. With some exceptions, logs cut in National Forests are not allowed to be exported to foreign areas.

The major focus of controversy respecting this system is that commercial lumber firms often feel that the Forest Service is much too conservative in terms of the size of the allowable cut. One sometimes encounters advertisements in the public press in which lumber companies charge that the U.S. Forest Service pursues a policy so conservative as to result in the waste of large quantities of what might otherwise have been harvested timber. The charge is also commonly made that large quantities of timber is left to the attack of insects and disease and that such trees ought to have been harvested.

There being at least two sides to any controversy one must not dismiss out of hand the complaints of the lumber firms. It is possible that on occasion, the Forest Service errs too far on the side of conservatism but it must also be recognized that there is also a fundamental difference in the way most commercial lumber firms look at a forest and the way the Forest Service looks at the same. In addition, some of the controversy currently prevailing in the Pacific tier of states (excluding Alaska) derives from the condition that some of the largest timber companies have cut their own lands at such a rate they do not now possess sufficient trees to keep their mills operating and are thus putting added pressure on the Forest Service to increase the allowable cut. A significant portion of the timber cut on the private lands has been exported, chiefly to the booming Japanese market, and the U.S. market has had to depend, to a considerable degree, on lumber from National Forest lands. The U.S. lumber price has been lower than prices in Japan and at this writing the United States is in an economic recession with a steep downturn in housing starts. This means a marked decrease in lumber demand for the time being and will reduce, for a time, some of the pressure to increase the allowable cut. But when the economy recovers one may expect this pressure to increase and more advertisements to appear in the press attacking the Forest Service for its "too conservative" limits of the allowable cut.

Another source of controversy is that of clear-cutting on National Forest lands (and private lands also) (Fig. 8.8). From a strictly short-term economic point of view, clear-cutting is the most efficacious way to harvest timber. This is particularly true if the stands to be harvested are even-aged stands, that is, stands of trees are of the same age. This can be compared to a grape crop. A farmer who can harvest all the grapes in a vineyard at the same time will have a lower cost than another farmer who must restrict harvest to only a few of the vines at a time and must go again and again to the field to complete the harvest. Similarly with trees, an even-age stand permits total harvest at a time, that is, a clear-cut. Regrowth after clear-cutting whether by natural reseeding or by replanting

**Figure 8.8**  Clear-cutting in coniferous forest, Washington.

(the latter is best to assure maximum regrowth of the desired species) results in even-age stands that, when mature, can be clear-cut.

If there are demonstrable positive economic aspects to clear-cutting why is it so often the object of controversy? The answer includes ecological and esthetic elements. Many forest managers believe that clear-cutting results in a too-serious loss of soil (sediment yield), a too-large interference in water run-off characteristics, too much perturbation of wildlife populations, and also creates unesthetic conditions when big blocks of forest are removed leaving ugly vacant patches behind until forest has a

chance to become reestablished. While the esthetic aspects may be a matter of personal preference the ecological questions cannot be so easily dismissed.

The fairly extensive literature respecting the environmental costs of clear-cutting suggest the following: clear-cutting under some conditions may not be significantly disruptive of ecosystems but may be markedly so under other conditions. In other words, it is not possible to present a single general case either for or against clear-cutting. It is apparent, from the research that has been done, that each site requires its own evaluation before it can be determined what the ecological effects of clear-cutting will be. There may also be differences in such effects at a given site depending on whether the trees are hardwoods or softwoods.

Arguments for or against clear-cutting, when made in public, too often appear to be based upon nonscientific information. It would greatly aid the complex issue if it were realized that there are circumstances where, from an environmental health point of view, clear-cutting is justified and that, conversely, there are situations where clear-cutting ought either to be greatly restricted or not permitted. Although a significant amount of research on the environmental effects of clear-cutting has been done, as already noted, much remains to be learned about site differences in specific forest regions of this nation.

It is unlikely that the varied public constituencies, with the exception of lumber companies, will ever be satisfied with other than a minor degree of clear-cutting in the publicly owned forests. The concept of trees as being just another agricultural crop may be a long time achieving public acceptance. The day may come, however, when public demand for wood products far exceeds the ability of the private lands to supply and such a situation might result in changes in popular views about how best to use the publicly owned forests of the nation.

Almost rivaling clear-cutting as an object of controversy is the practice of controlled burning in National Forests. Probably as a result of the intensive Smokey the Bear campaign mounted by the National Forest Service, the American public has been conditioned to believe that all fire in forests is undesirable. Moreover, this attitude is by no means confined to nonforesters and one finds many in the ranks of professional foresters who are very unsympathetic to the concept of controlled burning.

There has been a long-standing misunderstanding about the role of fire in natural ecosystems. The most widely (and perhaps until recently the exclusively) held view was that fire was always a negative influence in environments and, therefore, must be suppressed by all means possible. The terrible fires that swept over the abused forested areas of the nation in the late nineteenth and early twentieth century may well have provided the rationale for this fire-is-always-unnatural point of view. However, chiefly within the past two to three decades, there has been a growing awareness among ecologists that fire must be recognized as a natural environmental component of many ecosystems including forests and other types of woody vegetation.

Unfortunately, recognizing the natural role of fire in forests does not immediately lead to the means by which this understanding can be made a part of forest management. The reasons for this are chiefly economic, esthetic, and traditional resistance to the idea that fire is a needed tool for forest management. Nevertheless, there are ample data to indicate clearly that in many and perhaps most coniferous forests in North America fire is one of the most important agents producing and maintaining the forests. Moreover, a successful program of fire suppression, including putting out fires set by lightning strikes, may result in greatly increased dangers of highly destructive fires because of fuel accumulation or ecological succession to tree species perhaps not seen to be as commercially desirable as a fire-maintained tree species mix.

The role of fire in the ecology of forests can be better understood if one first recognizes that the term forest fire does not identify only one kind of fire. Fires vary according to many factors, of which fuel accumulation, nature of the fuel, weather conditions—especially humidity and wind speed and direction—play important roles. The more frequently fire occurs in a forest the less fuel there is to burn and hence the less heat and damage to the ecosystem. There are three types of forest fire: (1) surface fire (2) soil fire, and (3) crown fire (Fig. 8.9).

**Figure 8.9** Crown-fire in coniferous forest, Idaho.

When fuel is scarce a fire will most likely burn slowly and only on the surface. This will not be a particularly hot fire and will produce minimal impact except that it will tend to select *for* seedlings of species that can live through such fire and *against* seedlings of species that cannot survive fire. In general, conifer species are better adapted to fire of this nature than are hardwood species. Soil fire involves not only the surface litter (fuel) but also the organic debris (humus) in the upper part of the soil. This is often destructive of seedlings of all plant species and also exposes the soil to accelerated erosion. Crown fire is fire that moves through the forest crown and can be exceedingly destructive. The destructiveness will be heightened if there are large quantities of fuel on the ground. If ground-level fuel is scarce crown fire may enhance the growth rates of seedlings if they have escaped the fire above. However, a combination of a soil, surface and crown fire will cause major and long lasting impacts on a forest ecosystem.

Thus, under natural conditions, many and probably all of the wild coniferous forests of the United States were frequently cleaned of debris by random lightning strikes that set fires of limited intensity and of limited areal extent. Today, paradoxically, in some of the "best managed" forests the fire hazard frequently reaches high and potentially very destructive levels.

In the discussion above emphasis has been given to trees but a discussion of National (or other publicly owned) Forests would be incomplete without some comment on shrublands. In many parts of the Southwest, including much of the central and southern parts of California, large areas of public lands are covered by shrubs of many species. With minor exceptions, these shrubs are of no value at present for wood or other raw materials but they do constitute one of the region's most valuable resources because of their importance in watershed protection. One of the most extensive of the shrub formations is chaparral, which covers hundreds of thousands of hectares, particularly in California. Not all of the shrublands are within National Forest holdings but a large portion is. It strikes some visitors as odd to see signs along the highway announcing that one is entering or leaving a National Forest when not a tree is in sight! Management of these shrublands is extremely difficult principally because they are very subject to fire. The distribution of chaparral is coincidental with a Mediterranean climate, which implies winter precipitation and a summer drought. Fuel accumulation in the chaparral is fairly rapid and, paradoxically, the longer fire is suppressed the greater the danger there will be of very major fire. Chaparral is apparently a fire climax ecosystem, that is, it is an ecosystem that owes, to some extent, its distribution and species composition to fire. Of course, a primary part of the ecological picture is the annual drought.

Chaparral species were present millions of years before humans arrived in the region and thus natural fire, probably set by lightning, has been the chief source of ignition throughout geological history. The advent of humans some 20,000 or more years ago may have increased the frequency of fire. At present, in spite of many efforts to reduce to zero human-caused chaparral fire, conflagrations of anthropogenic origin frequently sweep through portions of these shrublands causing large ecological and economic losses (Fig. 8.10).

Although lacking many of the esthetic attractions of forests, shrublands have their charms and attract not only the home builder but also hikers, bird-watchers and, too often, persons careless with smoking materials. A major requirement, therefore in the management of chaparral is the restriction of smoking and use of open fires during what is termed the fire season each year. However, as noted above, the greater the success of fire suppression—including putting out lightning-set fires—the

**Figure 8.10**   Wildfire in chaparral.

greater the annual accretion of fuel. This is particularly serious where there are human habitations but is also of great importance where the principal use of the land is for watershed protection. One must add to the latter protection against mud slides because one of the sequels of chaparral burns is that in the following winter enormous masses of earth often rush off the steep slopes causing the loss of homes and other property below.

Humans have not learned to live with the chaparral. It may be that there is no acceptable means whereby we can live within such areas or even adjacent to such areas. Given the established fact that fire is a necessary component of this ecosystem, and that long-term (say more than 15 years) successful fire suppression will most likely result in major conflagrations, suggests that fire must be deliberately used to manage this resource. This is not a new idea and controlled burning experiments have been conducted in a number of locations in recent years. However, this is a costly process and can be applied to only a small portion of the total chaparral area and probably not at all to areas adjacent to human settlement. The absurd lack of awareness of the environmental hazard of living within this ecosystem can be seen in many locations. Even after great fires sweep parts of the brush destroying homes and sometimes even lives people quickly return and rebuild their often highly flammable structures.

## MANAGEMENT OF PRIVATE FORESTS

The principal aim and objective of owners of privately owned tree resources is to obtain the maximum possible profit or economic benefit from such ownership. Unlike the U.S. Forest Service, private owners do not have to attempt to satisfy a wide range of constituencies.

The ecological rules for sound management are the same for private as well as public forest resources but within those limits there is still a considerable range of options available to the private owner not available to the manager of publicly owned forest.

One important aspect of private ownership is the size of the holding and another is the kinds of trees on the holding. In the eastern United States, east of the Mississippi River, many private holdings are little more than woodlots from which the owner removes wood chiefly for fuel. Such woodlots are often a part of a farming operation. If such woodlots contain valuable hardwood species these may be sold to individuals who will cut them down and remove the logs to a mill for processing. In the Southeast some private holdings are of great size, these usually being planted to pine and managed as a crop. The trees are harvested on a regular rotation basis with much of the wood going to paper pulp mills although some is utilized for lumber, plywood and other purposes.

In the western United States, as in the East, the size of individual holdings vary greatly. However, hardwood is seldom of importance. Small holdings may be kept chiefly for their esthetic value but if sufficient merchantable timber is present this may be sold to a commercial lumber company. In contrast are the large holdings of a few very big corporations that manage huge forested tracts scattered in many parts of the region.

One of the most controversial aspects of forest management on private lands is clear-cutting, which has been described earlier. Although it might seem that it is a private matter as to whether or not to clear-cut on one's own land it becomes a public issue when or where it is believed that such cutting will cause accelerated soil erosion that might affect the biology of publicly owned streams or might hasten the siltation of water impoundments. This is a matter of such widely held concern that one frequently encounters advertisements defending clear-cutting as a sound and beneficial practice.

There is no all-embracing answer to the

question of whether or not clear-cutting is a justifiable or nonjustifiable practice. The available data indicate that the answer is almost always very site bound, that is, the answer will depend on the specific site that is the object of discussion. Although there are many general ecological similarities between forests it can also be said that each local site is almost as distinctive as a human thumbprint and thus must be evaluated on the basis of its own unique characteristics. Some of the variables that must be examined before it can be determined if clear-cutting is a sound ecological practice in a given location are climate, slope, nature of the soil, nature of the tree species, probable regrowth time after harvest, and wildlife habitat.

Why do commercial lumber companies generally favor clear-cutting? The answer is basically an economic one. In commercial forests maximum economic returns can usually be obtained if even-age stands of timber can be harvested. Furthermore, this allows planting of tracts of predetermined size and permits cutting and planting on a carefully worked out rotation system. Accelerated erosion associated with clear-cutting (which involves not only the transport of sediment per se but also the possible eutrophication of streams and lakes into which the soil is carried) can be significantly reduced in at least some situations by not allowing a given even-aged stand to exceed a size that tends to produce soil loss rates disturbing to adjacent or linked ecosystems (Figs. 8.11, and 8.12).

Although considerable research has been conducted on ecological questions relating to clear-cutting many questions remain to be investigated. It is possible, for example, that the present policy against clear-cutting in most National Forests might be modified if it could be shown (as some have suggested) that under some circumstances the general ecological well-being of a forest would be improved by clear-cutting. However, it might also be dis-

**Figure 8.11** Even-age stand of conifers in the Clark National Forest, Missouri.

covered that the present policy is the best one to follow.

## Problems Common to the Management of All Forests

Pests and disease attack private and public forests without regard to ownership and collectively cause an annual loss of timber and wood valued at hundreds of millions of dollars. While it is unrealistic to attempt to save all the timber and wood from pests and disease the loss is presently so large that greater success must be achieved in the future if we are to have an assured supply of wood products.

This is not to suggest that nothing is being done to protect our trees. A reading of trade

**Figure 8.12** Stand of uneven-age conifers.

journals and professional journals would suggest that most of the time and effort of forest managers is devoted to fire, pest, and disease control! Like other conflicting attitudes between the managers of private and public forests, there are disagreements as how best to achieve the ends of protecting the forests against the above-named dangers.

The problem of understanding the role of fire as an ecological factor in forests has been discussed earlier in this chapter. Therefore the remarks here deal chiefly with pests and disease.

Trees are sensitive to the attacks of many organisms most of which are insects belonging to two orders: Lepidoptera (butterflies and moths) and Coleoptera (beetles). Insects play a natural role in the forest ecosystem the most important aspect of which is to remove dead or

dying trees by consuming them and thus making space for regrowth as well as helping in the process of decomposing the dead or dying trees and releasing the nutrients they contain to the ecosystem. Sometimes, however, trees that are healthy and comparatively young are the object of attack and if the numbers of the attackers are great enough severe damage to an otherwise healthy stand can result. It is this latter situation that concerns forest managers most.

Trees are also subject to the attacks of fungi and certain viruses. In general, healthy trees are able to fend off such attacks but this is not always the case and, as with insects, great loss of healthy trees can result.

Management against pests and disease is done in several ways. One is to harvest selectively trees that are beyond their peak years of health and are thus becoming the site for pest invasion. In the case of some diseases it may be possible to obtain some control by removing vegetation that acts as a host for the disease during some part of the life cycle of the disease-causing organism. However, when there are massive outbreaks in the populations of certain insect species the alternatives may be to accept the loss (which may be very great) or to counterattack using chemical and/or biological weapons.

At present, biological control of forest pest insects has not achieved other than marginal success and therefore much greater confidence resides in the application of chemical insecticides. Shortly after the end of World War II, DDT became generally available to forest managers and it soon came into wide use in the control of forest insect pests. Spraying insecticides from airplanes or from the ground made it possible to effect control of several se-

rious insect pests. However, when it was discovered that DDT was having an undesirable impact on the forest ecosystems, public pressure was brought on the federal government to prohibit such applications. This has become law and DDT (and related compounds) are not now allowed to be used anywhere in the United States unless specifically permitted by the Environmental Protection Agency. Such permission is rarely granted and the once common practice of massive applications of chemical insecticides of all types is in the past. Unfortunately, the insects remain and thus a great annual loss of timber continues.

Of the several major insect pests in the western forests none is more important in economic terms than bark beetles, which require trees to complete their life cycles. Adult female bark beetles eat their way through the bark of pine trees or other conifers and lay eggs in places they have prepared inside the trees. The larvae

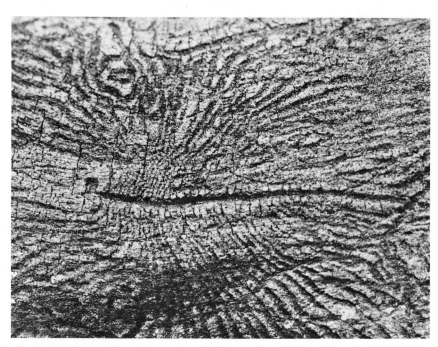

**Figure 8.13**   Damage done by bark beetles. Bark has been removed to show nature of damage.

feed on the tissues of the tree and if the larvae are sufficiently numerous they can kill within a few weeks what had been a healthy tree (Fig. 8.13). Although considerable research has been done on the ecology of bark beetles, still unanswered is the question as to what extent, if any, the population bursts are "natural" or are the result of human manipulations of coniferous ecosystems. Fire suppression may be contributing to this problem because this leads to the retention for longer periods of old and weak trees that seem to be the first site of an attack by these insects. After their numbers build up the beetles then invade healthy trees and with devastating results, insofar as timber loss is concerned. It is significant to note, in this context, that the principal control measure is to remove all overage, wind-downed, and otherwise unhealthy trees as well as downed limbs. This is material that was regularly consumed by fire until fire suppression became a basic element of forest management.

One other major insect pest, the gypsy moth, must be mentioned here because of its potential large-scale forest destruction (Fig. 8.14). Unlike bark beetles, this pest is not a native but was introduced into the eastern United States and escaped into the surrounding region where it quickly became a very serious pest in the forests and orchards of New England. The larvae eat leaves and because of the insect's abundance are able to completely defoliate large areas of forest in a short time. The economic loss caused by this ill-calculated introduction is beyond accurate computation. The chief means of control include the use of pheromones (sex attractants), which are used to lure males into traps; by spraying infested areas with the spores of a virus that only parasitizes a particular insect larva; and by the release of males that have been reared in captivity, sterilized by exposure to radiation and released to copulate with unsuspecting females. Unfortunately, males so treated are not as successful in finding mates as are untreated males and

**Figure 8.14** Larvae of Gypsy Moth eating leaves.

thus this method is not as effective as originally hoped.

Perhaps the most dramatic example of a fungal disase affecting trees is the chestnut blight, which, like the gypsy moth, was also introduced (this one by accident) to the eastern United States. The disease first appeared in New York City in the first decade of this century attacking the American chestnut, *Castanea dentata*. This beautiful tree formerly was common in and adjacent to the Appalachian mountains (Fig. 8.15). Its wood was highly regarded and was used for many purposes. Mature specimens might attain a height exceeding 35 meters and a trunk diameter of 3 meters. No really effective control measure against the fungus has been devised and thus one of the saddest common sights in some eastern areas are the still-standing skeletons of dead chestnut trees giving their mute testimony to human error (Fig. 8.16).

**Figure 8.15**  A healthy American Chestnut Tree.

**Figure 8.16**  American Chestnut Tree destroyed by Chestnut blight.

Although introduced pests pose a special set of problems relative to their control, the successful management of native pests seems to depend on our learning more about the ecological relationships of pests and forests and then to apply what we have learned. This may not always be easy to accomplish as witness the matter of fire. Any management program that only requires the use of exotic chemicals will have, at best, a relatively short success time. This is because resistant pest varieties will survive and reproduce and ultimately the chemicals will be all but useless. Although chemical insecticides must be used with great care and low frequency there are times when they may be the only mean available to knock down a pest population that, if not checked, will cause not only great economic loss but also very serious ecological perturbations in the forest. It is not likely that major population explosions of bark beetles occurred except rarely under natural conditions and therefore their current potential for forest disruption may be almost on a par with the disruptions caused by a too-frequent application of insecticides. We have got to recognize that, for better or for worse, all of our forest ecosystems are to some degree human artifacts. Even those areas we think of as wilderness are not really such if we interfere in any way with natural processes that includes fire suppression. Perhaps in no other area of our natural resources is there so great a need to recognize the fact of human ecological dominance and to accept the responsibilities that insight entails.

# FOREST MANAGEMENT AND CONSERVATION IN LATIN AMERICA

The forest resources of Latin America are chiefly hardwoods although in some areas softwoods are of actual or potential importance (Map 8.2). The picture for forest conservation and management in much of this region is not a positive one but many improvements have occurred in recent years and there are prospects that this trend will continue.

During the more than three centuries of colonial rule, during which time Spain and Portugal controlled vast territories (other European nations had much smaller territorial claims and the United States came late as a colonial power and has de jure control over only a few small islands in the Caribbean plus Puerto Rico), little thought was given to the proper management of the region's forest resources. On the contrary, if there was a uniform attitude vis-à-vis the forests it was to clear them for some economically useful endeavor. In the low latitudes, the mature forests are dominated by what may seem to be a bewildering number of hardwood species (Fig. 8.17). Relatively few of these species have even found other than a local market. In the earliest days of colonization in Brazil the most important commercial species was Brazil-wood (*Caesalpinia*), which was highly valued for the red dye that was made from the heartwood. Indeed, this wood gave the name to the country we know as Brazil. In Cen-

tral America one of the earliest commercial trees was logwood (*Haematoxylon* spp.), which could be made to yield black or blue dye. At a later date the timber value of such trees as tropical "cedar" (*Cedrella*) and mahogany (*Swietenia* spp.) came to be recognized. Pines occur naturally only as far south as Nicaragua (and on certain islands in the Caribbean) and oaks occur southward only into the northern Andes. However, where these trees did occur they were often highly regarded, even in the earliest colonial times, for lumber and fuel. The first major use made of wood other than the dyewood species was for mine timber, construction, and charcoal manufacture. It is not known if Indians manufactured charcoal in other than minute quantities prior to the European conquest of what is now called Latin America but there is no doubt at all that the magnitude of tree cutting for charcoal making greatly increased after the arrival of the Europeans and reached high levels in areas adjacent to mines where charcoal was used in smelting processes. Charcoal also became the universally preferred cooking and heating fuel until coal

**Figure 8.17** Tropical moist forest in eastern Puerto Rico.

and then petroleum products became more significant. However, even today, cutting wood for charcoal making remains an important activity in many rural areas and in Brazil, charcoal continues to play an important role in that nation's iron and steel industry. With rare exceptions, only hardwood is employed for charcoal. Softwood charcoal burns too rapidly to be of much value.

Mining during the colonial period also made heavy use of timber to shore up the drifts and

shafts of the mines and vast quantities of wood disappeared underground for such uses.

Cutting lumber for export to the world market has long been dominated by comparatively few species such as the two already mentioned and others such as rosewood and virtually all the most accessible trees were removed long ago.

As mentioned earlier, the softwood resource is relatively less abundant than the hardwood resource in this region. Mexico, Guatemala, Honduras, Nicaragua, and some Caribbean is-

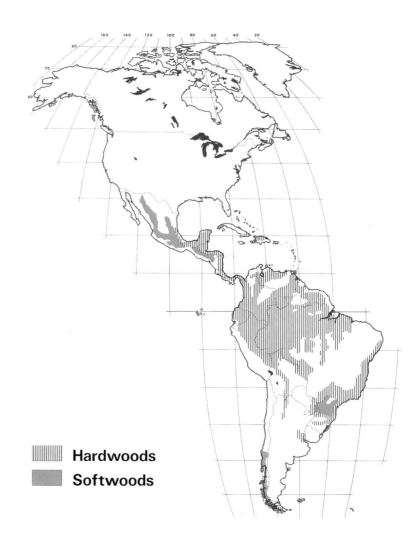

||||||| **Hardwoods**

▓ **Softwoods**

lands have fair amounts of pines. Brazil once had a fairly large and valuable resource in the Parana "pine," (*Araucaria* spp.), located mostly in the southeastern part of that nation. Uncontrolled cutting and destructive fires greatly reduced this resource but Brazil is now embarked on efforts to replant this valuable softwood timber tree. This conifer also occurs in other parts of southern South America most notably in parts of Chile but is seldom given the management it deserves.

In parts of northern Argentina and adjacent areas in other countries several tree species given the vernacular name of *quebracho* have been harvested for many years. These trees produce exceedingly dense wood suitable for many uses of which one is high-quality charcoal. Until other sources became available, certain species of *quebracho* were a major source of high-quality tannin and played a major role in the leather industry of this region. Although the economic value of the *quebracho*

**Map 8.2** Major hardwood and softwood resources of Latin America, Africa and southern Asia.

resource has been recognized for the better part of a century there has been little effort made to study the ecology of these trees nor to manage them properly. Like so much of the history of commercial timber exploitation in Latin America the *quebracho* resource has been mined rather than managed.

Of much greater danger to most of Latin America's forest resources is forest destruction. During the pre-Columbian era, most of the agriculture in the region allowed for the regeneration of forest after a comparatively brief period of clearing and cultivation (there were some exceptions to this, however, and severe forest destruction seems to have occurred in some places). The European introduction of cattle and other livestock started a train of events that gradually resulted in the increase of pasture at the expense of trees. In the twentieth century this conversion process has been exceedingly rapid and is chiefly in response to the rapid growth in human numbers and demand not only for meat but, increasingly, for the foreign exchange that the meat (beef) will earn in foreign markets. This phenomenon is particularly acute in Central America. This region is presently free of hoof-and-mouth disease and thus is permitted to ship fresh beef into the United States (something not permitted of most South American nations where this disease occurs and thus all meat shipments must be canned or similarly processed). The U.S. government limits the total amount of fresh beef that can be imported—in order to protect U.S. beef producers—but the quantity is great enough to have caused a rapid reduction of forest area in several Central American nations. As noted in the introductory remarks in this chapter, the human carrying capacity of forests is low as compared to croplands and pastures. The ecological/demographic truth in Central America is that forests can't support a population that approaches 20 million and is increasing at approximately 3 percent per year.

The nations of Central America have recently become aware that their often-times casual sacrifice of forests for economic returns in the short run might have negative economic (and ecologic) returns in the long run. A markedly stepped-up interest in forest management is now visible in several of these nations. However, human pressures may well thwart some or even most of the efforts now directed toward forest management.

Mexico has built up a commendable cadre of forestry experts but the destruction of that nation's forests has progressed so far that the tasks of management and reforestation strain all such efforts being made in that nation. Mexico has advanced forest legislation but there is often a lack of adequate enforcement. These difficulties arise in part because of inadequate funding and in part because of extreme human pressure on what is a too-limited resource in a nation having an estimated population of 64 million persons with an annual increase of at least 3 per cent. For many rural Mexicans, fuel wood (leña) and charcoal (carbón de madera) are the principal fuels used for cooking and heating. Not only is the forest resource overtaxed but also severe damage to watershed areas resulting in increased sedimentation behind the dams the nation requires for irrigation water and power production. Given the fact of Mexico's great wealth in natural gas it might be wise to pipe this to as many parts of the nation as possible and thus wean the people away from their traditional use of wood for fuel.

At present, the major site of forest removal is in the Amazon Basin of Brazil. This nation is committed to developing this region and believes that in order to do so it must construct a road net over the entire area. Without more than the most cursory previous investigation of the ecological consequences, Brazil has succeeded in pushing roads through and around much of the Amazon Basin. Accompanying this is a major program of forest removal to create

**Figure 8.18** Tree removal associated with the construction of the Trans-Amazon Highway System, Brazil.

vast new crop and pasture lands (Fig. 8.18). Thus far, the ecological consequences of tree removal on this grand scale are only partly visible, which allows for the expression of a large amount of emotion on all sides of the issue. At present no person seems to be able to state with any degree of precision what the long-term effects will be on the forest. That the native animals have suffered greatly has been established and data are accumulating to suggest that some serious soil erosion problems occur in at least some situations. It is being suggested that tree removal on this scale will interfere with the global carbon budget and in such a way as to cause a rise in atmospheric temperature, climate changes, and perhaps some impacts on middle latitude agriculture. As matters now stand, Brazil and the world must await the ecological results of this great unplanned and uncontrolled experiment in forest removal.

As with Central America and Mexico, most nations in South America now have forestry departments and a growing cadre of well-trained personnel. Thus, there will be no lack of sound forest information available to politicians in this region. Human population pressures coupled with increasing per capita demands for goods that often can be obtained only through importation will, however, make more difficult the task of all persons concerned with forest management in South America.

## FOREST MANAGEMENT AND CONSERVATION IN AFRICA

In many respects, the state of forest management in Africa today is a reflection of the degree to which the several colonial powers were interested in forest management prior to the wave of independence that swept the continent beginning in the 1950s. In general, the former British colonies had, to varying degrees, established mechanisms for the management of at least some of the forest resources. The French were almost as effective in this regard but the Belgian government tended to lag as did the Portuguese. The Germans were a colonial power on this continent too briefly to have exerted very much influence.

Possibly because of its fairly lengthy existence as a governmental unit (albeit with some changes that did not affect greatly the issue of forest management) South Africa has the most advanced forestry program at present. However, it should be noted that the colonial and even parts of the postcolonial periods in South Africa were marked by severe waste of the tree resources. Thus, while some of the work of the South African foresters is directed toward the management of wild forests a very large part of their attention is directed toward the establishment and management of exotic tree species. The most favored of these are species of Eucalyptus from Australia and pines chiefly from the Western Hemisphere.

Africa's most important environmental problem may be the rapid destruction of its forests. Few of these nations, south of the Sahara, possess a significant fossil fuel resource (an important exception is Nigeria) and wood is the only fuel vast numbers of people can afford to use (Fig. 8.19). This in itself would spell trouble for the forests but added to this pressure is the increasing need for more land for crops and livestock.

Most observers of the phenomenon of African forest destruction agree that it must be stopped but few persons have offered viable alternatives. Some of the suggestions put for-

**Figure 8.19** Gathering fuel-wood in Ethiopia. Scenes like this are general in many parts of Africa.

ward include subsidizing the purchase of fossil fuel (such subsidy being made by wealthy nations including OPEC), planting of rapidly growing tree species that can be harvested on much shorter rotations than is the case with many native African tree species, assisting in agricultural improvements that will lead to greater production on less land, encouraging adoption of improved livestock breeds so that more production will be obtained from less area, and adopting small-scale solar energy.

Unfortunately, almost all suggestions fail because of poverty, ignorance (rural populations tend to be largely illiterate), and strongly held cultural attitudes coupled with extraordinary cultural diversity within individual nations. As if these were not sufficient difficulties, few if any of the recently independent African nations have been able to achieve a national government sufficiently mature and stable to create the environments in which long-range planning is possible. The inexperience of government is paralleled by a youthful population that appears to be at the beginning of a human population explosion comparable to that which has been occurring in much of Latin America for the past three or more decades.

It is difficult for one to be optimistic about the fate of Africa's remaining forests. Their continued destruction can only increase rather than decrease the difficulties of these nations as they seek to achieve a higher standard of living for their people.

# FOREST MANAGEMENT AND CONSERVATION IN SOUTHERN ASIA

This section refers to the region including Pakistan on the west and Malaysia and the Philippines on the east but does not include any part of China.

The nation that dominates this region by virtue of its size and human population is India and the focus of comment will be on that country.

Prior to independence from Great Britain in 1950 (after having achieved the status of a dominion in the British Commonwealth in 1947) the colonial government had taken a strong interest in forest management and left behind the infrastructure for continued development of forest management in India.

Indian forest resources include both hardwood and softwood species, of which some have long been important in international commerce. Among these are teak (*Tectona grandis*), sal (*Shorea robusta*), and the Himalayan cedar or deodar (*Cedrus deodara*). Teak is one of the world's most valuable hardwood trees because not only is it a beautiful wood but is extremely durable and lends itself to a wide range of applications such as furniture and ship construction. It is a very slow-growing species and seldom reaches minimal harvest size in less than a century. The sal is also an extremely valuable hardwood species and is regarded by some as being as valuable as teak. The leaves of the sal are also important food for the lac insect (*Laccifer lacca*), from which shellac is made. The deodar is one of the world's most beautiful trees and may be seen planted as ornamentals in many places far removed from its native land. This is one of the three true cedars (*Cedrus*) the other two being the cedar of Lebanon and the Atlantic cedar. Deodar wood is easily worked and being aromatic possesses some limited insect repellant properties making it useful for chests, closet panels, and the like.

Besides the "famous" commercial trees of India there are many other valuable species used for timber and fuel. Management of Indian forests has long been hampered by ethnic complexity that here includes an extraordinary linguistic diversity, ignorance, and by the environment—crushing size of the human population. Although the annual rate of human population growth in India is less than for most of

Latin America and low latitude Africa the population base has attained such a large size that even a comparatively modest rate of increase is resulting in very large annual increments. This translates into very heavy pressure on the few remaining forest resources for fuel. Some parts of India are experiencing major soil erosion problems because of tree removal from slopes by impoverished farmers seeking more land to plant or, as elsewhere in India, for wood fuel. Most of India's citizens can't afford to purchase kerosene or other fossil fuel. In some parts of India wood has been scarce for decades and cow dung is the only fuel available.

A fairly large portion of southeast Asia has been a theater of war during the past couple of decades. Exceptions are Siam, Malaysia, and Indonesia. In the war-troubled countries forest management has been neglected and at times some forests were subjected to the use of defoliants in an effort to deprive enemy troops of cover.

Malaysia has a long-standing forest management program but in recent years the total forest area has been reduced as trees have been removed to establish or extend plantations of oil palm and rubber. The nation retains several relatively large areas in forest reserves but the meaning of the term reserve does not include the concept of a national park. Instead, the reserves are forested tracts that are managed for the purpose of future cutting or other commercial exploitation.

Indonesia, an island nation, has lagged in developing a viable forestry program. Rapidly increasing populations are impacting the remaining forest (which, as in Malaysia, is chiefly hardwood). The largest remaining stands of trees are located on the island of Borneo in the State of Kalimantan. West Irian (the western part of the island of New Guinea) and Sumatra still retain some significant forest resources but indiscriminate cutting, particularly on the latter island, is placing the future of the resource in doubt.

A growing and questionable trend in southeast Asia is the practice of removing the complex mixed hardwood forests and replanting to fast-growing tree species such as exotic pines. The argument most frequently advanced to support this practice is that native tree species have too limited a market and grow too slowly to make their management in plantations economically feasible. One must wonder, however, what the long-run ecological and economic effects will be in these highly simplified tropical ecosystems. Another problem is that over large areas in Indonesia, particularly, and to a lesser extent on the Asian continent, shifting cultivators have produced grasslands dominated by the coarse and economically useless *ladang* grass (*Imperata*). Such areas known as kogonales (sing., kogon) are not of economic value and planting trees (if such can be established) in such situations would be a definite improvement. In parts of Indonesia, the spread of *Imperata* is measurable in thousands of hectares per year.

## SUMMARY

Although trees are generally well regarded in present-day American society, humankind has had a very mixed and often destructive history with regard to them.

One possible reason for the love-hate relationship between people and trees is the fact that even under the most optimal ecological conditions forests have very low human carrying capacities and especially so when compared to grasslands that have been put to the plow or, more directly to the point, when compared to areas once forested but that have been cleared and turned to farming. This low human carrying capacity notwithstanding, forests are of immense importance to us and constitute a natural resource of inestimable value.

We, as a nation, have little cause for pride in the way our ancestors exploited the forest resources. Perhaps in no other aspect of the nation's natural resources does one encounter such a dreary history of wanton destruction.

Conservation of our forest resources began, in 1898, with the establishment of a federal agency, the Division of Forestry, which was administered by Gifford Pinchot. Unfortunately, this agency had first to confine its activities to the private sector because the passage in the previous year of the Forest Management Act had put a large share of the federal government-owned forest lands in forest reserves and under the control of the Department of the Interior. This situation was changed in 1905 when Congress established the National Forest Service as a division of the Department of Agriculture where it remains to the present day. Gifford Pinchot was made the head of the Forest Service and the policies he established continue to be influential. The emphasis was on sound management that included use, that is, timber harvest. This was strongly opposed by people such as John Muir but Pinchot's views carried the day as might be expected in a nation where a later president, Calvin Coolidge, was to assert that the business of the United States is business.

Since the founding of the Forest Service, there has been much federal legislation governing the management practices of the forest land under its control. Of the many Acts passed few have been more important, albeit more controversial in terms of interpretation, than the 1960 Multiple-Use Sustained Yield Act, which formalized, in legal language, what for decades had been the modus operandi of the U.S. Forest Service. However, this Act produced so much confusion as to its intent that a further piece of legislation, The National Forest Management Act of 1976, was passed to provide legal interpretation of the content of the 1960 Act.

Because the National Forests contain a major share of all the nation's wild-growing softwood resource it almost follows that there is friction between forest managers and the private lumber cutters who wish to obtain the largest possible quantity of timber to sell. In addition, the Forest Service is required by federal law to provide for the multiple use of the forests and the spirit of this legal requirement appears to relegate timber cutting to no more than equal status with other uses such as hunting, fishing, camping, hiking, watershed management, and the like. In the view of a highly vocal element in the commercial lumber industry, the Forest Service mismanages some of the forest because too small a cut of timber is permitted. In addition, this group frequently complains that too much emphasis is placed on selective cutting and too many restraints are placed on clear cutting. Although the latter is allowed in parts of the Northwest region, the commercial lumber industry would like to see the practice permitted in most if indeed not all National Forests.

Clear-cutting, the removal of all timber from a given plot at a given time, has economic advantages as compared with selective cutting where only certain trees may be felled at a given time. However, clear-cutting may lead to enormous soil loss, the silting of streams with loss of fish and other aquatic life, as well as to other undesirable ecological consequences. In defense of clear-cutting, it is true that this practice does not always result in major soil loss or other major ecological disturbances. However, there are few who would suggest that a parcel of land that has been recently clear-cut is other than an eyesore. This uglification of our National Forests seems to fly in the face of the requirement that such forests be managed for multiple use.

Also controversial is the use of controlled burning as a management tool in the National Forests. It has been gradually learned that fire is a natural ecological element in many if not all of our forests and particularly so in parts of the West. Lightning-set fire may well have been the chief means in earlier days of keeping fuel—dead limbs that lie on the ground, leaves, and other organic matter—from accumulating to such volumes as to provide the fuel for major and highly destructive forest fires. Modern-day attempts to suppress fires set by careless people have been extended to the suppression of lightning-set fire. So successful are these efforts that fuel often accumulates to dangerously high levels and when finally ignited and not put out immediately result in fires that cause enormous damage to forest ecosystems. Unfortunately, even if fire were to become generally accepted as a management tool, its actual use would be greatly restricted by the presence of numerous people and their permanent and temporary habitations within the National Forests.

Forests are subjected to the attack of insects and other organisms, which has led to the development of countermeasures by humans to protect the timber resource. Some of these such as the use of DDT have been banned from further use. There is no question that large timber volumes are annually lost to pests in our National Forests but it is also true that much of this loss should be seen as an aspect of the natural ecology of forest lands. It is true that some practices such as allowing trees to live past

their healthy prime and thus to become vulnerable to insect attack (and it is from such trees that pest populations may attack large numbers of healthy trees) do exist but this can be corrected by greater care in the selective harvesting of trees. The massive application of powerful insecticides should be employed only as the last resort and then only if the entire forest ecosystem is threatened with destruction, something that would rarely occur.

Forest conservation and management in much of the Third World is only in early developmental stages. There are some exceptions, but these are limited and the overwhelming picture is one of a rapid diminution in the total forest area chiefly as a result of the rapid growth of human numbers and the associated increased demand for farm and grazing land and for wood fuel. In general, a crisis situation now exists in much of Latin America, Africa, and Asia and no truly viable solutions to this situation have been advanced. The repercussions of this forest destruction are many and varied. The growing biological impoverishment affects not only the nations and regions immediately involved but also the entire global ecosystem.

# freshwater resources

## INTRODUCTION

People often take the freshwater resource as much for granted as they do the atmospheric resource. Water often seems to be so abundant as to require no more than casual thought with regard to its conservation and management. However, even in those parts of the United States where atmospheric precipitation is relatively abundant, clean freshwater is a threatened resource and more than one metropolitan area is finding itself hard pressed to provide adequate supplies for its citizens. In the southwestern United States high-quality freshwater is almost everywhere a scarce resource.

The uses to which freshwater is put are many and sometimes they conflict with one another and particularly so with regard to maintaining water quality. Among the more important uses to which freshwater is put are for drinking and food preparation and water for such use must be free of biological and chemical contamination. The human body consists chiefly of water and requires frequent renewals of this substance in order to survive. Persons engaging in fasts may sometimes go for astonishing lengths of time without food but must take water at fairly short time intervals.

Our need for water extends far beyond immediate physiological requirements and includes water for farming, manufacturing, waste disposal, cooling towers for nuclear generating plants, and many other applications. In order to better understand the nature and limita-

tions of the freshwater resource, the geographical and geological distribution of freshwater resources in the United States and the mechanisms that govern, to a large degree, atmospheric precipitation must be examined.

## THE WATER CYCLE

The gross movement of water between its three states—liquid, gas, and solid—is referred to as the water or hydrologic cycle (Fig. 9-1). Water enters the atmosphere as a gas produced by evaporation from oceans, lakes, ponds, streams, ground surfaces, vegetation, snow, and ice. Water vapor (gas) in the atmosphere changes to a liquid when atmospheric temperatures drop below the point where the contained water vapor condenses—this temperature being called the *dew point*. Condensation only occurs in the presence of hygroscopic particles or nuclei of various kinds. When water droplets attain sufficient size they fall as rain or hail. If the temperature where condensation occurs is low enough, that is, below 0°C, the water vapor does not first become a liquid but immediately is frozen into snow by a process termed sublimation. Rain, snow, and hail fall on all surfaces, which means that only a part of the total falls over land, the rest falling in oceans, lakes, ponds, and streams. After falling to the earth's surface water is returned by evaporation and transpiration to the atmosphere. The largest sources of water vapor are the oceans but all surfaces yield some water

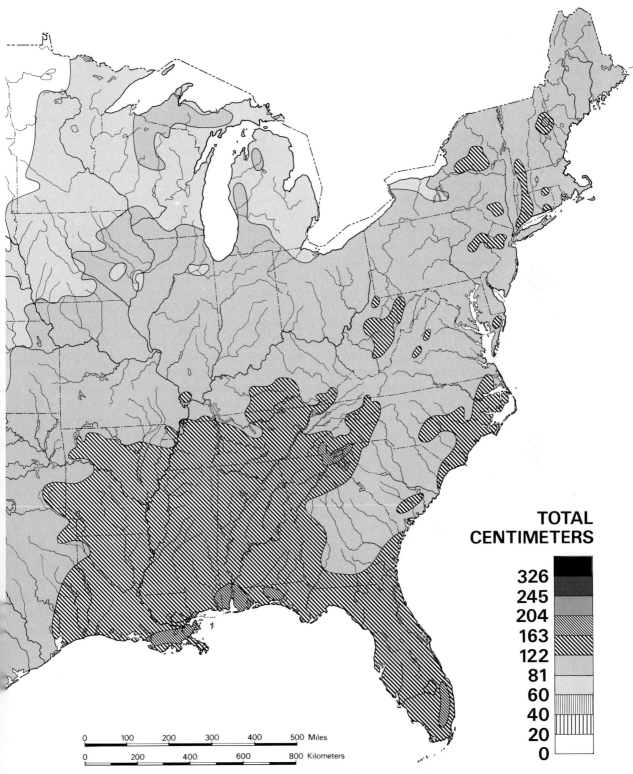

**TOTAL CENTIMETERS**

| | |
|---|---|
| ■ | 326 |
| | 245 |
| | 204 |
| | 163 |
| | 122 |
| | 81 |
| | 60 |
| | 40 |
| | 20 |
| | 0 |

0    100    200    300    400    500 Miles

0       200      400      600      800 Kilometers

**Map 9.1**   Average annual precipitation (centimeters) in the United States. (U.S. Atlas).

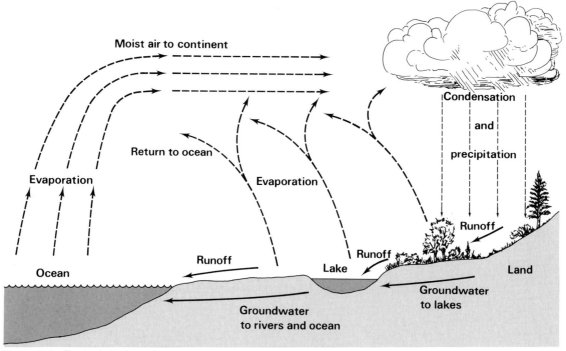

**Figure 9.1**   The hydrologic cycle.

vapor. However, areas distant from the oceans or located where atmospheric high pressure systems persist for long periods of time generally are poor source-regions for atmospheric moisture.

In the United States there are strong regional differences in average annual precipitation (see Map 9.1). The largest region of comparatively moist environments lies east of the 100th meridian and it is west of that meridian that many of the most serious problems of water scarcity occur in the United States. To be sure, there are some areas in the west that receive, on the average, large amounts of precipitation such as the western slopes of the Sierra Nevada, and the Cascade Range. However, a very large part of the western region can be characterized as arid or semiarid and precipitation amounts are often too low to support agriculture without artificial irrigation.

The sources of the freshwater we use may be divided into three categories: meteoric water, fossil water, and juvenile water. Meteoric water refers to surface and subsurface water derived from rain, hail, or snow. Fossil water is actually a form of meteoric water in that it was originally precipitated as meteoric water but came to be trapped in sedimentary rocks and then later buried under a cover of earth materials. Juvenile water is "new" water produced by chemical activities within the earth. Of the three "kinds" of water, meteoric water is far and away the most important insofar as a natural resource is concerned. Locally, fossil water is sometimes of temporary significance but such water sources are nonrenewable and once the fossil water has been extracted (pumped) there are no means by which the supply can be replenished. Juvenile water is rare enough to be a curiosity. One sometimes reads newspaper accounts of a "major discovery" of juvenile water but these "discoveries" almost always turn out to be conventional meteoric water resources.

## GROUNDWATER AND SOIL WATER

Much of the water we obtain is from surface supplies in lakes and streams. However, subsurface supplies are of major importance in almost all parts of the nation and particularly so in arid and semiarid parts of the west. Subsurface water may be divided into *soil water* and *groundwater.*

Soil water is the water that is found in the soil within the root zone of plants. The depth of such soil water is highly variable and subject to marked changes within time spans of days or hours. Frequently used measures of soil water are *field capacity* and *wilting point.* In a given field a soil is said to be at field capacity when the soil contains all the water it can hold in pore spaces after any excess water (*gravitational water*) has drained away. A quantity of water greater than field capacity, if retained for more than a brief time, creates a waterlogged condition which is almost always undesirable and damaging to most crop plants. The wilting point refers to the soil water condition when the moisture requirements of plants exceeds the available water supply in the soil and the plants begin to wilt.

Groundwater occurs in that upper portion of the earth's mantle that lies above an impervious layer of rock and in which all available pore space is occupied by water. This area is termed the *zone of saturation.* The top of the zone of saturation is the *water table.* The latter may occur at depths of many hundreds of meters or may extend to the surface of the earth (Fig. 9.2.) The depth of the water table in a given locality tends to fluctuate in response to .the seasonal amounts of water that reach the zone of saturation.

Any zone containing groundwater is an *aqui-* fer. Aquifers include unconsolidated soil materials as well as consolidated rocks such as sandstone. In a given locality there may be more than a single aquifer and thus more than a single water table. Where a water table coincides with the surface of the ground springs, streams, rivers, ponds, or lakes may occur. A particularly interesting type of aquifer is one that, if drilled into from above, results in a flow of water to the ground surface without the aid of pumps. This is an *artesian* aquifer and the well is an *artesian well* (Fig. 9.3). An artesian well can flow only so long as the rate of aquifer recharge is greater than the rate of withdrawal.

## WATER OWNERSHIP

Early European settlement of eastern North America was chiefly by persons who came from humid regions in which water could more or less be taken for granted and the laws respecting water ownership reflected that situation. Thus, the principal rule of water law in the most of the eastern United States was and is based on the doctrine of *riparian rights.* Basically, this doctrine asserts that anyone whose land adjoins a flowing stream has rights to utilize water from the stream. The riparian doctrine works rather well in regions where surface streams are frequent and carry reliable quantities of water. However, in regions such as much of the area west of the 100th meridian, the concept of riparian rights often conflicts sharply with the realities of surface water scarcity. Also, in the West, it frequently happens that soil suited to agriculture and human settlements do not coincide with the location of surface waters, thus water must be moved to where it is needed. There came to be established in the West the doctrine of *prior appropriation,* which asserts that the first user of a stream for beneficial purposes establishes a continuous legal priority for such water-use. Any water not appropriated by the first user can be appropriated by another user for beneficial purposes and so on

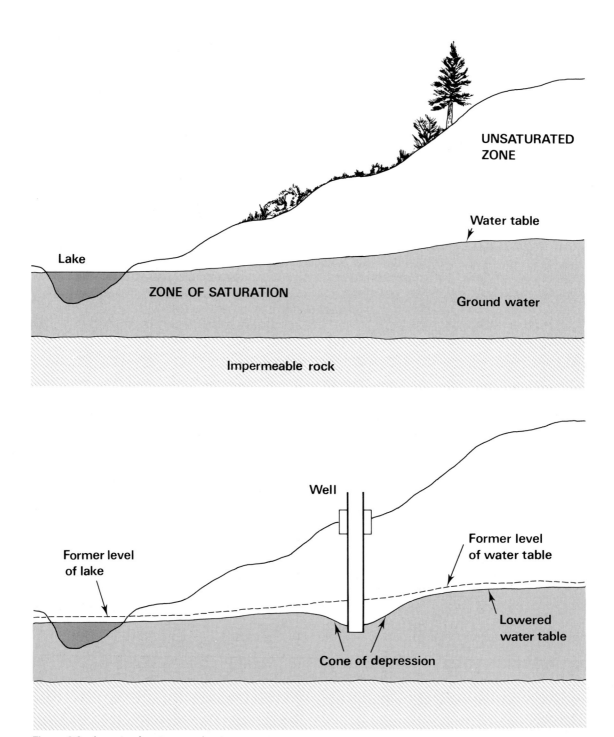

**Figure 9.2** Aspects of underground water resources.

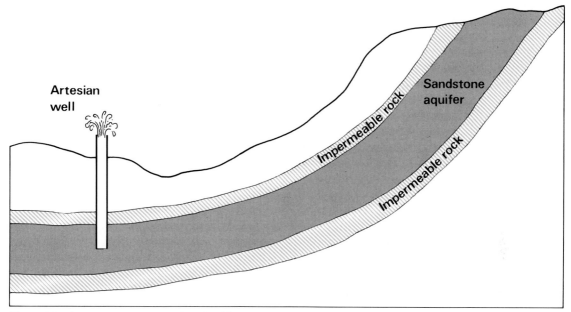

**Figure 9.3** Artesian well and associated aquifer structure.

until all the available water is appropriated. In some areas of the West (e.g., coastal Oregon and Washington) where water is sufficiently abundant the riparian doctrine is also applied (Map. 9.2).

In the dryer parts of the West water must be considered the most valuable of all natural resources since without a sufficient supply even the (sometimes) pure air cannot be enjoyed. It is not surprising, then, that litigation over water rights has long been a major aspect of water allocation in that region. Although prior appropriation may seem a fair and straightforward doctrine—especially to those fortunate persons who were first on the scene—this may be viewed by later potential water users as unfair. A complicating feature is that even where prior appropriation is the applied doctrine, courts may intervene and determine that later appropriators have a better claim to a given water supply than does the first appropriator.

Different laws prevail with regard to the allocation of the groundwater resource. English common law, upon which much of the U.S. legal system is based, holds that subsurface water belongs to whomever owns the land above such water and therefor that water may be used at any rate desired by the contiguous landowner. Such law does not take cognizance of the fact that, in most situations, the groundwater resource is a movable one and the aquifer containing the water is seldom restricted to a single property. Thus a person who pumps from "his" groundwater also pumps from the supply available to all the other persons who seek to obtain water from the same aquifer. The courts, until recently, have tended to accept English common law respecting groundwater use but in recent years there has been a trend toward more regulation over use of this resource. California, which depends heavily on groundwater to augment surface supplies, still has only limited control over groundwater use but other states have become more restrictive. Unfortunately, for much of the United States and not only the western region, overdrafts on the

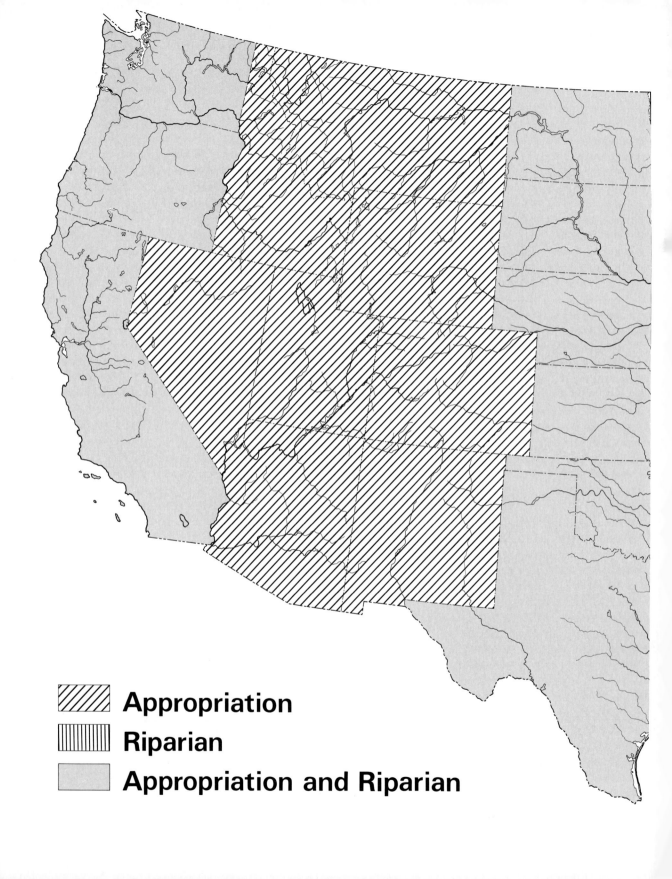

**Map 9.2 a&b**  Water rights in the conterminous United States.

0  100  200  300  400  500 Miles

0    200    400    600    800 Kilometers

groundwater resource have become frequent and unless this trend is reversed serious troubles will result (see discussions of this problem later in this chapter).

Our nation began with water ownership vested almost entirely in the private sector. However, the trend, particularly since early in the present century, has been toward ever-more public (government) ownership or at least control of the allocation of water. This development is due chiefly to passage, in 1902, of the Reclamation Act and the establishment of the Bureau of Reclamation (recently renamed the U.S. Water and Power Resources Service—WPRS). The influence of this Act of Congress and the Bureau the Act brought into being can scarcely be overstated. The Bureau of Reclamation undertook to control a significant part of the total runoff west of the 100th meridian through construction projects such as Hoover Dam on the Colorado River and the Grand Coulee Dam on the Columbia River. Chief justification for the activities of the Bureau of Reclamation was (and is) the belief that the private financial sector is unable to obtain the vast capital sums required for major water projects (which may or may not have been the case in every instance). This question has been rendered all but moot since passage of the Reclamation Act because this Act has all but usurped any possible major role that might have been played by the private sector.

In addition to federal water control, individual states also exercise considerable power and especially so in parts of the West. A notable example is California where some of the largest water diversion projects on earth have been instigated wholly or in part through state financing.

Perhaps the oldest form of public ownership of water supplies in the United States is by city and county agencies. Fairly early in the history of some eastern areas, cities found it necessary to obtain water supplies beyond their corporate limits.

Sometimes cities and counties have banded together to form a *water district,* a notable example of which is the Metropolitan Water District of Southern California. Membership in this quasi-governmental agency includes 127 cities and six counties. The MWD pumps from wells that it owns and contracts for and distributes water obtained from the Colorado River and northern California.

Another form of group ownership that may be more private than public is the *irrigation district.* Such districts were usually organized by farmers who invested funds sufficient to build a dam or dams and the system of canals and pipes required to distribute the water. Such districts may also provide water to urban areas if the supply is sufficient. Some irrigation districts are almost completely autonomous entities and conduct their affairs almost entirely free from government controls while others are essentially publicly owned utilities.

In conclusion, water ownership, in the United States, is a very complicated matter and is subject to modification in the courts. The frequent legal activities associated with water ownership probably speak more eloquently to the importance of this resource than any other phenomenon that could be cited.

## WATER MEASUREMENT

Water quantities are measured in a number of ways nationally and internationally. The United States tends to adhere to the English system of measure although there are some indications that along with the slow nationwide trend toward employing the metric system similar measures of water may follow. However, it is to be expected that several traditional aspects of water measure will prevail for a long time to come.

One of the most important water measures in the United States is the *acre foot.* An acre foot of water is the amount of water that will cover one acre of land to the depth of one foot and is equivalent to 325,851 gallons. As a rough rule of thumb, it requires about one acre foot of water to meet the household water needs for one year of a family of four persons. Major, as well as many minor, water apportionments in the United States and particularly west of the 100th meridian are usually given in acre feet.

Another frequently used measure is *second foot*. A second foot of water is the amount of water (usually stated in terms of cubic feet) that flows past a given point in one second. A second foot is equal to 449 gallons per minute (one cubic foot of water is equal to 7.4805 gallons) and 1.98 acre feet per day. Reservoir storage is commonly given in acre feet in the United States although in many other parts of the world the measure is in cubic meters (a cubic meter is roughly equivalent to 257 gallons and one acre foot of water is equivalent to 1233.5 cubic meters).

## WATER QUALITY

It may strike some readers as strange that water *quality* should be discussed before water *quantity* but this is being done in order to draw attention to the central importance of managing freshwater so as to maintain or even enhance the quality of the resource.

Having stated that water quality is of extreme importance we must now define the term water quality. Water quality is the nature of the biological and chemical characteristics of freshwater. Obviously, water quality evaluation tends to be focused on human needs and considerations and these include domestic, manufacturing, and agricultural elements.

Pure water, in the chemical sense, as we know, is $H_2O$. However, this degree of purity is seldom if ever encountered in the natural world and thus freshwater is usually a complex combination of chemicals in addition to $H_2O$. Moreover, even "laboratory pure" $H_2O$ is a chemical changeling in that it is a polymer—a compound that may have different atomic weights depending on the nature of the hydrogen and oxygen isotopes present.

Therefore, the water we most frequently use contains a variety of substances that are dissolved or carried in suspension. A certain amount of dissolved minerals of the right kind gives water a good taste—distilled water has a "flat" taste because it lacks these minerals. A certain amount of undissolved material in suspension is not necessarily harmful depending on the nature of the material although most people prefer to have their drinking water appear sparkling clear. Unfortunately, sparkling clear water is not a reliable indication that the water is biologically safe. Water in a mountain stream, for example, may be almost as clear as distilled water but can contain bacteria including those causing typhoid fever.

When water quality is discussed the focus of attention frequently moves quickly to water pollution. There are several useful definitions employed by different agencies but all have one element in common. Water may be said to be polluted when, through human acts, the biological and/or physical properties of the water are changed causing the water to be less useful and/or less safe for human use.

Our nation has a long history of unconcern—at least at legislative levels—for water quality and only in recent years have legislative bodies made serious efforts to protect the quality of much of the nation's water supply.

Water while being virtually the sine qua non for the support of life can also provide one of the chief media by which life-damaging elements can enter the human body. Perhaps because most of us now live in cities served by carefully controlled water distribution systems we have largely forgotten the not-very distant past when drinking water was often polluted in rural areas. As recently as the decade of the 1930s, for example, various governmental agencies still felt it necessary to instruct people where not to dig or drill a well with respect to the location of septic tanks or cesspools. Biological contamination of groundwater supplies drawn on for drinking water was once very common and, unfortunately, has not yet disappeared entirely. Farm folk often accepted "summer complaint," that is, gastrointestinal infections, as a natural phenomenon. How many infant children once perished in our nation because of biologically polluted water?

Our nation has been casual with respect to its surface waters and has employed lakes and rivers as dumping grounds for an enormous variety of organic and inorganic wastes. Some rivers, particularly in the northeastern and northcentral parts of the nation, became little more than open sewers into which virtually any type of solid or liquid waste was discharged or dumped. While one may sympathize with people in the Middle Ages having to live with open sewers running through their towns one can find scant reason to have sympathy for similar behavior in an age that has loudly and repeatedly proclaimed its scientific and social advances.

## BIOLOGICAL QUALITY

To be safe for drinking, water must be free of organisms that cause disease. Such organisms include viruses, bacteria, certain single-celled animals such as amoebas, which cause disentery, and flukes, which cause a variety of illnesses. It is usually not practical to routinely test a water supply for any and all possible pathogenic (disease causing) organisms so the usual procedure is to measure the frequency of an "indicator" organism such as the bacteria species, *Escherichia coli,* which is almost always present in the intestinal tract of humans and therefore is also present in human feces. Thus, the presence of *E. coli* in freshwater is an indication that human sewage has entered the water supply. The mere presence of *E. coli,* however, is not of itself an indication of unsafe water. A count is made of the (estimated) number of *E. coli* per 100 milliliters of water (equiv-

alent to 6.1 cubic inches) to determine if the number is within medically accepted limits. Although the legally accepted limits tend to vary around the nation, in general an average of 2000 *E. coli* per 100 milliliters of water is considered the upper safe limit. In public health parlance the population size of *E. coli* is given as the Most Probable Number (MPN) because a relatively small sample is used to determine the probable overall concentration of *E. coli.* Within the stated limits, the human body shows few if any pathogenic symptons from this organism. However, larger MPNs not only cause health problems to people drinking such water but these concentrations also indicate that fecal material levels are such that there might also be disease threats from other organisms. Total reliance on *E. coli* as an indicator of the biological quality of water may not be sufficient where there is a high probability for other pathogens to be present such as those causing typhoid fever or human cholera.

The safe biological quality of water is maintained or achieved through various means. Since a major aim is to prevent entry of pathogens into any water that might be used for drinking or other intimate purpose, disposal of human body wastes must be managed in such a way that pathogens are kept out of the drinking water supply. In most cities there is a never-ending problem with regard to the treatment of human wastes, the disposal of the treated *effluents,* and maintenance of a safe drinking water supply.

One of the major problems with sewage treatment is that it employs relatively large quantities of water as well as the fact that large quantities of water are required to convey sewage to a treatment plant. Water conservation frequently demands that this water be reused if at all possible and it is here that difficulty often occurs. To treat or process human sewage in such a way as to make the effluent biologically safe is a costly operation and because of this economic fact large quantities of sewage do not yet receive what many public health authorities deem necessary treatment in order to assure that the effluent water is safe for domestic reuse. Water not safe for human consumption may, however, be used for irrigation or in hydroponic agriculture but economic factors are not always such as to make such use feasible. The common practice is to give the sewage some treatment and then to discharge the resulting effluent into a conveniently located stream or lake. It then becomes the next user's problem to decontaminate the water before it is sent into water mains.

Although the difficulties are great and it is still often true that too large quantities of insufficiently treated sewage are discharged into streams and lakes, the technology of water purification is sufficiently advanced to prevent all but rare occurrences of water-borne disease in the United States.

Basically, water purification includes aeration and the addition of chemicals, usually chlorine. Aeration has the effect of destroying organisms that are anaerobic, that is, those organisms unable to survive in an oxygen-containing environment. Chlorine is a very effective and unexpensive destroyer of microorganisms in water. However, chlorine is presently under scrutiny as being a possible carcinogen (cancer-causing agent). One hopes that this chemical passes inspection because its effectiveness as a water purifier is very great. Other methods are also employed to enhance the biological quality of water although most of these are employed in relatively limited instances where economic considerations can be ignored.

Although one must be reasonable in one's judgment it nevertheless seems that there is no acceptable excuse for other than rare accidental biological contamination of our domestic water supplies. We have the technical means to do the required job. Only public indifference and narrow economic self-interest prevent achieving this goal.

# CHEMICAL QUALITY

Concern for the chemical content of water is fairly recent and may be divided into three categories (1) chemical content of domestic water, (2) chemical content of irrigation and industrial water, and (3) chemical content of water required by wildlife.

As noted earlier, drinking water, unless distilled, contains chemicals in addition to hydrogen and oxygen. The range and quantity of such chemicals may vary without presenting a health hazard. However, agricultural, manufacturing, and other activities have become sources for many kinds of unwanted chemical additions to water.

Prior to the Industrial Revolution, human-caused chemical pollution was rare but since industrialization—with its incessant technological changes—the chemical quality of water has been an object of concern. Unlike bacteria and viruses in human body wastes, sewage treatment plants are mostly *unable* to remove chemicals from waste water even though it is highly desirable to prevent entry of unwanted chemicals into the surface and groundwater supplies. Something of the magnitude of this pollution problem may be appreciated if it is realized that in addition to the thousands of chemical compounds already in daily use in this nation, each year brings additional hundreds of chemical compounds whose potential behavior in freshwater ecosystems is totally unknown even though many if not most of these chemicals are ultimately discharged into surface waters. Now and again a particularly dramatic instance of chemical contamination is given press coverage but thousands of chemicals whose potential toxicity is not known are present in our water supplies.

Two examples of chemical pollution receiving wide coverage in the news media are methyl mercury and polychlorinated biphynel (PCB). Mercury (Hg) was once thought to be inert in aquatic systems because it was believed that the chemical would sink into the mud at the bottom of a stream or lake causing no problems. However, it was later found that under certain conditions mercury is ionized and in this form (as a cation) it may enter food chains and if humans are a part of a mercury-contaminated food chain, such persons can become extremely ill. PCBs occur in many industrial chemicals and have been widely used and casually discarded for decades. Recently it has been determined that these chemicals are carcinogens and thus their presence in a domestic water supply at other than extremely low levels (parts per billion ppb) shouldn't be tolerated. This chemical is being found in many groundwater supplies and sometimes in such concentrations that environmental monitoring agencies require that further domestic use of the water be stopped. The example of PCBs points up a particularly difficult aspect of water chemical quality management: that some of the contamination has not come about through discharge of the chemicals into surface water but from discharge on the ground surface after which the chemicals percolated downward into the groundwater supply.

Cleaning up contaminated surface waters, although often a major task, is simple compared to the problems that must be faced with chemically contaminated undergound water supplies. At present there is no workable means of cleaning up such contamination and when a groundwater aquifer becomes chemically polluted the only recourse is to shut down the wells. The rate of water replacement in each aquifer is probably as unique as a human thumbprint and in most cases isn't known very precisely and thus, the rate(s) at which a given chemical will be flushed from an aquifer can't be determined. Therefor, for all practical purposes, a chemically polluted aquifer is lost for an indefinite and extended time to further safe human utilization.

It must be obvious that controls should be placed on the ground-surface discharge of chemical wastes. Only within the past few years has any serious effort been directed toward this issue and we are now in a situation where we are trying to find where and by whom chemicals have been dumped in the past. There is really no plausible excuse for this since it has been known for many years that groundwater can be contaminated from surface sources.

Another cause of chemical contamination of groundwater is nitrogen, or more specifically, nitrates, which have first been applied as fertilizer—usually in compounds such as ammonium sulfate $(NH_4)_2$ $SO_4$—and were later leached downward into the groundwater. High nitrate levels are being detected in several parts of the nation's groundwater resources and in some instances levels have been so high as to require the shutdown of wells. Nitrate $(NO_3)$ becomes nitrite $(NO_2)$ under certain circumstances and this latter is known to be a health hazard to infants.

Water, in order to be suitable for irrigation, must not contain so much dissolved minerals as to damage crop plants. There is no one upper limit for dissolved minerals because different crop plants, including tree crops, have differing degrees of tolerance for specific minerals or, as these are more generally termed, salts. Some examples of salt-tolerant crops are sugar beet, alfalfa (grown for hay), carrots, cabbage, and asparagus. Salt-sensitive crops include such examples as citrus, apples, pears, cherries, peaches, and plums. Some examples of moderately salt-tolerant crops are oats, wheat, corn, pumpkin, tomato, and certain varieties of cotton.

Mineral (salt) content of water available for irrigation together with climate and the salinity of the soil to be farmed largely determine the range of crops it is possible to grow in regions where irrigation is practiced. Although relatively little can be done to alter the quality of irrigation water (taken from surface or groundwater sources) prior to use, the quality of the *return flow* water can be affected. The term *re-*

*turn flow* refers to water that is returned to streams after use. Such water, in irrigated regions, is typically more saline than when it was first taken from a surface or groundwater source. This problem is discussed in greater detail later in this chapter.

For many manufacturing and industrial activities water of low mineral content is required and often in very large quantities. One example of such requirements is water used to produce steam to drive turbines in electricity-generating plants. Unless the water is almost free of mineral content, repairs must be made frequently in order to rid boilers, pipes, and other parts of the steam-producing mechanism of "scale," the mineral residue that accumulates when mineral-containing water is heated to produce steam. Often the available water is not suitable for steam production and must first be partially distilled. This is an expensive (energy intensive) process and therefor steam plants commonly have sophisticated recyling systems to reduce as much as possible loss of the expensive low-mineral-content water.

In some manufacturing activities the concern is with water "hardness." Water is said to be hard when difficulty is experienced in getting soap to make suds. The chemicals most often responsible for hard water are calcium carbonate ($CaCO_3$) and magnesium compounds. Water containing 120 parts per million (ppm) or more of these chemicals is considered hard. Hardwater is chiefly a problem associated with groundwater and particularly where there is much limestone in the subsurface geology. Water can be softened by distillation or by being treated in water softeners. The latter are usually ion exchangers employing table salt (NaCl).

## WATER POLLUTION CONTROL

Because in the past little or no economic cost accrued to water polluters there was no eco-nomic incentive to return water to surface or groundwater situations in as good a condition as when it was withdrawn for use. Although this has been cited frequently as an example of rapacious economic behavior, it was, in fact, sound economic practice for the individual farmer. The fault lay in the fact that government did not establish ground rules that would not only make pollution illegal but, more importantly, make it more economically costly to pollute water than not to do so. While it is true that manufacturing interests have generally resisted most governmental attempts to punish polluters with economic penalties the fact is that as long as the rules are applied equally to all so that the added cost impacts all water users equally and allows them to include these costs with the other costs of production there is little basis for honest complaint. In general, it is the economically marginal enterprise operating with inefficient technology that can't stay in business if required to make the added capital inputs required to comply with water quality regulation.

It is also argued, and with somewhat more validity, that compliance with water quality regulations, that is, regulations against water pollution, places a given industry in an unfavorable competitive position vis-à-vis the products of similar industries located in nations where water pollution is still tolerated. It would appear that where such cases can be thoroughly documented, the imported products of such industries should be subjected to a special water-pollution tariff that offsets any economic disadvantage such as the one noted.

Intelligent legislation respecting water pollution is a difficult enterprise and one that is likely to be resisted at the local level. However, many of the nation's more serious examples of surface water pollution involve rivers and lakes that include the territory of more than a single state or nation not to mention several cities or counties. Thus, regional and international cooperation is often required and, in some instances, nothing short of federal intervention will suffice to stop water-polluting activities.

It has only been since World War II that the federal government has given major attention to water pollution. The modern era of water quality legislation began with the passage, in 1948, of the Water Pollution Act and followed, in 1954, by the Water Facilities Act, which had as its principal aim the providing of a legal means by which the federal government could involve itself in issues concerning water quality. Other acts of Congress respecting freshwater quality were passed in later years until the landmark Water Quality Act of 1965. This enabling legislation marked the establishment of national standards for water quality and led to further federal legislation in this area—an activity that is still underway at federal and state levels. The principal effect of the legislation is to provide legal (economic) incentives to cease polluting streams and other surface waters. Currently, interest in pure water is being extended to include groundwater also. However, groundwater pollution often is a localized phenomenon and may often be controlled best at local or state levels.

## WATER QUALITY AND WILDLIFE

Maintenance of water quality for wildlife must be considered as a major concern of water management. Although many animals are more tolerant of certain types of water pollution than are humans it can be said that, in general, wildlife requires water almost as clean as do humans and, in addition, many aquatic animals are far more sensitive to slight changes in salinity than are people.

Two major groups of wildlife using freshwater are particularly sensitive to water quality, these being waterfowl such as ducks and geese and almost all strictly aquatic animals and particularly fish.

With regard to waterfowl, there is a need to provide them with extensive areas of water that can offer them a place to rest, nest, and feed. Suitable freshwater areas for waterfowl—and particularly for migratory species—have been greatly reduced in size and number during the past several decades. When waterfowl are forced to crowd together in unusual numbers on a sheet of freshwater they greatly increase their risk of becoming ill from such killing infections as that caused by the bacterium Salmonella. When not overcrowded, a single sick bird may not easily pass an infection along to others but when forced to congregate in too dense an aggregation an infectious disease can spread rapidly causing the deaths of large numbers of birds.

Salinity levels are often important for species of waterfowl that depend on aquatic plants for their food. Some of these plants are highly sensitive to other than comparatively low salinity levels and die if the salt content is increased.

Fish and other aquatic organisms are sensitive to the chemical and tamperature characteristics of the water they inhabit. Among the more important chemicals are dissolved salts and oxygen ($O_2$). Sewage and other kinds of organic waste tend to increase the oxygen demands of decay organisms (biological oxygen demand—BOD) and thus to reduce the amount of oxygen available to other organisms present. This may cause a stream or lake to suffer serious losses of those animal species whose oxygen requirements are greater than can be provided by the polluted water. This may not result in a lowered fish biomass per se but the species composition may change from highly valued species, such as trout having high oxygen requirements, to species sometimes referred to as "coarse fish." The carp is an example of a coarse fish and is known for its ability to tolerate relatively low levels of dissolved oxygen in the water it inhabits.

Other chemical changes, including changes in salinity, can have an impact on adult fish during the spawning season and the juvenile fish that manage to hatch may also be harmed. Each aquatic animal species has its own levels of chemical tolerances and often each life stage of an individual species has its own tolerances, (e.g., the juveniles of striped bass are far less tolerant of high salinity than are the adults).

Some aquatic organisms are as sensitive to water temperature as they are to water chemistry. As noted, there is a close relationship between water temperature and oxygen content. Thus, artificial warming of freshwater (or marine water) as it occurs in the discharge from nuclear power cooling towers, will reduce the potential amount of dissolved oxygen the water receiving the discharge can contain.

## DAMS

Most major dams are of one or two basic types—gravity dams and arch dams with the former being the more frequent of the two (Figs. 9.4, 9.5).

Gravity-type dams rely on their weight to hold back the water they impound. These dams are constructed in a variety of shapes and of varied materials and are formed so that the lowest part of the dam is also the thickest because this is where the greatest weight of the water occurs. These dams usually have a core of rocks or earth overlain by varying quantities of concrete with the greatest care being taken on the upstream side of the dam to prevent all but the most minimal amount of water leakage.

**Figure 9.4** Shasta Dam, a gravity-type structure.

**Figure 9.5** Hoover Dam, an arch-type structure.

Arch-type dams are elegant in design form and depend chiefly on cantilever action to withstand the pressures of impounded water. This type of dam is comparatively rare because it can't be used to span wide streams as can gravity-type dams which, in theory, have no upper limit as to size.

In the early days of the United States, dams were small and were financed chiefly from private sources. As the size, economic cost, and political complexities of dam construction increased there developed a marked trend toward public financing. Throughout most of the twentieth century, all large U.S. dam projects have been the products of governmental financing although actual construction may or may not have been done by a governmental

agency. The most important federal agency involved in dam construction is the Army Corps of Engineers.

The importance of the Army Corps of Engineers in the role of dam builders began with the passage of the Rivers and Harbors Act in 1927. This Act had as its principal aims the control of floods on America's rivers and the development and maintenance of harbors—inland and marine—in the United States. The job of achieving these aims was delegated largely to the Army Corps of Engineers.

The Army Corps of Engineers has been the frequent target of criticism by various groups, which have felt that this Army unit has been too desirous of damming America's rivers and has too broadly interpreted the meaning of flood control. However, other persons point out that in many instances regions once subject to devastating floods are now safe from such calamities.

Whenever possible, however, government-financed dams are built by private contractors as, for example, was the case with Hoover Dam on the Colorado River (Table 9.1).

## WATERSHED MANAGEMENT

Few better examples of getting the proverbial cart before the horse is afforded than the way much dam construction has been approached. The initial focus of attention and construction is almost always at the dam site with little attention being given to the watershed itself. The term *watershed* refers to the total surface and subsurface over which and through which water drains into a surface drainage system. Thus, the watershed of a given water impoundment is the surface and subsurface over which and through which water flows toward the dam. It is of the utmost importance that watersheds be managed with the aim of (1) maximizing the water available for impoundment and (2) reducing to a minimum the amount of sediment transported by running water into the water im-

Table 9.1
**Major water impoundments in the United States**

| River Basin | Name of Dam | Amount of Water Impounded ($10^6$ acre feet) |
|---|---|---|
| Colorado | Hoover | 29.75 |
| Colorado | Glen Canyon | 27.0 |
| Missouri | Oahe | 23.59 |
| Missouri | Fort Peck | 19.1 |
| Columbia | Grand Coulee | 9.7 |
| Missouri | Fort Randall | 5.7 |
| Sacramento | Shasta | 4.5 |
| South Fork, Flathead | Hungry Horse | 3.47 |
| Trinity-Klamath | Trinity | 2.45 |
| Stanislaus | New Melones | 2.4 |
| Tuolumne | Don Pedro | 2.0 |
| San Juan | Navajo | 1.7 |
| Bighorn | Yellowtail | 1.37 |

*Source:*   U.S. Bureau of Reclamation.

poundment. The best means of achieving these related aims is to maintain a vegetative cover that retards runoff of rainfall or snowmelt, which retards loss of soil.

Fire, in many types of watershed situations, can often be incredibly destructive of watershed quality. An extreme example of this is afforded by the chaparral vegetation of California. Many chaparral-covered areas are valuable watersheds and when subjected to wildfires become major sources of sediments with the arrival of winter rains. This is not to suggest that all fires in the chaparral or other watersheds are always harmful. Fire can and should be used as a management tool in chaparral and other vegetation types when such use is indicated but this must be done under very careful control. Regardless of the nature of the vegetative cover, wide-ranging *wildfires* will almost always have a sequel of major soil movements (e.g., major property damaging and life-threat-

ening landslides occur in parts of southern California during the winter in hillside areas that have experienced burns in the brushlands during the previous summer).

In those instances where a watershed is under the control of a single agency as for example the U.S. Forest Service, the task of management is somewhat less complicated than in the instances where more than a single agency or owner has responsibility for the watershed. Most of the discussion to follow will assume a situation where a single federal agency has title to all the land included within a watershed.

In general, good forest management equates with good watershed management since almost anything damaging to the forest will result in an increase of silt in the water flowing into a given impoundment. Thus, the vegetation ought to be as little disturbed as possible by fire, grazing, construction, and other activities. One will recall, however, from the chapter on forest conservation and management, that there is a legal requirement that National Forests must be managed for multiple uses. This requirement assures that something less than optimal watershed management can be achieved. Sources of disturbance include fires set accidentally, too much foot traffic (human and animal) over trails, too many people using and thus impacting available campsites causing loss of plant cover and soil compaction. It must be pointed out, however, that the impacts of multiple uses of watersheds are not uniform and vary from one situation to another. Very few quantitative generalizations can be used and each situation must receive its own thorough investigation before accurate determinations can be made as to the kinds and levels of uses that are permissible.

# MAJOR FEDERAL WATER CONTROL PROJECTS

Beginning in this century, the federal government has been engaged in the development of massive water control projects that have had profound effects upon the nation's economy as well as ecology. Two outstanding projects have been selected for description and discussion here: (1) The Tennessee Valley Authority (TVA) and (2) the Colorado River complex.

## The Tennessee Valley Authority

The Tennessee River, the principal tributary of the Ohio River, had a long history of destructive floods and, with the passage of the Reclamation Act in 1902, it became the first major American river system to receive attention from the Army Corps of Engineers. This interest centered not only on measures to affect flood control but also on the possibility of constructing ship canals around numerous shallow parts of the river to make the stream more useful for water transportation. The construction that followed, prior to the decade of the 1930s, was limited chiefly to canals although the desire to do something about the recurrent flooding remained a major object of investigation.

Opportunity for federal involvement in the entire Tennessee River watershed came during the economic depression of the 1930s. With the passage of the Norris Act in 1933, the federal government gained the means not only to control that entire watershed but also the means to do so under the aegis of a single federal agency, the Tennessee Valley Authority (TVA).

Probably no other similar venture by the federal government has raised as much controversy as did the TVA for this represented an invasion by the government into an area of resource development that previously had been chiefly in the private sector. Even now, decades after the initiation of this project, emotions still run strong pro and con and it may be that more time must pass before an unbiased assessment of the values of this huge project can be accurately determined.

The basic objective of the TVA was to tame the Tennessee River which, as indicated above, was known for its frequent and damaging floods. In order to achieve that end and also make the project economically self-sufficient the TVA was to be a major generator of hydroelectricity, which was to be sold cheaply in a large region suffering from a lack of economic development. Furthermore, in keeping with the multiple-use requirement of federally developed water resources, the TVA lake system was to become an important recreation complex (Map 9.3).

Thirty-three major dams and many smaller dams were constructed to restrain the floods and to generate electricity. This construction has extended over many years and includes the controversial Tellico Dam. Arguments over the Tellico Dam have focused on an endangered species of fish, the snail darter. It has been stated that construction of this dam will endanger this small fish but recent investigations have located populations of this species in streams that will not be affected by the dam construction. The Tellico Dam controversy is so bound up in political, economic, and biological charges and countercharges that an unbiased evaluation is all but impossible to obtain at this time.

The magnitude of the TVA development was and probably still would be well beyond the capability or desire of the private sector to achieve. Yet, it is this aspect of the TVA that strikes the most sparks of controversy. Does the federal government have the responsibility to engage in such projects even if the private sector cannot or will not? This question is not restricted to the TVA but is present wherever and whenever the federal government involves itself in the nation's natural resources.

## The Colorado River

The Colorado River defies most attempts to develop accurate numbers respecting the amounts of water it carries. The river drains an enormous area of about 627,000 km² in the United States to which must be added an additional approximate 5200 km² in Mexico. The

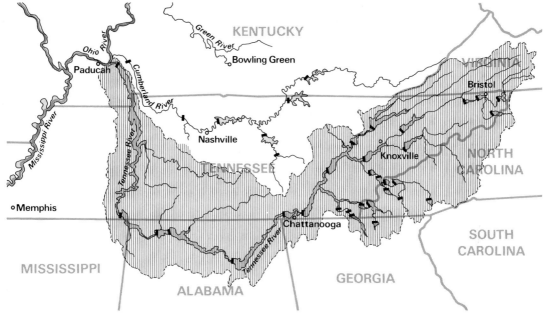

**Map 9.3**  System of water impoundments in the region of the Tennessee Valley Authority (TVA)

most important hydrological facts about the Colorado River are that (1) the water contains large quantities of dissolved minerals because it passes over and through rocks that contain large amounts of soluable minerals, (2) it carries a heavy silt load, (3) the annual flow volume is highly variable from year to year and the *average* annual flow, though commonly employed in planning, has little relevance to actual conditions, (4) passing as it does through some of the most arid parts of the nation makes of this river a hotly contested-for-resource and (5) this is an *international* river and requires that considerations beyond those of U.S. interests must or should be part of its management.

Interest in "developing" the water resources of the Colorado River date back at least to the last quarter of the nineteenth century when private groups diverted water from the river to irrigate some desert land in southeastern California. Over the years there were other privately developed diversions these also being for the

purpose of irrigating crop lands. Lack of sufficient means to handle the large quantities of silt carried by the river resulted in many difficulties with irrigation canals and associated construction. Ultimately, the various groups banded together and formed the Imperial Valley Irrigation District.

Major impetus for what might be termed megadevelopment of the Colorado River began with the interest of Los Angeles in the river as a source of water for an exploding urban population. Surveys were made by the city early in this century and during the waning days of the Presidential Administration of Calvin Coolidge, the *Boulder Canyon Project Act,* was signed. Early the next year, when Herbert Hoover was president, further presidential approval was given the project the major dam of which today bears Hoover's name. Hoover Dam was completed in 1936 during the presidency of Franklin D. Roosevelt and impounds 29.7 million acre feet in Lake Mead. This project produces hydroelectricity, provides for flood control and improved water quality below the dam (silt being trapped above the dam), makes water available for irrigation and urban uses regardless of the annual fluctuations of river-flow volume, and provides recreation facilities. The tamed river below Hoover Dam was further altered by impoundments to supply irrigation water to farmers and domestic water supplies to urban customers, the latter being developed by the Metropolitan Water District of Southern California. Water is brought from the Colorado River at Parker Dam via an aqueduct to the coastal region of southern California. Unfortunately, this water must be pumped because high country lies between the river and the urban market: pumping costs have soared recently with the increase in energy prices (see Map 9.4).

The annual flow of water in the Lower Basin of the Colorado River has been apportioned by court order as follows: beginning in 1985, Arizona is to receive $2.8 \times 10^6$ acre feet; Nevada is to receive $0.3 \times 10^6$ acre feet; California is to receive $4.4 \times 10^6$ acre feet; Mexico is to receive $1.5 \times 10;^6$ acre feet. The *official* figure for the average total annual flow of the Colorado River is $15 \times 10^6$ acre feet, which amount has been divided by court edict equally between the Upper and Lower Basins. Thus, the total apportionment for the Lower Basin exceeds by $1.5 \times 10^6$ acre feet the $7.5 \times 10^6$ acre feet apportioned to the entire basin. This excess amount, which exactly equals the amount due Mexico, must be obtained by *return flow,* that is, from water that has been used and then returned to the river and by other inflows, principally from Arizona rivers that are not computed as being a part of the "official" Colorado River flow-volume. This return flow water invariably contains more dissolved salts than it contained before use in irrigation and thus the quality of water delivered to Mexican farmers in Baja California has declined severely in recent decades. In order to alleviate a situation that resulted in the

salination of valuable farmland in Mexico, the U.S. government has constructed a desalination plant in Arizona near the confluence of the Colorado and Yuma Rivers. This is a very expensive "solution" to the water quality problem.

The Upper Basin of the Colorado is the site of other major water impoundment projects supported by federal funding. Chief among these is the Glen Canyon Dam behind which lies Lake Powell containing a maximum of $27 \times 10^6$ acre feet of water. Like Hoover Dam downstream, Glen Canyon Dam is multipurpose.

Three Damoclean swords hang over this enormous river basin development: (1) the unknown and probably unknowable future of climate in the river basin with special reference to precipitation, (2) useful life spans of the dams comprising the project since siltation reduces the storage capacity of every dam in the system, and (3) the still-not-adjudicated Indian water rights in the basin. Although the first two items will become issues only with the passage of many years this is not true of Indian water rights.

During the years when non-Indians were busy developing and apportioning the waters of the Colorado River the rights of the inhabitants present at the time of the first arrival of Europeans were largely ignored. This was shortsighted, if not irresponsible, because there existed a U.S. Supreme Court decision dating back to 1908, which held that Indians on a res[1] ervation had undiminished future water rights even though these may not have been used as soon as a reservation was created. Left out of the court decision was language that placed limits on the kind of uses to which the water might one day be put. In more recent years a quite different view has been developing: that the reservations are to be quasi-Indian nations or homelands in which the Indians may live and develop their own natural resources. Thus, instead of being assimilated or remaining on the

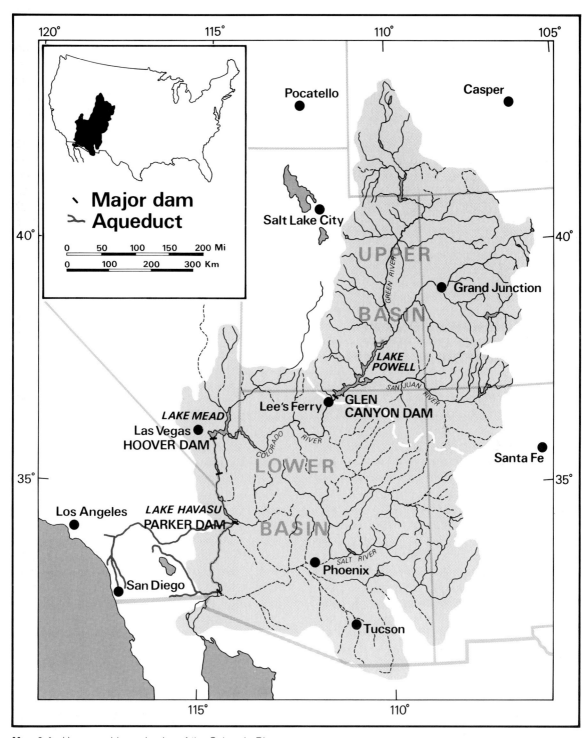

**Map 9.4** Upper and lower basins of the Colorado River.

reservations to scratch out a marginal farming/pastoral-based existence, more and more tribes are claiming the ownership of all the natural resources including water lying within the reservations.

The decades of legislative neglect by the U.S. Congress is in no small measure responsible for the current situation of which few Americans are aware. The various states that draw water from the Colorado Basin continue with their water plans as though the Indian question did not exist. However, until the Indian water rights are settled in the Colorado River Basin—and elsewhere in the West—water can be said to be apportioned only on a *provisional* basis.

## CONSERVATION AND MANAGEMENT OF FRESHWATER: THE CALIFORNIA EXAMPLE

The major water development schemes described in the previous section were essentially purely federal projects in that federal financing and development decisions were all or nearly all within the control of the federal government. However, the federal government may also act as a partner to a state especially when the latter is unable or unwilling to assume all the financial burdens of water development. The cooperation of federal and state agencies can be beneficial but such cooperation often produces conflicts requiring protracted litigation to settle. The cooperative approach to water development is very evident in California. Also there exists, almost side by side in some instances, privately developed water projects, state-financed water projects, federally financed water projects, and combinations of state and federally developed projects. Probably nowhere else in the United States are the conflicts associated with water development more complex than they are in California. Because of this and also because it is the most populous state with the highest annual income

from agriculture, of which a large part depends on irrigation, California will receive the focus of this section.

California, the third-largest state in the Union with an area of 410,756 square kilometers and the most populous with more than 22 million inhabitants, suffers because the local supplies of water in many areas are not sufficient to meet all the demand. Much of the history of the state can be written in and around the theme of water projects devised to supply rural and urban areas whose demands have been nothing less than explosive during most of this century. These demands are mostly located in places other than where local water resources are abundant and thus the state is the locale for water projects whose magnitude, in terms of quantities impounded, total length of distribution canals and people dependent upon the redistributed supplies are not equaled in any other individual state (see Map 9.5).

As was already pointed out in the discussion on the Colorado River, southern California was looking for water supplies early in this century and began the importation of Colorado River water to the coastal region of southern California in the years just prior to World War II. Those importations began only after another major project of water diversion from the Owens Valley, over 300 miles distant from Los Angeles, had earlier been completed (Fig. 9.6). Although it is the most populous part of the state, southern California lies almost entirely in an arid or semiarid region where the locally available water resource is so small as to be unable to support more than a very small part of the people living there.

To a considerable extent, the above situation is repeated in the northern part of the state. The largest concentration of population is centered in the San Francisco Bay area, but were it not for the construction of aqueducts and canals bringing water to that region only a much smaller number of people could be supported by the available local water supply.

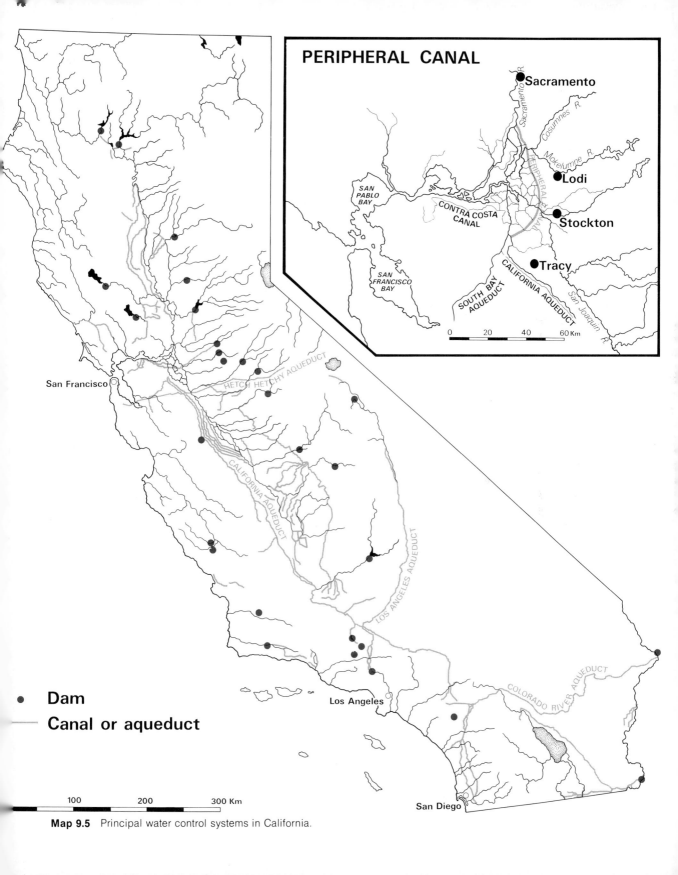

**PERIPHERAL CANAL**

Sacramento

Lodi

Stockton

Tracy

*Sacramento R.*

*Cosumnes R.*

*Mokelumne R.*

PERIPHERAL CANAL

SAN PABLO BAY

CONTRA COSTA CANAL

SAN FRANCISCO BAY

SOUTH BAY AQUEDUCT

CALIFORNIA AQUEDUCT

*San Joaquin R.*

0    20    40    60 Km

San Francisco

HETCH HETCHY AQUEDUCT

CALIFORNIA AQUEDUCT

LOS ANGELES AQUEDUCT

Los Angeles

COLORADO RIVER AQUEDUCT

• **Dam**

— **Canal or aqueduct**

San Diego

100    200    300 Km

**Map 9.5**  Principal water control systems in California.

**Figure 9.6** Owen's Valley, California. Cities, in this case Los Angeles, may obtain their water from sources located hundreds of miles distant.

The greatest water demand in California is not in the urban areas, however, but in the agricultural sector which consumes at least 80 percent of all water used in the state. Although agriculture is widely distributed throughout the state, the principal farming region is the Central Valley, this being composed of the Sacramento and San Joaquin Valleys (Fig. 9.7). Most of this enormously productive farm region depends on copious supplies of water stored behind dams located on the western slopes of the Sierra Nevada. Annual rainfall totals in the Central Valley are usually far too modest to support other than grazing and a few dry-farmed crops. The little irrigation that could be practiced in earlier days was where farms were located adjacent to rivers—and providing that the farms so located had established prior appropriation water rights thereto.

The first significant attempts to manipulate the surface water supply came during the gold rush period when water was needed to work gold placers (see chapter seventeen). Some of the canals dug during that period for the purpose of carrying water down from the Sierra Nevada to the gold "diggings" are still in use

but only for limited local domestic and agricultural uses. The next important attempts to manage the water resource came with attempts to prevent the floods that destroyed crops grown in the Central Valley. Like most rivers, the streams there had natural levees along their sides but these were not sufficiently high to prevent overflows during high water. Farmers banded together to construct higher levees on top of the natural features—an activity that continues even today.

Farmers in the Central Valley also were quick to learn that the winters are fairly short and rainfall not abundant and this is followed by a long, hot and dry summer. They were aware that unless they could obtain water for irrigation, farming was never going to be very important. Thus, irrigation districts were formed by private funding and others by a combination of private and public financing.

As the development of water for irrigation continued, urban demands were also being felt and in the early years of this century it was becoming apparent that local water supplies in the San Francisco Bay region were not sufficient to meet projected future needs. The city

**Figure 9.7**  Furrow irrigation, Central Valley, California.

of San Francisco reached eastward to the Sierra Nevada and, after much controversy, in 1923 flooded the Hetch Hetchy Canyon and led the stored water via aqueduct to the city. In the process they drowned a valley said to rival the beauty of Yosemite Valley. This was followed in later years by other Sierran water impoundments to provide water for the explosive growth of Bay area population. In addition to the city and county agencies, public utilities impounded Sierran rivers chiefly to generate electricity. The federal government, through the Army Corps of Engineers, became very active and particularly so in recent years as also is the case with the U.S. Bureau of Reclamation (now the WPRS). California has also financed large water impoundment schemes in the Sierra.

The need to coordinate the use and manage-ment of water derived from so many projects is self evident but has not been easy to achieve. Each agency tends to guard its water from regulation by others. Overlaying this development is the complex and conflicting laws governing water rights in the state. Both prior appropriation and riparian rights are recognized, although the former are frequently the most sensible given the fact that water is so often located at some distance from where it can be best employed whether it be for agricultural or other uses. The soils adjacent to Sierran streams are thin, have relatively low fertility, lie on steep slopes, and are easily eroded. The best agricultural soils lie in the Central Valley and only a limited area of these soils lies adjacent to a surface stream from which water could be drawn for irrigation. The amount of water available in valley rivers during the dry months of summer is not nearly enough to irrigate more than a modest fraction of the soil that is suitable for such water use.

The first major successful effort to coordinate water management in the Central Valley began prior to World War II. Although started as a state-financed project, funding was so difficult to obtain during the economic depression of the 1930s that the state turned to the federal government for assistance. The resultant scheme, the Central Valley Project, brought water to a vast area which previously could only be grazed or dry farmed. Immediately, conflict arose respecting the Reclamation Act of 1902, which states that individual land holdings benefiting from water developed by the expenditure of federal funds could not exceed 160 acres or double that amount for a married couple. However, in the San Joaquin Valley, for example, some huge land holdings benefited from this water and the owners of such land were and, in some cases, remain, the object of litigation. It must be realized that some of this land increased enormously in value after water was brought to it and, furthermore, the law does appear to clearly state what the acreage limitations are to be.

One is not dealing here chiefly with marginal family farms but mostly with large corporations that retain large legal staffs. Some of the landholdings have been declared illegal and the courts have required that they be broken up through sale. This has not always proved easy because if too large an amount of land is put on the market at one time there may be a depression in the price of land. The law also states that this land must be sold for its value *prior* to the receipt of federally developed irrigation water. However, it is not always clear that this proviso is honored. It has been and continues to be argued by the large landholders that the 1C0-acre limitation is archaic and should be revised upward. One reads of Congress strongly supporting such a revision—960 acres is commonly mentioned—of the acre limitation. Regardless of the possible justification for such an upward revision—there are arguments to be made for both sides of the issue—the fact remains that a fairly massive flouting of the water law has occurred in this region (and elsewhere in the West) and a citizen may rightfully question the propriety of allowing such acts to be rendered legally moot by permitting the persons involved to profit from law changes made after the illegal acts occurred.

More recently, another major water development and water transfer project was brought into being, the California Water Project, or as it is also known, the State Water Project (SWP). The aims of this project include the usual flood control, hydropower, irrigation, and recreation provisions but is really focused upon supplying irrigation water to the southern end of the San Joaquin Valley and water to southern California.

This is chiefly a state-financed project with the state funds being raised by the sale of bonds. The project, begun in the early 1960s, represents a major achievement in engineering but it is also an object of heated controversy.

There are so many facets to the controversy that only a few of the most important will be discussed here. First, there is strong sectional sentiment involved. It is widely felt in northern California that southern California is out to "steal" water that is the "property" of northern California. This attitude is directed mostly at a portion of the SWP that must be completed—according to many southern Californians—if sufficient water is to be delivered to the southern part of the state to fulfill contracts already signed. Also, according to the southern argument, beginning in 1985, "excess" water that has been obtained from the Colorado River will no longer be available to southern California as Arizona moves to take all of its $2.8 \times 10^6$ acre feet. This so-called excess amounts to approximately one million acre feet per year.

Much of this heated dissent is directed toward that part of the project called the Peripheral Canal (Map 9.5). This is a proposal to construct a canal around the eastern periphery of the confluence area of the Sacramento and San Joaquin Rivers (this area is known as the Delta) to transport water into the major canal that already sends the water to the southern end of the San Joaquin Valley and thence, by pumps, up over the Tehachapi Mountains to southern California. No single water issue in the state in recent decades has resulted in more public emotions and political activity than has the issue of the Peripheral Canal.

One of the basic elements of this controversy relates to the quality of water in the Delta and especially during years of drought—which in spite of California folklore to the contrary, is a frequent event—when water demands are greatest but water availability is low. Farmers in the Delta worry about saltwater intrusion into aquifers if there is insufficient head pressure created by too little freshwater flowing toward San Francisco Bay. Biologists and ecologists are concerned with the salinity of surface water, fearing that increased diversion of freshwater would allow more saltwater to intrude into the area and, thus, seriously impact aquatic animals and other life forms. Some farming groups in Central Valley support the canal while others align themselves with conservationists who oppose the canal. Particularly understandable are conservationists who fear the consequences of increased salinity in the Delta. Their efforts tend to focus upon obtaining legal restraints that will assure an adequate throughflow of freshwater during drought periods. Assurances have been given by the water agencies involved that this will be done but doubts remain.

Another major element in the controversy relates to water use by farmers. As noted earlier in this chapter, about 80 percent of the water used in California is employed in agriculture and chiefly for irrigation. Therefore, it seems self-evident that it is in the agricultural sector that the greatest potential for water conservation exists. Thus, many conservationists insist that there is already sufficient water flowing in existing canals to meet all present and projected water needs, north and south, if farmers were to upgrade their methods of water use. Although this is not the place to present a detailed discussion of the kinds of irrigation techniques used in California (and elsewhere in the United States) it may be noted that, with few exceptions, irrigation today often remains essentially unchanged from techniques developed hundreds of years ago in other parts of the world.

Little is known about the size of the costs that might be incurred in the Central Valley were any major modifications in irrigation methods to be developed and adopted. Most of the technological advances that have occurred are on the order of lining canals with concrete to reduce losses by percolation and paying greater heed to the actual water needs as well as timing of needs of crop plants.

It is frequently argued that water prices paid by farmers do not represent the true scarcity value of water and that the urban water users, by paying relatively higher costs for water, subsidize agriculture. There is no question that the cost of water per acre foot is far less to farmers in the Central Valley than is the cost for the same amount to urban users in the metropolitan centers of the state. It is often argued that water is so inexpensive to farmers in the Central Valley that they have little incentive to conserve it. This is something of an exaggeration because while the unit cost of water is far less than in San Francisco or Los Angeles, the large volume required makes water costs an important economic element in any farming operation and one seldom encounters wanton waste of water on any farm.

One area where water conservation in large quantities could be achieved would be by concentrating on crops having relatively low water requirements and abandoning the cultivation of crops having very high water demands such as cotton and rice. However, farmers are among the most independent of people and would probably resist by every possible means attempts to restrict their choices of crops grown. But does it make good sense for California to grow rice, which uses very large quantities of water, when parts of the southern United States can grow this crop where there are more abundant supplies of water? Or does it make sense to grow cotton under irrigation—there were an estimated 855,000 acres (346,154 hectares) of this crop in California in 1980—when there are alternative sources including imports for this fiber? When one also realizes that the federal government encourages the cultivation of many heavy water-demanding crops through acreage allotment programs and other measures one finds a definite basis for an examination of the whole issue of appropriate water use for irrigation.

One way often suggested by which desired conservation of water could be obtained is through a pricing system that reflects the true scarcity value of water. But how is this "true value" of water to be determined? Who is to make the judgment as to what is the best or optimal use of water on the farm or elsewhere? The sought-after ideal is a pricing system that will fully reflect the scarcity of water but that will not act as an unnecessary disincentive. At present, all pricing structures for water are patched-up entities reflecting the varied interests and pressure groups brought to bear upon the legislative process. In California, particularly, great care must be taken that water prices to farmers are not set so high as to significantly reduce the value of farm products.

Notwithstanding this, the human population

of California is overwhelmingly urban and the urban areas also contain important manufacturing units that together require a large and reliable supply of water. Thus, water management in California must not only contend with a sometimes vitriolic sectionalism but also with a conflict between agricultural and urban users of water. Although it might appear that this is only an intrastate matter such is not the case. The state of California contains approximately 10 percent of the nation's population and generates an important part of the nation's gross domestic product, a major component of which is food and fiber from the farms located in the state. Thus the outcomes of the water controversies in California will ultimately affect most of the nation's citizens.

## GROUNDWATER MANAGEMENT

The groundwater resources of our nation comprise a major portion of the total freshwater resource (Map 9.6). However, complex legal problems must be solved if this resource is not to be continuously overdrawn as is now the situation in most parts of the nation.

Like surface water law, laws governing the ownership and use of groundwater resources came to us chiefly from English common law. In this instance, the law stated that the water under the ground of a person's land could be used on the contiguous land or could be transported and used somewhere else. In some states, and notably in California, which has the largest individual share of the nation's groundwater resource, the law has been modified to limit use of groundwater to the land lying above the groundwater source. Although this is an improvement it does not restrict the *amount* of water that can be pumped. Unless further restricted, all the owners of farmland located above a groundwater basin may pump as rapidly as their means permit. This invariably leads to overdrafts on the water supply, that is, far greater amounts are removed than are replaced by the natural recharge rate.

The law regarding groundwater use often differs for urban utilities, which may be given rights that supersede those of earlier users of the groundwater. But this does not preclude overdrafts and such are vey frequent.

With the exception of fossil groundwater, the water underground is in a dynamic state and its abundance, as evidenced by the height of the water table, fluctuates over time regardless of the presence or absence of human interference such as by well drilling. The water underground is, as we saw earlier in this chapter, meteoric water that has moved via gravity to an aquifer. Water moves laterally in an aquifer in response to slope and hydrostatic or "head" pressure until it flows into lakes, ponds, streams, out on the surface in marshes, springs, or into the ocean.

The rate of water movement through a given aquifer is a function of the above noted variables plus the degree of porosity of the rock material comprising the geological structure of the aquifer. This structure is seldom uniform over more than a limited portion of an aquifer and thus it is impossible to state an average rate of speed for water movements in aquifers. Any removal of water from an aquifer will alter the previously existing equilibria. It can be expected that the average water table depth will decline as the rate of water removal increases; land subsidence may occur if sufficient volumes of water are removed (e.g., Mexico City and the L.A. Basin); the aquifer itself may undergo structural changes, which may reduce its future water-holding potential; along marine coasts saltwater intrusion may occur as has happened in the Los Angeles region.

Although groundwater (other than fossil water) is a renewable resource, from the point of view of the water user this may be a misleading concept because the rate of renewal, that is, the natural recharge rate, in most instances is less than the rate of removal.

It is possible to partially recharge some aquifers by diverting flood waters onto spreading grounds. These are specially prepared sites where water is prevented from running off and is allowed to percolate downward into the groundwater supply. Another method to affect added recharge is to pump reclaimed water down into an aquifer through specially drilled wells. Care must be taken that the bacteria in such water are removed by chlorination lest they clog pore spaces in the aquifer.

Whenever possible, groundwater supplies should not be used except when surface supplies do not suffice. However, there are many situations where groundwater is the only major source of irrigation water and, in addition, artificial recharging is not possible. This situation is well illustrated in a six-state region in the Great Plains.

Parts of Texas, New Mexico, Oklahoma, Colorado, Kansas, and Nebraska overlie what is known as the Ogallala aquifer. This aquifer is not generally uniform throughout the region in terms of porosity, water table height, head pressure, or water quality. The one uniform aspect that does exist is an overdraft so great that irrigation farming activity in the entire region of the Ogallala is threatened with a major reduction in the near future (Fig. 9.8). If water is not brought into the region from outside surface sources, what has been developed into one of the most important agricultural regions of the United States will revert from an irrigated corn farming area supporting 40 percent of the grain-fed beef marketed in our nation to a dry farming region with an enormous loss of productivity.

Virtually every problem associated with dependence on groundwater for irrigation is encountered in the region of the Ogallala. The most salient problem is that the annual water removal has been hundreds of times greater than the rate of recharge. In some parts of the aquifer the annual removal has been on the order of nearly 2 meters of water while the annual recharge rate has been no more than approxi-

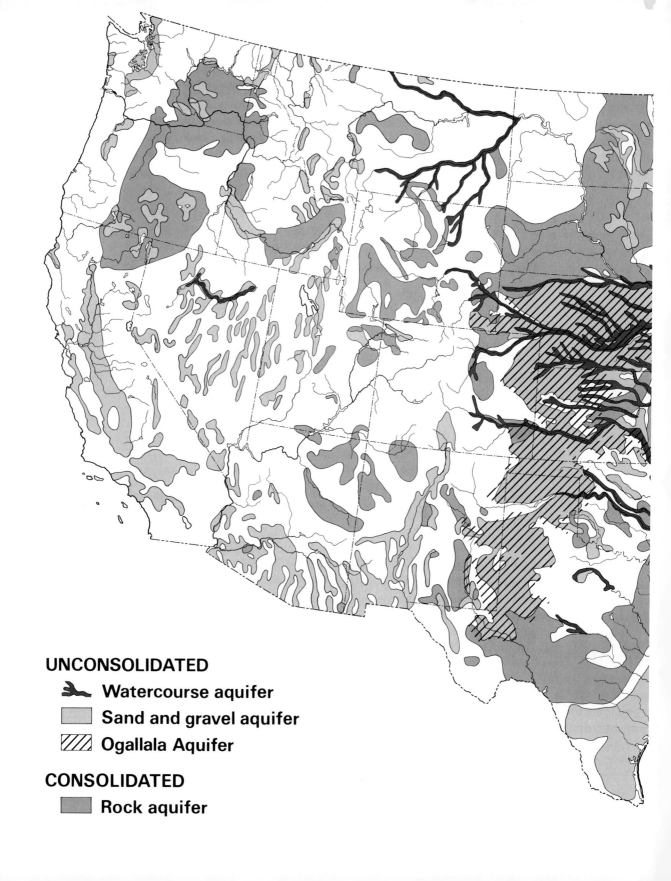

**UNCONSOLIDATED**

Watercourse aquifer

Sand and gravel aquifer

Ogallala Aquifer

**CONSOLIDATED**

Rock aquifer

**Map 9.6** Principal groundwater resources of the conterminous United States. The Ogallala aquifer is emphasised. (U.S. Atlas; U.S.G.S.).

0    100    200    300    400    500 Miles

0    200    400    600    800 Kilometers

**Figure 9.8**   Irrigation using water from the underlying Ogallala aquifer.

mately 5 centimeters. The Ogallala situation illustrates dramatically the fact that for all practical purposes wherever an aquifer provides most of the water used for irrigation, the groundwater is not a renewable resource. In the past, individual farmers pumped water from the Ogallala at whatever rate they could depending upon their individual desires. Now that the end is clearly in sight, efforts are being made to stretch out the use of the water that remains. There is no possibility for effective artificial recharges in this huge aquifer so the "solutions" include growing crops having low water needs, improving irrigation techniques, controlling well spacing, and limiting the amount of water that can be applied per year per acre to 2 acre feet.

California, as well as other western states (including those sharing the Ogallala aquifer) have been moving toward the development of groundwater management districts. These take different legal forms and often depend to a major extent on the honesty of farmers in order to

achieve adequate control over the use rate of groundwater. Many of the problems that have long troubled groundwater management derive from the already mentioned English common law plus inadequate knowledge of the geology and water behavior in specific aquifers.

Although water *quantity* is often the chief focus of concern when the groundwater resource is being examined, water *quality* is also of great significance. In the arid and semiarid western United States, virtually all groundwater contains a varied and often large quantity of dissolved solids (minerals) including boron, iron, sodium, manganese, magnesium, arsenic, as well as other minerals. To this array must be added chemicals of anthropogenic origin, that is, substances that are present in groundwater because of human actions.

In the eastern United States, the chief problems associated with groundwater resources are over-drafts and pollution. Water hardness is a problem where the groundwater is in contact with limestone or other calcium-containing rock. Although east of the 100th meridian annual rainfall and snowfall tend to be greater and more reliable than in many areas west of that meridian, the freshwater resource including the groundwater resource is in many places being overdrawn and water shortages are becoming an increasingly common feature. Part of the difficulty relates, however, to ancient and leaking delivery systems as is the case for New York City, and a lack of effective conservation measures in the larger population centers.

## THE GREAT LAKES

Among the nation's major water resources are the Great Lakes that are shared between our nation and Canada. From west to east they are Lake Superior, Lake Michigan, Lake Huron, Lake Erie, and Lake Ontario (Table 9.2). Of these only one, lake Michigan, is entirely within the borders of the United States. The natural drainage direction is from Lake Superior eastward to the St. Lawrence River and thence to the Atlantic Ocean.

Lake Superior owes its name to being the largest of the lakes having a surface area of approximately 82,414 square kilometers and it contains over 50 percent of the total water volume of the Great Lakes. The latter is due not only to a large surface area but also to this being the deepest (approximately 400 meters) of the lakes. By comparison, Lake Erie has approximately one-third the surface area of Lake Superior and a maximum depth of approximately 65 meters. One of the extraordinary features of this lake system is that lake levels have not varied much more than one meter over the past several decades. The principal uses to which this large volume of water is put include water transportation, water for domestic and manufacturing, sewer discharge, recreation, and commercial and sport fishing.

The outstanding objective for conservation in the Great Lakes is pollution control. Not only

Table 9.2
**The Great Lakes of North America**

| Name | Surface Area (km²) | Maximum Depth (m) |
|---|---|---|
| Lake Superior | 82,414 | 400 |
| Lake Michigan | 58,016 | 284 |
| Lake Huron | 59,596 | 231 |
| Lake Erie | 25,745 | 65 |
| Lake Ontario | 19,529 | 239 |

do millions of people live adjacent to the lakes but a significant share of U.S. as well as Canadian industry is similarly located. Some examples of the population in the U.S. shore region will point up the potential for pollution: Chicago, Illinois, approximately 3.5 million people; Milwaukee, Wisconsin, approximately 700,000; Detroit, Michigan, about 1.5 million; Cleveland, Ohio, about 750,000; plus many smaller cities having 100,000 or more inhabitants. Examples of heavy industries abound and include iron and steel, automobiles, and tire manufacturing, among many others.

The chief problem associated with the human population is sewage disposal. Even well-treated sewage, that is, sewage that has had virtually all pathogens destroyed, still contains great quantities of nutrients such as phosphates, which can have a serious impact on the lake's aquatic ecosystems resulting in lowered water quality and major biological changes. These come about because the nutrient enrichment causes accelerated *eutrophication*, that is, an increase in the nutrient content of the water as compared to the natural levels. This in turn affects *food chains* by stimulating the production of algae and certain bacteria that have quick turnover rates, that is, the bacteria have short life spans and thus huge masses of decaying microorganisms result, which require large amounts of oxygen as a part of the decomposition process. This biological oxygen demand (BOD) diverts oxygen from living organisms having high oxygen requirements. These latter organisms, such as trout, die and their numbers are replaced, at least in part, by other organisms having lower oxygen requirements such as carp.

Accelerated eutrophication of human cause is not a uniformly distributed problem in the Great Lakes. In general, the larger the lake the less the problem so far. The smaller lakes are more seriously affected as has been particularly the case with Lake Erie.

The problems associated with rapid eutrophication in Lake Erie have attracted so much attention that this lake has come to be "the horrible example" of Great Lakes pollution. Some published accounts have suggested that this lake is biologically dead. The truth, fortunately, is quite different. There are approximately 13 million people living on the Lake Erie watershed and the human body wastes, of this population, variously treated, were formerly dumped into the lake causing extremely rapid eutrophication. The main commercial fish species of the nineteenth century—such as lake trout—have now all but disappeared from Lake Erie but other species, once little regarded by commercial fishermen, are now taken in quantities about equal, in terms of weight, to the catches of earlier days. It is true that the value of this catch has declined because the species are less well regarded in the market place. What has happened is that the ecosystem(s) have undergone adjustments in response to the altered nutrient status and lowered amounts of available dissolved oxygen.

Another major factor causing changes in the fish species composition of the Great Lakes was the invasion of the sea lamprey, via the Welland Ship Canal, completed in 1829. Although a century passed before this fish was observed in the Great Lakes, it thereafter became such a predator of the lake trout as to threaten that species' continued presence in the Great Lakes.

Spurred by recent federal legislation—stim-

ulated in part by the actions of the United States-Canada International Joint Commission on the Great Lakes—the Great Lakes, and thus Lake Erie, are slowly ceasing to serve as the great sewer of that region. As fewer nutrients are permitted into the lake it is to be expected that oligotrophic conditions will return and with them the conditions required to support "quality" fish species still present in the other Great Lakes. The small surface area and limited depth of Lake Erie, which contributed to its accelerated eutrophication, will work to its benefit because it is expected that the lake will replace its water volume fairly rapidly with cleaner water. This is in sharp contrast with Lake Superior where it would take several centuries to replace polluted water after all pollution inputs had ceased. Laws controlling polluting activities have often not been well received in this region and especially in the case of some industries.

## DESALINATION

When confronting the shrinking freshwater resources in many parts of our nation it is not uncommon to read of suggestions for desalination of salt water as being the "solution" to water shortages in the future. Unfortunately, this does not offer a general solution because energy costs are far too great and will undoubtedly remain so as far as one can peer into the future. Desalination does have limited applications these being where no other freshwater is available and the considerable economic costs can be justified. The high energy requirements for converting water to steam are well known. Prior to the rapid rise in energy costs beginning in 1973–1974, desalination technology was advancing to the point where it appeared possible that this could be an economically acceptable source of freshwater for domestic uses, because the costs per thousand gallons (or per cubic meter) were not grossly larger than freshwater supplied from conventional sources.

However, at that time, the average price of a barrel of oil was less than $2 whereas the price later rose to above $30.

It makes far better economic sense to conserve conventional freshwater supplies than to indulge in fantasies of cheap water produced by desalination processes. It is pure folly to suggest that desalination could ever supply the great quantities of cheap water required for irrigation. There are possibilities for hydroponic uses of desalinated water because such agriculture is very conserving of the water supply but even here one suspects that only a few high-priced crops, such as cut flowers, could offer adequate returns on water desalination costs.

In the unlikely event that water desalination costs were lowered so that this process could become a significant source of freshwater for urban domestic use, another problem would have to be solved: the safe disposal of the enormous quantities of minerals that remain after water has been separated from its mineral content. Some of these materials could be marketed but the greater volume would have to be disposed of and most likely into the marine water from which the water was drawn. One could expect dislocations, at least locally, in the marine ecosystems that received these large and possibly toxic quantities of salts and other minerals. There would also be energy costs associated with disposal activities that would add to the costs of water desalination.

## RECYCLING OF WATER

With comparatively few exceptions today, water once used is discharged into convenient streams, lakes, or oceans. In reference to many rivers in the United States, water is withdrawn, "purified," used and returned to the river where it is repeatedly taken up, treated, used, and discharged by cities downstream until the river finally flows into the ocean. Recycling waste water instead of discharging it is now receiving growing attention.

A major potential source of recyclable waste water is sewage. Such water, if properly treated to destroy the pathogenic organisms it might contain, can be used for irrigation of crops. A number of problems prevent widespread use of such recycled water, the chief among these being economic costs, public acceptance, and the retention of toxic materials such as lead, cadmium, and other heavy metals. If water containing these and other toxic substances is used for irrigation it is possible that the plants will take up such large quantities of the metals as to make the plants unsafe for consumption by humans or their domestic animals. Experiments to solve this problem are being conducted but with only limited success. For example, it has been found that certain aquatic plants are very efficient in taking up some of these heavy metals thus making the decontaminated water safe or nearly so for agricultural and other uses. However, no acceptable solution has been found for the safe disposal of the metal-contaminated plants. Burning has been tried but this leaves a concentrated residue of toxic metals, which requires safe disposal.

## WATER CONSERVATION IN THE HOME

Major water savings are often possible to achieve in one's own home but the price of water is often set so low that there is little economic incentive to adopt conservation measures. It is frequently argued that it is unfair to set domestic rates so high that they will provide the principal incentive required for home water conservation. However, pricing can be so used if it doesn't unfairly injure those having modest incomes but forces affluent and major water consumers to pay increasing unit prices for amounts above certain set levels. Thus, a basic quantity of water could be available to all households (say one acre foot per four persons, which is the average in many areas) at modest prices. Successively higher quantities in excess of this lifeline amount would be charged at exponentially higher rates.

Unfortunately, water is used in much of the United States as though it were without limit and therefor a "free" good. Leaking water faucets go unrepaired, as do leaking water mains, and water is used to clean sidewalks and streets and to irrigate gardens and lawns totally unsuited to the ecological realities of water scarcity.

Southern California provides an outstanding example of this hydrologic myopia. Here is a region that would quickly die and return to the desert and semidesert that it was, were it not for the millions of acre feet of water imported each year. A foreign visitor to almost any part of this region where human settlement is most dense might easily conclude that far from being arid or semiarid this region enjoys a climate similar to that of northwestern Europe, that is, it receives abundant precipitation distributed throughout the year. Greeting the visitor's eyes would be thousands and thousands of hectares of green lawns and other vegetation requiring abundant water. In the evenings, especially, the gutters in many of the cities run full with irrigation water flowing off saturated garden soils. Streams, which on Geological Survey topographic maps are shown as intermittent—flowing only during the period of winter rains—are now permanent streams deriving their flow, during summer months, from the abundant supply of garden runoff water plus water drained and replaced from the nearly ubiquitous swimming pools that grace the region.

The green lawn is among the principal ecological anachronisms to be found in any arid or semiarid region. These are water consumers of great magnitude and must not be tolerated in future years as these regions struggle with the problems of obtaining sufficient water. Other vegetation must take the place of the thirsty plant species now grown and lawns must either disappear or become far less important groundcovers than they are at present.

It has been repeatedly demonstrated that the flush toilet is, in many homes, the principal element of domestic water consumption. Newly designed water tanks requiring less water are coming into use but people having older-style toilets can reduce water use without loss of efficiency by placing a solid object, having the volume of a common brick, in the water tank. Perhaps the next largest source of home water use (outside of the garden) is the shower. Improved shower heads that limit the flow of water but do not affect the cleansing efficiency are now easily obtained and can result in significant water savings.

So careless are the ways we use water in and around our homes in the United States that were all presently available means of conservation put into practice the size of the freshwater resource would be greatly increased. Add to this repair of the often-leaking delivery systems that cities have not repaired for decades and we would have another added quantity of water available to us.

## WATER CONSERVATION ON THE FARM

As noted earlier, irrigation in the West represents the largest use to which water is put in most of that region. Therefor, the possibilities for saving large quantities of water through conservation on the irrigated farm appear to be significant. However, until or unless the price of water to the farmer represents such an important part of the operating expenses that conservation becomes an economic necessity it may be difficult to affect major water savings in agriculture. This is not to say that most farms irrigate without thought to cost but it is also very obvious from past experience that, as in the case of the Ogallala aquifer, only when water becomes obviously scarce are measures adopted to maximize the benefits, vis-à-vis crop production, from the remaining water supply. By pricing water high enough the farmer receives a "signal" that it is a scarce resource and must be used with care.

An enormous amount of research has been conducted to determine the optimal water needs of specific crops grown under specific conditions of soil and climate. Although some of this research has focused upon the need to conserve water it has also focused upon the fact that over irrigation or irrigating at the wrong times can have counterproductive effects on crop production. The results of such research, if applied, tend to reduce water demand by farmers. The urban water user has a major interest in the issue of water conservation on the irrigated farm and especially where, as in California, the entire water resource has been integrated for management purposes at the state level and all citizens share, as it were, in a single water resource "pie." Seen thusly, water allocation is a "zero sum" game in that any amount used by one individual reduces the total amount available to all other individuals.

Irrigation water, as we have already noted, is subsidized by urban users who pay more per acre foot than do farmers. This can be an acceptable arrangement since the production values of agriculture contribute to the welfare of urban as well as rural inhabitants. However, such subsidies should not be tolerated when they result in placing an unfair economic burden on the urban water consumer as a result of the farmer viewing the water resource as a less expensive commodity than it really is, thus engaging in wasteful water-use practices.

Of equal if not greater importance with regard to water conservation in the region of irrigated farms in the West is the rapidly growing problem caused by *used* irrigation water containing large amounts of dissolved salts.

Recall that all water employed for irrigation contains varying amounts of dissolved minerals. Thus, when water is applied to fields for irrigation the mineral content of the soils is very likely to increase unless measures are taken to prevent such from occurring. One way to achieve this is to make certain that somewhat more water is applied to a crop than is required for the crop's needs. This "excess" or "tailwater" is allowed to drain away in ditches constructed for this purpose, which lead into larger drainage canals which themselves lead to rivers and thence to the ocean.

Drainage problems are frequently made worse by soil conditions especially when the topsoil is underlain, at shallow depths, by resistant layers of clay (*claypans*) or cemented minerals (*caliche*). Such situations easily become waterlogged and contaminated by mineral accumulations. Such topsoils, in the West, tend to contain relatively large amounts of minerals before they are ever irrigated.

Even where there are none or only limited impediments to downward movement of water in soils, as where deep alluvial soils occur without claypans or caliche layers, there may be a danger of contaminating the groundwater with highly mineralized irrigation water that has moved by gravity into the groundwater.

As these waters become more salty their suitability for irrigation or other uses declines sharply and they may become so contaminated by salts as to be useless. Where the natural water table is relatively high due to local obstructions to the downward movement of water in the soil, the addition of irrigation water may bring the water table so close to the surface, say within 2 meters, that the saline water can then move, by *capillary action*, upward to the root zone of trees, vines, or row-crop plants and either kill them or greatly reduce their productivity. The only known practical way to "solve" this problem short of the abandonment of irrigation—which may, in some cases actually be the best solution—is to lay pipe drains in the fields at varying depths beneath the soil surface depending on the local situation. The water, so drained, is led into a canal system that either leads the water into a river (and then to the ocean) or out on "waste" land where it is allowed to sink into the soil or evaporate. In the former situation there will be an increase in the salt content of the "natural" drainage of the river with possible negative effects on fish and other wildlife and on the quality of water delivered for urban or industrial uses. In the latter case, groundwater resources lying under the "waste" areas can become contaminated.

The problems recounted above occur in many parts of the West but probably with greatest intensity in the San Joaquin Valley of California. The conflicts developing there between irrigation farming, conservationists, and urban water users have, as yet, no generally acceptable solution. The WPRS (when still known as the Bureau of Reclamation) declared, in 1979, that approximately 400,000 acres (approximately 162,000 hectares) had been affected by artificially high saline water tables and that by the year 2080 the total could rise to 1.1 million acres (approximately 445,000 hectares).

This problem, in the San Joaquin Valley, ties in closely with the controversial Peripheral Canal. As already noted, much of that controversy is focused on the question of water salinity and saltwater intrusion. One must add to those concerns the growing perception by some farmers that the only "good" solution to preventing further saline increases in the Valley's groundwater is to drain highly saline irrigation "tailwater" into the system that includes the Delta—the major source of water for the California Water Project and part of the water for the Central Valley Project.

The value of agricultural products from this region is too great to permit serious consideration of shutting down irrigation activity. Also, the amount of invested capital is very large and those holding financial interests in irrigated lands constitute a powerful political force in California as well as in the nation's capital. Thus, a far greater drainage system than presently exists must be constructed so that saline waters will be disposed of in such ways as not to further lower the quality of Delta water. This can be accomplished only through the ex-

penditure of vast sums of money and the achievement of cooperation between farming groups and other sectors of the public. In the past it has been somewhat easier to obtain funding for water projects than it has been for achieving the necessary broad-based public cooperation.

## WATER CONSERVATION AND MANAGEMENT IN THE THIRD WORLD: SOME EXAMPLES

Virtually all the aspects of conservation and management of freshwater described in the previous part of this chapter are also applicable to Third World Nations. The chief differences are found not in kind but in degree and with especial reference to biological pollution. As in keeping with other chapters, no attempt is made here to be encyclopedic and only selected elements are brought forward to acquaint you with some of the kinds of issues and problems confronting some Third World regions.

### Latin America

The principal topics to be considered here include major water impoundments and biological contamination.

**MAJOR WATER IMPOUNDMENTS**  Parts of Latin America possess large potential and partially realized opportunities for major water impoundments. This is particularly true of the nations sharing the Amazon Basin—Venezuela, Colombia, Peru, Bolivia, and above all, Brazil. Mexico also possesses a fairly large potential although a significant share has already been developed. Only a few mainland Latin American nations are without some potential or realized water impoundments.

The uses to which major water impoundments are put varies but, in general, less emphasis is placed on multiple use than is the case in the United States. For example, recreation is usually given only minor, if any, consideration but electricity generation and water for irrigation are accorded great attention. In some nations, perhaps most notably Mexico, flood control is frequently a major consideration. In general, lesser-sized water impoundments are developed for urban uses and these are very numerous.

Until recently, Mexico seemed to be an energy-poor nation with regard to fossil fuels. Therefore, a great emphasis was given to developing the hydropower potential of that nation and with considerable success. Now that a large petroleum resource has been discovered hydropower may be viewed with less interest for a time. In contrast, Brazil, which has one of the largest undeveloped hydropower potentials in the world, is exerting considerable effort to develop this energy resource because, thus far, that nation has not made other than minor discoveries of petroleum, and the small coal resource it has is of poor quality. At present, Brazil's annual payment for imported petroleum is so great as to place a major strain on its economy and has contributed to the fact that Brazil—at this writing—has the largest foreign debt, estimated to be $80 billion, of any Third World nation.

All of the problems of watershed management described in the earlier parts of this chapter apply to Latin America but with even greater emphasis. In many nations where the growth of human population has been rapid, it has proven to be extremely difficult to apply the rules of sound watershed management for to do so could, in many instances, result in civil unrest among the peasantry as well as among the rural affluent classes. Thus, in many situations where dams have been constructed it is to be expected that the life expectancy of such will be much less than would be the case if proper protection of the watersheds could be achieved. The rapidity with which some reservoirs in Latin America silt-up after construction must cause any thoughtful person to be alarmed

and particularly so in those instances where the impounded water and generated power provide the foundation for greatly increased economic activities and associated human dependence. What is to become of these activities and the people they support when the aquatic foundation fails at some time in the future?

The ability to provide adequate supplies of sanitary water for domestic consumption has been only partially realized in urban and rural situations in many parts of Latin America. Considerable progress has been achieved in recent years and the number of cities—or parts of cities—having safe drinking water has increased. On the other hand, urban and especially rural inhabitants in many parts of this vast region are still without supplies of sanitary water. The available statistics for infant mortality (deaths that occur within the first year) in many of these nations list gastrointestinal disease as the leading cause of death. Among the poorly educated and informed, particularly, knowledge of the germ theory of disease is not frequent and thus little regard is given to the dangers inherent in sewage-contaminated water. Infants are not the only ones to suffer and it is not uncommon to find entire rural populations in some areas infected with a variety of intestinal parasites which, although the parasites alone may not be fatal, take a continuous toll on the energy and productivity of the persons so afflicted.

Exacerbating the situation with regard to the inadequate provisions for supplying safe potable water in urban areas is the flood of rural-to-urban migrants that has been taking place and continues to occur in almost every nation in this region. Thus, even the most conscientious governments may find it all but impossible to supply adequate quantities of safe water within a short span of time to the growing urban multitudes (e.g., Mexico City and São Paulo, Brazil). This problem is increased in many cases because most of these migrants bring with them to the cities habits that may have been marginally unsafe in the country but in the crowded situations of the cities may prove to be lethal.

All the great problems of water quality notwithstanding, many Latin American nations have made considerable progress in upgrading the quality of urban water supplies. The rapidly lowering rates of infant mortality, in several nations, is a partial reflection of these successful efforts.

## Africa

Unlike many parts of Latin America wherein industrialization has made great advances and challenges the agricultural sector for economic primacy, the economies of most African nations remain tied to the rural sector. This does not suggest that economic changes are not occurring and indeed it is the very drive to achieve economic change that is contributing markedly to water development in many parts of the vast continent. Unfortunately, this water development is not being achieved without environmental and societal costs and it is these and certain related phenomena that will be discussed briefly below (Map 9.7).

If one excepts the vast Sahara, the northeast "horn" region and the Namib-Kalahari region in the southwest, it appears from a map of Africa that most of the remainder of the continent is possessed of an abundance of large river systems. This appraisal is correct up to one important point, that being that most of the rivers have great seasonal variations in the volume of water they carry. This condition has spurred the construction of major dams and other water impoundment and diversion systems in a number of countries. Chief among these are the High Dam at Aswan on the Nile River (Fig. 9.9), the Kariba Dam on the Zambezi River, and the Akosombo Dam on the Volta River. In addition, there are some major irrigation projects, especially in the Sudan, that use water diverted from adjacent surface streams.

Most of the African continent appears to have poor fossil fuel resources, the chief exceptions to this generalization being Nigeria, Algeria, and Libya. Therefore, there has been much interest in developing the hydropower resources present in many of the newly emerged independent nations. The nation of Zaire contains within its borders most of the drainage of the

**Figure 9.9**   Aswan Dam, Egypt. This gravity-type dam impounds a maximum of 137 million acre feet of water.

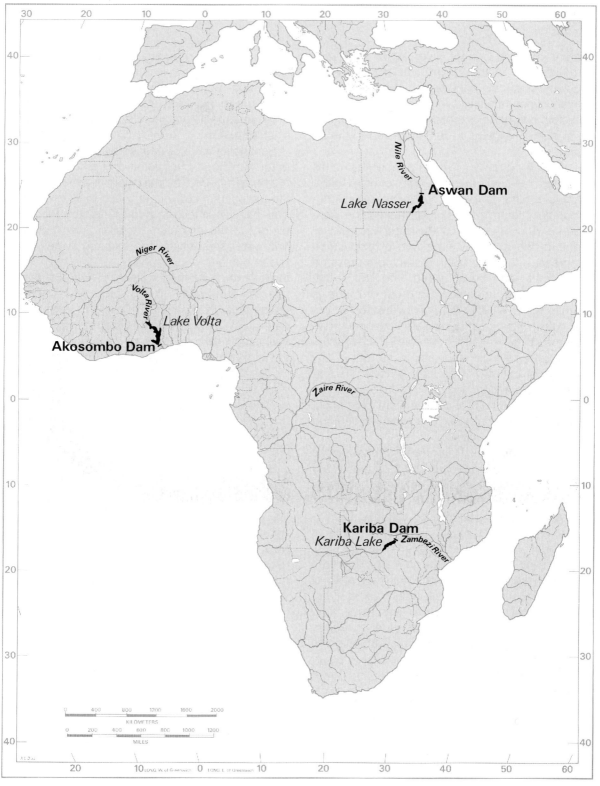

**Map 9.7** Principal water impoundments in Africa.

Zaire (formerly Congo) River, which itself represents one of the largest unrealized hydropower resources in the world. Although a relatively minor amount of development of this river system has been achieved, most of the potential energy remains to be harnessed in the future.

Viewed narrowly, it would appear that many African nations have a bright energy future ahead if other problems such as capital accumulation, technical training, raising the general level of education of the populace, and reducing the currently high rate of population increase—to name some of the more pressing problems—can be achieved. The fact is that the market for electricity in most of Africa is presently far smaller than the hydroelectric potential. To this must be added that some countries such as Tanzania have only a modest hydropower potential and lack fossil fuel in any important quantity. One can envision the day when some nations may be producers and exporters of electricity to other African nations but this will first require far more market demand than presently exists.

Some of the most important river resources in Africa are international and thus their management should, ideally, be by international commissions. The Nile River, to cite the principal example, is shared by Uganda, the Sudan, Ethiopia, and Egypt. Perhaps it is folly to seriously consider watershed management when such a multinational and major land area is involved. Nevertheless, such an attempt should be made because unless some effective control is achieved over at least some large parts of this vast watershed in order to reduce the siltation rate behind the High Dam, at some future time the lower valley of the Nile in Egypt will begin to decline for lack of water and power generated presently at the dam. Similar comment can be made for all the other major and minor water impoundments on this continent.

Although these major water impoundments have brought with them marked economic ben-

efits in the form of energy production and irrigation water they also have imposed various ecological prices. Chief among the latter is a widespread increase in certain water-related disease especially one called schistosomiasis or bilharziasis.

Schistosomiasis is caused by tiny flukes that enter the blood circulation and other parts of the human body. The pathogen is a member of the genus *Schistosoma* of which there are several species affecting human health. The life history of the organism includes both human and water-snail hosts. The parasite cycles between humans who void schistosome eggs via feces or urine into freshwater. If the correct snail species are present in the water, schistosome larvae enter the snails for a time and live there. Later, they leave the snails and, in the form of very small swimming creatures called a *cercaria,* move about in the water until a human wades there, bathes there, or otherwise makes body contact with the water, The cercariae are able to enter the body through the most minute crack or lesion of the body surface and having done so change again in form to the flukes that then invade many parts of the body.

Schistosomiasis is not a "killer" disease in that mortality rates are relatively low. However, this is an extremely debilitating disease and the victim, unless treated successfully, is condemned to a weakened life. It appears that the most serious clinical symptoms of this disease usually occur among children and the mortality rates also appear to be highest among children.

The relationship between water impoundments and schistosomiasis is that when fast-flowing water is slowed it often becomes optimal habitat for the snail species that play the vital role of intermediate host of the parasite. To this must be added the increased opportunities afforded people to make contact with water and the often total lack of understanding of the relationships between this disease and defecation or urination in surface waters. Medical treatment exists but is only available to a minor fraction of those who are infected. The best approach to this situation is by educating the people so that they will take greater care to deposit body wastes where they are least likely to contaminate water sources.

The following comments respecting major water impoundments in Africa, like many of the foregoing, do not relate to situations unique to that continent but they do reach such magnitude as to require a brief discussion. Whenever a river is dammed—no matter where or in what latitude—there will be major changes in the biology and chemistry of the water below and above the dam. The Nile River, for example, no longer flows all the way to the eastern end of the Mediterranean Sea. Thus the nutrients it once brought to those waters, which supported a fairly important marine fishery, are no longer present and the fishery there has greatly declined. In the Nile Valley, below the dam, the fields that for thousands of years were annually fertilized by the sediments carried by the Nile flood now no longer receive this benefit and artificial fertilizers must be applied.

In southern Africa, on the Zambezi River below the Kariba Dam, the former natural ecology that was adjusted to annual periods of flooding and drought has ceased to exist resulting in many changed ecological conditions. Although inadequately studied thus far, it is to be expected that marine ecosystems in the part of the Indian Ocean into which the Zambezi drains have been affected because of a decrease in the amount of nutrients delivered by the river.

The African water-impoundments experience appears to teach us that long-term conservation and management of these resources in Africa require more sophisticated preconstruction studies than has been the case in the past and that African nations must approach such studies and construction and later conservation and management on a basis of international cooperation. Unfortunately, other considerations, mostly of a narrow nationalistic scope, continually intervene to prevent such cooperation from taking place.

## SUMMARY

It is commonplace to divide living organisms into two major categories, aquatic and nonaquatic, but in fact, most life on earth is dependent on a constant supply of water. In the case of our own species, this dependence is so great that a person cannot survive without frequent intakes of freshwater. Our bodies consist chiefly of water and, in a way, we carry our freshwater ponds around with us. That "pond" needs frequent replenishment because of losses due to perspiration and the excretion of wastes. However, in spite of the immense importance of freshwater to human physiology and the important role played by water in agriculture, manufacturing, and other human enterprises, we frequently take this substance for granted.

The abundance and availability of freshwater in the conterminous United States varies regionally. In general, the Pacific Northwest and the region east of the Mississippi River usually receive abundant quantities of atmospheric precipitation. However, a large area, mostly west of the 100th meridian and excluding the Pacific Northwest, suffers from a lack of abundant rain and snow.

These regional variations in precipitation are reflected in water law. In general, areas that receive relatively abundant precipitation allocate water on the basis of riparian rights. This allows everyone whose land borders a surface source of freshwater to remove water for beneficial purposes. In areas where water is in limited supply relative to the actual or potential demand, the law of prior appropriation is followed. This law states that the first person to make use of a source of surface water may use all that he or she wishes provided only that such use be for beneficial purposes. If, after the first user takes what he or she needs, there is still water available, the next person to have used the water source may use all or part of the remainder provided it is for beneficial purposes and this continues until the entire supply has been appropriated. Although seemingly clear in its intent, prior appropriation may foster abuse—what, for example is a "beneficial" purpose?—and confers on the first user powerful rights that may not be acceptable to other persons at a later time. There are also areas in the West where both riparian and prior appropriation water rights are recognized.

Although water law respecting surface water is fairly well developed in the United States, this is not the case with underground water supplies. This source of water is overdrafted almost everywhere and state legislatures have been slow to correct this situation. Many of these underground reservoirs, termed aquifers, replace withdrawn water at very slow rates although sound conservation requires that the withdrawal rate does not exceed the recharge rate. Unfortunately, the recharge rates of most of the nation's aquifers are not known.

The federal government has been active in developing the nation's surface water resources as well as modifying river flows to reduce flooding and also to improve navigation. These efforts have often been viewed critically as wasting tax money or destroying natural ecosystems. The landmark federal water legislation was the passage, in 1902, of the Reclamation Act. This Act established the legal foundation for what later became a massive federal enterprise of dam building mostly west of the 100th meridian.

Although water quantity is of obvious importance equally so is water quality. The maintenance or upgrading of water quality must be a principal aim of water conservation and management.

Among the principal objects of achieving or maintaining water quality is to prevent freshwater from becoming polluted by sewage, factory wastes, toxic runoff from farmlands, or from any other sources that could lower water quality. It is relatively easy, in a technological sense, to maintain and even improve the quality of surface water and particularly water in flowing streams. Unfortunately, this is not true for water in aquifers. After an aquifer has been contaminated the water may not regain acceptable quality for years. At present, so little is known about the rates at which aquifers are flushed of contaminants that it is widely believed that once an aquifer is polluted it is permanently lost as a safe source of freshwater. This can be a calamity where aquifers supply a large share of the domestic water supply. Furthermore, while it may be comparatively easy to identify the source(s) of surface water contamination this is often not the case with contaminated aquifers because of an often considerable time lag between the discharge of a pollutant on the surface and the time it appears in the goundwater. In some instances the time lapse may be measurable in years and the person(s) responsible for the contamination can't be identified.

Water quality is also important in irrigation because it must not have so high a percentage of dissolved minerals as to damage growing crops. Furthermore, in the arid and semiarid West, great care must be taken to prevent mineral buildup in irrigated soils.

Prior to World War II, it was usually left to individual states and local jurisdictions to control water pollution. In general, this was not satisfactory. Thus, in 1948, the U.S. congress passed the Water Pollution Act to be followed, in 1954, by the Water Facilities Act. Other relevant federal legislation was also passed but it was often lacking in economic sanctions that would spur compliance. Then, in 1965, the Water Quality Act was passed setting forth national standards of water quality and providing the needed economic incentives to achieve compliance. Significant progress has been made, thanks to this and other relevant legislation. The general public appears to be strongly behind this national effort to clean up our water resources.

As we move toward improving the quality of our water resources we must also direct attention toward its more efficient use. Although the obvious limitations of water availability are most apparent in the arid and semiarid West, few parts of the nation can look on their local water supplies as being abundant. Parts of the East, for example, periodically experience water shortages. Some of this is due to inadequate storage facilities but, for example, as in the case of New York City, an antiquated and leaking delivery-tunnel system and marked waste of water in the city contribute to periodic water shortages. True, some of the water-shortage incidents have been exacerbated by unusual drought conditions in the watershed where the city obtains its water, but a sound program of water conservation that includes repair of the water delivery system and waste prevention is a necessity.

In the arid and semiarid West one may frequently encounter absurdities of water use or misuse. There is a seemingly endless array of suburban homes each with its lawn requiring water often imported from a great distance. Artificial lakes and ponds abound, and were one not aware of the actual water scarcity in this region one might well believe that it is an area of water surplus.

The largest savings of water must come from agriculture, which uses the greater part of the water in most of the western region. In California, for example, between 80 and 85 percent of all the water consumed in the state is used in agriculture. There are many possibilities for better water management on the farm but water prices are often so low to the farmer that there is inadequate incentive to treat water like the scarce resource it is.

In the arid and semiarid West water is clearly perceived as a resource without which the region cannot survive. Water development and water control are the foci of powerful political factions. Whoever controls water has great power; few issues stir as much heat and acrimony as do issues respecting water allocation and water development.

Complicating water development in the West is the fact that in many situations more than a single governmental agency is involved. Commonly, the federal government is associated with western water development that imposes acreage limitations on land benefited by such water. However, some corporate farms have for years ignored the acreage limitations imposed by the Reclamation Act and, as of this writing, they appear to be winning a much larger acreage limitation from congress and with no penalties for having ignored the 1902 acreage limitation.

Water problems in the Third World tend to mirror those of the United States except that the intensity of the problems often appear greater, particularly with regard to the biological quality of water. Millions of people do not have access to a safe drinking water supply, a fact that contributes importantly to widespread gastrointestinal infections and high rates of childhood mortality. A related irony is that where the quality of drinking water supplies has been improved one often encounters a surge in population growth. This latter is no justification for ignoring water quality but does lend emphasis to the need to limit births when the death rate falls or is expected to fall as a result of improved sanitation.

A large part of the Third World lacks fossil fuels and thus there is widespread interest in developing potential hydroelectric sources when such are present. In addition, the impounded water, as in the case of Egypt, may also provide needed supplies of water for irrigation. Thus, dam building is a major enterprise in many parts of the Third World. The benefits of these constructions may be large but it has also been shown that, in many instances, major ecological changes have occurred that negatively affects human health and that produce major changes in the ecosystems associated with altered river flows.

# marine biotic resources

## INTRODUCTION

Most of the earth's surface is not dry land but water. Approximately 97 percent of the water of the planet is contained in the marine environments. This vast area and volume of oceans and seas contains an enormous biomass of plants and animals of which a considerable share of the latter is harvested each year by humans. Most of the marine environments lie beyond the control of individual nations and thus constitute enormous "commons" where all too often, over the centuries, the biotic resources have been mined rather than managed. However, even in the waters under the legal control of governments the record of utilization has often been only slightly better and often very much worse.

The vastness of the seas and oceans has long led many people to believe that the biotic resources are inexhaustible and even today, when information on natural resources is far more widespread than in past years, the belief persists that the oceans still contain such huge reserves of fish and other animals as to be able to provide much larger contributions to the world's protein consumption than they have in the past. This belief, unfortunately, is not founded on facts and the facts are that, with relatively few exceptions, most of the world's important marine harvests are near their maximum permissible limits and some fisheries are exceeding the safe limits with danger to them lurking just ahead.

Perhaps these misconceptions about the biological productivity of marine waters are to be excused by the fact that until recent years, harvesters of the seas had little data on which to base their judgments about safe maximum catch size of the animals they gathered. Even at present, marine biology, although making impressive progress, is unable in many instances, to answer questions such as what is causing the anchovy catch in southern California waters to decline so sharply or what was (were) the cause(s) behind the collapse of the Peruvian anchovy fishery a few years ago. This is not to say that biologists do not have some rather shrewd ideas but proving them beyond doubt is often difficult.

Marine biologists, including marine fishery biologists, nevertheless, have advanced their studies to a point where it is no longer excusable to mine marine animal resources. More than enough is known, in the case of most fisheries, to be able to detect the signs that a given fishery is being overexploited and thus have time to adopt restrictions limiting the harvest amount. However, some nations do not expend sufficient money for fisheries research and even when data are available political pressures and economic pressures sometimes overrule the dictates of sound management. Also, it is the exception rather than the rule for commercial fisherfolk to view the work of biologists as being essential to the long-term health of commercial fishing.

Closely associated with marine fisheries

biology is the science of oceanography. Oceanography is the science of the physical and biotic characteristics of the oceans. Although this science can trace its origins back well into the nineteenth century it has only become of major importance in the twentieth century. Most industrialized nations engage in oceanographic research and the United States is in the forefront of such activities. In the United States, oceanographic research is conducted by universities and by governmental agencies, all of which cooperate as much as possible with one another. Oceanographic research is "big science" and requires large monetary expenditure. For this reason, the federal government is the chief funding agency for oceanographic research.

Marine fisheries biology is a specialized branch of oceanography and attempts to apply the results of basic research obtained by scientific investigations not always aimed at commercial application. In addition, marine fisheries biologists conduct much research aimed at achieving better understanding of the dynamics of the resources they study.

Oceanography and all the subdisciplines associated with it are complex fields of study. They all require sophisticated knowledge of physics, chemistry, biology and, of course statistical methodology. Although it is far beyond the scope of this book to discuss oceanography and marine biology in any detail it is necessary that certain basic features of these subjects be given a brief introductory examination in order that some of the discussions to follow will have meaning to the reader.

One of the most striking features of marine water is its lack of geographic uniformity in terms of such variables as salinity, temperature, dissolved oxygen, nutrients, light, current velocities and directions, and biological productivity.

Salinity, the amount of salts dissolved in a given volume of water, varies horizontally and vertically in the oceans. Locally, the greatest variations occur adjacent to the shoreline and particularly where freshwater enters via streams plus direct runoff from land surfaces. This zone is also subject to rapid changes of salinity when rainfall may dilute water close to the shore for brief periods of time. Surface salinity varies in the Atlantic and Pacific Oceans with the highest values, 36 to 37 parts per thousand occurring in the low latitudes and the lowest values 32 to 33 parts per thousand occurring in the higher latitudes. The Mediterranean Sea has even higher surface salinities and reach 39 parts per thousand during the summer months.

Water temperatures were the first of the several physical variables to have been measured and studied and these are still the most-often collected data. With few exceptions, water temperatures decrease with increasing depth but the rate of decrease varies from place to place and from time to time in any one place. Although the temperature of the upper part of the water is highest in low latitudes and lowest in high latitudes in the major oceans of the world, there are some notable exceptions to this generalization. The phenomena that most often alter this latitudinal temperature distribution are ocean currents and upwelling.

Major examples of ocean currents altering the latitudinal distribution of water temperature include the Humboldt (or Peru) current along the west coast of South America, the Benguela current along the southwest coast of Africa, the Canary current along the northwest coast of Africa, the Australian current along the west coast of Australia, and the California current along the West Coast of the United States and northwestern Mexico (Baja California peninsula). All of these currents transport cool surface water toward lower latitudes. By contrast, the Gulf Stream in the Atlantic Ocean transports warm water from low to high latitudes. (Map 10.1).

Upwelling is frequently associated with alongshore currents, that is, current movement parallel to a shoreline. Due to the deflecting effect of the earth's rotation and other physical phenomena water tends to pile up locally resulting in offshore (away from shore) currents being set in motion. Although such currents may extend only short distances from the shore they have the effect of setting up a rotation of water that brings cold water to the surface. This water may be enriched in dissolved oxygen as it nears the surface and contain relatively large quantities of dissolved nutrients and thus be capable of supporting a high level of primary and secondary production.

Water temperature per se is of great importance to most marine organisms. It also is very important because it largely determines the upper limit of dissolved oxygen possible for the water to contain, a fact having obvious biological significance.

Nutrients, organic and inorganic, are most abundant per volume of water adjacent to shorelines and particularly where surface streams enter the oceans. Areas of upwelling are also among the more nutrient-rich parts of the oceans. Ocean surface waters, located far from land, may be no more than deserts insofar as their nutrient status is concerned. It is important to keep this fact in mind when thinking about the oceans as places of supposedly unlimited potential for human food production. The Mediterranean, although nowhere distant from land, has a very low nutrient status in the upper parts of the water. This is due to the configuration of the very complex basin, a shallow "sill" at the entrance to the Atlantic which tends to impede the entry of relatively nutrient rich cool water, long summers and short winters that limit the runoff from the land and that therefore limit contributions of nutrients from that source. Relatively little is known about the deep waters of the Mediterranean.

Although life in the oceans is known to exist in environments where there is no measurable light (if one excludes the light—bioluminescence—produced by some animals) virtually all of the organisms harvested for human use are taken from the upper 200 meters of the oceans, that is, the zone where photosynthesis (primary production) is able to occur because there is sufficient sunlight. The 200 meters must be taken as the *approximate* lower limit because in many places the limit is far more shallow due to organic and inorganic substances in the water that prevent the passage of light to greater depths. This stratum is termed the *euphotic* or *photic* zone.

Primary productivity, and therefore secondary productivity, varies from one place to another in the oceans. In general, the areas of greatest productivity are to be found over continental shelves or where upwelling occurs. Also, water temperature plays an important role in the chemistry of seawater and determines to an important degree the amount of oxygen a given water mass can contain. Cool, well-oxygenated water containing an abundant supply of plant nutrients for algal growth will usually also be waters highly productive of consumer organisms of which many are the object of commercial interest.

Important questions regarding the chemistry and physics of seawater remain to be answered as, for example, the details of the carbon cycle in the oceans and the related question of carbon exchanges with the atmosphere. Nevertheless, oceanography has made great progress and a data base now exists that provides the insights needed to develop a truly scientific management of the ocean's resources. Increasingly, the major problems of conservation and management of the ocean's resources lie *not* in the areas of physical and biological sciences but in the areas of political and economic behavior.

**MARINE-HARVEST LOCATIONS** As mentioned earlier, marine productivity is not geographically uniform but varies from place to place. This section will list the principal marine-harvest locations and describe some of their characteristics.

There are many types of locations where ma-

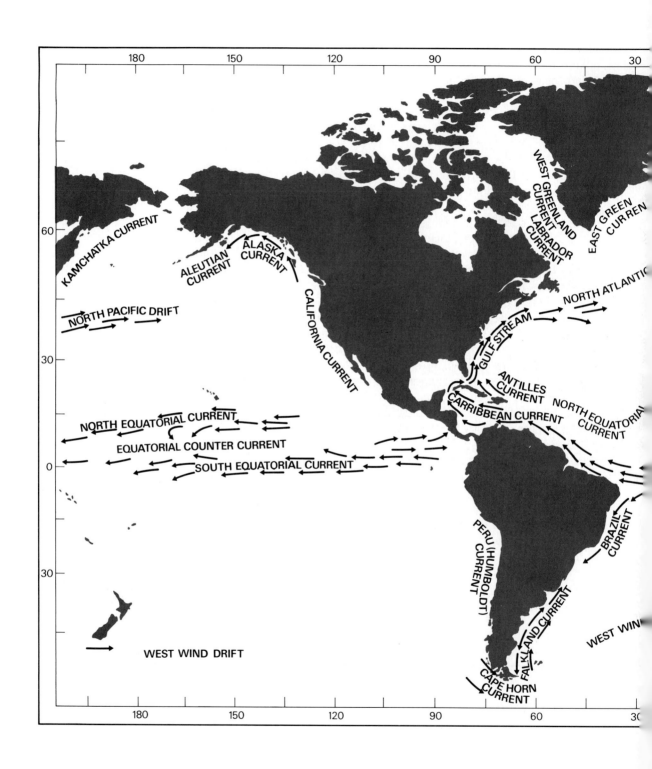

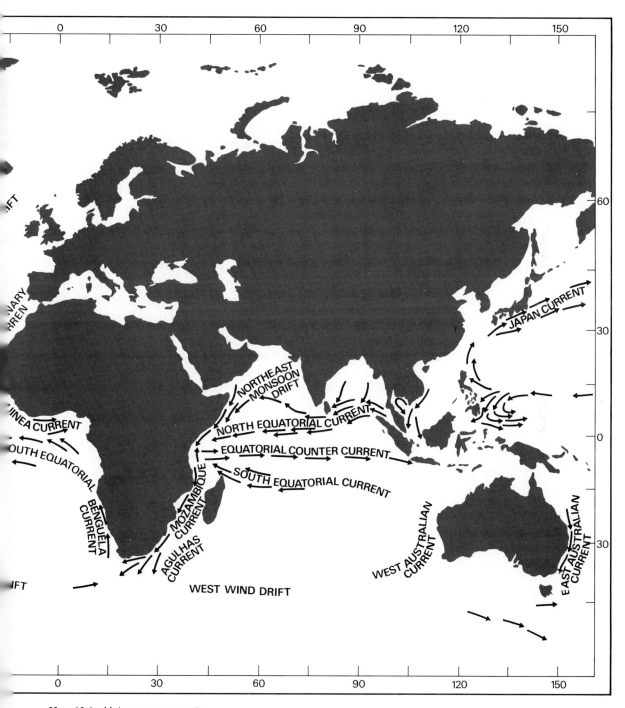

**Map 10.1** Major ocean currents.

rine waters are harvested but these can be included under a few major categories: estuaries, intertidal zone, neritic zone, benthic zone, oceanic zone.

Stated briefly, estuaries include situations where rivers meet and mix with seawater, the intertidal zone is the portion of the shore region (including estuaries) where the regular rise and fall of tides expose and then inundate the substrate; the neritic zone lies above the continental shelf. (The edge of the neritic zone varies from approximately 60 to 180 meters in depth depending on the water depth of the edge of a continental shelf.) At the edge of the neritic zone depths increase rapidly down to the benthic zone which may, in some places, exceed 3000 meters. Such great depths as just mentioned are referred to as the abyssal zone. The oceanic zone includes all the waters not included in the neritic zone and thus includes the just mentioned benthic and abyssal zones (Fig. 10.1).

**ESTUARIES**  Estuaries are located in all latitudes and although varying one from another in terms of specific physical and biological characteristics they share many properties in common placing them among the most productive of marine ecosystems (Fig. 10.2).

Salinity varies from season to season depending on the total amounts of freshwater flowing in and also daily as tidal changes carry salt water in and out. Temperatures also tend to vary over short periods of time and other variables subject to daily and seasonal changes include the depth to which light penetrates, and the amount of nutrients and the quantities of dissolved oxygen present.

With the exception of coral reefs, estuaries are probably the most productive of marine ecosystems. More to the point, estuaries are nurseries for many marine organisms. The eggs of many fish and crustacean species are laid in these ecosystems and the early (larval)

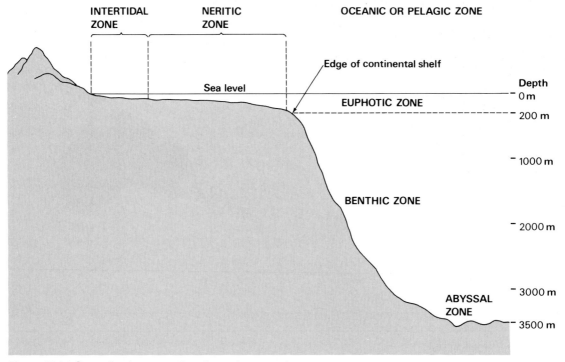

**Figure 10.1**  Generalized cross-section of a marine coastal area.

**Figure 10.2** Estuary, North Carolina.

stages of many organisms are passed in these habitats. Thus, it is no exaggeration to suggest that the continued viability of many important marine fisheries is dependent on the continued availability of ecologically healthy estuaries. Although the central role played by estuaries in marine ecosystems is widely known, estuaries are among the most misused of all marine ecosystems.

**INTERTIDAL ZONE** The intertidal zone is the zone where the bottom (substrate) is periodically covered and uncovered by seawater. Marine life is sometimes extraordinarily varied in this zone. In general, rock areas have the greatest animal diversity and biomass followed by mud areas and then by sand areas. Although this zone is seldom the focus of commercial fishing except on a limited scale the intertidal zone was probably the first marine area from which humans harvested marine animals and plants. In many parts of the world subsistence harvesting in this zone remains an important local activity. Chiefly because of its

easy access and limited area this zone is easily overexploited and damaged.

**NERITIC ZONE** The neritic zone includes all the water above continental shelves excepting the intertidal zone. This is the zone from which a large portion of the world's commercial fish catch is taken. In general, conditions are often nearly optimal for primary and secondary productivity because of a relative abundance of nutrients, light, and oxygen. Among the significant latitudinal differences in this zone is that in cool middle and high latitude areas fish species tend to be relatively few in number but have high biomass relative to the total number of species present. In warm, low latitude, areas fish species diversity tends to be high but the biomass of individual species is far less than is the case in cool neritic waters. Thus, it is in the cool waters of the world that one finds the major specialized fisheries employing boats and fishing gear designed to take perhaps only a single species. Such specialization is difficult or even impossible in warm, low latitude, neritic waters and boats and gear must often have a more general design if they are to be economically useful.

**OCEANIC ZONE** It is the upper or photic zone of the oceanic zone that is of greatest interest insofar as the harvest of marine organisms is concerned. These vast areas, as already indicated, are by no means uniform and the larger portion (as much as 90 percent according to some estimates) are only watery deserts where productivity is too low to be of interest to harvesters of the oceans.

The depth of this zone varies according to light penetration. The areas where penetration is deepest are usually the areas of lowest productivity since the clarity of the water is due to a lack of nutrients and microorganisms.

Several very important commercial fisheries are located in this zone among them being whaling, tuna, anchovies (some species), and marlin. In the minds of many persons, it is the oceanic zone that yields the largest portion of the annual harvest of marine organisms but this is not true. As already noted, it is the estuaries and the neritic zone that accounts for the greatest part of the world's marine fish catch.

**BENTHIC ZONE**   The benthic zone includes the area on and near the ocean bottoms beginning at the end of the neritic zone and extending downward to approximately 2000 meters. Depths greater than 2000 meters are referred to as the abyssal zone.

The benthic zone is characterized by a lack of light, enormous water pressures that increase rapidly with increasing depth, cool to very cold temperatures and having salinities, nutrients, and current velocities that vary greatly from place to place. The benthic zone is one of low productivity and is of limited importance for harvesting. The abyssal zone, although containing some of the most extraordinary forms of animal life in the oceans, is even less productive than the benthic zone.

**PRODUCTIVITY AND FOOD CHAINS**   As we have seen, productivity varies greatly from place to place in marine environments. The elements governing productivity are sunlight, nutrients, temperature, and dissolved oxygen. The flow of energy through marine ecosystems usually involves many energy transfers. The sum of such transfers may be visualized as a chain or web of interacting producers and consumers (see Fig. 1.1, Chapter 1). The most important primary producers are species of algae that float in the water. This collection of simple green plants is called phytoplankton and it is of critical importance to most marine food chains. Larger species of marine vegetation may also be important to the maintenance of food chains but it has been shown that in many cases the consumers of such are mostly species that are of little or no economic value. Almost as important as phytoplankton are the many species of very small floating marine animals called zooplankton.

As in any system involving energy transfers there is a loss of efficiency (entropy) between each transfer. Thus, in marine, as well as all other food chains, the shorter the length of the chain with respect to the species we wish to harvest the more efficient the fixation of energy we wish to utilize in the form of food or raw materials. The length of food chains from the planktonic beginning to the species we are interested in harvesting (the latter is not always the end of a food chain) varies from species to species. For example, with regard to anchovies the chain is short and we therefore are able to harvest what are sometimes very large usable quantities of fish. By way of contrast, swordfish feeding at or near the end of a fairly long food chain are not numerous and the total available harvest is tiny compared to the anchovy. Many of the most desired food-fish species occupy high trophic positions in marine ecosystems and their relative scarcity makes them expensive.

Large size in a marine organism does not always mean that it feeds at or near the end of a long food chain. The most outstanding example of this are the balleen whales, which feed relatively far down the food chain subsisting on a collection of small (but not minute) crustaceans called *krill* (Fig. 10.3). Now that these whales are becoming scarce there is growing interest in the direct harvesting of krill about which more will be said later.

We, as a species, harvest at a number of places in marine food chains but scarcely touch primary production. In Japan and a few other countries, large marine plants are harvested for food and are considered dietary delicacies. It has been suggested that phytoplankton be harvested and used directly as human food or used to feed animals that might then be eaten by humans. Although the total biomass of phytoplankton in the oceans is enormous it is almost always too small a percentage of seawater to make its harvest economically feasible.

Conserving and managing marine biotic resources has two major facets: (1) the conser-

**Figure 10.3** Close-up of euphausiids (krill). These small crustaceans usually vary between 10 mm and 25 mm in length.

vation of marine ecosystems and (2) the conservation and management of marine organisms.

## CONSERVING MARINE ECOSYSTEMS

Until recent years the general feeling was that the oceans were so vast that humans could have little significant impact upon their ecosystems. Although recognizing that occasional troubles occurred in estuaries and the neritic zone, the oceanic zone was dismissed as being all but immune to human impacts. Such views are incorrect and the public is becoming aware that, far from the all but indestructable ecosystems they were once thought to be, virtually all parts of the marine areas of the world are sensitive to human actions. Perhaps no other act than that of using the ocean as a garbage dump better exemplifies this traditional attitude.

There is no seaside human settlement that has not used the adjacent waters as a convenient dumping site for virtually every type of refuse produced by human settlements. The sight of refuse-filled barges towed by tugs and escorted by squadrons of gulls has been as much a part of the cultural landscape of New York as its famed skyscrapers and of San Francisco as its Golden Gate. This refuse, ranging from biodegradable wet garbage to chemicals so toxic that they could find no safe storage on land have been, for decades, consigned to the "safe" depths of the oceans (Fig. 10.4).

Of course, nobody asked such questions as to how this refuse behaved in food chains or where the materials went after being thrown into the water. After all, there was so very much seawater what possible harm could there be?

Wet garbage, vegetable refuse, probably does no harm and may even act as a fertilizer to stimulate some biological productivity.

**Figure 10.4** Tugboat in New York harbor pulling garbage-filled barges to be dumped offshore.

However, waste derived from factories of all kinds is another matter. Among these wastes have been and are substances known to be toxic in terrestrial and freshwater systems and thus must also be toxic in marine systems. So what is the justification for dumping such waste in marine waters? The answer is to be found in the widely held belief that the great volumes of seawater will dilute these chemical substances to the point where they could pose no threat to the environment or to us.

In recent years there has been a marked change in such attitudes in the United States and soon such disposal of wastes will be almost a thing of the past. Federal and state legislation now increasingly limit what may be deposited in marine waters and this includes the time-honored garbage barges: we will have to find other means of disposing of our garbage. Unfortunately, garbage scows will remain in use in many other parts of the world for a long time because this is a cost effective albeit biologi-

cally destructive means of disposing of one's urban and industrial wastes.

More ominous than traditional garbage are the cannisters of chemicals, nerve gas, and atomic wastes that have been given resting places on the bottom of the ocean.

There are many chemical compounds that once used cannot be used again and whose storage on land is difficult and costly. Almost as a matter of course many of these have been routinely placed in barrels and dumped offshore sometimes well within the neritic zone if this zone extends so far seaward as to make a haul out beyond the continental shelf to the benthic or abyssal zones appear uneconomic. These containers have relatively short lives because they are immediately subjected to the corrosive effects of seawater.

A recent addition to the refuse that has been and is being dumped in the marine ecosystems are nuclear wastes. During the early years of the "nuclear age" there was some marine dumping of nuclear wastes by the U.S. government agencies but this has been halted. However, other nations and particularly Great Britain and some other nations of Western Europe still view the seabed as a proper place to dispose of nuclear wastes. These countries are presently searching for what they believe will be safe disposal areas in the eastern Atlantic Ocean. There is also strong interest in the abyssal zone and particularly the very deep trenches that occur in some places with depths exceeding 10,000 meters.

The ocean has long been perceived by persons living nearby as an optimal site in which to dispose of sewage. This effluent is usually transported by canal, pipe, or other type of conduit to the marine environment. One of the earliest problems our species faced when it became settled into village life was that of disposal of human body wastes. For centuries the problem was (and in many places still is) solved by each person depositing his waste on the surface of the ground, hopefully somewhere outside the settlement but frequently not. As settlements grew in size this casual (and medically dangerous) means of disposal was found inadequate and one response was to channel the waste away into a nearby stream or, if near an ocean shore, into marine water.

It is one of the anachronisms of human technical achievement that the treatment and disposal of human wastes lags behind the level of achievement in many other fields of technology. Exacerbating this situation is the attitude of many otherwise informed and intelligent people vis-à-vis sewage treatment and disposal. This attitude may be summarized as one of indifference and unwillingness to support financing of available technology that would reduce actual and potential ecosystem harm from sewage (in chapter nine this problem was discussed with reference to freshwater resources).

There is probably no seaside city in the world that does not discharge most if not all of its liquid sewage into the ocean. This sewage is, chemically, a far different collection of substances than sewage was in the years the Romans developed what is thought to be the first major urban sewage system in the world, the *cloaca maxima*. Then sewage consisted almost entirely of human and animal wastes and its effect on marine systems must have been limited to enrichment. Today, sewage contains a large share of the liquid waste products of industry and even so-called domestic sewage, that is sewage derived from human habitations, is a chemical brew of such complexity as would cause a sorcerer's apprentice to pause for thought. Residues of medicines, cleaning agents, household chemicals—all these and others are part of the domestic sewage of any modern city. No one living knows what the total chemical content is of the factory-domestic sewage produced by cities all over the world and allowed to flow into the oceans.

Sewage treatment (see chapter nine) consists of attempts to reduce its content of pathogenic organisms (although viruses are all but immune to treatment). Frequently nothing is done to catch chemicals and remove them before they reach the ocean. Thus, among the thousands of substances that daily enter the oceans as a part of sewage, are heavy metals of which lead, cadmium, and mercuury are known to be highly toxic.

Thus far, in this discussion, a number of biological and chemical (including atomic) wastes have been noted and the inference given that these ought not be deposited in the oceans or at least not until we know much more than we do at present regarding the impact such materials might have on marine ecosystems. Nevertheless the idea may remain in the thoughtful reader's mind that, after all, the oceans are large and the total volume of wastes discharged must be too low to pose problems.

Perhaps the principal reason that we must be on guard against such reasoning is because of a phenomenon called the biomagnification or concentration factor. The concentration factor refers to the tendency of organisms to concentrate, in ever greater ratios, certain substances relative to the organism's body weight, as the substance moves through a food chain. A substance may occur in a very dilute concentration in seawater but, may reach very high levels of concentration as it is assimilated by organisms in the food chain. Some marine organisms are extremely efficient concentrators because they feed in such a way as to process a large volume of seawater or because they ingest a lot of minute food particles that contain toxic substances. An example of the former are bivalve molluscs. These so-called siphon feeders pump a lot of water through their feeding systems in a given time period and extract minute food particles in the process. They may thus also extract any toxic substances that are present in the water. These might include viruses (leading to problems such as hepatitis among human consumers) or heavy metals. A dramatic example of heavy metal concentration is methyl mercury, which is sometimes concentrated by bivalves and other marine organisms. When the level of concentration gets too high the unfortunate human consumer is severly poisoned.

An example of animals that are not siphon feeders but nevertheless feed by ingestion of large quantities of minute food particles are shrimp. These crustaceans are among the most sought-after creatures of the sea. Ordinarily very safe to eat, shrimp are known to be able to concentrate radioactive particles (radionuclides) if such are present in the food they eat. Thus, waters where the concentration of radioactive wastes derived from disposal or atomic testing appears to be very low and hence "safe" may, nevertheless, pose a problem if shrimp or other organisms capable of concentrating radionuclides are present.

Marine animals that feed at the end of relatively long food chains may be expected to be candidates for concentrating some undesirable substances. These may include DDT, mercury, and other chemical substances. A few years ago there was a considerable worldwide scare about mercury concentrations in swordfish and for a time these fish were not allowed to be sold in the United States. More recently it has been determined that the levels of mercury discovered in swordfish may not be significantly greater than were levels of mercury in sea fish before anthropogenic sources of mercury became important. This was determined, in part, through chemical examination of the tissues of fishes in museum collections that had been made many years ago. It is known that mercury is a widely distributed element in the earth's surface and has been washing into the sea for millions of years and thus it is to be expected that mercury would be present in fish tissues even if humans were not themselves responsible for this chemical getting into marine environments.

Although mercury levels in swordfish may represent no medical problem, prudence requires that a major research effort be made to identify the chemicals being introduced by every anthropogenic source into the oceans and to determine what happens to the ecosystems into which materials are dumped. Furthermore, prudence would dictate a conservative course that requires every effort be made to restrict use of the oceans as sites for waste disposal.

## Petroleum Pollution

This subject is discussed in chapter fourteen but it is nevertheless appropriate that it also be noted in the context of a chapter dealing with marine biotic resources. Petroleum "seeps" are a natural feature of some submarine situations. For example, in the Santa Barbara coastal region of California where much controversy surrounds further attempts to drill oil wells (a controversy that is owing in large measure to the blowout of an offshore oil well a few years ago, Fig. 10.5), some petroleum drains naturally from the seabed in that area. This is not to argue that

**Figure 10.5** Oil blowout in the Santa Barbara area, California.

oil well blowouts are ecologically safe but only to indicate that oil enters marine ecosystems in some places by other than anthropogenic agency. However, the huge international marine traffic in oil and oil-drilling activities on continental shelves have increased the possibilities for much greater quantities of oil to enter marine ecosystems than probably ever occurred under natural conditions. Tanker accidents as well as deliberate, albeit illegal, discharges of waste oil cause great damage to local marine life.

It appears that the greater share of anthropogenic oil discharge—accidental or deliberate—occurs adjacent to shore, that is, in the very locations where many of the most important marine fisheries are located and it may be expected that the damage, ecologic and economic, is far greater than it would be if such discharges occurred most often far out to sea and especially in those vast reaches of the oceanic zone where productivity is low to begin with.

Another source of oil contamination are drilling sites located offshore in the neritic zone. It is true that in the early days of offshore drilling for oil, methods were often careless and resulted in accidental oil spills. In recent years most oil companies attempt to use methods that reduce as far as possible the threat of a spill. Public opinion in the United States seems particularly strong in this area and even in foreign areas oil spills from drill sites are likely to be given wide coverage by the news media.

The most recent large-scale spill resulting from a drilling accident occurred in the Gulf of Mexico just off the Mexican coast in the Bay of Campeche. This well burst its controls and spewed enormous quantities of oil into the Gulf until, weeks later, it was subdued. The oil slick floated all the way north to Texas where, for a time, it posed a threat to parts of the local neritic ecosystems. Besides the poor publicity earned by such a spill there is an economic incentive to prevent them. With petroleum selling for more than $32.00 per 42-gallon barrel, a spill can represent a major economic loss.

The environmental impacts of oil spills are not always easy to evaluate due, in part, to the rapidity with which these events become environmental "media events." This is not to suggest that oil spills do not pose threats to marine ecosystems because they do but it must also be noted that the shrillness of some public responses to some spills appears out of keeping with the actual level of the ecological difficulties present.

Petroleum has leaked into marine ecosystems for millions of years and thus, at least in limited quantities, must be seen as a nonanthropogenic substance in some parts of the world's oceans. However, the *magnitude* of at least some anthropogenic oil spills dwarf anything known to occur in natural circumstances.

What are the principal known effects of oil spills? When they occur in the neritic zone the impact on the animal and plant life may be sudden and devastating. This includes effects on seabirds and shore birds. For a time a neritic community subjected to a large oil spill simply may be so injured by the deaths of so many creatures occupying varying places in the food chains that the system ceases for a time to exist as a functioning entity. The rate of recovery of communities subjected to a spill and the possible long-term genetic effects are major questions now receiving the attention of investigators.

It appears that the impact of a given oil spill will be determined, in part, by the volume of oil relative to the water volume, the rate and direction of the surface currents, the time of the year, and the chemical characteristics of the oil itself because petroleum is not a uniform substance.

Most large-scale spills occur in or near the neritic zone and thus the chances for at least local destruction of organisms is greater than on the high seas where winds and currents may disperse the oil before it reaches neritic zones. This is not to suggest that no damage results from oceanic spills or discharges. Many bird species and certainly some fish species might be expected to be harmed at least in the area of any spill.

The time of the year may be important because of breeding seasons and the presence or absence of eggs or larvae. Seasonality may also be important with respect to algal production and if this is true then disturbing this could have far-reaching effects even on ecosystems not immediately involved in a given spill.

Tests have shown that differing types of crude oil produce differing effects on biota. Also, petroleum is known to contain compounds that are carcinogenic (cancer causing) and this raises the presently unanswered question as to what this might mean for human health where the human consumption of contaminated species is concerned.

## Thermal Pollution

Nuclear power generating plants require large quantities of water as a coolant and for this rea-son, when possible, such plants may be located close to a source of seawater. The water, after serving its coolant function, is returned to the ocean, which has the effect of raising water temperature in the area where the hot water from the reactor mixes with cooler seawater. This phenomenon has received the somewhat inaccurate designation thermal pollution but since the term is now well established in use, it is retained here.

In general, the increased temperature will favor warm-water animal species and there may even be an increase in the production of some species. However, other species requiring the cooler water that previously occurred may be reduced in number or disappear. Particularly affected are the larval stages of some marine organisms that have very narrow ranges of temperature tolerance. Probably most generating plants sited to draw from and discharge water into the neritic zone will affect a comparatively local area providing there is a fairly strong movement of water by currents and wave action. The effects on ecosystems close to shore can be reduced by piping the hot water to well away from the shoreline although there will still be local heating of seawater no matter where the discharge occurs. Estuaries are poor places for the siting of nuclear power plants as are embayments where the mixing of water is slow. In these and similar situations the hot-water effluent might cause very considerable damage not only to the local marine biota but, through linkage, also to other marine ecosystems.

## Destruction or Modification of Marshlands

Marshlands have been disappearing at a rapid rate as they are converted to housing tracts, factory sites, and marinas for recreational boating. A prime example of this phenomenon is the coast of California. Salt marsh, once a fairly frequently encountered ecosystem, has become almost rare. In the San Diego area, for example, a once large marshy area adjacent to Mission Bay has been converted to a vast and admittedly attractive recreational area with the result that only a tiny remnant of marsh remains. There are many other examples along the coast and the few remaining marshes are looked on hungrily by "developers" who wish to convert them to marinas or housing subdivisions or both.

California, recognizing, albeit a bit belatedly, the threat to its shoreline, created a Coastal Commission, which must pass on all developments in the coastal zone. The Commission is frequently the object of attack by persons who feel that their rights to private property are not being respected. However, the Commission has had the effect of greatly slowing the process of coastal destruction that had progressed very far and serves to show that any citizenry, if possessed of sufficient will, can halt the destruction of what is one of the nation's most important resources.

## MAJOR MARINE FISHERIES OF THE UNITED STATES

The most convenient way to organize the data of any nation's marine fisheries is to group them according to the major places of occurrence. For the United States such a grouping might include the following: the Atlantic, Gulf, and Pacific regions with their subdivisions (Map 10.2).

### Atlantic Region

The Atlantic region includes all Atlantic waters under the control of U.S. law as well as oceanic regions visited by United States fishermen. The following subdivisions may be identified: New England including the Grand Banks, Middle Atlantic, Chesapeake Bay, and South Atlantic.

#### NEW ENGLAND AND THE GRAND BANKS

It is very appropriate that a discussion of United States saltwater fisheries should begin with this region because it is here that marine fishing first became important during the colonial period and it is here that the tradition of looking to the sea for a livelihood remains the strongest of any major fishing region in the United States. The principal fisheries in this region are located in the neritic zone. The Grand Banks are relatively shallow parts of this zone thus bringing the substrate closer to the photic zone than would otherwise be the case. This region has long been famed for its productivity of valuable market fish species such as cod, haddock, and flounders. Closer to shore, lobsters and a variety of molluscs are taken.

What makes this region so highly productive? This is a place where the warm waters of the Gulf Stream mix with cool currents moving from the north. This creates a considerable degree of turbulence bringing quantities of nutrients from the bottom of the neritic zone into the upper parts of the photic zone. The oxygenated waters from the north combine with the high nutrient content to provide the elements for a high level of primary and secondary productivity.

However, in spite of the enormous productive capacity of these waters, the animal resources cannot forever withstand the tremendous harvesting pressure that has been brought to bear in this region and particularly in recent decades. For many years codfish was the mainstay of the commercial catch and exceeded in total weight, all other species taken. Alas, the day came when, as a result of overharvesting, the catch of this fish declined and its place of primacy was taken over by flounders and other less desirable species.

This region has not been the fishing grounds of U.S. fishermen only. The nationals of many countries have long been accustomed to fish these waters. In recent years huge fishing vessels from the USSR took enormous quantities of fish from the region for consumption in that country. Most of the region lies beyond the traditional 3-mile to 12-mile limits claimed by na-

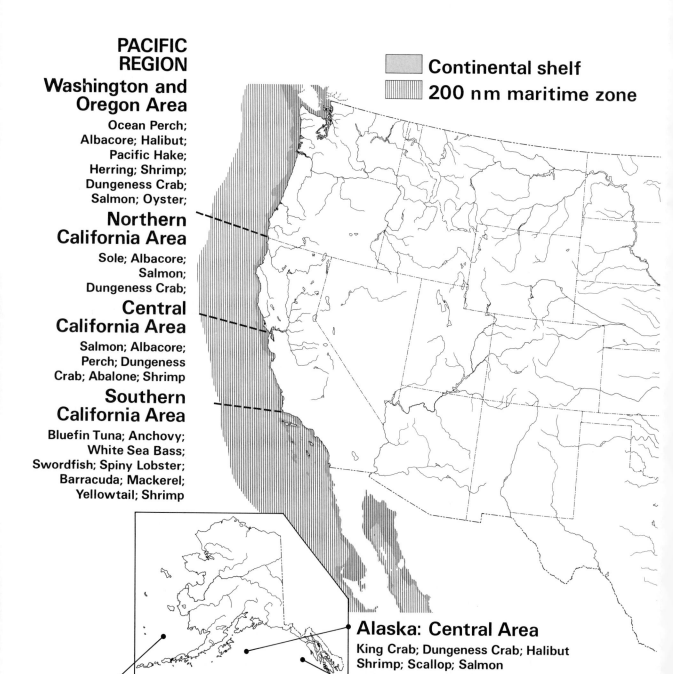

# PACIFIC REGION

## Washington and Oregon Area

Ocean Perch;
Albacore; Halibut;
Pacific Hake;
Herring; Shrimp;
Dungeness Crab;
Salmon; Oyster;

## Northern California Area

Sole; Albacore;
Salmon;
Dungeness Crab;

## Central California Area

Salmon; Albacore;
Perch; Dungeness
Crab; Abalone; Shrimp

## Southern California Area

Bluefin Tuna; Anchovy;
White Sea Bass;
Swordfish; Spiny Lobster;
Barracuda; Mackerel;
Yellowtail; Shrimp

Continental shelf

200 nm maritime zone

## Alaska: Central Area

King Crab; Dungeness Crab; Halibut
Shrimp; Scallop; Salmon

## Alaska: Southern Area

Salmon; Halibut; Dungeness Crab

## Alaska: Western Area

King Crab; Salmon; Halibut

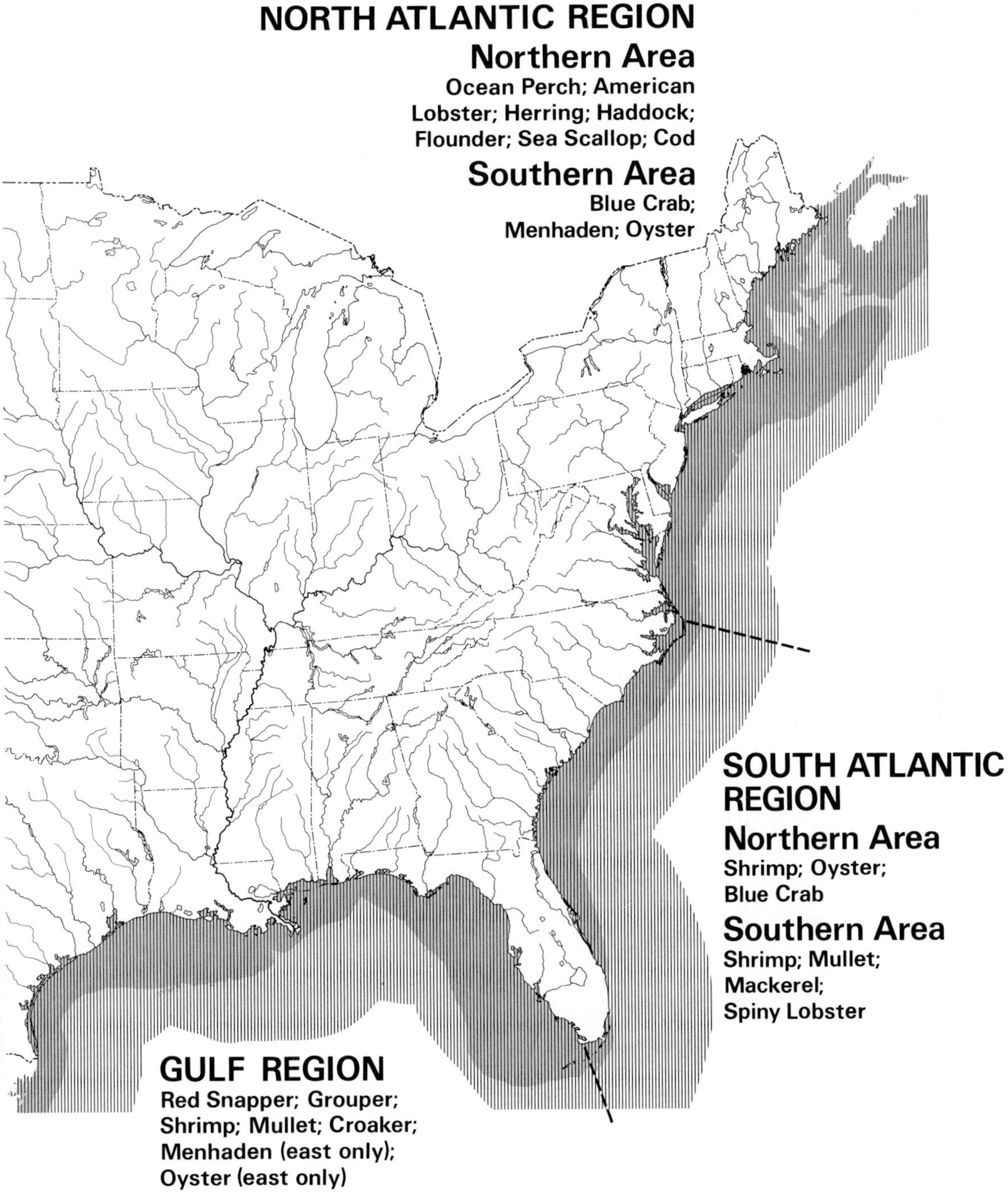

**NORTH ATLANTIC REGION**
**Northern Area**
Ocean Perch; American
Lobster; Herring; Haddock;
Flounder; Sea Scallop; Cod
**Southern Area**
Blue Crab;
Menhaden; Oyster

**SOUTH ATLANTIC REGION**

**Northern Area**
Shrimp; Oyster;
Blue Crab
**Southern Area**
Shrimp; Mullet;
Mackerel;
Spiny Lobster

**GULF REGION**
Red Snapper; Grouper;
Shrimp; Mullet; Croaker;
Menhaden (east only);
Oyster (east only)

**Map 10.2** Major marine fisheries of the United States.

tions and thus the fishing grounds were in international waters over which little conservation could be exercised (Fig. 10.6).

Recently this situation has changed dramatically with passage of an international Law of the Sea which, among many other provisions, allows a nation to claim up to 200 miles offshore as its territorial waters insofar as the natural resources are concerned. This has put much of this subregion within United States (or Canadian) jurisdiction. At the time of this writing, the United States allows foreign ships to fish in this region after first being licensed to do so. The catch size and means of harvest are controlled and subject to close inspection. This

appears to have reduced some of the more outrageous actions once reported to occur but too much damage is still occurring.

It is not enough to limit harvest totals: there must also be a strict limitation on the use of fishing gear that will unduly disturb the marine environments in which the fishing takes place. The Soviets and nationals of other countries frequently employ enormous trawl nets that are dragged, that is "trawled," in such a manner as to rip up the bottom of the neritic zone creating enormous chaos in the ecosystems. It is thought by some marine biologists that such destruction not only takes many years to heal but that the damage is not limited to the sites where the

**Figure 10.6**  Trawler in operation on the Grand Banks. The net is beneath the water and is connected to the ship by cables visible in the stern area.

great nets have passed. This type of harvesting ought really be called by a more appropriate designation such as *raubwirtschaft* (robber economy).

Although not an unmitigated blessing, the Law of the Sea finally provides the United States with the incentive it has heretofore lacked to protect this great source of marine animals. Unfortunately, foreign megatrawlers are still permitted to operate in this region. That this is in some measure a political as well as a fisheries' management decision is suggested by the fact that the damage caused by these harvest methods is well documented but it is considered a politically sensitive matter to maintain a tight control over the activities of foreign ships fishing this region. Recently the Soviet vessels had their fishing rights taken from them, not because of their fishing methods but because of their military invasion of Afghanistan.

Not all the other fishermen in this region, United States nationals or others, are in harmony with the prospect of greater controls being exerted over their fishing activities. Here, as in all commercial fishing regions, there is often a lack of effective communication between the regulators and the regulated. Also, there is the natural resentment that will be present whenever one's accustomed actions are restricted. It is in the best interests of U.S. fishermen to cooperate closely with federal fisheries' personnel in order to reestablish the fish populations in this region and to assure that harvests do not exceed the sustained yield capacity of the fish resource. In the past, fishermen may have had too little opportunity to contribute to federal decision making but this is now being overcome and is, of course, a *sine qua non* for any truly cooperative efforts between government and fishermen.

**MIDDLE ATLANTIC NERITIC ZONE** This zone extends from southern New England to Chesapeake Bay. A wide range of fish and crustaceans are harvested from this region, but it has been overfished for years by both United States boats as well as by foreign vessels. With regard to the latter, it has been chiefly the Soviets who have been the most destructive. This region yields a very long list of commercially valuable marine animal species but dominating the list are menhaden, (fished not for food but for oil and other products), flounders, whiting, and the succulent scallop (a mollusc).

These waters, including as they do some of the world's busiest shipping lanes and adjacent to one of the world's most populated areas, are subjected to many kinds of pollution. Any management program of the fish resources in this zone must include major efforts to reduce the pollutant load.

**CHESAPEAKE BAY** Few are the Americans for whom the name of Chesapeake Bay does not conjure up visions of oysters on the half shell, bounteous harvests of fish, succulent clams and soft-shelled crabs. This vision, although now a bit flawed, still retains much of its factual basis for this region, although small, remains one of our nation's very important marine harvest grounds.

The high level of productivity of the waters of this region can be attributed to the many rivers draining into the bay, shallow water allowing light penetration to the bottom, and waters cool enough to be relatively rich in oxygen.

Unfortunately, this extraordinary natural marine fish farm has been abused almost beyond belief by pollution of virtually every known type. The levels of pollutants have reached such heights that many persons who once delighted to dine on the bay's oysters will no longer do so. These molluscs are filter feeders and can concentrate toxic substances quite easily thus making them particularly dangerous if harvested from polluted water. There is now a multistate effort underway, combined with federal support, to lessen the rates of pollution and to completely eradicate the types of pollutants that cause the deaths of fish and other species and/or that might cause human illness if ingested with seafood.

In addition to the very serious matter of pollution is the problem of overharvesting the marine resources. This region has been the object of numerous scientific studies designed to determine the size of commercial fish stocks and thus to establish catch limits necessary to maintaining a sustained yield harvest. It is to be hoped that in the future harvest limits and pollution control will result in a fishery that deserves the high regard it once possessed.

**SOUTH ATLANTIC SUBREGION** This subregion extends from Cape Hatteras—of shipwreck fame—southward to the southern tip of Florida. The Gulf Stream—misnamed because it does not originate in the Gulf of Mexico but rather in the eastern Caribbean—flows northward in this zone more or less paralleling the coast until the latitude of Cape Hatteras where it swings away from the coast. It seldom invades the near-shore zone but flows a short distance away and thus relatively cool water is found in the inshore part of the neritic zone and rather warmer Gulf Stream water in the outer neritic zone. Productivity in the Gulf Stream is lower (as one would expect) than in the cooler in-shore waters but in the zone of contact between cool and warm water there are often concentrations of fish species highly regarded by both commercial and sport fishermen. Although encompassing a much greater area and volume of water than does Chesapeake Bay, the annual dollar value of the catch from this subregion is usually less than for Chesapeake Bay.

A wide variety of marine animals is taken here including menhaden, red snappers, mullet, sea trout, scallops, crabs, and shrimp.

Though not entirely free from pollution, this area has been spared the major pollution disasters so often visited on subregions to the north. This is not to suggest there are no pollution problems but the chief management

problem is the size of the annual harvest. Overfishing has afflicted most of the commercial fisheries of this subregion. The demand for some of the species, for example, red snapper, often far exceeds the level of a sustained yield harvest and the temptation to overfish the resources is often strong.

## Gulf Region

The Gulf region includes the waters of the Gulf of Mexico and extends from southernmost Florida on the east to the Texas-Mexico boundary on the west.

This is a region blessed by conditions that produce an enormous production of shrimp—which is the dominant fishery of the region—as well as a wide range of other harvestable marine animals. Of the latter, menhaden dominates the catch according to size of catch although not by value. Food-fish species are similar to those taken from the south Atlantic subregion.

Of great importance to the production of the shrimp is the discharge of the Mississippi River, which brings enormous quantities of nutrients to Gulf waters. Also of importance in this regard are many smaller rivers that discharge into the Gulf from western Florida to southernmost Texas. Indeed, these rivers and the shallow waters of the Gulf of Mexico—the neritic zone extends for many kilometers from the shore—and abundant estuarine ecosystems combine to produce optimal ecological conditions for a variety of shrimp species. Although dwarfed in terms of weight caught by many other marine animals, the Gulf shrimp catch is one of the most economically valuable of all U.S. fisheries. For this reason, the Gulf shrimp fishery has been the object of intensive and detailed research for many years and much has been learned about the biology of these organisms (Fig. 10.7).

Among the many important facts regarding shrimp biology that have been discovered is that each species has unique habitat require-

**Figure 10.7** Shrimp boats, Louisiana.

ments. Although possibly caught in the same shrimp trawl net at the same time, one species is known to bury itself each day in the bottom and then only in certain kinds of material while another species does not hide in such a manner but migrates daily between different ocean depths (called diel movement) seeking the deeper water during the daylight hours and rising to middle depths after dark. Some species spawn their eggs out into the ocean while other species carry their eggs attached to them for a time.

There are important differences in growth rates and ages of reproduction between shrimp species. Most species attain a legal commercial size well before the females are sexually mature and the age of attaining minimum legal catch size or of sexual maturity varies from one species to another.

Although they may not appear capable of other than limited migration, it has been discovered that some Gulf shrimp species may move from 100 to nearly 300 kilometers from their nursery areas to the areas where they appear in commercial harvests. This means that in order to spawn these animals must return over similar distances to estuaries. The varied biology of the shrimp species comprising the commercial catch in this region makes management and conservation a difficult task.

The *bete noire* of this fishery is overharvesting. Until recently, a significant part of the Gulf shrimp catch was taken in international waters and thus was not subject to legal control. Indeed, some U.S. based shrimp boats operated as far away as the Bay of Campeche in waters the fishermen considered international but which Mexicans considered to be Mexican waters. This sometimes volatile issue (resulting in gunfire and alleged loss of human life on some occasions) has been solved by the new Law of the Sea, which placed this and similar areas under the legal jurisdiction of the Mexican government.

Similarly, much of the water formerly beyond the control of the U.S. government is now within our nation's jurisdiction and this can only have a beneficial effect on the long-range prospects of this fishery. This conclusion is often not shared by shrimp fishermen but this fishery has long suffered from a *raubwirtschaft* mentality engendered in large measure by the fact that so much of the resource lay beyond any legal control.

Many fisheries in the Gulf have been plagued by oil pollution. This has become a particularly serious problem since the petroleum industry began to drill in the neritic zone and often many kilometers from the nearest land (see chapter fourteen). The volume of marine shipping has increased greatly in the last few decades which, in addition to increasing the pollution, has stimulated harbor construction detrimental to estuarine as well as inshore neritic ecosystems. These activities adversely affect the shrimp and other marine animal species that require these habitats in order to maintain their populations.

## Pacific Region

The Pacific region includes the marine area from northwestern Alaska south to the United States-Mexican border. This large region may be subdivided into the following subregions: Alaskan, Puget Sound to San Francisco Bay, and San Francisco Bay to the United States-Mexico border.

**ALASKAN SUBREGION** This region has become one of great significance to the American marine fisheries. Although still in the early stages of scientific study the subregion is known to support high levels of primary and secondary productivity and particularly adjacent to and south of the Aleutian Islands where water temperatures are lower than in many parts immediately to the north of these islands.

In the early days of commercial fishing salmon was the primary catch. Indeed, it wasn't until this region had been overharvested that major attention was given to the commercial potential of other marine animal populations. Of lesser total value but at one time far better known in the popular mind was the fur seal harvest, which was concentrated in the Bering Sea north of the Aleutians and about which more will be said later.

The Alaskan salmon fishery once presented such a piratical image that it drew the attention not only of conservationists but also of authors such as Rex Beach, who immortalized some of the aspects of these activities in his book, *The Silver Horde*. If ever there was an example of mining the resources of the sea without thought of the future, it was this fishery. Yet despite mistreatments of this resource, it is still in existence, albeit with annual catches of less than half those recorded for the 1930s, and salmon still provide the largest tonnage of any of our commercially harvested marine food fish and are exceeded in dollar value only by shrimp! In the decade of the 1930s, Pacific salmon was often considered to be a relatively inexpensive fish to eat. Today however, these fish have become so expensive that it is currently not unusual to see them retailing for more than $5 per pound.

What were the chief causes of the decline of this fishery? The answers to that query can be summarized under overharvesting (and particularly of juvenile individuals), lack of effective legal fishing controls, absentee ownership of the canneries (most of the salmon was canned), general lack of knowledge regarding the biology of these fish, and interference with spawning.

Salmon belong to the anadromous fishes, that is, fish that spend most of their lives in saltwater but which must return to freshwater to spawn. Management of such fish obviously is complicated by this duality of aquatic habitats and is further complicated by the fact that Alaskan salmon species migrate far out into the Pacific during their adult years. This means that at least some salmon populations will at times occur even beyond the new 200-mile limit and other populations perhaps will spend some time in waters claimed by one nation and some time in waters claimed by another nation. This is the case with at least some of the salmon populations in the area under discussion and has led the United States and Canada to conclude agreements designed to regulate the international aspects of this fishery.

It is difficult to single out the factor most requiring attention in the management of salmon but proper conservation of the spawning streams must rank very high. If such streams are denied the fish, or if such areas are so modified as to reduce the chances of more than a few fish successfully spawning, the future of the fishery will be placed in jeopardy. Mining, dam building, and logging, which results in an increased erosion of soil into the spawning streams, and pollution from sawmills and paper pulp mills are among the important phenomena that affect spawning.

The allowable age class of the catch is of very great management importance because too great a removal of sexually immature individuals will result in a lowered future population regardless of what other measures may be taken to manage the fishery. The age of maturity varies from species to species. Pink salmon, one of the species taken commercially, require two years to attain sexual maturity while some other species may require three or four years. In most instances the age-class problem can be met successfully by limiting the lower mesh size of the nets used in commercial salmon fishing. It also is of critical importance that a sufficient number of adults be allowed to enter their home streams and spawn. This can be greatly aided by restricting human access to the mouths of rivers and by keeping commercial fishing at a distance sufficient to assure that enough fish run the gauntlet of nets and get into the rivers to mate.

In recent decades other marine animals have become commercially important in Alaskan waters. These include halibut (subject to international management between the United

States, Canada, and Japan), Alaskan pollock, Pacific herring, Pacific cod, ocean perch, and king crabs. Because these are more enlightened times and governmental controls are much more elaborate and effective than in the days of the early salmon fishery one may expect proper management of the fishery resources in this subregion. The new Law of the Sea will be of particular benefit for it is no longer possible for foreign megatrawlers to mine this area as was previously happening.

**FUR SEALS** One of the dramatic conservation stories of an earlier day is that of the near extinction and recovery of the northern fur seal, *Callorhinus ursinus* (Fig. 10.8). This mammal breeds each year on the Pribilof Islands in the southern Bering Sea and ever since the discovery of these islands by hunters in the latter part of the eighteenth century has been the object of human hunters. Governed as a part of Russia until the purchase of Alaska by the United States in 1867 the Pribilof seals were hunted to the point where their continued existence was doubtful. This uncontrolled hunting was brought to a halt in 1911 with the signing of an agreement between the United States, Great Britain, Japan, and Russia, which recognized the long history each nation had in harvesting this resource (Canada then being a dependency of Great Britain could not be a legal signatory to the treaty). The treaty restricted the annual harvest and required that the harvest be shared with the nations participating in the treaty. This latter has undergone some changes since 1911 but the basic components remain more or less the same. The United States assumes full responsibility for conservation and management of the herd and establishes what each year's harvest number will be. Usually only males are allowed to be killed (all harvesting is done by government employees) but in some years a small number of females are also taken in order that favorable sex ratios are maintained in the herd. At the time when

**Figure 10.8** Northern Fur Seals (*Callorhinus ursinus*).

the first treaty was signed there were an estimated 130,000 northern fur seals remaining. By 1935 the herd size had increased to an estimated 1.5 million.

The allowable harvest varies each year. For example, 96,000 animals were taken in 1961 but in 1970 the total was 42,228 animals. Differences between years are attributable to changing numbers within age classes, especially the number of young bachelor seals unable to find a mate, bachelor seals being the principal age class harvested.

Although an account of the commercial harvest of sea mammals would not be complete without mention of the sea otter and whales the former is considered below in the San Francisco to Mexico subregion and whales are given separate treatment later in this chapter.

**PUGET SOUND TO SAN FRANCISCO BAY** Although a broad range of marine animal species are harvested in this subregion there are few major fisheries if weight of the catch be the sole criterion. However, salmon, perch, bottom fish such as sole, many species of rock fish, crabs, large shrimp, clams, and abalone are among the commercially valuable species taken. One of the most notable examples of a fish reserved strictly for sportfishermen is the striped bass, an anadromous species introduced into Pacific waters in the latter part of the nineteenth century. This fish attains weights in excess of 40 kilograms but most of the examples caught are smaller. Although this fish was once taken by commercial fishermen this was stopped in this century and the striped bass is the chief prize sought by noncommercial fishermen and women in and around the San Francisco Bay area. These fish regularly range as far north as Coos Bay in southern Oregon and as far south as the Salinas River in California (Fig. 10.9).

One of the major concerns of the California Department of Fish and Game is the management of the marine sport fishery of California, particularly striped bass. The spawning grounds in the San Francisco Bay region, which is here taken to include the lower parts of the Sacramento and San Joaquin Rivers (known as the Delta region, see chapter nine). As previously noted in chapter nine, there is great and growing concern that too little water will be discharged from the two major river systems into the delta area and thence into San Francisco Bay. The spawning requirements of

striped bass are quite precise and it is feared that even minute changes in salinity of the water in the major spawning regions of this species will cause a major decline in the number of fish and even their possible extinction where they are now most abundant in California.

San Francisco Bay suffers from many other actual and potential environmental problems. The shape of the bay and the movement of water within it assures that it can be easily polluted if great care is not taken to avoid such a condition. Unfortunately, until recently, little thought was given to the biological health of this extraordinary embayment with the result that effluent from factories and sewers flowed without restraint into the bay. It is a measure of the underlying ecological resilience of much of the bay that animal life continued to exist. What has happened in some of the areas studied is that there have been changes in species composition and, in some cases, even an increase in the total animal biomass. In addition, there has been an exchange, in some instances, of harvestable species for species of little or no value to humans. Recognition of the threat to the future biological viability of the Bay led various citizens' groups to sponsor legislation that is bringing about conditions that more and more resemble those reported from early days before factories and sewers threatened the life systems.

**SAN FRANCISCO BAY TO THE UNITED STATES MEXICO BORDER** After the city of San Francisco is passed there are only relatively small coastal settlements until the Santa Barbara to San Diego megalopolis is encountered. Some of these smaller settlements derive a partial livelihood from the sea but even the once-important fishing center of Monterey is today oriented more toward tourism than toward harvesting the ocean. Monterey, once the "sardine capital" of the United States bears mute testimony to what can happen to a marine resource and the fortunes of people who depend on it when the resource is exploited be-

**Figure 10.9** Catch of Striped Bass (*Morone saxatilus*) in California.

yond its capacity to maintain a biomass of harvestable size.

Cannery Row in Monterey was devoted to processing and canning the seasonal catch of Pacific pilchards ("sardines") brought to the docks. Pacific pilchards were also harvested as far north as British Columbia but the California harvest was dominant in terms of total weight taken. After the record year of 1937 annual harvests began to decline and eventually the fishery failed. In 1967, commercial fishing for the Pacific "sardine" was halted but their stocks have not recovered and they remain far too scarce to support even a minor commercial fishery.

It has been suggested that the collapse of this fishery may not have been the result of overharvesting but was because of a natural collapse of the population. This kind of phenomenon is known to occur in nature and cannot be ruled out in the case of this fish species. However, one may be permitted to also come down on the side of overexploitation as the cause. The singular lack of management in this fishery was notable and even if that contributed but a part to the collapse it ought not be forgotten lest the next time when another species is involved we take the position that sudden collapses of fish populations are only natural.

Some of the major prizes of both commercial and sport fishermen along this coast are molluscs belonging to the family haliotidae, otherwise known as abalone. In the early days of European settlement in California, some species of abalone were abundant on rocky substrate in the intertidal zone along the coast. Although some tribes of California Indians had harvested this resource they appear not to have seriously affected abalone populations. Commercial exploitation began in the nineteenth century but did not become important until the twentieth century. Soon these creatures became too scarce in the intertidal zone for commercial harvest and it became necessary to dive for them. This is a luxury food that can be

afforded by relatively few persons but nevertheless is attractive to commercial fishermen. Catch limit and size of individuals is carefully controlled to help preserve the remaining resource. At present there is a growing and very heated controversy about the importance of the once nearly extinct southern sea otter (*Enhydra lutris nereis*) as a predator of abalone (Fig. 10.10).

The sea otter formerly ranged from the Aleutian Islands south along the Pacific coast to a little below the United States-Mexico boundary. Russian hunters began to exploit this resource in the Alaskan region during the latter part of the eighteenth century. As the northern herds were reduced to levels no longer justifying hunting effort the Russians, along with hired Aleut Indian hunters, moved southward hunting the otters along the California and Baja California (Mexico) coasts until the California coast passed into U.S. control. Hunting of sea otters continued until prohibited in the U.S. waters in 1910. At that time it was feared that all of the southern otters had disappeared but a small herd was discovered in the Monterey area in the 1930s. Since then, otters have increased until they are today considered by commercial abalone fishermen to be a major pest because they compete for abalone!

From Point Conception just north of Santa Barbara to the Mexican border there is a fairly intensive harvesting of the neritic zone by both commercial and sport fishermen. The commercial harvests include a wide range of fish species.

One of these important commercial species is the northern anchovy, *Engraulis mordax,* which is distributed from British Columbia to the southern tip of the Baja California peninsula. Only from Monterey southward, however, is the species harvested in large quantities. Three main uses are made of this harvest: (1) canned for human food, (2) fish meal and oil, and (3) live bait for commercial fishermen.

Quite aside from the immediate commercial

**Figure 10.10** Sea otter (*Enhydra lutris*), California coastal region.

importance of this anchovy is the importance of the species in marine ecosystems. It is believed, for example, that the anchovy is the principal food of many of the predator fish species that are the object of commercial and sport fishermen. It has also been established that at least one bird species, the brown pelican, depends chiefly on this species of fish for food.

With the demise of the sardine fishery attention increasingly focused on the commercial harvest of anchovies. The size of the annual catch is limited by the authorities each year. In 1978–1979 the allowable commercial quota was 52,500 tons, which the commercial fleet (consisting of purse seiners) was just able to achieve. The difficulty in reaching the limit allowed, suggests to some observers that the allowable harvest is too large. Most of this feeling comes from the persons who catch live anchovies for sale for sport fishing boats, which use the fish for bait.

The size of the allowable catch of anchovies is determined by measuring the size of the egg and fish larvae biomass in marine waters. The allowable catch for 1979–1980 was set at 56,100 tons, an amount considered by many sportfishing interests as being excessive. The arguments tend to focus on the validity of the sampling methods used. Even some biologists have been heard to say that they lack confidence in the prevailing statistical methodology employed. Further complicating the situation is the fact that Mexican fishermen are exploiting this species in Mexican waters and without any restrictions as to size of annual harvest. Although it is not presently known how much of the total biomass of this species moves between U.S. and Mexican waters there is a widespread opinion that an appreciable amount of anchovies does so move and that unless Mexico can be persuaded to reduce its present unrestricted harvest its anchovy fishery will not only fail but also that of the United States. However, some biologists scoff at this idea pointing out that the anchovy has a very high rate of egg production and grows to maturity in one year and is thus able to rapidly reestablish its numbers should there be overharvesting during one or a few years.

The position of some biologists as just given

is correct as to fecundity but a cautious person would have to recognize that only a few aspects of anchovy biology are well known and no one knows for certain what the *biological potential* of this species actually is. The high level of fecundity may, in fact, indicate that the species requires this as well as a large adult, egg, and larval biomass in order to survive. Little is known about egg and larval predation and thus some of the assurances of safety based on fecundity alone appear derived from intuition rather than from emperical data.

In any case, the northern anchovy provides us with an example of how conflicting uses, conflicting appraisals, and international harvesting of a marine resource can result in very difficult management problems almost beyond human ability to resolve.

The major human impacts in this subregion are the already noted overharvesting and water pollution.

## THE UNITED STATES— GENERAL COMMENTS

In 1976 Congress passed the Fishery Conservation and Management Act. Among the several provisions of this legislation, which assures a federal role in all fisheries decisions, is the provision that regional marine fisheries be managed by *consortia* consisting of federal and state agencies. Partly because of its newness and partly because of a reluctance to accept the intrusion of the federal government this Act remains fairly controversial in many groups whose interests are in the commercial or noncommercial harvest of marine organisms. Although it may yet be too early to properly evaluate the Act it does appear to be a major step in the right conservation direction. This legislation owes its origin chiefly to the Law of the Sea, which has given nations control of resources out to 200 miles from a nation's shore line. The federal government suddenly found itself in possession of the resources not only of

much of the nation's neritic marine zone but often large swaths of the oceanic zone right down to and including the benthic zone. The potential for conflicts in interests between state and federal government are considerable and especially so in the instances where species range within traditional state zones and the new federal zones.

One of the major management problems has been and remains a lack of funds for research needed to discover the best ways to manage many of the nation's fisheries. Of course just throwing money in this direction should be avoided, but all too often there is a lack of proper boats and gear, not to mention trained personnel, to do the kinds of studies required if our marine fisheries are to be put on a scientific management basis.

Another serious issue is the question as to which species may properly be converted into fish meal, oil or some other nonfood product. In the case of menhaden, there is no such choice because the fish is all but inedible. If it is to be harvested it must be for meal, oil and other products—*providing* that the size of the harvest does not threaten other species that depend on menhaden for food. But what about other species, such as the already discussed northern anchovy, which are excellent human food? Is it in the best interests of our nation to permit any part of that resource to be converted into chicken feed or oil? Before answering the question keep in mind that edible (to humans) animal protein is one of the world's scarcest important resources.

We need to establish priorities in this area and these can and should be establised only after all constituencies have been consulted. Too often it is the best-funded groups that manage to control too many aspects of the nation's commercial harvest of marine biotic resources.

There must be better communication with the general public that presently tends to ignore almost all issues regarding the management of our marine resources. This attitude is partly due to a mistaken belief that the size of the marine animal resource is so great that there is no need for personal concern. Indeed, many persons believe that the marine waters under our control are yielding only a modest percentage of the total potential harvest. This is untrue and the unfortunate fact is that almost all of our current fisheries are being overharvested or harvested at about the limit commensurate with a sustained yield. We, as a nation, cannot look to the sea as a major increased future source of animal protein. With better management, with more restriction of foreign harvesting in our waters and with more judicious use made of the animals we do harvest we can increase somewhat the food value of the annual catch (Table 10.1).

Although the gear employed is vastly different than that used by paleolithic fishermen, marine harvests almost everywhere remain a *gathering* operation. The possibilities for farming the estuarine and parts of the neritic zones appear ever brighter as research progresses. However, even this idea is not new, witness oysters that have been cultivated in many places for many years. It is important to note that most such efforts to farm the sea (maricul-

ture) are directed toward raising luxury products such as oysters or lobsters.

## THE THIRD WORLD— GENERAL COMMENTS

One of the characteristics of Third World nations is that a significant percentage of the human population does not receive sufficient high-quality protein in the diet. It might be said that aside from general economic poverty, it is this lack of protein that is the prime criterion for determining if a country has Third World status or not. Animal protein production should first go to satisfy the nutritional requirements of Third World citizens and then be exported.

Exporting prevails because of the Third World's desperate need to obtain foreign exchange. Many fisheries products are easily sold to the affluent nations able to pay the price for high-quality protein. Before this issue of protein export is discussed further, we will first review the general picture of marine fisheries in the Third World by examining the following topics: productivity, foreign investment, and government investment.

Table 10.1
**Examples of recent United States marine fish harvests (weights in metric tons)**

| Fishery | 1965 | 1970 | 1975 | 1980 |
|---|---|---|---|---|
| Cod, Atlantic | 16,329 | 24,041 | 25,401 | 53,524 |
| Flounder | 81,647 | 76,658 | 73,483 | 98,430 |
| Haddock | 60,782 | 12,247 | 7,257 | 24,948 |
| Halibut | 18,144 | 15,876 | 9,525 | 8,618 |
| Menhaden | 782,908 | 833,256 | 817,835 | 1,132,632 |
| Salmon, Pacific | 148,326 | 185,975 | 91,626 | 278,508 |
| Clams (meats) | 32,205 | 44,906 | 51,256 | 43,092 |
| Crabs | 151,955 | 125,646 | 138,800 | 237,231 |
| Scallops (meats) | 10,433 | 4,989 | 6,350 | 13,608 |
| Shrimps | 110,678 | 166,470 | 157,398 | 154,223 |

*Source:* Adapted from *Statistical Abstract of the United States*, Department of Commerce, 1981.

## Productivity

As we have already seen, productivity and especially primary productivity, is highly variable from place to place and thus there is a kind of geographical lottery with regard as to which nation has poor marine biotic resources and which has good resources. Almost every nation with a marine coast will possess some fishery resources and a rather large percentage of these nations has a shrimp resource which, in today's international market place, is almost as salable as petroleum. Those nations favored by cool along-shore currents as are countries on the west coast and southeast coast of South America, the southwest and northwest coasts of Africa, and the east coast of southeast Asia possess marine biotic resources of importance. By contrast, the east coast of Africa and the coasts of the nations bordering on the Indian ocean, all but the southeast part of the east coast of South America, the Caribbean region, and the tropical Pacific, border on warm waters whose productivity is frequently modest and seldom productive of large biomasses of comparatively few fish species as is the case in cool waters. This last is often compensated, in part, by a high species diversity (more than 600 fish species have been recorded from the Bay of Panama, for example), but while this diversity may not hinder development of a commercial fishery directed to local markets it is often a decided hindrance to the development of specialized commercial fisheries directed toward export. Cutting across these generalizations are shrimp species that may occur in very large masses in warm as well as comparatively cool waters. In warm waters where there is an abundance of food as often is the case just beyond where rivers flow into the ocean shrimp populations may support important commercial activities.

One of the most productive of marine areas, if not *the* most productive area in the Third World region, lies along the west coast of South America. There, in the Humboldt Current, pri-

mary productivity is capable of supporting an enormous biomass of fish which, until a few years ago, was dominated by the Peruvian anchovy, *Engraulis ringens,* about which more will be said later. Cool waters along the shores of other nations also provide a part of the requirements for high productivity and all these areas have well-developed fisheries.

It is one thing, however, to speak of primary or secondary productivity in the general terms as has been done here and quite another to be able to determine what such productivity is in any given locale. As we have already seen, in the United States where fisheries biology has made many important advances, there remain serious difficulties with respect to the development of statistical techniques that will permit formulation of reliable estimates of the maximum allowable catch of a given marine animal. The problem is many times greater in most of the Third World because very little research on primary productivity has been done and the few investigations that have been made are seldom of sufficient duration to provide for the discovery of the variations that can be expected to occur and to identify the chief factors that influence the observed variations in primary and secondary productivity.

A person looking through bibliographies dealing with fisheries in the Third World might be led to believe that they have received the kind of attention just said to be generally lacking. A closer scrutiny of the publications, however, will reveal the fact that many of the studies were conducted to determine the approximate size of the biomass of a given species of animal and on the bases of those data assumptions are made as to what the size of the annual harvest might be. One usually searches in vain for information about what might be expected to happen to a given marine ecosystem if a given species is harvested at any given biomass level or quantity. The emphasis is usually on discovery of "underused" or latent fishery resources, the testing of various fishing gear and methods to determine the most efficient types, and analyses of the financial requirements of developing a particular fishery. In short, marine resources are frequently approached as though they were a nonrenewable mineral resource rather than a renewable resource requiring careful study before any large commercial fishing enterprise is developed. A lack of basic ecological perceptions is, unfortunately, all too often the hallmark of the literature dealing with the development of marine fisheries in the Third World.

This situation exists owing, in part, to the desire to increase foreign exchange earnings and in part to the long-established *raubwirtschaft* approach to resource exploitation in many of these nations.

## Foreign and Governmental Investment.

The lack of in-country capital to obtain modern boats and gear as well as modern processing plants has often led to foreign investment and occasionally foreign domination of Third World marine fisheries, resulting in a condition where there is a strong tendency for the foreign-owned boats and equipment to overharvest the resources. Governments have frequently found themselves unable to adequately enforce their laws governing the harvests. In recent years, the trend has been somewhat away from foreign domination and toward the establishment of government-controlled corporations that may allow private fishermen to operate albeit under tight harvest controls but to enforce government control in the international marketing end of the operations. Although not always operated as well as it should be, this move away from foreign control is a necessary first step toward creating the conditions wherein conservation and management of marine fisheries become possibilities. Sometimes there is conflict between a nation's marine scientists and the government agencies controlling the size of the harvest. A notable example of this was provided by Peru.

**ANCHOVIES, BIOLOGY AND POLITICS: THE PERUVIAN EXAMPLE** One of the most celebrated and controversial cases of conflicting views respecting what caused the collapse of a major fishery is afforded by Peru and the Peruvian anchovy fishery. Because this story is so illustrative of the many cross-currents present in virtually every major Third World marine fishery oriented toward export it will be described in detail here.

As noted earlier in this chapter, the cool waters of the Humboldt Current are able to support a high level of primary and secondary productivity. A major example of the latter has been, until recently, the enormous biomass of the Peruvian anchovy whose distribution extends beyond the 2360 kilometer long coast of Peru but was concentrated in the latter's waters.

Prior to the 1950s, this enormous biomass was a classic example of a latent resource in that it was scarcely touched by commercial fishermen, although it did serve as the food source for millions of seabirds and various species of predatory fish. Then in response to a rapidly growing world market demand for fish meal and fish oil for animal feed supplements, fertilizer, and various industrial uses, harvest of the anchovy began.

Beginning with a few hundred thousand metric tons per year the annual harvest rapidly grew exceeding 3.5 million metric tons in 1960, and, in the peak year of 1970, 12.3 million metric tons. This fishery took Peru from the status of a minor fishing nation to number one among the world's nations in terms of weight of the catch and provided Peru with large amounts of desperately needed foreign exchange since almost all of the harvest was exported (Fig. 10.11).

Almost from its inception the fishery was subject to governmental regulation and government officials, recognizing the need to have

**Figure 10.11** Haul of anchovies, Peru, prior to the collapse of the resource.

nomic pressure with the result that little effective restriction of the fishery actually occurred. The danger signals were there. For example, while the size of the annual harvest increased during the 1960s and up to the record year of 1970, the catch per boat and catch per man hour effort was declining, that is, more and more boats were catching progressively less per boat.

Disaster struck in 1972. In that year the normal water conditions were interrupted by a phenomenon called the el niño current (the Christ-child current because it occurs near Christmas) which took its swing southward along the Peruvian coast bringing, as it always does, warm water of lower productivity and creating a temporary but major shock to the normal equilibria of the coastal ecosystems. The el niño current has been the object of a number of studies because its advent has always been known to create biological havoc wherever it occurred. Unfortunately, the el niño current occurs at irregular and unpredictable intervals. There is nothing abnormal about the el niño current and it must be seen as a phenomenon to which the marine life in the region long ago adjusted. Perhaps a part of the adjustment was the extraordinary productivity of the anchovy in that this may have been the evolved behavior to assure survival during the incursion of the warm and nutrient-poor water (Map 10.3).

The abnormal condition was, of course, the enormous toll being taken of the anchovy fish resource. It is easy for nonbiologists to assume that any species with a large population is more or less safe from overexploitation. However, there is absolutely no biological law that large numbers always confer a biological potential that will permit recovery from sharply lowered populations. The 1971 catch slightly exceeded 10 million metric tons but the biological trouble signs were sufficiently evident in the form of sharply reduced numbers of eggs and larvae in the zooplankton as to cause the biologists to

sound biological data on which to determine management procedures, established the Instituto del Mar del Perú (The Peruvian Marine Institute) to conduct research. During the earlier years after the foundation of the Institute there was not always good cooperation between the biologists and the government and especially so when it was not infrequently suggested that the allowable harvest was greater than the stocks could bear if the goal was a sustained yield. Biological facts conflicted with eco-

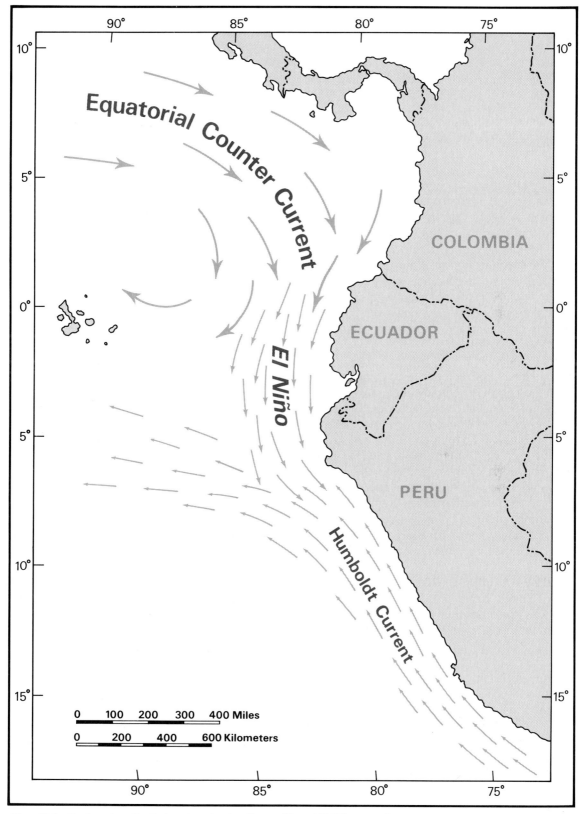

**Map 10.3**  Northwestern South America showing the position of El Niño current.

express alarm. Their alarm was justified for in the very next year the total harvest fell to about 4 million metric tons and continued the slide until the annual catch total resembled that of the first years of the fishery. An armada of boats and nets was capturing the last of the resource.

In December, 1978, the Instituto del Mar del Perú gave notice that continued fishing of anchovies could result in the extinction of the species. A furore quickly developed between the Instituto and the military junta ruling the nation. The public reason given for the furore was that the Instituto had no right to publicize its position but the real reason was the pressure on the financially strapped government to earn more foreign exchange. However, this time biology prevailed and a total ban on anchovy fishing ensued for 1978.

There remained, however, a large investment in boats and factories to be amortized and fishermen required employment as well as the workers in the fish meal factories. Therefore, intensive fishing for another species, the Peruvian sardina, was begun. In 1977, over one million metric tons of this sardina were harvested and converted to meal and oil. Will the anchovy recover to its former abundance? Will the sardina also be overharvested? These and other questions remain to be answered. But one lesson has been relearned: even the largest marine biotic resources have a harvest limit.

## SHRIMP—A LIVING GOLD MINE OF THE SEA

Before World War II, shrimp consumption was confined chiefly to areas not far from where they were caught and people living more than a couple of hundred kilometers from the coast seldom dined on these crustaceans. With the development and rapid diffusion of quick freezing technology it became possible to market shrimp very widely and particularly so in the United States where frozen foods gained a wide acceptance. This crustacean is relatively easy to prepare and is quite versatile being acceptable both as appetizer and en-

tree. The demand for shrimp boomed in the United States with the result that shrimp rushes akin to gold rushes began in the marine waters of virtually every nation where there was a possiblity of occurrence of a shrimp resource. Unfortunately, the mining analogy also extends to the manner in which these animals have often been harvested. An almost total disregard for basic research coupled with high harvest pressures have combined, in case after case, to produce overexploitation. World demand for shrimp has continued to rise and with it the price they bring and this tends, in the short run, to offset the economic effects of a diminished catch. An examination of shrimp fishing statistics will often result in discovery of shrimp fisheries where the annual harvest size has been trending downward but the dollar value has continued to rise. Early danger signals of overharvest of shrimp include declines in the average size of the shrimp being caught indicating that the most fecund younger individuals on which future harvests depend are being harvested instead of older less fecund individuals (the older shrimp also have slowed or stopped their growth and thus are no longer converting primary productivity to meat biomass), declines in catch per boat per hour and declines in harvest on a per-fisherman per-hour basis. It does not require a sophisticated education to perceive these danger signals, although it may take some training in statistical methods to demonstrate the mathematical validity of the perceived dangers.

To reiterate, shrimp fisheries in the Third World are so frequently overexploited because of the need for foreign exchange. This pressure conflicts with the requirements of how best to manage a fisheries resource. It is frequently all but impossible for biologists to be heard when the interests of government officials, entrepreneurs, and workers dependent on the shrimp catch conflict with moderate attempts to manage the shrimp resource.

Not infrequently, foreign capital is involved

in these fisheries and because of tax laws that allow rapid depreciation of boats and equipment there is frequently no incentive to take a long-range view of the shrimp resource because the greatest financial returns will accrue to the boats able to harvest the largest quantities of shrimp in the shortest time. Thus, from a financial point of view, the investment can be returned along with good profits before the resource collapses. Like a variation of a Ponti scheme, however, as more and more entrepreneurs are attracted to the fishery it is discovered that only the first on the scene reap a large economic reward and eventually the fishery, if pressures on it are not reduced, must collapse. When this latter occurs it is not unusual to read in the newspapers that the cause of the collapse is due to testing of atomic weapons, a mysterious disease, or by an act of God: anything but the fact that the fishery was overexploited.

Some argue that the difficulties that ultimately accrue to a Third World nation's fisheries when they are over utilized is a matter for only politicians and economists to worry about. Nothing could be more inaccurate. The loss of these fisheries is a loss of income to the citizens of these nations and a loss whose duration depends on the magnitude of damage done to a given fishery. Properly managed, these fisheries will provide food and income for a nation's citizens almost indefinitely.

**EXPORT OR FOOD AT HOME?**  In the opening paragraph of this section we asked whether a Third World nation ought first satisfy its protein needs before marine animal resources are allowed to be exported. This question has generally been left unanswered other than to suggest that it is a government's responsibility.

However, even if decision makers had all the facts, there would still be problems. Some fishery resources such as the anchovy are not presently widely acceptable as human food in the nations where the resource is harvested.

Other resources such as shrimp, are not widely consumed in the nations of origins because of its high price. The price of shrimp is partly a reflection of the world market price, but it is also a reflection of the fact that modern shrimp fishing techniques, while very efficient, are expensive and thus impose a relatively high cost on harvest activities.

In situations where the resource either is not acceptable as food or where it would be a costly luxury food whose demand would be far less than the (biologically) allowable harvest there could and should be an export of the resource. Shrimp therefore, could be converted to purchasing high-quality protein that is less expensive than shrimp.

## BEYOND THE 200-MILE LIMIT

In the oceans beyond the 200-mile limit now claimed by the world's nations is a vast "commons" over which there is little legal restraint with regard to harvests. The vastness of this area continues to give strength to the myth that equally vast biotic resources exist only waiting to be harvested. With few exceptions, most of the area is one of low productivity and thus offers no significant harvest opportunities. One important exception is whaling, discussed as follows (Map 10.4).

### Whaling

The first organized commercial whaling seems to have begun in the Bay of Biscay in the twelfth century. This was shore based and it was from the shore the whalers set out in row-boats to kill whales, which were then towed to land where they were tried (cooked) for their oil. The tongues were first removed, salt cured, and sold widely as a delicacy. The whale fishery gradually became one in which the whales were processed at sea and as local whale populations were overexploited, the fishery shifted northward until whaling was concentrated in the

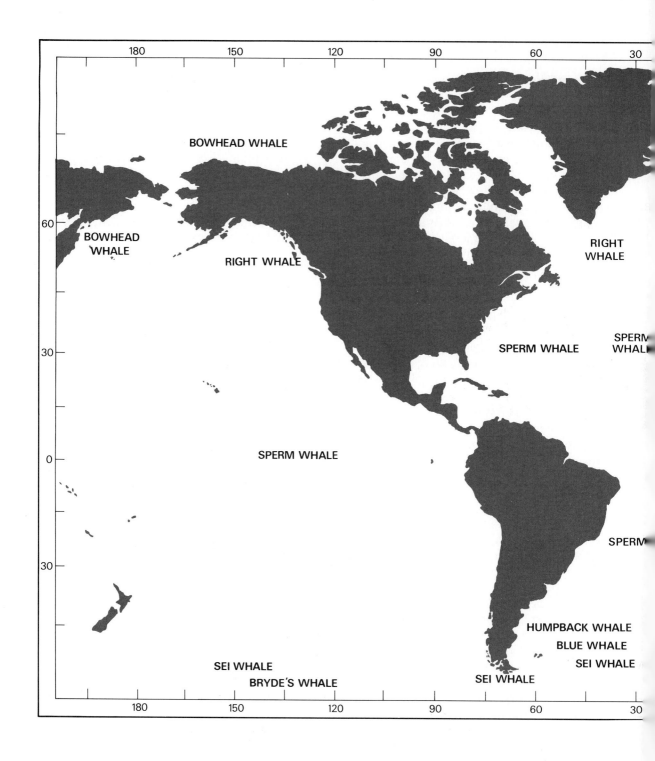

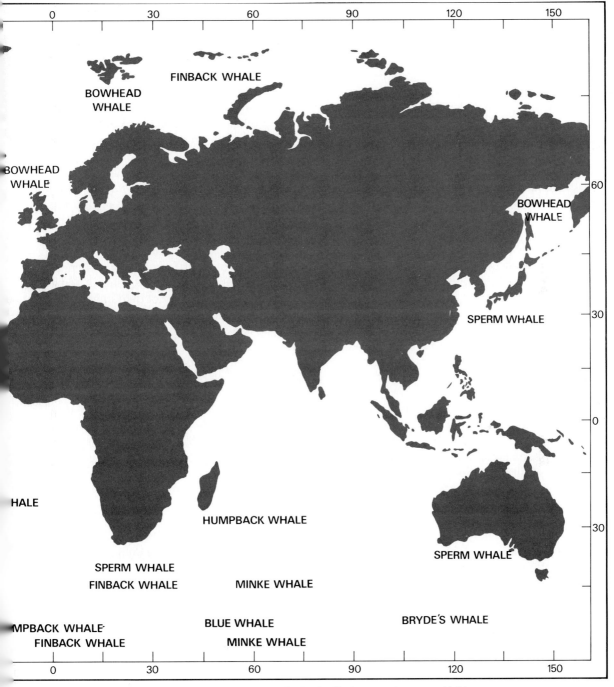

**Map 10.4** Past and present whaling grounds. Whale distributions as shown are highly generalized.

Northern Atlantic around the island of Spitzbergen.

A second commercial whaling complex began in the New England colonies. This was also originally a shore-based fishery but gradually ships were adapted to processing the whales at sea. This fishery, unlike the European fishery that was based on whalebone whales, came to specialize on the sperm whale so named because of the large quantities of clear oil—spermaceti—contained in the head of this animal. This oil is an excellent illuminant burning with a bright clear flame and, until cheap kerosene drove it out of the market place in the nineteenth century, was the most highly sought after illuminant then available. Sperm whale oil also has many unusual properties among which is its ability to retain its lubricating qualities under conditions of high temperature. Because of this and other properties, sperm whale oil was, until recently, a major component of automobile transmission fluid—but we are getting a little ahead of the story.

Returning to the European whale fishery, we discover that well before the end of the nineteenth century the arctic whale stocks had so diminished, because of overexploitation, that commercial whaling had declined sharply. For many years mariners had noted, in their log books, the presence of whales in far southern waters and thus in 1904 an antarctic whale fishery was begun.

The antarctic whale fishery employs fleets consisting of fast killer ships and factory ships on which the whales are processed. Aircraft are used for locating whales as are other mechanical aids. An important aspect of this fishery was its early focus on the blue whale, which until the invention (by a Norwegian) of the Svend Foyn harpoon gun, would not be taken because the blue whale like other members of its group (*rorquals*) sink when killed. The Svend gun employs a hollow but strong line connected to the harpoon. This is fired into a whale like a cannon, a small bomb in the head of the

harpoon explodes, killing the animal, and then compressed air is pumped into the dead animal via the hollow line blowing it up like a huge balloon thus preventing it from sinking.

Many nations have particpated in the antarctic and other whale fisheries in this century although for most of the time there was a predominance of Europeans.

During the early decades of the modern mechanized whale fishery there was no regulation of the catch size and each year in the Southern Hemisphere summer, there was an unrestrained rush to kill and process as many whales as was humanly possible. Although the main focus was on the blue whale, with annual catches exceeding 12,000 individuals in some years, other species were not disdained. Biologists, as well as some persons engaged in the whaling itself, began to express the fear that the whale stocks were being overharvested. This was largely an intuitive—albeit sound—judgment because almost nothing had been learned about the biology of these great mammals. However, because the judgment was largely intuitive in the early days there was little real effort directed toward control of the harvest. It was not until 1931 that the League of Nations (forerunner of the United Nations) agreed upon an International Convention (treaty) designed to limit the harvest of whales. Lacking any real authority to enforce the convention, however, it was ignored by the whalers. Later an International Whaling Commission was established for the purpose of regulating the annual catch. From its first meeting in 1949, this Commission sought to establish the allowable whale catch each year. The blue whale was chosen as the unit of measure and the total annual catch was given thenceforth in blue whale units until stopped because the blue whale no longer figured in the catch since it had become almost extinct (1 blue whale = 2 fin whales = $2\frac{1}{2}$ humpback whales = 6 sei whales). Each year the Commission presented its allowable catch and each year the whaling fleets of the nations signatory to the Convention proceeded to ignore it. The allowable catch was, by public admission, usually too high itself but represented an attempt each time to compromise biology with greed in the oceanic commons.

Not surprisingly, whale stocks declined under the onslaught and first one and then another nation withdrew from the fishery because of economic problems associated with the declining size of the whale stocks. Today, Japan remains the only nation with a major-sized whaling fleet—although minor whaling still occurs in some other nations. Thus, it is Japan that is presently the object of a worldwide campaign to "save the whale." This is somewhat unfair, because Japan did not become a major factor in the oceanic whale fishery in the antarctic until well after the major harvests had been made by ships belonging to the fleets of other nations.

Blue whale numbers have declined to the level where some biologists doubt that this species will be able to make a comeback. The reproductive rate of the blue whales is low and it may be that the remaining number is less than the threshold of the species' biological potential. The blue whale has been given complete international protection. It remains to be seen if this came too late to save the species.

Sperm whale populations have also suffered greatly and while the United States has banned all use of sperm whale oil this ban is not in effect in many other nations and thus a market continues for this animal.

Available data suggest that the stocks of all whale species that have been subject to harvest are very low and that a moratorium on all whaling should be instituted until such time stocks have recovered enough to support a carefully controlled harvest. Japan is presently strongly resisting any attempt to curb her whaling activities and in the absence of any international mechanism to halt that nation's whaling activity it is probably futile to complain

about it. There is the possibility that Japan cannot exert enough pressure on the remaining whale resource to seriously affect its future survival. There is no clear answer because precise whale population data are lacking.

It might be noted that one whale species, the grey whale, did make a comeback after becoming very scarce and then being given complete protection. Unfortunately, there is no way to determine if this rebound from a much reduced population would be typical of all whale species. We must wait and see and hope that in the meantime the whale harvest will be modest relative to the size of remaining stocks.

## Krill: A New Major Food from the Sea?

With the exception of sperm whales, the whales that are or were hunted in the antarctic ocean are krill feeders. Krill is an old whaling term for the many shrimp like crustaceans found in the cooler oceans of the world, with particularly heavy concentrations in the Antarctic. Now that humans have greatly reduced one of the major predators of krill it is being widely suggested that we replace the whales and harvest the krill ourselves for food and raw material.

The suggestion is not without merit in that preliminary explorations have established that in some places and at some times krill concentrations are large enough to be worth harvesting. There are some major problems that have to be overcome, including uneven geographic distributions in the horizontal direction, complicated diel movement that may allow for concentration in depths accessible to nets for a space of time and then movement to depths beyond the reach of presently available commercial gear, concentration of green algae, which give the animals an unappetizing appearance and odor, and a lack of reliable data regarding the true size of krill stocks. It is quite important that there be reasonably accurate estimates of krill stocks if they are not to be overexploited but present estimates range so widely that there is no sound data base for managing the resource.

Most of the harvestable krill occur in international waters and if whaling provides any useful example it may be that krill will go the same way as the whales if sufficient market demand can be developed. That it was Soviets who pioneered in the exploration of krill as a harvestable resource may not bode well for the future of these animals. The Soviet government has shown itself capable of the extremes of ruthless harvesting of marine resources virtually everywhere their boats have fished in international waters.

The ideal course to follow would be to establish an effective international commission to study krill and whose recommendations regarding harvest quantities would have the force of law. Progress in this direction is being made. In 1976 an international meeting was held at Woods Hole, Massachusetts, to evaluate what was known about the marine biology and natural resources of the southern ocean (Antarctic) and to suggest lines of investigation. That resulted in a program called Biological Investigations of Marine Antarctic Systems and Stocks (the acronym is BIOMASS). The first expedition was conducted during the Southern Hemisphere summer of 1980–1981.

One hopes that a new chapter will be written with regard to the use of the antarctic marine resources but one is also aware that unless every nation honors the regulations, however elegant they may be written, krill too may go the way of the whales.

## SUMMARY

Although the marine area is huge and far exceeds the total land area only relatively limited parts are sufficiently productive as to make them important locations for commercial-scale fishing. In addition, most of the long-established commercial fisheries are either being overexploited or are being used very close to the safe upper limits.

The principal locations of commercial fisheries are the neritic zones (continental shelves), estuaries, and limited parts of the oceanic zones. The chief controlling factors governing the size of the animal biomass are the availability of nutrients in conjunction with ample light to foster maximum primary productivity. These conditions occur most frequently on continental shelves and in estuaries.

Marine ecosystems are far more fragile than many people believe and this is particularly true of estuaries and the neritic zones. Even the oceanic zone, far removed from land, can be seriously impacted by human activities. One of the oldest and still most serious threats to marine ecosystems is their use as sites for dumping and discharge of all manner of wastes. This practice may have deleterious effects on marine life and make some of the animals unsafe for human consumption. The accidental or deliberate spilling of petroleum has emerged as a major source of environmental concern and especially so when this occurs in the biologically rich neritic and estuary zones.

The marine shore is an attractive site for the installation of nuclear power plants having large cooling-water requirements. Discharge of heated water back into marine ecosystems affects marine life by favoring species adapted to warm water but may be lethal to species that cannot tolerate the changed temperature.

Managing marine fisheries so as to prevent overexploitation of commercial species is a major goal but often difficult to achieve. Part of this difficulty lies in a frequent inadequacy of data but there are often political difficulties as well.

The United Nations Conference on the Law of the Sea has led to the establishment of a 200 mile-zone offshore in which each nation has sovereignty over the natural resources within the zone. In 1976 the federal Fishery Conservation and Management Act was passed in response to the establishment of the 200-mile zone and gives the federal government a new role in marine fishery management. This management role functions in the form of consortia between federal and state agencies. Although it is still too early to make an evaluation of this system it appears to provide the necessary framework in which conservation and management of our marine natural resources can best be achieved.

Many Third World nations have a marine environment as part of their territory but few of these nations have established even the rudiments of sound fisheries management procedures. In general, emphasis is placed on increasing the catch of exportable species with little regard being given to assuring that there will be fish to harvest in the years ahead.

Some observers have suggested that Third World nations ought to make strong efforts to retain animal protein for sale at home rather than to export it. This argument stems from the fact that most if not all Third World nations have large numbers of citizens who do not receive adequate animal protein in their diets. However, there are many cultural and economic problems preventing such a course of action.

With the establishing of the 200-mile limit, many Third World countries will be in a position, for the first time, to develop much needed fishery management programs. However, it remains to be seen if the opportunity will be seized or ignored.

Out beyond the 200-mile limit lies the great oceanic "commons," which has been exploited by many nations. The most common example is that of whaling. Since the beginning of commercial whaling in the Bay of Biscay centuries ago down to the present moment, whaling has been marked by repeated overkill and by a growing list of whale species hunted to the verge of extinction. In spite of many attempts to prevent this from continuing there has been only limited success. Whales provide us with nothing that cannot be obtained from other sources. Nevertheless it appears that they will be hunted until they become so scarce that economics rather than a sense of moral decency brings whaling to an end.

Can the oceans, that is, all the marine ecosystems, be saved from further degradation by humans? The answer seems to be "yes" for there are no technical limitations preventing this from being accomplished. If enough people in enough parts of the world demand the necessary changes we can alter the trend toward marine ecodestruction. Progress is being made in the United States. Other nations, as they become aware of the serious implications of using the oceans as dump sites or exploiting them without regard to the biological limits, should increasingly fall into line. However, this will not come about unless ceaseless national and international attention is drawn to the need to conserve and manage the world's marine ecosystems.

# wildlife conservation

## INTRODUCTION

One often encounters the term *wildlife* in stories dealing with one or another aspects of conservation. Although in wide use, the term has a rather imprecise application. Some persons employ the word to designate the mammals and birds that are sought by hunters and trappers while others construe the word to mean all wild birds, mammals, and other animal taxa. Some have included wild vegetation along with animals. It is not entirely clear as to when and by whom the term wildlife was first used but it seems to have come into general usage after the first decade of this century and was and is mostly employed with reference to birds and mammals sought by hunters and trappers. The latter application of the word has been the one most often employed by government agencies charged with "game management" as well as by many private organizations of hunters and conservationists. In this chapter, the term wildlife is applied to all animals—vertebrates and invertebrates—that are not strictly aquatic.

Including as it does such a broad array of animals, the term wildlife will be subdivided as follows:

Game birds.

Game mammals.

Furbearing mammals.

Nongame birds and mammals.

Vertebrates other than birds and mammals.

Invertebrates.

## HISTORY OF EXPLOITATION OF GAME BIRDS AND MAMMALS IN THE UNITED STATES

Prior to the arrival of Europeans in the region of what is now the United States, many native Americans (Amerinds) depended on the wild animal resource for food and hides. Hunting in this region dates back many thousands of years—possibly more than 30,000 years according to some investigators—and it was not until perhaps 4000 years ago that hunting was no longer the principal concern of *some* of the native Americans, these being tribes that had adopted agriculture. Even in these latter instances, however, hunting usually remained an important activity because there were no domesticated animals—other than the dog—that could supply meat. Given this long history of hunting and trapping one might expect that the game bird and mammal resource was reduced in abundance even to the level of actual scarcity. That, however, did not happen for when the first Europeans arrived they encountered an extraordinary variety and abundance of game birds and mammals. If there is a theme common to most of the reports of the early explorers it is the abundance of deer, bison, fur-bearing mammals, ducks, geese, quail, and other creatures of the hunt.

In the early years of European settlement, pioneers were too few and their firearms too inefficient to have caused very much impact on the game birds and mammals but with the passage of time, the number of Europeans increased as did also the numbers and efficiency of their weapons. One then begins to read accounts of people complaining about the local diminution in the abundance of deer and other animals—although the numbers still remaining might strike an observer today as representing abundance!

The early period of European settlement was marked by subsistence hunting with relatively little meat being sold. However, market hunting later developed and particularly adjacent to the larger settlements. Market hunting ultimately reached large and often alarming levels and was not brought under effective control until many years after independence from England.

Market hunting contributed to the eventual extinction of the passenger pigeon (*Ectopistes migratorius*) and led to the near extinction of that monarch of the prairies, the American bison or buffalo (*Bison bison*). Because these two animals represent many of the social and ecological aspects of unregulated market hunting in the United States their stories will be retold here.

## The Passenger Pigeon

Were one to select a single game bird to serve as an example of the extraordinary abundance of some animal species at the time of European entry into North America it would be difficult to find a better example than the passenger pigeon. This bird once bred in a vast forested region bounded on the west by the prairies, on the north by southern Canada, on the east by the Atlantic shore and as far south as northern Mississippi. Their total number from one year to another varied but some individual flocks were estimated to contain more than two million birds (Fig. 11.1). Migrating flocks, in some years, reached astonishing numbers and there are published accounts of flocks that "darkened" the sky. These high numbers did not occur every year and the records suggest a possible cyclic rise and fall in population numbers. Just what the principal factors controlling the reported population variations were are unknown and probably never will be determined.

It is known that Indians exploited this resource and rather heavily, and even destruc-

**Figure 11.1**   View of Fort Erie with migration of wild pigeons, 1804. A contemporary watercolor by Edward Walsh.

tively at times, but it appears that this exploitation was not sufficient to have seriously impacted the species' populations. Sometime during the nineteenth century market hunting of passenger pigeons began to assume a large scale. This hunting took place chiefly during the nesting season because it was at that time the birds were concentrated in large numbers in relatively local areas: some nesting sites encompassed many square kilometers and included an estimated two million or more adult birds. The dead birds were shipped in barrels by rail to the larger cities in the Eastern United States. Because of the huge numbers of birds destroyed each year it was long believed that it was this alone that caused the bird to become extinct. However, in more recent years, investigators have suggested that hunting was but one important contributing factor.

Perhaps the single greatest contributor to passenger pigeon extinction was the destruction of the forests on which the birds depended for food and nest sites. As is noted in the chapter on forests, tree removal to increase land available for agriculture took place on a large scale and this must have greatly reduced the habitat available to this bird. It has also been suggested that an epizoötic contributed to the extinction—an epizoötic being an animal disease that reaches epidemic proportions. Although there is little if any supportive evidence for this idea, attention has been directed to the incredible concentrations of birds in the nesting colonies and the fact that it is not uncommon for epizoötics to occur whenever there are very high concentrations of animals in a limited area. Of great relevance also to this question of extinction is the fact that these pigeons were usually slaughtered during the nesting season, which meant that not only great numbers of adults were killed but also nestlings starved in vast numbers and untold quantities of eggs in nests did not hatch.

Although it is important to recognize the possibility of multiple reasons for the extinction of this bird it is difficult, after looking at the record of the great slaughter and the massive reduction of habitat, to believe that human acts were not the root causes of the extinction that occurred "officially" on September 1, 1914 when the last passenger pigeon died in captivity in the Cincinnati Zoological garden.

## The Bison or American Buffalo

The bison (*Bison bison*), like no other large native mammal, characterizes, in the public mind, the once great abundance of game mammals on this continent. The principal geographic range of these animals was from near the shores of the Gulf of Mexico northward into Canada and perhaps into Alaska although there is controversy about the latter. On the east it almost reached the Atlantic shore and in the west, while concentrated on the grass east of the Rocky Mountains, bison were recorded from extreme north-east California and parts of eastern Oregon and Washington. It appears to have been totally absent only from Arizona and possibly Nevada. It extended south of Texas into a limited area of northeastern Mexico (Fig. 11.2).

There are many estimates of the population size of this animal at the time of the first European entry to North America, in fact there is what might be termed a special subgenre of wildlife literature in North America that has dealt, over the years, with the question "how many buffalo were present when the white man first arrived?" The figure most frequently encountered in scholarly sources is that there were approximately 60 million animals.

Before the European arrival, this animal was a stable resource for many of the Indian groups that shared the bison's ecosystems. Although the Indian hunter was skilled he did not possess the technical means to do more than modestly harvest the bison herds and there is only limited evidence that the Indians overexploited this resource in pre-European times.

**Figure 11.2**   Herd of buffalo (*Bison bison*).

The first bison seen (or at least recorded as being seen) by a European was a specimen or two in the zoological park of Moctezuma in Tenochtitlán, the Aztec capital (now Mexico City), in the early sixteenth century. Soon, other Europeans, chiefly Spaniards, exploring the southern United States, were encountering this animal in the wild.

Reduction of the bison herds began early after European settlers invaded the easternmost part of the geographic range of the ani-

mal. According to one authority, Martin Garretson, the beasts had become extinct in Pennsylvania by 1800. The same authority gives 1815 as the last known date for a buffalo in West Virginia and by 1825 the animal had become almost extinct in all of its former range east of the Mississippi River. The animals had been killed for the hides—called "robes"—for their meat and sometimes for their tongues, which were considered a delicacy. Another factor was habitat destruction principally caused by the conversion of grasslands to farms. It is also true that large numbers were killed simply because they were not tolerated by the farmers, bison being not only competitors for the available grass but they are also large and, to some people, frightening animals.

The wave of slaughter flowed westward with the tide of settlement and the movements of trappers and hunters. Large-scale commercial hide hunting had become well established on the plains prior to the Civil War. Because the hides are "prime," that is, in peak condition, only during the cold winter months it was also possible to ship varying numbers of tongues to market without much risk of spoilage. Buffalo meat too found its way onto the menus of many restaurants although it was often considered "gamey" in flavor and fetched only a modest price.

The extension westward of the transcontinental railroad west of the Mississippi River began in 1851 and although this marked a great beginning in developing a surface transportation net in the West it also marked the beginning of what is surely one of the most unpleasant chapters in the history of the wanton destruction of native North American mammals. What had already been overexploitation of buffalo now escalated into a mammoth slaughter. Hunters were hired by the railroad companies to provide meat for the construction crews and these hunters not only fulfilled the contractual responsibility but also shipped thousands of robes and tongues east to an eager market. The Civil War, 1861–1865, caused a temporary reduction in the slaughter but with the cessation of hostilities of man against man in the South the bison slaughter resumed on the plains.

The magnitude of the buffalo slaughter almost defies one's efforts to convey it. The carnage suggests a major war rather than the activities of hunters. Tons of rotting buffalo carcasses were left on the prairies during the winters because only the hides, tongues and some meat were recovered. Millions of robes existed in those years, yet today they are so rare as to be treasured collector's items.

After about three decades it had become evident to all but a few that the once great herds were no more and that the bison might be approaching extinction. Perhaps no individual was more effective in bringing this truth to public attention than William T. Hornaday. He published, in 1889, a detailed account of what had happened to the buffalo and pleaded for its total protection. By this time it was no longer very profitable to kill these animals although a few hunters remained, who, if not checked, would have soon accounted for the last living buffalo. There was also another group still making a profit, the bone gatherers. So great was the quantity of these bones that they were accumulated into railroad car quantities and shipped off to bone-meal factories.

Hornaday, and others, caught the attention of the federal government—almost too late. In 1894, the U.S. Congress passed a law giving total protection to the then remaining buffalo whose total number did not exceed 1000 animals. It was a stroke of luck that this number was not lower than the lowest critical number from which the species could recover, for recover it did although, as everyone knows, never to approach its former abundance. Today there is serious talk of ranching buffalo particularly on shrublands that have a carrying capacity too low to make them attractive for raising domestic livestock.

Beginning in the colonial era, market hunting for game birds and mammals was a widespread activity and only occasionally regulated to any effective extent. Such hunting was often necessary on the frontier before a reliable supply of meat could be produced by domesticated animals. Unfortunately, market hunting often continued long after the actual need for such meat had disappeared. Over the years commercial hunting techniques became more efficient, that is, more lethal. This is well illustrated by market hunting for waterfowl and deer.

During the fall and winter migrations of ducks and geese—as well as other water birds—market hunters would attract large numbers of birds to areas where the hunters had thrown grain. After the birds had gathered in such a place the hunters would fire what can best be described small cannons capable of killing, as well as wounding, hundreds of birds at a single firing of the piece. Vast numbers of birds were thus obtained for urban markets and probably equally large numbers were left to die after having been wounded and could no longer fly nor otherwise take care of themselves.

A favorite method of shooting deer was to attract them to salt put out for this purpose and then to "jack lamp" them after dark, that is, to use a bright lantern to blind the animals after which they were easily shot. Deer meat—venison—often appeared in butcher markets and was frequently offered for sale in restaurants.

Game bird and mammal populations cannot withstand unmanaged commercial exploitation and thus great decreases in the numbers of commercially hunted creatures became common and so alarmed biologists and others that eventually all commercial hunting (except trapping for furs) was brought to a halt in the United States. Much of this regulation was achieved only after some years had passed in the twentieth century.

Not all commercial hunting was for meat as has already been shown in the case of the buffalo. Trapping mammals for their fur was once an extremely important economic activity in North America and comprised a very important economic element in the pioneer period of this region. Although trapping continues today, it no longer even approximates its former importance. The abundance and distribution of many of the important furbearing mammals have been greatly reduced. On the other hand, that foundation of the early fur trade, the beaver (*Castor canadensis*), although no longer found in some of its former haunts, is doing very well and at

times becomes so numerous in some areas as to become troublesome (Fig. 11.3).

Other commercial hunting, now completely outlawed, was directed at certain birds for their feathers. During the late nineteenth and early twentieth centuries fashion decreed that women's hats be decorated with bird feathers and as a result enormous numbers of birds, usually during the nesting season, were shot for their plumes.

Another traditional aspect of hunting, subsistence hunting, must be noted here. Shooting for the "pot" is the oldest type of hunting anywhere. During much of the pioneer period being a skilled hunter was considered an important attribute. Often it was only through the skill of a hunter that meat appeared on the pioneers' table. However, as with market hunting, this type of game animal exploitation became less and less important as the production of domesticated animals increased. Nevertheless, a strong tradition of subsistence hunting in many rural areas of the United States has carried over to the present day. As long as this is conducted within the limits set by law it is a good use of game meat. Unfortunately, in some rural parts of the country some hunters believe that the local game belongs to the local inhabitants and can be taken whenever the locals choose to do so. During periods of unemployment or other economic stress the level of illegal hunting sometimes increases in rural areas.

Game management today is largely motivated by the view that hunting is chiefly recreational although it is recognized that the meat thus harvested is a welcome bonus of the hunt. For most urban hunters, the costs of hunting, which includes fuel, lodgings, weapons, ammunition, guides, and the like, are so high that there can be little thought that this is a cost-beneficial activity in the accepted economic sense.

Thus far the discussions have focused on game birds and mammals. This is appropriate because, until recently, it has been this group

**Figure 11.3** Beaver (*Castor canadensis*) and dam.

of animals that has received the major share of attention from wildlife managers and hunters. However, there are many species of vertebrates and invertebrates that have not been the object of the hunter but that have been affected by human activities.

One of the major concerns of American conservationists has long been that of the protecting rare species of birds and mammals. Among the birds, one of the earliest objects of concern was the California Condor (*Gymnogyps californianus*) (Fig. 11.4). To this might be added the whooping crane (*Grus americana*) (Fig. 11.5),

the ivory-billed woodpecker (*Campephilus campephilus* ssp.), and a number of other species. The condor and the whooping crane are still with us though probably not for long. The ivory-billed woodpecker may already have passed into the oblivion of extinction since it has not been sighted for several years.

More recently concern has been shown for animals that only a few decades ago were often considered not worth attention because they had no "no economic value." These include reptiles, amphibians, and many invertebrates—particularly certain species and sub-

**Figure 11.5**  Whooping Crane (*Grus americana*).

**Figure 11.4**  California Condor (*Gymnogyps californianus*).

species of butterflies (Lepidoptera). Many representatives of the just-named groups are very rare and have been given all the protection that the law can provide.

Other elements of the history of wildlife use, abuse and latter-day management in North America are the concepts *predators* and *pests*. These are related to one of the most controversial aspects of game management in North America.

Beginning with the earliest settlement by Europeans there was an all-out attack on virtually any animal species thought to be a predator of game or domesticated animals. A similar attack was mounted against species that competed, or appeared to compete, with *Homo sapiens* for his crops. Little if any consideration was given to the ecological roles that the predators played in the world ecosystems. Among the animals classified as predators were wolves and coyotes (Fig. 11.6), mountain lions (Fig. 11.7), bobcats, weasels, skunks, virtually all birds of prey and especially hawks, falcons, and eagles. Until recent years, many states and counties paid cash "bounties" for each predator killed.

Some states published "blacklists" of birds that were considered to be pests and these could be killed at any time and in any number. Some of these were introduced species such as the European sparrow and the starling but native birds were also included in such lists.

In the last couple of decades there has been a marked shift in traditional attitudes and today it is generally recognized that the predators and many of the so-called pests are to be protected if "desirable" wildlife and associated habitat are also to be properly managed. California, for example, no longer pays a bounty on mountain lions and this beautiful cat is now given careful protection. It is thought that around 600 mountain lions are needed in deer habitat throughout that state to help manage the deer herds.

Old ideas die hard, and it must be noted that some individuals and groups are not happy with the changing views of wildlife managers respecting predatory animals. At this writing, a very heated controversy is occurring in sheep-raising country in the West because many, and probably most, sheep ranchers are absolutely convinced that coyotes take a heavy toll of their herds and particularly of their annual lamb crop. There is no question that coyotes do take sheep and sometimes in such numbers as to represent a serious economic loss to the rancher. It is also known, however, that this condition does not occur everywhere in the sheep ranges and thus an all-out war against the coyote everywhere does not appear justified. Some cattle ranchers are of the opinion that coyotes kill many calves but, when pressed, at least some of these men and women will admit never having observed such a kill made and that it is likely that coyotes seen feeding on dead calves were eating animals that had died from some other cause.

Predators are natural parts of wild and many semiwild ecosystems and thus require the same careful study, attention and management as any other animals present. Traditional anthropocentric views respecting predators have no place in today's wildlife management.

## MODERN-DAY WILDLIFE MANAGEMENT

Although the kinds of animals considered to be a proper part of wildlife conservation and man-

**Figure 11.6**  Coyote (*Canis latrans*).

**Figure 11.7**  Cougar or Mountain Lion (*Felis concolor*).

**Figure 11.8**  Bobwhite quail (*Colinus virginianus*).

agement, as indicated earlier, have greatly increased over the early years of management, the focus is still on the species that are the principal objects of hunters and therefore, discussion will begin with game birds and game mammals.

## Game Birds

Game birds are frequently divided into upland game birds and waterfowl. The upland game bird species in North America are numerous and include native and introduced kinds. The most important native species are doves (*Zenaidura* spp.), bobwhite quail (*Colinus virginianus*) (Fig. 11.8), California valley quail (*Lophortyx californica*) and other quail species, band-tailed pigeon (*Columba fasciata*), woodcock (*Philohela minor*), and the turkey (*Meleagris gallopavo*) (Fig. 11.9). The most important exotic species include ringneck pheasant (*Phasianus colchicus*), hungarian partridge (*Perdix perdix*), chukar partridge (*Alectoris graeca*).

Waterfowl species are far more numerous than upland game bird species and little purpose will be served here to attempt to list them all. The species most frequently killed most years are mallard (*Anas platyrhynchos*), canvasback (*Aythya valisneria*), teal (*Anas* spp.), Canada goose (*Branta canadensis*), plus a few others (Fig. 11.10).

## Upland Game Bird Management

The principal object of management is to produce the largest possible harvestable crop of healthy birds. This is achieved by maintaining

**Figure 11.9**  Wild turkey (*Meleagris gallopavo*).

**Figure 11.10** Canada Geese (*Branta canadensis*).

and/or improving the habitat and this is accomplished through maximizing available plant cover for protection and the maximization of food, water supplies, and breeding habitat.

Such a management program, to succeed, requires that farmers, ranchers and other landowners cooperate by adopting practices that help to provide food and cover. Quail and bobwhite, for example, require an abundance of low-shrub cover and if this is not available populations will suffer. A farmer or a rancher can greatly enhance the numbers of these birds by taking care to allow a certain amount of brush to remain on his or her property and, where brush clearance is required, to pile the cut material in places not otherwise used. In many parts of the West water is often a serious limiting factor in what otherwise is good quail habitat. Fairly simple and inexpensive "guzzlers" can be constructed to provide a reliable supply of water where none existed previously.

Food can be increased by planting certain plants whose seeds are eaten by quail.

Pheasants and partridges, although exotic to the United States, respond well to good management practices. In the case of pheasants, little more is needed than large areas of wheat fields where the birds not only obtain cover but abundant food. The partridges have established populations in some of the most rugged areas in the nation and management consists chiefly of enhancing water supplies and, as with all game birds and mammals, carefully regulating the hunting pressure.

## WATERFOWL MANAGEMENT

Waterfowl management, like upland game bird management, has as its primary aim the production and maintenance of the largest possible healthy biomass of harvestable birds. This task is difficult to achieve with this group of animals because almost all the species are migratory and management requires international cooperation in order to be effective.

As indicated on Map 11.1, there are five principal migrational routes or "flyways" followed by migratory waterfowl in Central and North America. The breeding areas are located at the northern ends of the flyways and the southern ends are wintering sites where breeding does not occur. Although some of the southward migrating birds fly all the way to South America, it has been established that most of the migrating ducks, geese, and swans winter in Mexico. Thus, essentially three countries—Canada, the United States, and Mexico—must cooperate if there is to be effective conservation of these birds in North America.

Formal international agreement began in 1916 with the conclusion of a treaty between Canada and the United States. Mexico joined in 1936 and since then there have been various treaty revisions. Formulating a treaty that is sensitive to varied national needs has not been easy nor has the application of its provisions always been satisfactory in the eyes of all three signators.

Canada provides a considerable share of the breeding grounds as does the United States. Mexico supplies a wintering ground as also does the United States. Hunting seasons are arranged so that the birds are not shot during the breeding season. Thus, the legal hunting season occurs during the winter months. The breeding areas in Canada are increasingly characterized by reduced expanses of water and an increasing scarcity of food. In the United States, suitable breeding areas were formerly abundant but have decreased in number and area to a great extent during this century. The decreases have been due to agricultural development, water diversion for purposes other than waterfowl habitat, and the like. Wintering and breeding areas must have water sufficient to meet the needs of the birds. In the United

States both fresh and saltwater areas serve as sites for wintering waterfowl. In Mexico this is also true although saltwater is far more important than freshwater. However, even under the best of conditions, freshwater suitable for wintering waterfowl was not abundant in that nation and recent years have witnessed the reduction of such sites as land has been drained for agriculture.

Habitat and allowable kill are among the principal concerns of those engaged in migratory waterfowl management in the three-named countries. Of the two, habitat is the greater problem because hunting is extremely well regulated in Canada and the United States and, although leaving something to be desired, there is no major problem in Mexico with respect to the number of ducks and geese killed each year (although one sometimes reads press accounts stating the opposite). It must also be pointed out that the largest numbers of ducks and geese are killed in the United States each year. Maintaining waterfowl numbers, therefore, is to a very large extent dependent upon maintaining adequate habitat.

The problem of maintaining suitable habitat is present in all three countries. In Canada and the United States, the once great expanses of intermixed prairies and waterholes have shrunk dramatically as a result of "reclamation" for agriculture. Although this process has been most marked in the United States, Canada has by no means escaped it. The wintering grounds in the United States and Mexico have also suffered greatly. In the United States many freshwater sites have vanished or are drastically reduced in areas. Many salt marsh sites that once harbored huge flocks of wintering ducks and geese have been filled in for building space or are polluted. Similarly, in Mexico, what had always been a limited freshwater habitat is now much reduced in some instances, almost to the vanishing point. It is critical to the survival of millions of ducks and geese that adequate-saltwater areas in Mexico (and the United

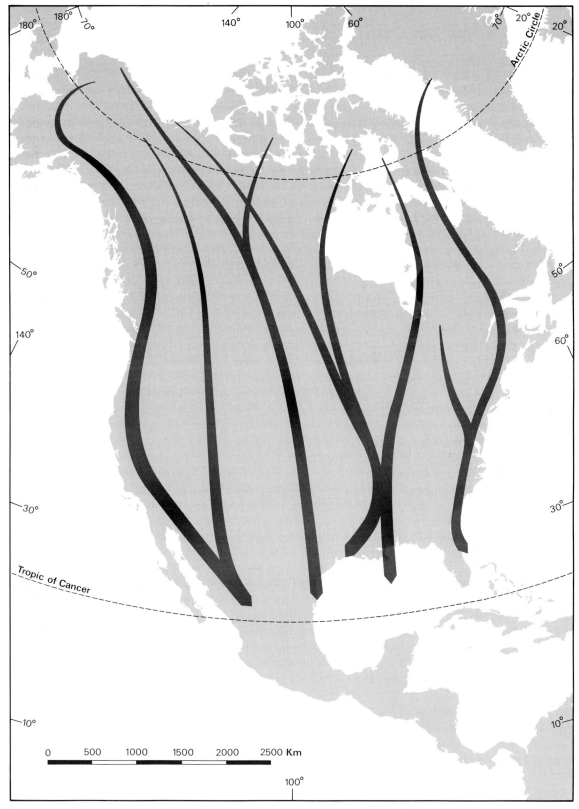

**Map 11.1** Principal flyways followed by migrating waterfowl in Canada, the United States and Mexico.

States) be managed for waterfowl. This sometimes conflicts with other interests such as petroleum exploitation along the Gulf of Mexico shore in southern Mexico and the Gulf coast of the United States.

It is not enough to provide habitat for the wintering birds. There must also be places where the birds are absolutely safe from the hunters guns at all times and, furthermore, these places ought to provide adequate food for the birds. The United States now has a fairly extensive system of wild-fowl refuges that are administered by a variety of local, state, and federal agencies. Although this collection of refuges looks impressive on a map of the United States it is, in fact, less than adequate for those birds that require marsh habitat for shelter, food, and breeding. Some ducks such as mallards and pintails, and some geese, take shelter in the refuges by day and invade harvested fields after dark to feed on grain that has fallen to the ground. These birds will survive for some time to come. However, many other species must have the food only the marshes provide and may have to go into nonprotected areas to get it and thus they suffer a higher kill rate.

Habitat, then, is the key that will set the limits to migratory waterfowl populations and thus the permissible kill. Misplaced sentimentality with respect to hunting may result in birds starving to death or being subjected to epizoötic episodes. As is so frequently the case over much of the world, humans must substitute for the predators that once helped maintain populations within the carrying capacities of available habitats. However, as suitable breeding and wintering habitats shrink, so too must the size of the allowable kill. This may appear self-evident but nevertheless eludes the understanding of many hunters who seek some other cause to account for the diminution of wildfowl numbers. Even if the total habitat area were maintained at the present level the annual allowable kill must fluctuate in response to the annual variations in habitat carrying capacity and reproductive success.

The economic value of sport hunting for ducks and geese, especially in the United States, is considerable amounting to many millions of dollars each year spent on guides, equipment, travel, and other related expenses. However, for those who thrill to a flight of ducks coming into a set of decoys, talk of the economics of hunting is irrelevant.

# GAME MAMMALS (GENERAL)

It is usual to divide game mammals into two groups: small game and big game. The species falling into one or the other categories tend to do so on the basis of tradition rather than by application of metric criteria.

## Conservation and Management of Small Game

The principal small game animals of the United States are squirrels, rabbits, and hares. In some areas, raccoon and opossums are important.

Squirrels occur in many parts of the United States but only certain arboreal species are generally considered to be small game. Ground squirrels, although abundant in many parts of the West, are seldom shot except as objects of pest control (Indians considered ground squirrels to be good food but this did not carry over into European hunting patterns). The most important of the arboreal squirrels insofar as hunting is concerned, occur in woodlands and forests east of the Rocky Mountains. Several arboreal species occur in the West but only one, the western grey squirrel, is hunted and only to a limited degree. The eastern species, the grey squirrel, now has available to it a much reduced habitat due to tree removal over the past several centuries but nevertheless has managed to survive and even to be fairly abundant in parts of its present range. As long as its habitat requirements are provided and hunting pressure is not too great these interesting mammals will remain a part of the sylvan—and urban—scene for a long time to come.

Rabbits and hares come very close to being ubiquitous in much of the conterminous United States. More exactly, rabbits occur in a wide range of ecosystems coast to coast while hares (*Lepus* spp.), are found mostly west of the Mississippi River (so-called jackrabbit) and the northern edge of the nation (snowshoe hare). Although hares are sometimes hunted for their meat, by far the greater hunting pressure falls on the native rabbits all of which belong to the genus *Sylvilagus*. And of all the species of belonging to the just-named genus it is the eastern cottontail (*S. floridanus*) that figures most importantly as a small-game mammal. Adaptable to many habitats, not too fussy a feeder and having a high reproductive rate—up to three litters per year—there is little danger of these creatures becoming scarce. Indeed, the chief problem of management is that they are sometimes cyclically more numerous than can be supported by the available food supply.

The raccoon (*Procyon lotor*), occurs in many habitats in the United States although the animal generally favors oak woods if such are available. These nocturnal carnivores are hunted for meat and fur although, judging from comments made by raccoon hunters, it is really the thrill of an after-dark chase led by hounds that is what this particular hunting is all about. Providing that adequate habitat is maintained and hunting pressure regulated this highly adaptable animal maintains its numbers very well. It adapts easily to urban environments and may become a pest at times by ripping off portions of roof to obtain a denning site.

Opossums (*Didelphis marsupialis*), North America's only native marsupial mammal, have long been well regarded by some rural folk in the southern United States. If an animal be captured alive, after having been "treed" by a dog, it might then be caged and fattened be-

fore being sacrificed for the pot. Although once confined to areas east of the Rocky Mountains, this mammal has been introduced into the Pacific coast region and is now well established in parts of California, Oregon, and Washington but is not much hunted in that region. So adaptive to human-modified environments is this mammal that it poses no problem for wildlife managers except that it may become a problem by eating the eggs and juveniles of certain wild birds.

## Conservation and Management of Big Game

The principal big-game animals of the United States are white-tail deer (*Odocoileus virginianus*), mule deer and black-tail deer (*Odocoileus hemionus*), pronghorn or antelope (*Antilocapra americana*), wapiti or elk (*Cervus canadensis* spp.), moose (*Alces alces*), mountain lion (*Felis concolor*), peccary (*Tayassu tajacu*), and bears (*Ursus* spp.) (Figs. 11.11 to 11.15).

As with the animals already discussed in this chapter, regulation of hunting and provision for proper and sufficient habitat are also the keys to conserving and managing the big game animal resource. Although the list of big game animals for the United States is impressive actually only three forms—white-tail deer, mule deer, and black-tail deer—comprise the major share of the total annual harvest by hunters. Of these three, the white-tail deer is the most important in terms of total biomass harvested. This is followed by mule deer and then the black-tail deer. White-tail deer are found chiefly east of the Rocky Mountains although they also occur in the Pacific Northwest. They favor moderately disturbed woodland and forested habitats where the preferred food is most abundant. This is a deer species that can actually profit from some human-induced disturbance of its habitat. White-tail deer are frequently found in areas where two or more ecosystems, mature or otherwise, blend into one another. Such sit-

**Figure 11.11**  Mule deer (*Odocoileus hemionus*).

**Figure 11.12**  White-tail deer (*Odocoileus virginianus*).

uations, termed *ecotones,* are so important for white-tail deer that it is sometimes called an "ecotonal species."

In some parts of the present-day range of white-tail deer the major problem is to keep its populations low enough to prevent starvation of the animals during the winter. It is absolutely essential to the well-being of many deer herds (whatever the species) that there be a harvest most years by hunters. Allowable kill limits are determined by making careful counts of the herds in districts to be hunted and an assessment of the condition of the carrying capacity of the deer range. One problem that must frequently be faced by the managers is that often too many females survive. The tradition of shooting only male animals (bucks) is so ingrained in the thoughts of American hunters that

**Figure 11.13**  Elk or Wapiti (*Cervus canadensis*).

**Figure 11.14** Moose (*Alces alces*).

it is only with some difficulty that they can be induced to shoot females (does). The doe problem might not exist were it not that humans have either destroyed or greatly reduced the

populations of natural deer predators over much of the white-tail range. It must be noted, in this context, that North American deer are polygamous.

Many people feel revulsion when contemplating the hunting of deer. Perhaps no other animal in the ethnozoological fantasies of modern-day Americans has such a hold on the public mind. This has been engendered in great measure by the work of animated cartoonists and the writings of certain authors whose efforts are directed toward children and even adults. Deer are frequently anthropomorphized in these productions and this tends to make the work of wildlife managers more difficult than it need be. It might be argued that animal cartoons in which animals speak and carry on more or less like humans has had a beneficial effect by stimulating interest in wildlife and wildlife conservation. However, it seems unlikely that this fantasy approach to wildlife can really provide the sound basis for public cooperation with the professionals charged with wildlife management.

## Fur-bearing Mammals

If this section were being written 100 to 150 years ago it would probably require a chapter all its own, so important was fur in the economy of North America at that time. As every student of American history knows, fur trappers opened up to exploration large areas of North America and furs, particularly beaver pelts, were one of the most sought after wild products on the continent. However, times and fashion change and although furs are still used for human garments and decoration, many of the pelts so employed are raised on so-called fur ranches where quality and color can be controlled. There is still a market for wild-trapped furs but nothing like it was in the past. Among the fur-bearing mammals that have figured in the American wild-trapped fur industry are beaver (*Castor canadensis*), mink (*Mustela vison*), muskrat (*Ondatra zibethica*), pine marten (*Martes*

**Figure 11.15** Collared peccary or javelina (*Tayassu tajacu*).

*americana*), fisher (*Martes pennanti*), wolverine (*Gulo luscus*), raccoon (*Procyon lotor*), otter (*Lutra canadensis*), wolf (*Canis lupus*), wildcat (*Lynx rufus*), lynx (*Lynx canadensis*), and bear (*Ursus* spp.). Trapping is done in the winter months when the furs are in their best condition or, as trappers say, prime. Trapping has long been and still remains a source of income for farmers but there is little organized commercial trapping today in the United States. In Alaska trapping is locally significant although individual incomes from this activity tend to be modest.

In recent years there has been moderate to significant rejection of wearing furs on the part of many people. Although the mink coat remains an important status symbol, such fur is mostly ranch raised and includes colors that only rarely occur among wild mink. Various synthetic fabrics having the look and feel of fur have made great inroads into the fur-apparel industry, thus greatly reducing the potential market for all but a few kinds of fur.

Management of fur-bearing mammals requires that attention be given to maintaining suitable habitat and restricting the annual catch to levels of sustained yield. Trapping pressure is seldom a problem these days and the famed beaver, once reduced to dangerously low numbers is now frequently so common as to become a local problem. The fisher, apparently always comparatively rare, is slowly recovering from what once looked like inevitable extinction.

## RARE AND ENDANGERED SPECIES

From almost the beginning of an identifiable conservation movement in the United States concern has often focused on trying to save rare and endangered species of animals. However, until quite recently such concern has usually been directed at only a single animal species at a time and often only a vertebrate that

seemed to command widespread public interest and sympathy (e.g., the bison). This narrowness of vision has changed markedly in the past few years and concern for rare and endangered species of animals now includes creatures that, in some cases, are known only to a relatively few biologists. Concern for animal life today includes many invertebrate taxa as well as vertebrate forms. This has sometimes stimulated derisive public comment and especially so when large sums of money and major construction projects are involved.

These who suspect that conservation is foolish sometimes appear justified—to themselves—when they read that a major effort is to be made to preserve a rare butterfly or a rare subspecies of salamander. However, quite aside from the moral question involved, there can be few ecologically informed persons who do not subscribe to the view that human-caused extinctions are usually not in the best interests of maintaining ecosystem viability. One reads often that extinction is a natural feature of nature—which is true—and that therefore human-induced extinctions are to be accepted as natural which they are not because all too frequently there is no replacement by another species. *Extinction with replacement* is natural but the almost random extinctions caused by the destructive acts of our species is an entirely different matter.

There is also the moral issue with respect to saving rare and endangered animals and it may well have been this concern that led the United States to enact, in 1973, the *Endangered Species Act* (and also to be signatory that year with many other nations to a convention sponsored by the International Union for the Conservation of Nature and Natural Resources, to control trade in threatened wildlife), which has been amended from time to time to include tighter restrictions or to shift an animal species from one category to another (Table 11.1). Many of the animals on this list are of no economic value and some are so rare that they occupy tiny

Table 11.1
**Endangered and threatened wildlife, 1981**

| Endangered Species | Mammals | Birds | Reptiles | Amphibians | Fish | Invertebrates[a] |
|---|---|---|---|---|---|---|
| World total | 256 | 210 | 68 | 13 | 44 | 36 |
| United States | 15 | 52 | 7 | 5 | 29 | 33 |
| | | | | | | |
| Threatened Species | | | | | | |
| World total | 24 | 3 | 12 | 3 | 12 | 6 |
| United States | 3 | 3 | 8 | 3 | 12 | 6 |

*Source:* Adapted from *Statistical Abstract of the United States,* 1981.
[a] Probably does not even approximate the actual numbers.

areas scarcely larger than a large urban lot. As has been indicated earlier in this book, humans do have a moral responsibility for the living things around them, such responsibility being part of the price of being a reflective primate that has achieved ecological dominance in most of the world. Just because our fellow creatures have traveled along evolutionary pathways different from our own does not give us license to treat them with disdain and carelessness. All life must command human respect or no life will command human respect.

## URBAN WILDLIFE

It may appear strange to have a topic heading of urban wildlife but a moment's reflection will perhaps show that it is appropriate. Most Americans, some 75 to 80 percent, live in urban areas and only a relatively small fraction are able to leave the city for the countryside except on rare occasions. If all wildlife were confined to nonurban areas this would make for a dreary urban environment. Fortunately, however, most if not all urban areas do have wildlife and sometimes an extraordinary range of species.

Parks, of course, are obvious places to see many bird species and even such densely populated areas as New York City boast parks where resident and migratory birds can be seen. Mammals—other than dogs and cats—

are rather rare in many cities although in Los Angeles, for example, deer, coyotes, gray foxes, skunks of two genera, ground squirrels, woodrats, and other native rodent species as well as rabbits and hares are sometimes abundant within certain parts of the city where habitat conditions are suitable. Reptiles and amphibians frequently manage to find urban areas suited to their needs and may be more abundant than many persons realize. Invertebrates have managed rather well in our towns and cities some of which we could perhaps do without. One of the most delightful of the invertebrate groups is the Lepidoptera (moths and butterflies) that grace gardens and parks and respond with increased numbers if their nectar plants and food plants for their larvae (caterpillars) are made available.

Until now there has been rather little attention given to the management of wildlife in our urbanized areas but this neglected subject deserves to be given more recognition than it has received.

## WILDLIFE CONSERVATION PROBLEMS IN THE THIRD WORLD

Although virtually all parts of the world have animal species that are rare and or endangered, it is in the Third World that these conditions loom greatest in terms of total species involved. Why is this the case? Many reasons can be identified but three are outstanding: (1) most of the Third World countries lie in the low or tropical latitudes where animal species diversity is very high, (2) rapid human population growth is affecting habitats resulting in widespread forest destruction or practices that tend to reduce wild animals in favor of farming and livestock, and (3) there is often strong international demand for wild animals and parts of wild animals (e.g., hides and horns).

Of major concern at present to the international fraternity of biologists is the likelihood that human-caused extinctions in the moist tropics is already occurring at a fairly high rate and actually may be accelerating. No one has devised a precise estimate of the numbers of animal species and subspecies that are disappearing month by month but the general consensus is that the rate is high enough to be a very serious matter. Most of these are extinctions of invertebrate animals.

In the popular mind, the greatest concern regarding animal extinctions is directed toward species of vertebrates and especially the larger mammals and more colorful birds. More than one international organization (e.g., the World Wildlife Fund and the International Union for the Conservation of Nature and Natural Resources) fashion much of their public appeal for funds around this widespread concern for the larger wild animals.

Most of the concern for wildlife protection comes not from inhabitants of the Third World nations (although there are persons in those nations who are vitally concerned) but from persons living in the industrialized nations. This results in some problems that all too often are either ignored or dismissed as unimportant. Specifically, it is the perception of more than a few educated citizens of the Third World that the developed nations, having reduced their own wildlife to what are often little more than remnant populations, now wish to turn large parts of the Third World into giant zoological parks.

Why, from the viewpoint of a citizen of Kenya, for example, should that nation expend great effort and expense to maintain herds of wild animals? The only argument that can be expected to have widespread and lasting acceptance is an economic one (e.g., to attract tourists). Appeals based solely on esthetic arguments are likely to be acceptable to only a few persons.

The government of Kenya has come to appreciate the economic value of big game animals as an attraction for tourists. Kenya, being particularly poor in many natural resources (e.g., fossil fuel, hydroelectric potential, and many metals), sees wildlife as a renewable resource that can attract, almost indefinitely, tourists with "hard" currencies from many parts of the world.

However, Kenya's government must contend with some of its citizens whose views are not particularly sympathetic to the development of this tourist resource. Some of these persons argue that it is undignified for a modern country to be dependent on tourists for its economic well-being and add that an influx of tourists also means an influx of ideas that may not be compatible with African cultural ways. Others argue that it is undignified for a country to maintain large zoological parks for the amusement of tourists and that such areas are better used for grazing livestock or crop production. As though these conflicting ideas were not enough to contend with, there is wide disagreement as to how the wildlife resource should be managed even if it be agreed that its highest economic use is to attract tourists. Thanks, to a large extent, to the sentimental anthropomorphization of animals by many western animal lovers the task of properly managing wildlife in some parts of Africa, and most notably Kenya, is made more difficult than it should be. A case in point is the elephant population in Tsavo National Park in Kenya (see chapter twelve). Although the female African elephant has a rather long gestation period—approximately 22 months—and a cow usually produces only one calf at a time, this animal nevertheless has the reproductive capacity to exceed the carrying capacity of almost any local area. In times past elephants were almost always on the move, seldom remaining long enough in a given locale to become environmentally destructive. The growing human presence in Africa assures now that this freedom to wander is no longer possible. Thus, if elephants are to be confined to park areas their numbers must be kept in check lest they do great damage to the parks and thus to themselves. The fight between the informed wildlife managers who correctly perceive the need to kill a certain number of elephants each year in order to protect the elephants as well as the park has collided with the sentimental—and non-African—view that killing elephants is a high crime.

In Africa, as in many other situations in the world, humans must assume the role of predator and/or population controller. Misguided sentiment only results in greater environmental destruction and often a threat to the continuance of the very species the people seek to preserve.

It is obvious that most of the stimulus for African wildlife protection originates from sources outside the continent. It would seem to follow that since it is foreigners who want this preservation it is foreigners who ought to pay the not inconsiderable economic costs that are often involved. Yet, in most of the international appeals for funds to save this or that species of animal one never sees included the costs of paying farmers for not increasing the area of their crop lands or herders their area of pastures.

All of the world's developed nations now recognize the need to supply monetary aid to Third World nations but almost no recognition has been given to the need to subsidize the efforts required to preserve endangered animal species. This can be an expensive business and, as the Third World finds itself in difficult finan-

cial conditions related to rapidly growing populations and soaring bills for imported energy, it is naive to expect that they will wholeheartedly expend scarce monetary and other resources for the protection of rare and endangered species.

A major thrust of the International Union for the Conservation of Nature and Natural Resources has been the curtailment of international trade in wildlife. This is a worthy effort and merits support but it should be realized that some of the species of animals protected by international conventions governing the trade in wildlife are species that, if properly managed and harvested, could be a renewable source of income in parts of the Third World. Seen not through the eyes of a Westerner devoted to saving the wild animals but through the eyes of a local Kenyan, for example, those international conventions may appear as one more example of imperialistic big-brotherism. Thus, all too often ways are found to ignore the law and an illegal trade in wildlife flourishes. This is certainly the case in Kenya where all hunting was made illegal. The result has been to increase the number of illegal hunters, involve more people in corrupt practices, and a furthering of contempt for efforts designed to protect and manage the wildlife resource.

Unless and until the common people are consulted and made to feel a part of wildlife conservation and management in most Third World countries, there may be scant time left for the survival of wild animals in such nations.

## SUMMARY

The first colonists in what was to become the United States of America encountered such a wealth of game birds and mammals that the myth of limitless animal resources was early established and long persisted before being put to flight. The colonial experience was reinforced during the process of the nation's westward expansion for, repeatedly, incredible numbers of animals were encountered.

Market hunting plus trapping of fur-bearing mammals were present almost from the inception of the colonial period and were to continue for many decades and, with regard to trapping, down to the present day. Given the reckless abandon that characterized many decades of hunting in the United States it can only be seen as remarkable that far more species did not become extinct or were brought to the edge of extinction than has proved to be the case. Extinctions have occurred, such as the passenger pigeon that once was counted in the millions and near extinction as for example the bison.

Market hunting was still widely allowed in the early years of this century but is now outlawed in all states. Trapping for wild fur-bearing mammals is still conducted, albeit under strict legal controls, but this activity is of minor economic and ecological importance today.

The chief interest in most wildlife management programs today is the maintenance of the largest possible stocks of game birds and mammals, that is, species that are sought by recreational hunters. Although these efforts, by and large, have been successful, it is unfortunate that so much emphasis has been placed on the narrow spectrum of animal species hunters seek rather than on the entire range of animal species. This situation is undergoing a change, albeit slowly, as a new generation of wildlife managers trained in the concept of the ecosystem perceive that all animals and their affective environments require management attention.

Although most game mammals are managed on a state-by-state basis as is also true of upland game birds such as quail and doves, migratory waterfowl fall under the legal control of the federal government. In turn, the U.S. government is signatory to an international treaty, along with Canada and Mexico, which appor-

tions responsibilities among the three nations vis-à-vis hunting seasons, species, and kill limits permitted. Unfortunately, there is no provision to assure that adequate waterfowl habitat will be maintained, and the growing reduction of suitable habitat is seriously affecting the populations of migratory waterfowl.

Ought there be a major reduction or even cessation—for a time—of duck and geese hunting? Certainly, the animals so obtained do not serve any significant dietary need because they cost far more to shoot than an equal amount of meat costs in the market. However, hunters are well organized into national groups possessing considerable political power—a fact that must be considered when discussing conservation and management of migratory waterfowl.

In keeping with the growing public awareness that humans have a moral responsibility to all forms of life, federal legislation (and much state legislation as well) has recently been enacted to protect rare and endangered species of animals and not only those that might seem most obvious but also insects, fish, reptiles, plants—in short virtually all forms of life that seem to require protection if they are not to become extinct through human actions. The nation seems to be adopting the premise that all life must command respect or no life will command respect.

Third World nations often find it extremely difficult to conserve their wildlife and especially those species for which there is a commercial—often international—market. Many types of hides, horns, and other animal parts are eagerly sought after much to the detriment of the affected species. Increasingly, nations are passing legislation designed to halt this traffic but as long as a market exists the slaughter will continue. Among the areas most seriously threatened are the Amazon basin, tropical African countries, and parts of southern Asia.

Looking over the world at present, there seems to be a race on against and toward extinctions of a great number of animal species many of which are known only to a few biologists and many totally unknown. Running in the race is a growing international commitment toward respect for life in all of its forms but the frontrunners are human population growth, human ignorance, and avarice. Which one will win? Unfortunately, no matter the outcome of the race, the world will at best become poorer by dozens and perhaps thousands of species now living on it.

# parks and preserves

## INTRODUCTION

Many people when asked what they think is the chief object of conservation will answer by saying it is to set aside parks and preserves for the preservation of wild nature. No other aspect of natural resource conservation commands the widespread lay interest that parks and preserves do and it is not surprising that it is also this aspect of conservation that seems to most frequently arouse the strongest emotions and most disparate assemblage of concepts and views.

The idea of the park (however defined in actual practice) is so generally held to be a desirable attribute of civilized society that few persons will openly oppose the establishment of a given park since to do so may seem tantamount to casting aspersions on the basic values of society.

Yet, when one examines various issues relating to park formation, including something so basic as a working definition of what a park or preserve is, one often comes away with a sense of some confusion about the phenomena that we call parks and preserves. It will aid our understanding of some of the problems of definition and concepts if we take a brief look at the history of parks here and in other parts of the world.

## HISTORY OF PARKS

Insofar as Western traditions are concerned, the idea of setting aside a piece of land to which there could only be limited access and limited use seems to have first occurred in the Middle East many centuries ago. It may be that it was the Assyrians who first implemented the idea of the park and their concept of such was to be more or less the standard until fairly recent times. That is, a park was an area set aside for hunting by a limited number of people belonging to the ruling elite. Such parks may have been the response to a growing scarcity of game animals for otherwise there would have been little reason for the creation of such entities. The park-as-hunting-preserve for the elite came down through centuries little changed and are what we would today call hunting reserves.

Relatively detailed records of parks in England date back to the time of the Saxon invasion (1066). William the Conqueror was an avid hunter as were many if not most of the men of that day since hunting was generally equated with virility and prowess in battle. This association of male prowess—machismo—continues, in many parts of the world, to be a potent element in maintaining hunting as a sport. This is not to say that women did not also engage in hunting but for centuries it was not considered a proper activity for ladies to hunt other than small game or to take part in what were little more than carefully staged ritualized slaughters. In the latter instance, hunts for large mammals were arranged so that the beasts would be driven near to where women sat as spectators and in front of whom the animals would be killed—by men.

In English law, a park had the specific meaning of an enclosed area in which the game belonged to the king who could permit its being hunted by others if he so desired. A forest was a similar area but, unlike a park, possessed a staff charged with its maintenance. A chase was a hunting ground not bounded by fencing. Hunting within a chase might be done by someone other than the owner of the land. Over the years these and related terms have tended to lose their preciseness of meaning so that today, in England, the term park is employed to include a variety of lands set aside in whole or in part for many reasons other than hunting.

After the passage of centuries during which parks—however defined—were the recreation grounds of the powerful, a new trend developed whereby such parks were presented to the public. Among notable European examples of this largess is the great *Parque Retiro* of Madrid and the *Bois de Boulogne* (Fig. 12.1) of Paris. In both instances, the parks were the former playgrounds of royalty. In similar fashion, English royalty has turned over to the public a number of formerly private parklands.

The United States, lacking both a tradition of royalty and a tradition of private hunting preserves, came to the establishment of parks by somewhat different pathways. The park type for which this nation is best known is the national park and so discussion will begin with that (Map 12.1).

The first national park, Yellowstone, was set aside by an act of Congress in March 1872 (Fig.

**Figure 12.1**   The Bois de Boulogne, one of the major urban parks of Paris, France.

12.2). Roderick Nash, a historian, has shown that the original idea for Yellowstone Park lay not in the desire to preserve wilderness per se but principally to protect the spectacular geysers for which the park is still well known. It was only later, after the official founding of the park, that its wilderness attributes came to be widely known and appreciated. Part of the language of the Act setting Yellowstone aside has a peculiar beauty: "(the park is set aside) as a public park or pleasuring ground for the benefit and enjoyment of the people." Specific lan-

**Figure 12.2** Yellowstone National Park.

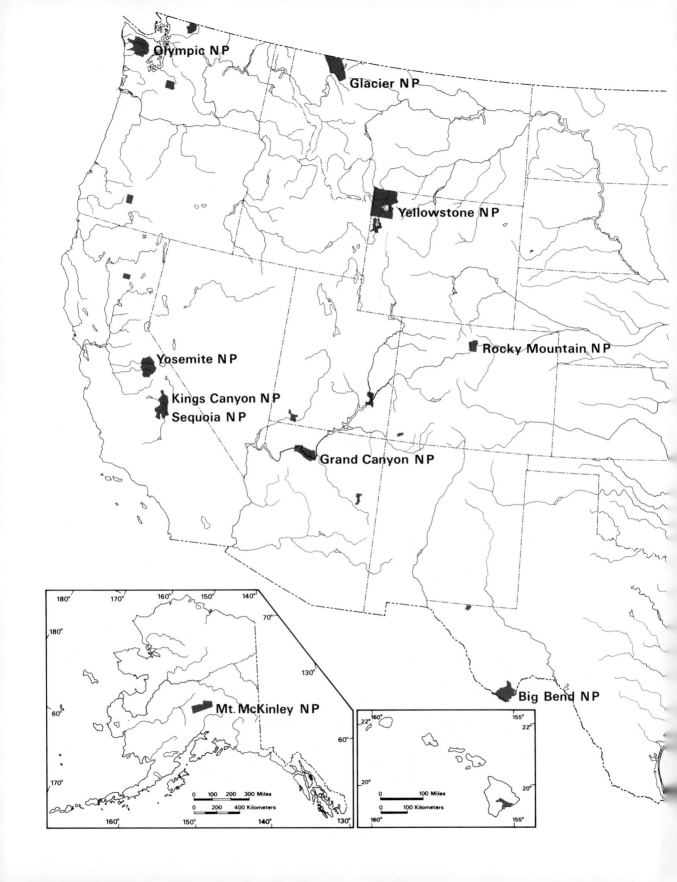

**Great Smoky Mountains NP**

**Everglades NP**

| 0 | 100 | 200 | 300 | 400 | 500 Miles |

| 0 | 200 | 400 | 600 | 800 Kilometers |

**Map 12.1** National parks in the United States.

guage was included to assure that all features were to be preserved in their natural condition, which leads one to conclude that a person or persons involved in drafting the Act thought beyond the geysers. As historian Nash pointed out, however, there was widely varying opinion as to just what functions the park would serve and to what degree tourist facilities should be developed within the park. Furthermore, not everyone was happy with the notion of withdrawing so much land from public development. One extraordinary feature is that more than 100 years later this remains the largest national park in the conterminous United States (888,708 hectares or 2,221,773 acres).

As more national parks were established, it became necessary to increasingly formalize their management, which in the earliest period was the responsibility of the Secretary of the Interior. Thus, in 1916, the National Park Service was created and made a part of the Department of the Interior. The Park Service—as it is generally termed—has the responsibility of managing not only the national parks but also all other designated federal parks that include, besides the national parks, national monuments, national recreation areas, national seashores, national lakeshores, national preserves, natural areas, national military parks, national battlefield parks, national memorial parks, national historic sites, national memorials, national parkways, and national capital parks.

An especially significant piece of federal park legislation, the Antiquities Act, was passed in 1906. This act permits the president of the United States to establish national monuments by decree thus avoiding the possible pitfalls of congressional approval. This act allows the president to act quickly to save, from commercial exploitation, areas that might otherwise be lost to the nation if the more leisurely congressional legislative route were followed. The degree to which presidents have availed themselves of this act has varied considerably since

its passage. From 1906 through 1940 a total of 60 national monuments were established (not including those which later became national parks). From 1941 through 1978 a total of 30 such entities was declared. However, the largest number of national monuments ever established was declared in 1978 during the presidency of Jimmy Carter who set aside as national monuments the following areas in the state of Alaska: Gates of the Arctic, 3,818,624 hectares (9,432,000 acres); Noatak, 2,348,178 hectares (5,800,000 acres); Wrangell-St. Elias, 4,827,125 hectares (11,923,000 acres); Denali, l,616,599 hectares (3,993,000 acres); Lake Clark, 1,186,235 hectares (2,930,000 acres) plus a few others. In 1980, The Alaska National Interest Lands Conservation Act changed the status of the above to other categories but all are administered by the National Park Service.

Major federal park legislation occurred in 1964 with the passage of the Wilderness Act. This represented the culmination of efforts that can be measured in decades although it was only from 1957 onward that serious legislative efforts developed. The Wilderness Act makes permanent all the wilderness, wild, and canoe areas that the U.S. Forest Service had so classified a month or more prior to the passage of the Act. The Act also allows the National Park Service to set aside as wilderness areas pieces of land of 5000 acres (approximately 2000 hectares) or more that do not yet have roads through them or in them. The purpose of the Wilderness Act is to preserve the "primeval" natural conditions of an area designated as wilderness, that is, an area that: "(1) generally appears to have been affected primarily by the forces of nature, with the imprint of man's work substantially unnoticeable; (2) has outstanding opportunities for solitude or a primitive and unconfined type of recreation; (3) has at least five thousand acres of land or is of sufficient size as to make practicable its preservation and use in an unimpaired condition; and (4) may also contain ecological, geological, or other features of scientific, educational, scenic, or historic value."

Other provisions of the Act, however, leave open the possibility of disturbances this being where such uses as grazing, and mining rights were established prior to the passage of the Act. It remains to be seen how easy or how difficult it will be in the future to weaken the intent of the Wilderness Act. Its passage through Congress was sometimes marked by bitter controversy most of which came from the commercial community, which saw future opportunities for resource exploitation being sharply curtailed. There were also arguments to the effect that too much land was being frozen into preservation that could only be enjoyed by a small number of our citizens, that is, those who like to camp and partake of the pleasures afforded by wild areas. This latter argument must be given consideration for it is a fact that very few persons will enjoy such areas firsthand. It would seem then, that justification for the preservation of wild areas must also include their scientific value as is included in the language of the Act. However, quite valid criticism has been leveled as to the actual scientific use that has been made of the already existing national parks. The justification for setting aside parks and preserves often focuses on their scientific research value but surprisingly little work of such nature has as yet been done.

Perhaps the best justification for setting aside wilderness areas as well as national parks and all other areas of preservation is that we have a moral responsibility to do so. There are those who would challenge this position by saying that it is based on personal values and is therefor invalid. But isn't such an argument weak and of little merit when it is realized that much of the "glue" that holds any society together and makes life worth living is composed of values.

The National Park Service is not the only federal agency charged with the responsibility for the management of parks and preserves. The other agencies are The Fish and Wildlife Ser-

vice (Department of the Interior), Bureau of Land Management (Department of the Interior), Forest Service (Department of Agriculture), Bureau of Outdoor Recreation (Department of the Interior), and Department of Defense.

The greatest surprise on the above list may be the Department of Defense. Although the principal mission of that Department relates to military matters it does have under its control approximately 12 million hectares (30 million acres) and the several branches of the military follow programs and procedures designed to protect the environment including identification and protection of officially designated endangered species of plants or animals. Some parts of the lands controlled by the Department of Defense are made available to the civilian public for recreational use if such does not compromise military needs.

## Other Parks and Preserves

Although dominant in the realm of parks and preserves, the federal government is by no means the only entity that has been active. States, counties, cities, and other agencies have also played and continue to play important roles in the establishment and management of parks and reserves. Virtually every state in the United States has at least one State park. Nationwide there are county parks by the hundreds and city parks must number in the thousands. There are also "natural" areas that have been set aside by universities for preservation and study. One such is the Natural Land and Water Reserves System of the University of California. This system presently includes various examples of wild ecosystems native to the state. They have been acquired by a combination of gifts and matching grants from foundations as well as a limited amount of funds from the state of California.

Most state parks are for the purpose of providing outdoor recreation for the public and while there are often restrictions as to the environmental disturbances allowed the parks are generally too small to serve any preserve function. These parks are often located in places where urban populations can reach them easily and thus serve a very important recreational need. During the summer months, many such parks are continually utilized to the limits allowed resulting in conditions not unlike those the people were ostensibly attempting to escape.

County parks are are almost entirely of the picnic—sometime camping—type and their public use is often very heavy. Such parks may include or retain some natural features of vegetation and wildlife but often these are minimal.

City parks range widely in size and contained features. It is interesting that two of the largest city parks, Central Park in New York City and the Golden Gate Park in San Francisco, are located on sea coasts. Los Angeles, California, also can boast of a large park, Griffith Park, but very much of the area is in steep terrain and brush and therefore not available to most people. However, unlike Central and Golden Gate parks, Griffith Park contains an impressive collection of plant and animal species native to the chaparral vegetation.

Most city parks are fairly modest in size and some are very small ones referred to as "vest-pocket parks." The latter may occupy a site that is smaller than the area of a standard city building lot.

## PARKS AND PRESERVES: OBJECTIVES FOR ESTABLISHMENT

During the latter part of the nineteenth century when our nation was passing rapidly from a land with a western frontier to a land that was almost totally under human control it became evident, as we have already seen, that unless something of the natural lands was saved none would remain in a few years. Thus, the varied intellectual streams of environmental concern tended to come together in a feeling of urgency that the principal requirement was to save representative or unique natural areas from commercial exploitation. This sense of urgency has been the chief stimulus down to the present day—and although it has served its purpose well—some of the strongly held assumptions are now coming under scrutiny by the scientific community. This is not to suggest that we ought not to have saved what has been saved, but it is to assert that henceforth more ecological reasoning must accompany efforts directed toward the establishment and management of all "natural" parks and preserves.

To begin, we still do not have an adequate understanding of the ecological status of many and probably most of our federal parks and preserves. This situation derives from several factors of which one is the already mentioned lack of scientific investigations and a general but inaccurate belief that most of our national parks (all categories) are essentially wild places mostly untouched by human agency. This takes us back to some of the language quoted earlier in the 1964 Wilderness Act, which defines a wilderness area as one having been "primarily affected by the forces of nature, with the imprint of man being scarcely unnoticeable." These conditions are probably seldom met outside of Alaska. The concept of the "virgin wilderness" does not equate with many of the known facts of the history and prehistory of human occupancy in the conterminous United States. People have been present in this area for at least 12,000 years, and probably far longer, and it is a virtual certainty that human-set fire has been an ecological force of varying degrees of significance over this considerable span of time. In addition, hunters and gatherers and farmers in prehistoric times affected the ecosystems in a host of other ways. It is of no moment to argue (sometimes unsoundly) that these people lived in "harmony" with their environments. By their presence and actions the ecosystems they occupied were altered. We still know too little about the details of these changes but some are beginning to emerge and especially with regard to fire, which was widely employed by hunters to drive animals in desired directions.

The coming of the European was a highly destructive period not only for the nation's ecosystems but also for the native human inhabitants. The latter were either exterminated or brought to the edge of extermination in a short time and the ecology they had previously developed vis-à-vis the ecosystems they had occupied and used also disappeared in whole or large part.

The Wilderness Act, as well as many other elements of environmental legislation, contain elements of this myth of the "pristine wilderness," an entity that may have been rare when the first European set foot in what is now the conterminous United States. We must attempt to determine, as precisely as possible, the nature and extent of human-caused-disturbances in our National Parks and preserves if we are to develop the accurate models on which to base our future procedures for park management.

Of even greater importance than the question of relative pristineness is the question as to what the optimal sizes and geometric configurations parks and preserves should have in order to assure that a maximum degree of plant and animal protection will occur as far into the future as possible. It may appear foolish to pose such a question in view of the fact that many protectionists believe that their principal task is to save *any* piece of noncultivated or otherwise exploited nature regardless of size or configuration. However, recent research into the dynamics of the biogeography of islands is leading many to believe that it is time that serious consideration be given to the question of the optimal size of parks and preserves.

This is not the place to detail current and recent island biogeographical research, so suffice it to say that the aspects of the theory that concerns us most are the following: (1) area size and shape do act to restrict the number of species possible to live on an island, and (2) distance from the nearest source(s) of recruitment of replacement species is a major determinant as to which species can or will reach a given island. Some of this is no more than a restatement of long-observed natural history. The two elements just noted are beginning to occupy the attention of biologists concerned with the ecological effectiveness of nature preserves.

Every park or preserve is, to some degree, an island if we do not define an island solely as an entity surrounded by water. Ecologists recognize as an island any area surrounded by different ecological conditions. Thus, for example, a small range of mountains rising well above a surrounding plain and isolated from other similar heights is an island at least in its upper portions in that the ecological conditions existing at those higher elevations are isolated from similar ecological conditions located elsewhere. Thus, the organisms that require the environments provided by the higher elevations are insular organisms as are organisms located on land surrounded by water.

Stated in the simplest terms, the larger the area preserved the greater the number of species of animals and plants it will be able to retain over long time periods. It has been observed, for example, that when a large area of forest is removed leaving only a relatively small forest stands remaining, for a time there are more animal species remaining in the forest remnant than will ultimately be accommodated at the "equilibrium state." The space and other requirements of even the more common vertebrate animals is so often inadequately known, however, that at present it is usually impossible to predict just what species will remain and which ones will become extinct in a given ecosystem remnant. Even less is known about the area requirements of even the most common invertebrate species nor is much known about the dynamics of most of these organisms on a species-by-species basis when habitat area is reduced or increased.

All of the foregoing difficulties notwithstanding, island biogeographical theory does require that we give attention to the question of what we intend to preserve in a given proposed preserve-area and to what degree we can hope to succeed. We also must face the issue of whether the time-honored approach of saving whatever we can save and worry later, if at all, about ecological viability may not survive the close scrutiny that is sure to be brought to bear on future preservationist's efforts as well as upon areas already set aside for preserves.

It has long been a truism in wildlife preservation that one should focus efforts on habitat preservation, and, if such is successful, the animals one wishes to save will be saved. Unfortunately, this view takes one only part way to the core of the matter. It is more correct to say that what one must try to do is preserve entire ecosystems and that the number and variety of such systems ought to be large enough to accommodate, on a more or less perpetual basis, all plant and animal taxa present when a given reserve is set aside. That ideal can seldom be met now in the United States with the exception of Alaska where it appears that the larger parks are of sufficient size to allow the continued presence of all plant and animal life for a very long time to come.

Older parks may or may not possess the size attributes and/or access to areas where replacement species are present and are able to disperse into the park or preserve when ecological space (niches) become available. Yellowstone National Park, which may appear to be large enough to permit virtually all species present at its creation in 1872 to have survived unmolested, nevertheless, is not large enough to provide a winter grazing ground for its elk population. These animals must, therefor, leave the park and be subjected to the risk of being killed, quite legally, by hunters outside the park.

Perhaps the key test of any major park or preserve is whether or not it is large enough to support populations of the top predators (e.g., bears and wolves) in sufficient numbers to permit the predators to play their ecological roles. In some parks, and most notably Yellowstone with its population(s) of grizzly bears, the problem is not one of sufficient area or ecological conditions but the interplay between humans and grizzly bears. The latter know little fear of humans and thus are very dangerous animals as occasional news reports tragically indicate. The problem is how to allow humans to view these great beasts while at the same time keeping bears and people apart. In other parks in the western United States brown bears may be present and while not as large as grizzlies can nevertheless pose a hazard to humans when the bears become too "friendly."

The biggest native cat of North America is the cougar (if we exclude a minute remnant population of jaguars in southern Arizona). This animal can and should be accommodated whenever large parks are planned in areas that include the species' natural geographical range.

Wolves, once present in every state of the conterminous United States and Alaska, are today becoming rare or are extirpated over most of their former range (excepting Alaska). Long the object of concerted attack by individual ranchers as well as state and federal agencies, these large carnivores had little chance of surviving except in the least settled and remote areas (Fig. 12.3).

Attitudes respecting predators have been changing in recent years and no longer is there the once common spectacle of private and government forces arrayed together in efforts to rid the land of all of these animals. Of course, it is foolish to suggest that grizzlies and humans could coexist today in California or that wolves should be given carte blanche to the domesticated animals of our nation. However, it is within the national parks that justification for the preservation of these large predators can

**Figure 12.3** Gray wolves hunting over snow.

be and should be made. Furthermore, in instances where there are human/predator conflicts in such parks, the modifications should come in the area of human behavior even to the extent of keeping humans—except park managers and scientists—completely apart from the animals. The spectacle of people feeding bears along the roadways in Yellowstone is a ridiculous one. Park authorities do attempt to control difficult bears by removing them to remote parts of the park or by depriving them of access to garbage. However, the public really needs some education as to their proper roles and actions in the parks. There seems to be little justification for permitting human behavior in national parks that is appropriate to a mechanized amusement park.

## PEOPLE/PARK MANAGEMENT

As our nation became more mobile, thanks to the automobile, once relatively isolated national parks came increasingly within range of the traveler from any part of the United States. This has justified, in one measure, the setting apart of land in national parks but, in recent years, this very ease of access has created problems certainly not envisioned when the Congress of the United States set aside the first national park as a "pleasuring ground" for the people.

Pleasuring grounds they have become. With regard to those who visit the parks to derive the spiritual and intellectual pleasures there are few problems. However, as though the national parks were in some bizarre way microcosms not only of wild nature but wild human nature in the last half of the twentieth century, many of the parks now face growing problems of environmental pollution and crime. Nowhere is this better illustrated than in Yosemite National Park (Fig. 12.4).

This magnificent park is located between the two major urban clusters in California—the San Francisco Bay Region and Los Angeles. Most park visits are confined to a relatively small area in the southern sector where there are lodges and stores catering to visitors and spaces for campers and their vehicles. Smog is now frequent in this part of the valley. So heavy is the summer demand for the park that one must sign up well in advance in order to gain entrance

**Figure 12.4**   Yosemite Valley in Yosemite National Park.

(Fig. 12.5). The crowning indignity is that crime, sometimes of a violent nature, is occurring with ever greater frequency and park rangers find themselves reluctantly cast in the role of police. Illegal use of narcotics appears to be common as is public drunkenness. Theft—something once unheard of—is now frequent.

One possible solution to these problems is to keep all private vehicles out of the park and to move all commercial installations outside as well. Visitors would enter the park in special vehicles (e.g., buses) and only those persons prepared to camp in tents could remain overnight. All others would set up in their camping vehicles or take rooms in lodgings in facilities provided outside the park. This and other suggested solutions have met with strong resistance but, given the *raison d'etre* of national parks, it may be that the only way they can be saved is by adopting measures governing ac-

cess that will assure that the parks, and not some sordid remnant, will be available in the future. Fortunately, most of Yosemite's area is not easy to penetrate even on foot and this major part seems less endangered although foot traffic has become so heavy in some areas as to cause some environmental degradation. There are growing quantities of litter left by backpackers even in the most remote areas of the park and it has been indicated that water pollution occurs in some streams that appear to be pure although they may in fact be contaminated with human body wastes.

Fortunately, a growing number—still small, however—of backpackers are striving to achieve minimal environmental disturbance. This is an ideal worthy of achievement and possibly the only one that will allow the future use of what appears on park maps as isolated areas.

**Figure 12.5**   Crowded conditions in Yosemite National Park.

There remains the problem of the large number of national park visitors. If we can accept that park access is, in the terms of economists, a scarce good perhaps we should begin formulating an ecologically and societally sound basis for the allocation of access to the national parks. This may seem cold blooded but it will be far more cold blooded in the long run to ignore the problem. Here is an area where the informed citizen should work with relevant specialists as well as legislators to develop the required rules for park access. Perhaps each of us, as a benefit of citizenship could be granted, at birth, a certain number of park visits per national park. Those persons not wishing to use their visit rights could give them away or sell them to persons who wished to use the parks more frequently. Such a system would have the virtue of alerting the general public to the fact that national parks are limited in area, irreplaceable, and of enormous material and nonmaterial value to our nation. Such a system might also provide the intellectual stimulus for

the inclusion in elementary and secondary education of the fundamentals of ecology, biology, and resource conservation and management in a crowding nation and crowding world.

## MANAGEMENT OF NATIONAL PARKS

Current procedures relevant to the management of our national parks reflect, to some extent, recent developments in ecological research. However, as in any science, applied ecology tends to lag significantly behind the insights developed by theoretical ecology and this is true for our national parks where, in various instances, the discoveries of research ecologists are not always applied because the findings conflict with some strongly held traditional attitudes respecting how the ecosystems of the parks are to be managed. Behind much of the traditionalists' position is the view, already noted, that the ecosystems of the parks are essentially pristine and that the focus of management must be to prevent every kind of disturbance. One aspect of these conflicting views is that of the ecological role of fire in forests and brushlands. The traditional position is that all fires should be suppressed but there is abundant evidence to indicate that fire, at varying levels of intensity and frequency, is necessary to maintain the ecological viability of many forest and brush ecosystems. Unfortunately, this insight is difficult to apply because of the mind set widely held that fire is always bad. As we have seen in the chapter on forests, if fire is successfully suppressed for long periods of time large amounts of fuel accumulate on the forest floor and these accumulations, if ignited, can result in terribly destructive fires. We saw that under natural conditions, lightning-set fire, in a number of cases, seems to have been frequent enough to assure that very low accumulations of fuel could develop thus greatly restricting the damaging effects of fire when it occurred. Furthermore, fire plays a role in plant succession and it is to be expected that any human manipulation of fire frequency will necessarily result in ecological changes. This is not to suggest that human-set fires resulting from careless behavior should be permitted. Instead, it is to suggest that controlled burning may have to become an essential management technique in many national parks.

In parks where the former large predators are lacking, it may be necessary to cull deer herds by shooting in order to prevent an ecologically destructive overpopulation from developing. This culling must include does as well as bucks although public sentimentality often rejects this idea. In parks where large predators remain the best management course may be to allow predators and prey to interact in a natural fashion with human intervention occurring only when ecological balances appear to be about to be destroyed to the detriment of the animals.

## URBAN PARKS

Quite different in their basic purposes as compared to national parks are parks in urban areas. The urban park is such an ubiquitous feature of our landscapes that we often give them little thought, this being especially true of those cities where a highly mobile population tends to be focused on recreational areas distant from the city core.

As noted in earlier paragraphs, some of the largest urban parks in Europe owe their existence to having first been the play areas of royalty and then were later given to the people for their pleasure and recreation. In the United States, urban parks owe their existence to both the gifts of private citizens and the purchase, with tax monies, of land by civil authorities.

The two best known urban parks in the United States, Golden Gate Park and Central Park, came about by a combination of personal vision on the part of a few individuals and the cooperation of civil authorities and groups of interested citizens.

Central Park, located in the island borough of Manhattan, is not the largest park in New York City—at least four other New York City parks are larger—but it is by far the best known. Its 342 hectares (846 acres) lie in the midst of some of the most densely settled land in the United States (Fig. 12.6). Many famous persons were associated with the design of this great park the most outstanding of whom was Frederick Law Olmstead. By day the park accommodates thousands of citizens. Many find the trees, grass, squirrels, and other amenities a priceless island of nature in the midst of the mad pace of the city. Unfortunately, after nightfall many parts of the park are not safe for the innocent visitor and police find it all but impossible to prevent a variety of illegal activities. This nocturnal problem is now true of many of our nation's urban parks.

Golden Gate Park is a magnificent green

**Figure 12.6**  Central Park, N.Y., looking to the north.

rectangle about 3 miles long and ½ mile wide encompassing 412 hectares (1017 acres) (Fig. 12.7). The person chiefly responsible for the landscaping—which is outstanding—was John McLaren. Busy by day, this park too becomes unsafe after nightfall.

For size alone, Griffith Park in Los Angeles with its 1738 hectares (4253 acres) stands near the head of the list. Much of the terrain of this park is so steep that it is not usable for most recreational activities. However, enough near level land exists to make this a very popular park. Again, after dark is not the time for a visit.

Lest it be thought that the measure of excellence of city parks is size alone, let it be said that while large parks are desirable in that they can accommodate a large number of people engaged in a variety of pursuits and also offer the greatest scope for landscaping that can convey a sense of wildlands, small urban parks

**Figure 12.7**   Golden Gate Park, San Francisco, California.

are also of great importance to the quality of city life. For many urban dwellers and especially the very young as well as the elderly the local park—if there is one—offers the only really accessible area for outdoor rest and recreation. In areas where apartment dwelling is the rule such parks are ecological and psychological necessities for persons of all ages. It is being increasingly suggested that in the future fewer Americans will own their homes and that more and more persons will live in apartments. If this proves to be the case the need for local accessible parks will be even greater than in the past. If our cities are to be inhabitable in the future they must be well supplied with parks of the right sizes and locations to accommodate human needs.

One of the most exciting recent developments in urban park design, size, and location has been taking place in New York City. Best described as the "vest pocket park movement" the supporters of this idea press the view that cities need—and can obtain—small urban spaces that can be transformed into miniparks that serve the needs of pedestrians and local residents (Fig. 12.8). The idea, when first brought forward, did not immediately win acceptance by officialdom which had long been wedded to the American ideal that bigger is best. Nevertheless, with perseverance, this group of dedicated individuals gradually won over supporters to the idea and today the city—especially Manhattan—is the possessor of a number of such vest pocket parks. They are marvels of what can be accomplished in limited space and their acceptance by the people has been of a high order. These little parks also seem to convey the message that perhaps we, as a nation and a people, are at last adjusting our thinking to post frontier realities albeit somewhat tardily. It also suggests that we are at last making peace with our urban environments realizing that for better or for worse we have become an urbanized nation.

**Figure 12.8** Vest pocket park in New York City.

Greater use of existing urban parks for education is something that could be done. Too few schools seem to recognize the ecological laboratories that even the most simple parks provide. Students can learn the names and geographical proveniences of the plantings and the names and biological characteristics of the birds and other animals present. Even the smallest vest pocket park in New York City has sparrows and pigeons both of which have interesting stories regarding their places of origin and time of introduction to the United States and elsewhere. Their populations fluctuate, in part, in response to the food provided them by people and this could form the basis for any number of school study projects.

Probably the greatest need for parks is felt by children. This seems to have been under-stood much longer in Europe than in the United States but, of course, Europe's wildlands disappeared much longer ago. Unfortunately, in the United States the possibility of automobile mobility seems too often to substitute for the action required to take a child to a local park. In many West Coast cities, for example, one finds that there is often a preponderance of European-born parents pushing their little children on the swings or talking with friends while watching their children play. Americans seem to be discovering that perhaps the occasional distant trip to the country does not substitute for frequent trips to a local park. An urban child who has not had a large amount of park experience while growing up is surely a deprived child. It is to the children of our nation that we must dedicate much of our future efforts to establish urban parks (Fig. 12.9).

## PARKS AND PRESERVES IN THE THIRD WORLD

Wealthy nations, and especially the United States, whose wealth includes large areas still not completely brought into the sphere of economic exploitation can afford to set aside land in national parks and find the financial support necessary for their maintenance without producing significant strain upon the national economy. Far different is the situation with almost all Third World nations where land for farms and livestock is often in short supply and funds for park maintenance can be obtained only by taking away money from other often desperately needed services. These severe limitations notwithstanding, the record of many Third World nations has been outstanding with regard to the establishment of national parks and preserves. However, the problems of maintenance are often great and without the technical and financial assistance of wealthier nations there is doubt as to how many of the extant as well as planned national parks will survive this century.

**Figure 12.9** Urban parks need not be large in order to provide grass and trees in addition to play areas for children.

## Parks and Preserves in Latin America

Although a limited number of national preserves were set aside prior to the establishment of Yellowstone Park, it was only after the advent of that park that something like the beginning of a national park movement came into being in Latin America. For quite a number of nations in that region, the establishment of national parks has occurred only during the last 10 to 20 years.

The difficulties of establishing and maintaining national parks and preserves in Latin America are similar to those already noted for the United States but with some additional elements. These last include economic poverty, increased demand for land to be used not for preserves but for farms and grazing land, and a general lack of a widespread public concern for conservation. One result of these and related problems is that in some countries there are more parks listed than exist in actuality. That is, the parks have been officially decreed but in the absence of appropriated funds for park guards, park signs, and all the other aspects of management these are no more than "paper parks," in that they appear on documents and on maps but otherwise do not exist.

Many Latin American nations are experiencing rapid increases in human population. This means that more land is required to produce food for national consumption and raw materials for export. Thus, in tiny nations such as Costa Rica possessing an already high population density and an annual population growth rate exceeding 2 percent plus a crushing foreign debt load, the pressure to get all available land to produce agricultural and animal products for internal and external markets is understandably great. It is, therefore, a remarkable achievement that Costa Rica has set aside more than 129,000 hectares in parks and preserves.

In contrast, Brazil can set aside some very large parks and not make much of an impact on the total land area of the nation. Brazil's human population is concentrated within 200 kilometers of the Atlantic coast and it is within this coastal zone that Brazil has been most active, thus far, in establishing national parks although some have recently been established in the Amazon Basin.

The wealthier nations of Latin America (e.g., Brazil and Venezuela) can probably find the funds necessary to properly manage the parks that are established. However, the poorer countries, which are in the majority, often can't supply the needed funds. This fact brings us to the question as to why and for whom these parks have been or are to be established.

The obvious answer is that the parks have been or will be established to protect ecosystems and that these parks, like Yellowstone, are also to be pleasuring grounds for the people. With regard to the former there is no cause for dispute but this is not the case with the latter. In the United States a very large middle class has financial resources available to it to defray the costs of visits to the national parks. Also, a largely literate population has the opportunity for vicarious enjoyment of national parks through the purchase of published materials. Latin American nations, in general, do not have large middle classes and thus the potential clientele for national parks is relatively limited in size.

It is often from wealthy nations outside this region that the stimulus comes for the establishment of major parks and preserves. Much of this outside stimulus is generated by organizations dedicated to the conservation of wild areas. Perhaps the most influential of these has

been the International Union for the Conservation of Nature and Natural Resources (IUCN), which is based in Morges, Switzerland. The IUCN works through private and national governmental agencies and through the United Nations and has become a powerful element in the recent two or three decades of park establishment in the Third World—as well as the developed world.

The IUCN has worked particularly hard to provide basic guidelines for what a national park should be. The following definition was promulgated in 1969: "A National Park is a relatively large area 1) where one or several ecosystems are not materially altered by human exploitation and occupation, where plant and animal species, geomorphological sites and habitats are of special scientific, educative and recreational interest or which contains a natural landscape of great beauty and 2) where the highest competent authority of the country has taken steps to prevent or to eliminate as soon as possible exploitation or occupation in the whole area and to enforce effectively the respect of ecological, geomorphological or aesthetic features which have led to its establishment and 3) where visitors are allowed to enter, under special conditions, for inspirational, educative, cultural and recreative purposes." It can be seen that much of the language of the definition bears a close resemblance to the language contained in the U.S. Wilderness Act of 1964.

A major object of IUCN activities is to stress the critical need for providing adequate protection to national parks. Also, and this is a vital point, the IUCN will not recognize as a national park any *preserve* no matter how large if the public is excluded from it. Thus, we see that there is basically a three-pronged thrust here: (1) preservation of wild areas that are to be kept free of exploitation, (2) that such areas be given the means for proper maintenance, and (3) that the public be given access. In short, a mirror of the national park policy that has been evolving in the United States ever since the establishment of Yellowstone.

A large part of Latin America lies within the tropics (which are here defined to include all the area between the Tropics of Cancer and Capricorn as well as areas poleward in which killing frosts are rare or nonexistent) and a major concern among many conservationists, living outside this area, is for the forested ecosystems that are presently being removed at a rapid rate (see chapter on forests). Most of this forest conversion is in response to the increasing need for farm and pasture land. Although this cutting is almost universal in tropical Latin America its impact is most readily seen in Central America. Unless there is a significant reversal of current trends in that region—and there appears little hope for this—only relatively small and isolated forest-islands will remain there by the end of this century.

To conclude this section, it is not enough just to provide the stimulus for the establishment of national parks and preserves in the economically hard-pressed nations of Latin America. There must be continuing outside sources of funds to these nations if such park and preserve establishments are to survive the pressures noted above. Such financial support should not only be sufficient to properly manage the parks and preserves but also to provide sums to the national treasuries equal to the sums lost to the economy by not having such lands in farms or pastures. Up to the present, foreign conservationists, understandably, have concentrated their efforts on getting land put into parks and preserves. However, many of these exemplary efforts will come to nothing if the economic requirements are not considered and provided for. A dispassionate observer of the current foreign efforts to get poor nations in Latin America (and elsewhere) to set aside lands in parks and preserves might wonder if all this is being done not for the principal benefit of the Third World nations but for the current and future benefit of the foreign conser-

vationist-biologist community to use and enjoy for research and other purposes. This may appear to be an unkind comment but it must be made because it is precisely in this light that of these well-meaning efforts are viewed by some of the citizens of nations in Latin America and elsewhere. The first of two major conservation tasks in Latin America—the establishment of national parks and preserves is well on the way to achieving success. The second major task—foreign funding for the support of the parks and preserves—has scarcely gotten underway.

## Africa

Unlike most of Latin America where the national parks are known to relatively few living outside of the region, many of the national parks of Africa are known to large numbers of persons not living in that region and some these parks are the object of major touristic interest. Most African nations possess at least one recognized national park and some nations such as Kenya, Tanzania, and South Africa have well-deserved international reputations for their parks and game reserves. Among the more outstanding are the following.

1  Kruger National Park in South Africa, with an area of 1,817,146 hectares, was established in 1926. Kruger National Park attracts thousands of visitors each year to see a wide range of large and small animals.

2  Tsavo National Park in Kenya, established in 1948. The 2,080,000 hectares comprising this park contain an extraordinary array of the larger game mammals of East Africa.

3  Serengeti National Park, Tanzania, established in 1951 and contains 1,295,000 hectares. As large as this park is it still doesn't provide all the area required by many of the migratory animals it contains (Map 12.2).

Kenya and South Africa, particularly, are aware of the economic value of their national

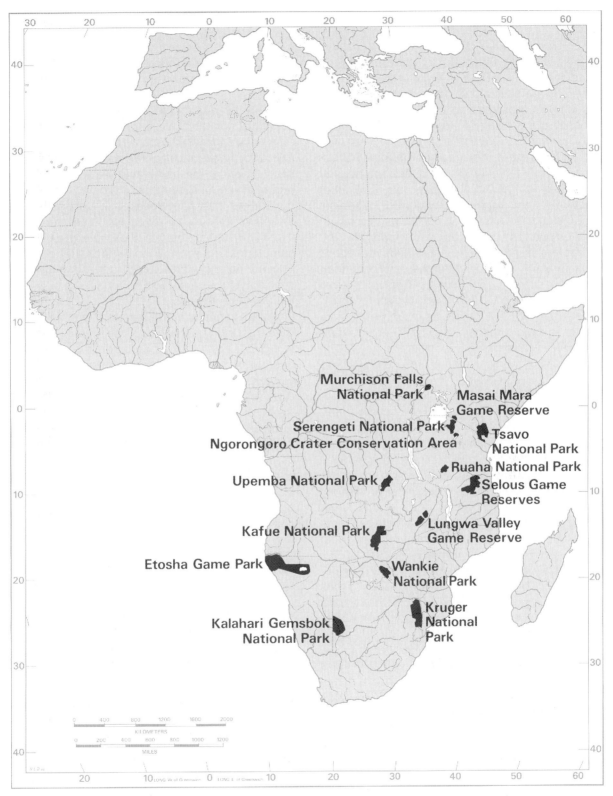

**Map 12.2** Major national parks in Africa.

parks and use the parks to attract tourists to their countries to spend hard currencies. Other nations are becoming increasingly aware of the economic possibilities of attractive national parks and it is to be expected that the trend toward park establishment will continue.

Unfortunately, there is a growing conflict between conservationists and the increasing numbers of land-hungry rural folk. The latter often do not appreciate why they ought not graze their livestock or plant their crops on lands that they thought were theirs to use. The problem is particularly acute with respect to pastoralists and it is often these folk, by their cutting of trees and burning of pastures, that the greatest threat is posed to park integrity. Lest these folk be viewed as villains it must be kept in mind that they often have no viable alternatives to park encroachment if they are to provide for themselves and their families. The problem is exacerbated by a widely held view among the rural (and not a few urban) inhabitants that parks and reserves are colonial remnants since many of them were established during the colonial period. Fortunately, African governments have not only picked up where the colonial powers left off but in some instances have extended the total areas under protection.

There can be no doubt, however, that there is presently a growing contest between park protection and the rising rates of population increase in many if not most African nations. Before this century is over more than one major park will be seriously compromised by this growing human tide. Another factor, as yet little studied, is warfare. It is generally understood, for example, that soldiers in Uganda, during the infamous governance of Idi Amin, occasionally went on killing sprees in some of that nation's national parks. It is to be expected that the growing incidence of guerilla warfare in Africa will negatively affect more than a few reserves and parks. To all this must be added the widespread illegal trade in animal parts. Animal skins and rhinoceros "horns" find ready mar-

kets in many parts of the world in spite of the large number of nations now forbidding such trade.

It may be that economic necessity and not scientific concerns will prove to be the chief element protecting the parks and preserves of Africa for unlike most of the national parks of Latin America, the parks and preserves of Africa offer the tourist uniquely exciting views of a world that has all but ceased to exist outside the parks not only of Africa, but elsewhere in the world. Latin America lacks the great assemblages of large mammal herds that occur in many parts of Africa and it is these magnificent animals that attract the tourists . . . and their hard currencies.

Sound scientific management of the parks is burdened with problems not the least of which has been some misunderstanding about the role of fire in many African ecosystems. For years it was the conventional ecological wisdom to view fire—all fire—as something to suppress if the ecosystems of the parks were to be preserved. More recently, however, the fact that fire constitutes an important and necessary element in many African ecosystems has come to be appreciated although application of that knowledge remains difficult. Another problem has been that no matter how large a park might be it may still be insufficient to contain, in perpetuity, all the animal species that try to occupy it. Many of the larger mammalian herbivores in Africa are migratory and so long as there was land available for this their populations presumably remained in balance with the ecosystem's carrying capacity. However, when confined to parks even as large as Tsavo there is a tendency for some species to reproduce beyond the park's carrying capacity. The animal most noted for this is the African elephant. It is being gradually appreciated that even large forested tracts can support relatively few of these magnificent beasts and if overstocking occurs great damage to the forest will result, which seriously affects the elephant populations. Thus, in order to protect some areas from such destruction, elephant herds must be maintained at ecologically permissible levels, which can only be done by control shooting. This latter is too often viewed by animal lovers as cruel and inhuman although far more cruel is the slow starvation of elephants unable to obtain sufficient food.

Most African nations are poor and can't always be expected to be able to perform all the costly tasks associated with sound park management. If the ecosystems of many parts of this continent are to be saved for future generations to see and appreciate it is absolutely necessary that the wealthier nations of the world contribute financially to the effort.

## Asia

For those who believe that dense human population precludes the establishment of national parks, Japan stands as a stunning refutation. In this tiny island nation of 372,000 square kilometers (somewhat less than the area of the state of Montana) with a population of approximately 115 million persons, approximately 26,000 square kilometers have been set aside in national parks and preserve areas. It must be pointed out, however, that only about 10 percent of the total park area meets the IUCN criteria but even so this is an outstanding achievement. The fact that the Japanese people are generally very well educated and have a long history of appreciation of wild places and wild nature contributes much to this success and may, indeed, be the chief factors for this achievement.

The Republic of India, with its nearly 650,000,000 inhabitants and approximately 3,186,000 square kilometers, lacks the educated populace of Japan, and also unlike Japan, India is chiefly a rural nation in that scarcely more than 20 percent of the population is urban (in contrast, Japan's urban population is approximately 76 percent of the total population). Most of the literate portion of In-dia's population live in urban situations meaning that the greater share of the rural population is either illiterate or nearly so. Of even greater significance is the large population base, which increases at about 2 percent each year. Thus, every two years India adds to its population a sum greater than the population of California (approximately 23 million), the most populous state in the Union. Because the bulk of this increase occurs in rural areas the pressure to obtain more farmland and pasture also increases exponentially each year. Thus, it must come as no surprise that India has few national parks and preserves (termed "sanctuaries" in India) and that their total area represents a far smaller percentage of the national territory than is the case with Japan.

It appears that many of the so-called national parks and sanctuaries of India are subject to a variety of exploitive activities and even where such are strictly forbidden they are still apt to occur. This is not surprising in the light of the rural poverty of this nation and the enormous and growing population pressure already noted. Making the task of management even more difficult is that fact that, in India, the individual states have the sole right to establish "National" parks and sanctuaries. The central government does attempt to offer guidance and encouragement but given the enormous economic and social problems of the nation it is perhaps remarkable that any interest is directed toward parks. Although no longer rich in large numbers of the big game mammals for which India was once famous, remnants do survive and if provided with protection could be of major interest to tourists.

## SUMMARY

Parks and preserves have a long world history. In the earliest period they were chiefly for the use of social elites but this later evolved toward a broader societal use until today, in many parts of the world, most parks are available to the general public.

In the United States, parks and preserves are important parts of the nation's recreation facilities as well as being places where elements of wild nature receive varying degrees of protection. Outstanding among the parks of America is the system of national parks that began in 1872 with the establishment of Yellowstone National Park, which remains, to this day, the largest national park in the conterminous United States. There are also various state park systems and a multitude of regional, county, and city parks in the United States. As the population of our nation has grown and become intensely urban, parks and preserves have assumed ever greater importance to us.

Use pressure on many of the national parks has reached levels where some of the very things people go to them for are threatened. Increasingly, there are urban problems to contend with such as automobile-caused air pollution, drug abuse, and other similar activities. How are these parks to be managed so that all who wish to visit them may do so and, at the same time, assure that only minor ecological disturbances will occur? These two aims are often incompatible in at least some parts of some of the national parks. Another question raised frequently is how much, if any, commercial activity ought to be allowed in the national parks? At the outset of its establishment, Yellowstone Park had commercial activities some of which were even encouraged by the federal government. Today, there is a growing sentiment for moving all commercial activities outside of the parks but this is often resisted by the would-be affected commercial enterprises.

When first established, there was little if any thought that the national parks would be the sites for scientific research. Today there is a widespread opinion among biologists and others that research ought to be a primary activity in these parks. On balance, remarkably little biological research has as yet been done within

them, even though no small amount of public justification for the establishment of still more national parks is the need for areas where research on wild ecosystems can be conducted.

It would appear, in several respects, that our national parks are approaching a crossroads with regard to how they are publicly perceived and how they are to be used. Many interests, both private and public, are represented but the trend appears to be strongly in the direction of achieving less ecological disturbance and less commercial activity within park limits and achieving an increase in the scientific research conducted within the parks.

Only a relatively small fraction of the nation's total population will ever visit a national park. By far the greater share of our population lives within a short walking or commuting distance of an urban park. While the largest urban parks may receive the most attention in printed sources even the smallest urban parks, some less than a city building lot in area, provide valuable amenities. Important to all age groups as they are, urban parks may be of chief value to the urban child. It may be among the more important of adult responsibilities to assure that adequate urban parks are available for children and that parents regularly take their children to them. This appears to be a growing trend in the United States and one that mirrors an older European pattern.

The United States and other developed nations are by no means unique in having parks and preserves. A growing number of Third World nations are setting aside national parks and other preserves but virtually all these nations experience serious difficulties in doing so.

Among the more serious problems that these nations encounter is the conflict between a growing population with its demand for more land and the government that tries to set park land aside in perpetuity. Another major problem is financing park establishment and maintenance. It may be relatively easy to declare a given area a park but extremely difficult to obtain the money to pay for private land encompassed by the park or to pay for park development and administration. In nations where there are potential major tourist attractions as, for example, the large herbivorous mammals in Kenya and Tanzania, these may provide the financial means to establish and maintain national parks. However, in contrast, many national parks in Latin America do not possess the spectacular natural features that attract large numbers of tourists and such parks must be financially subsidized. Because, by definition, most Third World nations are economically poor, obtaining sufficient in-country funds to support national parks may be impossible. Since no small part of the stimuli to establish national parks and preserves in the Third World come from biologists and conservationists in the developed world it would seem that a substantial amount of financial support should also come from the same source. However, this has not generally been the case: biologists and conservationists are not themselves usually possessed of other than modest funds. Nevertheless, if there is not to be a serious loss of scientifically invaluable parks and preserves in the Third World in the years ahead, some means must be found to assist these nations, on a permanent basis, in saving the parks and preserves already established as well as others that ought to be established. This is a race against human population growth. Unless international economic support is forthcoming for Third World national parks, population growth will win. If this happens, not only will the individual nations suffer irreversible biological impoverishment but the entire world will be similarly affected.

# energy resources: introduction

No other nation has approached our country in its current per capita use of energy and unless some extraordinary breakthrough in science and technology occurs no other nation is likely to duplicate the twentieth century use of energy in the United States. This extraordinary level of consumption coupled as it once was with what appeared to be limitless quantities of inexpensive energy allowed our nation to live a thermodynamic fantasy—a dream from which the nation is now being awakened.

The awakening began in 1973–1974 when the Arab component of the Organization of Petroleum Exporting Countries (OPEC) embargoed shipments of crude petroleum to Western nations in retaliation for support given to Israel in the Israeli-Egyptian war. Following the embargo, OPEC forced a series of huge rises in the price of crude oil. In 1970, the price per barrel of the highest grade of Arabian oil ("Arabian Light") was approximately $1.20. In mid-1982 the price was $34.00 per barrel with some variation among OPEC members. Within a decade, therefore, energy costs soared in the United States from nominal to burdensome. In those developing nations lacking their own petroleum resources, the price rise has been all but ruinous and many of those countries have increased their foreign indebtedness to alarming degrees.

With the rise in petroleum prices came a new regard for energy costs in the United States which has already manifested itself in a rapidly expanding market for small automobiles giving better gasoline mileage than did their larger predecessors. There is also growing interest and activity in home insulation, construction designed to conserve energy, and household appliances designed to use less energy. That some success has attended these efforts is shown by the reduced nationwide consumption of petroleum during recent years. This reduction, however, is still insufficient to assure prevention of future energy dislocations in the United States economy.

Much confusion has accompanied the "energy crisis" and the public is to be excused if it sometimes adopts a cynical view of the exhortations made to conserve energy and most specifically energy produced by petroleum. One source of this cynicism is that from time to time, since 1973–1974 there have been temporary oil gluts that have received great media attention. When these have occurred there has been little or no decrease in the pump price of gasoline nor in the price of heating oil or other home energy bills. The public is often of the opinion that it is being made to pay more than it should for petroleum products. Evidence presented that Europeans and others pay far more for gasoline than we do in the United States seldom serves to allay to the feelings of distrust.

Is there *really* an energy crisis? The answer is no and yes. The reason for the ambivalent answer is that the question is improperly phrased. A better-phrased question might be "is there a shortage of energy-producing resources in the United States?" The answer to that question is *no*. However, if one asks "is there a problem or problems in making the energy resources *available*," the answer is *yes*. The United States has enormous coal resources sufficient to provide a large part of the nation's energy requirements for centuries but, in order to mine, transport, and combust such huge quantities of this resource we would have to accept a number of major environmental impacts. Thus, we face not a crisis of energy because of a lack of resources but a potential environmental crisis were we to affect a major expansion in the use of coal.

To continue with the question "is there an energy crisis?" your attention is directed to nuclear power. There is a widespread feeling in the United States that nuclear power is too dangerous to use and that no new nuclear reactors should be constructed. Thus, what of itself is a major potential source of energy becomes unavailable or only limitedly available because of considerations having nothing to do with the abundance of nuclear fuel.

## TERMS AND CONCEPTS

Energy is the capacity to perform work. Various measurements are employed to describe the amount of work performed in a given situation and this energy "language" must be understood. Two of the more frequently used terms are British thermal units (Btu) and kilocalories (kcal). In the United States, power companies tend to employ the Btu most often. *A Btu is the amount of energy required to raise the temperature of one pound of water from 14.5° to 15.5° Fahrenheit (F) at normal sea level atmospheric pressure*. When Btu's are employed to describe the power production of major population/industrial areas the term *quad* is commonly employed. A quad is one quadrillion Btu's ($10^{15}$ Btu). A kilocalorie is the amount of heat required to raise one kilogram of water one degree Celsius (from 15°C to 16°C) at normal

sea level atmospheric pressure. One kilocalorie (1 kcal) is equivalent to 3.968 Btu.

Physical scientists employ still other measures of energy for example, dynes, ergs, and joules. In many nations other than the United States and the United Kingdom the joule is being used with ever-greater frequency. This unit of energy is also commonly employed by scientists in all nations. A joule (the name is a memorium for a British scientist, James Joule) is a very small unit of energy: 1000 joules are equivalent to only 0.9484 Btu.

Energy statistics are also given in terms of (British) horsepower and watts. These two values are commonly employed in the United States, the former to describe the power potential of a given piece of machinery like an auto engine and the latter as a measure of the quantities of electricity produced or consumed. One British horsepower is the amount of energy required (or expended) to move 33,000 pounds the distance of one foot in one minute. One-horsepower is just about equal to 746 watts. When the watt is the measure employed it is common to see kilowatt used, this being 1000 watts. For very large electrical energy units the term megawatt is used, this being equal to 1 million ($10^6$) watts. Recently, the term megawatt has been giving way to the use of quad.

One of the significant concepts respecting energy is that of energy conversion efficiency (ECE). By ECE we refer to the amount of useful work compared to the amount of heat that is produced by a given energy conversion. The concept we are noting here relates to the second law of thermodynamics, which states that in *any energy transfer some of the energy is lost to heart*. There is no such thing as a 100 percent efficient energy transfer; the heat produced in any transfer is lost and cannot be reconstituted in the same concentrated quantity as the energy that originally produced the heat. This latter phenomenon is referred to as *entropy*, which can be stated non mathematically as the tendency for energy to move from an ordered (concentrated) state to a disordered (nonconcentrated) state. Taking the long-term view, we must recognize that even the chief source of energy to our planet, the sun, is subject to the second law of thermodynamics and thus its future is not unlimited. However, lest this cause any alarm, keep in mind that some billions of years must still pass before there will be a diminution in the sun's energy output great enough to affect life on our planet.

The most significant long-term source of energy available to us may be the sun. In fact, it is somewhat misleading to distinguish solar energy from, say, coal, petroleum or hydropower. There would be no coal nor petroleum were it not for the solar-powered plant and animal productivity of millions of years ago. Such fuel sources are really fossil sunshine. The electricity that can be generated by falling water owes its existence to heat (energy) received by the earth and which evaporates moisture, transports it by air movement (the result of differential atmospheric heating by sun energy) to where the moisture returns to earth in the form of rain or snow. Plant biomass, now more and more looked to as a source of energy, would not exist without the energy coming from the sun. So, in effect, a large part of the energy we use is actually solar, no matter by what other terms we refer to it. During the twentieth century the United States and most other industrial nations have been living on the stored (fossil) sunshine accumulated over millions of years. Such energy is nonrenewable (short of millions of years) and thus ultimately this energy source will become too scarce to supply other than a small fraction of our needs.

Must the planet one day have an energy system based chiefly on current reception of solar energy? Perhaps this may be the case and certainly a far greater use of solar energy will be made in the years ahead. However, quite apart from the highly controversial use of nuclear energy, some alternatives may exist to a total future reliance on direct solar energy. One of these possibilities is hydrogen. This element exists in almost unlimited (from a utilization point of view) quantities and there is reason to be optimistic that what appear to be relatively minor technical problems can be solved in order to make hydrogen a major world source of energy in the twenty-first century.

Perhaps what we ought to keep uppermost in our thinking about available energy options is that just because we humans made a major commitment to fossil fuels beginning with coal and then later adding petroleum and natural gas doesn't mean the world must end because these fuels will ultimately become too scarce and hence too costly to provide for our principal energy needs. To think thusly is evidence of a lack of imagination and a lack of confidence in our ability to carry on. However, this is not to suggest that we are relieved of the necessity to think about energy conservation and especially about the question of what is the most desirable level of future consumption of energy.

Some of the advocates of continued exponential increases in energy production argue that to do otherwise would risk increased unemployment and especially among the less skilled members of the labor force. This position has a certain intuitive attraction to it for it seems logical that an increase in energy consumption is prerequisite to an increase in available jobs. However, a counter argument can be made that increased energy supplies tend, at least in some instances, not to create jobs but to reduce jobs. A prime example of this is modern agriculture, which is an *energy intensive* activity requiring only a small percentage of our nation's total labor force to produce the food we use or export. Thus, it can also be argued that if it is employment we are concerned about insofar as it is influenced by energy consumption then labor-intensive rather than energy-intensive activity is the direction in which to go. A moment's reflection on the latter suggestion, however, leads to the realization that this is precisely the situation most poor countries find themselves in today and few of those countries prefer such a condition.

Giving each side of the debate its due, one must be aware that some of the advocates of continued growth in energy production and consumption occasionally appear naive and environmentally insensitive. Some of those who most strongly advocate a halt to the growth of energy production and a severe limiting of the means by which energy will be produced sometimes appear to be pressing quasi-metaphysical views rather than views related to the "real world."

We must be alert for the catch words of both arguments. The advocates of unlimited energy growth sometimes refer to any and all detractors as "econuts" or the environmental "lunatic fringe" and the more ardent advocates of a steady state vis-à-vis energy consumptions refer to their opposites as advocates of "growthmania." While there is clearly a basis for debate, confusion often arises because the elements of the debate are seldom separated but are jumbled together in grand confusion, these being (1) personal value systems and (2) the pragmatic aspects of energy conservation. Although our principal concern lies with the pragmatic aspects of energy conservation, one would be naive indeed to believe that that is all that must concern us. The question of personal value systems may well prove to be the principal focus around which the energy debate is ultimately resolved.

Many of the concerns voiced in the United States regarding energy tend to be extremely parochial. Often overlooked is that any debate about energy must include not only the United States and the rest of the already industrialized nations but also the billions of persons living in the Third World. With the exceptions of the favored few Third World nations that possess large petroleum resources, the remainder of this group of more than 100 sovereign states faces energy problems of dismaying magnitudes.

Arguments about steady states of energy consumption and the like have no particular relevance for these nations where the human population is increasing at rates above 2 and sometimes 3 percent per year and in which the demand for consumer goods increases even more rapidly than does the population. One of the more important tasks of the citizens of the United States is to begin to think about energy on a global scale rather than solely on a national scale. Only when we accomplish this and incorporate its results into our various plans for future energy development will there be a chance for sound long-term energy conservation within the United States.

## HISTORY OF ENERGY PRODUCTION AND CONSUMPTION

For all but a small portion of the total time our species has been in existence, it has depended for energy on the work performed by people. The first important nonhuman energy source was supplied by large domesticated animals such as cattle and horses. Although there is some disagreement among authorities as to precisely when the first of these animals was domesticated it appears that none was domesticated earlier than 10,000 years ago and not for thousands of years afterward did their use become very widespread.

Although the discovery of how to make fire predated animal domestication by thousands of years, the use of fire to produce energy capable of doing useful work is much more recent and dates from the late seventeenth century. In 1698 a stream-driven water pump was invented which, though very fuel inefficient, was the first or among the first heat-driven engines to find a serious application. Other inventions involving fire and steam followed and it was the well-known James Watt who, in the eighteenth century, made of steam an energy source that was to transform the world and make possible the Industrial Revolution. These early steam engines used wood for fuel but as this became increasingly scarce in England and Europe it was replaced by coal. It must be stressed that while steam power was making great strides it was doing so almost entirely outside of a rural context. The latter was to remain dependent on the energy of the horse, ox, and human muscles for quite a while longer.

Employment of wind to perform useful work probably was first done to propel sailing vessels. The use of sails was present in Egypt by at least 2500 B.C. Windmills seem to have a more recent origin having been recorded first in Western Europe in the twelfth century. These windmills were employed to mill grain and, in the case at least of the Netherlands, to pump water. In recent years there has been a growing interest in wind as a means of generating electricity.

Water-generated power on a scale to be other than a curiosity seems to have first made an appearance in parts of Western Europe in the twelfth century and was associated with the mining industry. For centuries, water power was used to turn wheels, which in turn could be geared to turn stones to mill grain, raise and lower stamps to crush metal ore, and to manipulate bellows to smelt or soften metals. Water-power sites were, obviously, highly valued and great skill was developed in making use of these energy sites. Today, water power remains of major importance although it is only rarely employed to turn an old fashioned water wheel. Instead, falling water is often directed into turbines whose blades are made to spin and produce what we call hydroelectricity. It might be noted here, however, that more than a few opportunities still exist for useful application of the "old fashioned" water wheels.

The heat (energy) property of coal was known for many centuries before this material became an economically significant source of energy. The first important use was in England and this later spread to the continent of Europe and far beyond. The use of coal met with considerable resistance for a long time, however, because its immediate precursor, charcoal, was seen as being far superior.

Charcoal can be made from any wood, but hardwood is almost always preferred because the resultant product burns slowest and is less bulky per energy unit. The time and place of discovery of the properties of charcoal are not known nor is it known as to where or when actual charcoal making was first accomplished. However, this material was known and valued (and manufactured) long before the Industrial Revolution. Charcoal is still an important energy source today and particularly so in many Third World nations.

Petroleum and natural gas have been known since ancient times although their use as important energy sources is less than a century old. Petroleum was first used commercially to produce kerosene and only later, toward the very end of the nineteenth century, did it begin to assume significance as a major source of energy. It was not until about World War I that oil-fired ships and the automobile thrust petroleum into an important role in the international energy scene.

Widespread use of natural gas is even more recent than the use of petroleum for energy. Unlike liquid oil, natural gas is not easy to transport from well head to distant markets and until the necessary pipeline technology was developed enormous quantities of natural gas was "flared," that is, it was burned away into the air, unused. Even today huge quantities of natural gas are flared continuously in some of the largest oil fields in the world because of the problems of processing and transporting this resource to distant markets.

The most recent major addition to the world's energy resources is nuclear fuel. The so-called atomic age began with the pioneering research on radioactivity by Marie Curie, née Sklodowska, and Pierre Curie at the very end of the nineteenth century and during the early years of this century. That the radium and other radioactive substances investigated by this duo of scientists might be the source of enormous exploitable energy was not immediately perceived but by the 1930s research was being performed in various places that led to the conclusion that it might indeed be possible to release what was then only theorized to be huge quantities of energy.

The first major application of a human-devised release of atomic energy was in the form of a fearsome weapon. This occurred at Alamogordo (literally, fat cottonwood tree), New Mexico, on July 16, 1945. On August 6, 1945, an atomic bomb was dropped on Hiroshima, Japan, and on August 9, 1945 another bomb was dropped on Nagasaki. Extensive development and testing ensued, after the war, of more sophisticated atomic weapons of greater explosive yield. In addition to the United States, nations known to possess atomic weapons capability at the present time include Great Britain, France, Soviet Union, China, and India. It is generally accepted that virtually any nation can construct at least a crude atomic bomb if it has the desire to do so.

A current focus of nuclear research in the United States and certain other "atomic" nations is the production of electricity in nuclear-fueled power plants. The number of nations included in this array far surpasses the nations known or suspected to possess atomic weapon capability.

## HISTORY OF ENERGY USE IN THE UNITED STATES

The earliest colonial period was marked by the use of human and animal power—the latter being chiefly supplied by oxen, which later gave way to horses and mules. Water power also became significant wherever a suitable site was located close to a settlement or, vice versa where a settlement could be sited adjacent to a water power source. Windmills were rare or nonexistent in the early years. Wood was

the preeminent fuel for heating, cooking and, in the form of charcoal, for metal working. By the early nineteenth century, however, coal began to supersede charcoal and also increasingly, water power. The former was due chiefly to a rapid adoption of the steam engine although the steam engine was often to be fueled by wood well into the nineteenth century.

Coal and steam were the energy "kings and queens" of the nineteenth century. Steam engines were driving ships of many sizes, railroad locomotives, and, toward the end of the century, a wide range of heavy farm machinery. Personal transportation was by horse or on foot throughout the nineteenth century.

In 1859, the first commercial oil well was drilled in Pennsylvania and from this modest beginning rose the enormous petroleum industry of the twentieth century. The first use of this petroleum was for kerosene or, as it was then more generally known, mineral oil. Toward the end of the century, other petroleum-derived products came into use but gasoline did not attain significance until the widespread adoption of the automobile and other applications of the internal combustion engine in the twentieth century.

Steam-driven electrical generators came into existence in the latter part of the nineteenth century in some of the larger cities and this form of energy spread at various rates of speed around the nation. It was not until the twentieth century that electricity became generally available and in sparsely settled areas it remained rare until the decade of the 1930s when rural electrification programs sponsored by the federal government made electricity available to many such areas.

Throughout much of this energy revolution, however, horses and mules remained the chief nonhuman source of energy on the nation's farms. It was not until the early 1930s that these animals gave way to tractors and it might be said that the age of mechanization of American farms is only a matter of a few decades. The urban picture was different in that shortly after World War I the automobile, streetcar, and truck had driven horses from the cities and from all but the smaller towns.

With the development of the necessary pipeline technology, natural gas began to be distributed at ever-greater distances from its places of origin, chiefly in Texas, and by the 1940s a considerable national network of such pipelines was in place. This has been added to frequently so that few places in the nation are without access to natural gas.

The most recent chapter of U.S. energy production and use is the development of nuclear power plants. At present most of these plants are located in the eastern United States but there is a rapidly growing resistance by a variety of organizations to the construction of any more such facilities.

The growth of per capita energy consumption in the United States dating from the beginning of this century is an astonishing story and especially so when it is compared with most other nations. During the middle of the 1970s, for example, the annual per capita consumption of energy in the United States was approximately 332 million Btu ($332 \times 10^6$ Btu). For India the comparable figure was 5 million Btu ($5 \times 10^6$ Btu). West Germany and Japan, both considered economic powers had, respectively, per capita energy consumptions of about 158 million Btu ($158 \times 10^6$ Btu) and about 98 million Btu ($98 \times 10^6$ Btu). This enormous difference in the per capita consumption of energy between the United States and other highly developed nations—not to mention the Third World—is frequently the object of international concern since it appears to some observers, many of whom are our allies and friends, that we not only consume more than our fair share of the world's energy resources but also waste a great part of it.

In less than a century our nation went from relatively low per capita energy consumption and a horse and buggy society to a nation that consumes energy like no other (Table 13.1). However one may feel about this, one thing should be kept in mind: at the present time there is no known energy source or collection of sources or envisioned sources that would make energy available to more than a tiny fraction of the world's population at a level equal to the current per capita use in the United States (Table 13.2).

Table 13.1
**Per capita energy consumption, United States**

| Year | Total of all Energy (including hydro-electricity, etc.) Total $10^{15}$ Btu | Per Capita $10^6$ Btu | Petroleum Total $10^{15}$ Btu | Per Capita $10^6$ Btu | Natural Gas Total $10^{15}$ Btu | Per Capita $10^6$ Btu | Coal Total $10^{15}$ Btu | Per Capita $10^6$ Btu |
|---|---|---|---|---|---|---|---|---|
| 1950 | 33.9 | 223 | 13.5 | 89 | 6.0 | 39 | 12.9 | 85 |
| 1955 | 39.7 | 240 | 17.5 | 106 | 9.0 | 55 | 11.5 | 70 |
| 1960 | 44.1 | 245 | 19.9 | 111 | 12.4 | 69 | 10.1 | 56 |
| 1965 | 53.0 | 274 | 23.3 | 120 | 15.8 | 81 | 11.9 | 61 |
| 1970 | 66.8 | 328 | 29.5 | 145 | 21.8 | 107 | 12.7 | 62 |
| 1975 | 70.7 | 332 | 32.7 | 154 | 20.0 | 94 | 12.8 | 60 |
| 1980 preliminary | 76.3 | 343 | 34.3 | 154 | 20.4 | 92 | 15.7 | 71 |

Source: *Statistical Abstract of the United States*, 1981.

Table 13.2
**World and United States energy consumption (in $10^6$ metric tons of coal equivalents)**

|  | 1960 | 1970 | 1975 | 1979 |
|---|---|---|---|---|
| World total | 4019 | 6512 | 7529 | 8706 |
| United States | 1447 | 2204 | 2284 | 2506 |
| U.S. percent of total | 36.0 | 35.0 | n.a. | 28.8 |
| | | | | |
| Energy source | | | | |
| Solid fuel | 2049 | 2272 | 2397 | 2738 |
| Liquid fuel | 1293 | 2279 | 3348 | 3834 |
| Natural gas | 593 | 1293 | 1581 | 1846 |
| Electricity | 85 | 155 | 223 | 288 |

Source: *Statistical Abstract of the United States*, 1981.

One sometimes reads or hears that what we need most in the United States is to go back to a simpler day of low per capita energy consumption when most of the energy needs were supplied by human or other animal muscle. However appealing this might appear to be, it is highly unlikely that this will come to pass for the basic reason that such energy sources could not begin to supply even a small fraction of the energy we need. It requires about 10 people working one hour to produce the energy equivalent of one horsepower and a single liter of gasoline will produce energy that is about equal to 30 hours of adult human labor. To convert any large part of our economic system from the current energy-intensive to human labor-intensive would require, among other things, a social revolution of a dimension probably without equal in human history.

There are geographical areas in the world, however, where labor-intensive instead of energy-intensive conditions still prevail. These occur, almost without exception, in Third World nations where lack of capital and large human populations make this use of human labor necessary. Where such conditions prevail it is sometimes desirable that there not be any ma-

jor substitution of energy-intensive activity for labor-intensive activity because to do so would result in even larger numbers of unemployed persons as well as greatly exacerbating the already large impact, on the economies, of costly imported fossil fuel. Even in the most developed countries there are some elements of the economies that might be better off were there a greater degree of labor intensity than is presently the case. However, energy intensity is so widely and uncritically regarded as the sine qua non of development that contrary views seldom receive a hearing.

With regard to animal power in the United States, one must recognize that unless there is a major revolution in our value systems this source of energy will remain modest. However, animal power remains important in many developing nations and may be expected to continue so, in many instances, not necessarily because these nations lack the means to convert to machines but because this energy source is more compatible with the ecologies and economies of such countries.

## SUMMARY

Beginning about a couple of decades ago, the United States discovered the obvious—that energy resources are finite and with that discovery the term "energy crisis" entered the American vocabulary. Other parts of the world had much earlier made the same discovery and had appropriately adjusted their energy consumption. The United States, having long been the possessor of enormous quantities of fossil fuel resources as well as an almost unlimited access to world sources of fossil fuels, behaved as though energy was endlessly and inexpensively abundant. We are painfully learning that this is not so and are beginning to adjust our uses of energy accordingly albeit with too many stops, starts, and tentative federal support of new energy technologies.

We are a wasteful nation with regard to virtually every natural resource we use and nowhere has this been more true than with energy resources. Nevertheless, we still possess a remarkable amount of fossil fuel resources one of which, coal, is abundant enough to supply most of our needs for several centuries to come. We could and should embark on a national energy conservation program but, thus far, there has been little political will to do so. Such a program, if carefully designed, would permit continued economic expansion but would also require that many currently wasteful uses of energy be stopped. It is most likely that energy conservation in the United States will proceed about as rapidly as the cost of energy becomes an increasingly visible and painful item in private and public budgets.

There is really little chance that our nation will go back to what some believe was a "simpler time" when a large share of the energy used was supplied by human and animal power. This could only be accomplished by achieving a social revolution of unprecedented dimensions. So, we must accept that we will remain dependent on relatively large quantities of energy per capita to make our civilization work. But, we must also decide on what kind of energy producing and consuming civilization we are to become. In the past, we have allowed forces to carry us along serene in the mistaken belief that we were riding an endless wave of cheap energy and allowed others to make the energy-use decisions. It is time now that such decision making be democratized at least to the degree that there be widespread public debate and discussion. The fate of our energy future is far too important to be determined solely by "experts" and politicians.

# energy resources: part I

## INTRODUCTION

The first nonregenerative energy resource humans used to a major extent was coal and now, after nearly two centuries of such use, coal is still important and may attain even greater importance in the future than it enjoys at present.

The major use of coal is for the production of electricity—about 50 percent of all coal burned in the United States goes for this use—with other amounts going for the production of coke used in iron and steel manufacture and for the production of chemicals.

Coal is the partially carbonized remains of vegetation that was first deposited in marshy situations millions of years ago and, with the passage of many years, was compressed and chemically modified to produce the different coal types we find today.

The first major stage of preservation of plant material produces *peat.* The formation of peat can be quite rapid with depths of several meters accumulating in the space of only 10,000 years. The process of peat formation continues to occur in our time although the annual increment in any given place is almost too small to measure. Most of the peat beds that exist today are found in the Northern Hemisphere in places where there are short cool summers and long, cold or cool winters and where impaired surface drainage favors the accumulation of partially decayed vegetation. It is believed that similar conditions must have prevailed in past geological time when the great coal beds were undergoing their earliest formation.

Peat, when first removed from a peat bed, contains a high percentage of moisture and must be allowed to dry before it can be burned. Even when dry it has a low Btu-to-volume ratio and therefore is not presently used on a large scale. It has long been used in some parts of the world, Ireland for example, as an inexpensive fuel. It is sometimes used to fuel electricity generating plants and perhaps its best-known use is in the production of Scotch whiskey. The world's peat resources are considerable but this energy source is not likely to be of major importance in the foreseeable future (Fig. 14.1).

When peat is compressed by growing accumulations and if the depth of such accumulation is great enough—the peat undergoes a slow concentration of the components that can be used for energy production. That is, with the passage of time—and sufficient heat and compression—there is a reduction of moisture and volatile materials and *lignite* is formed. Lignite, or "brown coal" has a low Btu content compared to the other major types of coal and for this reason is not mined unless there are no other suitable energy sources available. With continued compression *subbituminous* coal is formed followed by bituminous and then anthracite coal. Bituminous coal is the best all-around coal type for it is suited to many applications including the fueling of electricity generating plants and for manufacture of coke used in iron and steel smelting. Subbituminous coal is not suited to the production of coke but serves well in electricity-generating plants. Anthracite, the most highly carbonized of all coal

**Figure 14.1**   Cutting and stacking peat in Ireland.

types, serves best as a domestic heating fuel because it burns with a fairly clean blue flame. Anthracite is too scarce to be of use in either the generation of electricity or the production of coke.

Coal sometimes occurs at the surface where it has been exposed by earth movements and erosion and coal also occurs down to depths in excess of 2000 meters. In the United States, most of the known coal deposits of economic value occur between the surface and 1500 meters depth. The depth at which a given coal deposit exists will largely determine the type of mining that will be used to extract the coal.

Coal deposits that lie within 50 meters of the surface may often be most easily mined by *surface* or *strip mining* (Fig. 14.2). Such deposits usually have a quantity of soil and sedimentary rocks lying above them. This material is called *overburden* and must be removed before actual extraction of the coal is possible. The over-

burden is deposited in *spoils banks* adjacent to the *coal seam* that will be stripped. Stripping is usually accomplished by huge buckets operated in conjunction with a dragline. The mined coal, after some processing, is loaded in trucks or railroad cars and transported to market. Strip mining for coal is the most controversial mining technique employed, this being due to actual or possible environmental damage caused by this kind of coal extraction.

The other type of coal recovery is by underground mining. This usually involves vertical *shafts,* which are sunk to the level(s) of the coal stratum or strata and lateral *drifts* are made away from the shafts through the actual coal seams. Underground mining is more costly than strip mining but must be resorted to when the coal lies at depths too great to permit economic strip mining. One type of underground mine may not involve the use of vertical shafts. This is done when a coal seam is exposed in a

**Figure 14.2** Strip mining for coal in Ohio. The dragline "Big Muskie" weighs 12,247 metric tons and is 138 meters in length, overall.

canyon wall so that a *drift* can be run in from the canyon wall. This sometimes can be the most economic type of underground coal mining but the necessary geomorphological conditions are not often found.

The United States has a very large coal resource (Map 14.1). As the map indicates, the greater part of the existing reserves consists of types of bituminous coal but there is also a large quantity of lignite. Estimates of the size of the coal resource vary from source to source although there is, overall, relatively close agreement. The estimates followed here were made by Averitt in 1969 and appear to correctly represent the size of this resource. According to this estimate, the United States has approximately 1.5 trillion metric tons of mineable coal including lignite. It is important to make the distinction between *mineable* coal and coal *resources*. The former refers to the quantity that can probably be recovered given the current state of mining technology and costs whereas the latter refers to all the coal thought to be in the ground regardless of technological or economic limitations. The size of the known reserves of any mineral resource is always

partly the function of price (i.e., market conditions) and available extraction technology.

The first coal fields (deposits) to have received intense exploitation in the United States were those located mostly east of the Mississippi River. Today, the major part of the *unmined reserves* is located west of the Mississippi River in the Rocky Mountain region. Many of these western coal deposits are suitable for strip mining.

How long will our coal resources last? That is a question frequently asked but the answers, almost as frequently, vary. Basically, any answer must consider the probable rate at which we will mine this resource which, in turn, depends on widely varying estimates as to how large a share of our total energy production will be produced by coal in the future and how much coal we will export to other nations. The estimate of our use of coal for energy production hinges in part upon projections of how much electricity we will be using in the future and what the foreign market demand for coal will be. Individual estimates tend to vary considerably. Perhaps the pivotal question is what environmental price are we willing to pay for

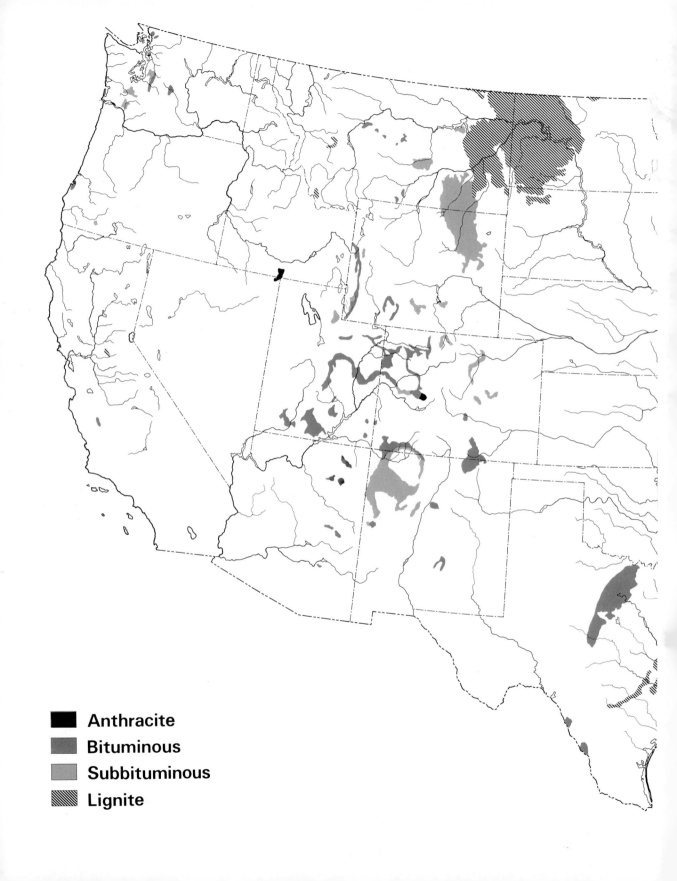

Anthracite

Bituminous

Subbituminous

Lignite

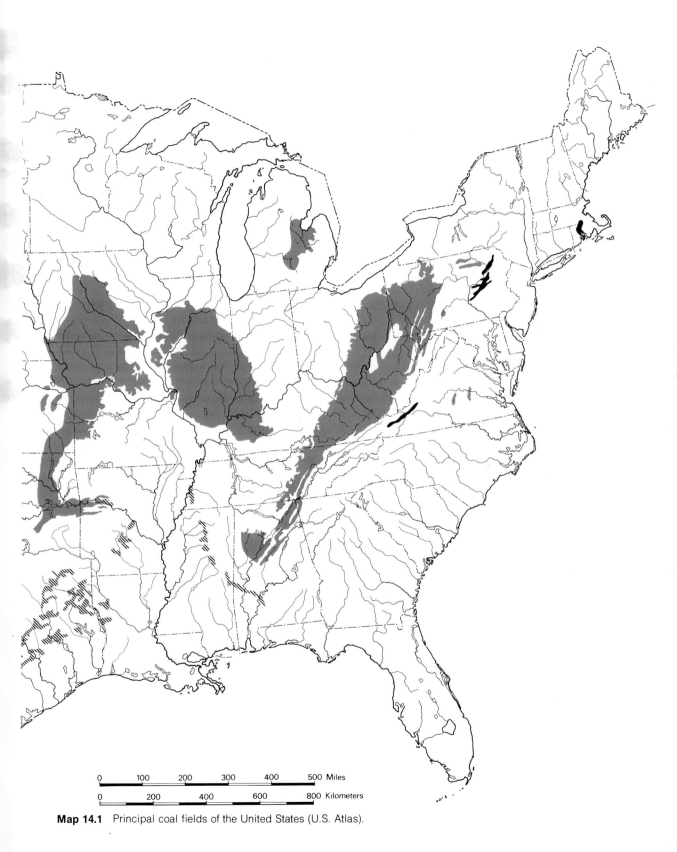

**Map 14.1** Principal coal fields of the United States (U.S. Atlas).

coal-generated electricity and increased export sales of coal.

At this writing (1982), petroleum has become relatively abundant in the international market place, a condition that tends to decrease national interest in accelerating the rate at which we exploit our coal resources. There has been a slowing of the annual increase in per capita electricity consumption that greatly affects the amount of bituminous coal that is mined. Environmental regulations governing coal mining and coal utilization also influence the annual rate of coal extraction. Subject to so many influences, it is not surprising that there are sometimes wide variations from one year to another in the quantity of coal mined. In recent years the annual national production of bituminous coal has been approximately 640 million tons. At that average rate of extraction, we have coal sufficient for several centuries. Were that rate to be tripled or even quadrupled, we could still look forward to more than a century of abundant coal supplies.

We often think of coal as being useable only in the solid form but it can be processed to make coal gas which can be distributed by pipe line like natural gas. Coal gas is produced by heating coal to a temperature high enough to drive off the hydrogen and methane the coal contains. Coal gas contains about one-half hydrogen and one-third methane along with a variety of other gases such as nitrogen and carbon dioxide. The high hydrogen content makes coal gas a very explosive mixture but one that can be managed safely. Coal gas was formerly used in many parts of the United States until abundant supplies of natural gas became available. As the natural gas resources of the United States appear to be on the wane and the cost of natural gas escalates we may expect to hear more, in the future, about coal gas. Coal can also be processed to produce petroleum-like materials that can then be refined to produce gasoline, diesel oil, and the like.

There is no question about the abundance and versatility of "king" coal. Why, then, aren't we energy self-sufficient through all out exploitation of this resource? The answer is to be found in the spheres of economics, politics, and environmentalism, all three of which will be discussed in the next section of this chapter.

## ECONOMIC CONSTRAINTS ON THE USE OF COAL

Coal must compete in the market place with every other type of energy resource. Although extremely abundant, as has been shown, coal can be costly to mine, process, and deliver to market. Underground mining is considerably more expensive and dangerous than strip mining and although the latter form of coal extraction often receives the greater part of public attention more than 50 percent of all coal mined in the United States is by underground activity.

Developing a new underground mine is expensive and may take up to eight years before actual production can begin. During this time there may be no return on investment which, in the case of a large underground mine, may represent many millions of dollars. On the other hand, a large underground mine may be productive for 50 or more years. Another major cost, in addition to capital costs, is labor which has risen markedly since World War II. In the case of strip mines, the yield of coal per hour of labor is usually significantly greater than the comparable yield from underground mines and it is this fact, coupled with usually sharply lower initial capital costs, that makes strip mining so attractive and the reason that most projections about future development of our coal resources are based principally on strip mining. However, it must be noted that underground mining has become highly mechanized thus increasing output per worker/hour.

Beginning in 1973 when the price of petroleum rose sharply the economics of coal mining changed making this energy resource more attractive for investment. However, it must be kept in mind that the well-head cost of petroleum produced in most OPEC nations and, particularly Saudi Arabia, is so low that these nations could lower the price of crude oil and suddenly render uneconomical the exploitation of a significant share of the presently economically useful coal deposits in our nation. Although it is not likely this pricing action will occur the mere fact that it could casts a shadow of instability over coal mining. This is particularly true for many underground mines where even a slight softening in the demand and, hence, lowering of the market price for energy would make the mines uneconomical to operate and could force temporary or permanent closure of them. Thus, it may be that if coal is to assume the preeminent place in energy production in the United States special governmental involvement assuring a profitable market for coal producers would have to be devised. However, this is not likely to occur because to do so would ignore the fact that energy resources are global resources and there is now essentially one huge global energy market. Attempts by the U.S. government to manipulate coal (or other energy prices) might be counterproductive insofar as the nation's long-term economic interests are concerned. Coal, then, may be a "king" but it currently lacks a kingdom.

## COAL AND POLITICS

It is almost self-evident that any major energy resource is subject to domestic as well as international political influences and this is true of coal. We must also be aware that the present status of coal as an energy source in the United States, while important, does not reflect its preeminent energy role prior to World War II when the nation's railroads and electrical generating plants were largely coal fired nor, to take this back even farther in time, to the last quarter of the nineteenth century up to and just beyond World War I. In those earlier years, coal had no

serious competition from other energy sources and occupied a position more closely akin to that occupied today by petroleum. Beginning in the 1920s, petroleum began to make large inroads into the coal market and especially with regard to diesel-powered machinery in ships, trains, and trucks, and in the substitution of oil for heating where coal once reigned almost unchallenged.

Domestic politics have entered most significantly with respect to mine safety, labor relations, and during times of national military emergencies. Confrontations between the federal government, mine owners, and mine workers constitute a major part of the fabric of American industrial history. During the early years of the twentieth century, coal mine owners came to be regarded by many persons as rapacious exploiters of labor and natural resources. It was this image, in part deserved and in part invented, that contributed to the federal government involving itself in the control of coal pricing during World War I. Although the rationale behind this action appears to have been a desire to assure the stable production in wartime of the energy the nation needed it seems, in the event, also to have created considerable confusion and a lasting enmity between all the players. Major conflicts arose between the federal government's attempts to control coal prices and the desire of the soft coal mine owners to obtain higher coal prices. A detailed study of this and related conflicts by J. P. Johnson shows that, contrary to the widely held public view of the time, there was not a soft coal cartel, or in the language of the times, a coal trust. The chief purpose of detailing this matter here is that it illustrates the more or less continual conflicts in the American political arena between the consuming public that wants cheap energy and the owners or producers of energy who seek to maximize profits. It also draws attention to the fact that far from being a cartel, soft coal mining was almost as open a free-for-all as some might wish for. Unfortunately, this openness and lack of cooperation often led to wasteful overproduction, careless and dangerous mine operations, and instability in most all aspects of the production and sale of soft coal.

## COAL AND THE ENVIRONMENT

Coal mining and coal-use constitute some of the most environmentally disruptive activities in which humans engage. However, it is only in recent years that these long-recognized truths have received the attention they deserve. Today, the environmental costs of coal extraction, processing, and combustion are no longer ignored and have become a major element in determining the economic future of any coal deposit as well as the future importance of coal in the nation's energy picture. Note also that it is in the area of environmental considerations, broadly defined, that most aspects of coal conservation and management are to be found.

## HEALTH AND SAFETY

In order to grasp the role of coal in human affairs and human welfare properly one must go back to the years when the Industrial Revolution in Great Britain had completed the transition from wood to coal as its principal source of energy. Coal mining was then exclusively underground.

We think today that coal mining is the work of adult males—although women are joining the ranks of miners in increasing numbers—but in the first half of the nineteenth century coal mines in Great Britain employed children. A report of 1842 details the employment of children as young as five years old in underground coal mines under the most apalling physical conditions. In one mining district it was stated that children began work in the mines at age seven, very commonly when they were age eight, and generally when they were nine. One witness described the employment underground of a three-year-old boy.

Of course, adult males were also employed and they often constituted the major part of the mine labor force. Girls and women were also employed in the mines and were not exempted from the most arduous of tasks among which was the carrying, on their backs, of sacks of coal from the mine face up to the surface, this being accomplished by scaling a series of ladders. Then they commonly carried 100 to 150 pounds of coal at a time and worked 12-hour shifts.

No safety precautions were taken with the exception of the development, in the early nineteenth century, of miner's lamps that would not ignite the "fire-damp" (methane gas), which often occurs in coal mines as the result of the decomposition of coal in the presence of water and air. Given the callous and even brutal disregard of the time for the welfare of miners it must be assumed that adoption of this invention was stimulated chiefly to prevent the great economic loss that can occur with a mine explosion.

Underground coal mining is one of the most dangerous occupations undertaken today even after considerable care has been taken to improve mine safety. In the early days of coal mining in Great Britain it was hazardous beyond belief. In addition to methane gas, which not only can cause powerful explosions but can asphyxiate the unwary, coal dust was (and remains) a great hazard because it is highly explosive. We also know today that prolonged breathing of coal dust can lead to a pulmonary disease called "black lung." Mines were also very unsanitary because workers commonly stayed below for up to a half a day or more and thus voided urine and feces in whatever tunnels or unused drifts that were at hand. This led to a health problem commonly known as "miner's worm," which is the common hookworm, *Anclyostoma* spp. . Mines are not the natural habitat of this serious intestinal pest and occurred in such places only because of the toilet habits of miners. The law now requires that miners have regular and adequate access to toilet facilities but in earlier times no thought was given to this matter.

Health and safety in the coal mines remain as serious issues even today although conditions are immeasurably better than those just described. Miners continue to die from explosions, are maimed in accidents, and too often live out their lives impaired by black lung disease. The most recent major federal legislation respecting safety is the Mine Safety Act of 1969. This is administered by the Mine Safety Health Administration. Thanks in large measure to this legislation and its effective enforcement, coal mine fatalities in the United States have been sharply reduced (133 in 1980 as compared to 233 in 1970). But no matter how much care is taken, underground coal mining will always be a dangerous occupation.

A large part of this nation's coal reserves lie in situations suited to strip mining and therefore most of the occupational hazards associated with underground mining are not factors to consider with this type of coal-extraction activity. However, when costs permit, that is, when market conditions are favorable, it is to be expected that underground coal mining will expand and given the trends of energy requirements we may be assured that human costs will continue although at levels far below those which prevailed in earlier decades.

# ENVIRONMENTAL COSTS OF MINING

Most environmental impacts associated with coal mining are tied to strip mining although underground mining is not entirely free of these problems. Most of the following comments relate to strip mining but attention will be drawn to any instance relevant to underground mining.

Probably no other type of mineral exploitation causes more general public attention than does strip mining and especially strip mining for coal. Unlike underground mining where most of the altered geology is hidden from public view a strip mine is there for all to see and the sight is one that can delight few other than those having a financial interest in the extraction of coal. It can be argued that one's personal sense of landscape esthetics offers no acceptable basis for allowing or disallowing strip mining. However, there are environmental impacts associated with such mining that all must accept as serious and requiring consideration. These impacts include water pollution, destruction of soil that is a part of the overburden, disruption of surface and subsurface ecosystems, possible disruption of previously existing subsurface water flows and, in parts of the semiarid West, the massive export of scarce water.

## Water Pollution

In the eastern United States, where most of the strip mining for coal has so far taken place, the most common complaint of ecologists and others concerned with healthy environments is the often profound and biologically destructive changes that take place in water chemistry in areas that have been strip mined. Chief among these changes is the greatly increased acidity of the water. Much eastern coal has a high sulphur content and the mine wastes are exposed year after year to rain and melting snow, leaching out sulphur that then comes into contact with the air and forms sulfuric acid, $H_2SO_4$. This process may extend over many decades in a given site thus contaminating surface and subsurface waters.

There is no absolutely foolproof system available to prevent these events after an area has been strip mined but acid leaching can be greatly reduced by what is termed *basic reclamation*. This consists of pushing the mine debris and overburden back into the mined strip, compacting this to some degree, and then spreading soil on top and planting the area to grass. So-called *full reclamation* involves an attempt to restore the land as it was prior to mining including the surface configuration and natural vegetation. Of course none of these methods, however conscientiously applied, actually restores the land to its previous ecological condition.

It is sometimes stated that full or even basic reclamation costs too much to make coal competitive with petroleum. Studies have been conducted that suggest this is not always the case. Also note that it is unlikely that a coal mining company will understate the probable costs of reclamation. The major question here is how much deterioration of water and associated resources—including the esthetic resources—we are willing to accept in the name of energy availability. Before we can begin to answer that question we must realize that we are often so far removed, geographically from the mining sites that our answers may lack a degree of relevance. By contrast, not only are the owners of coal deposits interested in achieving their economic ends but so too are the miners. Remember that we are talking not just about profits but also about jobs and families. The level of acceptable environmental impact, say, of a resident of San Francisco where coal provides little of the energy consumed or employment in that area may be different from residents of parts of West Virginia where coal mining offers virtually the only viable economic activity.

In the western United States most of the coal has a relatively low sulfur content—one of the reasons that there is so much interest in this resource—and thus acid water pollution problems are not expected to be serious. However, a study has shown that in those areas receiving less than an annual average of approximately 250 millimeters (10 inches) of precipitation probably cannot be reclaimed because this scant water is insufficient to allow for reestablishment of viable ecosystems. Great attention is presently focused on the environmental im-

pacts of western strip mining and perhaps one can be cautiously optimistic that environmental harm will be kept to a minimum. The degree to which this is achieved will undoubtedly be influenced by events in the global energy market and particularly events associated with the oil of the Middle East.

## Pipeline Transport of Coal

In the eastern United States, water availability is not often a problem with respect to strip mining but this is not the case in the western region where most of the future strip mining for coal is expected to take place. The latter region receives limited annual precipitation and the amounts tend to vary greatly from one year to another. The problem is not that the mining per se requires a great amount of water for it does not. The problem is that of possible pipeline transportation of the coal to where it will be used to generate electricity.

In past years the railroads transported most of the nation's coal to market—the remainder went by water. However, studies have shown that today the most inexpensive means of transport might be in the form of *coal slurry*. Such a slurry consists of powdered coal suspended in moving water. This can be pumped and sent by pipeline to where it is to be burned. Enormous quantities of water would be used in this process—water that would have to come from sources already well known to be modest in amount. Should such a use of the available water be made, local agriculture and stock raising would be affected as would the biological and chemical composition of the remaining drainage.

## ENVIRONMENTAL COSTS ASSOCIATED WITH BURNING COAL

It is with the combustion of coal that one encounters the most serious objections to its increased employment in energy production and it is here that most of the technological problems are found that must either be solved or at least reduced before there can be an environmentally safe national and international expansion of the burning of coal.

## Air Pollution

Far and away the most serious aspect of coal burning is air pollution. This concern is not new for it goes back in time many centuries. King Edward I of England (d. 1307) imposed the penalty of death on any person convicted of burning coal, so great was his and general public feeling against the use of this fuel. Later, but still centuries ago, when coal burning had become general in Great Britain the soot and smoke that hung over the industrial areas was often noted in the literature of the time. It was long ago (correctly) assumed that coal smoke was unhealthy but aside from the edict noted above and some later weak and very sporadic legislation, coal smoke was accepted as part of "the price of progress."

Although many early objections to coal use were based chiefly on the unpleasant smell of coal smoke we now know there are far more serious elements involved. These include soot and other particulates, release of sulfur that may form sulfuric acid, carbon monoxide (CO), and carbon dioxide ($CO_2$). It has been suggested that a major conversion to coal use would also increase the content of ionizing radiation in the atmosphere adjacent to coal-fired plants because some coal contains minute quantities of radioactive materials. At present, however, it appears that the previously listed hazards are far more immediate and demanding of attention.

## Soot and Particulates

Coal soot is chemically complex and contains many compounds of which some may be carcinogens. Some of these substances interfere with gaseous exchanges in the lungs and while this may not be an important consideration for healthy individuals, persons suffering from pulmonary, heart, or other health problems are affected.

Coal soot and other particulates smudge the exposed surfaces of buildings. This can be seen in such cities as Paris, London, and New York where programs for cleaning soot-covered building facades are underway. Some of the buildings now show, for the first time in over a century, aspects of beauty long ago covered up by the residues of coal burning. Of course, in order to affect such a cleanup coal burning must cease or means be employed by which particulates are trapped before they leave the site of coal combustion.

## Sulfuric Acid

Much of the coal that is presently used to fire electrical generating plants contains fairly large quantities of sulfur that are released into the atmosphere where it may combine with water to form sulfuric acid ($H_2SO_4$). This acid may then fall in accompaniment to rain and this "acid rain" may, in turn, negatively affect fresh water ecosystems and other parts of the environment. Like soot and particulates, sulfur emissions can be greatly reduced by installation of the proper equipment in the smoke stacks of plants burning coal.

## Carbon Monoxide

Carbon monoxide is produced whenever a carbon-containing substance is burned. This is an odorless and colorless gas and when in sufficient concentrations, can cause severe physical harm or death to humans and other air-breathing organisms. Even relatively low concentrations of CO in the atmosphere may impede human-response time in emergency situations. Although the harmful effects of CO are well known there are no means presently available to control CO emissions at coal-burning plants. Fortunately, CO tends to dilute rapidly in the atmosphere and thus dangerous concentrations are usually very limited in time and area.

## Carbon Dioxide

Carbon dioxide is produced by the combustion and decomposition of all carbon-containing matter and therefore is a natural component of the atmosphere. Moreover, unlike carbon monoxide, $CO_2$ is not poisonous although it can be asphyxiating when there is insufficient oxygen ($O_2$) present to breathe. Although $CO_2$ is not poisonous this chemical compound is produced in large quantities by the combustion of coal and other carbon fuels including petroleum, wood, and peat and thus is causing great environmental concern. This concern is related to the role that $CO_2$ plays in the heat balance of the sun-earth-atmosphere system.

Most of the solar radiation that enters the earth's atmosphere is in the form of shortwave energy and some of this passes through the atmosphere directly to the earth's surface. However, clouds and particulate matter in the air reflect about 30 percent of this shortwave radiation immediately back into space and there are other losses but approximately 46 percent reach the earth's surface. A small percentage, about 3 percent is immediately reflected as short wave energy but the remainder, approximately 43 percent, is absorbed at the surface. Some of this latter energy is fixed by green plants by the process called photosynthesis. The remaining absorbed energy is re-radiated as *longwave energy*. Longwave energy is fairly easily "captured" for relatively brief periods of time by clouds, water vapor, and carbon dioxide. It is the latter that appears to play the largest role with respect to retention of heat in the atmosphere.

As mentioned earlier, carbon dioxide is a normal component of the earth's atmosphere. The concern is how much more can be added by human acts before there would be changes in the weather and climate caused by changes in the temperature of the atmosphere. This concern is not of recent origin. A Swedish scientist, S. Arrhenius, raised this question in 1896 and suggested that an increase of $CO_2$ 2.5 to 3 times its then present level might cause air temperatures to rise as much as 8° to 9°C and produce mild climates in the northern high latitudes and melt the icecaps.

More than 80 years later, the question is again being raised and given considerable research attention. There is no argument that $CO_2$ is increasing in the atmosphere chiefly as a result of burning fossil fuels. There *is* considerable argument as to the degree and direction of climatic and weather changes associated with this increase in atmospheric $CO_2$.

Models are being developed and refined in an effort to obtain answers to these and related questions, However, much remains to be learned of the carbon cycle although its broad outlines have long been understood. Particularly difficult at present is the question of air/ocean carbon exchanges. There is fairly general agreement that increased inputs of $CO_2$ into the earth's atmosphere will have climatic consequences great enough to influence agriculture and thus world food production. Unfortunately, the magnitude, direction, and geographic locations of the changes cannot presently be determined with any acceptable degree of precision. Carbon dioxide cannot presently be economically removed from the emissions produced by burning carbon-containing fuel.

## PETROLEUM

Petroleum, or oil as it is also commonly known, is a complex assemblage of hydrocarbons containing a number of other substances in varying quantities. Sulfur is usually the most important impurity in terms of pollutant content and of difficulty in refining crude oil.

The origin of petroleum is the result of the

past accumulation of vast quantities of partially decayed minute plants and animals that were buried with sediment and then trapped in geological structures so that the oily material could not escape (Fig. 14.3). It requires millions of years of accumulation and entrapment under precisely correct geological conditions in order to produce deposits of economically useful size. Thus, we say that this is a nonregenerative energy resource although in terms of geological time there is regeneration but this is at a rate so slow as to be of no value or relevance to human needs.

Crude oil has wide ranges of physical characteristics and these are all well recognized in the oil business. Most highly prized are the light or "sweet" crude oils and least valued are the heavy or "sour" crude oils. The former contain a minimal amount of sulfur and a maximum amount of components that can be refined most easily into gasoline. The sour crudes are most difficult to refine, have a lower portion refinable to gasoline and are least desirable for use where air pollution related to sulfur dioxide emissions is a particular problem, which happens to be true of much of the United States.

Crude petroleum can also be extracted from tar sands, oil shale, and coal and refined into virtually the same range of products as can ordinary crude oil. These sources of oil will be discussed in detail later.

## Location of Petroleum Resources in the United States

As can be seen on Map 14.2, oil in commercial quantities has been found in many parts of the United States. However, the principal region is located in Texas and adjacent areas and in southern California. The other significant oil producing area in the United States is near Prudhoe Bay, Alaska.

The first successful drilling for oil was in Pennsylvania but there is now only relatively modest production from that area.

## World Oil Resources

The known major oil deposits of the world are shown in Map 14.3. Note how these are concentrated among a few countries and particularly note the fact while many Persian Gulf countries possess this resource in abundance dozens of other countries have no oil or such modest quantities as not to justify inclusion on the map. You should also note those nations that are members of OPEC (Organization of Petroleum Exporting Countries). Not all significant exporters of oil are members of this cartel, the most notable such exception being Mexico. Also of particular interest is the location of many of the major oil deposits in the Soviet Union. Many of these are located distant from the major population (consuming) centers, and the individual deposits tend not to be on the scale of those of the Middle East nor the larger ones in Texas and California.

## History of Oil Use in the United States

The history of petroleum use in the United States parallels the rise of the automobile to become the dominant means of personal transportation. Prior to the early twentieth century, the major use of petroleum was for the production of kerosene which, in the last half of the nineteenth century, took from whale oil the principal world market for illuminating oil. In addition to gasoline, heating oil challenged successfully the position in the market place formerly occupied by coal and also took over from coal the fueling of locomotives and steamships. In more recent years, a remarkable and still-growing number of chemical products derived from oil form the basis of a multibillion dollar petrochemical industry. Of the many valuable oil-derived products, plastics have been most significant in transforming many aspects of our daily lives.

Although gasoline consumption had reached what had appeared to be impressive levels be-

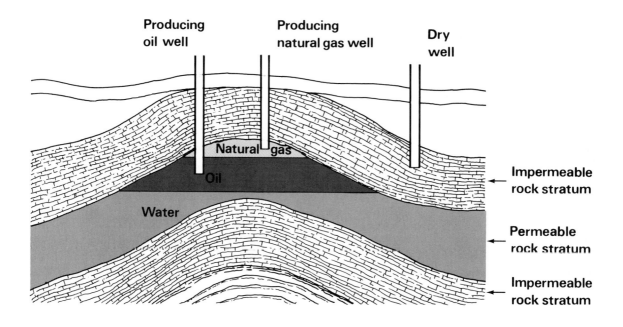

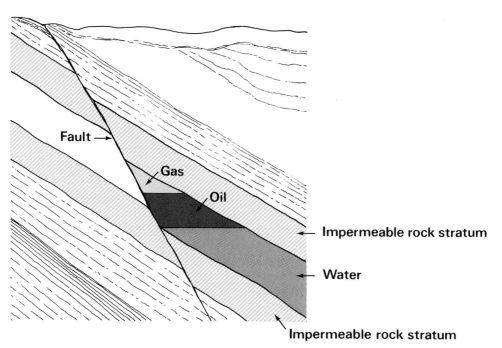

**Figure 14.3** Geological structures—folds and faults—in which oil and natural gas are sometimes encountered.

fore World War II it was after that conflict that the consumption of gasoline and other petroleum-derived products rose to spectacular heights in the United States and other industrialized parts of the world. In 1950, the United States consumed about one billion barrels of gasoline but by 1978 the annual consumption had risen to 2.7 billion barrels. Even more spectacular in terms of the overall increase in petroleum consumption was the use of distillate fuel oil, which is also known as diesel oil and heating oil: in 1950, the consumption in the United States amounted to only 75 million barrels but in 1978 the consumption was approximately 12.5 billion barrels. This last illustrates the incursion made by diesel fuel and heating oil into the market formerly dominated by coal. It can therefore be seen that it has been chiefly since World War II that the "age of petroleum" arrived in the United States. This pattern of increased consumption has been duplicated in the rest of the industrialized world although, on a per capita basis, far below that of the United States.

**THE SEARCH FOR AND DISCOVERY OF PETROLEUM DEPOSITS** Petroleum, not uncommonly, seeps to the surface and such places have long been exploited by humans. Primitive peoples are known to have used such sources—which usually are in the form of tar because the more volatile fractions have been lost to evaporation—for medicine, caulking boat seams, and other limited applications. There are indications that in some parts of the world shallow wells were occasionally dug to reach oil but the quantities so obtained were minuscule. When more modern interest developed in petroleum as a source of inexpensive illuminating oil (kerosene) it was the oil and tar seeps that first attracted the attention of well drillers.

In the early days, beginning with the first recorded well in 1859 in Pennsylvania, drilling equipment was extremely crude by present-day standards (Fig. 14.4). Only very shallow drilling depths were possible and oil deposits, to be productive, could not exceed more than a few hundred meters in depth. Such shallow fields (in oil-producing parlance a deposit of

**Figure 14.4**  Early oil field in Pennsylvania.

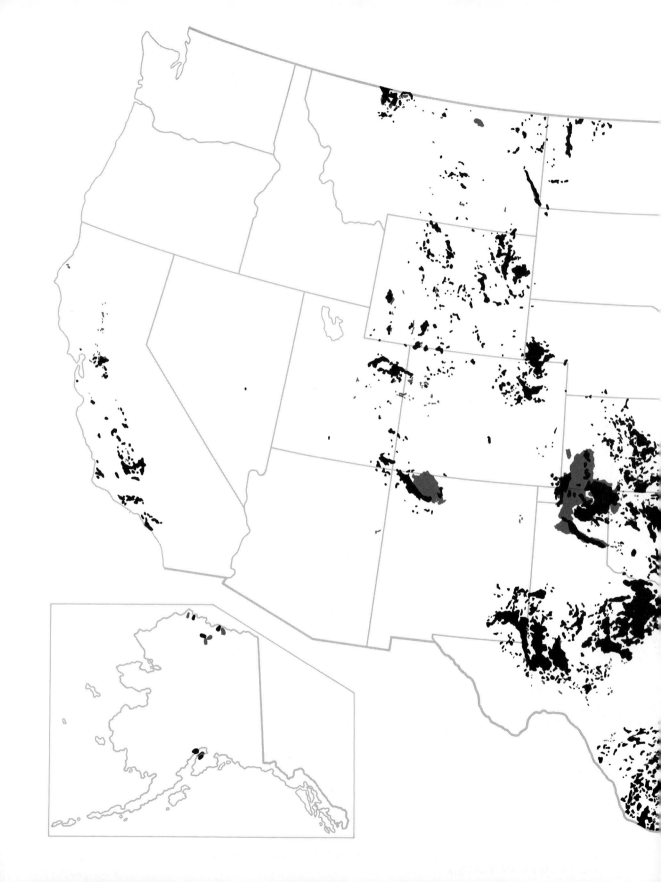

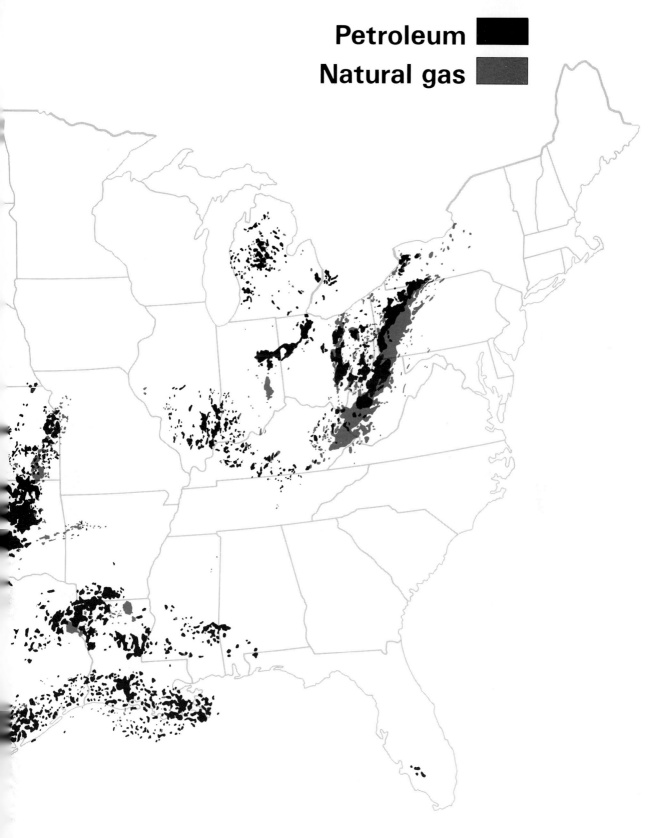

**Map 14.2** Petroleum and natural gas fields of the United States (adapted from the U.S. Atlas and Department of Energy).

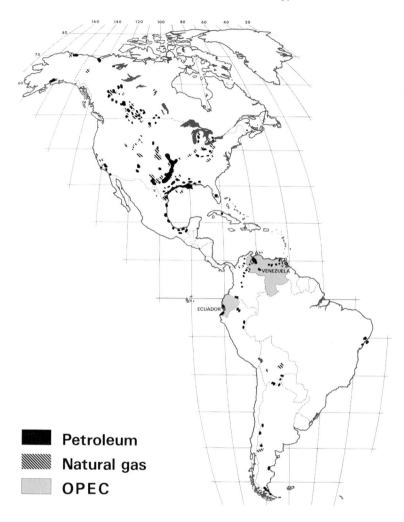

**Petroleum**
**Natural gas**
**OPEC**

oil is a field and the term is used interchangeably in this chapter) tended to contain only modest quantities and it soon became evident that drilling to greater depths would be required and equipment was gradually developed to accomplish this. However, the basic drilling system—called a cable tool system—made drilling very slow and still greatly limited the depths to which a well could be drilled. The technological innovation that made more rapid

and much deeper penetration possible was the rotary drilling system. This has been improved on frequently and today wells drilled in excess of 5000 meters are not rare and depths of more than 6500 meters have been attained (Fig. 14.5).

Although the problems of attaining great depth were formidable ones to overcome they were no greater than the problem of drilling direction. Unless kept under careful control at all

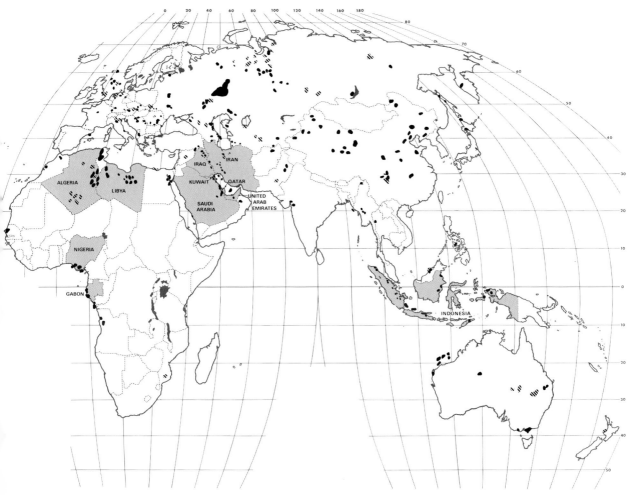

**Map 14.3** World petroleum and natural gas resources. OPEC members are named. The area of a given field as shown on the map is not always indicative of the size of the reserve in that field.

times an oil well drill will wander off in undesired directions. This is obviously wasteful of time and money and reduces chances of success. Thus *directional drilling* techniques were developed, which permit extreme accuracy of the drilling direction. This also made possible *slant drilling* whereby a single drill site or platform can be used to drill more than a single well by directing each drilling operation away from its neighbors.

As noted earlier, drill sites in the early days of the oil age were usually determined by oil or tar seeps at the surface. This gave way, in time, to a more sophisticated search for underlying *geological structures* that would have the greatest possibility of containing oil. Referring again to Figure 14.1, it will be seen that *anticlinal* structures offer the best possibilities for the underground entrapment of oil. There are also other situations such as an area of *faulted*

**Figure 14.5** A modern oil-drilling operation.

strata that allow entrapment in parts of the faulted area. These latter situations can be valuable but are especially difficult to drill since the oil collections tend to be very disjunctly distributed.

How are likely geological structures located? Some persons operate on intuition and will drill if they have a feeling that somewhere, beneath the surface, there is oil. Although not at all scientific it must be admitted that some enormous oil finds have been made following this approach. However, drilling is so expensive that the prudent will employ all available and affordable scientific techniques to aid in the search. Chief among these are seismic exploration, gravimetric analysis, plus good general geological detective work that pieces together various data to form a picture of the possibilities.

*Seismic exploration* makes use of the fact that sound waves can be directed downward into the earth. The speed of return of the "echoes" is a function of the depths that the sound reaches and rebounds to the surface from resistant rock strata. By igniting a carefully located set of explosive material and recording the echoes on tape it is possible to draw, with

fair precision, the shape of the hidden underground geological structures.

The force of gravity is not constant over the earth, this being due to variations in density of the earth's crust. Gravimetric forces that differ from the prevailing local conditions are referred to as *gravity anomalies*. Not all such anomalies indicate possible oil-bearing structures but some do. When these are located, further geological exploration such as seismic techniques may help to determine the likelihood of oil being present. One of the useful attributes of gravimetric analysis is that it can be conducted from specially equipped aircraft and thus large areas can be explored in a relatively short time. In areas difficult to penetrate by land as, for example, many parts of the Amazon Basin, this is the only practical means by which gravimetric analysis can be conducted.

After a promising geological structure has been located and financing for drilling has been arranged the next step is to assemble a drilling crew and all the necessary equipment. Then a large and very solid platform is constructed on which all drilling work will take place. If the well is being drilled offshore in the ocean a drilling platform costing millions of dollars will have to be constructed and floated into position. The term for the beginning of actual drilling is "spudding-in." Oil business publications take careful note of the wells that are spudded-in each week.

A rotary drill is used and a drill bit of specially hardened steel bores its way down into the earth. The deeper the drill bit penetrates the greater the oil and natural gas pressures will be when and if oil is encountered. That favorite oil well drilling scenario of Hollywood movies, the "gusher," is seldom encountered today and then usually only by accident (Fig. 14.6). In the early days of oil well drilling, gushers, that is, uncontrolled high-pressure flows to the surface of oil, natural gas, and water, were fairly common. This resulted in a great waste of the resource and also created a major fire hazard especially where there was a large quantity of natural gas and light crude oil. Even today, oil well fires occur and may require days to extinguish. *Blowouts*—as gushers in offshore wells are called—occur but usually only because of a failure of pressure-control equipment or a misjudgment of the pressures to be encountered.

If success has attended the drilling effort in a hitherto undiscovered oil field, this first well is subjected to a series of tests to determine what its rate of sustained production is likely to be. Some new wells produce at very high rates for a brief time and then suddenly decline. Before more drilling in the area is undertaken assurances must be had that further search will be adequately rewarded.

The level of oil well drilling activity at a given time tends to reflect market conditions. When oil prices are low relative to drilling costs, drilling activity decreases. Conversely, when market prices are high relative to drilling costs, drilling activity also increases as has been the case in recent years in the United States and especially since the federal government decontrolled the price of "new oil."

It must be kept in mind, however, that vir-

**Figure 14.6** Oil Gusher . . . once a common phenomenon but now rare.

tually all the easily accessible oil in the United States has been located and all the increased drilling activity is at even greater depths in geological situations of increasing—and hence chancy—complexity or on offshore sites where huge initial investments must be made prior to any drilling activity.

## CONSERVATION AND MANAGEMENT OF PETROLEUM

There are five principal foci for the conservation and management of petroleum resources:

(1) drilling procedures, (2) oil field management procedures, (3) refining procedures, (4) transport by tankers, and (5) consumption of the final products.

## Conservation during Drilling

As mentioned earlier, oil well "gushers" are now considered accidents. During any drilling operation great care is taken at all times to monitor the pressure in the well and to assure that all counterpressure measures are in place and either functioning or ready to function should they be needed. As drilling approaches or enters oil-bearing strata that also usually contain natural gas, the pressure in the well increases. As this happens drilling becomes slower and slower and greater and greater attention is given to the gusher preventing features. So successful are these efforts that a gusher or blowout today is usually given considerable press coverage. Of course, some or even most of the press attention is due to the fact that a blowout often has the capacity to cause great environmental damage, this being especially true if this accident occurs at a marine drilling operation.

An accident of this nature occurred in 1969 in the offshore oil field near Santa Barbara, California, and received enormous attention in press, television, and in scientific circles. Emotions on all sides of this accident ran so high that it is not easy to discern fact from fiction but the following appraisal of the environmental effects appears to be accurate.

Seabirds and shorebirds of many species that happened to be in the area where oil was liberated suffered greatly. These birds had their feathers soaked with crude oil and, in addition, often accidentally swallowed oil. No accurate toll of loss of bird life is available but certainly hundreds perished after the accident. Marine aquatic life, vertebrate and invertebrate animals, and plant life was affected to varying extents. Where there were heavy accumulations of crude oil the impact, for a time, was very great with the local loss of many individuals.

Beaches were also affected by large quantities of thick crude oil and thus sand-dwelling organisms were killed in the areas where the oil came ashore.

Assertions were made by some persons that a more or less permanent ecological Armageddon had occurred. Countering this pronouncement were comments that the whole matter had been overblown by environmental "extremists" and that essentially nothing of ecological importance had occurred. After the passage of a few years it now appears that the local ecosystems have recovered from the spill. The present safety record respecting drilling operations and blowouts is a generally good one. It is simply more economic to operate in as safe a fashion as possible. Moreover, in the United States, state and federal agencies take a very dim legal view of carelessness. In addition, and at least as influential, are the numerous conservation groups that keep sharp watch over drilling operations.

## Oil Field Conservation and Management

Perhaps at first glance one may wonder how there could be any conservation or management aspects to an oil field after it has been successfully drilled. Actually, it is in this very aspect of oil production that many of the most important conservation/management activities take place and where some of the most challenging problems remain to be solved.

A major if not the primary concern in the management of an oil field is that it not be over–drilled. This has often been difficult to achieve, particularly in the United States, where more than one oil company is active in a given field. Also, there has been no guarantee that limited ownership, especially in the past, of an oil field would assure limited drilling. Why the need to limit drilling? The answer lies in how oil is gotten out of an oil field once the field has been drilled. In virtually all oil fields—the chief exception being some deposits of very heavy crude—there is a certain quantity of natural gas present and this, until released by one or more oil wells, exists under pressure. This pressure can be used to help force oil through the porous rock to well "exits" and thence all or part way to the surface. Thus, fundamental to good oil field conservation/management is assuring that maximum use is made of this pressure in order to help extract the maximum quantity of oil possible. Even though pressures may not be sufficient to raise the oil to the surface the main importance of maintaining good pressure is to force oil through the sedimentary rock to where the oil can escape through wells even if the latter requires that the entire lift be done by pump action. One of the first tests made of a new discovery is to ascertain oil field pressure and to note the effect on this pressure as oil is lifted at different rates of speed. Also, great attention is paid to the well cores obtained while drilling to see how porous the oil-bearing stratum is. The more compact the rock, that is, the lower the porosity, the greater is the need to maintain maximum possible gas pressure in order to assure maximum extraction of oil. Based on such analyses, determination is then made as to the number of wells that should be drilled in a field. In the early days of oil well drilling in the United States, most if not all fields were overdrilled with an attendant wasteful loss of pressure, and therefore, a great loss of oil. Even under the best of geological and management conditions no more than 30 to 40 percent of the total oil present in a given field is lifted to the surface. Thus, the vast bulk of *discovered* oil in the world is still in the ground and will remain there unless techniques are discovered to get the oil out.

What was discussed under oil field pressure above is termed *primary recovery*. Added means may be used to increase production and these are termed secondary recovery techniques. These include (1) reinjection into the oil-bearing strata of natural gas that comes to the surface with the oil. This involves separate holes drilled at varying distances from wells and into which the gas is forced at varying lev-

els of pressure. Essentially what this does is to replace lost gas pressure. (2) Injecting water under pressure down specially drilled holes that again has the effect of maintaining or increasing pressure on the field.

One sometimes hears of tertiary recovery techniques but so far these are chiefly in the experimental stage. Some experiments include explosions set off within the oil-bearing area to jar loose oil that is being tightly held in the rock strata, pumping very hot steam under pressure to soften heavy oil so that it will move more readily to wells, and setting fires underground to force oil through strata and also to soften heavy oils to make them flow more readily.

Other aspects of oil field management relate to oil spills and to air pollution. Oil spills may seem of no consequence if they occur on land (marine spills were discussed earlier) but this is not the case. Oil spills can seep downward and contaminate aquifers and therefor must be prevented. Crude oil contains volatile substances and particularly so in the case of the light or sweet crudes. Therefor, where an oil field is located adjacent to human settlement or where any atmospheric situation can lead to smog every effort must be made to assure that a minimum quantity of hydrocarbon vapors is allowed to escape. This is a particularly important matter in such places as southern California where producing oil fields are found in heavy urban settlements.

Last, but not least, is the need to maintain safety conditions that keep the fire hazard as close to zero as humanly possible. Crude oil is highly flammable and oil field fires can be extremely destructive. Again, producing oil fields in or near human settlement must be given the most stringent protection against fire.

## Conservation during Refining Procedures

Oil refineries were once major sources of air pollution in the United States and remain such in many parts of the world where there are no regulations governing emissions from refineries. The principal emissions from uncontrolled refineries are hydrocarbons and these, as noted in the chapter on atmospheric conservation, are often major components of smog. Control of such emissions requires the installation of special equipment plus application of procedures in the refinery designed to restrict the escape of hydrocarbons into the atmosphere. To the problem of smog should be added the unpleasant odors that often come from oil refineries and although these cannot be reduced completely proper measures will make living conditions downwind much more pleasant than would otherwise be true.

Oil refineries are heavy users of water. Conservation requires that water not be wasted and should be reused whenever possible. Because many processes require water with minimal quantities of dissolved solids, some water must be treated before use. This water is usually reused as often for obvious economic reasons. Water, both fresh and salt, can be polluted by careless refinery procedures and today both state and federal laws require that proper measures be taken to prevent such pollution.

Refinery safety is an important aspect of management. Oil refineries typically contain within them or in adjacent tank "farms" quantities of highly volatile and, thus, highly explosive, liquids. Refinery fires are extraordinarily dangerous to human safety, refinery installations and, of course, to any adjacent structures.

## Transportation by Tankers

One of the more astonishing aspects of the petroleum trade in the last few decades has been the advent of giant oil tankers so large that they are capable of carrying 300,000 tons or more of oil at a single time (more than two million barrels) (Fig. 14.7). Although not all of the international oil-tanker fleet consists of giant vessels such ships pose enormous environmental hazards because should they be wrecked the quantities of oil spilled create toxic conditions that may extend over many hundreds of square kilometers of the ocean surface (Fig. 14.8). Should a wreck occur adjacent to a shore the possibilities for ecological damage are many and varied. Therefore, extreme caution must govern the navigation of oil tankers—large and small—and while accidents occur and are

**Figure 14.7**   Large oil tanker capable of transporting 2,001,860 barrels at a time.

**Figure 14.8** Wreck of the oil tanker Torrey Canyon off the south coast of England in March, 1967.

given wide coverage in the news media the fact is that only a small fraction of oil transported in tankers is liberated into marine and shore environments by shipwrecks (Map 14.4).

Although one can assume that most ship captains will attempt to navigate their vessels in a safe manner, a similar degree of confidence cannot be entertained with regard to the unlawful but all-to-frequent custom of pumping the bilges of oil tankers when they are at sea. The bilges are the bottommost interior part of a ship and it is here that all manner of waste accumulates that must, from time to time, be got rid of lest it reduce the transporting efficiency of the vessel. The legally *approved* method is to pump the bilges into shore-side tanks or other safe containers while the vessel is still in port. However, this is fairly expensive so to save money many a captain is instructed by his shipowner to pump the bilge at sea. Catching

such violators is often difficult and most go undiscovered. The occasional discovery of violators is usually achieved by actually observing the illegal operation or by testing an oil slick created by bilge pumping and matching its chemical "fingerprint" to the oil remaining in the bilges of a suspect tanker. Some of this illegal behavior is "justified" by the mistaken belief that the oceans are so vast that they can't possibly be harmed by the addition of the contents of a single oil-contaminated bilge. Lost to view, apparently, is that when hundreds of captains adopt the same attitude the cumulative deluge of oil becomes a major source of toxic substances capable of impacting large parts of the oceanic ecosystems.

Recent experimentation involving the use of bacteria that feed on petroleum and that can be introduced into bilges to convert toxic petroleum into nontoxic substances is showing

**Map 14.4** Major oil tanker and liquid natural gas routes.

promise. However, judging by the fact that illegal bilge pumping continues it seems that general adoption of this measure has not yet occurred.

## Conservation of the Final Products

When the public thinks about oil conservation it is usually gasoline that is being considered, although diesel fuel and home heating oil as well as the heavier products used to fire the boilers of electricity generating plants are also included. Often questionable, however, to the thoughtful person is the actual need for such conservation, especially, as not infrequently occurs, if there is a world "glut" of crude oil—not to mention the fact that the United States, at this writing, produces a little over half of the oil it consumes.

Unfortunately, the federal government sometimes appeals for oil conservation for a reason that can be seen by many to be not true—that we must conserve oil so that we won't run out of this natural resource. There is scant danger in the next two decades of our running out of oil because the supply, domestic and foreign, has become exhausted. The age of oil may be approaching an end but that end lies sometime in the early part of the next century (see later section, How Much Oil Is There?). If this is the case is there any reason or reasons to conserve oil? The answer is *yes* and the reasons follow.

A major reason to control our consumption of oil in the United States is to reduce the outflow of money to pay the import bill. The huge sums of money required to pay for petroleum imports are relatively recent phenomena and owe their origins to the price explosions that began in 1973. Before then, although our level of imports was great, the cost per barrel was modest. This is no longer the case and OPEC's success in raising the price of petroleum again and again has resulted in an enormous transfer of wealth from the United States (and other nations, also,

but the United States leads the way in the size of the expenditure) to OPEC. This has affected our economy in a multitude of ways almost all of which are harmful to some degree. At the very least, money that might otherwise have been invested in new enterprises in the United States or the expansion and modernization of already established enterprises has been diverted abroad. A much larger part than ever dreamed possible of our annual national cash flow is diverted to OPEC. True, some of the members of OPEC, most notably Saudi Arabia, reinvest substantial amounts of this money in the United States but most of this investment is short-term, which can be liquidated quickly. This imparts an undesirable measure of instability in that this high degree of liquidity, if exercised, could destabilize our financial markets.

Another important reason for conservation of oil is related to the one just given. Our nation does not wish to allow, year after year, a major imbalance of payments, that is, we want to recover, through foreign sales of our goods, as many as we can of those petrodollars we send abroad. Although every foreign sale of any goods or service contributes to this end, increasingly it has been agriculture that is called on to perform the bulk of the task. In this respect, the United States may be likened to an enormous "banana republic" except that instead of exporting bananas to pay our oil import bills we export enormous quantities of wheat, corn, soybeans, and other agricultural produce. The implications here are serious because we also must produce adequate food for our own needs. This means that we are forcing our fragile soil resources to produce at levels that may increase the already unacceptable levels of soil erosion, soil compaction, and loss of tilth. Also, there are increased applications of energy-costly, factory-produced fertilizers. The United States justly prides itself in its fine agricultural production but it is doubtful if our future national interests include a decades-long overexploitation of our soils resources.

A third major reason for conservation relates to national defense. This is a murky area, however, because the federal government has invoked this reason more than once over the past half century or more and not always based on reasoning that stands up to close scrutiny.

For example, during the presidential administration of Dwight D. Eisenhower, limits were placed on the import of foreign oil in order to "protect domestic oil producers who might be driven out of business by less expensive foreign oil." The rationale was that in time of war we would have a healthy national oil industry ready to supply the nation's needs. This somewhat convoluted reasoning ignored the obvious fact that if defense interests were the paramount consideration, then the best procedure would have been to conserve our national oil reserves while availing ourselves of then low priced foreign crude. Why not proceed the same way now? The answer is that since Eisenhower's day, we have become increasingly dependent on foreign crude oil to meet our demands and that crude oil, as we all know, is definitely not inexpensive. Reduction of oil use therefore, is desirable in order to reduce our foreign dependence on supplies that would likely be interrupted or completely interdicted in time of war.

There is yet another important reason and this has to do with other importing nations and particularly those to which our nation is closely tied economically. Unrestrained use of oil by us has both short- and long-term effects on the price and availability of this resource. To the extent that we can relieve pressure for upward movement of oil prices we can help to reduce the impact of oil importation on the economies of most of the Third World nations, not to mention European nations and Japan where dependence on foreign oil sources is almost complete. The chief long-run consideration is that

by avoiding needless consumption, the total world supply will be stretched out for more years thus allowing greater time to develop alternate energy sources.

Because oil is a global resource, and because no non-Communist industrialized nation is self-sufficient in this resource, it follows even in the case of the United States, with its considerable national production, that not all aspects of potential lowered consumption lies within the sole control of consuming countries. Thus we turn our attention to OPEC.

The 13 nations comprising OPEC (see Map 14.3 for a list of OPEC members) are by no means in close accord respecting the most desirable approach to the conservation of their oil resources. Generally, the organization breaks down into two broad categories: a group whose members wish to lift as much oil as possible in as short a time as possible and to receive the very highest prices the market will tolerate and a second group comprised of nations wishing to maintain what they perceive as a moderate position relative to pricing and wishing to lift their oil at a rate that permits a stretched-out time span for extraction of oil from their oil fields. What are the reasons for these sharp opposing differences?

The group wishing for rapid removal and highest possible prices are mostly nations whose known oil resources are relatively limited. To stretch out removal time, in their view, is to run the increasing risk of having to compete in price with alternative energy sources as they come on line in the future. By getting the oil out as fast as possible and at prices reflecting the fact that in the near term there is no real substitute for oil it is hoped that a maximum economic return will be realized. Added to this is the fact that most, if not all, of these nations—Libya and Nigeria are notable examples—have overambitious development plans that require enormous cash flows in the short term to pay the bills. Indeed, in spite of what seems to be incredibly large amounts of money going to some of these nations more than one has experienced problems in meeting its international financial obligations.

The second group, the nations wishing to hold prices down and to stretch out the total time of production, are those having large reserves of oil—the most outstanding of which is Saudi Arabia. By their line of reasoning, oil prices must be kept high enough to pay for desired development within the exporting nations but low enough so that it will not become economically attractive for the consuming nations to invest in the development of alternative energy sources to the extent that the market for oil is challenged. Time works on the side of the development of alternate energy sources and against the economic interests of Saudi Arabia with its enormous oil reserves. Another important part of this argument is that rising energy costs are inflationary and have a weakening effect on the value of money used to purchase oil. Because the U.S. dollar is the principal medium of international exchange, inflation of this currency results in an actual lowering of the value received for oil unless the price is raised to accommodate losses due to dollar inflation. The latter becomes self defeating because the dollars earned must be used to purchase imported goods that are being forced up in price due to inflation. Also, the inflation of the dollar tends to reduce the value of dollar-denominated investments of which Saudi Arabia possesses a large quantity. A stable dollar, then, along with oil prices that do not result in the development and widespread adoption of competing forms of energy are among the more important conservation aims of Saudi Arabia and other members of what we here have been calling the second group within OPEC.

There is not total accord within Saudi Arabia for maintaining relatively high daily production. There is considerable sentiment—outside the Saudi royal family—to reduce the daily oil production to something well below recent levels. One argument offered to support this position is that too much money flows into Saudi Arabia to allow for the best possible rate of investment in the nation's infrastructure and, thus, a great deal of purchasing power is lost. Furthermore, goes the argument, it is in the nation's best interests to stretch out the time over which the oil is removed thus assuring for the greatest possible time span an income to the nation. An adjunct to this argument, and one being acted on at present, is that instead of selling all its crude oil production, the nation should engage in refining operations because the profits will be greater. Also, there should be a petrochemical industry that also would, it is argued, increase the nation's economic returns. These arguments seem to ignore the potential for development of alternate energy sources to reduce the future market for petroleum and also overlook the enormous difficulties of gaining access to world markets for refined products and the products of petrochemical plants.

Returning the discussion to the United States, one can identify many ways that petroleum conservation can be achieved at the level of the consumer. Although a number of ideas are discussed below, one, market mechanisms, will be given the major emphasis chiefly because this is not only an effective way to achieve conservation of petroleum but it is also frequently the object of heated controversy.

By market mechanisms is meant that the price for the raw and refined products should be allowed to reach levels that truly reflect the degree of petroleum scarcity. According to this reasoning, widely held among some American economists, the highest or best use will be made of oil if the true value as represented by an uncontrolled price is affixed to crude or refined petroleum. Also, according to this view, this will permit the smoothest possible flow of the "scarce good" from producer to consumer. The conservation is "built in" because price acts as a braking mechanism on use, which is to say that the demand for oil is elastic. A major difficulty with allowing uncontrolled market conditions to allocate gasoline, fuel oil, and diesel oil, as well as any other refined product that figures significantly in the nation's energy supply picture, is that inequities can develop that work considerable hardship upon those sectors of the population whose need is great but who may be unable to pay the price demanded. It is this consideration plus the fact that virtually every consumer of energy wishes inexpensive and abundant energy that price and distribution dislocations have often occurred as the federal government has tried to manipulate market forces so as to achieve a better social distribution of energy. Perhaps even in a democracy, there should be some governmental control over market forces respecting the pricing of energy but it also appears that this must be used with care lest serious short and long-term supply dislocations occur as a result of economic disincentives that discourage investments required by the energy producing industry.

Because approximately one-half of all petroleum use in the United States is in the form of gasoline it is obvious that a major restraint on petroleum use might be achieved by a successful effort to reduce gasoline consumption. One way this might be achieved is through taxation, which would make gasoline so expensive that people would only use it for essential purposes. European governments have taxed gasoline very heavily making the per liter cost well above prevailing prices in the United States. However, in Europe, the automobile has never come to occupy the all-pervasive transportation role that it has in the United States. Large parts of the European work forces ride to work in public transportation or walk or bicycle there. In parts of the United States and particularly the West, public transportation is poorly developed and residential areas are not concentrated and are seldom located adjacent to where people work. Thus, a major tax increase

to lessen the use of gasoline would injure, disproportionately, people who must use their cars to get to work and to perform the other myriad tasks that are required today. The wealthy could shrug off the increased cost as being negligible and would be unlikely to reduce their use of gasoline.

The procedure that *has* received government approval is setting a national speed limit of 55 miles per hour on the highways for all vehicles. It has been shown, in repeated testing, that as a vehicle's speed increases beyond 45 miles per hour its consumption of fuel increases at an increasing rate. However, there is widespread opinion that the 55 mph limit is too low. In some parts of the West where settlements are few and far between traveling at 55 mph on a modern interstate highway that was engineered for speeds of 70 mph can be a trying experience for many drivers. Some elements of the long-haul trucking industry, which uses mostly diesel-powered vehicles, complain that their trucks operate most efficiently at speeds greater than 55 mph because of gear and axle ratios. Similarly, some car owners argue that the smaller fuel-efficient cars ought to be allowed a greater speed limit than the larger "gas guzzlers." All this illustrates the fact that no law attempting to restrict highway speed limits will meet the satisfaction of all elements of the driving public.

There is no question that an enforced 55 mph limit would reduce the nation's consumption of gasoline not to mention a decrease in highway accidents resulting in death. Aside from the humane attributes of reducing highway accidents is the major reduction in economic losses associated with such accidents. Carpooling has been stressed as a good means to achieve fuel saving. Where pooling can be done effectively this is to be encouraged and is a contributor to gasoline conservation.

So far, the most significant savings in gasoline seems to have come about as a result of the shift from large fuel-inefficient autos to smaller more fuel-efficient autos. There is a direct and inescapable relationship between a car's weight and the amount of fuel it consumes. This shift to smaller cars is a response to the marketplace. That is, as the price of gasoline rose and represented an ever-larger portion of family costs, small cars began to replace large cars. Unfortunately, it isn't always clear if, over the long run, the family actually is ahead financially with the purchase of the smaller cars offered for sale. However, it appears that for most families, attention is directed toward the more visible monthly costs of gasoline rather than other and less visible costs of operating a motor vehicle, which works to the advantage of gasoline conservation.

The other two largest users of petroleum are electricity-generating plants and space heating. The former are important particularly in many coastal areas of the United States. The electricity so generated is used for a myriad of purposes and it is here that potentially great savings in petroleum use can be achieved.

Americans are frequently wasteful of electricity and this is chiefly due to the fact that in past years we seldom paid its true cost. This habit, however, is coming to an end because the prices of fuel in the United States are now being allowed to rise to world market levels. This will not necessarily mean a lowering in our material standard of living but it does mean that we will treat this form of energy with the economic respect long accorded it by almost every other nation. Increased electricity costs may cause some economic dislocations. An example may prove to be the manufacture of home air conditioning units and particularly those of the window type, which have been acquired in large numbers in the United States. These devices have made summer in the city and suburb bearable to millions. However, they are also, collectively, among the largest consumers of electricity and during summer months utility companies find themselves hardpressed to supply the needed electricity.

Americans are not prepared to go back to the sweltering days before air conditioning but they can achieve the same present-day comfort at the work place and at home by requiring that all buildings from private residences to the largest factories and office skyscrapers be designed to be energy efficient. This doesn't require years of research. On the contrary, the architectural and engineering elements of this are very well known. However, until the recent rise in energy costs, it was often not deemed cost effective to construct energy-efficient buildings, Even today, whether it be a private residence or a major building, the added costs of achieving energy efficiency are retrieved only after the passage of several years.

Retrofitting homes that were constructed during the era of cheap energy may often not be cost effective in under five or more years depending on what is done, the type of house construction, and the geographic location. Various tax incentives have been offered to encourage such retrofitting but, in general, one must be patient for the economic returns if such be the primary motive. Happily, for some people, such modification of their homes is done in the spirit of helping to achieve the goals of energy conservation and the economic gain— albeit long term—is of secondary concern.

Americans must change their ideas about what is a comfortable air temperature. We tend to overheat our work and personal living spaces and also to heat areas when no one is present. The "sense" of what is a comfortable temperature, to some degree, is an acquired trait albeit one not easily altered if recent experience in the United States is an accurate indicator. Attempts by the federal government to reduce work-place temperatures have met with varying degrees of acceptance with many persons feeling it an invasion of their personal "rights" as well as working a hardship on them. However, one may expect that as energy costs rise we will see a greater acceptance of lower temperatures and an adjustment in the nature of the clothing we wear. It is absurd to heat an entire house, for example, when only one or a few rooms are occupied. It may be foolish to heat the one room if the person in it would be comfortable by putting on a sweater or a heavier pair of pants.

Solar energy (discussed later in chapter sixteen) is frequently touted as "free" energy. It seldom is because of the cost of equipment and its installation but solar energy is "free" if one gets in the habit of opening curtains and other sun-blocking devices on windows having an equatorward exposure during the hours when there is sunshine. Similarly, by blocking off the sun's rays during the warm part of the year a house that is reasonably well insulated can be made to remain fairly cool without air conditioning equipment—a fact known and employed for centuries in many parts of the world where summers are very hot.

This energy awareness will most likely increase in the United States at about the same pace as the rise in the costs of energy. There seems no way to get around the phenomenon that the price of energy is a potent mechanism for achieving conservation.

## HOW MUCH OIL IS THERE?

The most pressing question with regard to the petroleum resource is how much is there? Given the obvious importance of these questions one might expect that a precise answer is readily available. Such is not the case, however, as we shall see, and all nations operate to some degree in an Alice in Wonderland world of petroleum statistics.

Since early in this century there have been conflicting estimates regarding the size of the nation's petroleum resources and of the time that the resource would last given various rates of extraction. There was concern in early years of this century that the nation was then about to exhaust its oil resources. One scholarly writer suggested, in 1910, that at the then-annual rate of oil use in the United States we would run out

of oil in 90 years but if the rate were to increase even modestly we would be without oil by 1935. In 1909 the United States used a total of approximately 175 million barrels of oil. This may be compared to our present annual use (including imports) of approximately 5.5 *billion* barrels of which about half is provided by domestic production. The prediction alluded to above was not irresponsible for it was based on then-existing known oil fields and then-existing ideas about the likelihood of future oil discoveries. However, vast new oil field discoveries were subsequently made and there developed a widespread attitude that we could safely extrapolate forever into the future the past rate of oil field discoveries. Those who suggested otherwise were often dismissed as pessimists and, indeed, the record of discovery seemed to support the position of the optimists. However, there is a limited number of geological structures in which oil and its congener, natural gas, have been concentrated into quantities of economic significance.

Not all of the mistaken optimism may be accounted for by the past success in locating new fields. It is one of the more peculiar features of oil conservation in the United States that the federal government has had to depend largely on data supplied by private oil companies in order to determine the size of the nation's oil resource. The U.S. Geological Survey has made some contribution but not at all sufficient to permit the government to make totally independent reliable assessments. The justification for this, according to the private oil firms, is that such data are private property and must be protected lest competitors make use of information that might be economically detrimental to the firm(s) that developed the data. Thus, the U.S. government has often had to operate with insufficient information and sometimes with quite misleading information as, for example, when the major oil producers in the past assured the federal government that the United States possessed far larger oil resources than was actually the case. Our national interests require that the federal government be given access to *all data* respecting oil and any other important natural resources located within our national territory for how else can a credible national conservation program be mounted?

The reluctance of oil companies to freely supply data, notwithstanding, there has been no lack of attempts by individuals to estimate the quantity of oil remaining in the national territory. Generally, these attempts are based on such data as the number of wells drilled, the total number of feet drilled, and the yield of oil compared to the number of feet drilled. Also, taken into account are the obvious lack of medium-depth structures remaining to be drilled and the added costs of the very deep drilling required to reach structures that may or may not contain economic quantities of hydrocarbons. In this same line of consideration are the costs and difficulties associated with oil exploration in offshore locations, in the north slope of Alaska, and other difficult-to-exploit situations.

The current consensus is that no matter how diligent the drilling of exploration wells may be, and accepting what appears to be reasonable rates of success, the U.S. production of crude petroleum from drilled wells has passed its peak and there will be a diminishing quantity of oil obtained from in-country sources.

Before we can proceed further with the question of how much oil is there we must examine the terminology and concepts used to describe the size of the oil resource. Remember that the total quantity of oil in a given oil field does not represent the amount that can be lifted. Only rarely is as much as 30 percent of the total in a given field recovered—the rest remaining underground for lack of a means for getting it out. Thus, when talking of *oil reserves* one speaks of that quantity of oil that can be lifted given the nature of the oil field and the available

technology. The key estimate is proven recoverable reserves for this represents oil that can be lifted given the best data available about the field, market conditions, and available technology. Any estimates given beyond the one just mentioned are relatively unreliable. It is in the estimation of probable or potential reserves that imaginations are sometimes overworked. On the other hand, a petroleum geologist with well-established credentials for making conservative estimates of the potential production of new fields may be well worth listening to. There is much art still mixed in with the science of oil field estimations. Oil fields that have a fairly regular geological structure throughout offer the best possibilities for accurate appraisals providing sufficient exploration work is conducted. Oil fields that are much faulted and have generally complex and irregular geological structures so that oil (and gas) occur more or less randomly make accurate estimates of reserves very difficult to achieve. An example of such a field is one recently located in the Bay of Campeche and now being rapidly developed by Mexico. An example of the former is much of the producing and potential producing areas of Saudi Arabia. The last is also true of some of the very large fields of Texas that for years have produced almost half the annual U.S. domestic production of oil.

There is no close agreement even among the experts as to how much recoverable oil remains within U.S. territory, nor is there agreement as to how much recoverable oil there is worldwide. With regard to the international scene the probabilities for accuracy are not great and, thus, we may expect wide-ranging estimates to appear not only in the popular news media but also in professional publications. Part of the reason for this situation is that there is often a lack of basic geological data and because large areas have not yet been drilled thus allowing a freer rein to the imaginations of some of the estimators.

What most concerns us here is the issue of how long the present reserves, as well as the most likely new discoveries in our national territory, will continue to supply a significant part of our oil need. The answer will depend on a number of elements of which the following are most important: the amount of oil we use each year, the degree to which we are able to adopt oil-energy substitutes, and the degree to which we stress imports of oil over the consumption of domestic crude.

No matter how frugal we become with regard to oil use the future life of this resource as the chief supplier of this nation's energy is measurable in terms of a few decades. Remember that oil is an international resource and that the United States is only one of many oil consumers. We must also be aware that the Third World, most nations of which are oil importers, will make increasing demands on the world's oil supply as populations increase and as economic development moves ahead albeit at relatively low annual rates of increase.

As pointed out earlier in this section, an important aspect of twentieth-century petroleum use has been one of confounding the predictions that oil was running out and would soon be in short supply. However, times have caught up with what were once judged the sour views of pessimists and we must begin to adjust our thinking to accommodate the reality of a world that by the midpoint of the twenty-first century will no longer be relying on oil for more than a minor part of its energy production.

With such a prospect clearly in view one might ask: Why bother to conserve a resource that not only is finite but whose predicted future contribution is so limited with respect to time? Some of the answers to this query have already been presented but will be repeated here, in part, for added emphasis.

Our nation must reduce its imports of petroleum in order to reduce the high outflow of dollars that have national and international destabilizing effects on the economy; we must reduce our oil use so that there is a greater quantity available to other nations whose dependence on imported oil is total or almost so; we must reduce our imports of oil so that we cease forcing our soil resources to produce crops for export to help pay our oil import bill.

To the above list might be added that we and the entire world must conserve oil in order to provide the lead time required to develop alternate energy systems that will produce the quantity of energy required by the world. Although it is being argued in some circles that it is coal that will bridge the "gap" between the end of the age of oil and the beginning of some still ill-defined "brave new world," we have seen that such a massive increase in the use of coal would entail major environmental costs of which at least one, the $CO_2$ increase in the atmosphere, would be global in its impact. Coal undoubtedly will supply part of the "gap" because it is abundant and therefore will be used. However, we must not forget that for all its shortcomings, oil remains an extraordinarily flexible substance with respect to transportability and application and no viable substitute is yet available to us.

In conclusion, there can be no single answer posed to the question stated at the beginning of this section. The amount of oil remaining depends on future oil discovery success, future rates of national and international consumption, the development of techniques that will permit a greater percentage of oil recovery than has thus far been possible, as well as on other variables. The world does appear to be adjusting to the fact that the petroleum resource is limited and that it must be used with greater restraint than has been the practice in the past. Thus, one might reasonably estimate that petroleum will continue to be sufficiently abundant to meet our nation's, and much of the world's, energy requirements for at least three and perhaps as many as five decades ahead.

This is the time we have in which to develop alternate energy production systems.

## NATURAL GAS

Natural gas occurs alone or with petroleum. Typically, natural gas is positioned above a petroleum deposit as seen in Fig. 14.3. Natural gas consists of various chemicals of which methane, $CH_4$, is the most valuable fuel component. There is also a liquid portion that can be processed and marketed as propane or butane. This last is widely used as bottled gas in areas where pipelines for the transport of natural gas have not been laid. Natural gas can be cooled and compressed to form liquid natural gas (LNG).

### Distribution in the United States

The principal areas of natural gas fields are almost coincident with the oil fields. This is due, of course, to the fact that oil and natural gas occur in almost identical geological conditions. Note that the location of the natural gas fields are usually far from the major urban populations and manufacturing centers—a fact to which we will return.

Until recently, there was very little exploration to find natural gas. Today, natural gas is becoming more and more the principal object of exploration because of its versatility, transportability, strong market demand, and clean-burning qualities as compared to oil and coal. It is believed that major gas finds may await discovery in the Rocky Mountains, the Appalachians, in a zone offshore in the Gulf of Mexico and in the north slope of Alaska.

No major population center in the United States is today without a piped-in supply of natural gas (Map 14.5) and there are plans to further extend service although the high costs of pipe manufacture and pipe laying will impose restrictions on this. There is also hope in some circles that what is believed to be a major natural gas resource in Alaska's north slope

will be piped south through Canada to the "lower 48" (as the conterminous United States are known in the state of Alaska). The projected cost of this undertaking—perhaps $40 billion—makes financing very difficult. However, should the price of energy rise further, means may be found to achieve this construction although some estimates (early 1982) suggest that the wholesale price may exceed $14 per thousand cubic feet, which compares with the average current price of about $3.50 per thousand cubic feet.

Very deep drilling in some areas may yield significant quantities of gas but probably not enough to meet more than a relatively modest part of the current total energy demand of our nation.

### Distribution Worldwide

Natural gas is known to be present in many parts of the world and at least in some instances in what appears to be large quantities. Large parts of the globe have not yet been explored for hydrocarbons and some of these areas may one day become important natural gas producers. At present the major known gas fields are located in the Middle East with the leader probably being Saudi Arabia. Another nation, Algeria, has made major gas discoveries that will become an important element in the world energy market in the near future. Mexico's new oil field in the Bay of Campeche contains a large natural gas component. Indonesia similarly has what appears to be large natural gas resources.

The principal problem with regard to the marketing of natural gas *overseas* is that unless the water distance is fairly limited, as for example between the gas fields of the North Sea and Europe's mainland, the gas must be processed into LNG and transported in costly specially designed LNG vessels able to maintain the low temperatures and high pressure required to keep the gas in a liquid state (Fig. 14.9). The conversion of natural gas to a liq-

**Figure 14.9** Ship designed to transport liquid natural gas (LNG) at minus 162 degrees Celsius.

low but in the gaseous state the danger is very high and people living near a proposed LNG terminal port are usually adverse to having such ships discharge their LNG cargoes in their vicinity.

Unfortunately, there are very few situations along our nation's coastlines where a combination of safe anchorage for vessels and safe distance from human settlement are combined. Even where settlement is very sparse as is sometimes the case where an LNG terminal is proposed, public resistance may still make such development all but impossible.

## HISTORY OF THE USE OF NATURAL GAS

It may be one of the all-time ironies of natural resource use that natural gas, now one of the most highly valued of the world's energy resources was, until recently, wasted and allowed to burn away into the air unused. Even today, enormous volumes of natural gas are continuously burned off—"flared" is the term used—in the oil fields of Saudi Arabia and other oil-producing regions because there is no nearby market for the gas. Some of the gas is reinjected to maintain pressure on the fields but the rest, after separation from the oil, is flared away.

The waste of natural gas in the United States in past years seems all but unbelievable today as we face rapidly escalating prices for this excellent source of energy. It has been estimated that just prior to 1910 the United States was wasting, at a minimum, one billion cubic feet ($10^9$ ft$^3$) of gas per day. Repeated efforts were made to require oil field producers to stop this behavior but this was, for the most part, resisted until the 1930s when the development of natural gas pipeline systems made profitable the marketing of this energy resource. Much of the prior waste could have been prevented by requiring that oil field operators reinject the gas

uid state is energy costly and thus, from a strictly thermodynamic viewpoint, very inefficient. The transport of LNG and its conversion back to gas are dangerous operations. The ships are, in a sense, floating bombs and every precaution must be taken to prevent sparks or fire that could ignite the gas. In the compressed and chilled state the danger is fairly

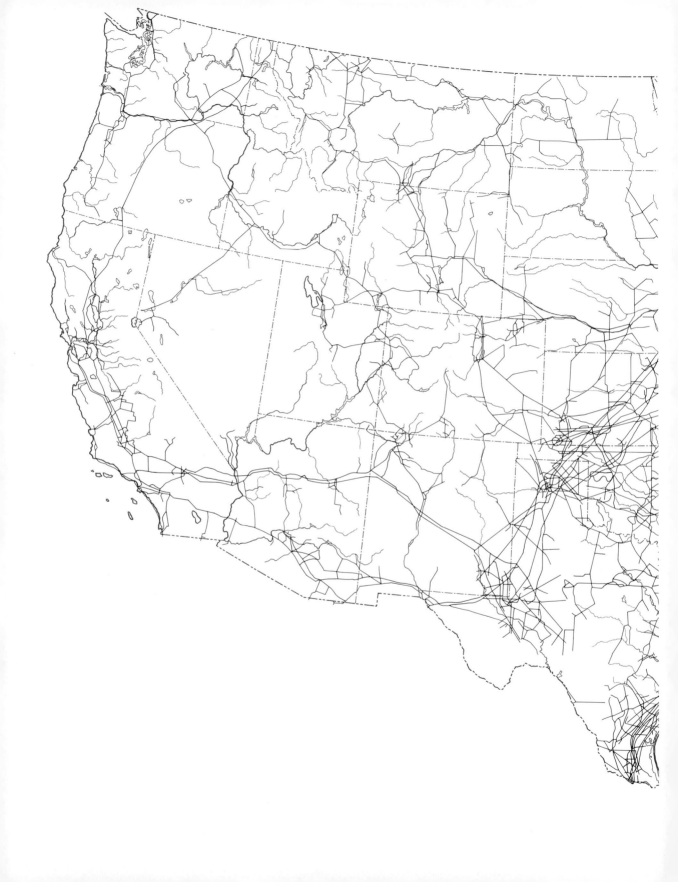

**Map 14.5** Natural gas pipeline-net in the conterminous United States. (U.S. Federal Power Commission).

into the geological strata from which it had come.

The most blatant aspect of this waste of gas often occurred when a well drilled for oil struck only natural gas and instead of capping the well the gas was allowed to escape into the air. Sometimes the gas ignited and there is an instance where a single well burned for 20 years and in the process gradually decomposing the adjacent rock and ultimately creating a lake of fire. There can be little acceptable justification for this waste.

As you read this, enormous quantities of natural gas are being flared in the world's oil fields for "lack of a market." Although one might expect that LNG will become increasingly produced and sold in the future, it appears that long before this comes to pass billions upon billions of cubic feet of gas will be lost forever.

There are other sorry aspects to this story of current waste. Natural gas is a major feedstock for the manufacture of factory-produced nitrogen fertilizer. The irony here is more than apparent—a Third World struggling to produce more food but becoming less and less able to pay the soaring price for nitrogen fertilizer while the feedstock for that fertilizer burns off over oil fields for "lack of demand."

Some, not all, natural gas deposits contain a small quantity of helium. Helium is an inert gas for which there are many industrial applications. Being inert it is particularly useful wherever a gas is needed that poses no danger of explosion. The major known world concentration of helium is in parts of Texas. The federal government, beginning with World War I, initiated a program of helium recovery. Unfortunately, however, private oil and gas companies have little economic incentive to do this partly because the production would exceed the current market demand. All excess helium would have to be stored for future use in underground sites. It appears that the only way such conservation could be accomplished would be for the federal government to subsidize the separation of helium from natural gas and to undertake the task (and cost) of storing the gas against future use. A National Commission to study helium conservation has been established but little progress has been made.

The highest concentrations of helium in natural gas wells is about 7.5 percent. Helium is considered to be fairly well concentrated when it represents 1 to 1–4 percent of natural gas. By comparison, helium represents only about one part in 186,000 in the earth's atmosphere and this low level of concentration makes recovery from that source very uneconomic.

## SYNTHETIC FUELS

Much attention has recently been devoted to the subject of *synthetic fuels,* a term often shortened to synfuels. Synthetic fuels are those that have been derived from the conversion of carbon-containing raw materials principally coal, tar sands, and oil shale. Usually the resultant fuel product is petroleum although gas in large quantities can also be produced. Perhaps the basic reason that so much attention has been given to synfuels in the United States is that this nation and adjoining Canada possess huge supplies of the raw materials from which enormous quantities of fuel might be extracted providing that certain economic and environmental problems are solved.

The government of the United States has vacillated on the issue of governmental financial support for the development of synfuels. Motivated by a perhaps impossible-to-achieve desire to attain national energy self-sufficiency the government, at times, has made various sums available for research and the development of pilot synfuel plants. At other times, seemingly fearful that to support this nascent industry is to engage in socialistic practice, financial support is lessened or withdrawn. When there are threats of foreign-imposed limitations being placed on our ability to import all the oil we want there is increased sentiment for a rapid development of a synfuel industry. However, let the oil supply situation become relaxed and such sentiments are less frequently expressed. This is not the kind of market atmosphere to which private capital is likely to be attracted and it may be that insofar as the development of a synfuels industry is concerned there will have to be large-scale financial participation by the federal government with the justification being that this industry is to be principally a standby adjunct to oil importation should cutoffs of the foreign supply require this production. Some observers are openly critical of the soundness of the economics of synfuel production as long as a very large world "conventional" oil resource is still available and one that will remain so for at least a few decades. Countering this argument is the assertion that at the very least, many years will be required before a major synfuel industry can be developed, that is, one that would be able to make a significant contribution to the nation's energy needs.

The chief constraints on the development of a major synfuel industry may prove to be more environmental than economic. Furthermore, even the most enthusiastic estimations of future synthetic fuel production indicate production totals equal to about 15 percent of our present oil consumption. One must keep in mind that synfuel *production* is not to be confused with the total amounts of oil said to be available prior to mining and processing. During World War II the Nazi government, cut off from oil supplies, made an all-out effort to develop a synfuel industry in order to keep their war machine alive. Utilizing lignite coal, this production did not exceed 45 million barrels of oil per year. This amount is about equal to approximately three days of current oil consumption in the United States. Of course we possess far richer and more easily processed synfuel sources than did the Nazis but it is well to keep in mind that synfuels will not substitute for more

than a small percentage of the quantities of oil we presently use.

## Oil from Oil Shale

Although the principal source of petroleum at present is in liquid form, huge quantities of oil are "locked up" in a rock known as *oil shale.* The United States has what is generally believed to be the world's largest oil shale re-shale resource with estimates as high as $2.4 \times 10^{12}$ barrels. Most of the shale oil resource in the United States is located west of the Mississippi River (Map 14.6) in areas of low precipitation.

The oil occurs in a type of sedimentary rock called shale. Shale consists of fine layers of clay-mud or silt and when broken tends to do so in thin horizontal laminations. Some shale contains organic matter from which petroleum can be derived and this is what is referred to as oil shale. However, the oil does not occur in these rocks in a liquid form but as a solid substance called *kerogen*. When kerogen-bearing shale is heated to 425° to 510°C, the kerogen decomposes to crude oil, natural gas, and a residuum containing carbon and shale rock. This rendering of oil from shale is termed *pyrolosis* or *destructive distillation*. The oil thus obtained can be refined in the same manner as oil lifted from an oil field (Fig. 14.10).

Because of the enormous quantities of oil thought to be present in the oil shale deposits of the United States there is great interest in exploiting this natural resource. However, very little oil is being produced from shale at present and there is often disagreement as to the probable future contribution this energy resource will make to the nation's energy supply.

In order to make shale oil extraction profitable (at present) shale deposits must contain a minimum of 25 barrels of oil per ton of rock. Thus, there are large quantities of oil shale that can't be exploited given today's market price for crude petroleum. As the real cost of energy increases these less rich deposits *may* be-

**Map 14.6** Oil shale and tar sand resources of the United States and Canada (U.S. Department of Energy).

come economical to exploit. There are large known areas of oil-rich (i.e., kerogen-rich) shale but even these are not yet exploited to any important degree. The limitations are principally environmental in nature although the large capital investments required also constitute a partial deterrent.

The environmental constraints relate chiefly to water availability, water pollution and proper disposal of the enormous amounts of waste rock that will accompany any large-scale oil shale development. Most of the known oil shale deposits in the United States occur, like much of the still-to-be exploited surface coal deposits, in the West in places that receive limited quantities of precipitation. Thus, oil shale exploita-

**Figure 14.10**   Mining oil shale in Colorado.

tion conflicts with other present or potential use of the scarce water resource. And, no matter how careful the operation, it is certain that some water pollution will occur in the surface flow and/or in the groundwater.

Perhaps of even greater concern is the question as to how best to handle the waste rock. Any oil shale plant of economic significance with respect to the amount oil produced will yield enormous volumes of waste rock. It has been established, furthermore, that this waste will have a volume as much as 50 percent greater than that which was removed from the mine for processing. This is because the grinding, application of heat, and other aspects of processing increases the volume of the rock. So it is not a simple matter of putting the rock back into the place from which it was excavated. Care must be taken to contour the returned waste in such a way the landscape is

not made ugly nor subject to accelerated erosion of the soil that has been returned and placed above the waste and planted to grasses suitable for livestock feeding.

Some estimates envision an annual production, in 20 years, of two billion barrels a year. If such a goal is attained or even closely approached the problem of waste disposal will be great. It is sometimes suggested that most of this oil shale exploitation will take place in areas far removed from human settlement and where there is little of value in the landscape to worry about. That is an obviously spurious argument and should be disregarded. This is not to say the oil shale resource should be ignored—it is far too valuable. But we must be on guard lest there be repeated out on the High Plains another episode of destructive resource exploitation that has already been too much a part of the history of our nation.

It would seem that when we reach the point of having to seriously consider large-scale exploitation of oil shale and tar sands (see below) we ought to ask ourselves some hard questions about the suitability of the ways we intend to employ this environmentally and economically costly addition to the energy supply. For example, is it really desirable to alter the ecology of large areas and employ large quantities of scarce water to supply energy to energy inefficient structures, to run inefficient window air conditioners, or to light billboards and overilluminate public and private spaces?

### Tar Sands

Oil also occurs associated with some porous sandstone deposits located at or very near the surface of the ground. This oil is very heavy and must be mined rather than pumped. The United States has only a small tar sand resource but Canada has what are believed to be quantities equal to double the original conventional crude oil deposits in the United States. The largest such deposits are the Athabasca tar sands, which are located chiefly in the Canadian province of Alberta. Until recent years, only a limited amount of oil was produced from tar sands and this on an experimental basis. The chief limitation was cost, but with the rise in the world price of crude oil exploitation of the tar sands have become more economically attractive. Unfortunately, getting a large production from this resource will take considerable time as well as very large investments. Climate is also a major problem because the deposits freeze in the winter making mining during that season all but impossible. The sandy material also quickly ruins the dredge buckets, which must be repaired frequently and at high cost. All these problems nonwithstanding, given the continued rise in energy prices this resource will figure more importantly in the future than it does at present. Perhaps the most serious limiting factor to all-out tar sand exploitation is that of the major environmental changes that are associated with this mining. Restoration of the mined areas will be impossible and it is questionable as to what degree Canadian citizens will wish their landscape made ugly to satisfy the energy demands of their southern neighbor, the United States, to which most of the oil produced is destined.

### Oil and Gas from Coal

Although the principal interest in coal is as an energy source in its solid state, coal lends itself to the production of synthetic fuels including oil and gas. Virtually every type of coal may be used to produce synfuels but bituminous coal with which this nation is still well supplied is also said to be the best coal grade for synfuel production.

Coal gas is nothing new and, in fact, the first gas lighting that appeared in cities was accomplished by the production and piped distribution of coal gas. Coal gas must be processed in order to increase its Btu content and also be "scrubbed," that is, it must have unwanted components such as sulfur removed before it can be distributed. Once fully treated and processed, coal gas may be employed the same way as natural gas. One often-cited advantage of coal gas is that it can be produced and processed near the mine site and the gas can be transported by pipeline to market thus greatly reducing energy transportation costs. Unfortunately, all the environmental problems described in the discussion of coal mining relate also to *coal gasification*. There are, to be sure, some experimental developments that would permit coal gasification without having to mine the coal. However, it is still too early to predict what, if any, value these approaches will have respecting the future of large scale coal gasification.

By various methods collectively termed *coal liquifaction,* coal may be made to yield petroleum. At present, all the available techniques suggest that such oil will not be able to compete in price with other synfuels not to mention conventional petroleum. However, given the enormous coal resources of the United States it may be that one day well in the future coal may provide a small but useful quantity of oil for national use.

# SUMMARY

Coal, the first fossil fuel to be utilized in large quantities is still, several centuries later, an energy resource of major world importance as well as being of actual and potential great importance to the United States.

Coal mining is hazardous to the environment, to human health, (especially underground mining) and to the atmosphere when it is burned. Nevertheless, so abundant and versatile is this energy resource that there seems little doubt it will continue to make significant contributions to our nation's energy requirements for a long time to come.

Although most of the coal mining in the United States has been conducted east of the Mississippi River, the greater share of the nation's coal reserves lie in the West and particularly within the Rocky Mountain region.

Coal may be burned in the form of chunks, as a slurry of pulverized coal mixed in water, or it can be converted to coal gas. It can also be made to yield petroleum. Coal would most likely provide most of the nation's energy needs were it not that it has had to compete unfavorably, until very recently, with cheaper petroleum and natural gas. However, as the price of coal becomes more attractive environmental concerns associated with its mining, processing, and burning have worked to raise questions about the role coal will play in the nation's energy future. The great abundance of the coal resource in the United States illustrates the fact that there is not an energy crisis per se, if such be defined narrowly in terms of available energy resources. The real issue is whether or not we as a nation are prepared to pay the high environmental costs of air and water pollution that will accompany a major increase in coal utilization.

At present, petroleum is still the most important source of energy we consume although its days of supremacy appear to be numbered to not more than a half dozen decades—if that long. The brief age of petroleum, which provided the means for an unprecedented expansion of energy use in the United States and other parts of the world, will be seen by future historians as a brief incident in the flow of human history. Nevertheless, we live in the critical time when that age is drawing to a close and therefore are required to make the multitude of painful adjustments needed to develop an economy based on other energy resources. We can stretch out our own petroleum resources by better oil field management. We must do all possible to minimize the consumption of petroleum fuel not only to make national and international supplies last as long as possible, but also to ease the outflow of dollars to pay for oil imports and to lessen the pressure to raise still further the international price of oil.

Natural gas, in many respects, is the most desirable of all fossil fuels in that it is the cleanest burning of all of them. It also has many uses in chemical manufacturing as for example the production of nitrogen fertilizer. All this notwithstanding, there has been, and continues to be in some parts of the world, a criminal waste of this resource. The waste alluded to here is the practice of "flaring" natural gas in oil fields, that is, the setting afire of gas issuing from a well and allowing the gas to burn night and day, wasting away into the air, because there is no market for it. Under almost all conditions, such gas can and should be reinjected into the strata from which it came or it should be piped to exhausted oil fields and injected and stored until needed. The U.S. similarly wasted enormous quantities of natural gas in the past but today this energy resource is treated with greater respect as its price spirals upward.

Great popular press as well as scientific attention has been given recently to the so-called synfuels. These include mostly products that can be derived from coal, coal shale, and tar sands. Coal, as already noted, can be processed to make gas and oil. Oil shale, if heated sufficiently, can be made to yield petroleum as can tar sands. The United States has great resources of coal and oil shale and Canada has great reserves of tar sands. However, at this writing (1982) there has been a rapid diminution of federal support for synfuel development largely as a result of a modest decline in the world price of petroleum. This points up the powerful role played by the international price of energy with respect to energy development decisions in our nation. It may be a mistake to back-and-fill before every price change in petroleum. However, there are also significant environmental issues associated with any major synfuel development in the United States not the least of which is the requirement for large quantities of freshwater in a region where this is a scarce resource.

# nuclear energy

## INTRODUCTION

With the detonation of the first atomic bomb at Alamogordo, New Mexico, in 1945, there began a new era of energy production. Although the first use to which atomic energy was put was to kill or maim human beings and the next immediate application was the development of more sophisticated nuclear weaponry, rapid strides were soon made toward development of a technology capable of translating the energy released by fission reactions into electricity.

Heat is produced when the nuclei of fissionable material such as uranium 235 ($^{235}U$) are forced apart, that is, fissioned. Uranium occurs, as do many other chemical elements, in varying forms that, although having the same atomic number, differ in their atomic mass. These variations, or chemical species, are called *isotopes*. The differences in the atomic mass of isotopes are due to varying numbers of neutrons in the nuclei—the number of protons in the nucleus of a given element being constant. Uranium 235 is an isotope of uranium that has characteristics making it suitable for use in nuclear power-generating plants.

In conventional nuclear power plants in the United States $^{235}U$ is the most commonly employed fuel but before it can be used it must be enriched, that is, concentrated, by separating it from an accompanying heavier isotope, $^{238}U$. The latter is more abundant than the former but cannot be used in conventional reactors.

The first commercial nuclear power plants proved to be relatively wasteful of $^{235}U$ thus generating concern that this fuel would soon be exhausted unless other nuclear power technologies were developed and adopted. It is now possible to retrofit these older reactors in such a way as to increase their efficiency which by 1988, according to some estimates, could be as much as 23 percent over the present. Some of the concern regarding the rapid rate $^{235}U$ resources were being used has also dissipated because of a much slower development of nuclear power plants in the United States than had been earlier projected.

Nevertheless, interest among some scientists and commercial energy firms remains strong to develop other fission technologies that would have the effect of stretching out the available supplies of nuclear fuel. One major focus of this interest is upon "breeder" reactors. These reactors are to be designed to utilize plutonium 239 ($^{239}Pu$). This isotope of plutonium has been described as the most toxic substance known and it is also among the materials used in modern nuclear weapons. Breeder reactors are so named because they "breed" nuclear fuel while burning (fissioning) nuclear fuel. A breeder reactor may be designed to first burn $^{235}U$ and then burn the $^{239}Pu$ it produces during the former operation, and then, still later, burn the $^{239}Pu$ it produced ("bred") while burning $^{239}Pu$. These reactors may also burn $^{239}Pu$ fuel, which is produced as part of the fission reaction in conventional reactors using $^{235}$U. However, before this can be done it must be separated through *reprocessing* of the spent fuel after removal from the conventional power plant.

The great toxicity of plutonium 239 and its importance to weaponry led the United States to declare a moratorium on the commercial reprocessing of spent fuel in the United States and to refuse to reprocess spent fuel produced in the conventional reactors of other nations. Only Great Britain and France (as of mid 1982) have *commercial* reprocessing facilities other than the United States. This moratorium was extended to include the U.S. military but this latter restriction may not stand much longer.

There are two fundamental types of nuclear steam generating plants regardless of the type of fission process employed. These are *boiling-water reactors* and *pressurized-water reactors.*

Boiling-water reactors are designed so that the heat of the fission reaction is transferred to water in direct contact with the fuel rods. The steam thus produced is led into other parts of the generating plant where it turns generators to produce electricity. Pressurized-water nuclear power plants (which also are the kind employed on nuclear powered ships and submarines) do not boil the water in the reaction chamber (where the water is kept from contact with the fuel rods) but heats it under high pressure after which it is passed away in pipes from the chamber to a heat exchanger where the water, now at a lower pressure, becomes steam after which it is sent to the generator (turbine).

The history of nuclear power generation is a short story. It was not until 1970 in the United States that the energy industry became convinced that nuclear-generated electricity could be made competitive in cost with coal, oil, or gas-fired generating plants. This assumption has often been challenged it being argued that all the costs associated with the development of nuclear-generated electricity are not taken into account including the economic costs associated with long-term management of waste products produced by nuclear power plants.

Nevertheless, it did appear in the first few years of the 1970s that nuclear generating plants, by the end of the century, would be supplying an appreciable amount of electricity to the nation's energy grid (Fig. 15.1). After only a few years, however, the United States found its drive toward nuclear energy being brought almost to a halt.

By 1977, the United States had 64 commercial nuclear generating plants most of which were located east of the Mississippi River. The world total for the same year was 204. By 1980 the total for the United States was 75, but construction of new nuclear reactors had all but halted and great difficulty was being experienced in finishing those begun earlier in the decade and bringing them "on line" to add their electricity to the national supply of energy (Table 15.1). The nuclear power industry, which only a short time before had been so optimistic, was all but extinct insofar as new plant additions were concerned. Uranium, which had sold for as much as $49 per pound, was selling

Table 15.1
**U.S. nuclear energy production**

|  | 1965 | 1970 | 1975 | 1980 (prelim) |
|---|---|---|---|---|
| Operating reactors | 10 | 19 | 51 | 75 |
| Capacity, $10^6$ kWh | 0.9 | 6.5 | 39.8 | 56.5 |
| Percent of total electrical generating capacity | 0.4 | 1.9 | 7.8 | 9.2 |

*Source: Statistical Abstract of the United States, 1981.*

**Figure 15.1** Nuclear power plant located on the shore of Lake Michigan.

(in late 1981) for as low as $25 per pound and with no immediate prospect for an increase in price (Map 15.1).

The reason for this extraordinary reversal in the United States was the growth of public fear that nuclear power plants were directly and indirectly too dangerous to be allowed to increase. Few other recent phenomena, with the possible exception of the U.S. involvement in Vietnam, have led to such a strongly held negative public opinion.

## HAZARDS OF PRODUCTION

Public demonstrations against the use of nuclear energy were rather unfocused—although there was never a lack of published antinuclear material—until March 28, 1979, when an accident occurred in a pressurized-water nuclear reactor near Middletown, Pennsylvania. The actual site of the reactor was Three Mile Island located in the Susquehanna River and thus the incident quickly became internationally known as the Three Mile Island Nuclear accident (or, frequently, nuclear "disaster") (Fig. 15.2). The accident resulted in the venting of a small quantity of radioactive gas to the outside atmosphere. Fuel rods in the reactor core suffered damage and for a time it was feared that a *meltdown* might occur. Had the latter actually occurred, a major and extremely serious emission of radiation might have taken place. A chaotic mess of serious radioactive dimensions did develop *inside* the plant, this being composed of damaged fuel rods, contaminated water, and radioactively contaminated walls, surfaces, and other materials. Cleaning this up will be slow and very expensive: the cleanup is estimated to cost more than the construction of the plant itself.

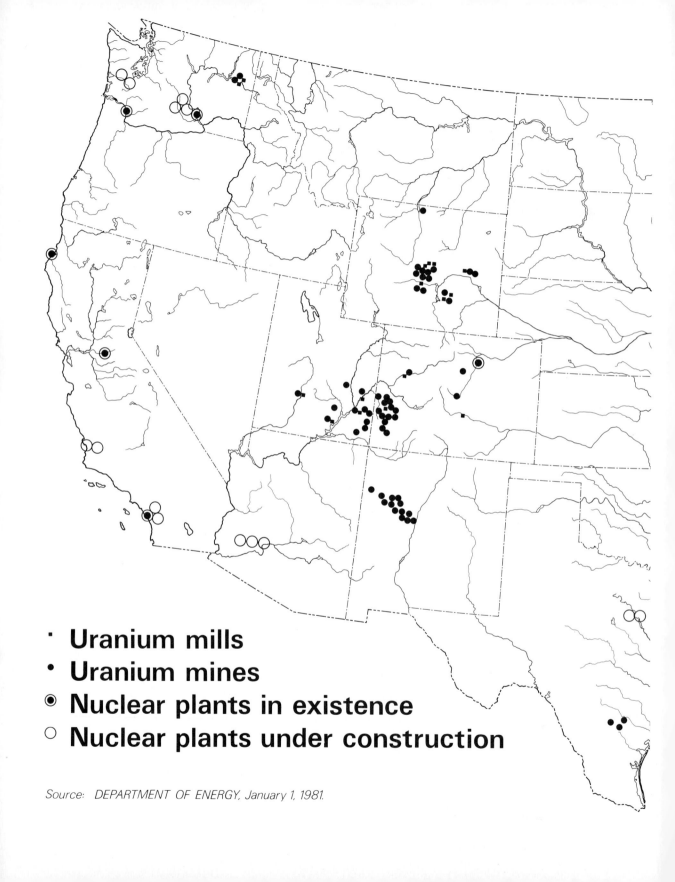

· **Uranium mills**

• **Uranium mines**

◉ **Nuclear plants in existence**

○ **Nuclear plants under construction**

*Source: DEPARTMENT OF ENERGY, January 1, 1981.*

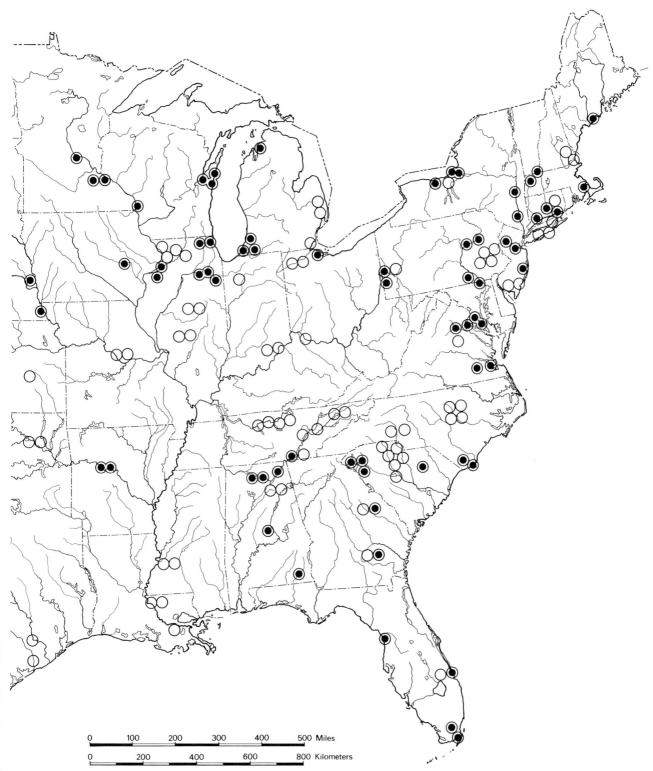

**Map 15.1** United States uranium resources and locations of on-line nuclear power generators (U.S. Department of Energy).

**Figure 15.2**    Three Mile Island Nuclear power plant.

This event was given intensive and extensive coverage by the news media and had the effect of galvanizing much public opinion in opposition to further development of nuclear power. Major public demonstrations took place in different parts of the country and whether based on hard data or on fear alone it soon became evident that a major turning point in the use of nuclear power had taken place.

An important source of difficulty with regard to this fear of nuclear power is that much of the language and concepts of nuclear physics *appears* to be beyond the grasp of the ordinary citizen. However, regardless of the basis of the fears expressed by the public, nuclear power production does carry with it some risks and the public, however poorly informed it may be as to the scientific details of fission and nu-

clear power generation, is correct in demanding achievement of the highest degree of safety before allowing any further expansion of the nuclear power industry.

Many of the *advocates* of all-out expansion of the use of nuclear power generating plants have tended to gloss over some of the real dangers associated with such a decision. Many of those *opposing* such power generation tend to describe the potential hazards in highly emotional terms thus detracting from the credibility of their positions.

The principal potential hazards of nuclear power plants are meltdowns and explosions, emissions of radioactive materials from the plant into the outside environment, unsafe disposal of waste materials including obsolete plants, and the already mentioned reprocessing of fuel rods including plutonium separation and its possible use in weaponry.

Starting with meltdowns and explosions and emissions of radioactive materials it can be pointed out that up to this writing (mid 1982) only one meltdown has occurred in the United States and that was confined to the special containment vessel designed for this purpose. Three Mile Island seems to have *approached* the point of meltdown (and there was a partial failure of the system to contain radioactive gas). There was no explosion there nor has there been an explosion in any nuclear power facility in the United States. The Three Mile Island incident was a compound of faulty design, inadequately trained personnel, and a lack of adequate communication between the plant and outside scientific centers where the accident could have been much more quickly monitored than was the case. The particular tragedy of the Three Mile Island incident is that from a pure technology standpoint it should not have happened. The fact that it did in spite of so many public statements about the safety of such plants eroded the public's confidence to a marked degree. That accident notwithstanding—and one must remember that there was no human injury associated with the incident—the safety record of nuclear plants in general has been outstanding. Furthermore, with the technological advances in recent years the safety of *new* plants ought to be even better. Unfortunately, there is a more limited basis for optimism regarding some of the older plants.

Since 1976, the federal Nuclear Regulatory Commission (NRC) has been engaged in an inspection program of commercial (and other) nuclear power plants and its findings often do not inspire a feeling of confidence. Instead, one may conclude that there was too great a rush to adopt this new technology before adequate design standards were achieved and before there was a sufficiently detailed training of management personnel and plant work forces. Most ominous of all, perhaps, is the number of plants where radiation control was said to be substandard. Of 44 generating plants judged to be substandard in some way in 1977, 8 were cited for inadequate control of radiation. Although the Three Mile Island plant was not listed as having inadequate radiation control it was cited as having weaknesses in safeguards, quality assurance, and emergency planning. Several plants were said to have had inadequate cooperation with the NRC. In order that there be no other Three Mile Island incidents it is imperative that (1) reactor design be adequate, (2) that all personnel be properly trained and regularly examined to make certain that skills are maintained at a high level, (3) that the NRC play an active and controlling role in all nuclear power plant developments and operation, and (4) that top NRC personnel be appointed in such a way that their jobs are nonpolitical with as much autonomy as possible. Obviously, only the very best scientists are to be considered for NRC posts.

## HAZARDS OF WASTE DISPOSAL

We come now to what many view as the most serious problem respecting nuclear power generation—the safe disposal of nuclear wastes. These wastes are produced in reactors and in reprocessing plants, and obsolete reactors themselves are waste requiring disposal. The wastes consist of many isotopes having varying radioactive half-lifes. It is this feature which causes greatest concern because it is known that some of the radioactive waste products have half-lifes of many thousands of years (a half-life is the time required for one half of the atoms of a given mass of radioactive material to disintegrate. A given isotope having a half-life of 10,000 years still has one-half the original mass of radioactive isotopes at the end of 10,000 years, one-quarter after another 10,000 years, one-eighth after another 10,000 years and so on). Some of the wastes will emit lethal quantities of radiation for hundreds of thousands of years. As of this writing, no universally accepted method has been devised for the safe permanent storage of these wastes.

In 1979 it was estimated that more than 250,000 cubic meters of liquid radioactive wastes were being kept in "temporary" federally supervised storage facilities. In spite of some public statements to the contrary, wastes so stored will continue to accumulate unless a breakthrough occurs in the technology and sociology of safe waste storage. Suggestions as to how to safely store the waste are numerous and include first sealing in glass, then in a metal container and then placing the container deep in an abandoned salt mine, firing the waste off into space, and dumping the wastes into the sea. The suggestions (excluding the obviously fanciful one of firing the waste off into space) tend to break down into two components: (1) containerization, and (2) storage site. Both components must work to perfection if safe disposal is to be achieved.

Although most of the published discussions treat with the *technology* of waste disposal little is said about the *sociology* of safe disposal. If one first reflects upon the fact that many of the wastes that must be stored have half lifes exceeding 10,000 years and thus will be "problems" for hundreds of thousands of years and then one reviews the past ten thousand years of human history which includes just about all the time since the invention of agriculture, one can't be optimistic that for the next 10,000 years and probably several hundred thousand years (or several times the total number of years that *Homo sapiens* has been present) people will behave in an unprecedentedly responsible manner to protect stored nuclear wastes from escaping confinement or to move them should leaks and other problems occur. Even should we grant that waste disposal *technology* will be adequate can we lien the future of our and other species, a future that will depend on a degree and persistence over time of responsible human behavior for which there is no historical precedent? There is even the possibility that such responsible behavior could be achieved by the creation of a technological police force that would itself pose grave dangers to the freedom of the societies they were charged with protecting from the dangers of nuclear wastes.

Among the more frequently mentioned sites for disposal are salt deposits and the floor of the oceans. Salt deposits are attractive because they contain a minimum of water and tend to be geologically stable over relatively long periods of time. Such sites are known to exist in the United States, particularly in New Mexico. It is not surprising, however, that New Mexico officials are generally opposed to their state being used for the storage of atomic wastes. It may prove to be politically impossible to store radioactive wastes anywhere in the United States on a permanent basis. Thus, interest is turning more and more to the oceans.

Far too little is presently known about the geology of the ocean floors and especially with reference to the specific elements that relate to the feasibility of the ocean floor being used as a site for safe disposal. Most of the published suggestions for seabed disposal do not include any provision for permanent monitoring of the disposal sites. Disposal is usually thought of in terms of burial and some attempt to seal-off the sites. Although oceanbed disposal may one day prove acceptable no such disposal should be permitted until far more is known about potential dangers and limitations than is known at present. Unfortunately, it appears that some European nations are already planning to go ahead with oceanbed disposal.

In 1945, and for a few years afterward, the United States was the only nation possessing the technology required to make a nuclear bomb. But the nuclear genie, once released from the bottle, could not be returned and soon we were joined by other nations, which now include Great Britain, France, the Soviet Union,

China, and India. Other nations undoubtedly possess the knowledge and the capability for creating a nuclear explosive device. It has been suggested that virtually any country could, if it so wished, build a crude atomic bomb. The geographic proliferation of nuclear generating plants is even more widespread and includes, in addition to the bomb club named above, Israel, Japan, West Germany, Spain, Mexico, Brazil, Argentina, and probably other nations also. Soon it will become a cachet for a nation to possess a nuclear generating capacity.

All current nuclear reactors depend on heat released by fission, but there are international research efforts underway directed toward developing a *fusion* reactor. When the nuclei of hydrogen atoms are forced together—something that can occur only under conditions of extraordinary high temperatures—great energy is released. Temperatures required for fusion rival those of the sun, which is itself a great nuclear reactor. Achieving sufficiently high temperatures, that is, 10 million degrees Celsius or more, can be achieved by combining the material to be fused (i.e., hydrogen) with a fission-produced explosion that yields the required high temperature.

Although the technical problems requiring solution are many there appear to be three principal ones that have thus far prevented achievement of a commercially viable fusion process: (1) more energy, so far, must be expended to achieve fusion than is yielded by fusion, (2) inability to contain the super heated gas or *plasma,* (3) providing means adequate to heat the fusionable material on a sustained basis.

Earlier optimism about the availability of energy produced in fusion reactors has cooled but interest remains strong. Were fusion reactors to be made technically and economically acceptable the amount of energy available would be almost unlimited. Such reactors would use deuterium ($^2$H) (an isotope of hydrogen) and hydrogen, of course, is an all but unlimited re-

source. It has sometimes been suggested that fusion reactors would pose no hazards because any failure would instantly lower the temperatures required to create fusion reactions. However, such reactors would produce large quantities of tritium ($^3$H), which although having a low level of radioactivity, would have to be carefully stored lest it get into living systems since it behaves exactly like its chemical congener, hydrogen. Questions have also been raised about other possible sources of danger such as radioactive contamination of the generating plants. Given the still highly experimental stage of fusion research, it may be premature to raise an alarm. However, the public should keep apprised of developments in this area and especially so when the time arrives, probably not before the twenty-first century, when efforts are begun to construct electrical generating plants using fusion reactors.

## SUMMARY

As we have seen, nuclear power generation carries with it risks to which even the most ardent advocates of such power generation admit. A major question seems to be the nature of the risks and the human responses to them. It is in this area that emotion sometimes seems to part company with science and statistical probability. It appears that which worries many people is that the risks associated with nuclear power plants are of a new and mysterious nature. Americans seem to accept that approximately 50,000 highway deaths occur each year as well as the hundreds of thousands who die from other controllable causes. But even though the risks of injury or death from nuclear power plants are so low as to be statistically insignificant the public perception of the risks is quite different.

Thus society, perhaps unwittingly, is positioning itself at one of those historic crossroads where the choices made will largely determine the direction of material culture far into the future. If the nuclear option is discarded it would seem that within a comparatively short time we must begin to consume great quantities of coal or retreat to a far less energy intensive society than we have at present. That there is public sentiment for the latter course is obvious. It is also very evident that there is public sentiment against such a course being adopted.

Already discernible is a growing, albeit unstructured, debate in the United States and the world respecting the choices of energy path-

ways we should follow in the future. With regard to material aspects of living there probably can be no more transcendental issue than the one posed in this debate. The answers should come chiefly from the collective value judgments of citizens. This is the first time in human history when the masses have been in a position to reflect on the nature of available energy pathways and also to be able to influence the choices made.

# energy resources: part II

## INTRODUCTION

Although fossil fuels—oil, coal, and natural gas—are at present overwhelmingly important to the United States and the world's energy supply, other energy sources offer varying degrees of promise of supplying large parts of the energy required in the future when fossil fuels become too scarce to provide more than a modest fraction of the energy demand.

Among the actual or potentially important nonfossil (and nonnuclear) fuel resources are hydropower, wood and other kinds of biomass, wind, direct solar energy, hydrogen, the oceans, and geothermal energy. In the United States today, only hydropower, among this array, contributes significantly to the nation's energy supply, but the other listed sources offer varying possibilities of becoming important in the future.

## HYDROPOWER

Water resources are discussed in detail in chapter nine but the use of running water for energy production has been separated from that chapter and included here because of the importance of water as an energy source.

The utilization of running water to perform work is ancient and many ingenious water-driven devices have been invented. The water wheel seems to have first been developed in the Mediterranean region. This use of water (Figs. 16.1, 16.2) became very widespread and

water wheels are still to be seen in use in some parts of the world. It was not until the latter part of the nineteenth century, however, that running water was first used to generate electricity and it is this use that is the most important today and it is on this that the discussion to follow is focused.

The United States has made rapid progress in this century in developing the nation's hydroelectric potential (Map 16.1). Most such developments have been in conjunction with other uses of water (e.g., irrigation, flood control, and recreation). Recent technological advances make it possible to transmit electricity hundreds of kilometers from the place of generation. Research underway points in the direction of a further increasing of the transmission distance.

Few major hydroelectric installations in the United States are used for the sole purpose of generating electricity and thus each installation requires a careful balancing of the competing water uses. This is particularly the case where the water is also used for irrigation. In dry years severe competition may result between those needing the water for agriculture and those demanding more electricity. This difficulty is avoided to some degree at some installations by the use of *pumped storage*. This requires at least two water impoundments positioned close to one another. The special impoundment is located as far above (higher) the main storage reservoir as possible. During the day or night when electricity demand is less than the generating capacity this unused en-

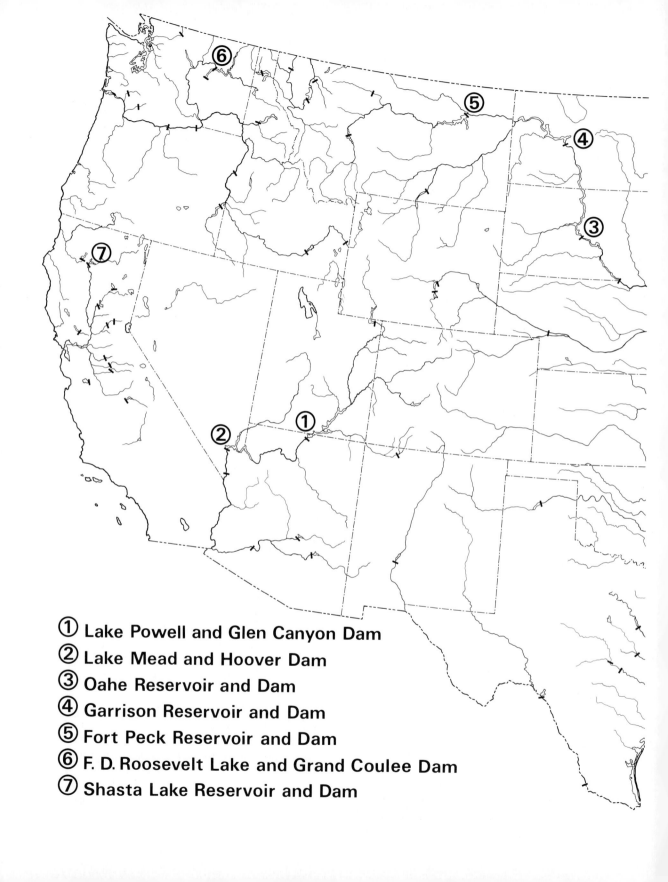

① Lake Powell and Glen Canyon Dam
② Lake Mead and Hoover Dam
③ Oahe Reservoir and Dam
④ Garrison Reservoir and Dam
⑤ Fort Peck Reservoir and Dam
⑥ F. D. Roosevelt Lake and Grand Coulee Dam
⑦ Shasta Lake Reservoir and Dam

**Map 16.1** Major hydropower installations in the United States.

**Figure 16.1**   Overshot water wheel.

ergy can supply power to pumps to send water into the special reservoir from which it can be drained through generators when there is the highest demand for electricity.

A major complicating element in the generation of hydroelectricity is that the diurnal as well as seasonal demands do not remain constant. Three types of electricity demand are generally recognized by power companies: base load, cycling, and peaking. *Base load* refers to power stations that operate continuously, *cycling* refers to power plants that generate electricity only between dawn and midnight (the hours of highest demand) and *peaking* refers to plants that run only in the late afternoon and early evening when the peak demand in private residences, including apartments, occurs. Thus, it can be seen that *installed electrical generating capacity,* if adequate to meet peak demands, must always exceed the demand levels of certain other parts of the day or night. The demand nadir usually occurs between midnight and dawn when most people are sleeping (Fig. 16.3).

The problems of water conservation are discussed in detail in chapter nine so only a very brief comment will be made here and specifically with reference to hydropower dams. Although hydropower installations are expensive they are usually very efficient being able to convert up to 90 percent of the energy of falling water, as it passes through turbines, into useful energy (electricity). However, even the best-planned dams have finite life expectancies. The

**Figure 16.2** Wheel of pots, northern India.

principal life limiting phenomenon is the accumulation of water-carried sediment deposited in the impoundment area above a dam. This can be retarded by control of disturbances on the watershed (see chapter nine) and by the construction of dams upstream whose function is to catch debris before it reaches the main impoundment. With regard to expected dam life in general, no firm estimate can be given because every situation is unique with respect to rates of siltation, size of the impoundment basin and so on. Some dams "die" after a few decades but others may have a life expectancy of two or even three centuries. But no dam lives forever and thus our concept of hydropower as a regenerative energy source must be tempered by this realization.

The United States is estimated to have developed a little more than one-third of its total hydroelectric potential. Projected future construction costs loom very high, however, and it is not a certainty that the resultant energy production will be cost competitive with coal or even oil. Fossil fuel power plants offer greater flexibility of use because it is easier to raise and lower electrical output than is the case with many hydroelectric installations.

Recently hydroelectric installations in the United States have been providing about 15 percent of the total energy consumed by the nation. Many experts do not see this as increasing in the years ahead and some even suggest there will be a diminishing contribution from this source by the end of this century. These latter assessments tend to be based on assumptions as to how much we will or will not

**Figure 16.3** Turbine part being lowered into position in a Grand Coulee hydropower installation.

increase our total consumption of energy. This is an extremely volatile aspect of consumer behavior and it is possible that the relatively high per capita increases in energy consumption that have occurred in recent years will soon decline.

The uncertainty respecting the size of future demand is well known to engineers and others whose task it is to plan for future energy-producing installations. Such plants, regardless of how powered, require lead times of up to 10 years to come on line yet there are relatively few experts who feel confident of any prediction made for 10 years ahead given the many social and economic uncertainties that exist. Should the people of the United States decide to embark on a course of effective energy conservation it would appear that little added

electrical generating capacity would be needed in the next couple of decades.

There is increasing concern among some environmentalists that the *ecological* costs of some dams is too high to justify additional construction. These concerns tend to focus on the impact on aquatic ecosystems, fish spawning success, the flooding of fertile soil and the destruction of "wild rivers" much valued by outdoor enthusiasts. It should also be noted that some large water impoundments appear to be responsible for an increase in local earthquakes.

## WOOD

Wood was probably the first form of inanimate energy employed by humans. The earliest uses of wood were for cooking and space heating. Later when the heat properties of charcoal were discovered (probably independently in several places) wood became and remained the major heat source our species commanded for many centuries. Coal and then oil and natural gas later combined to relegate wood energy to a minor place in the energy production of industrialized nations although wood fuel continues to be important in many of the nonindustrialized parts of the world.

Wood, as a possible significant source of energy, is today being examined in the United States and some other nations. Particular interest is being directed toward the use of wood wastes generated by sawmill operations or wherever wood or timber is harvested for purposes other than fuel production. There is also a rapidly growing interest in developing *energy plantations* where fast-growing trees can be harvested at relatively short time cycles and processed into some easily usable form such as *wood chips*. Special machinery has been developed for the purpose of harvesting entire trees and rapidly reducing them to tiny chips that can be used for such purposes as boiler fuel for the production of electricity in steam-generating plants.

In those parts of our nation where wood supplies are abundant and where constraints on harvest are sufficiently limited as to allow utilization, wood may *locally* become a moderately important component of the energy supply system. However, these areas tend to be located where the growth rate of trees is relatively slow because of short, cool summers and long, cold winters. An important exception is the southeast where growth rates are high for such trees as pines and thus harvestable fuel is available on 20- to 30-year cycles. At present prices, however, this wood is far too costly to be burned and is mainly used for paper pulp and timber. Of course, *timber residues* can be and are often saved and utilized for fuel—sometimes in the lumber mills themselves to generate steam to operate plant equipment.

In the western United States and Alaska there are vast timbered areas as well as areas once timbered but now in second growth to which some persons point as possible sources of fuel wood. Since much of this land is owned by the federal government there would likely be formidable and effective public efforts to restrict attempts to harvest this wood for large-scale energy production. In addition to the political difficulties there are economic constraints. Wood harvesting requires a considerable expenditure of energy including the costs of processing the harvested wood and transporting it to market. Particularly in the case of Alaska, the costs of transportation may preclude use of the forests for energy production. This applies to some degree also to the more isolated parts of timbered Canada although wood fuel might contribute to some of the energy requirements of that nation. However, as long as Canada enjoys large oil and oil-sand reserves as well as major undeveloped hydroelectric potentials wood energy will most likely remain only a modest contributor to that nation's total energy supply.

Wood burning to heat residential space remains, in the United States, the largest energy use to which wood is put, and as the prices of fuel oil and natural gas escalate, wood becomes a more attractive alternative. However, only in those parts of the United States where the proximity to wood sources makes transport costs competitive or where the consumer is able to harvest and transport the wood himself or herself over modest distances can wood be considered an economical alternative to fossil fuel use. Wood-burning fireplaces are generally very inefficient because most of the heat goes up the chimneys. However, there are improved fireplace designs available and well-engineered wood burning stoves that greatly increase the amount of heat sent into the area desired to be warmed.

Contrary to widely held opinion, wood burning is an air-polluting activity of considerable significance and particularly where such fuel is used in abundance. Environmental Protection Agency-sponsored studies indicate that burning wood may emit more carcinoma-causing particles than oil or natural gas and may be on a par with burning coal. Also, burning wood emits more $CO_2$ than does oil or natural gas. At this writing there is relatively little regulation governing wood burning but should the use of this fuel continue to increase, such regulation will probably become necessary and widespread. Some cities in the United States do have regulations that govern the times when wood may be burned. Some other cities are becoming very concerned about this source of air pollution especially some urban areas in the northeast where in the past there has been almost complete dependence on imported oil for winter heating. Some towns in that region now experience major air pollution caused by wood smoke.

The public may be excused if it finds this current alarm about wood smoke strange because for centuries wood supplied virtually the only source of extra heat in winter. Perhaps all wood smoke is not the same in terms of toxicity since all wood is not the same chemically. Assuming, however, that wood smoke is a significant health hazard there is technology available to greatly reduce particulate emissions by assuring that more complete combustion takes place. Unfortunately, these stoves and furnaces are much more expensive than traditional wood stoves and thus do not enjoy a large market. The long-run interest of some northeastern areas—and perhaps some other parts of the nation as well—may be best served by regulating the types of stoves or furnaces used. This would reduce air pollution and extend the wood supply since less would have to be burned per stove or furnace to achieve a useful yield of heat.

Experimentation is underway to achieve the development of furnaces that can extract far more Btu from wood than the best of present-existing furnaces do. As these developments are brought into the manufacturing phase we will see a much better use made of fuel wood than is now the case. Also, the economics of wood for energy (steam production in electrical generating plants) might also be altered so that wood could compete successfully with fossil fuels in the market place.

## WOOD ENERGY IN THE THIRD WORLD: SOME EXAMPLES

Although the future significance of wood as an energy source in the United States and other wood-rich industrialized nations remains questionable, this is not true for many Third World nations where fossil fuel is lacking and hydroelectricity, if available, is too costly for large numbers of the people to use. Much attention has been focused upon the global fossil fuel "energy crisis" but for hundreds of millions of people—far more than the total population of the industrialized nations—wood is the principal fuel used and the rapidly growing shortage of wood in many such nations is a source of increasing national and international alarm.

Much of this alarm is not directed toward the looming wood shortage per se but toward the environmental damage that is often associated with fuel-wood harvest. Some nations have attempted to legislate fuel-wood harvest controls but these, in general, have met with little success. There are too many people dispersed over large areas to effect control. In addition, governments being unable to provide the other fuel at affordable prices sometimes find it easier to ignore the ecological problems associated with fuel wood harvesting.

Many of the affected nations lie in the low latitudes and within moist climates where the forests contain hardwood tree species suitable for charcoal manufacture. Charcoal when burned produces considerably more heat than firewood. By processing wood into charcoal, much greater quantities of heat energy per unit volume and weight of fuel can be obtained, which lessens transportation costs per heat unit. Charcoal making is a widespread practice in Third World nations possessing suitable hardwood resources. Unfortunately, the techniques of production are often so primitive that a large fraction of the potential energy value is lost. Highly efficient but relatively expensive ovens are available for the efficient production of charcoal but are not in general use.

If wood fuel is to continue providing the principal share of inanimate energy used by many Third World countries in the coming years, much of the fuel must ultimately be produced from plantations of rapidly growing tree species. Experimentation to identify suitable tree species is currently underway as is also research into more efficient ways to combust wood. Unfortunately, such progress as is being made appears to fall far short of compensating for the ecological damage associated with rapid removal of tropical forests. Foremost among the varied aspects of ecological damage are accelerated soil erosion, flash flooding, loss of plant and animal diversity, and possible long-term effects on soil structure and fertility. In much of the Third World the fuelwood crisis is, therefor, also an ecological crisis not exceeded in severity by numerous "ecological crises" with which the industrialized world is more familiar.

## PLANT AND ANIMAL BIOMASS CONVERSION

In the previous section, wood as an energy source was discussed. Strictly speaking, wood should be considered under the heading *biomass conversion* but to do so complicates not only an understanding of the problems of wood use for energy but also the use of other forms of plant and animal materials as energy sources.

Of particular interest is the conversion of animal manure and agricultural wastes into *biogas*. Biogas is the term widely used for the gas—mostly methane ($CH_4$)—produced by certain bacteria feeding on wastes in an oxygen-free environment. The methane content of biogas averages about 50 to 70 percent of the total gas produced by the bacterial action, and unless treated, does not equal the Btu content of natural gas. On average, there are 540 to 700 Btu per cubic foot of biogas as compared to 1000 to 2200 Btu per cubic foot for natural gas. Biogas may be used directly from the producing units called *digesters* if, for example, it is to be burned in a small gas stove. It may also be used to fuel stationary gasoline engines after making a simple carburetor modification. However, in the latter case and in all instances where the gas is used to power machinery it is usually desirable to "scrub" the gas first in order to rid it of certain corrosive properties and other gases it may contain.

As might be expected, biogas is particularly attractive in poorer Third World nations where all or most fossil fuel is imported. However, is there a place for biogas fuel in the United States?

According to figures released in 1972 by the U.S. Bureau of Mines, about 1.3 trillion cubic feet of methane gas ($1.3 \times 10^{12}$ ft$^3$) could be recovered from all types of methane-producing wastes available on farms. The technology to produce this gas is available now but there has not been any great rush to take advantage of it. Thus, it appears that a significant amount of energy is going to waste on the farm that could be utilized. The reasons for this lack of enthusiasm have not been systematically investigated but it does appear that the traiditional reliance on gasoline, diesel fuel, and electricity acts as a partial block to trying something new. While it is true that some farmers make modest use of biogas in limited engine conversions and claim savings in energy costs it isn't yet clear how far such energy conversions can be scaled upward to operate cost effectively on large-scale farms.

A curious aspect of biogas use is the fairly recent discovery by some cities that their old dumps, with the passage of time and the work of anaerobic bacteria, have become sources of biogas. To tap this resource wells are drilled and the gas led off to scrubbers and then to where it is to be used.

Often in the news in the United States and abroad is the use of crop plants to produce alcohol which, in turn, can be used in internal combustion engines. Almost any plant source can be used for such production but only plants containing a relatively large amount of sugar and/or starch are really suitable. The material is fermented and then distilled to produce ethyl alcohol or as it is also known, ethanol, $C_2H_5OH$. Ethanol may be used unblended or may be mixed with gasoline to make *gasohol*. In spite of some local regional enthusiasm for gasohol encouraged for a time by the federal government, gasohol has not found wide acceptance in the United States. It is highly questionable as to whether or not ethanol production on a scale large enough to be a factor of importance in the U.S. energy supply system is economically or ecologically sound. Ethanol production costs are relatively high although large scale plants might bring these down. However, a more serious question to consider is that of using valuable soil, fertilizer, and energy resources to produce alcohol for fuel. Were the United States in a position of having to import all its energy needs perhaps such a course might have to be accepted regardless of the ecological consequences and economic costs but, even then, only after all other conservation measures had been adopted.

Brazil, especially, has received much attention for its drive to produce huge quantities of ethanol to replace as much as possible its large importations of oil. Less attention seems to have been given to the growing disillusionment of car owners using ethanol fuel. They have found it difficult to get engines started especially in southern Brazil where fall and winter can be quite cool and drivers have also discovered that engine life, because of corrosion, is shortened when ethanol is burned. In addition, questions are being raised in that country as to the economic wisdom of large-scale farming to produce ethanol.

In the United States, a certain amount of currently wasted crop materials might economically be converted to ethanol and this might find a limited-application on or near farms and ranches. But, as stated earlier, large scale *ethanol farms* do not appear to be either ecologically or economically sound for the present or foreseeable future.

## WIND POWER

The wind is free . . . or is it? Although air movement is accomplished by the sun through differential heating and cooling of earth and water and, thus, wind of itself is free; the *harnessing* of wind energy is by no means so. Use of the wind to propel boats and ships and to turn the wheels and gears and other apparatus of mills is centuries old but both fell into decreased use when other energy sources became available. The great wind-driven clipper ships of an earlier day gave way to steam power and the picturesque windmills of Holland have almost disappeared from that and other regions where they were used to mill grain or pump water having fallen prey to steam or internal combustion engines. A major reason for the nearly complete demise of the use of wind-power is the *lack of reliability* of wind and that limitation remains the most serious obstacle to wind again becoming an important energy source.

Nevertheless, there is growing interest in harnessing wind energy. Most current research is concentrated on developing more efficient ways to convert wind energy into electricity, better ways to *store* electrical energy, and the identification of the best windy sites where major wind-power installations might be placed.

Although sometimes forgotten, wind energy has long played an important role in parts of the U.S. West where it is used to lift well water to livestock tanks and sometimes to supply people with a water supply. Crude though these windmills may appear they are well adapted for their tasks being ruggedly constructed and easily repaired. However, they are inadequate as potential electricity generators because of small wind-blade diameters, blade weight, and other inefficiencies.

The windmill generators being developed today often bear scant resemblance to the windmills of the West being designed with the aid of wind tunnel studies, computer simulations, and the application of sophisticated engineering techniques unknown even 50 years ago (Fig. 16.4). However, all the technology possible will not alter the fact that winds almost never blow continuously and never continuously at the same speed. There is, at present, a lack of quantitative data respecting windy areas and data for more than a year or two for a given site are very rare. Before the economic costs of large-scale installations can be justified, years of studies are required to identify and evaluate promising sites. Wind velocities need not be very high to be useful—some cur-

**Figure 16.4** This wind-driven turbine is capable of generating 2,000 kilowatts at wind speeds of 40 km per hour and above.

rent windmill generators can operate at speeds as low as 12 km/hr: very high wind velocities can be more destructive than useful. What is the most desirable are winds of moderate velocity in the range of 30 to 40 km/hr that blow nonstop most of the time.

Even the best wind sites are not likely to provide continuously useful wind velocities and thus wind-generated electricity most likely will be used as an adjunct to more conventional energy sources. Through use of available switching devices, wind-generated electricity can be fed into the electricity grid allowing fossil fuel-fired plants to reduce their generation and thus save fuel.

The large-scale *storage* of electricity in batteries is possible although this is still very costly and not likely to find wide use until battery technology improves and far lower costs are achieved. In short, wind-generated electricity will have to be integrated with other electricity-generating plants in order to be of significant value.

The present start-up capital costs for installing state-of-the-art wind machine generators is relatively high and there is still too little experience in most regions to determine how soon capital costs can be recovered and whether the electricity produced will be cost competitive with fossel fuel-fired plants or with hydroelectricity. All such considerations may prove less relevant than that of making certain that we utilize all possible in-country energy resources, and especially such low environmental impact ones like wind energy, in order to reduce reliance on foreign sources of energy.

## DIRECT SOLAR ENERGY

The day must come when we, like plants, will have to rely on our ability to capture, directly, the energy provided by the sun. This energy is often described as "free" but it is not because of the costs of harnessing it.

The simplest and, at modest scales, the least expensive way of using solar energy is to heat water for home use (Fig. 16.5). The necessary installations are by no means inexpensive and it may require the passage of several years before savings are obtained over the cost of more conventional energy sources. This *caveat* notwithstanding, it is in the nation's overall energy interests to give strong encouragement toward achieving widespread adoption of solar-water heating devices. It is well established that water heating presently consumes a large share of all energy consumed in the United States, which is to say that an appreciable part of the fossil fuel we burn is used to produce hot water. No part of the United States could not provide some relief from fossil fuel use by employing solar water heaters but it is in the "sunbelt" where this would be most practical because there are so many days per year where enough solar radiation is received to heat water at least part way to the desired temperatures.

Like wind power, solar radiation is not constant in quantity at a given location. Various experimental approaches to overcoming this problem are underway but even in the absence of suitable solutions there is still justification for installation of solar water heaters in many parts of our nation. Some states offer special income tax advantages for persons who make such investments and it might be in the nation's best interest were this plan adopted by the federal government.

Heating water to produce steam and then using this to generate electricity is possible but still too costly to compete in the market place with electricity generated by fossil fuel. French engineers and scientists have done important work on solar heaters and there is at least one installation where extraordinarily high temperatures are obtained through use of many mirrors that focus the sun's rays onto a very small area. Temperatures of 3300 degrees Celsius have been obtained. Of course this is much

**Figure 16.5** A large roof-top installation of solar energy collector panels for the purpose of heating water for a commercial establishment.

hotter than required for steam generation and is mentioned here to indicate the fact that there is no basic *engineering* problem preventing the collection of the sun's rays to create high temperatures.

Besides the current relatively high costs of such large-scale solar plants is the problem that after dark there can be no generation of heat. However, solar plants could be tied into other generating systems (e.g., hydroelectric or fossil fuel), and when the sun isn't present the other plants could replace the energy supplied by the solar plant during the day.

The use of mirrors is very attractive because they can be made to reflect almost 100 percent of the radiation that strikes them onto a desired place. Unfortunately, even very thin dust films on the mirrors reduce their reflective properties by a large percentage and no efficient means

has been developed to keep a large array of mirrors in top reflecting condition. It is in the very places where solar power seems most attractive, namely deserts and semi deserts, that dust is a major problem and one that must be corrected if solar plants are to be other than engineering curiosities.

The direct conversion of sunlight (photons) into a flow of electricity was first accomplished many years ago and devices that do this are called *photovoltaic cells* (Fig. 16.6). Although the basic physics are well understood there remain serious technical difficulties in being able to produce such cells at costs competitive with other means of generating electricity. Should the costs of manufacture be substantially reduced photovoltaic cells would probably become an important means of supplying electrical energy.

**Figure 16.6** Close-up view of an array of photovoltaic cells capable of producing 100 kilowatts.

## THE OCEANS

Still experimental are efforts to harness the power of tides, waves, and the vertical thermal differences in marine and some lake environments. Some parts of the world experience broad diurnal tidal ranges that can be taken advantage of, at some sites, by damming at high water and allowing the water to drain through generators on the lowering tide. At the other end of the tidal cycle it is possible to direct the rising tide to pass through generators.

All of which is attractive except there is a *still-stand period* at the end of each high or low tide period. Thus far, the most ambitious attempt to harness tidal power has been done by the French. This plant, however, is viewed chiefly as an experimental activity and as such, has provided much useful information about the potentials of tidal power.

There are relatively few sites on this planet where tidal conditions as well as suitable dam sites combine to be of potential use for a tidal power plant. Many of these sites are too distant from electrical energy markets to make them economically attractive. Thus, tidal power will not make other than modest energy contributions and especially in the United States, which has a scarcity of appropriate sites.

Harnessing the wave action of the ocean to generate electricity appears possible. Hawaii is particularly interested in these possibilities—that state must import all of its fossil fuel—and this may be the first state where wave-generated electricity becomes significant. It isn't yet clear as to what kinds of conservation problems might arise with a wave-action generating plant. One might expect, however, that any environmental disturbances would be restricted to the immediate site and would not affect adjacent marine ecosystems.

It has long been known that there are vertical thermal differences in the oceans and also, seasonally, in many lakes. Ways are being sought to convert these thermal differences into electrical energy that is economically competitive. Thermal differences (gradients) must be at least 20°C and these do not occur everywhere. They occur most frequently in low-latitude oceans (as, for example, in the ocean near Hawaii). At present, the major problem seems to be in achieving a plant that can withstand occasional high winds and rough seas and remain fixed in place. Some lakes may also prove to be appropriate for this technology but not many possess the necessary temperature gradient and there are seasons when the thermal gradient breaks down for a period of time that would temporarily render the plant nonproductive. Thermal gradient energy appears to have considerable potential in sites where thermal, storm, water current, and market conditions combine to make installations feasible.

## HUMAN AND ANIMAL ENERGY

In our preoccupation with the megasources of energy we may overlook the oldest forms of energy humankind has used and still depends on for much of the work that is accomplished—human and animal energy. Today, human and animal energy are often dismissed as unimportant or where such are still an important part of the total expenditure of energy, as being a sign of backwardness. This is unfortunate for it tends to spur adoption of fossil-fueled machinery to perform tasks that might as well or even better be performed by humans and/or their domesticated work animals. The widespread adoption of fossil fuels brought, for a time at least, vast rewards for some nations. But millions on millions of people were unable to share in the pioneer period of such adoption and now often find that their belated efforts to do so only exacerbates already serious economic troubles. Thus, there is beginning to be a reassessment, albeit modest, of human labor-intensive activities where such may be the only economically sane approach to achieving economic stability. This isn't to suggest that there ought to be a swing back to some mythic day before machines became prevalent, but that the all but universal denigration of human energy needs to be reexamined.

Animal energy particularly, deserves greater attention. A workhorse, for example, can perform in 1 hour the work that requires as much as 10 hours for a human worker to produce. Mules (horse-donkey hybrids), were collectively, the single most important source of power on American farms until the late 1920s when tractors with internal combustion engines swept mules and horses from the farm scene. Horses, mules, oxen, and water buffalo remain important energy sources in various parts of the world. There appear to be possibilities that these animals could once again be brought back into some of the agricultural systems of even the most developed of nations but so set is the notion that only fossil-fueled machinery is efficient this reintroduction may be very slow in occurring.

## HYDROGEN

Of all the "new energy" options that appear to have a strong potential for supplying large parts of the energy consumed in the next century and beyond, *hydrogen* ranks at or near the top. For all practical considerations, hydrogen is available in unlimited quantities. Hydrogen is a highly explosive gas—as was dramatically shown by the Hindenburg disaster—and thus requires very careful handling. However, gasoline also is a highly explosive material—a fact not preventing its use.

Hydrogen can be separated from water by several known means of which one, electrolysis, is presently the most favored although it is not energy efficient. Making hydrogen gas available for uses now filled by petroleum-derived fuels poses several difficulties if efficient and inexpensive availability is to be achieved. The gas can be compressed and stored in cylinders, or it can be chilled to very low temperatures when it becomes liquid thus allowing a larger volume to be stored in a given space. It can also be stored by allowing it to be absorbed by certain metals such as lithium from which it can be retrieved as a gas when required. All of these methods are not without problems but none appears impossible of being solved.

Some persons advocating that a major effort be made to adopt widespread use of hydrogen fuel assert that when combusted hydrogen produces only water. This is true if it is combusted, only in the presence of oxygen for if ordinary atmosphere is used nitrogen oxides, which are serious air pollutants, will be created. Thus it might be that oxygen tanks would have to accompany any engine fueled with hydrogen. Availability of oxygen would be no problem since it would be one of the two elements produced by the electrolysis of water, $H_2O$.

Hydrogen is said to cause certain metals to become brittle when long exposed to the gas and there may well be other difficulties of a similar nature to be solved. Nevertheless, based on currently available information, it seems reasonable to expect that hydrogen might one day fuel electrical generating plants and perhaps large vehicles such as trucks. If sufficient effort were directed toward solving some of what are essentially engineering problems of storage and portability it might be possible to fuel any vehicle and possibly even aircraft with hydrogen.

## GEOTHERMAL ENERGY

It has long been known that the interior of this planet is hot and that even at relatively minor depths temperatures are appreciably greater than those at the surface. Although it varies from place to place, on average the temperature of the earth's mantle increases at the rate of approximately 30°C per kilometer of depth. In some locations water penetrates to depths where it is heated to well above the boiling point and if this very hot water reaches the surface it may do so as steam as, for example, the famous Old Faithful geyser in Yellowstone National Park. In other geological situations the presence of such heated water does not become evident until a well has been drilled into it. This geothermal energy can be used to generate electricity when the proper conditions are present.

Geothermal energy is often described as a renewable resource and is so treated here. In fact, so little is known about the probable longevity of geothermal fields at present that most specialists are hesitant to make other than general estimates as to the energy yield or life span of any given geothermal situation (Fig. 16.7).

Nevertheless, it does appear that this resource warrants detailed study. There is one geothermal-generating plant operating in the United States, this being located in the Sonoma Valley of California. Iceland uses its extensive geothermal resource chiefly to heat space in

**Figure 16.7** Commercial geothermal plant located about 75 miles north of San Francisco, California.

homes and other structures. Italy, since early in this century, has made some use of its geothermal resource as have also, for example, New Zealand, China, the Soviet Union, and France.

One of the problems of using this energy re-source in some situations is that the hot water contains a high percentage of unwanted min-erals some of which are very corrosive to the pipes and other parts of a geothermal-gener-ating plant. Then there is always the problem of what to do with the hot water—unless it is the hot water that is being piped into homes for heating. If discharged into surface streams the aquatic life may be poisoned. Even under the best of conditions, geothermal plants tend to emit various gases including water vapor into the atmosphere: this might not be a problem in isolated areas and where the amount of water is relatively minor. Where large quantities of hot water is removed from a geothermal field there is the possibility of *land subsidence* unless the used water is reinjected into the field from which it was taken.

It is far too early to determine what contribution geothermal energy can make to the United States or to the world. With added exploration and more geological study as well as further development of technologies capable of handling the associated environmental problems it is possible that geothermal energy will be able to make a modest and medium-term contribution to the nation's energy supply. However, the sometimes overenthusiastic depiction of this resource as being of such size as to provide an appreciable part of near-term energy demand seems unjustified by current scientific evaluations of the geothermal resources.

## SUMMARY

A question being asked with increasing frequency is whether or not there is a "solar energy age" just ahead. The answer will be determined by many things including what further commitment is made, if any, to the use of coal and to nuclear energy. Should it be decided that neither coal nor nuclear energy are acceptable large-scale substitutes for petroleum then one might suggest that the answer to the question about solar energy be in the affirmative. However, there remains a multitude of technical problems that must be solved as well as the overcoming of what, at present, are major economic obstacles before the direct reception of the sun's rays provide us with the major share of the energy we need.

However, there are other kinds of solar energy that are already used or that offer promise for the future. Among these are hydropower, which already supplies us with energy; wood; plant and animal biomass (in addition to wood); and wind. At present, hydroelectricity provides about 15 percent of the nation's energy consumption and some experts are of the opinion that this figure is not likely to be increased because of environmental and economic constraints on further development of our hydro-energy potential. Wood, that ancient fuel, still plays a role in the U.S. energy picture but a minor one. This could be increased to some limited extent but probably not to where it supplied more than a minor part of the total energy consumed.

Conversion of plant and animal biomass, including animal manure, into usable energy is possible. Many plant parts can be fermented to produce ethanol; manure and other plant wastes can be used to produce biogas. The production of energy from these sources can be increased in the U.S. but it is not clear as to what part they might play in our total future energy requirements. It is certain the large quantities of potentially useful plant biomass are presently not utilized but this may be due in some measure to economic constraints as well as lack of interest in using the resource.

Wind energy, though not free as some would have us believe, offers an interesting albeit limited source of energy. The constraints on development are economic as well as physical in nature. Costs of installations are still comparatively expensive and the number and location of suitable windy sites are limited. Since the wind seldom blows all the time, wind-generated electricity must be fed into an electrical grid that allows for an on-off contribution from wind generators. Nevertheless, this remarkably clean source of energy should be developed as far as conditions allow.

Solar energy, in all its forms, are especially attractive to many Third World nations because so many of them lack adequate supplies of fossil fuel and find it economically destructive to purchase their energy requirements in the international market place. However, most of the same economic constraints noted for the United States are present in the Third World. With regard to plant and animal biomass, products such as biogas already play a role in the energy consumption of some Third World nations and this could be significantly increased. If the scale is kept modest, there are possibilities for the application of techniques to use direct solar insolation as, for example, simple and inexpensive solar cookers. Wood remains a major energy source for many Third World nations but this is contributing to severe impacts on the remaining wood resources. There must soon be a shift to wood fuel plantations where such are environmentally sound choices.

Among the other energy options that should be noted are hydrogen and geothermal. Hydrogen is so abundant that there is no theoretical limit to its use but there are still a number of difficulties preventing its widespread use, among which production costs, difficulty of storage, and explosiveness rank highest. How-ever, there does not seem to be any problem that can't be solved one day. In addition to its abundance another significant aspect of hydrogen is that it burns clean providing sufficient oxygen is present during combustion.

Geothermal energy is a limited resource in the U.S. and elsewhere. However, where conditions permit, this energy source can make a modest contribution to the U.S. energy needs. Unfortunately, geothermal is not an environmentally "clean" source because the hot water, usually highly charged with minerals, is usually discharged above ground after use in a generator. Furthermore, where there have been large-scale withdrawals of underground steam, subsidence of the ground has sometimes occurred.

While one ought to be cautious before adopting any proposed solar or other innovative energy development, we should also adopt a fairly adventurous attitude and be willing to give all suggestions a full hearing. It may be on one or more still new and speculative developments that the world will one day depend for most of the energy it consumes.

# mineral resources

## INTRODUCTION

Whatever else may characterize the time in which we live it is certain that our profound dependence on a broad array of minerals is enough to make this a distinctive period in human history. Of course it would be an oversimplification to speak of an age of minerals but the concept has merit in that it helps to focus on an aspect of conservation that often receives too little attention. While it is true that abundant affordable energy is critical to the functioning of modern industrial society it is no less true that there is a similar critical need for many minerals.

Although the United States can entertain the possibility, albeit ephemeral, of achieving something close to "energy independence" this is not remotely possible with regard to a host of minerals without which our economic system could not long survive (Map 17.1, Map 17.2).

Not only does the United States import 50 percent or more of 20 or more kinds of minerals but a number of these are critical to our steel industry. Among the latter are chromium, cobalt, tantalum, manganese, and titanium. These metals are *ferroalloys* since they are combined with iron and other materials to produce steel (Table 17.1). Also of great importance is the fact that many of these materials are obtained from some nations not known for their political stability and/or friendliness to the West.

Minerals are nonrenewable resources but it does not follow that there is no basis for their conservation and management. In the pages ahead, various means by which minerals can be conserved and managed will be discussed.

Table 17.1
**Iron and ferroalloys**

| Metal | Principal Source Areas |
| --- | --- |
| Iron ore (principal reserves) | Brazil, U.S.S.R., India, Australia |
| Manganese | Brazil, India, U.S.S.R., South Africa |
| Molybdenum | United States, Canada, U.S.S.R., Chile |
| Cobalt | Zaire |
| Chromium | South Africa, U.S.S.R., Zimbabwe, Zambia, Philippines, Turkey |
| Nickel | Canada, U.S.S.R., Cuba |
| Tungsten | China, U.S.S.R., Korea, United States |
| Vanadium | United States, South Africa, Namibia, Finland |
| Tantalum | Brazil, U.S.S.R., Zambia, Zaire |

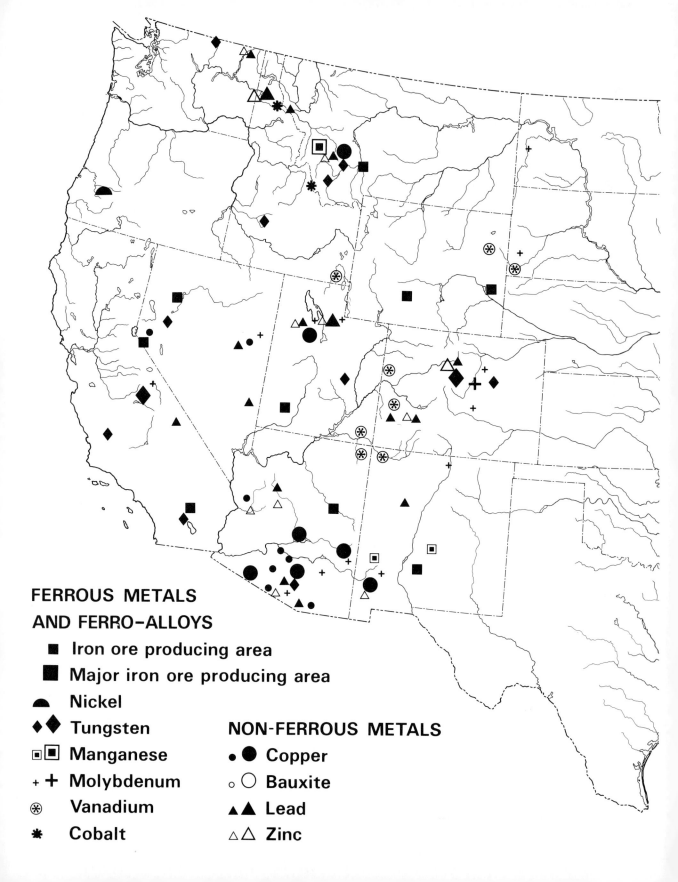

FERROUS METALS
AND FERRO-ALLOYS

■ Iron ore producing area

■ Major iron ore producing area

◗ Nickel

♦◆ Tungsten

▫▣ Manganese

+ ✚ Molybdenum

✳ Vanadium

✲ Cobalt

NON-FERROUS METALS

•● Copper

∘○ Bauxite

▲▲ Lead

△△ Zinc

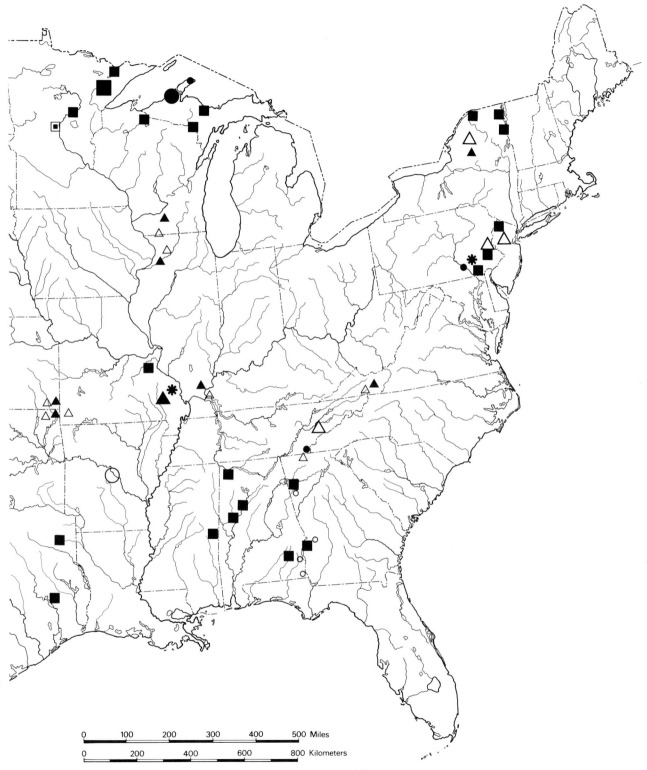

**Map 17.1** Ferrous and non-ferrous metal resources of the United States.

0    100    200    300    400    500 Miles

0         200        400        600        800 Kilometers

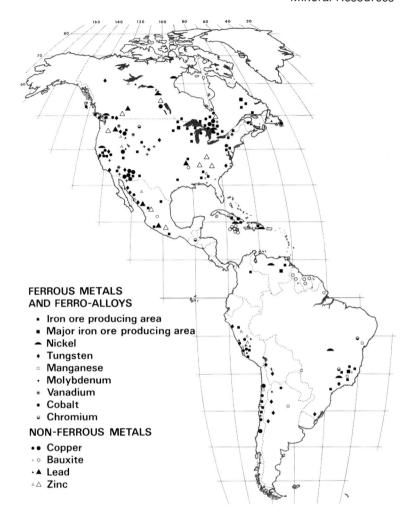

**FERROUS METALS
AND FERRO-ALLOYS**

- ▪ Iron ore producing area
- ▪ Major iron ore producing area
- ▲ Nickel
- ♦ Tungsten
- ▫ Manganese
- + Molybdenum
- ✳ Vanadium
- • Cobalt
- ◦ Chromium

**NON-FERROUS METALS**

- • Copper
- ◦ Bauxite
- ▴▲ Lead
- ▵△ Zinc

## MINING AND SMELTING

Mining is such an ancient activity that no one can be certain as to where it began. Most likely, mining did not have a single geographical point of origin. Earliest mining was nothing more than selecting desired types of rocks for weapons and tools from among the gravel of stream beds or seashores. The first mining for metals is also lost in the mists of prehistory. The first *organized* use of metal seems to have been associated with copper. The ore of this metal occurs in many places over the earth but only rarely in an almost pure form known as *native copper.* Native copper is very soft. Perhaps by accident it was learned that copper when alloyed (mixed) with other substances such as arsenic or tin produced a far harder metal suitable for spearheads and other uses. This alloy, called *bronze,* became so important in some parts of the Old World that this period has been named the Bronze Age. However, before bronze could be widely adopted the technology of *metal smelting* had to be developed. Smelting is the application of heat to metals and ores containing metals to cause the metal to melt.

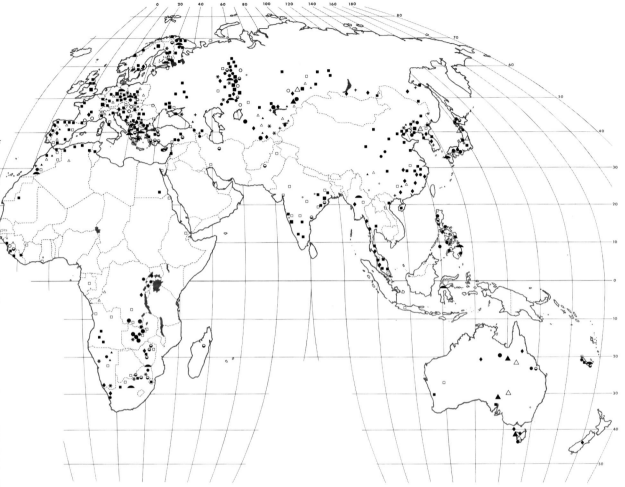

**Map 17.2** Ferrous and non-ferrous metal resources of the world.

Pure copper melts at 1080°C and tin melts at the comparatively low temperature of 232°C. These—and even higher—temperatures can be attained in charcoal-burning furnaces. Mining during the Bronze Age was confined chiefly to surface ores but some tunnel mines of shallow depth have been discovered.

The Bronze Age was superseded by the *Iron Age.* Early iron mines were developed in the limited situations where iron ore was very rich, that is, where the ore contained 60 percent or more of the metal. Iron almost never occurs in a pure elemental form and thus even the earli-

est iron smelting produced not pure iron but various iron alloys over which the fabricator had almost no control. Smelting iron also posed greater problems with regard to the production of sufficient heat since iron melts at 1535° C. However, this temperature can be attained in a properly designed charcoal-burning furnace. Iron is superior to bronze because it can be given an edge it will retain much longer than bronze and the metal itself can be made much harder than bronze by hammering red hot iron, which has the effect of driving minute quantities of carbon into it (this having come from the charcoal) and, while still very hot, being thrust into water and cooled very rapidly (quenching). This latter causes the iron to retain the changed physical structure it acquired wh.le being red hot. By alternately heating, hammering, reheating (annealing), and quenching, the metallurgists were able to create a valuable material, *steel.* As already noted, iron usually occurs mixed with other elements or compounds and it so happened that in some locations in the Mediterranean region and western Europe, the native iron ores contained traces of such metals as magnesium which, when alloyed in the furnace produced a quality of steel especially prized for its ability to take and retain a very sharp edge.

For many centuries, in spite of technological advances in metallurgy, the yield of metal from mining and smelting processes was very small when compared to the present day. Nevertheless, mining and associated activities continued to make gains in technical sophistication and long before the advent of the Industrial Revolution most of the basic types of surface mining and underground mining had come into use.

One of the oldest forms of surface mining is placer mining, which involves the separation of

metal from alluvial deposits of gravels and other materials. This can be done in a simple fashion by *panning* or it may be accomplished through the use of expensive floating dredges. Metals most commonly placer mined are gold, tin, and platinum.

Another type of surface mining is the *open-pit mine.* This form of surface mining can be developed where there are very large ore deposits located at or near to the surface of the ground and that can be exploited by excavating a successively larger pit. Today, the world's largest copper, iron, and aluminum mines are of the open-pit type (Fig. 17.1).

Underground mines for metals vary from shallow "drift" tunnels that follow an original surface discovery a short distance into the ground to mines that are huge complex labyrinths of shafts and lateral drifts and that may reach hundreds of meters in depth—so deep, in fact, that it may be very difficult to supply sufficient cool air to prevent the collapse of miners by heat prostration.

All types of surface mining cause some environmental disturbance. Placer mining tends to alter the chemistry and biology of the water downstream from the mining site and in the case of dredges will also leave behind *tailings*

**Figure 17.1**  Open pit copper mine, Arizona.

**Figure 17.2** Hydraulic mining tor gold.

in conical piles that persist for decades if not centuries. One form of placer mining no longer allowed in California—*hydraulicing*—sent so much soil debris downstream as to interfere with shipping on the Sacramento River (Fig. 17.2). Increased flooding during the winter season was also one of the results of this highly destructive form of mining. Even the most humble gold panning mine sites may retain traces of activity decades and even centuries after the mining activity ceased. Open-pit mines are ugly to behold and unless precautions are taken dust from such operations is blown over areas well removed from the actual mining site.

The environmental impacts of underground mining vary considerably with the nature of the metal being mined but all such mines will have mine *spoils* or *tailings* associated with them and such are invariably unsightly (Fig. 17.3). More important is that in some instances these wastes leach toxic chemicals into surface and groundwaters with undesired biological results.

Conservation at a mining site involves not only the adoption of measures to protect the environment as much as possible, as has been suggested in the comments above, but also the adoption of measures to assure that there will be a minimum waste of the metals being mined. A general trend in mining over the past century, and particularly in the most recent decades, is the development and application of techniques to assure that the greatest possible amount of metal is recovered from a given mine.

Closely related to conservation within the mine is conservation of the ore once it has been removed and is processed. Smelting, to cite one of the major aspects of ore processing, has increased in efficiency very much in recent years this being due in no small measure to having to process lower-grade ores (Fig. 17.4). The lower the grade of ore, that is, the lower the metal content per ton, the greater is the need to extract as much of the metal as possible. This need is further increased by the fact that *mining is an energy-intensive activity*. Not only has the cost of energy been rising rapidly but ever greater quantities of energy have to be used to extract a given quantity of metal such as copper or iron from increasingly lower grade ores.

Not all metals are extracted from their ores solely by smelting. Various chemical processes are employed when the desired metal(s) are naturally combined with other materials that are either not desired or not separable unless the complex is subjected to chemical treatment.

Every type of ore smelting operation poses a threat to the environment because of the discharge of polluted air sometimes containing, as in the case of lead, highly toxic substances or by discharge of toxic wastes into adjacent streams where, in the worst cases, virtually all

**Figure 17.3**  Mine spoils, Colorado.

life will be destroyed. Recent legislation in the United States is reducing the frequency and severity of such formerly common practices.

Most of this discussion about mining has been directed to the metallic minerals. Although metals do occupy extremely important positions in the spectrum of mineral resources, the nonmetallic minerals are also very important. We use so many different kinds of nonmetallic minerals that only some of the most important will be listed here: salt, sulfur, clays, boron, sand, gravel, phosphates, limestone, gypsum, industrial diamonds, and gemstones.

Sand, gravel, limestone, and gypsum comprise the basic raw materials for the production of concrete without which much of our modern road and building construction would not be possible. The mining of these minerals often entails the modification of large areas because comparatively large volumes of material are required. Stone, particularly marble, is mined in several parts of the nation. The *quarries* from which the stone is removed often fill with water after quarrying (mining) has ceased and such sites may be a danger to the unwary and particularly to children. Sulfur and salt mines are usually underground and environmental disturbances are usually limited to the mine sites. Salt is also obtained in large quantities by using the sun's energy to evaporate water containing salt. Environmental disturbances are very local in these types of exploitations.

## THE UNITED STATES: MINERAL RICH OR MINERAL POOR?

Our nation occupies a paradoxical position respecting mineral resources. We are second only to the Soviet Union in possession of non-fuel minerals but our consumption is so great that since the 1920s we have been net importers of many of these minerals. Although available estimates vary as to future levels of importation, it does appear that by the end of this century we will have an annual import bill for imported minerals that will rival, in size, our recent annual costs of petroleum imports. However, many factors could operate to alter the amount of future metal imports in either direction. For example, the major shift from large metal-consuming automobiles to smaller cars plus a possibility that people will keep cars longer before acquiring new ones *and* the fact

**Figure 17.4** Metal smelter in operation.

that a growing share of the U.S. auto market has been captured by foreign producers is having and will continue to have a depressing effect on our nation's demand for iron, ferroalloys, and nonferrous metals such as lead, zinc, copper, and other metals used by American automobile manufacturers. On the other hand, increased defense spending for metal consuming armaments of all kinds could result in demands that offset some of the declines in demand caused by changes in other sectors of the nation's economy (Table 17.2).

Closely related to these concerns is the question as to how large our nation's metallic mineral reserves are. In spite of the fact that sizeable mining and mineral exploration in this country date back to well over a century, it is believed by some persons in the mining industry that many large mineral discoveries remain to be made. Challenging this view are persons who believe that most of the important discoveries have already been made. This might seem to be an unimportant difference of views but behind these positions lies the desire to gain access to certain government lands now off limits for mineral exploration and the fears of some conservationists that such exploration will lead to degradation and destruction of areas already set aside to be protected.

Even if we restrict our inquiry as to how large our mineral resources are to known deposits we still encounter difficulties in arriving at a precise answer. The chief reason for this is economics. As already noted, the size of a proven resource is judged not solely in terms of the actual quantity judged to be present but also in terms of the relationship of production costs to the market price. Thus, our proven mineral reserves could grow or shrink even if there were no further exploration or removal. As was noted earlier, there has been a trend in mineral processing technology that allows for the economical processing of abundant, albeit ever-lower, grade ores. It is to this fact that the more optimistic point when it is suggested by others that we, as well as the world, may be rapidly approaching a time when we shall have exhausted most of our mineral resources. The more pessimistic assert that *energy costs* will ultimately put a cap on the utilization of ever leaner ores and that we must not count only on technology to compensate for the shrinking supply of richer ores.

It is absurd to speak of the danger of actually totally exhausting the supply of metallic minerals. The *marketplace* regulates consumption, to a major degree, and this mechanism will almost assuredly choke off demand well before a given metallic resource is all used up. We also often overlook *substitution* as a factor in

Table 17.2
**Some important nonferrous metals**

| Metal | Major Sources |
| --- | --- |
| Copper | United States, U.S.S.R., Chile, Zambia, Canada, Zaire |
| Lead | U.S.S.R., Australia, Canada, United States, Mexico |
| Zinc | Canada, United States, Australia, Peru |
| Aluminum (ore) | Jamaica, Surinam, Guyana, U.S.S.R., Australia |
| Platinum | U.S.S.R., Canada, South Africa |
| Tin | Malaysia, Bolivia, U.S.S.R., China, Thailand |
| Mercury | Spain, Italy, U.S.S.R., Mexico, United States, China |
| Gold | South Africa, U.S.S.R., Canada, United States |
| Silver | Mexico, Canada, Peru, U.S.S.R., United States |

the probable future availability of a given metal resource. Plastics, for example, have been substituted for many auto parts once made of metal. Although it is not currently popular in some conservationist circles to suggest that future technology will provide some alternatives to present-day metal needs it is absurd to dismiss that as a possibility. The error is to place all of one's reliance on technology to correct all of the resource availability difficulties we might expect to encounter. History does provide us with a basis for some optimism and indeed, one might ask what our present state of technology might be had it been determined in the Bronze Age that because high-grade copper ore and alloys were being rapidly exhausted there was no other alternative but to return to the Stone Age? Surely there is a reasonable basis for the inclusion of some confidence in our continued ability to manipulate mineral resources to provide us with the goods we desire?

However, we must confront the fact that our nation depends almost entirely on foreign sources for certain metals that we presently consider critical for the functioning of our economy. Substitutes may be found for these metals but this will take time and considerable financial investment. If our desire is to become less dependent on foreign suppliers then more research must be directed toward the development of substitute materials and processes. However, the pursuit of "mineral independence" ought to be tempered with an awareness that we can't return to the condition prevailing at the beginning of this century when our nation could claim to be essentially self-sufficient with regard to all the raw materials we required. The desire to return to those halcyon days may be understandable but if pursued as federal policy would lead not only to frustration but, in the process, could cause great damage to protected natural areas and lower the quality of our lives. For better or for worse, there is now a *global economy* and our future as well as the future of other nations lies not in a back-to-a-moated-nation movement but rather in achieving workable humane economic relationships between nations.

Related to this is a question often raised in this and other nations: Does the United States have the right to consume more minerals per capita than any other nation on earth? It has become an international cliche to ask "is it right for about one-sixth of the world's population to consume more than 30 percent (or some other relatively large percentage) of the world's current production of natural resources?" This raises a host of questions including the question as to how acceptable at the *global level* is the market place as the chief means of allocating scarce metal resources.

The industrialized nations are sometimes loud in their criticism of the United States with regard to our per capita consumption of natural resources and the impact we thereby make on world market prices. This criticism is understandable and not without merit. However, one must be aware that these nations are themselves attempting to increase their industrial outputs and thus some of their complaints seem to derive from not having succeeded quite as well as we have in the world marketplace. One also notes that although the United States is frequently described as "wasteful" one need not be a particularly astute observer to note that the often-condemned behavior is international. It would seem that vulgarity and "wasteful" consumption is a trait common to most if not all cultures and may be limited in expression more by economics than by personally or nationally held values.

Although we may accept that the industrialized nations must be prepared to accept the rigors and disciplines of the marketplace it is more difficult to accept this view with respect to the poor nations of the world. It seems to some observers that it is Kafkaian to demand that poor nations take their chances in the marketplace and accept without complaint their limited ability to compete there for scarce goods. It is ironic that many of these Third World nations are the chief suppliers of the minerals competed for by the wealthy nations. It might appear to some observers that these poor nations could organize into cartels like OPEC and thus obtain higher prices for their minerals. Although such efforts have been attempted, particularly with regard to aluminum, they have not thus far succeeded. However, the point is that many Third World nations do not possess mineral wealth or any other natural resource wealth except their soils, which must not only produce for the internal market but also products for export. These nations can't hope to develop other than minimal manufacturing activities (e.g., soft drink bottling, food processing, alcohol manufacturing, tobacco products, and light assembly of such things as bicycles) because they can't afford to purchase the raw materials not to mention the needed capital goods for larger scale enterprises.

It may appear that the United States should reduce immediately the amounts of its importation of minerals and thus free up supplies for the Third World. However, few useful results for the Third World would occur were we to adopt such a course unless the action were a part of a globally agreed-to scheme and was coupled with a host of other measures making it possible for Third World nations to actually use the increased minerals made available to them. Were the United States to adopt unilaterally what some might perceive as a moral position by cutting back on our imports of minerals we could expect that (1) market prices would fall and (2) other industrial nations would take advantage of the increased supply of lower-priced minerals to increase their consumption of them, whereupon market prices would again increase. Although we might for a short time bask in the warmth of our "moral" behavior, the Third World nations depending on income from mineral exports would suffer economic, political, and other difficulties because of the lower prices obtained for their mineral exports in the world marketplace. Lest this appear conjec-

tural note that during every economic recession in the United States the world price for copper, aluminum, lead, zinc, cobalt, and other major metallic minerals has declined, thus bringing hard economic conditions to the exporting Third World countries.

Any significant altering of the present world distribution of minerals (as well as many other natural resources) can't be achieved unless cooperative international efforts are brought to bear on the enormously complex problem of determining what constitutes an equitable world distribution of scarce goods. Although it may be granted that for poor countries the economic maxim that the marketplace is the best mechanism available for the optimal distribution of scarce goods, in this case it is neither humane nor politically safe. It is also unsound to suggest that simplistic unilateral reduction of mineral imports (or many other imported natural resources) constitutes an acceptable alternative.

Third World nations are increasing the intensity of their complaints respecting what they receive for their exports (be they mineral or other) and the much higher prices they are required to pay for imported goods. Allowing for frequent poor management on the part of the leaders of many of these countries, the fact remains that the nations have incurred large and rapidly growing foreign debts and their ability to borrow the sums necessary for development has become increasingly difficult. It must also be kept in mind that without significant exception Third World nations expect one day to have industries that require, among other things, metals of various kinds. If these nations, beset by increasing debt burdens and increasing difficulties attending capital accumulation, are not given relief from market-established prices of raw materials that they require for development they can only look forward to more poverty, more political unrest, and an ever-widening gulf between their living standards and the living standards of the developed world.

It is far beyond the scope of this book to suggest ways by which the foregoing difficulties might be overcome. However, the problems will most assuredly increase and it is among the important responsibilities of all educated and informed members of a democratic nation to stimulate debate and discussion toward the end of achieving the humane and politically stable world that can't possibly be attained if the marketplace is allowed to be the principal if not sole arbiter by which resources are distributed internationally.

## STOCKPILING

Concern for mineral—and especially metal—availability in the United States is frequently focused on the so-called strategic minerals, that is, those that are most required for industry and particularly those used in the production of military goods. As already noted, some of the most important of these are the ferroalloys some of which must be obtained entirely or in substantial measure from foreign sources many of which are often politically unstable and thus present the specter of interruptions in supply.

Aside from seeking substitutes within our national borders for such imports, the fact remains that for such metals as platinum, cobalt, manganese, and chromium there are no satisfactory substitutes now available and such may not become available for many years. One response to this has been for the federal government to establish stockpiles of these and other resources whose supply might be threatened by political disturbances in foreign areas. The U.S. government has been operating a stockpiling program for many years, the chief justification for which is to assure ample supplies during a period of war.

Several difficulties attend the stockpiling of metals. Chief among these are costs to taxpayers, deterioration of the quality of stored metals and the economic threat posed by the market "overhang."

The expenditure of tax money is always subject to public scrutiny and it has been argued that the metal stockpiling program costs more than it is actually worth to the nation. However, prudent behavior requires that some substantial effort be made by the government to protect the nation against the possibility of a supply cut off.

Most metals oxidize if unprotected and are also subject to other forms of deterioration unless care is given to them. This can be fairly costly and most certainly, in a given short term, tends to increase the unit costs of the metal above what the price is in the marketplace. However, the stockpile exists precisely to protect against the time when the metal is not available perhaps at any price in the marketplace.

Most troubling of all for many persons is the "overhang" aspect of stockpiling. The term "overhang" or "market overhang" is employed by commodity traders to identify large quantities of a commodity that are known to exist although not being traded, but which could quickly be placed onto the market and thus depress prices. Although the *raison d'etre* for federal government stockpiling is to protect against an interruption of imports it is true that some metals are held in such large amounts that some exporters as well as importers are fearful that a disorderly market could result if, for political reasons, the federal government should decide to "dump" large quantities suddenly onto the market. This aspect of stockpiling can't be completely corrected but the history of our government's behavior vis-à-vis sales from the stockpile—with a few exceptions—is one that should keep such fears to a minimum.

## RECYCLING

Metal mining and processing, as previously indicated, are energy-intensive activities. Therefore, every effort should be made to reduce energy consumption associated with metals production. Equally important, every effort, commensurate with good economics, should be made to reuse scarce metals, or metals whose smelting energy cost is high, for as long and often as possible. Recycling of metals is not a particularly new activity because some metals have been the object of recycling for centuries as for example mercury, gold, and silver. Iron and steel products have been recycled for many decades as have lead, zinc, and copper. Much more recent is the interest and activity in aluminum recycling but aluminum has been of major economic importance only in this century.

Although the list of recycled metals appears to be rather impressive, it should be noted that with the exception of gold, silver, and mercury, the percentage of recycled metal to total metal used remains comparatively small. Huge quantities of metals are discarded in landfills every year and there is as yet no economical method available to recover these materials. A considerable portion of wrecked automobiles is recycled for the steel they contain but great numbers of autos are not so utilized. The price of scrap metal varies according to market conditions and when the price on nonscrap is low the scrap price may fall so low as to be of little interest to scrap collectors. At such times larger than usual quantities of scrap metal may be discarded where they can't later be reclaimed. The economic costs of collecting, processing, and shipping scrap metal are significant, and if nonscrap prices are low it may sometimes not be possible to make a profit by recycling metals.

At present, there is great and still growing interest in recycling aluminum, which is used in many applications. Most of the aluminum recycling activity is currently focused on retrieval of beverage containers. The United States imports almost all of the aluminum it consumes—a quantity that has been increasing very rapidly in the past couple of decades. Aluminum smelting is extremely energy intensive. However, very much smaller amounts of energy are required to melt aluminum cans and other aluminum objects. Thus, recycling of aluminum is

highly desirable because of (1) the great quantities of energy that can be saved, (2) the lessened reliance on an imported aluminum (ore or finished aluminum) and (3) less litter to contend with in our environments.

A major and as yet unsolved problem associated with metal recycling is that of efficient collection of scrap. At present, a large share of the metal recycling activity depends on more-or-less casual *ad hoc* collecting efforts. Better organization, such as having people separate their trash and trucks having compartments in which metals and other valuable waste could be separated, might be one possible way to increase collection efficiency. However, it will most likely be the marketplace that will ultimately provide the impetus for the development of efficient large-scale metal recycling. Until there is a greater economic incentive and legal requirements to achieve a high level of metal recycling, this is not likely to occur. As metals become more costly in real terms there will be heightened efforts to reclaim as much as possible for reuse.

## SUMMARY

One of the distinctive features of our time is the extraordinary dependence of our economy on a wide array of minerals. Another equally significant and closely related feature is that few if any industrialized nations are totally self-sufficient in the minerals they require. The United States has changed in little more than three-quarters of a century from a condition of almost total self-sufficiency to having now to import 50 percent or more of at least 20 different kinds of metallic minerals some of which—like cobalt, chromium, and manganese—are critical to our ability to manufacture special kinds of steel.

Mining is an energy-intensive activity as well as being an impacter of the environment at mining sites and where the minerals are processed in smelters. Mining is the ultimate nonrenewable use of a natural resource insofar as its primary acquisition is concerned. However, by recycling, many mineral resources can be used and reused for protracted periods of time. Recycling has tended to be most significant where scarce and precious metals are involved or where energy costs of recycling are significantly less than those of primary production. We and other nations must rapidly become even more sophisticated with regard to the recycling of minerals if major shortages of some are not to occur in the near future.

Mineral resources point up the importance of looking at natural resources on a global scale. With the possible exception of the Soviet Union, the industrialized nations of the world must import large fractions of many of the minerals they require. A large portion of these come from Third World nations which, with few exceptions, would like to be able to process the min-

erals that they now export in raw form into more valuable and hence more profitable products. However, they are usually frustrated in this desire through lack of capital and technical ability. Furthermore, there are many Third World nations that lack mineral resources but would like to engage in manufacturing activities that require mineral resources. Again, these nations lack capital as well as the technical cadres necessary to achieve such a goal. At present, the developed nations command the world marketplace for minerals and set the price for them. It would appear that some equitable method should be developed to overcome this example of the tyranny of geography if not for reasons of human decency then for reasons related to the encouragement of economic and, hence, social stability in the Third World.

# suggested readings

## CHAPTER ONE

Burch, W. R., Cheek, N. H., Jr., and Taylor, L. (Eds.), *Social Behavior, Natural Resources, and the Environment*. New York, Harper & Row, 1972.

Clapham, W. B., Jr., *Natural Ecosystems*. New York, Macmillan, 1973.

Daly, H. E. (Ed.), *Toward a Steady-State Economy*. San Francisco, W. H. Freeman, 1973.

Falk, R. A., *This Endangered Planet: Prospects and Proposals for Human Survival*. New York, Random House, 1971.

Forrester, J., *World Dynamics*. Cambridge, Massachusetts, Wright-Allen, 1971.

Hardin, G. and Baden, J. (Eds.), *Managing the Commons*. San Francisco, W. H. Freeman, 1977.

Heilbroner, R., *An Inquiry Into the Human Prospect*. New York, Norton, 1974.

Lake, L. (Ed.), *Environmental Mediation: The Search for Concensus*. Boulder, Colorado, Westview Press, 1980.

Meadows, H. D., Meadows, D. L., Randers, J., and Behrens, W. W., *The Limits to Growth*. New York, Universe, 1972.

Mishan, E. J., *The Economic Growth Debate*. London, Allan & Unwin, 1977.

National Academy of Sciences, *Resources and Man*. San Francisco, W. H. Freeman, 1969.

Odum, E. P., *Fundamentals of Ecology* (3rd ed.). Philadelphia, W. B. Saunders, 1971.

Simmons, I. G., *The Ecology of Natural Resources*. New York, Halsted, 1974.

Smith, V. K. (Ed.), *Scarcity and Growth Reconsidered*. Baltimore, Johns Hopkins University Press, 1979.

Van Dyne, G. M., *The Ecosystem Concept in Natural Resource Management*. New York, Academic Press, 1969.

Young, O. R., *Natural Resources and the State*. Berkeley and Los Angeles, University of California Press, 1981.

## CHAPTER TWO

Harding, W., *The Days of Henry Thoreau*. New York, Knopf, 1965.

Hays, S., *Conservation and the Gospel of Efficiency: The Progressive Conservation Movement, 1890–1920*. Cambridge, Massachusetts, Harvard University Press, 1959.

Leopold, A. S., *A Sand County Almanac*. New York, Oxford University Press, 1949.

Marsh, G. P., *Man and Nature*. New York, Scribners, 1864.

Nash, R., *Wilderness and the American Mind*. New Haven, Yale University Press, 1967.

Nash, R. (Ed.), *The American Environment: Readings in the History of Conservation*. Reading, Massachusetts, Addison-Wesley, 1968.

Udall, S., *The Quiet Crisis*. New York, Holt, Rinehart and Winston, 1965.

Worster, D., *Nature's Economy*. San Francisco, Sierra Club, 1977.

## CHAPTER THREE

Beaujeu-Garnier, J., *Geography of Population*. London, Longmans, 1966.

Bogue, D. J., *Principles of Demography*. New York, Wiley, 1969.

Borgstrom, G., *Too Many*. New York, Macmillan, 1969.

Brown, L. R., *Resource Trends and Population Policy: A Time for Reassessment*. Washington, D.C., Worldwatch Institute, 1979.

Eckholm, E., *Losing Ground: Environmental Stress and World Food Prospects*. New York, Norton, 1976.

Georgescu-Roegen, N., *The Entropy Law and the Economic Process*. Cambridge, Massachusetts, Harvard University Press, 1971.

Grayson, M. J. and Shepard, T. R., Jr., *The Disaster Lobby: Prophets of Ecological Doom and Other Absurdities*. Chicago, Follett, 1973.

Hardin, G. (Ed.), *Population, Evolution, and Birth Control: A Collage of Controversial Ideas*. San Francisco, W. H. Freeman, 1969.

Maddox, J., *The Doomsday Syndrome*. New York, McGraw-Hill, 1972.

Mudd, S. (Ed.), *The Population Crisis and the Use of World Resources*. Bloomington, Indiana University Press, 1964.

Ridker, R. G. (Ed.), *Population and Development*. Baltimore, Johns Hopkins University Press, 1976.

Salk, J. and Salk, J., *World Populations and Human Values*. New York, Harper & Row, 1981.

Singer, S. F. (Ed.), *Is There an Optimum Level of Population?* New York, McGraw-Hill, 1971.

United Nations, *Demographic Yearbook*. New York, United Nations, Annual.

## CHAPTER FOUR

Dasmann, R. F., Milton, J. P., and Freeman, P. H. (Eds.), *Ecological Principles for Economic Development*. New York, Wiley, 1973.

Dolman, A. J. (Ed.), *RIO Reshaping the International Order: A Report to the Club of Rome*. New York, Signet, 1977.

Hofstadter, R., *Social Darwinism in American Thought*. (Rev. Ed.), Boston, Beacon Press, 1955.

Makhijani, A. and Poole, A., *Energy and Agriculture in the Third World*. Cambridge, Massachusetts, 1975.

Georgescu-Roegen, W., *The Entropy Law and Economic Process*. Cambridge, Massachusetts, Harvard University Press, 1971.

## CHAPTER FIVE

Baron, R. A., *The Tyranny of Noise*. New York, St. Martin's Press, 1970.

Brodine, V., *Air Pollution*. New York, Harcourt Brace, 1973.

Kellogg, W. W. and Schware, R., *Climate Change and Society*. Boulder, Colorado, Westview Press, 1981.

Landau, R. (Ed.), *Air Conservation*. Washington, D.C., American Association for the Advancement of Science, 1968.

National Research Council, *Odors from Stationary and Mobile Sources*. Washington, D.C., National Academy of Sciences, 1980.

Singer, S. F., *Global Effects of Environmental Pollution*. New York, Springer Verlag, 1970.

Sugden, T. M. and West, T. F. (Eds.), *Chlorofluorocarbons in the Environment: The Aerosol Controversy*. New York, Halsted Press, 1980.

Williams, J. (Ed.), *Carbon Dioxide, Climate and Society*. New York, Pergamon, 1978.

Williamson, S. J., *Fundamentals of Air Pollution*. Reading, Massachusetts, Addison-Wesley, 1973.

## CHAPTER SIX

Bennett, H. H., *Soil Conservation*. New York, McGraw-Hill, 1939.

Bridges, E. M., *World Soils*. London, Cambridge University Press, 1970.

Foth, H. D. and Schafer, J. W., *Soil Geography and Land Use*. New York, Wiley, 1980.

Held, R. B. and Clawson, M., *Soil Conservation in Perspective.* Baltimore, Johns Hopkins University Press, 1965.

Jacks, J. V. and Whyte, R. O., *The Rape of the Earth: A World Survey of Soil Erosion.* London, Faber, 1939.

Jenny, H., *The Soil Resource: Origin and Behavior.* New York, Springer-Verlag, 1980.

Papadakis, J., *Soils of the World.* Amsterdam, Elsevier, 1969.

Sanchez, P. A., *Properties and Management of Soils in the Tropics.* New York, Wiley, 1976.

United States Department of Agriculture, Soil Survey Staff, *Soil Taxonomy.* Washington, D. C., USDA Handbook No. 436, 1975.

Watters, R. F., *Shifting Cultivation in Latin America.* Rome, United Nations Food and Agriculture Organization (FAO), 1971.

# CHAPTER SEVEN

Atherton, L., *Cattle Kings.* Bloomington, Indiana University Press, 1961.

Bartlett, R. A., *The New Country: A Social History of the American Frontier, 1776–1890.* New York, Oxford University Press, 1974.

Bogue, M. B., *Patterns From the Sod: Tenure on the Grand Prairie.* Springfield, Illinois, Illinois State Historical Society, 1957.

Clawson, M., *The Bureau of Land Management.* New York, Praeger, 1971.

Costello, D. F., *The Prairie World.* New York, Thomas Y. Crowell, 1969.

Dobie, J. F., *The Longhorns.* Boston, Little-Brown, 1941 (plus later eds.).

Driver, H. E., *Indians of North America.* Chicago, University of Chicago Press, 1969.

Foss, P., *Politics of Grass.* Seattle, University of Washington Press, 1960.

French, N., *Perspectives in Grassland Ecology.* New York, Springer-Verlag, 1979.

Gates, P. W., *Landlords and Tenants on the Prairie Frontier.* Ithaca, New York, Cornell University Press, 1973.

Humphrey, R. R., *Range Ecology.* New York, Ronald, 1962.

Kraenzel, C., *The Great Plains.* Norman, Oklahoma, Oklahoma University Press, 1955.

Robbins, R. M., *Our Landed Heritage.* (rev. ed.) Lincoln, University of Nebraska Press, 1974.

Schlebecker, J. T., *Cattle Raising on the Plains, 1900–1960.* Lincoln, University of Nebraska Press, 1963.

Steinbeck, J., *The Grapes of Wrath.* New York, Viking Press, 1939 (plus many editions since).

Stoddart, L. A. and Smith, A. D., *Range Management.* New York, McGraw-Hill, 1955.

U. S. Department of Agriculture, *Grass: The Yearbook of Agriculture.* Washington, D. C., U. S. Dept. of Agriculture, 1948.

Weaver, J. E., *North American Prairie.* Lincoln, Nebraska, Johnson, 1954.

Weaver, J. E. and Albertson, F. W., *Grasslands of the Great Plains.* Lincoln, Nebraska, Johnson, 1956.

Webb, W. P., *The Great Plains.* New York, Grosset & Dunlap, 1931.

# CHAPTER EIGHT

Brown, S., Lugo, A. E., and Liegel, B. (Eds.), *The Role of Tropical Forests on the World Carbon Cycle.* Springfield, Virginia, National Technical Information Service—U. S. Department of Commerce, 1980.

Bruges, R. L. and Sharpe, D. M. (Eds.), *Forest Island Dynamics in Man-Dominated Landscapes.* New York, Springer-Verlag, 1981.

Clawson, M., *Forest for Whom and for What?* Baltimore, Johns Hopkins University Press, 1975.

Davis, K. P., *Forest Fire: Control and Use.* New York, McGraw-Hill, 1959.

Eckholm, E., *Planting for the Future: Forestry for Human Needs*. Washington, D. C., World-watch Institute Paper No. 26, 1979.

Edlin, H. L., *Trees and Man*. New York, Columbia University Press, 1976.

Frome, M., *The Forest Service*. New York, Praeger, 1971.

Haden-Guest, S. (Ed.), *A World Geography of Forest Resources*. AGS Special Pub. 33, New York, Ronald Press, 1956.

Myers, N., *Conversion of Tropical Moist Forests*. Washington, D. C., National Academy of Sciences, 1980.

Preston, R. J., Jr., *North American Trees*. Cambridge, Mass., MIT Press, Third Edition, 1976.

Reichle, D. E. (Ed.), *Analysis of Temperate Forest Ecosystems*. New York, Heidelberg, Berlin, Springer-Verlag, 1970.

Richards, P. W., *The Tropical Rainforest*. New York, Cambridge University Press, 1952.

Smith, W. H., *Air Pollution and Forests*. New York, Springer-Verlag, 1981.

Spurr, S. H. and Barnes, B. V., *Forest Ecology* (3rd ed.). New York, Wiley, 1980.

U. S. Department of Agriculture, *The Outlook for Timber in the United States*. Washington, D. C., U. S. Government Printing Office, 1973.

U. S. Department of Agriculture, *Yearbook of Agriculture, Trees, 1949*. Washington, D. C., U. S. Government Printing Office, 1949.

U. S. Department of the Interior, Forest Service, *Timber Trends in the United States*. Washington, D. C., U. S. Government Printing Office, 1965.

U. S. Interagency Task Force on Tropical Forests, *The World's Tropical Forests: A Policy, Strategy, and Program for the United States*. Washington, D. C., Department of State Publication 9117, U. S. Government Printing Office, 1980.

Wood, N. C., *Clearcut*. San Francisco, Sierra Club, 1971.

Zivnuska, J. A., *U. S. Timber Resources in a World Economy*. Baltimore, Johns Hopkins University Press, 1967.

## CHAPTER NINE

Ackerman, E. A. and Lof, G. O. G., *Technology in American Water Development*. Baltimore, Johns Hopkins University Press, 1959.

Dunne, T. and Leopold, L. B., *Water in Environmental Planning*. San Francisco, W. H. Freeman, 1978.

Hundley, N., Jr., *Water and the West*. Berkeley and Los Angeles, University of California Press, 1975.

Jackson, W. T. and Paterson, A. M., *The Sacramento-San Joaquin Delta: The Evolution and Implementation of Water Policy*. Davis, California, California Water Resources Center, University of California at Davis, 1977.

Kahrl, W. L. (Ed.), *The California Water Atlas*. Sacramento, State of California, 1979.

Leopold, L. B. and Langbein, W. B., *A Primer on Water*. Washington, D. C., Department of the Interior, 1960.

Mandel, S. and Shiftan, Z. L., *Groundwater Resources*. New York, Academic Press, 1981.

McKee, R. *Great Lakes Country*. New York, Thomas Y. Crowell, 1966.

Moss, B., *Ecology of Fresh Waters*. New York, Halsted Press, 1980.

Kneese, A. V. and Bower, B. T., *Managing Water Quality: Economics, Technology, and Institutions*. Baltimore, Johns Hopkins University Press, 1968.

Otis, D. S., *The Dawes Act and the Allotment of Indian Lands*. Norman, Oklahoma, Oklahoma University Press, 1973.

Russel, C. S. (Ed.), *Safe Drinking Water: Current and Future Problems*. Baltimore, Johns Hopkins University Press, 1978.

Russell-Hunter, W. D., *Aquatic Productivity*. New York, Macmillan, 1970.

Seckler, D. (Ed.), *California Water: A Study in Resource Management*. Berkeley and Los Angeles, University of California Press, 1971.

Sheridan, D., *Desertification of the United States*. Washington, D. C., U. S. Government Printing Office, 1981.

U. S. Department of the Interior, Bureau of Reclamation, *Colorado River System Consumptive Uses and Losses Report, 1971–1975*. Washington, D. C., U. S. Government Printing Office, 1975.

U. S. Water Resources Council, *The Nation's Water Resources, 1975–2000*. Washington, D. C., U. S. Government Printing Office, 1978.

Utton, A. E. and Teclaff, L. A. (Eds.), *Water in a Developing World*. Boulder, Colorado, Westview Press, 1978.

Wright, J. C., *The Coming Water Famine*. New York, Coward, 1966.

## CHAPTER TEN

Bardach, J., *Harvest of the Sea*. New York, Harper, 1968.

Bell, F. W., *Food From the Sea: The Economics and Politics of Ocean Fisheries*. Boulder, Colorado, Westview Press, 1978.

Council on Environmental Quality, *Ocean Dumping: A National Policy*. Washington, D. C., U. S. Government Printing Office, 1970.

Crutchfield, J. A. (Ed.), *The Fisheries: Problems in Resource Management*. Seattle, University of Washington Press, 1965.

Friedheim, R. L. (Ed.), *Managing Ocean Resources: A Primer*. Boulder, Colorado, Westview Press, 1979.

Geyer, R. A. (Ed.), *Marine Environmental Pollution*. Amsterdam, Elsevier, 1981.

Glantz, M. H. and Thompson, J. D. (Eds.), *Resource Management and Environmental Uncertainty: Lessons From Coastal Upwelling Fisheries*. New York, Wiley-Interscience, 1980.

Hardy, A. C., *The Open Sea: Its Natural History*. Boston, Massachusetts, Houghton Mifflin, 1965.

Hood, D. D., *The Impingement of Man on the Oceans*. New York, Wiley-Interscience, 1971.

Ketchum, B. H., Kester, D. R., and Park, P. K. (Eds.), *Ocean Dumping of Industrial Wastes*. New York, Plenum, 1981.

Livingston, R. J. (Ed.), *Ecological Processes in Coastal Marine Ecosystems*. New York, Plenum, 1979.

Marx, W., *The Frail Ocean*. New York, Coward, 1967.

Mathews, L. H., *The Natural History of the Whale*. New York, Columbia University Press, 1978.

M'Gonigle, R. M., and M. W. Zacher, *Pollution, Politics, and International Law: Tankers at Sea*. Berkeley and Los Angeles, University of California Press, 1981.

Middleditch, B. S. (Ed.), *Environmental Effects of Offshore Oil Production*. New York, Plenum, 1981.

Odell, R., *The Saving of San Francisco Bay: The Role of Citizens in Environmental Planning*. Washington, D. C., The Conservation Foundation, 1972.

Palmer, H. D. and Gross, M. G. (Eds.), *Ocean Dumping and Marine Pollution: Geological Aspects of Waste Disposal*. New York, Academic Press, 1979.

Ross, D. A., *Opportunities and Uses of the Ocean*. New York, Springer-Verlag, 1980.

Smith, J. (Ed.), *"Torrey Canyon" Pollution and Marine Life*. London, Cambridge University Press, 1970.

Steele, J. H., *The Structure of Marine Ecosystems*. Cambridge, Massachusetts, Harvard University Press, 1974.

Stommel, H., *The Gulf Stream—A Physical and Dynamical Description*. Berkeley and Los Angeles, University of California Press, 1965.

United Nations Food and Agricultural Organization, *Yearbook of Fisheries Statistics.* Rome, Food and Agricultural Organization, Yearly.

U. S. Fish and Wildlife Service, *Fishery Statistics of the United States.* Washington, D. C., Dept. of Commerce, Issued Yearly.

## CHAPTER ELEVEN

Dorst, J., *A Field Guide to the Larger Mammals of Africa.* New York, Houghton Mifflin, 1970.

Craighead, F. C., *Track of the Grizzly.* San Francisco, Sierra Club, 1979.

Dasmann, R. F., *Wildlife Biology.* New York, Wiley, 1964.

Gabrielson, I., *Wildlife Conservation.* New York, Macmillan, 1959.

Garretson, Martin, *The American Bison: The Story of its Extermination as a Wild Species and its Restoration under Federal Protection.* New York, New York Zoological Society, 1938.

Giles, R. H., Jr., *Wildlife Management.* San Francisco, W. H. Freeman, 1978.

Guggisberg, C. A. W., *Man and Wildlife.* New York, Arco, 1970.

Johnsgard, P. A., *Ducks, Geese, and Swans of the World.* Lincoln, Nebraska, University of Nebraska Press, 1978.

Leopold, A., *Game Management.* New York, Scribners, 1933.

Leopold, A. S., Butierrez, R. J., and Bronson, M. R., *North American Game Birds and Mammals.* New York, Scribner, 1981.

Myers, N., *The Sinking Ark.* Oxford, Pergamon Press, 1979.

Roe, F. G., *The North American Buffalo: A Critical Study of the Species in its Wild State* (2nd ed.). Toronto, University of Toronto Press, 1970.

Shorger, A. W., *The Passenger Pigeon, its Natural History and Extinction.* Madison, Wisconsin, University of Wisconsin Press, 1955.

Temple, S. A. (Ed.), *Endangered Birds: Management Techniques for Preserving Threatened Species.* Madison, Wisconsin, University of Wisconsin Press, 1978.

U. S. Department of the Interior, *Rare and Endangered Fish and Wildlife of the United States* (rev. ed.). Washington, D. C., Bureau of Sport Fisheries and Wildlife, 1968.

Weller, M. W., *Freshwater Marshes: Ecology and Wildlife Management.* Minneapolis, University of Minnesota Press, 1981.

Ziswiler, V., *Extinct and Vanishing Animals.* Heidelberg, Springer Verlag, 1967.

## CHAPTER TWELVE

Bush, R., *The National Parks of England and Wales.* London, Dent, 1973.

International Union for the Conservation of Nature and Natural Resources, *Second World Conference on National Parks.* Lausanne, Switzerland, IUCN, 1974.

International Union for the Conservation of Nature and Natural Resources, *United Nations List of National Parks and Equivalent Reserves.* Brussels, Hayez, 1971.

Ise, J., *Our National Park Policy: A Critical History.* Baltimore, Johns Hopkins University Press, 1961.

Schofield, E. A., *Earthcare: Global Protection of Natural Areas.* Boulder, Colorado, Westview Press, 1978.

Seymour, W. N., Jr., *Small Urban Spaces.* New York, New York University Press, 1969.

Shomon, J. J., *Open Land for Urban America.* Baltimore, Johns Hopkins University Press, 1971.

U. S. Department of the Interior, National Park Service, *Preserving our National Heritage.* Washington, D. C., U. S. Government Printing Office, 1977.

## CHAPTER THIRTEEN

Berkowitz, D. A. and Squires, A. M., *Power Generation and Environmental Change.* Cambridge, Massachusetts, MIT Press, 1971.

Conant, M. A. and Gold, F. R., *The Geopolitics of Energy.* Boulder, Colorado, Westview Press, 1978.

Cook, E., *Man, Energy, Society.* San Francisco, W. H. Freeman, 1976.

Fisher, J. C., *Energy Crisis in Perspective.* New York, Wiley, 1974.

Folder, J. M., *Energy and the Environment.* New York, McGraw-Hill, 1975.

Ford Foundation, *Exploring Energy Choices.* Washington, D. C., Ford Foundation Energy Project, 1974.

Georgescu-Roegen, N., *Energy and Economic Myths.* New York, Pergamon Press, 1977.

Gibbons, J. H. and Chandler, W. U., *Energy: The Conservation Revolution.* Plenum, 1981.

Hollander, J. M., Simmons, M. K., and D. O. Wood (Eds.), *Annual Review of Energy.* Palo Alto, California, Annual Reviews Inc., published each year.

Lovins, A. B., *Soft Energy Paths: Toward a Durable Peace.* Boston, Massachusetts, Ballinger, 1978.

Merrick, D. and Marshall, R., (Eds.), *Energy-Present and Future Options.* New York, Wiley-Interscience, 1981 (Vol. 1).

Schurr, S. H. et al., *Energy in America's Future: The Choices Before Us.* Baltimore, Johns Hopkins University Press, 1979.

Wilson, C. L., *Energy: Global Prospects 1985–2000.* New York, McGraw-Hill, 1977.

## CHAPTER FOURTEEN

Academy Forum, National Academy of Sciences, *Coal as an Energy Resource: Conflict and Consensus.* Washington, D. C., National Academy of Sciences, 1977.

Averitt, P., *Coal Resources of the United States January 1, 1967.* Washington, D. C., U. S. Geological Survey, Bulletin 1275, 1967.

Betancourt, R., *Venezuela: Oil and Politics.* Boston, Houghton Mifflin, 1979.

Blair, J. M., *The Control of Oil.* New York, Pantheon, 1976.

DeGolyer and MacNaughton, *Twentieth-Century Petroleum Statistics.* Dallas, Texas, DeGolyer and MacNaughton, 1978.

Ezra, D., *Coal and Energy: The Need to Exploit the World's Most Abundant Fossil Fuel.* New York, Halsted Press, 1978.

Green, A. E. S. (Ed.), *Coal Burning Issues.* Gainesville, Florida, University of Florida Press, 1980.

Hawley, M. E. (Ed.), *Coal Part 1: Social, Economic, and Environmental Aspects.* Pennsylvania, Dowden, Hutchinson & Ross, 1976.

Hunt, J. M., *Petroleum Geochemistry and Geology.* San Francisco, W. H. Freeman, 1979.

Johnson, J. P., *The Politics of Soft Coal.* Urbana, University of Illinois Press, 1979.

Lewis, J. L., *The Miner's Fight for American Standards.* Indianapolis, Bell (c. 1925).

McCleskey, C., *The Government and Politics of Texas.* Boston, Little-Brown, 1975.

National Research Council, *Surface Mining: Soil, Coal, and Society.* Washington, D. C., National Academy of Sciences, 1981.

National Research Council, *Helium: A Public Policy Problem.* Washington, D. C., National Academy of Sciences, 1978.

Pennsylvania State University, Institute for Research on Human Resources, *The Bituminous Coal Industry: A Forecast.* University Park, Pennsylvania, Pennsylvania State University Press, 1975.

Sampson, Anthony, *The Seven Sisters.* New York, Viking Press, 1975.

Singh, J. J. and Deepak, A. (Eds.), *Environ-*

*mental and Climatic Impact of Coal Utilization.* New York, Academic Press, 1980.

Tugwell, F., *The Politics of Oil in Venezuela.* Stanford, California, Stanford University Press, 1975.

Wali, M. H. (Ed.), *Ecology and Coal Resource Development* (2 vols.). New York, Pergamon Press, 1979.

Williamson, I. A., *Coal Mining Geology.* New York, Oxford University Press, 1967.

Wilson, E. and Hunt, J. (Eds.), *Petroleum in the Marine Environment.* Washington, D. C., National Academy of Sciences, 1975.

Wolfe, D. (Ed.), *Fate and Effects of Petroleum Hydrocarbons in Marine Organisms and Environments.* New York, Pergamon, 1977.

## CHAPTER FIFTEEN

Cottrell, A., *How Safe is Nuclear Energy?* Exeter, New York, Heineman, 1981.

Fritz, M., *Future Energy Consumption of the Third World with Special Reference to Nuclear Power.* New York, Pergamon, 1981.

Gaines, L., Berry, R. S., and Long, T. V., *TOSCA: The Total Social Cost of Coal and Nuclear Power.* Boston, Ballinger, 1979.

Inglis, D. R., *Nuclear Energy: Its Physics and its Social Challenge.* Reading, Massachusetts, Addison-Wesley, 1973.

Johansson, T. B. and Steen, P., *Radioactive Waste from Nuclear Power Plants.* Berkeley and Los Angeles, University of California Press, 1981.

Nuclear Energy Policy Study Group, *Nuclear Power Issues and Choices.* Cambridge, Massachusetts, Ballinger, 1977.

Osterhout, M. M. (Ed.), *Decontamination and Decommissioning of Nuclear Facilities.* New York, Plenum, 1979.

Sills, D. L., Wolf, C. P., and Shelanski, V. P. (Eds.), *Accident at Three Mile Island.* Boulder, Colorado, Westview Press, 1981.

Teller, E., *Energy From Heaven and Earth.* San Francisco, W. H. Freeman, 1979.

Union of Concerned Scientists, *The Nuclear Fuel Cycle* (rev. ed.). Boston, Massachusetts, MIT Press, 1975.

## CHAPTER SIXTEEN

Boyce, S. (Ed.), *Biological and Sociological Basis for a Rational Use of Forest Resources for Energy and Organics.* Asheville, North Carolina, U. S. Forest Service, 1979.

Earl, D. E., *Forest Energy and Economic Development.* Oxford, Clarendon, 1975.

Ekholm, E., *The Other Energy Crisis: Fuelwood.* Washington, D. C., Worldwatch Institute Paper No. 1, 1975.

Flavin, C., *Energy and Architecture: The Solar and Conservation Potential.* Washington, D. C., Worldwatch Institute Paper No. 40, 1980.

Hayes, D., *Rays of Hope: The Transition to a Post-Petroleum World.* New York, W. W. Norton, 1977.

Howell, D., *Your Solar Energy Home: Including Wind and Methane Applications.* New York, Pergamon, 1979.

Inglis, D. R., *Wind Power and Other Energy Options.* Ann Arbor, University of Michigan Press, 1978.

McDaniels, D. K., *The Sun: Our Future Energy Source.* New York, Wiley, 1979.

Metz, W. D. and Hammond, A. L., *Solar Energy in America.* Washington, D. C., American Association for the Advancement of Science, 1978.

Ross, D., *Energy From the Waves.* New York, Pergamon, 1979.

Smith, N., *Wood: An Ancient Fuel with a New Future.* Washington, D. C., Worldwatch Institute Paper No. 42, 1981.

Tillman, D. A., *Wood as an Energy Resource.* New York, Academic Press, 1978.

White, D. E. and Williams, D. L., (Eds.), *As-*

sessment of Geothermal Resources of the U.S. 1975. Washington, D. C., U. S. Geological Survey Circular 726, 1975.

World Bank, Renewable Energy Resources in the Developing Countries. Washington, D. C., World Bank, 1980.

## CHAPTER SEVENTEEN

Cameron, E. N. (Ed.), The Mineral Position of the United States, 1975–2000. Madison, University of Wisconsin Press, 1973.

Flawn, P. T., Mineral Resources. Chicago, Rand McNally, 1966.

Greever, W., Bonanza West: The Story of Western Mining Rushes, 1848–1900. Norman, Oklahoma, Oklahoma University Press, 1963.

McDivitt, J. F., Minerals and Men. Baltimore, Johns Hopkins University Press, 1965.

National Research Council, Mineral Resources and the Environment. Washington, D. C., National Academy of Sciences, 1975.

National Research Council, Reserves and Resources of Uranium in the United States. Washington, D. C., National Academy of Sciences, 1975.

**Accelerated Soil Erosion** Soil erosion occurring at a rate greater than normal and usually caused by human acts.

**Acre Foot of Water** The amount of water required to cover one acre of land to the depth of one foot. Equal to 325,851 gallons.

**Aerosol** Any small particle, solid or liquid, less than 10 microns in diameter and capable of being airborne for long periods of time.

**Albedo** The reflectivity of a surface. A white surface such as snow has a very high albedo but that of a black surface is very low.

**Allowable Cut** The amount of timber the U. S. National Forest Service allows to ·be cut in any season in a given National Forest.

**Altruistic** An act or acts performed for the benefit of another person or group.

**Anadromous Fish** Fish species that spend part of their lives in saltwater but must return to freshwater to spawn.

**Anthracite Coal** The hardest coal type recognized. Characterized by a high carbon content and relatively low content of volatile substances.

**Anticline** A geological structure usually composed of sedimentary rocks that have been folded in an archlike structure the apex of which is directed away from the earth's center.

**Aquifer** An underground porous stratum of consolidated or unconsolidated earth materials capable of containing water in the available pore spaces.

**Arabian Light Crude** The most valuable type of crude oil produced in Saudia Arabia and is the standard for high-grade crude oil in some other parts of the world.

**Arable Land** A widely used but sometimes misleading term that may denote land suitable for crops only or may also include land suited to pasture use.

**Arboreal Animal** Any animal that lives on or within trees or requires trees for a significant part of its life needs.

**Arithmetic Population Density** The simplest population measure determined by dividing the total human population into the total land area of a region or nation.

**Artesian Well** A well that flows to the surface without pumping being required.

**Atmosphere** The globe-encircling envelope of gas of which only the lowest stratum, the troposphere, contains sufficient oxygen to support most life on this planet.

**Benthic Zone** The bottom or substrate of marine ecosystems.

**Biogas** A gas produced by the decomposition of organic materials by certain bacteria. The gas contains significant quantities of methane gas, $CH_4$, but at concentrations much less than does natural gas.

**Biological Oxygen Demand (BOD)** The oxygen demand made by decomposing organisms in aquatic environments.

**Biomagnification** The tendency for certain substances to become more concentrated in organisms as the substances move through a food chain. Also referred to as the *concentration factor*.

**Biomass** The total quantity, usually measured in wet weight unless stated to the contrary, of all the plants and animals in a given place at a given time.

**Biomass Conversion** The conversion of plant or animal biomass to a form or forms suitable for energy production as for example, biogas or ethanol.

**Biome** The largest terrestrial ecosystem it is convenient to recognize. For example grasslands, tropical rainforest.

**Bituminous Coal** The soft coal type found most suited to a wide range of industrial uses including iron and steel making and fuel for steam-generating plants.

**Breeder Reactor** A nuclear reactor that "breeds" or produces more fuel than it consumes.

**British Thermal Unit (Btu)** The amount of heat energy required to raise one pound of water one degree Fahrenheit.

**Caliche Layer** A layer of hardened material, often of high calcium content, which frequently occurs at shallow depths in soils developed under arid climatic conditions.

**Canopy, Tree** The total area covered by the top or crown of a tree. A *closed canopy* is one where the tree crowns meet to form a continuous cover.

**Capillary Action** The wicklike action in the upper soil that moves water against gravity to the surface where it evaporates.

**Capital, Flight of** The phenomenon whereby money is sent out of a country in an attempt to avoid internal economic difficulties that might result in a loss of wealth on the part of those participating in the action.

**Carcinogen** A cancer-causing material or substance.

**Carrying Capacity** The upper limit of numbers of living organisms sustainable within a given ecological situation.

**Cation Exchange Capacity** The capacity of a given soil to move cations to sites where they are available for plant nutrition.

**Celsius, Degree** A system of temperature measurement named after Anders Celsius. Zero degrees Celsius is the temperature at which pure freshwater begins to freeze and 100 degrees Celsius is the temperature at which the same kind of water begins to boil (both at 760 mm barometric pressure). Usually abreviated to °C.

**Chaparral Vegetation** A woody, evergreen shrub- to low-tree vegetation that covers large areas of southern and central California. This vegetation type is found in almost all similar, that is Mediterranean, climate areas in the world although it goes by a number of other names.

**Clay Pan** A hard, water-resistant stratum of clay that often is found in soils in semiarid and arid climates. These pans make irrigation difficult as there is a tendency for the soils to become waterlogged.

**Clearcutting** The often controversial practice of cutting all the timber in a given area resulting in the exposure of the soil to possible accelerated soil erosion.

**Coal Seam** Any stratum of coal.

**Continental Shelf** The portion of a continental plate that extends varying distances offshore underwater. As a rough measure, the edges of the continental shelves lie near 200 meters depth.

**Contour Plowing** The act of plowing at right angles to a slope rather than parallel to a slope.

**Controlled Burning** The act of using fire, under controlled conditions, to reduce the accumulation of combustible plant detritus in forests, woodlands, and shrublands before it becomes dangerously large.

**Coppice** A second-growth forest or woodland. Wood produced in such situations is referred to as coppice wood.

**Damoclean Sword** A situation where potential grave harm may occur that is restrained only by a minor impediment. Derived from the story of Damocles, a court flatterer who so irritated his king, Dionysius 1, that the king seated Damocles beneath a sword suspended by a single human hair.

**Decibel** A measure of sound. Actually, it is a measure of air pressure, which is then described in terms of sound.

**Decomposers** All the organisms present in an ecosystem that break down or decompose dead organic material.

**Decreasers** Plant species in grasslands that are highly desired by grazing animals but that are unable to withstand other than the lightest grazing pressure before decreasing in abundance.

**Demography** The study of human population.

**Derived Savanna** Tropical grasslands brought about by human actions, usually forest removal, and hence derived from another type of ecosystem.

**Desertification** The process whereby semiarid areas adjacent to deserts are transformed into desert. Although all the causes of desertification are not yet known it is well established that human actions such as overgrazing of livestock are major contributing factors.

**Destructive Distillation** Heating a material such as coal or wood to cause volatile components to be driven off as gases. Another term for this is pyrolysis.

**Diversity** Usually refers to the total number of plant and animal species present in a given area. May also refer to ecological diversity with reference to variations in the physical and biotic components of a given situation.

**Ecological Diversity** See Diversity.

**Ecosystem** A unit of interacting physical and biotic elements that together form a system in which there are ordered or regulated flows of energy and apportionments of the available food materials (nutrients).

**Ecotone** A place where two or more ecosystems come together. Sometimes referred to as the "edge." Such situations often support more animals of certain species than do any single one of the adjacent ecosystems.

**Effluent** Any liquid discharge from a factory, storm drain, sewer, or other human-controlled source.

**El Niño Current** The periodic south-moving invasion of the Pacific equatorial counter current along the northwest coast of South America. This brings an invasion of warm water, of relatively low dissolved oxygen content, into cool, well-oxygenated water often resulting in a catastrophic loss of animal life.

**Energy** The capacity for performing work.

**Entrepreneur** A businessperson.

**Entropy** The tendency for energy to move from an ordered to a disordered state.

**Environmentalism** The most recent phase of the American conservation movement.

**Estuary** In general, any situation where inflowing freshwater meets and mixes, to varying degrees, with saltwater.

**Ethanol** Alcohol produced by the fermentation of sugar.

**Euphotic Zone** The uppermost stratum in water where there is sufficient light to support photosynthesis. The depth of this zone is highly variable.

**Even-age Timber Stand** An area in a forest characterized by having trees of the same or nearly the same age. This condition may be the result of a fire that destroyed all the trees allowing for the burned area to recover from seedlings developing at the same time. It is more common today to encounter even-age stands that are the result of clearcutting.

**Eutrophication** The enrichment of water by nutrients capable of increasing primary productivity. This is a natural phenomenon but also one that is frequently brought about, on a large scale, by human actions and which may result in reducing water quality.

**Extirpation** The total removal of a plant or animal species or subspecies from a particular area and usually as a result of human acts.

**Fahrenheit, Degree** A measure of temperature devised by Gabriel Fahrenheit. Zero degrees represents the temperature of an equal mixture of snow and salt. The temperature at which freshwater begins to freeze is 32 degrees and the temperature at which water begins to boil is 212 degrees. Usually abbreviated F.

**Ferroalloy** Any metal, such as manganese, that is mixed with iron to produce steel.

**Field Capacity** An irrigation term for the condition of a field when all the pore spaces in the root zone are filled with water. If more water is applied it will pass through to the subsoil below.

**Fire Climax** A vegetation type, such as chaparral appears to be, that owes its existence entirely or largely to the occurrence of fire.

**Fish Meal** An oat meal like product, odorless and containing high percentages of nutrients suited for animal and human nutrition, produced from almost any type of fish.

**Fission** The process whereby the nuclei of certain materials such as uranium 235 are forced apart, liberating energy.

**Flaring Gas** Burning off natural gas in oil fields.

**Folk taxonomy** Nonscientific but often very sophisticated folk systems of biological or physical nomenclature.

**Food Chain** The chainlike arrangement of living organisms in ecosystems composed successively of primary producers and consumers.

**Forest** A collection of trees and other vegetation in which most of the canopy is usually closed.

**Fossil Fuel** Any concentration of carbon-containing substances and particularly coal, petroleum and natural gas, which are suited to the production of energy.

**Fossil Water** Water that was trapped at varying depths in the ground, in past geological time, in aquifers which no longer can be replenished since they no longer communicate with a source of water.

**Geothermal Energy** Any source of potentially usable heat from within the earth. Usually restricted to hot water (including steam).

**Green Manure** The use of green plants (which have been planted and then plowed under) as a nutrient or other desired addition to the soil.

**Green Revolution** The great increases in the production of certain crops accomplished largely through the application of plant genetics. Refers chiefly, although not exclusively, to the increased production of such crops as wheat and rice in certain Third World nations.

**Groundwater** Water contained within aquifers in a given place. May be located at shallow or very considerable depths.

**Habitat** The environment favored by an organism or in which an organism occurs.

**Hardwood** Any wood with a dense grain. This term is applied rather generally but such woods as oak, maple, and teak are typical hardwoods.

**Hectare** A unit of land measure far more widely used in the world than the British-U. S. acre. A hectare is approximately equivalent to 2.47 acres.

**Horsepower** A unit of energy equal to the amount of power required to move 33,000 pounds one foot per minute.

**Hydrocarbon** A compound containing hydrogen and carbon. However, the term is also applied to petroleum and natural gas, for example, even though these substances also contain nonorganic substances.

**Hydrologic Cycle** The cycling of water in its liquid, solid, and gaseous states into and out of the atmosphere.

**Hygroscopic Particle** Any particle present in the atmosphere that is capable of absorbing or retaining water.

**Increasers** Grassland plant species that have a tendency to increase in numbers when subjected to moderate grazing pressure.

**Infant Mortality** Termination or loss of life between the time of live birth and the first birthday of a human child.

**Internal Combustion Engine** An engine that derives its motive power through the controlled combustion of gases within confined, that is, internal chambers (i.e., cylinders).

**Intertidal Zone** The place at the sea edge where there is a diurnal or semidiurnal alternating exposure and covering of the substrate by tidal action.

**Invaders** Plant species, often toxic to livestock, which invade overgrazed grasslands.

**Ion** An atom that has either lost or gained one or more electrons from the outer ring and thus has respectively, a positive or negative charge.

**Ionization** The process whereby an atom becomes an ion.

**Isotope** A species of an element having the same atomic number as the "parent" element but differing from it in its atomic mass.

**Juvenile Water** "New" water produced by chemical actions usually at some depth within the earth.

**Joule** A measure of energy. This is a very small unit of energy: 1000 joules = 0.9484 Btu.

**Kerogen** The material contained in oil shale that can be removed and processed into petroleum.

**Kilocalorie** A thousand small calories. The amount of heat required to raise the temperature of one kilogram of water one degree Celsius.

**Kilowatt** One thousand watts.

**Krill** Common name given to small marine crustaceans that resemble shrimp. They occur in large numbers in some areas and particularly so in antarctic waters.

**Laissez Faire Economy** An economy free from governmental restrictions.

**Lapse Rate of Air Temperature** The increase or decrease in air temperature that occur along an altitude gradient. Usually, there is a decrease in temperature with an increase in altitude.

**Latent Resource** An entity in the environment that at present may have no use or market but that might have such in the future under changed economic and/or technological circumstances.

**Latifundia** Very large private landholdings such as has characterized many parts of Latin America since their imposition in colonial times.

**Lignite Coal** Also known as brown coal. Lignite is softer than bituminous coal and is not as well regarded for most industrial applications.

**Liquid Natural Gas (LNG)** The product produced for ship transport by compressing and lowering the temperature of natural gas.

**Market Overhang** A situation where a commodity is in abundant supply but not in the marketplace but that could be placed there on short notice thus causing prices for it to weaken. The mere presence of such an overhang may cause prices to be lower than they would be in its absence.

**Marketplace** In economic terms, the free and open vending and purchase of goods and services where the prices are established by supply and demand rather than by fiat.

**Megawatt** A million watts.

**Meltdown** When the cooling system or other

controls fail to regulate the rate of the fission reaction in the core of a nuclear reactor the fuel rods and associated structures in the core are subject to great heat and may melt, an accident producing grave consequences.

**Mercantilism** The economic philosophy that it is in a nation's best interest for the government to foster international trade but only to the extent that the preponderance of economic gain should accrue to the stronger country.

**Meteoric Water** Water derived from rain, snow, and hail.

**Methane** $CH_4$—the major component of natural gas.

**Methanol** $CH_3OH$. Often called wood alcohol because it is frequently obtained by the destructive distillation of wood.

**Mores** Human behavior governed by tradition or custom rather than by formal legal sanctions.

**Natural Levee** A river tends to deposit, along its margins, more material than it does in the center of the flow and this leads to the development of banks higher than the usual river level except at flood stage. These banks are natural banks or levees as contrasted with human-made levees, which are usually raised on natural levees.

**Natural selection** The central element of Darwin's explanation of how plant and animal evolution is accomplished. This states that various environmental forces work on individuals in such a way that those best adapted to the conditions will have the best chance to survive and reproduce, that is, they will be naturally selected for survival.

**Neritic Zone** Essentially the same as the continental shelf in terms of location.

**Oil Shale** Sedimentary rock containing relatively large quantities of kerogen which can be extracted and processed into petroleum.

**Oligotrophic** Any body of water having a low nutrient status.

**Ore** Rock or earth material containing a metal in actual or potentially sufficient concentrations to be worth commercial exploitation.

**Overburden** The earth and stone material lying above a mineral resource located at a relatively shallow depth.

**Overdraft of Groundwater** Removal of groundwater from an aquifer at a pace greater than the recharge rate of the aquifer.

**Particulates** Small liquid or solid particles emitted from such sources as factories, internal combustion engines and certain electricity-generating plants.

**Peat** Partially decomposed vegetal matter that, if allowed to accumulate, may evolve into lignite and other types of coal. Peat has a low Btu content per volume as compared to bituminous coal.

**Pedology** The scientific study of soil.

**Petroleum** A complex hydrocarbon from which a multitude of useful products is obtained as well as being the principal energy resource in most of the developed world.

**Photochemical Smog** A type of air pollution resulting from the reaction of sunlight on nitrogen oxides in the atmosphere.

**Photosynthesis** The process by which light acts on water and carbon dioxide in the presence of chlorophyll to synthesize carbohydrates required for plant nutrition.

**Photovoltaic Cell** A device capable of converting the sun's rays into an electrical current.

**Plankton** The assemblage of eggs, larvae, small adult animals and plants such as algae, which are moved about in the water chiefly by the action of currents. The animal component is termed zooplankton, the plant component is termed phytoplankton.

**Plow Pan** A water-resistant stratum in the soil

that comes about as a result of plowing always at or near the same depth.

**Pore space in Soil** The spaces between individual soil particles. Pore space is important for the proper aeration and drainage of soil.

**Primary Production** The total production, through photosynthesis, in an ecosystem. Also termed gross primary production.

**Primary Recovery of Oil** Oil that is removed from an oil field without recourse to measures to increase the "natural" recovery rate.

**Prior Appropriation Water Rights** The doctrine that gives the first claimant to a water source the right to use all that that person wishes provided it is for beneficial ends.

**Quad** A measure of energy equivalent to $10^{15}$ Btu.

**Radioactive Half-life** The time required for a given amount of a radioactive substance to have its mass reduced by one-half through radioactive emissions.

**Raubwirtschaft** Literally, a robber economy. Used to describe any especially wasteful or destructive exploitation of natural resources.

**Return Flow** Water that has been passed over a field for irrigation and that has not percolated into the soil but has flowed away into a surface stream.

**Riparian Water Rights** The doctrine that asserts that a land owner may use water from streams or lakes on which his/her property borders.

**Salination or Salinization of Soil** The process(es) by which the mineral content of a soil is increased often as a result of poor irrigation techniques and/or the application of highly mineralized water to the soil.

**Savanna** Usually restricted to mean a grassland in the low latitudes.

**Secondary Oil Recovery** Application of measures to recover oil in an oil field from which no further amount can be obtained by con-

ventional primary recovery methods. Secondary recovery may involve the injection of water or natural gas to increase the pressure on the field or some other method aimed at recovering some of the remaining oil.

**Second Foot of Water** A flow rate equal to one cubic foot per second past a given point in a stream.

**Second Growth** The tree or brush growth occurring after the first or primary harvest. Actually, this term is applied to all regrowth of trees or shrubs even though such might represent dozens or more harvests since the first one.

**Second Law of Thermodynamics** This states that as energy moves through a system it becomes increasingly diffuse and is lost to heat, that is, entropy.

**Selective Cutting** Cutting only those trees that are deemed ripe or otherwise suited to being harvested and leaving all others as undisturbed as possible. See clearcutting.

**Selective Grazer** Any herbivore that first eats the plants it likes best and proceeds, successively, to those it likes next best.

**Sink** A general term applied to situations where a substance or energy enters a situation or place in which it remains for a lengthy period or from which it may not be retrievable. Is also used as a pejorative term, as for example, characterizing the urban lawn as an energy "sink."

**Slurry** Any liquid—often water—in which solids are held in suspension through constant movement of the liquid.

**Softwood** Wood whose grain is not dense and thus has a relatively low specific gravity. Examples include pine and fir.

**Soil** The shallow discontinuous surface layer of combined organic and inorganic substances and living organisms that forms the principal growth medium for many nonaquatic plants.

**Soil Horizon** A particular stratum in a soil distinguished from other soil strata by color, chemical content, biotic content, and other relevant features.

**Soil Profile** The total assemblage of all soil horizons in a given soil.

**Spoils Bank** Waste materials such as overburden from a mining operation.

**Stocking Rate** The number of animal units best suited to a given grassland situation.

**Strip Mining** Surface mining, usually for coal.

**Subsidence, Land** The collapse or subsidence of land caused by the removal of water, oil or other materials underground.

**Sustained Yield** Harvesting a renewable resource at a rate that permits repeated harvests at similar yield levels for protracted periods of time.

**Synthetic Fuel or Synfuel** Fuels produced from oil shale and tar sand; also the production of oil and gas from coal.

**Tar Sand** Sandy deposits containing large quantities of oil in the pore spaces.

**Temperature Inversion** Ordinarily, air temperature decreases with an increase in altitude. However, this condition may be inverted so that the temperature increases, up to a certain altitude.

**Terrestrial Radiation** Heat (energy) radiated from the earth of which most is of a longer wavelength than is solar radiation. Hence, it does not pass as easily as does solar radiation through the earth's atmosphere, a fact of great significance to the overall heat balance of the earth.

**Third World** Nations that are characterized as underdeveloped.

**Tilth** The ease or difficulty with which a soil can be worked by plows or other agricultural instruments.

**Timber Residues** Various "waste" products resulting from all aspects of timber processing but which are increasingly seen as an energy source, albeit of modest dimensions.

**Upwelling or Coastal Upwelling** The pronounced upward movement of water along certain coasts, which may stimulate increased productivity through the transport into the euphotic zone of nutrients and cool water.

**Watershed** The total surface and subsurface areas over which and through which water flows into a drainage basin or water impoundment.

**Water Table** The top of the zone of saturation in an aquifer.

**Wilderness** Areas that have been minimally disturbed by human actions.

**Wildfire** A major fire in brush or tree cover burning totally out of control and often the result of exceptionally large accumulations of fuel on the soil surface.

**Wilting Point** The time when the water demand of a plant begins to exceed the water available to it in the soil.

**Woodland** An area where trees, although relatively abundant, do not form a closed canopy.

**Zebu** A breed of cattle of southeast Asian origin that has been widely introduced into tropical lands and particularly so in Latin America.

**Zeitgeist** A German word referring to the prevailing spirit or intellectual quality of a given time.

**Zero Population Growth** The stabilization of the human population at some level instead of allowing a continued increase to occur.

**Zero-sum Game** A game or situation in which the size of the possible winnings is constant and thus a win must be balanced by a loss of equal size.

**Zone of Saturation** That portion of an aquifer in which all available pore spaces are occupied by water.

# photo credits

Figure 11.2: Allan D. Cruickshank/Photo Researchers.

Figure 11.3: Jen & Des Bartlett/Photo Researchers.

Figure 11.4: John Borneman/Photo Researchers.

Figure 11.5: Allan D. Cruickshank/Photo Researchers.

Figure 11.6: Joseph Van Wormer/Photo Researchers.

Figures 11.7, 11.8, and 11.9: Leonard Lee Rue III./Photo Researchers.

Figure 11.10: George Laycock/Photo Researchers.

Figure 11.11: Harry Engels/Photo Researchers.

Figure 11.12: Leonard Lee Rue III.—National Audubon Society/Photo Researchers.

Figure 11.13: Allan D. Cruickshank—National Audubon Society/Photo Researchers.

Figure 11.14: Len Rue, Jr.—National Audubon Society/Photo Researchers.

Figure 11.15: Leonard Lee Rue III.—National Aubudon Society/Photo Researchers.

## chapter twelve

Figure 12.1: Ph. Charliat/Rapho-Photo Researchers.

Figure 12.2: Warner F. Clapp—National Audubon Society/Photo Researchers.

Figure 12.3: Dale P. Hansen—National Audubon Society/Photo Researchers.

Figure 12.4: C. G. Maxwell/Photo Researchers.

Figure 12.5: U.S. Department of the Interior.

Figure 12.6: Skyviews Survey, Inc.

Figure 12.7: Dick Powers/Leo deWys.

Figure 12.8: J. W. Cella/Photo Researchers.

Figure 12.9: Dr. Charles F. Bennett.

## chapter fourteen

Figure 14.1: J. Slaughter/United Nations Photo.

Figure 14.2: USDA—Soil Conservation Services.

Figure 14.4: Courtesy Gulf Oil Corporation.

Figure 14.5: Courtesy Aramco.

Figure 14.6: Courtesy Gulf Oil Corporation.

Figure 14.7: Courtesy Mobil Oil Corporation.

Figure 14.8: United Press International.

Figure 14.9: Courtesy Brooklyn Union Gas Company.

Figure 14.10: Kent & Donna Dannen/Photo Researchers.

## chapter fifteen

Figure 15.1: Department of Energy.

Figure 15.2: Bill Pierce/Woodfin Camp.

## chapter sixteen

Figure 16.1: Bruce Roberts/Photo Researchers.

Figure 16.2: Marc & Evelyn Bernheim/Woodfin Camp.

Figure 16.3: U.S. Department of the Interior.

Figure 16.4: Department of Energy, photo by Dick Peabody.

Figure 16.5: Department of Energy, photo by Aratex.

Figure 16.6: Department of Energy.

Figure 16.7: U.S. Department of the Interior, Geological Survey.

## chapter seventeen

Figure 17.1: Bucky Reeves—National Audubon Society/Photo Researchers.

Figure 17.2: The Bettmann Archive.

Figure 17.3: Maurice & Sally Landre—National Audubon Society/Photo Researchers.

Figure 17.4: Paolo Koch/Photo Researchers.

# index